Jihadi Terrorism, Insurgency, and the Islamic State

Front Cover Image: Islamic State recruits graduating from the Shaykh Jalal ad Din training camp in November 2015 in what is likely the eastern province of Nangarhar, Afghanistan. The Wilayah Khorasan branch of the Islamic State was established in January 2015 and conducts operations primarily in Afghanistan and Pakistan. This image and others related to this training camp were released by the Wilayah Khorasan in November 2015 via social media (#ISIS #Khurasan) for propaganda purposes [Image Courtesy of the Foundation for Defense of Democracies' *Long War Journal*]. The Islamic State of Iraq and the Levant (formerly al-Qa'ida in Iraq) has been designated a Foreign Terrorist Organization (FTO) by the U.S. Department of State since 17 December 2004, https://www.state.gov/j/ct/rls/other/des/123085.htm.

Jihadi Terrorism, Insurgency, and the Islamic State

A Small Wars Journal Anthology

Dave Dilegge and
Robert J. Bunker, Editors

Copyright © 2017 by Small Wars Foundation.

| ISBN: | Softcover | 978-1-5245-7772-8 |
| | eBook | 978-1-5245-7773-5 |

All rights reserved. No part of this book may be reproduced or transmitted in any form or by any means, electronic or mechanical, including photocopying, recording, or by any information storage and retrieval system, without permission in writing from the copyright owner.

Print information available on the last page.

Rev. date: 02/16/2017

To order additional copies of this book, contact:
Xlibris
1-888-795-4274
www.Xlibris.com
Orders@Xlibris.com

CONTENTS

Acronyms xv

Foreword: The Islamic State (IS) as a Complex Adaptive System
        Gary Anderson.. xxvii

Introduction: Jihadi Terrorism, Insurgency,
        and the Islamic State
        Robert J. Bunker and Dave Dilegge xxxi

Jihadi Terrorism, Insurgency, and
the Islamic State in Context

Chapter 1:   Legitimate Deliberate Democracy in Transition:
              Failure in the Democratization of Iraq by the
              United States from 2003-2014
              Daniel Tyler Brooks 1

Chapter 2:   Confusing a "Revolution" with "Terrorism"
              Eric C. Anderson 16

Chapter 3:   Reconsidering Religion, Reconsidering Terrorism
              Alexs Thompson 41

Chapter 4:   Ignored in Asia: The ISIL Threat
              David L. Edwards 52

Chapter 5:   Missing Political Front in Afghanistan
              Clark Johnson 59

Chapter 6: Unmasking the Executioner:
What This Gesture Means and How It Can Help
in the Fight Against ISIS
Holly Hughson 74

Chapter 7: Boko Haram's Resiliency Spells
Trouble for West Africa
Jeff Moore..83

Chapter 8: Urban Siege in Paris:
A Spectrum of Armed Assault
John P. Sullivan and Adam Elkus 91

Chapter 9: The ISIS Beheading Narrative
Doyle Quiggle..107

Chapter 10: ISIS For The Common Man
Keith Nightingale 114

Chapter 11: Nigeria's Critical Juncture:
Boko Haram, Buhari, and the Future of the
Fourth Republic
Matthew Blood..123

Chapter 12: On Self-Declared Caliph Ibrahim's May
2015 Message to Muslims: Key Problems of
Motivation, Marginalization, Illogic, and
Empirical Delusion in the Caliphate Project
Paul Kamolnick 135

Chapter 13: America's New Strategic Reality:
Irregular World War
Jeff M. Moore 149

Chapter 14: Al Shabaab Resurgence
Arnold Hammari 153

Chapter 15: A War With ISIS is a Battle Against Ideologies
Chelsea Daymon..162

Chapter 16: Interview: Thinking About ISIS
in Strategic Terms
Robert C. Jones..169

Chapter 17: ISIS and the Sex Factor
Thomas McNamara...183

Chapter 18: Why is Turkey Attacking the
Kurdish Militants Instead of ISIS?
Feryaz Ocakli..187

Chapter 19: Status Quo in the Sinai
Daniel Glickstein and John Miller............................191

Chapter 20: Islamism, Islamofascism, and Islam?
G. Murphy Donovan..195

Chapter 21: The Problem with Proxies:
Ideology is No Substitute for Operational
Control
Yelena Biberman and Orr Genish............................200

Chapter 22: Why ISIS is Winning in Iraq
Johnny Lou and Patrick O'Connor..........................210

Chapter 23: Disrupting the MFO: ISIS in Sinai
Matthew J. McGoffin 217

Chapter 24: Mujahideen: The Strategic Tradition
of Sunni Jihadism
Brett A. Friedman 221

Chapter 25: Friday the 13th in Paris
G. Murphy Donovan..236

Chapter 26: The Starfish Caliphate:
How ISIL Exploits the Power of a
Decentralized Organization
Stewart Welch...240

Chapter 27: Jihadist Narratives:
    Democratized Islam and Islamic Nation Building
    Caleb S. Cage...246

Chapter 28: Justifying Jihad:
    A Case Study of Al-Shabaab and Boko Haram
    Daniel Pesature 262

Chapter 29: ISIS is Not a Terrorist Organization
    Ajit Maan..277

U.S.-Allied Policy and Counter-Jihadi
and Counter-Islamic State Strategies

Chapter 30: Adam Smith's Invisible Hand vs. The Taliban:
    Bottom-Up Expeditionary Diplomacy in Fragile
    States—Best Practices from the Civilian Surge in
    Afghanistan
    Melinda Hutchings 283

Chapter 31: AFPAK Hands:
    A Template for Long-Term Strategic
    Engagement?
    Mike Coleman, Jim Gannon, Sarah Lynch
    and Reggie Evans 315

Chapter 32: What Is the Counter-Daesh Strategy?:
    A "Cohenian" Exercise
    Kevin Benson..325

Chapter 33: Narrative: The Critical Component of Counter-
    Terrorism Strategy
    Ajit Maan..334

Chapter 34: 'Confronting ISIS in Libya:
    The Case for an Expeditionary
    Counterinsurgency'

Nader Anaizi, Frederick H. Dotolo, III and
Merouane Lakehal-Ayat 339

Chapter 35: The 21st Century Answer to "Burning their
Crops and Salting their Fields": Interdicting and
Destroying The ISIS Financial Network
Greg Kleponis and Tom Creal 355

Chapter 36: "Channeling": The United Kingdom's Approach
to CVE-A Plan Americans Deserve But Will
Never Receive
Ryan Pereira 361

Chapter 37: Cultural Heritage Preservation and Its Role for
Paving the Way Toward Peace
Marc A. Abramiuk and Wilem S. Wong 373

Chapter 38: It is Time to Reassess How the US Conducts
Detention Operations in the Current Fight and
the Need to Incorporate our Regional Partners
in the Future—Insurgents are Not Traditional
Enemy Prisoners of War
John Hussey 384

Chapter 39: Global War on Terrorism: How Does the
United States Military Counter and Combat the
Worldwide Spread of Islamic Extremism?
Richard K. Snodgrass 396

Chapter 40: Deconstructing ISIS:
SWJ interview with William McCants on The
ISIS Apocalypse: The History, Strategy and
Doomsday Vision of the Islamic State
Octavian Manea 409

Chapter 41: How to Defeat the Islamic State: Crafting a
Rational War Strategy
Anthony N. Celso 418

Chapter 42: Defeating ISIL in the Information Environment
Alan Dinerman 435

Chapter 43: Information War with the Islamic State in Iraq
and the Levant: An Indirect Approach
Brian Russell 440

Chapter 44: Reevaluating General Order 1X
Tom Ordeman, Jr. 447

Chapter 45: Talking to Tyrants, Sharpening Axes
Robert Murphy 461

Chapter 46: Finding the ISIS Center of Gravity:
Why Does It Have to Be So Complicated?
Ian Bertram 465

Chapter 47: Basing Stabilisation Efforts on Evidence of What
Works: Lessons from Afghanistan
Jon Moss 471

Chapter 48: Defeating the Abu Bakr al Baghdadi Gang:
A Realistic Strategy
Huba Wass de Czege 488

Chapter 49: Kurdistan: The Permanent Solution to Daesh
Joshua A. Perkins 521

Postscript: Ten Endgames of an Effective
Counter-Insurgency Against IS
Joshua Sinai 533

Notes 537

Notes on Contributors... 643

ABOUT SMALL WARS JOURNAL AND FOUNDATION

Small Wars Journal facilitates the exchange of information among practitioners, thought leaders, and students of Small Wars, in order to advance knowledge and capabilities in the field. We hope this, in turn, advances the practice and effectiveness of those forces prosecuting Small Wars in the interest of self-determination, freedom, and prosperity for the population in the area of operations.

We believe that Small Wars are an enduring feature of modern politics. We do not believe that true effectiveness in Small Wars is a 'lesser included capability' of a force tailored for major theater war. And we *never* believed that 'bypass built-up areas' was a tenable position warranting the doctrinal primacy it has held for too long—this site is an evolution of the MOUT Homepage, Urban Operations Journal, and urbanoperations.com, all formerly run by the *Small Wars Journal's* Editor-in-Chief.

The characteristics of Small Wars have evolved since the Banana Wars and Gunboat Diplomacy. War is never purely military, but today's Small Wars are even less pure with the greater inter-connectedness of the 21st century. Their conduct typically involves the projection and employment of the full spectrum of national and coalition power by a broad community of practitioners. The military is still generally the biggest part of the pack, but there a lot of other wolves. The strength of the pack is the wolf, and the strength of the wolf is the pack.

The *Small Wars Journal's* founders come from the Marine Corps. Like Marines deserve to be, we are very proud of this; we are also conscious and cautious of it. This site seeks to transcend any viewpoint that is single service, and any that is purely military or naively U.S.-centric. We pursue a comprehensive approach to Small Wars, integrating the full joint, allied, and coalition military with their governments' federal or national agencies, non-governmental agencies, and private organizations. Small Wars are big undertakings, demanding a coordinated effort from a huge community of interest.

We thank our contributors for sharing their knowledge and experience, and hope you will continue to join us as we build a resource for our community of interest to engage in a professional dialog on this painfully relevant topic. Share your thoughts, ideas, successes, and mistakes; make us all stronger.

"...I know it when I see it."

"Small Wars" is an imperfect term used to describe a broad spectrum of spirited continuation of politics by other means, falling somewhere in the middle bit of the continuum between feisty diplomatic words and global thermonuclear war. The *Small Wars Journal* embraces that imperfection.

Just as friendly fire isn't, there isn't necessarily anything small about a Small War.

The term "Small War" either encompasses or overlaps with a number of familiar terms such as counterinsurgency, foreign internal defense, support and stability operations, peacemaking, peacekeeping, and many flavors of intervention. Operations such as noncombatant evacuation, disaster relief, and humanitarian assistance will often either be a part of a Small War, or have a Small Wars feel to them. Small Wars involve a wide spectrum of specialized tactical, technical, social, and cultural skills and expertise, requiring great ingenuity from their practitioners. The *Small Wars Manual* (a wonderful resource, unfortunately more often referred to than read) notes that:

Small Wars demand the highest type of leadership directed by intelligence, resourcefulness, and ingenuity. Small Wars are conceived in uncertainty, are conducted often with precarious responsibility and doubtful authority, under indeterminate orders lacking specific instructions.

The "three block war" construct employed by General Krulak is exceptionally useful in describing the tactical and operational challenges of a Small War and of many urban operations. Its only shortcoming is that is so useful that it is often mistaken as a definition or as a type of operation.

***

Small Wars Journal is NOT a government, official, or big corporate site. It is run by Small Wars Foundation, a 501 (c)(3) non-profit corporation, for the benefit of the Small Wars community of interest. The site principals are Dave Dilegge (Editor-in-Chief), Bill Nagle (Publisher), Robert Haddick (Managing Editor) and Peter Muson (Editor). Dilegge, Nagle and Haeddick, along with Daniel Kelly, serve as the Small Wars Foundation Board of Directors.

The views expressed in this anthology are those of the author(s) and do not necessarily reflect the official policy or position of the Department of the Army, the Department of Defense, the Federal Bureau of Investigation, the Department of Justice, or the U.S. Government, or any other U.S. armed service, intelligence or law enforcement agency, or local or state government.

Acronyms

ABC	American Broadcasting Company
ACS	Assistant Chief of Staff
AD	Anno Domini
ADMM	ASEAN Defense Minister's Meeting
ADRP	Army Doctrine Reference Publication
AFB	Air Force Base
AFISMA	African-led International Support Mission to Mali
AFPAK	Afghanistan-Pakistan
AIHRC	Afghan Independent Human Rights Commission
AIT	Advanced Individual Training
AJPME	Advanced Joint Professional Military Education
AK	Avtomat Kalashnikova (Automatic Weapon of Kalashnikov)
AKO	Army Knowledge Online
AKP	Adalet ve Kalkınma Partisi (Justice and Development Party)
AMISOM	African Union Mission in Somalia
ANDF-P	Aghan National Detention Facility in Parwan
ANGLICO	Air Naval Gunfire Liaison Company
ANSF	Afghan National Security Force

AOR	Area of Responsibility
AP	Associated Press
APC	All Progressives Congress
APH	Afghanistan-Pakistan Hands
AQAA	Al Qaeda and its Affiliates and Adherents
AQAP	Al Qaeda in the Arabian Peninsula
AQI	Al Qaeda in Iraq
AQIM	Al Qaeda in the Islamic Maghreb
ASEAN	Association of Southeast Asian Nations
ASI	Additional Skill Indentifier
ASIS	American Society for Industrial Security
ASVAB	Armed Services Vocational Aptitude Battery
AUMF	Authorization for the Use of Military Force
BA	Bachelor of Arts
BBC	British Broadcasting Corporation
BCE	Before the Common Era
BG	Al Baghdadi Gang
BOLC	Basic Officer Leader Course
Brig Gen	Brigadier General
BS	Bachelor of Science
BSE	Bachelor of Science in Engineering
CA	Civil Affairs
CAMS	Certified Anti-Money Laundering Specialist
CAP	Combat Air Patrol
CAST	Center for Advanced Studies on Terrorism
CBC	Canadian Broadcasting Corporation
CBS	Columbia Broadcasting System
CENTCOM	Central Command
CERP	Commanders Emergency Response Program

CFE	Certified Fraud Examiner
CGSC	Command and General Staff College
CHAS	Central Helmand Archaeological Study
CIA	Central Intelligence Agency
CJCS	Chairman of the Joint Chiefs of Staff
CJIATF	Combined Joint Interagency Task Force
CJOA	Combined Joint Operations Area
CJTF	Civilian Joint Task Force
CJTF-HOA	Combined Joint Task Force-Horn of Africa
CNN	Cable News Network
COCOM	Combatant Command; CCMD is the newer official acronym
COG	Center of Gravity
COIN	Counter Insurgency
COL	Colonel
CONOPS	Concept of Operations
CORDS	Civil Operations and Revolutionary Development Support
CPA	Coalition Provisional Authority
CPT	Captain
CT	Counter Terrorism
CTL	Company Landing Team
CVE	Countering Violent Extremism
DAIL	Directorate of Agriculture, Irrigation, and Livestock
DC	District of Columbia
DCI	Director of Central Intelligence
DDA	District Development Assembly
DDOS	Distributed Denial of Service
DDR	Disarmament, Demobilization, and Reintegration

DEA	Drug Enforcement Administration
DIME	Diplomatic, Information, Military, and Economic
DLAB	Defense Language Aptitude Battery
DLI	Defense Language Institute
DLIFLC	Defense Language Institute Foreign Language Center
DOD	Department of Defense
DOS	Department of State
DR	Doctor
DST	District Support Team
DV	Dependent Variable
EFT	Electronic Fund Transfer
EG	Exempli Gratia (For Example)
EMS	Emergency Medical Services
EU	European Union
EUBAM	European Border Border Assistance Mission in Libya
FAO	Foreign Area Officer
FBI	Federal Bureau of Investigation
FGS	Federal Government of Somalia
FIFO	First-In, First-Out
FIR	Futurist in Residence
FLN	National Liberation Front
FM	Field Manual
FMF	Foreign Military Financing
FOB	Forward Operating Base
FSA	Free Syrian Army
G-7	Group of Seven

GBP	Great Britain Pound
GDP	Gross Domestic Product
Gen	General
GIA	Armed Islamic Group
GIGN	Groupe d'intervention de la Gendarmerie nationale
GIRoA	Government of Islamic Republic of Afghanistan
GIS	Global Information Systems
GNC	General National Congress
GO	General Order
GoI	Government of Iraq
GPS	Global Positioning System
HDP	Peoples' Democratic Party (Halkların Demokratik Partisi)
HMEP	Helmand Monitoring and Evaluation Programme
HPRT	Helmand Provincial Reconstruction Team
HQ	Headquarters
HUMINT	Human Intelligence
IA	Initial Assessment
IA	Iraqi National Army
ICSR	International Center for the Study of Radicalism and Political Violence
ICT	Information and Communications Technology
ICU	Islamic Courts Union
IDLG	Independent Directorate of Local Governments
IDP	Internally Displaced Person
IED	Improvised Explosive Device
IISS	International Institute for Strategic Studies
IMET	International Military Education and Training

IMoLIN/AMLID	International Money-Laundering Information Network/Anti-Money-Laundering International Database
IN3	Internet Interdisciplinary Institute
INTERPOL	International Police (International Criminal Police Organization; ICPO)
IP	Iraqi Police force
ISAF	International Security Assistance Force
IS	Islamic State
ISR	Intelligence, Survelliance, and Reconnaissance
ISI	Islamic State in/of Iraq
ISI	Inter-Services Intelligence
ISIL	Islamic State in/of Iraq and the Levant
ISIS	Islamic State of Iraq and al-Sham
ISIS	Islamic State in/of Iraq and Syria
ISO	Islamic State Organization
IT	Information Technology
IV	Independent Variable
JAM	Jeesh Al Mahdi
JCISFA	Joint Center for International Security Force Assistance
JCS	Joint Chiefs of Staff
JDAL	Joint Duty Assignment List
JP	Joint Publication
JN	Jabhat al-Nusra
KDP	Kurdish Democratic Party
KGH	Kiernan Group Holdings
KM	Kilometer
KRG	Kurdistan Regional Government
KS	Kansas

KSA	Kingdom of Saudi Arabia
LLM	Master of Laws
LPIND	Language Proficiency Indicator
Lt	Lieutenant
LTC	Lieutenant Colonel
Lt Col	Lieutenant Colonel
LTTE	Liberation Tigers of Tamil Eelam
MA	Master of Arts
MAAWS	Money As A Weapon System
M&E	Monitoring and Evaluation
MAGTF	Marine Air-Ground Task Force
MAJ	Major
MBTA	Ministry of Borders and Tribal Affairs
MEB	Marine Expeditionary Brigade
MENA	Middle East and North African
MEU	Marine Expeditionary Unit
MFO	Multi-National Force and Observers
MHIA	Minister of Hajj and Islamic Affairs
MI	Military Intelligence
MISO	Military Information Support Operations
MISTI	Measuring Impacts of Stabilization Initiatives
MITT	Military Training Team
MMAS	Master of Military Art and Science
MNJTF	Multinational Joint Task Force
MoIC	Ministry of Information and Culture
MOS	Military Occupational Speciality
MP	Military Police
MRRD	Ministry of Rural Rehabilitation and Development
MS	Master of Science

MUJAO	Movement for Oneness and Jihad in West Africa
MWD	Military Working Dog
NATO	North Atlantic Treaty Organization
NCO	Non-Commissioned Officer
NGO	Non-Governmental Organization
NOC	National Oil Company
NSS	National Security Strategy
NYC	New York City
NYPD	New York City Police Department
OEF	Operation Enduring Freedom
OIF	Operation Iraqi Freedom
1LT	First Lieutenant
OPSEC	Operational Security
OR	Oregon
ORHA	Organization for Reconstruction and Humanitarian Assistance
OSD	Office of the Secretary of Defense
PA	Pennsylvania
PACOM	Pacific Command
PDIA	Problem-Driven Iterative Adaptation
PhD	Doctor of Philosophy
PKK	Partiya Karkerên Kurdistanê (Kurdistan Workers' Party)
PLO	Palestinian Liberation Organization
PM	Prime Minister
PME	Professional Military Education
PO	Psychological Operations
POMEPS	Project on Middle East Political Science

PPD	Presidential Policy Directive
PRT	Provincial Reconstruction Team
PUK	Patriotic Union of Kurdistan
RAID	Recherche, Assistance, Intervention, Dissuasion
RAND	Research and Develoment
R-CA	Representative California
RCLF	Reional, Culture and Language Familiarization
RCT	Regimental Combat Team
RIAD	Radio-In-A-Box
ROTC	Reserve Officer Training Corps
SACREUR	Supreme Allied Commander Europe
SAF	Syrian Air Force
SCAP	Supreme Commander of Allied Powers
SF	Security Force; Nigerian
SF	Special Forces
SIGAR	Special Inspector General for Afghanistan Reconstruction
SJA	Staff Judge Advocate
SMA	Strategic Multi-Layer Assessment
SME	Subject Matter Expert
SNA	Somali National Army
SOF	Special Operations Forces
SOFA	Status of Forces Agreement
SoIz	Sons of Iraq
SOMO	State Organization for Marketing of Oil
SOP	Standard Operating Procedure
SP	Sinai Province
SS	Schutzstaffel
SSA	Security Sector Assistance
SSP	Security Studies Program

SSR	Security Sector Reform
START	Study of Terrorism and Responses to Terrorism
SWAT	Special Weapons and Tactics
SWCS	Special Warfare Center and School
SWJ	Small Wars Journal
TA	Targeted Audience
TFG	Tranisitional Federal Government
TMAF	Tokyo Mutual Accountability Framework
TRAC	Terrorism Research and Analysis Consortium
TRADOC	Training and Doctrine Command
TX	Texas
UAE	United Arab Emirates
UBL	Usama bin Laden
UK	United Kingdom
UMEP	Uruzgan Monitoring and Evaluation Programme
UN	United Nations
UNDOF	United Nations Disengagement Force
UNESCO	United Nations Ecuational, Scientific and Cultural Organization
UNODC	United Nations Office on Drugs and Crime
UNSOA	United Nations Support Office for AMISOM
US	United States
USA	United States Army
USACAPOC	United States Army Civil Affairs and Psychological Operations Command
USAF	United States Air Force
USAFA	United States Air Force Academy
USAID	United States Agency for International Development

USAR	United States Army Reserve
USBATT	United States Battalion
USCENTOM	United States Central Command
USDA	United States Department of Agriculture
USG	United States Government
USMC	United States Marine Corps
USMCR	United States Marine Corps Reserve
USPACOM	United States Pacific Command
USSOCOM	United States Special Operations Command
USSR	Union of Soviet Socialist Republics
VA	Virginia
VBIED	Vehicle Borne Improvised Explosive Device
VEO	Violent Extremist Organization
VSO	Village Stability Operations
WWII	World War Two
YPG	People's Protection Units

Foreword

The Islamic State (IS) as a Complex Adaptive System

Gary Anderson

Washington, DC

May 2016

Before crafting a strategy against an opponent, it is important to try to understand him. This anthology is an attempt to understand the Islamic State (IS) as a complex adaptive system that has no single center of gravity. As such, it must be viewed from a number of perspectives to be understood.

The IS is waging the first truly global hybrid war. As such, it has a number of manifestations. In Syria and Iraq, it is waging state-on-state near-conventional war employing a regular army. It controls ground, has a functioning government, and collects taxes. Overseas, it functions a quasi-empire with Waliyah, or provinces, that swear loyalty to it in Libya, Central Africa, and the Philippines. However, it also runs insurgencies in places as diverse as Europe and the Sinai Peninsula. To the extent that it is a state, it is a state sponsor of terrorism of a kind that has struck from Paris to California.

To some extent, most of America's big wars have been hybrid in nature. The American Revolution, the Civil War, and World War II saw conventional conflict that was intermixed with unconventional warfighting methods. Irregular combat, insurgency, and terror were used as tools by both sides. Vietnam was no exception to that rule. Our first Gulf War (popularly known as OPERATION DESERT STORM) may be the last purely conventional conflict that we will ever fight.

In its most dangerous manifestation, the IS controls two major cities in two separate countries defended by a fanatical army that will use urban combat on a Stalingrad scale replete with complex tunnel systems; its warriors will fight among the civilian population in an effort to force attackers to destroy the city to save it. This forces the loose coalition aligned against the would-be caliphate to make the hard choice of waiting them out and allowing them to use their considerable resources to fund world-wide mischief elsewhere, or conducting urban blood baths.

Even if Mosul and Raqqa are liberated in a series of conventional campaigns, the hydra will not be destroyed. The IS cells throughout the world will declare the urban defenders to be martyrs and fight on. No single strategy will finally wipe out ISIS as a movement. It will need to be attacked at multiple points with a variety of approaches. Not since the Cold War have we been faced with an enemy that needs such a diverse and multi-pronged strategy to be defeated. Unfortunately, since 2009, the senior leadership of our country has denied that it is in a global war against radical Islam; even the use of the term in anathema.

This anthology analyzes the many manifestations of the IS, and discusses its strengths and weaknesses. Not all of the authors agree on the proper approaches or even the nature of the problem. However, informed readers who may be crafting a revised approach to defeating the IS can analyze them and make intelligent choices regarding the true nature of the enemy and how to defeat it. Leadership decapitation and denial of financial resources alone won't work against complex, adaptive systems; they are Darwinian. From a leadership perspective, the slow and stupid are targeted fairly effectively. However, dead leaders are replaced by younger and more agile individuals. Economically, there are always banks to be robbed and rich people to be kidnapped for ransom. Such systems need to be attacked at multiple points by multiple means to overwhelm them. This book helps to identify the strong points and vulnerabilities of this complex and adaptive foe.

Complex, adaptive systems can be defeated no matter how evil and ruthless they are. Nazi Germany was defeated because it was attacked on many fronts with multiple tools. The coalition against it was imperfect, but it had an agreed upon end state. It used tools as diverse as strategic bombing and resistance movements in occupied territories as well as overwhelming conventional force. Ultimately, however, there was a steely determination to totally destroy the Nazi evil and never to let it rise again. We lack that today, but the essays in this book should convince us of why we should return to that ethos. We Americans did not truly realize the extent of the evil we were facing until well into the war. Thanks to modern technology, we know the extent of the IS evil; but, to date, we have lacked the will to confront it head on.

Unfortunately, the people who really need to read this book in the near term probably won't. Our current leaders believe themselves to be the "smartest guys in the room." They have created a long-term strategy designed not to see its final outcome until after they are gone. In the unlikely case that it works, they can take credit in their memoirs; if it doesn't, it is the new guys' fault.

It is the next administration that will hopefully benefit from this anthology. After January, 2017, the new civilian leaders and their military advisors will have a clean slate to write on. They will have a lot of reading to do and hopefully this book will be on their short list.

Introduction

Jihadi Terrorism, Insurgency, and the Islamic State

Robert J. Bunker and Dave Dilegge

Claremont, CA and Largo, FL

October 2016

This work is the third *Small Wars Journal* anthology focusing on radical Sunni Islamic terrorist and insurgent groups. It covers this professional journal's writings for 2015 and is a compliment to the earlier *Global Radical Islamist Insurgency* anthologies that were produced as Vol. I: 2007-2011 (published in 2015) and Vol. II: 2012-2014 (published in 2016). The initial anthology was principally Al Qaeda network focused with the second one providing pretty much equal coverage to both the Al Qaeda and Islamic State networks. Both of these two volumes also showcased additional *SWJ* writings on other radical Sunni and jihadist themes and together presented over one hundred chapters and over 1,500 pages of professional analysis provided by dozens of our journal's contributors over a seven-year period.[1]

This anthology, which offers roughly six hundred and fifty pages of additional analysis, follows the same general conceptual breakdown as the earlier works and is divided into two major thematic sections—one focusing on jihadi terrorism, insurgency, and the Islamic State in context and the other focusing on U.S.-allied policy and counter-jihadi and counter-Islamic State strategies. Given the rapid expansion of the Islamic State since the establishment of the Caliphate in June 2014 and the increasing threat global threat it represents to the U.S. and its allies, this work is dominated by writings focused upon it and its network constituents.[2] Hence, this anthology is being called *Jihadi Terrorism, Insurgency, and the Islamic State* with no mention of Al Qaeda within the title. Still, writings focused on other Sunni radical Islamist concerns as well as the Al Qaeda network itself are also represented in quite a number of its roughly fifty chapters.

The chapters themselves begin with an essay (Ch. 1) by Daniel Tyler Brooks who at the time of the writing of his essay was a U.S. Army Captain—with 2 deployments supporting Operation Iraqi Freedom—in a graduate program in international studies at University of Denver. He has since been awarded an M.A. and is presently a student at the Command and General Staff College (CGSC), Fort Leavenworth, KS. His chapter explores the failure of democracy taking root in Iraq as a component of the US policy of 'nation-building' during the 2003 to 2014 period. Iraq is an interesting case study in that it was an authoritarian state which post-invasion seemed to have a somewhat bright future. Brooks explores the decision points on the path to the democratization process and argues that this process failed for two important reasons. First, the Sunni Arab population of Iraq remained disenfranchised and viewed democratization as an illegitimate form of governance that both threatened its core interests and delivered few public goods. Second, the US failed "…to impose forcefully western cultural mores that are prerequisites for deliberate democracy." From the perspective of this anthology, the first reason for failure is of primary importance because it allowed the Islamic State to draw upon disenfranchised Sunni populations in Iraq for its initial recruiting base. This situation has not significantly changed, with Iraqi governance increasingly being viewed as co-opted by Shia and Iranian interests. The final chapter (Ch. 49) is by Joshua A. Perkins who at the time of its writing was an Armor officer with a graduate degree in political science—national security and diplomacy specialization—from the University of West Florida. His short essay discusses the advantages of the US backing the establishment of a Kurdish state—Kurdistan—as a permanent counterbalance to the Daesh (i.e. the Islamic State) threat in Iraq and Syria. Additional advantages would be the geo-political balancing of Iranian aspirations in the region as well as limiting Shia influence in Iraq and Syria while keeping the Assad regime weakened. Turkish obstacles to a Kurdish state would be significant—which the author downplays—and such a new sovereign entity would likely only further promote two major coalitions in the region, with Russia firmly backing the Shia and Assad alliance and Israel and Saudi Arabia most certainly backing the Kurds.

Some of the individual chapter highlights of this anthology in the jihadi terrorism, insurgency, and the Islamic State in context section of the work are those by Holly Hughson, Doyle Quiggle, Johnny Lou and Patrick O'Connor, and Ajit Maan. Holly Hughson—an international humanitarian aid SME and University of St. Andrews alumna—in her essay (Ch. 6) analyzes the components of an Islamic State execution video (the 5th of a murdered Western hostage) released in November 2014. Of note in the video is the fact that the IS executioners were unmasked. The essay analyzes the reasons and context behind why the executioners were unmasked and discusses some IS vulnerabilities that could thus accordingly be exploited. Dr. Doyle Quiggle, a professor to forward deployed U.S. troops overseas and anthropology of war researcher, writes in his article (Ch. 9) on the beheading narrative of the Islamic State. He draws upon Regina Jones' more generalized beheading typology—based on the four categories of judicial, sacrificial, presentational, and trophy—and discusses them within the specific context of IS usage. Johnny Lou and Patrick O'Connor provide us with a more insurgent and ground combat focused work (Ch. 22) that analyzes Islamic State territorial victories in Iraq stemming from the earlier de-Baathification policies of the U.S. These authors, both researchers at the Chicago Project on Security and Terrorism—University of Chicago, argue that, as a result, IS troops have acquired far better tactical military skills than Iraqi governmental soldiers, using the Battle of Ramadi in May 2015 as an example. Finally, in the contribution (Ch. 29) by Dr. Ajit Maan—an internarrative identity and counter-terrorism recruitment specialist—she posits in this short piece that labeling the Islamic State is as a terrorist organization is inaccurate and limits U.S. policy options to defensive counter terrorism (CT) responses. Rather, she seeks to have IS labeled an insurgent group with territorial ambitions that should be addressed by military, and presumably COIN, strategies in coordination with other nations and Kurdish forces in the Syria and Iraq area of operations.

Chapters of note in the U.S.-allied policy and counter-jihadi and counter-Islamic State strategies section of the anthology include those by Kevin Benson, Ajit Maan, Greg Kleponis and Tom Creal, Octavian Manea, and Anthony N. Celso. Dr. Kevin Benson, a retired U.S. Army Colonel and a seminar leader at the University of Foreign Military and Cultural Studies—Fort Leavenworth, KS, discusses elements of the Obama Administration's counter Daesh/IS strategy in his short essay (Ch. 32). He does this by linking it to the Eliot Cohen model of strategy drawing upon assumptions, ends-ways-means, and stated risks, priorities, and a theory of victory. Dr. Ajit Maan provides an additional essay (Ch. 33) in this anthology that explores the use of the narrative for counter terrorism strategy purposes. Her focus is on the use of a 'strategic narrative' against IS which contains military and developmental narrative and counter terrorism narrative components. Greg Kleponis and Tom Creal, a retired USAF Colonel and PhD candidate with the University of Bolton, UK and a Forensic Accountant and Panel Expert to the UN, respectively, contribute an article (Ch. 35) on interdicting and destroying the Islamic State's financial network. They argue that this is the 21st century equivalent of 'burning crops and salting fields' and is a capability that needs to be applied to terrorist entities like IS which more closely resemble organized criminal organizations than political or military organizations. Octavian Manea, a frequent SWJ contributor and editor with the Romanian weekly magazine *Revista 22* (22 Magazine), in his essay (Ch. 40) interviewed William McCants, the author of *The ISIS Apocalypse*. Much of that interview provides a contrast between IS and Al Qaeda Central from which it evolved and splintered off. Dr. Anthony N. Celso, an Associate Professor of Security Studies at Angelo State University, in his work (Ch. 41) provides an alternative war strategy—distinct from the Obama Administration *low cost/minimum risk* containment policy—that can be utilized against the Islamic State. This alternative war strategy would focus upon providing a counter response to the IS *remain* and *expand* strategy that is facilitating the growth of the Caliphate by attacking IS vulnerabilities linked to state building and its apocalyptic and transnational Takfirist ideologies and brutality.

All of these chapters, and many more not discussed, are placed in context by the front and end pieces to the anthology. The book begins with a foreword by Col Gary Anderson, USMC (Ret.) who has held numerous positions including that of being the first Executive Director of the Center for Emerging Threats and Opportunities (CETO), Potomac Institute—which operates as a stand-alone branch of the Futures Assessment Division of the Marine Corps's Futures Directorate at Quantico, Virginia. His foreword discusses how the Islamic State should be viewed as a complex adaptive system in order to devise strategies against it. It also equates the inherent evil nature of the contemporary Islamic State with that of Nazi Germany existing over seventy years ago and explains the utility of this anthology for the incoming civilian leaders and military advisors of the next presidential administration coming into office in January 2017. The foreword is then followed by this introduction which has provided a short overview of the anthology and will next describe the context that the Islamic State existed within during the 2015 time period. This is facilitated by drawing upon pre-existing IS time line and map resources. It has been written by the editors of this work who have law enforcement CT (counter terrorism) support and military HUMINT (human intelligence) expertise, respectively. Dr. Joshua Sinai—a CT Principle Analyst with Kiernan Group Holdings (KGH)—then provides the postscript to this work. That essay highlights ten interrelated COIN (counter insurgency) end game strategies that can be effectively utilized against the Islamic State. The work also contains a detailed acronyms listing in the front section as well as a notes section following the chapters and postscript. The final sections of the anthology contain information on its contributors and on the two *Global Radical Islamist Insurgency* anthologies that were previously published.

Prior to reading *Jihadi Terrorism, Insurgency, and the Islamic State* some additional contextual information is being offered here related to the Islamic State during the 2015 period. This additional context can best be provided by means of a time line of the major Islamic State activities that took place when the anthology essays were written. This timeline represents a much abbreviated 2015 overview of a more expansive and detailed one spanning 2004 through mid-2016 produced by Cameron Glenn—a Senior Program Assistant, Iran & Middle East Programs, U.S. Institute of Peace—in cooperation with the Wilson Center:

> **Jan. 7:** Two gunmen, Saïd and Chérif Kouachi, attack the offices of French satirical newspaper Charlie Hebdo in Paris, killing 11 people. A third assailant, Amedy Coulibaly, carried out a synchronized attack on a kosher supermarket, taking hostages and killing four people. Coulibaly reportedly declared allegiance to the Islamic State.
>
> **Jan. 26:** Kurdish fighters, with the help of U.S. and coalition airstrikes, force out ISIS militants from the Syrian border town of Kobani after a four-month battle.
>
> **Feb. 4:** ISIS releases a video of Jordanian military pilot Moaz al Kasasbeh being burned alive.
>
> **Feb. 15–16:** Libyan militants allied to ISIS release a video showing the beheading of 21 Egyptian Christians, who had been kidnapped on January 12. Egypt launches airstrikes in Libya in retaliation.
>
> **Feb. 25–26:** ISIS militants abduct at least 200 Assyrian Christians in northeastern Syria. The U.S.-led coalition launches airstrikes in the same area.
>
> **March 20**: ISIS-linked militants bomb two mosques in Sanaa, Yemen, killing 137 people.

April 5: ISIS militants seize the Palestinian refugee camp of Yarmouk in Damascus where more than 18,000 people reside.

April 19: ISIS posts a video showing militants from its Libyan branch executing dozens of Ethiopian Christians.

May 17: ISIS takes over Ramadi, Iraq.

May 20: ISIS seizes the ancient Syrian city of Palmyra.

May 21: ISIS militants take full control of Sirte, Libya—Muammar Qaddafi's hometown.

May 22: ISIS claims responsibility for the suicide attacks on a Shiite mosque in eastern Saudi Arabia, which killed 21 people and injured more than 100.

June 17: Kurdish fighters expel ISIS from the strategic Syrian town of Tal Abyad on the Turkish border.

June 22: Kurdish forces take full control of Ain Issa, a military base, from ISIS militias.

June 26: ISIS fighters kill at least 145 civilians in an attack on Kobani, Syria. The same day, ISIS-linked militants attacked a Shiite mosque in Kuwait, killing 27 people and injuring more than 200.

June 27: ISIS claims responsibility an attack on a Tunisian resort in Sousse, where 38 people were killed and 39 were wounded—most of them foreigners.

July 1: ISIS fighters carry out simultaneous assaults on military checkpoints in Egypt's northern Sinai Peninsula, killing dozens of soldiers.

July 20: A suicide bomber with links to ISIS strikes a cultural center in Suruç—a Turkish border town near Kobani—killing at least 30 people.

Aug. 6: ISIS claims responsibility for a suicide bombing on a Saudi Arabian mosque that killed at least 15 people, including 12 members of Saudi police force, in Asir province, near the south-western border with Yemen.

Sept. 30: Russia begins airstrikes in Syria. It claims to target ISIS, but U.S. officials allege that many of the strikes target civilians and Western-backed rebel groups.

Oct. 6: ISIS kills at least 25 people in a series of car bombings in Yemen's two largest cities, Aden and Sanaa.

Oct. 9: ISIS makes significant gains in northwestern Syria, seizing six villages near Aleppo.

Oct. 15: Iraqi forces recapture the Baiji refinery, the largest oil refinery in the country, from ISIS.

Oct. 22: A member of a U.S. special operations force is killed during an ISIS hostage rescue mission in northern Iraq - the first American to die in ground combat with ISIS. Twenty ISIS fighters are killed during the mission, and six more are detained.

Oct. 31: Sinai Province, Egypt's ISIS affiliate, claims responsibility for bombing a Russian passenger plane over the Sinai Peninsula, killing all 224 on board.

Nov. 12: ISIS claims responsibility for suicide attacks in Beirut that killed 40 people.

Nov. 13: Kurdish forces seize Sinjar, Iraq from ISIS.

Nov. 13: ISIS carries out a series of coordinated attacks in Paris, killing 130 people.

Nov. 15: France ramps up its airstrikes on ISIS targets in Raqqa, Syria.

Dec. 1: Defense Secretary Ashton Carter announces that U.S. special operations forces would be sent to Iraq to support Iraqi and Kurdish fighters and launch targeted operations in Syria.

Dec. 2: A married couple allegedly inspired by ISIS kill 14 people in San Bernardino, California.

Dec. 10: U.S. officials announce that airstrikes killed ISIS finance minister Abu Saleh and two other senior leaders in Tal Afar, Iraq.

Dec. 27: Iraqi military forces seize Ramadi from ISIS.[3]

As can be seen above during the January through December 2015 period, two major themes related to the Islamic State are evident. The initial one is terrorism based and portrays the willingness of this group to promote direct attacks by its network constituents on civilian populations in not only the Middle East but farther afield including Europe and the United States. Many of these attacks move beyond traditional gun and bomb type incidents and are more ritualistic and barbaric in nature including the use of mass beheadings and immolation. The follow-on theme is that of territorial conquest and the taking of major cities in Iraq, Syria, and even Libya. While Caliphate expansion setbacks are evident during 2015—with a number of Kurdish successes and the Iraqi liberation of the Baiji refinery and later Ramadi at the end of the year—IS during this period was still primarily in its territorial expansive phase and willing to actively target French, United States, and Russian interests and nationals in addition to its much closer enemies.

Of these two themes, the later one—essentially *Hijrah* (immigration to the Caliphate and its expansion) focused—is still dominant. While the Islamic State has long been designated a FTO (Foreign Terrorist Organization) by the U.S State Department, it has since evolved defacto into a quasi-sovereign state challenger (albeit criminal) to the Westphalian form. Instead of only having the capacity to field small terrorist and insurgent cells, it had by 2015 grown in size to field a full blown terrorist army. This army was composed of not only local Sunni recruits but included thousands of foreign nationals from Europe and other locales formed into mechanized and light infantry units numbering in the tens-of-thousands of fighters, coordinated by a relatively centralized government based in Raqqa, Syria. It is this 2015 manifestation of the Islamic State—still expansionist in nature and having the initiative in much of Syria, Iraq, and even Libya—that the writings in this *SWJ* anthology are focused upon.

For additional reader context, an ISIS sanctuary map created by John Lawrence, an analyst with the Institute for the Study of War (ISW), is being provided below. It provides an end of 2015 snapshot of IS control (in black), attack, and support zones in Syria and Iraq:

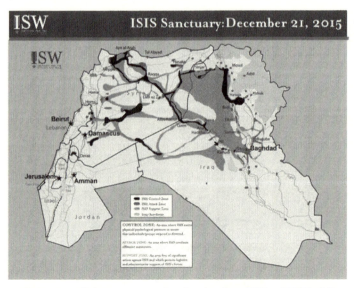

Courtesy of the Institute for the Study of War (ISW) [4]

The IS control, attack, and support zones in Syria and Iraq were marginally changed from June 2015 when an earlier IS sanctuary map was produced by the ISW [5]. Loss of direct IS control (in black) North of Aleppo and East of Baghdad was evident while IS control along the Eastern crescent between Mosul and Hijwa and around Hijwa itself was noticeable as was IS seizure of territory in Southern Syria west of Derra. Where greater territorial expansion is evident is from an earlier January 2015 IS sanctuary map that was produced. The map is provided below and portrays far less direct IS territorial control than the later December 2015 map as the Caliphate would begin to expand and solidify its conquests both deeper into Western Syria and in Central Iraq:

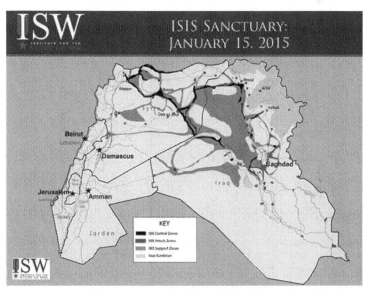

Courtesy of the Institute for the Study of War (ISW) [6]

It is hoped that the reader will find *Jihadi Terrorism, Insurgency, and the Islamic State* a useful addition to the *SWJ* anthologies focusing upon radical Islamist groups. This ongoing series of anthologies will likely see the creation of a follow on anthology of 2016 *SWJ* writings on this important topical area released later in 2017 to get this series more up to date and timely in its publication schedule.

Jihadi Terrorism, Insurgency, and the Islamic State in Context

Chapter 1

Legitimate Deliberate Democracy in Transition: Failure in the Democratization of Iraq by the United States from 2003-2014

Daniel Tyler Brooks

First Published 4 January 2015

"The first principle of republicanism is that the *lex majoris partis* is the fundamental law of every society of individuals of equal rights; to consider the will of the society enounced[i] by the majority of a single vote as sacred as if unanimous is the first of all lessons in importance, yet the last which is thoroughly learnt. This law once disregarded, no other remains but that of force, which ends necessarily in military despotism."—Thomas Jefferson to Alexander von Humboldt, 1817. ME 15:127

"Bear in mind this sacred principle, that though the will of the majority is in all cases to prevail, that will, to be rightful, must be reasonable; that the minority possess their equal rights, which equal laws must protect, and to violate would be oppression."—Thomas Jefferson: 1st Inaugural, 1801. ME 3-318[ii]

Why did Democratization fail in Iraq? This question is important because as the United States continues to maintain a preponderance of power in the world, it is expected that the US will continue to pursue the development of democracies throughout the world in accordance with ideas contained in the Bush Doctrine informed by Democratic Peace Theory (Fiala, 2007, p. 28). Understanding how the democratization of Iraq failed could be instructive to future endeavors towards democratization throughout the world, and provide an understanding of some of the factors that contributed to the rise Islamic State of Iraq and the Levant (ISIL) which may be useful in resolving the current regional crisis. Legitimacy Theory of Deliberate Democracy states that for a government to be considered legitimate,[iii] it must be inclusive of all social groups, and additionally that legitimacy is a prerequisite for a democracy to succeed (Cohen, 1997, p. 69). My specific thesis is that in order for the democracy in Iraq to succeed (Dependent Variable, or DV) post-US occupation, the Iraqi government (GoI) must be inclusive (Independent Variable, or IV) of all interest groups in Iraq, specifically the ethno-sectarian groups that represent the Shia, Sunni Arab, and Sunni Kurdish populations in Iraq. My assumption is as follows: As of August, 2014, Democratization of Iraq has in fact failed in Iraq with the rise of the Islamic State of Iraq and the Levant (ISIL) as a regional power.

The first major decision point for US Policy Makers following the successful defeat of Saddam Hussein's Army was what to do with the defeated Iraqi military forces. Prior to the invasion of Iraq, then Defense Secretary Donald Rumsfeld, along with planners in the Office of Special Plans, developed the occupation strategy of De-Ba'athification upon defeat of all Iraqi military forces (Rathmell, 2005, p. 1021). The logic behind this policy was rooted in the idea that for the sake of legitimacy of democracy in the post Saddam Iraq, the Ba'athist regime had to be totally dismantled from top to bottom (Terrill, 2012, p. XII). The ruling elite in Iraq was predominately Sunni Arab (approximately a 15-20% minority); however, it was in this group of people that the preponderance of the education, institutional knowledge, infrastructure support, political elite, and security forces resided (Stradiotto, 2004, p. 18). Upon disbanding the Iraqi military, police force, and the firing of Ba'athist Party members (the majority of which was made up of Arab Sunnis) in GOI positions, suddenly, the former ruling elite found themselves unemployed (Terrill, 2012, p. 39). As democratic government is a matter of majority rule, Sunnis across Iraq feared that any democratic system would always divide upon sectarian lines with the formerly oppressed Shiite majority (approximately 60-70%) creating a new, oppressive rule in the opposite direction (Eland, 2005, p. 47). Immediately following de-ba'athification and disbanding of the Iraqi police and military, looting and chaos immediately followed (Green, 2009, p. 614).[iv] US ground forces were ill-equipped at maintaining key infrastructure and rule of law in the state of anarchy that was created, and US military commanders had to immediately resort to martial law. Newly unemployed, Arab Sunnis felt disenfranchised by the new democratic political system being developed by the transitional government, and with political and military expertise and military caches at their disposal, the Sunnis turned to the only avenue they felt could resolve their grievances: insurgency (Damluji, 2010, p. 73).

Consequently, when the first Parliamentary elections occurred in 2005, Arab Sunnis, under the influence of tribal sheiks, boycotted the elections, with only 2% of Sunnis in Anbar Province voting compared to a 60-70% Shiite voter turnout throughout Iraq (Mingus, 2012, p. 679). There was a strong sense of cynicism throughout Sunni tribes that the new government was not going to be representative of them because of their status as not only a minority, but also as the previous oppressors of the Shiite who now had the majority power in the new status quo (Mingus, 2012, p. 679). The unfortunate result was a self-fulfilling prophecy, as few Sunni leaders were elected to positions of political power, and the GoI, under the majority rule of the Shiite elected leaders, favored polices that favored Shiite over Sunni ones even in the formation of the Iraqi Constitution, which was not imposed by the US Government and was drafted and was voted on by an Iraqi Constitutional Review Committee (Hamoudi, 2007, p. 1316). As time progressed, blood feuds took hold between Shiite and Arab Sunni communities, leading to an uptick in sectarian violence (Green, 2009, p. 612). The most prominent factions of the Sunni insurgency aligned itself with Al Qaeda in order to obtain external support and funding, creating Al Qaeda in Iraq (AQI) under Abu Musab al-Zarqawi (Damluji, 2010, p. 74). Meanwhile, the most prominent radical Islamic Shiite militias banded together into the Jeesh Al Mahdi (JAM), under Imam Muqtada Al-Sadr and supported externally by Iranian Quds force, in an effort to regionally balance Sunni AQI and fight against what some radical Shiites saw as Western Cultural Imperialism through the US democratization of Iraq (Eland, 2005, p. 47).

The amount of violence in Iraq reached an all-time peak by 2005 (Green, 2009, p. 614). Sunni tribesmen in Anbar Province began to cry out to their sheiks to do something about the rising ethno-sectarian violence. Sunni tribal sheiks affiliated with the 1920s Revolutionary Brigade began coming in conflict with Sunni members of AQI in a turf war over criminal activity.[v] These sheiks reached out to local US army commanders for parlay, and the results was the beginning of the Sunni Awakening (Sahwa) Councils which sought a local grassroots security solution for the sectarian violence (Green, 2009, p. 617). The Sahwa councils gave way to security partnerships between US Commanders and Sunni tribal sheiks, as well as paving the way for the end of Sunni boycotts of future GoI elections. The popular movement was to be the catalyst for an amazing turn around in favor of US COIN efforts, as the ideas generated in Anbar province began to spread among Sunni tribes across Iraq with the implementation of the US Surge advocated by General David Petraeus (Biddle, 2012, p. 10).

By December, 2006, Field Manual 3-24 (Counterinsurgency), which had made significant circulation throughout the Army and Marine Corps in draft form up to this point, was finally published. The work was supervised by a research team headed by none other than General David Petraeus. Gen Petraeus, capitalizing on the success in Anbar Province with the Sahwa councils, decided that the best way to bring the disenfranchised, unemployed, former Ba'athist Sunnis back into the fold was to create Sunni dependency on the local GoI. The primary method was to pay local Sunni sheiks to provide militias at the rate of $300 per guard a month to pull local security on their own villages (Biddle, 2012, p. 12). Even the name of this new force, "Sons of Iraq" (following the name "Concerned Local Citizens") was a master stroke, as it invoked images of patriotism likened to the US Revolutionary War organization, "The Sons of Liberty (Biddle, 2012, p. 12)." In spite of criticisms that the strategy essentially paid AQI leaders "protection" money, the true genius of the technique was that it created a system of accountability among sheiks and local US commanders in the form of using money as leverage, or as US Army doctrine called it, "Money As A Weapon System" (MAAWS) (Petraeus, 2009, Para 1-153).[vi] When an incident of violence occurred in a tribal Sunni sheik's area of responsibility, US commanders simply threatened to cut the pay of the sheik's tribesmen, or to cancel the contract and go to a rival.[vii] Gen Petraeus doubled down on the early indicators of success caused by the SoIz and was able to convince a skeptical US Congress to authorize funding for the US Surge in 2007 (Khedery, 2014, p. 1). With the additional US troops and SoIz, Gen Petraeus focused combat power on securing the local national population in conjunction with the reconstituted Iraqi national army (IA) and police force (IP). The result was a staggering reduction in violence across all of Iraq (Biddle, 2012, p. 12).

By 2009, there was a sense in Iraq that Democracy might actually take hold and work. Iraqi security forces were gaining prestige among the population, rule of law was beginning to provide an alternative to ethno-sectarian violence, and Sunni politicians were getting elected and passing more representative laws and furthering more inclusive policies. Sunni voter turnout percentages exceeded that of the Shiite for the 2010 Parliamentary elections, as the Sunnis learned from their mistake in boycotting the 2005 elections, and supported the more moderate Iraqi National Movement Party led by former Prime Minister Ayad Allawi against the incumbent State of Law Coalition under Prime Minister Nouri Al Maliki (Mingus, 2012, p. 684).[viii] During the formation of the new government, Ayad Allawi had the largest number of seats, with 91 parliamentary seats verses PM Maliki's 89 (Dodge, 2013, p. 248). Prime Minister Nouri Al Maliki refused to step down and stalled the Iraqi parliament into deliberations to form a new government for the nine months that followed.

For several reasons, the US government chose to not pressure PM Maliki to step down, and the result was the disillusionment of the Sunni population who had been willing to give democracy a chance (Khedery, 2014).[ix] I conducted an interview with former US Ambassador to Iraq (2009-2010) Christopher Hill, the current Dean of the Josef Korbel School of International Studies at the University of Denver, and asked him about the various reasons why the US did not pressure PM Maliki to concede to PM Allawi.[x] Dean Hill asserted that it is a mischaracterization of US policy, and his position in particular, to suggest that the US wanted PM Maliki to remain in power following the 2010 election (Hill, 2014). In fact, US leaders in Iraq actively tried to two avenues to effect a democratic change in leadership in Iraq. The first of which was encouraging PM Allawi to petition the smaller Shia parties to achieve majority support against PM Maliki's party (Hill, 2014). Iraqi parliament was not controlled by a two party system, with a total number of seats exceeding 300, resulting in neither PM Allawi nor PM Maliki from having an actual majority; unfortunately, the Iraqi Constitution did not sufficiently describe what method Parliament should pursue in the formation of a government without a single party achieving a solid majority (Hill, 2014). Consequently, the solution generated from within parliament was ad hoc, and the result was that PM Maliki garnered majority support from the smaller Shia controlled parties for his party to retain power while PM Allawi squandered his time and political capital protesting abroad (Hill, 2014). US leaders pursued a second option of attempting to find another leader within Maliki's Dawa party that could relieve PM Maliki, but no suitable alternative existed that could garner the party's political support (Hill, 2014). There was no "top cover" from the Obama Administration to resort to any coercive or incentive methods to entice PM Maliki to concede and retire from politics, and with PM Maliki's confidence in his ability to secure third party support, he had little to reason to feel as though he needed to step down and accept any US offer (Hill, 2014). Ultimately, Former Ambassador Hill suggested that the Iraqi constitution was ill-conceived, and did not provide a sufficient system to protect Sunni rights and give them sufficient influence to effect a peaceful regime change (Hill, 2014).

The Democratization of Iraq failed on 22 December, 2010 when Iraqi parliament approved PM Maliki's new government in spite of PM Allawi's party having the most seats. From the 2010 elections until US forces redeployed from Iraq in December of 2011, PM Maliki successfully expanded the powers in the office of Prime Minister by consolidating control of Ministry of Interior and the Ministry of Defense under the office of the PM, effectively turning the IA and IP into his own praetorian guard (Dodge, 2013, p.7). PM Maliki then returned to a policy of de-ba'athification through purges of Sunni leadership throughout the GoI, looking back to previous US De-ba'athification efforts and Iraqi de-ba'athiciation law as justification for banning prominent Sunni politicians from running for government office and arrested some on charges of sedition (Terrill, 2012, p. 53-54). Additionally, PM Maliki failed to honor promises made to integrate SoIz into government security and civilian jobs. The Sunnis felt betrayed by democracy, and turned back to violence, except this time, instead of turning to AQI, the Sunni turned to an even more radical organization: The Islamic State in Iraq (ISI), led by Abu Bakr al-Baghdadi, a former AQI leader released in 2009 from Bucca following the US decision to turn the prison system over to the GoI (McLaughlin, 2014, p. 1).[xi] The "Democracy" of Iraq no longer maintained legitimacy with the Sunni population.

An alternative hypothesis is that democratization in Iraq failed because Radical Islamist ideologies dominated the local culture of Iraq post de-ba'athfication and that a Western democratic system would never have worked in the country due to being incompatible with regional cultural mores that naturally rebel against Globalization.

My research suggests that this hypothesis is insufficient to suggest a necessary outcome, and ironically, fears among US policy makers regarding Muslim perceptions of Western Cultural Imperialism actually retarded US efforts to establishing a sustainable democratic system in Iraq (Pei, 2003, p. 54). In policy discussions, the Bush Administration made comparisons that Iraq would become a model for democracy throughout the Middle East, much as Post-WWII Germany and Japan had for Europe and Asia (Dobbins, 2006, p. 153). Some academics criticize this comparison due Iraq's lack of a homogenized national identity, and lack of established institutions (Bellin, 2004, p. 598). Regardless of the criticism from academics on the validity of the comparison between post-WWII Japan/Germany with Iraq the historical lessons those two occupations provided were not actually followed in the occupation and democratization of Iraq in several critical ways; the first of which was that in Iraq, the US did not establish the authoritarian leadership of a US Occupation commander as the de facto head interim government (Bellin, 2004, p. 603).[xii] General Douglas MacArthur and General George S. Patton, in Japan and Germany respectfully, served as the provisional head of government for both of their regions until satisfactory democratic constitutions could be established. Both generals additionally had the wisdom to use the privilege of their position to resist the insistences of politicians back in Washington DC to seek revenge against party members from the former regimes. Following the Potsdam Declaration, Gen MacArthur left the Japanese emperor in power, while placing only key members of his staff on trial for war crimes, leaving critical government institutions and infrastructure running (Thompson, 2008, p. 177). General Patton in Bavaria-Germany, who was infamously questioned as to why he did not aggressively pursue de-nazification, compared the US Democratic and Republican parties (choosing one or the other is the political reality of being an American) to the Nazi party (the only political reality of being a German) and implied that not all Nazis were complicit in atrocities (Blumenson, 1974, p. 780-787).[xiii] Gen Patton went on to suggest that these former Nazis were necessary partners in post war development (Blumenson, 1974, p. 780-787).

Even in those days, such pragmatism came at a cost, as General Patton was relieved by General Eisenhower shortly after making his politically chaffing statements (Blumenson, 1974, p. 780-787). Both Gen MacArthur and Gen Patton understood that for democracy to take root in their countries, the first thing that had to be maintained was security and infrastructure, and if that meant keeping the status quo in power for the short term to avoid alienating the key power brokers, so be it. Secondly, came the forming of a constitution and democratic deliberations. In the development of the Japanese constitution, Gen MacArthur had originally hoped that the Japanese people would frame a sufficiently democratic constitution on their own; however, after several drafts continued to mimic the Meiji Constitution of 1889, General MacArthur vetoed the document for the final time, and appointed two US legal officers from his staff to draft the constitution unilaterally and presented it to the Japanese leadership (Bellin, 2004, p. 603). The lesson here is that the occupying commander had to force the democratic system to be followed until it was internalized by the Japanese people. Cultural differences are just a matter of tailoring language and messaging; MacArthur understood how to be a forceful Shogun to the point of imposing democracy, and was revered as if he were a "god" by the Japanese people for it (Manchester, 1978, p. 550-552).

In any discussion about Imperialism and Globalization, there inevitably comes a point where assumptions about mores and relative values of certain Western beliefs concerning the development of other countries become a focal point. There is a sense in the academic literature that Western paternalism and exceptionalism is amoral at best and immoral at worst in the sense that it seeks to impose values of one powerful culture on another less powerful culture (Thompson, 2008, p. 163). While it is understandable when anthropologists (who are very concerned with the appreciation of cultural aesthetics, job security, and the preservation of untainted populations to study) mourn the death of cultures, there is a temptation in the study of comparative Culture, Politics, Religion, Philosophy, etc to suggest that all views are of equal moral validity, a practice commonly referred to as Moral Relativism. The pitfall in this line of reasoning is that in situations like Iraq, decision makers (and the academics who advise them) sometimes place too much value on respecting the culture of the host nation. I recognize this statement is offensive to some and counter-intuitive for most. What must be remembered, above all is that development is not an end unto itself, but instead a means to an end. In the case of post-invasion Iraq, the end was to stabilize the region by ending anarchy and martial law within the state of Iraq, establishing a democratic government, and creating a state that could defend itself militarily from regional external influencers.[xiv] To talk about means without ends, we are not talking about strategy, and the "Build it and they will come" mentality in practice becomes "Build it, and it will become a ruin that testifies to your lack of purpose."[xv]

Within members of the State Department and among some senior commanders, there was a certain cognitive dissonance in that the US shouldn't force Western ideas of how to do democracy on the Iraqis, but instead let them make their own decisions in regard to the development of their own democratic government. There was a lack of self-awareness among decision makers and academics in that the very act of imposing democracy upon a culture that was used to authoritarian regimes, was to impose cultural values (Thompson, 2008, p. 175-176). To pursue a course of action that involves imposing a system of government without imposing the mores that underpin it is to act in an immoral manner by spending blood and national treasure to establish a society that is doomed to fail from the very start. There are several moral underpinnings of a democratic society (verses an authoritarian one) that must be accepted by the governed as a minimum in order for a democratic system to survive and properly function: [1] Inclusive government (all sects can effect change by effective non-violent avenues) (Stradiotto, 2004, p. 8); [2] Tolerance of opposing ideas (freedom of expression) (Cohen, 1997, p. 75); [3] Willingness regularly to change status quo (democracy is dynamic) (Gutmann, 2009, p. 6); [4] Subjugation of public will to majority rule (Brooks, 2009, p. 52); [5] Minority Rights (Brooks, 2009, p. 52); [6] Military subordination to civilians and allegiance to the ideals of the state (rather than the state head);[xvi] [7] Fair Enforcement of Rule of Law ("blind" justice) (Moon, 2009, p. 121); [8] Right to Property (Locke, 1690; Chap V-24); and [9] Separation of church and state.[xvii]

Systematically, these mores have to be embedded into the charter (or Constitution) of a democratic country, and maintained by a system of checks and balances (Moon, 2009, p. 121). The residual of these mores suggests a system of democracy that is not actually democracy, but instead a Constitutional Republic.[xviii] Additionally, these values must be reinforced by whatever instruction is provided by the occupying nation through advisement, or imposition when the "correct" conclusion isn't drawn by the host nation partner on their own accord (Bellin, 2004, p. 606).[xix] Failure to do so, however morally reprehensible the imposition of values on another may seem, is to build a democracy on a foundation of sand. The Founding Fathers of the United States Government in their Enlightenment philosophy, were successful in distilling the justification for democracy into a set of three universal principles: "Life, Liberty, and the Pursuit of Happiness."[xx] If you had asked a random Iraqi on the street what he really cares about, it generally comes down to "I want to be able to make a decent living for my family, and I want my children to be safe and happy." This common ground between Westerners and Iraqi citizens was where the strategy of getting the Iraqi population to internalize Western mores should have begun.

There is a Western moralist assumption, and one may call it Western arrogance, but explicitly stated, the Western assumption is that cultures that infringe on individual liberty and human rights any more than is necessary to prevent anarchy are immoral.[xxi] The assumption may be challenged, but the challenger must identify a more palliative, practical moral alternative assumption before asserting alternative moral imperatives.[xxii] Consequently, to whatever extent possible, when it aligns with Western national interests, the West should seek to influence the cultural mores of states and societies that are historically oppressive, and the United States should seek to ensure that cultural backings of tyranny are neutralized. Much to the dismay of the anthropologists who may see the assimilation of tribal and national cultures into a Western ideal as a bad thing, to the extent that it creates peace, the imposition of Western values on "Less Developed" cultures (to the extent that they are not Westernized) is worth the cost. The word "impose" has a negative connotation in the context of cultural imperialism, but if the democratization of Germany and Japan made the world safer by gutting their need and desire to seek world domination, all while advancing human rights and freedom within those countries, then whatever "evil" is in the slaying of their previous nationalist leanings is worth whatever weight the act adds on the Western collective conscience. In Japan, the successful democratization of the country was in large part due to the imposition of democracy under the watchful, and benevolent eye of the totalitarian leadership of the Supreme Commander of Allied Powers (SCAP), General Douglas MacArthur (Stradiotto, 2004, p. 10). Likewise, dismantling sectarianism in Iraq, or at least creating a system that reigns it in or marginalizes it through tribal inclusion in non-violent government institutions, is worth the imposition of Western mores on tribal identities and traditions. One method of the imposition could have been to create a House of Commons and a House of Sheiks (or House of Lords) as a bicameral legislature when the parliamentary system was designed with the creation of the Iraqi Constitution, and until mores were internalized, the US could have maintained oversight with a "SCAP" in place with veto power to be used in extreme cases.

In Iraq, does United States Imperialism make the world any better off than the forms of Imperialism that preceded it? Insofar is as US foreign policy advances individual liberty and human rights throughout the world in its pursuit of national interests by using democratization where applicable, the answer is yes. Whether or not the invasion of Iraq was in US National interests or the Middle Eastern Regional interests is a question for a different article, but the point is that once the deed was done and Saddam was overthrown, democratization in the aftermath was in the best interests of regional and international peace strategy for the US.[xxiii] By democratization, a stable Republic would have been sufficient, as long as all sectarian groups maintained an ability to resolve grievances and effect legislative change. An ideal measure of effective governance in the case of Iraq would have been once popular vote resulted in a peaceful regime change in favor of minority sects; e.g. the measure for Iraq was the 2010 elections.

Does the United States always advance individual liberty and human rights in the pursuit of its national interests? Democratization is part of the solution to questions of US moral superiority in Imperialist and Globalization models, not part of the problem. Historically, US Imperialist policies have on occasion preferred pro-US dictatorships over Anti-US democracies in the pursuit of national interest, which, empirically, has the power to potentially overthrow Democratic Peace Theory[xxiv] as a sound predictive model. However, in and of itself, this historical evidence is insufficient to damage the justification of the US using democratization as a sound strategy for promoting human rights in its pursuit of global primacy and hegemony.[xxv] In its moral application for the sake of world stability, the Bush Doctrine, when examined as an imperialist doctrine, should have been advanced as more of a political and economic endeavor rather than military one. Military imperialism is not a sound strategy for any great power in a world of nuclear proliferation, and is certainly not a moral one regardless of intentions when viewed with an eye toward the historical military endeavors of world domination.[xxvi] US influence of Globalization and the transition from global institutions and societies to a future global democratic government should be the strategic aims of the Bush Doctrine in application by the US. Imperialism is no more evil than a kitchen knife is evil; it is how imperialism is pursued and what end state the individual using it as a strategy has as the ultimate objective that can be considered just or unjust. The Cold War of the 21st century is a battle between three things: 1. Control over the structure of a World Government emerging out of International institutions, 2. Political Influencers of said emerging world government, and 3. Ideologies that threaten to undo emerging world government by pushing the world back towards international anarchy.

In conclusion, the democratization of Iraq failed for two critical reasons: US failure to legitimize the democratic government with the Sunni Arab population of Iraq, and US failure to impose forcefully western cultural mores that are prerequisites for deliberate democracy. Had the United States taken a more pragmatic approach to maintaining the Sunni status quo in the short term following the defeat of Saddam's army, the US could have prevented the Sunni insurgency from arising in the form of AQI. Additionally, US failure to force Iraqi leadership to follow the Iraqi constitution in regard to the 2010 election doomed the government to lose the legitimacy the US had fought hard to secure following the Sunni awakening and surge. Had the US government appointed a "SCAP" like in post-WWII Japan, with the power to oversee and have final editorial and veto power over the Iraqi constitution and its enforcement, the democratization of Iraq may have succeeded given the time and patience required for Iraqis to internalize democratic mores. If the timeline seems open ended, one should consider instead the course of action that was actually taken in Iraq; it has yet to be seen exactly how many years the US spends in the Iraq region before the current conflict is resolved. Did the US ever even have such a man with the wisdom and civic virtue necessary to perform such a task in the manner of General Douglas MacArthur? Perhaps General David Petraeus could have provided the appropriate leadership had he been appointed to such a position.

The Arab Spring erupted not long after US withdrawal to Kuwait in December of 2011, and revolutions throughout the Middle East further destabilized authoritarian governments in places like Libya and Syria. Without strong US leadership in response to these popular uprisings, power vacuums developed, and Syria became a haven for Al Baghdadi's Islamic State to seize territory, and gain legitimacy among Sunnis in Iraq who are seeking a means of autonomy from the failed democracy in Iraq. With Al Baghdadi's self-appointment as caliph and successful seizure of territory across the Middle East, the Islamic State in Iraq and the Levant (ISIL) is emerging as a power competing for legitimacy in the region. While understanding the events that gave rise to this new "state" is informative for understanding its motives and aspirations, what we don't know now is to what extent the structure of the Iraqi government contained in the Iraqi Constitution has contributed to the creation of ISIL and what the past has to offer in regard to how US policy should address the emerging threat of ISIL. Even now, as General Austin discusses attempting to create a new Sahwa in Anbar province as a strategy against ISIL, US policy makers must consider how the breach of trust between the US/GoI and the Anbar Sunnis following the disbanding of the SoIz and the 2010 election presents a formidable challenge to regaining the social capital necessary to replicate the success of the Sahwa (Barnes, 2014). Additionally, policy makers must consider how the 2006 Sahwa also benefited from General David Petraeus' Surge Campaign, which is currently not an option for the battle with ISIL under President Obama's "No boots on the ground" policy. As the US begins another long conflict in the Middle East, perhaps if we wish to continue the Bush Doctrine's method of democratization under the leadership of the Obama administration, we must consider what went wrong in the last application, verses perhaps learning the wrong lessons by assuming that the democratization of Iraq was doomed from the outset. Otherwise, any half measures we take in dealing with this threat may simply create the next one.

Chapter 2

Confusing a "Revolution" with "Terrorism"

Eric C. Anderson

First Published 19 January 2015

That the world should be so simple Washington could "bin" offshore challenges in a small set of categories that expedite planning and policy options. The Cold War dichotomy made life in the Pentagon a much simpler affair. You were either "communist" or you were not. In the wake of Gorbechev's failure, you were a "rogue" state, or not. Osama Bin Laden only served to further add a category, "terrorist," or not. This dichotomous sorting process made it relatively easy to explain policy options to the American electorate and direct the expenditure of taxpayer blood and treasure. Iraq, "rouge," Afghanistan and all things al-Qaeda "terrorism." Respond appropriately. Iraq meant deployment of large conventional force and time spent with boots on the ground. Afghanistan and al-Qaeda, pin-point targeting and late night visits to remote locales with black helicopters and US Special Forces. But what happens when the problem does not fit into the bins?

Welcome to the Islamic State of Iraq and Syria (ISIS), otherwise known as the Islamic State of Iraq and the Levant (ISIL) or the Islamic State.[i] The new caliphate—Washington's latest "terrorist." Pull out the drones, tag the troops who can arrive without drawing attention, and fly 2,700 sorties in 30 days. Mission achieved. Well, maybe not.

What happens when your "terrorist" has 30,000 armed recruits, is occupying territory the size of West Virginia and has proclaimed an ideology that includes establishing a formal government with an identified constituency and offers a school curriculum? What does it mean when they control the regional wheat supply, are poised to do the same with fresh water, and essentially own the electric power grid? Are they still "terrorists"? Webster might have thoughts to the contrary. I certainly do.

The ability to challenge an existing regime with an organized armed force, focused on sustained operations, occupying terrain and imposing a new government might be more appropriately declared a "revolution." And requires a very different response than rooting out "terrorists." Ask King George. Ask Louie the 16th. Ask Batista. Ask the former Shah of Iran.

Revolutions are hard. They do not succumb to link-analysis—find your individual adversaries via who they communicate with—or precision strike. A movement with thousands of men and women under arms is not terrorism that can be rooted out by flying remote control missions with armed, unmanned airframes from Nevada or Idaho. This requires a "presence," and not one that is "rented"—see the Hessians—but rather is ready for a sustained engagement that demonstrates a willingness to die in the name of preserving a competing ideology. Welcome to Iraq and Syria. Welcome to Yemen and Mali. Welcome to Somalia and Nigeria. It appears we are on the cusp of a brave new world that will make your skin crawl unless medieval judicial standards were a ready practice in the adjacent neighborhood. And Washington is seemingly unwilling to embrace this new reality.

Not that one can blame decision makers for seeking the most cognitively straightforward assessment. The human mind is, in most cases, attuned to avoiding complexity and employing proven solutions. We seek familiar patterns and recoil when things deviate from the expected. Newspapers call this "headlines." In the Intelligence

Community it is called "indications and warning," a means of preparing the policy maker or war fighter for events that might not turn out as desired. Welcome to ISIS.

That is to say, we are witnessing an evolution in the threat environment confronting the U.S. Intelligence Community, policy makers, and war fighters. The terrorism-focus that largely predominated in our campaign against al-Qaeda, the Taliban and Sunni uprisings in Iraq is being outpaced by a transition in many of these organizations' *modus operandi*. In the case of certain al-Qaeda elements—particularly al-Qaeda on the Arab Peninsula, al-Qaeda in the Islamic Maghreb, al-Shabaab, and the Islamic State of Iraq and Syria. In each of these cases the primary focus no longer appears random acts of terror intended to disseminate a message that otherwise might be ignored or forgotten. These groups, and very specifically ISIS, have stepped from terrorism into revolutionary movements. That is to say, they are busily engaged in the process of seizing territory, establishing a form of governance, implementing a new ideology, and brutally putting an end to opposition and the old regime.

One could argue we are witnessing a return to the French Revolution—a violent uprising that may give way to Robespierre's "Reign of Terror"—in this case the imposition of a draconian version of Sharia law. Just as the monarchies of Europe were not prepared for the "new" France, despite having witnessed the American colonialists break with Great Britain, we now contend the U.S. National Security apparatus is not recognizing the implications of powerful entities willing to declare the rise of a new caliphate. This is a problem—unlike terrorism—that cannot be addressed with the intellectual tools or kinetic options that seemingly succeeded in decapitating Bin Laden's vision for al-Qaeda.

To explain the depth of this problem and facilitate an understanding of the type of organizations emerging in this new threat environment, this text will focus on the rise of ISIS by outlining the events that gave rise to its formation, examining its ideology and governance strategy, and then turning to a consideration of its potential courses of action. In accomplishing that task we also hope to lay out the implications for the

U.S. intelligence, policy, and war fighting communities. Ultimately, the goal is to make clear we are witnessing the rise of new non-state actors who appear to have little interest in observing the dictates of, or even maintaining, the Westphalian system that shaped existing international mores and modes of behavior.

A Brave New World?

The U.S. national security apparatus periodically needs a call to heed the sea changes taking place within the Westphalian "system." In the opening round of the Cold War it was George Kennan's long cable from Moscow, subsequently published under a pseudonym in *Foreign Affairs*. Kennan's argument that: "The possibilities for American policy are by no means limited to holding the line and hoping for the best. It is entirely possible for the United States to influence by its actions the internal developments, both within Russia and throughout the international Communist movement…" gave rise to the policy of "containment" and led to a U.S. Intelligence Community, Defense Department and national security strategy suited to the perceived greatest danger—Moscow's global ambitions.[ii]

Kennan's ideas had greater staying power than even the Union of Soviet Socialist Republics—the term "containment" periodically appears in Chinese literature evaluating Washington's approach to Beijing's reappearance on the global stage—but was poorly suited for the world that emerged during the 1990s. So, seemingly, was the U.S. national security collective. The Intelligence Community shed employees and went in search of a mission; the Defense Department worried a threat of suffering deep budget cuts; and, politicians sought to realize a "peace dividend" in the face of an apparently much more benign threat environment. Bin Laden and al-Qaeda would bring an end to that perceived erosion in attention, capabilities and policymaker imagination.

Arguably, the next fundamentally formulative document for the national security community as a whole was the *9-11 Commission Report*. In a document totaling 585 pages, the report's authors called for a new national security strategy, a revision of the Intelligence Community's operating procedures—to include establishing a Director of National Intelligence—and a press for the policy makers to seek greater unity in their efforts. Broad ambitions, but for a nation engaged in a Global War on Terror," a clarion call that resulted in significant changes.

The *9-11 Commission Report*, in many senses as aspirational as Kennan's work, created a national security apparatus that seemed to be remarkably adept at defeating terrorists before they could execute attacks on the homeland. It also appeared to lend cohesion to National Security Council deliberations that facilitated a "whole of government" approach to addressing al-Qaeda and other untoward actors who came to the fore in Afghanistan and Iraq. What it did not do, however, is prepare the Intelligence Community, policy makers, or war fighter for the emergence of non-state revolutionary entities with the ability to seize large swaths of territory—think of ISIS in Syria and Iraq or AQIM in Mali.

This article will attempt to start that conversation. While I harbor no delusion of being as smart as George Kennan nor as broadly staffed or experienced as the 9-11 Commission, it now is time to begin the intellectual transition away from the War on Terrorism and turn to the threat of increasingly powerful non-state actors that could begin redrawing national boundaries and challenge the international norms that have prevented World War III. The last line is not in jest—given the religious identification of these non-state revolutionaries, there is a very real possibility of igniting a conflict that pits Islam against any other competing religion. A recipe for disaster.

What is Terrorism?

We are perhaps best served by starting with what is terrorism. Sadly, even in the wake of spending over a decade battling "terrorism" there is no agreed upon definition. Suffice it to say, at one point the Intelligence Community even classified its definition and refused to share with the general public. So here's what one will find in explaining the phenomenon we have been battling since the anarchists started their campaign at the end of the 19th century. Given the consequences of Arch Duke Ferdinand's assassination, it should not be surprising the first official—that is outside a dictionary—definition appeared in Article 1.1 of the League of Nations' 1937 Convention for the Prevention and Punishment of Terrorism. In that document, the collected wise men declared "acts of terrorism" were "criminal acts directed against a State and intended or calculated to create a state of terror in the minds of particular persons or a group of persons or the general public."[iii] What's missing here, of course, is why the act of terror was committed in the first place.

This is no minor oversight. As more than one author has noted, "one man's terrorist is another's revolutionary." Or, as attorneys pithily remark, good luck in separating "terrorist organizations" from "liberation movements." Please recall that Osama Bin Laden and the nascent Taliban were celebrated mujahedeen—freedom fighters—before they launched an assault on the West for the perceived endless infidel presence in the home of Mecca and Medina. In any case, the Soviet Union spent a decade attempting to crush "Charlie Wilson's War." A just campaign from Washington's perspective, a terrorist nightmare according to Moscow. This suggests a requirement for further refinement of our terms.

In 1991, Edward Luttwak, then the strategy chair at the Georgetown Center for Strategic and International Studies, and Stuart Koehl, a professional military analyst, jointly published *The Dictionary of Modern War: A Guide to the Ideas, Institutions and Weapons of Modern Military Power*. A hefty tome, weighing in at nearly 700 pages, the book is an effort to precisely define the history, issues, and tools confronting Washington and the Western world. These two prestigious authors, however, apparently have difficulty in discerning the difference between a terrorist and revolutionary. Here's their definition of "terrorism:"

> The use of violence against civilians by covert or clandestine organizations for political purposes.... By bombings, shootings, kidnappings, hijacking, and assassinations, terrorists seek to lower public morale, reduce confidence in official authorities and institutions, obtain concessions, and force governments into acts of repression which they hope will lead to a popular *revolt*.[iv]

Helpful, in that we are led to believe this is not a state-actor or uniformed force, but a bit confounding in that the term *revolt* inherently implies revolution, and the targets, "official authorities and institutions" are two of the three areas Chalmers Johnson—as we shall see—constitute the type of change a revolutionary is intent on accomplishing.

Back to the United Nations. In 2002, that body set about drafting the *Comprehensive Convention on International Terrorism*. Accordingly, the diplomats suggested—they have still not agreed in a vote—that terrorism is identified when:

1. Any person commits an offence within the meaning of this Convention if that person, by any means, unlawfully and intentionally, causes:
(a) Death or serious bodily injury to any person; or
(b) Serious damage to public or private property, including a place of public use, a state or government facility, a public transportation system, an infrastructure facility or the environment; or
(c) Damage to property, places, facilities, or systems referred to in paragraph 1 (b) of this article, resulting or likely to result in major economic loss, when the purpose of the conduct, by its nature or context, is to intimidate a population, or to compel a government or an international organization to do or abstain from doing any act.

Again, the problem is how to discern between the terrorist and the revolutionary, and who gets to make that decision. Which drives us forward to 2004. Here we find the United Nations Security Council engaged in a semantic waltz that comes up with the following word play in Resolution 1566:

> Criminal acts, including against civilians, committed with the intent to cause death or serious bodily injury, or taking of hostages, with the purpose to provoke a state of terror in the general public or in a group of persons or particular persons, intimidate a population or compel a government or an international organization to do or to abstain from doing any act, which constitute offences within the scope of and as defined in the international conventions and protocols relating to terrorism, are under no circumstances justifiable by considerations of a political, philosophical, ideological, racial, ethnic, religious or other similar nature.

A vague hand wave at attempting to categorize particular forms of activity as outside the realm of politically acceptable…so long as you are a member of the existing governmental structure and frown upon upstarts who would replace the status quo with a different version of governance. Then revolution becomes a "criminal act." Washington, as one might suspect, has had its own problems in defining terrorism. Here is the official Federal Bureau of Investigations solution:

> 18 U.S.C. § 2331 defines "international terrorism" for purposes of Chapter 113B of the Code, entitled "Terrorism:" International terrorism means activities with the following three characteristics:
> - Involve violent acts or acts dangerous to human life that violate federal or state law
> - Appear to be intended (i) to intimidate or coerce a civilian population; (ii) to influence the policy of a government by intimidation or coercion; or (iii) to affect the conduct of a government by mass destruction, assassination, or kidnapping
> - Occur primarily outside the territorial jurisdiction of the U.S., or transcend national boundaries in terms of the means by which they are accomplished, the persons they appear intended to

intimidate or coerce, or the locale in which their perpetrators operate or seek asylum

And then we have the Department of Defense:

The calculated use of unlawful violence or threat of unlawful violence to inculcate fear; intended to coerce or to intimidate governments or societies in the pursuit of goals that are generally political, religious, or ideological.

Followed by the State Department—which buries this in an annex to its annual report on terrorism:

Section 2656f(d) of Title 22 of the United States Code defines certain key terms used in Section 2656f(a) as follows:
(1) The term "international terrorism" means terrorism involving citizens or the territory of more than one country;
(2) The term "terrorism" means premeditated, politically motivated violence perpetrated against non-combatant targets by subnational groups or clandestine agents; and
(3) The term "terrorist group" means any group practicing, or which has significant subgroups which practice, international terrorism.

Not satisfied with this collection of definitions—but with a nod of approval for the Department of Defense approach—in his seminal text, *Inside Terrorism,* Bruce Hoffman offers his own effort at delineating the difference between such activity and criminal or revolutionary movements. To that end, Hoffman argues terrorism can be identified through five key attributes:

1. Terrorism is political in aims and motives
2. Terrorism is violent or threatens violence
3. Terrorism is designed to have far-reaching psychological repercussions

4. Terrorism is conducted by an organization with an identifiable chain of command or cell structure—whose members wear no uniform or insignia
5. Terrorism is perpetuated by a subnational group or non-state entity[v]

Hoffman goes on to contend we can now define terrorism as "the deliberate creation and exploitation of fear through violence or the threat of violence." And, he seeks to refine the definition by contending terrorists seek to have "psychological effects beyond the immediate victim," "[one] designed to create power where there is none," or, he continues to "consolidate power where there is very little."[vi]

The bottom line, any organization that engages in armed revolt against an existing regime can almost automatically be characterized as a terrorist plot. But is that helpful? Well if one wants to circumvent or avoid the War Powers Act this is good stuff. Congressional blessing for employment of the Department of Defense's impressive capabilities is typically hard to acquire. The last official United States government declaration of war against a foreign power took place in 1942. There has been subsequent Congressional approval of the use of force—recall the 1964 Gulf of Tonkin Resolution or the January 1991 Congressional vote approving military action against Saddam Hussein. But Bin Laden and al-Qaeda created a new problem, how to go to war with a non-state actor? The solution was the Authorization for Use of Military Force (AUMF), passed as Senate Joint Resolution 23 by the United States Congress on 14 September 2001.

There is little argument this was an expedient and widely accepted means of meeting an immediate threat. The bill passed in the House of Representatives with 420 ayes, 1 nay and 10 not voting. The Senate was equally cooperative, 98 ayes, 0 nays, 2 present/not voting. Very similar legislation was rolled out for the subsequent 2003 attack on Iraq. Introduced in Congress on 2 October 2002, in conjunction with the Administration's proposals, House Joint Resolution 114 passed in the lower chamber by a vote of 296-133, and passed in the Senate by a vote of 77-23. The White House had a powerful political tool in its kit and was unlikely to abandon the option, regardless of comments made on the campaign trail.

Which Begs the Question—What is a Revolution?

But what happens if you are confronting a revolution. Let's return for a moment to the issue of cognitive processing. Depending on one's education and upbringing—culture, entertainment, national myths, religion—terms take on mental images that are hard to eradicate or override. Ask Americans about terrorism, and visions of the collapsing Twin Towers in New York flash through the psyche. Ask them about revolution, and a picture of George Washington or Thomas Jefferson pass through the synopsis. For intelligence analysts, this "background" tends to engender "mirror imaging" or flash evaluations. No need to ponder through this, "I know what 'terrorism' is and is not." In the same vein, "I know what a 'revolution' is and is not." Think, however, if you were born and raised in Cuba after Castro came to power. Now what is a revolution? Take the same perspective and apply it to an Iranian born and raised after 1979. What is a revolution? What does it accomplish? Who are the heroes?

This renders important the definition of "revolution" for academics, intelligence analysts, policy makers, and war fighters who must motivate forces in dangers' way. Academics want an "ivory tower" value-free term. Intelligence analysts should seek the same, but are often influenced by their audience—policy—to come up with something more communicative to the desired reader. (Analysts seek approval from the audience, just like novelists.) And the war-fighter wants visions of George Washington or Simon Bolivar. So what do we get?

Semantically, we run into the same problem apparent during an investigation of what constitutes terrorism. Thomas Jefferson was famous for writing to James Madison, that, "I hold it that a little rebellion now and then is a good thing, and as necessary in the political world as storms in the physical." Jefferson, however, does not spell out what that rebellion would look like. Interestingly, Alexis De Tocqueville is equally vague in *Democracy in America*. The closest he comes is in Volume Three of the tome, when the following appears:

> Every revolution enlarges the ambition of men. That is above all true of the revolution that overturns an aristocracy. …. In this first exaltation of triumph, nothing seems impossible to anyone. Not only do desires have no bounds, but the power to satisfy them has almost none. In the midst of this general and sudden renovation of customs and laws, in this confusion of all men and all rules, citizens raise themselves and fall with unheard of rapidity; and power passes so quickly from hand to hand that no one must despair of seizing it in his turn.[vii]

This at least offers hint at the strum and angst associated with revolution, but I highlight the fact De Tocqueville is particularly focused on the toppling of the *ancien regime* and suggests the new would-be rulers are more than a bit chaotic in their bid to establish a new order. This chaos is suggestive of an opposition that is not completely in synch on their ambitions or end state. Also of note, De Tocqueville free admits such revolutions can come the barrel of a gun and may not always end in a democracy—leading one to suspect he is looking back on the French revolution as much as he is discussing the outcome of George Washington's efforts.

A more contemporary academic effort to parse out "revolution" begins in 1962 with a paper published in *Political Science Quarterly*. Titled "Revolution: A Redefinition," the author, Peter Amann, opens with the admission, "There is no 'true' definition of an abstraction"—in this case "revolution."[viii] Nonetheless, this is a political scientist at work, so Amann makes a stab at wrestling with the alligator. His first step is to set forth conditions for a revolution—starting with a sovereign state, "a political organization exercising, or able to exercise, a monopoly of armed force, justice and administration over a given area and population. Add to that, he continues, the argument this monopoly on power "depends largely, not on the consent of the governed, but on their habit of obedience, whatever its motive."[ix] So we have moved beyond De Tocqueville's focus on aristocracy and can now take aim at all forms of the governmental status quo. And arrive at a definition of revolution, "a breakdown, momentary or prolonged, of the state's monopoly of power, usually accompanied by a lessening of the habit of obedience." As for the duration of such events, "revolution prevails when the state's monopoly of power is effectively challenged and persists until a monopoly of power is re-established."[x]

I hasten to point out at this stage Amann makes no qualifications concerning the revolutionaries' attire (recall Hoffman's definition of "terrorism" included an assumption such groups would be without uniform) nor does he spell out or subscribe particular tactics to a revolution. Rather Amann declares the revolutionaries may vary from small groups to a large element of the population and that the "most obvious hallmark" of their deserving the title is the exercise of military force.[xi] Amann does not spell out what constitutes "military force." Is it shooting at Red Coats from behind stone walls? Is it fighting Batista from the hills and jungle? Or is it direct symmetric contact with the armed forces protecting the status quo? All tactics are fair game in such a situation—but one thing is clear, the revolutionaries are seeking to create fear and exploit same by operating in an environment where there is little to no power, or they would already be out of business. So perhaps Hoffman has not saved us with his definition of "terrorism," as Amann's "revolution" looks remarkably like the same phenomena.

So let's move forward with the conversation, turning now to Chalmers Johnson's text, *Revolution and the Social System*. As a political scientist, Johnson sought to define revolution as change, effected by use of violence, to a government, regime, or society.[xii] (Back to Tocqueville.) The phraseology is important here. As a subsequent scholar explains, "society" is community collective consciousness concerning means of cohesion, "regime" is the existing political power arrangement—from constitutional to monarchy—and "government" is the bureaucratic institutions used to exercise political power. More importantly for our conversation, "violence" is differentiated from "force." "Violence," we are told, is force "used with unnecessary intensity, unpredictability, and usually destructively."[xiii] Now Johnson's definition of "revolution" takes on a much broader scope, particularly as to Hoffman's contention that "terrorism" is identified by the "creation and exploitation of fear through violence or the threat of violence." Seems that Johnson's "revolutionaries" do exactly the same thing.

Revolution and the Social System becomes, arguably, more helpful in separating "terrorism" from "revolution" in Johnson's six typologies of a revolt. The first, *Jacquerie*, finds the peasants massed outside the walls with torches and pitchforks at the ready.[xiv] In this form of revolution, Johnson argues, the mass is acting in the name of the church and king with the intent of removing local or national elites—i.e., the Taliban. The second, *Millenarian Rebellion*, trods down a similar path, but adds an inspirational leader with a utopian dream—think Mullah Omar, Osama Bin Laden or al-Baghdadi.[xv] The third type, *Anarchistic Rebellion*, is a reactionary response to change, harkening back to the "good old days."[xvi] Potentially, the Salafist movement in Egypt.

Which brings us to Johnson's fourth "revolution" typology, *Jacobin Communist*. This he defines as: "A sweeping fundamental change in political organization, social structure, economic property control and the predominant myth of social order, thus indicating a major break in the continuity of development."[xvii] In his 1966 essay, "Theories of Revolutions," Lawrence Stone decrees this is a "very rare" phenomenon that can only occur within "a highly centralized state with good communications and a large capital city, and its target is government, regime and society."[xviii] Rare, perhaps in 1966, but what we have now watched, at least transitorily, occur in Afghanistan, Egypt, Iran, Iraq, Syria, and possibly Tunisia. The same may be underway in Nigeria and Yemen. The problem here, of course, is that Chalmers Johnson's label—*Jacobin Communist*—pulls the analyst off target. We mirror image Marx, not the Prophet Mohammed.

Type five is the *Conspiratorial Coup d'Etat*.[xix] This falls in the realm of work done by Edward Luttwak, who penned *Coup d'État: A Practical Handbook*.[xx] It only falls into the "revolutionary" category as such events may cause fundamental change in society, regime and government. Consider, for instance, Qaddafi coming to power in Libya or Saddam Hussein taking the reins in Baghdad. Finally, Johnson holds out for *Militarized Mass Insurrection*. In this case we are looking for a guerilla war founded on an ideology not military strategy, as the revolutionaries are dependent upon popular support and solace.[xxi] Here we find examples like Mao in China, potentially the Muslim Brotherhood in Egypt, and Hezbollah in Lebanon.

All of which is to say, Chalmers Johnson offers a clearer perspective on what might be considered a revolution and overlays the academic's heuristic devices, but then opens the door to pulling the ISIS campaign into his fourth typology. Leaving us again to beg for a definition of "revolution" that steps clearly outside the boundaries of "terrorism.

The next significant academic attempt at this problem comes in 1972, when Isaac Kraminick publishes "Reflections on Revolution: Definitions and Explanation in Recent Scholarship." Kraminick opens his discussion on the subject with the apt warning: "There are few concepts over which there has been so much contention as that of revolution...Few things are so ambiguous."[xxii] That admonition laid before the reader, Kraminick plunges in, coming away with what appears to be a refined definition of the central concept. His first stab comes in the form of guiding historians seeking to separate "simple" internal social strife from a sea change. To that end, he suggests we consider a revolution as something with, "a particular direction and purposive orientation to the change; a novel structuring of society, a new and millennial order must be sought."[xxiii] As examples he offers the "great historical revolutions"—English, French, Russian—and modern—China and Cuba. He also notes "revolution is a cultural phenomenon involving fundamental changes in norms and values."[xxiv] This looks mightily like what we are seeing with the ISIS campaign, a transition from the sectarian, nondenominational "liberal democracy" in Iraq or Assad's dictatorship in Syria, to a secular regime guided a council seeking to meet the dictates of the *Koran* as they understand the words of the Prophet.

Kraminick, however, is not finished, six pages later, he adds further elucidation. Focusing on the political elements within such a sea change he argues, "Revolutions are the substitution of one governing elite for another….Revolution is thus an event primarily found in the political arena; governments, elites, and the masses are the players and power is the fruit of victory."[xxv] We would note he does not restrict the players to uniformed forces or other established governments or states. Rather, that these are simply potential participants. ISIS has its own elite, al-Baghdadi, a spiritual head with a PhD in political science, and a number of formerly well-placed Baathist party members who are suspected of serving to guide the military campaign. As for the masses, 30,000 armed militants did not only come from the upper crust of Iraqi or Syrian society—to say nothing of the foreign fighters who have drifted in from Europe and even the United States.

Not surprisingly, Kraminick steers us back to that now-departed seer, Samuel Huntington. Drawing upon Huntington's *Political Order in Changing Societies,* Kraminick offers the following quote from the Harvard professor:

> A full-scale revolution involves the destruction of the old political institutions and patterns of legitimacy, the mobilization of new groups into politics, the redefinition of the political community, the acceptance of new political vales and new concepts of political legitimacy, the conquest of power by a new, more dynamic political elite, and the creation of new and stronger political institutions.[xxvi]

Given this definition, it is easy to argue there was no revolution when Saddam was removed from office. Instead, the existing elite, to use a very broad sense of the term, assumed governmental functions and went about practicing politics in a manner Saddam would have surely recognized. ISIS threatens to undo all of that and bring in a new crop of leaders, cultural values, and a very different justification for recognizing its political legitimacy.

Let's move on by returning to Luttwak and Koehl's *Dictionary of Modern War*. While they do not provide an explicit definition of "revolution," the two scholars make this observation on what they find to be "revolutionary war:"

> Armed conflict between a government and opposing forces, wherein the latter rely mainly on guerrilla warfare and subversion rather than formal warfare. The revolutionary side operates by establishing a rival state structure which embodies a political ideology, and which is intended to replace the existing order….the covert 'administration' collects taxes, conscripts, and information—all of which can be extracted from the population even if the government is in apparent military control of the area in question. These resources are supplied to the guerrilla arm, which strives to erode the government's control and undermine its prestige. That in turn facilitates subversion (propaganda + terror) to extend the reach of the covert administration, which sustains the guerrilla.[xxvii]

This is ISIS in practice as we know it today. And raises a vexing observation. Following this definition of "revolutionary war," one is drawn to conclude terrorism is a tactic employed by revolutionaries, it does not, *ipso facto*, make them terrorists.

This conversation is briefly resumed in 1996, when Clifton Kroeber publishes an essay titled, "Theory and History of Revolution." Plowing through a mountain of academic writing on the subject, he comes to the conclusion most definitions have employed the following three terms: "brief," "violent," and "successful."[xxviii] (It seems losing revolutionaries are not allowed retain the honorific adjective in histories written on their efforts—was Che Guevara a "terrorist" or a "revolutionary"? Depends on if you are asking Hollywood or Washington.) One can argue if "brief" is truly a fitting term—recall our own revolution took eight years and Mao was on the road much longer than that—nonetheless, we are on to something here, particularly the catch phrase "violent." In any case, Kroeber steers us to a much simpler definition with few modifiers or semantic qualifications. "Revolution and revolutions," he argues, "signify all demands, suggestions, and attempts at radical change—and, in addition, all unplanned changes equally basic." He goes on to observe, "Revolutions signify drastic, fundamental changes in their full depth, duration, and complexity."[xxix] Now we have arrived at the situation in Iraq and Syria as ISIS pushes toward Baghdad.

Finally, a nod to the most recent attempt to separate revolution from terrorism. The most recent version of the US Army's Field Manual 3-24, "Insurgencies and Countering Insurgencies," seeks to avoid this definitional nightmare by instead focusing on "irregular warfare," "a violent struggle among state and non-state actors for legitimacy and influence over the relevant population(s)." As an "insurgency," it is described as "a struggle for control and influence, generally from a position of relative weakness, outside existing state institutions."[xxx] One could contend this is just intricate verbal sparring, but there is a point to be taken from these two definitions, neither implies a fundamental change in regime, society or government within the conflict. But even the US Army cannot avoid eventually pigeonholing "revolution." In Chapter Four of the guide to solving the American armed services' seeming most perplexing problem of the 21st Century we are told:

> A revolution is a popular insurgency with plans to overthrow a government and transform its society and government from one form of government to another. Revolutions generally evolve from a rebellion, but in revolutions popular support comes in the form of a fully mobilized population, which differs from simply passive or active support. A fully mobilized population is part of a revolution and it is generally seeking fundamental lasting change in a society's political, economic or social order.[xxxi]

Oh, to be fair, a "rebellion" is defined a scant ten lines above this statement. A "rebellion (also known as an insurrection)," according to the US Army, "may be fomented by a group that challenges state control." The difference between "revolution" and "rebellion" is that the population only offers "passive" support to the latter.

Now we are back to splitting semantic hairs. The US Army's definition of "revolution" is remarkably similar to that offered by Chalmers Johnson, but we must be able to discern between a "passive" and "full mobilized" population or we will be looking to counter a "rebellion." Reading a bit further, it would appear one wants to be confronted with a "rebellion" and not a "revolution." "Rebellions," the US Army holds, are illegal acts that can be prosecuted as a crime by virtue of the fact they are an effort to "incite, assist or engage in violent acts against a constituted government." "Revolutions," on the other hand, are a far more dicey proposition as this type of conflict requires an effort to "reintegrate the mobilized population and not only reintegrate members of the insurgency."[xxxii] Two things to immediately take away from the US Army doctrine here, first, there is no mention of "terrorism" in either "rebellion" or "revolution," and we have no idea of how to decide what qualifies as a "passive" versus "fully mobilized" population. The operational planner is on his or her own for that decision.

Time to return to the situation in Iraq and Syria for a moment. Within the Sunni population in both nations we find a disenfranchised population who see little purpose in acceding to the existing regime. I could contend the two sitting governments at least safe-guarded their property rights, but that was a tenuous guarantee at best. Neither Baghdad nor Damascus was holding out the promise of equal representation within the "democracies" they supposedly practiced, so "civil rights" were also tenuous for the Sunni. Perhaps, then, they are no longer "passive," but instead a source of support for the opposition— willingly or unsubtly compelled. This explains the 30,000 under arms working for ISIS and strongly nudges an analyst toward employing the term "revolution" as opposed to "terrorism;" making al-Baghdadi a modern-day George Washington, a situation that causes cognitive dissonance in capitols from Riyadh to Washington.

A Potential Way Forward

In conversations with policy makers and war fighters it quickly becomes clear they have little patience for the academic or intelligence community's preoccupation with factual minutia and contentious debates over terminology. "Tell me what time it is, don't build me a clock," was a favorite phrase of one now-retired National Intelligence Officer. Inevitably, the analyst would forget this guidance and resume a description of cutting gears and tuning movements, a course of action that frequently ended with yelling in the front office and demands for more "competent" persons to work the problem. Having no desire to go in search of a new occupation, I recommend the following as a definition of "revolution." It is a movement of sufficient size to form a shadow government, challenges the existing regime with a new ideology, seeks to replace the sitting government and presents an alternative to standing cultural or social norms. This is the American "rebellion" the French revolution, Lenin coming to Saint Petersburg, Mao finishing the "Long March," and Castro riding a jeep into Havana. In contemporary times it could have been the Taliban, the Muslim Brotherhood's failed bid to rule in Egypt, AQIM in Mali or Ennahda as it struggles to govern in Tunisia.

In contrast, "terrorism" is the employment of violence intended to shock a target population by a group or organization that is not positioned to serve as a national governing body in the event these activities result in a collapse of the ruling elite. Here we have the 19th Century Anarchists, West Germany's Baader-Meinhof Gang, Italy's Red Brigades, Ilich Ramírez Sánchez (Carlos the Jackal), Timothy McVeigh, and al-Qaeda as originally crafted under Osama Bin Laden's tutelage. These are organizations with a political message but no apparent thought to long-term staying power. They would clear the way for a new government and perhaps a different social order, but do not seemingly want to be responsible for the mundane task of constituent services and diplomatic niceties. Which begs the question, what is Hamas or Hezbollah? A revolution or terrorist organization? Questions that are beyond the scope of this work, but illustrate the difficulty in drawing clear lines between "revolution" and "terrorism." For political reasons it is sometimes more expedient or convenient to have fuzzy definitions—at least so long as one is not drawn into the possibility of having to kinetically dispatch or dispel the "troublemakers." "Revolutions" suggest a need for heavy munitions and boots on the ground—an operational plan that requires winning hearts and minds. "Terrorists" imply a more transitory target,[xxxiii] normally handled by police forces and discrete use of explosives.

And so we are back to the dilemma of where to "bin" ISIS/ISIL/ the Islamic State. This is no minor concern, as the *Washington Post* has ably demonstrated for its readership. In the week following beheading of two journalists and the Obama administration's debate over ramping up airstrikes, the newspaper started almost every article on ISIS with the adjective "terrorist." The reporters were in good company. Here's what the President of the United States called the Islamic State on 10 September 2014: "Tonight I want to speak to you about what the United States will do with our friends and allies to degrade and ultimately destroy the terrorist group known as ISIL."[xxxiv] But look what happens in the week following the Chairman of the Joint Chiefs of Staff's testimony before Congress.

To set the stage, let's return to General Dempsey's remarks. He is sitting before the Senate Armed Forces Committee on 16 September 2014 following a request to explain how the administration plans to defeat this new threat. In his response we find this description of ISIS:

> I want to emphasize that our military actions will be part of a whole of government effort that works to disrupt ISIL financing, interdict the movement of foreign fighters across borders, and undermine the ISIL message...

> ISIL will ultimately be defeated when their cloak of religious legitimacy is stripped away and the populations on which they have imposed themselves reject them. Our actions are intended to move in that direction.
>
> This will require a sustained effort over an extended period of time. It is a generational problem. And we should expect that our enemies will adapt their tactics as we adjust our approach.[xxxv]

The terminology Dempsey employs to describe the Islamic State looks remarkably familiar to the verbiage used to define a "revolution." There is no discussion of "terrorism," this is about "messaging," stripping away "legitimacy," and a "generational" problem. In other words, we have something very different than the rise of al-Qaeda in Iraq; this needs more than an F-16 pilot with good intelligence and smart munitions.

President Obama seemingly made the same transition within a ten-day period. Speaking with Steve Kroft on *60 Minutes* 28 September 2014, the President described the Islamic State as: "sort of a hybrid of not just the terrorist network, but one with territorial ambitions, and some of the strategy and tactics of an army."[xxxvi] This verbal footwork came a little late in the game. On 23 September 2014, a day after the US air campaign began over Syria, the *Washington Post* was no longer starting its articles with the "terrorist" Islamic State, but had moved its readership on to the term "political Islam." This transition brings its own baggage.

"Political Islam," one quickly discovers upon wading into the literature, is one of the most nebulous terms an academic or journalist can employ to define a public movement or organization. In a book published in 1997, *Political Islam,"* Joel Beinin and Joe Stork offer this attempt at explaining the phenomena:

> We term the movements examined in this volume 'political Islam' because we regard their core concerns as temporal and political. They use the Koran, the hadiths (reports about the

words and deeds of Muhammad and his companions), and other canonical religious texts to justify their stances and actions.[xxxvii]

Not terribly helpful. "Political Islam" in this context is anything that is window dressed with the terminology or mythology of the *Koran* and related writings? Yes, that does indeed seem the case. Writing on the same subject six years later, Graham Fuller declares, "I use the terms 'political Islam' and 'Islamism' synonymously." He then goes on to state, "An Islamist is one who believes that Islam as a body of faith has something important to say about how politics and society should be ordered in the contemporary Muslim world and who seeks to implement this idea in some fashion."[xxxviii] Other academics offer similar vague pronouncements.[xxxix]

We are stuck in an endless "do-loop" here in the sense "Political Islam" is like Justice Potter Stewart's definition of "pornography," "I know it when I see it." To wit, I offer the following, "political Islam" is the practice of justifying one's form of governance by arguing your ideology is based upon the *Koran* and other Muslim foundational documentation or mythology. The reason for taking such a course of action is entirely logical. As Moorthy Muthuswamy writes in *Defeating Political Islam,* "If an individual wants to capture, control, and rule a land and its people; it is hard to think of a better way than to declare oneself so close to the almighty God as to be the sole purveyor of his 'revelations'."[xl] Taken from this perspective, the ISIS decision to wrap themselves in the cloak of the Prophet makes complete sense. The revolution they are bringing is made more palatable for the masses as it is justified in the name of Muhammad and Allah. This appeal to a higher authority worked for the leaders of the Muslim conquests from 634-750, and for the Christian Crusaders three hundred years later.

Which brings us back to the issue of how to respond the Islamic State?

In response, we point to an article Alireza Doostdar, a professor of Islamic Studies at the University of Chicago Divinity School, wrote in early October 2014. Using the quirky title, "How Not to Understand

ISIS," Doostdar bids caution in trying to "bin" the Islamic State as yet another example of Islamic revival and fundamentalism. Doostdar is not dismissing the influence of "Salafi Islam" on the movement, but he notes there are other factors at play. For instance, "What we call ISIS is more than just a militant cult. At present, ISIS controls a network of large population centers with millions of residents, in addition to oil resources, military bases, and roads. It has to administer the affairs of the populations over whom it rules, and this has required compromise and coalition-building, not just brute force."[xli] Furthermore, he continues, lacking a "good grasp of the motivations of those who fight for or alongside ISIS" we have simply subscribed to an argument it is driven by religion. But, he notes, ISIS emerges from a decade of "war, occupation, killing, torture, and disenfranchisement" in Iraq, and more recently in Syria. Thus, he argues, we should not be surprised by the ISIS brutality—it is not Islam that brings forth this behavior, "it is a whole ecology of cruelty spread out over more than a decade."

Doostdar further complicates the situation in his attempt to unearth the allure for foreign fighters who join ISIS. He admits it could be visions of the utopian caliphate, but it is equally possible they are motivated by "compassion for suffering fellow humans or of altruistic duty."[xlii] This is an unsettling proposition for Western audiences that have been shocked by beheading clips on U-Tube and television footage of an entire town being subjected to apparently random shelling. This is "compassion" or altruism?" Again we return to the issue of relative definitions and personal perspective. What seems compassionate to one—dog ownership—may be cruelty to another—for example, members of People for Ethical Treatment of Animals.

So how do we respond to ISIS? It will take more than kinetic shock and awe. The argument this is a revolution suggests a hearts and minds campaign, a sustained presence on the ground, and a plan for the future. Nation building has to be part of the dialogue. We are now in a "whole of government" problem and the Department of Defense is but one tool in the repair kit. The alternative option is to let ISIS carve its own space within the Middle East. To establish the Caliphate and be weighed down with the administrative burden of governing and providing constituent services so as to maintain a veneer of legitimacy. (Recall al-Anbar revolted against al-Qaeda in Iraq when its members "over-stepped" the tribal leaders' bounds, ISIS will likely find the setting no easier to control.)

This latter option is enticing. It would save billions of dollars that are currently being expended on munitions and aviation fuel. However, it sets a discomforting—to say the least—precedent. If ISIS wins in Syria and Iraq—essentially trifurcating Iraq and carving away half of Syria—what message are we sending to AQAP in Yemen, to AQIM in Mali, to al-Shabaab in Somalia, and Boko Haram in Nigeria? Does this open the door to a Confederation of the Caliphate that then seeks to follow in the footprints of the 7th Century Muslim conquest? These are the questions one should ask as you proceed through the essays that follow. We are on the cusp of a "brave new world" and the paradigms that served us so well in the Cold War and Global War on Terrorism may no longer be an appropriate framing mechanism.

Chapter 3

Reconsidering Religion, Reconsidering Terrorism

Alexs Thompson

First Published 20 January 2015

Abstract

This article suggests that a new definition of religion is necessary to properly conceptualize and develop policy in response to violent religious behaviors. It is argued that religion is frequently, even if indirectly, presumed to be peaceful theological window dressing that can be ignored in addressing religious violence. Military and political leaders, for example, forbid troops from entering religious building for fear of offense with little regard for missed opportunities for engagement. Such a perspective leads commanders and analysts to be stuck describing terrorists as evil monsters with no real mechanism of understanding how religion can be alluring because of its advocacy of violence. There is a frequent discussion, for example, about whether Islam is fundamentally violent. In what follows, a new perspective on religion is offered that recognizes and prioritizes the fact that religions like Islam can sanction violence in ways that are ultimately local and intoxicating. Rather than relying on terms of convenience like terrorist and evil, this new perspective on defining religion offers a more nuanced approach to responding to religious violence.

Introduction

In 2008 while deployed to Fallujah, Iraq, I found that Imams were frequently described as the primary fuel for violence in al-Anbar province. Accordingly, military and diplomatic leaders tended to avoid and isolate religious leaders from important discussions about rebuilding stable Iraqi communities. Religious leaders were understood to be forces of discontent who needed to be marginalized if Iraqis were to ever realize a thriving society. Given the important historical role that religious leaders have played in Iraqi history, I designed a data collection plan to test whether religious leaders were preaching violence and stoking the flames of insurgency. With the help of my teammates and various military units, we were able to gather reports from tens of thousands of Friday sermons.

We discovered that over 80% of the sermons we analyzed were neutral to the Iraqi government and the United States; approximately 10% were positively disposed towards the Iraqi government and the United States, and less than 5% were openly hostile to the United States and the Iraqi government. Rather than finding a preponderance of violent sermons, we found those sermons to be primarily concerned with religious and social justice issues. For example, we were able to find an imam who was preaching against the disruption of the food supply chain by terrorist elements. By engaging that religious leader, we were able to make substantial changes to development priorities, security procedures, and contract awards with the effect of increasing local Iraqi involvement in rebuilding their own society. What follows are three erroneous principles that guided our analyses and two principles that were gleaned from our study of those religious sermons.

Religion is Not Peaceful

When analysts face improbable situations like religiously motivated beheadings or rape, they default to name calling because religion is so frequently avoided and misunderstood. Muslim terrorists are described as evil monsters because there is little understanding of their religious motivations. Appeals to 99 virgins for those who martyr themselves, for example, is scoffed at as opportunistic, juvenile, and unconvincing: window dressing for deeper, more important social issues. The intersection of religion and violence tests the limits of analysis because there has been little explanation of how religion can be alluring *because of* violence. When young men and women speak enthusiastically about their desire to kill themselves in the name of God, it is significantly easier to investigate their economic status and declare that they are too poor to understand the implications of their behavior then to trace the religious justifications for such decisions. Analysis of these types of events gets stuck describing how bad the perpetrators are and how they are poor representations of their religious tradition. Accordingly, policy recommendations are most frequently focused on how to acquire more guns and more money to dissuade and, if necessary, eliminate those who make such decisions.

Defaulting to terms like monster and evil or ignoring religious is based on a predilection to understand religion as constructive and peaceful. Terrorists are monsters because they bastardize religious traditions that would otherwise build communities and strengthen social bonds. Terrorists, like werewolves and vampires, are perversions of the visage and aims of the societies from which they emerge and which they terrorize. It is helpful to recognize that religion neither *is* peaceful nor violent and terrorists are not monsters, but products of their religious environments. Terrorists, for example, are drawn to religion because it affords an opportunity to exact religious justice and institute a more perfect world. So long as those terrorists are explained away as miscreants who violate the principle of peaceful religion it will be much easier to avoid and misunderstand religiously motivated violence than engage it. Religious leaders in Fallujah, while I was there, were ignored not only because they were erroneously understood to be fomenting an insurgency, but because they were seen as unable to use their religion to bring about peace. If religion was the cause of violence and could not be leveraged to build peaceful communities, religion was ineffectual.

Religion is Not Window Dressing

Religion is one of the most difficult topics from which to collect data because of cultural sensitivities. The adage discouraging the discussion of politics or religion in polite conversation is well attested notwithstanding the fact that political science has a long history of sophisticated theories. It remains possible to speak in fairly abstract and specific terms about political realism and political economics, for example. Religion tends to lack such a rich syntax for theoretical, public discourse. This is true in spite of the fact that religion continues to influence human behavior at every level.

Individuals who commit acts of violence in the name of religion are frequently analyzed as psychologically unstable, socially deviant, and economically disadvantaged. Religion, as an actual cause for violence, is frequently left ignored and unanalyzed. When religion is identified as the cause of religious behavior, the arguments are usually simplistic accusations against "them" by "us". Those who put effort into analyzing violent events frequently preserve a type of privileged status for religion, writ large, even if individual religions are labeled as violent. The contact point between religion and violence for sophisticated analysis is frequently one of confusion. Analysts are understandably disgusted and angry when they observe violence perpetrated in the name of a particular religion and seek to explain away the religious aspects of the actors and apply deeper, more important motivations for such behavior such as sociological factors. There are frequent calls for moderate religious leaders to admonish their violent counterparts with the expectation that the truth of that religion supports moderation and peace-building.

In effect, religion is treated as mere window dressing for an explanation of violence; those who perpetrate such violence do not understand their true religion. Policy implications of this perspective tend to encourage nation-building, inter-religious dialogue, and psychoanalysis. It frequently happens that even when perpetrators of violence point to religious texts as the motivation for their behavior, analysts default to psychological and sociological explanations. Religious explanations for violence become untouchable, inexplicable, and beyond the pail of productive policy discussions.

But religion cannot be ignored when analyzing religious violence. While in Iraq, my military and political commanders avoided local religious leaders because they did not have the knowledge to attack what those commanders understood as the key cause of violence in the region. They treated religious language and religious leaders as critical variables that ought not be engaged. For example, representatives of the US-led coalition were forbidden from entering any religious buildings. Religious buildings in the communities where I worked were social buildings where problems were solved, resources were distributed, and relationships were solidified. Our commanders were motivated by a sense that Iraqi problems were tribal, economic, and political even though our enemies and our partners understood religion to be the keystone issue. Islam, in that case, was not window dressing that could be avoided. This does not mean, however, that Islam *is* violent, but that serious analysts must be able to frame violence in particularly Islamic terms without ascribing that violence to every Muslim everywhere.

Religion is Not Theology

Another reason religious leaders were ignored while I was in Iraq was that religion is often mistaken for theology and few people understand theology of their or other religious traditions. Theology, as the study of God, is concerned with how human communities theorize a divine being. When confronted with claims of purported divine authority, it can be tempting to find competing texts that reject violence in Islam and preach tolerance and moderation. When that happens, however, the discussion devolves into a contest about who has the proper interpretation of divine will. At the conclusion of our study of religious leaders in Fallujah, I sat one day with a group of people who emerged from our studies as key communicators and partners in spreading stability. As we discussed ways of undermining the influence of violent actors, the discussion turned to whether the Qur'an can be used to justify killing innocent Muslims. One Imam mentioned a Qur'anic passage that requires special accommodations for Christians and Jews.

Other Imams chimed in with other Qur'anic passages that advocated violence that gave the terrorists what they needed to justify their actions. We came to agree that theology—the study of texts—could not resolve the fundamental issue at stake. Our research team, as a result of that encounter, came to understand that another prevailing misunderstanding of religion is that it is synonymous with theology. Theological awareness is important, but on both sides of any disagreement, the validity of an argument is not the ink on a piece of paper, but the traditions that authorize the use of one type of verse over another. Those who perpetrate religious violence have their own theological systems that does not need to accord with other religions or even with others within their religious tradition.

Theological engagements can lead to greater understandings of various theological perspectives, but they do not usually lead to the cessation of religious violence. Terrorists are unlikely to be persuaded that they misunderstand their theological tradition because one or another outside observer is able to quote the Qur'an. If the study of religion is understood to be the study of theology, observers rightly back away from direct engagement with religious leaders and resort to emotional descriptions of terrorists and their violent actions. When understood correctly, religious justifications for violence are not primarily found within religious texts, but in the complex lived experiences of those who choose to commit those violent acts.

Religion is an Analytical Category

Stripped of its frequent assessment as window dressing that is focused on peace-building and theology, religion takes on a very different image. Religion, from this perspective, can be understood as a theoretical term that requires more careful definition if religious violence is to be conceptualized and handled correctly. Religion, let us say, describes a class of human behaviors that are similar only because they have been defined as similar. "Religion" is a term of convenience created by analysts to make it easier to describe vastly different phenomena. Religion is an analytical term—a heuristic device—that attempts to lump together human behaviors that appeal to the divine for their justification.

Jonathan "J.Z." Smith, a pioneer in the study of religion, wrote: "Religion is solely the creation of the scholar's study. It is created for the scholar's analytic purposes by his imaginative acts of comparison and generalization. Religion has no independent existence apart from the academy." Smith's point was that analysts—academics in his estimation—ought not conduct their work as if all religious events can be analyzed by the same criteria. When writing an academic paper or presenting to a similarly theoretically-minded audience it might be useful to compare "religion" across cultures, but that comparison is *for some purpose*. Most frequently, that purpose is to explain how religious events should be conducted.

Terrorists are frequently compared to their non-violent counterparts to justify why the terrorists' theology is incorrect. Analysts and commanders tend to create an empirical equivalency between religious phenomena rather than recognizing that equivalency as analytical. This is to say that one's ability to compare a Muslim terrorist with a moderate Muslim is only possible because outsiders want to be able to lump

"Muslims" into one category and construct that category as peaceful. But those two groups are Muslim only insofar as the term Muslim helps outsiders figure out how to stop terrorists. It is useful to talk about Islam and Muslims as theoretical categories, but those theories have done little to thwart the appeal of terrorist ideologies. It is time, then, to refashion one's understanding of religion.

Religion is Self-Authorizing

Given these observations, let us suggest that religion is a closed system of language that authorizes itself. Rather than ignoring religious components of religious violence or defaulting to peace and theology, it might be useful to understand religion as primarily a system of language that defines its own reality. Violent religious groups rely on themselves to legitimize their behavior. It is not necessary to defer to interpretations of religious texts offered by other groups or bend to legislation. This allows violent religious groups to interpret well-known passages in radically new ways. Traditional methods of interpreting texts become irrelevant because new religious movements assume the right to interpret texts in ways that they authorize. They may be called heretics by outsiders, but they refer to themselves as reformers and visionaries.

In other language systems, there is a necessary dialogue with external groups. Theorists of political science and economics, for example, are still bound by academic history and social customs. What makes religion different as an analytical category is that it requires no external authorization to assert its theories. Religious groups can justify their violent behavior by pointing to other texts and individuals, but they can also exclusively authorize their behavior internally. Religious groups certainly can engage their wider communities, but they are organized to eschew social trends in favor of religious principles.

Religious groups are frequently, at their foundation, utopian groups whose purpose is to change society even when that society does not want to be changed. Religion *need not* accord with social norms if its stated aims are in jeopardy. This aspect of religion, more than its appeal to the divine can drive a reformulation of one's understanding of religion. Rather than simply referring to terrorists as monsters, for example, it might be useful to describe them in their own terminology. Monsters are otherworldly and lend themselves to fantastical descriptions. Terrorists, when reimagined as part of the continuum of human behavior, expose themselves to sustained analysis.

Analyzing Religious Violence

The recent rise in popularity of ISIS in Iraq and their supposed inspiration for the most recent attacks in Paris are a fitting example. Labeling ISIS as Islamic, Salafist, extremist, violent, barbaric, backwards, and evil may have descriptive and cathartic value, but those terms offer little insight from which to build effective policy. If one analyzes ISIS as a utopian group, however, the calculation changes. That is, if analysts take a break from demonizing terrorists and consider them in their own terms, it is more likely that the effects of ISIS can more clearly be understood and, hopefully, mitigated.

ISIS is a utopian movement that has come together as champions of a just society. Their violent behaviors are authorized through compelling language that refers to a golden era of Islamic rule. If one takes seriously the actions and words of those who support ISIS, one hears traces of a historic call for a better society, a more just society, one in which individuals are able to achieve their highest potential. Terrorists of this sort become a group that metes out the most extreme and awful punishment only on those who deviate from the utopian ideal. Their message is appealing because it uses violence to instill the most desirable form of human community. The fact that *we* find them abhorrent is irrelevant.

Those who perpetrated the beheading in August 2014 and the attack on Charlie Hebdo in January 2015 are not unique because they appeal to the divine nor because their actions are "religious." Terrorist organizations in general achieve their impact on communities because they create compelling linguistic frameworks that cannot be dismantled by external factors. ISIS, like Al-Qaeda, is not simply a military force that can be bombed into submission or a social movement that will be replaced by a new fad. There are certainly military, diplomatic, and economic aspects of their success, but its distinctive feature, the reason it has caused such a policy problem, is that it is a closed system of language that cannot be bombed, talked, or bought out of existence. Members of ISIS that arrive from the United States, Europe, and the United Kingdom are not simply disaffected, uneducated, poor young males; the utopian society described by ISIS is, let it be said plainly, alluring.

The number of deaths and the amount of destruction in places like New York, Fallujah, and Paris have frequently been quantified to justify military action and moral disgust, but it has done little to explain the ability of terrorist language systems to persuade individuals around the world to join their cause. The goal of a new analytical perspective, however, would not be for *us* to create a utopian society for *them*, but to support competing narratives for a stable society.

Conclusion

When I deployed to Iraq, many analysts were persuaded that religious leaders were the primary cause of insurgency because so much of the violence was being perpetrated in the name of religion. The commanders and analysts with whom I worked spent a great amount of energy ignoring and perpetuating misunderstandings of religion in general and Islam in particular. Through detailed study we discovered that indigenous religious leaders were not a determinative cause of religious violence, but that they could be helpful in building stable communities. Once we were able to redefine our understanding of religion, integrate religious leaders, and focus our attention on the narratives promulgated by violent religious groups, our efforts were significantly more effective.

Rather than countering theological arguments, for example, we directed our attention to specific people, locations, and issues that drove narratives of religious violence. Our interactions with local religious leaders were focused on understanding the local arguments of terrorists in their communities and we abandoned a broad, theoretical understanding of terrorists and terrorism. We began to understand that our use of the terms insurgent and terrorists were primarily to help us talk to one another, but that those terms did not adequately describe the communities in which we were working. Iraq in 2008 may not be the Iraq or Paris of 2015, but theoretical considerations about the confluence of religion and violence remain important.

Chapter 4

Ignored in Asia: The ISIL Threat

David L. Edwards

First Published 21 January 2015

Introduction

In February 2014, Abu Bakr al-Baghdadi declared the establishment of a caliphate, known commonly as the Islamic State of Iraq and the Levant (ISIL). This was a significant pronouncement in the Islamic faith, as a caliphate is traditionally known as the formation of a sovereign state to lead the devote Muslims. Since February 2014, ISIL has acquired large swaths of Iraq and Syria, killed and misplaced thousands of people, forged alliances, obtained substantial numbers of recruits and financing, and wreaked havoc across the globe. In September 2014, then Director of the National Counterterrorism Center, Matthew G. Olson, stated that "ISIL views itself as the new leader of the global jihad" (2014). While ISIL supporters are emerging across the world, absent is a focus on the organization's presence and activities in Asia. As a result, particular attention should be paid to the Asia Pacific.

The Asia Pacific region possesses a significant Muslim population, to include the world's most populous Muslim nation-state: Indonesia. Additionally, between 1979-1989, Asia observed its citizens travel to the Middle East to participate in terrorist activity during the Soviet Union occupation of Afghanistan. Furthermore, a substantial number of organizations and individuals within the Asia Pacific region have pledged allegiance to ISIL. The most notorious of the allegiance pledging organizations include Abu Bakar Bashir, a leader of Jemaah Islamayah; Abu Sayyaf and the Bangsamoro Islamic Freedom Fighters, two Filipino terrorist groups. Therefore, a strong connection exists between Asian extremism and ISIL.

What role will ISIL play in the United States Pacific Command area of responsibility? Asian support for ISIL will largely be based in Southeast Asia, which possesses the largest Muslim population in the region and will manifest through Asian nationals traveling to the Middle East, the secondary effects of these travels, and finally through a resurgence of terrorist activity in the Asia Pacific region. To suppress the Asian-ISIL influence requires the formation of a combatant command coordinating council, an increase in regional partnerships, and an increase in Intelligence, Surveillance, and Reconnaissance (ISR) and intelligence sharing.

Asian Nationals Travel to the Middle East

The most immediate reality of Asian support for ISIL is the traveling of its citizenry to the Middle East. These individuals are providing sizeable contributions to the organization's activities. As this activity crosses various geographic combatant commands, the formulation of a combatant command coordinating council is necessary to properly address and combat this issue.

Many from Asia are traveling to support ISIL in the Middle East. In July 2014, Veryan Khan, editorial director of Terrorism Research and Analysis Consortium, reported that approximately 500 fighters had traveled to the Middle East from the Asia Pacific region (Regencia 2014). In September 2014, Admiral Samuel Locklear, Commander of the United States Pacific Command (PACOM), estimated that 1,000 fighters had traveled to Iraq and Syria from the Indo-Asia Pacific. He continued, "That number could get larger as we go forward" (Locklear 2014). In the span of only two months, the number of fighters from the Asia Pacific doubled. Since September, ISIL has received numerous pledges of allegiance from both individuals and organizations, to include Nigeria's Boko Haram, Egypt's Ansar Beit al-Maqdis, Libya's Majlis Shura Shabab al-Islam, and the Philippines' Abu Sayyaf and Bangsamoro Islamic Freedom Fighters. In late October 2014, the United Nations (UN) published a report that declared, "Numbers since 2010 are now many times the size of the cumulative numbers of foreign terrorists fighters between 1990 and 2010—and are growing" (Ackerman 2014). Given the expanded nature of public support across the globe for ISIL since September, and this most recent UN report, it may be assumed that the number of Asian fighters traveling to the Middle East continues to climb.

The Asian ISIL fighters are actively engaged in the organization's activities. In May 2014, Ahmad Tarmimi Maliki, a Malaysian member of ISIL, led a suicide bombing mission in Iraq that killed 25 Iraqi soldiers and himself; another Malaysian died while fighting in Syria and was proclaimed a martyr by the Pan-Malaysian Islamic Party; three Malaysian women allegedly traveled to Syria to provide sexual support to the ISIL fighters; Robert "Musa" Cerantonio, an Australian, traveled to the Philippines to recruit for ISIL. Cerantonio is also very active on social media and as of July 2014 he had over 6,700 followers on Twitter and YouTube. He also maintained a Facebook page, which, prior to its deletion by Facebook personnel, had over 3,000 likes—making Cerantonio the "third most 'liked' person online among 'western jihadists in Syria'" (Regencia 2014). Haja Fakkurudeen Usman Ali, a Singaporean, left his family and traveled to Syria to join ISIL, while another Singaporean, traveled to the region to join her husband and two teenage children already in the Middle East (Ibid.). Numerous accounts identify Asian nationals fighting alongside ISIL from Indonesia, Malaysia, Singapore, Philippines, and Australia.

These developments cause consternation for the United States Pacific Command (PACOM) and Central Command (CENTCOM). ISIL has engendered the support of organizations across the globe, which crosses all of the geographic combatant commands. To properly combat such an issue requires the formation of a combatant command coordinating council, which will at a minimum include the geographic combatant commanders and will fall under the auspices of the National Command Authority. This body will serve as a forum to bring the combatant commanders together to discuss transnational issues, such as terrorism, piracy, illicit trafficking, humanitarian assistance and disaster relief, and others that span multiple combatant commands. Additional organizations or agencies can be brought in as necessitated topically. For example, for countering terrorism, the National Counterterrorism Center; Special Operations Command, which has the operational lead for combating terrorism; Transportation Command; and Strategic Command, would be likely members of the coordinating council. This council would ensure a holistic approach to each transnational issue and access to all Defense Department assets.

Secondary Effects

Historicity paints a daunting picture of the Asian landscape upon the return of the ISIL experienced Asian fighters. The emergence of a single enemy to the Asian Pacific community provides a unique opportunity for partnership building to placate the region of this existential threat.

The Asia Pacific region is rightly concerned about the number of fighters traveling to the Middle East, as these individuals will return with unique firsthand knowledge of terrorist activities, logistics, recruiting tactics, economic support, networking, and methodologies. Between 1979-1989, Asia supplied the Middle East with nearly 800 fighters during the Soviet occupation. Subsequent to the 800 fighters' return, those combat experienced Asian fighters, "form[ed] extremist groups of their own, including the notorious al Qaeda-linked organization

Jemaah Islamiyah," stated Southeast Asian expert Joseph Chinyong Liow (Liow 2014). Jemaah Islamiyah was responsible for the Bali bombing in 2002 and the Australian Embassy bombing in Indonesia in 2004. Additionally, Filipinos that traveled to the Middle East in the 1980s for the same purpose returned to the Philippines and formed the terrorist organization Abu Sayyaf, which is known for its violence (Regencia 2014). These terrorist organizations remain active to date and are the by-product of a mere 800 fighters. As of September 2014, the estimated number of Asian fighters that have traveled to support ISIL was in excess of 1,000–with numbers likely rising. What will be the by-product of this generation of Asian fighter?

This threat provides fertile soil for the growth of partnership building. In his most recent posture statement, Admiral Samuel Locklear, Commander of PACOM, stated, "A sustained effort to build and enhance the capacity of our allies and partners is the cornerstone of our counter terrorism strategy in South and Southeast Asia" (2014). Recent PACOM activity has demonstrated the importance of leveraging existing forums for partnership building, such as the Association of Southeast Asian Nations (ASEAN). The most important proposed activity for partnership building is a follow-on to the ASEAN Defense Minister's Meeting (ADMM) Counter-Terrorism Exercise, which was conducted in September 2013 and brought together the ten ASEAN nations and the eight "Plus" countries. This engagement served as a substantial leap forward in partnership building, yet the formal realization of ISIL did not occur until February 2014. As such, a follow-up engagement that highlights existing realities is necessary. Furthermore, an increase in International Military Education and Training (IMET) and Foreign Military Financing (FMF) where ISIL threats exist, such as Indonesia, Malaysia, Philippines, and Singapore will demonstrate U.S. support to the region and inculcate combating terrorism expertise in the region. The ADMM Counter-Terrorism Exercise, IMET, and FMF will concurrently provide the greatest opportunities to build partner capacity in Asia Pacific and lead to combating secondary effects of Asian ISIL fighters returning to the region.

Resurgence in Asia Proper Terrorist Activity

In addition to the threat of Asians traveling to the Middle East and those returning home with newfound skill sets, ISIL has experienced support from Asia proper. Many nations have witnessed their citizens supporting ISIL while remaining in-country. This presents an interesting dilemma where ISR and intelligence sharing prove salient solutions.

Dr. Rodger Shanahan, an international relations expert at Lowy Institute for International Policy, stated that ISIL poses a serious threat to the democratic governments of Indonesia and Malaysia (2014). In addition to Asian jihadists traveling to the Middle East, there is a large contingent of local Asian supporters that have pledged their allegiance to ISIL, to include Abu Bakar Bashir, a leader of Jemaah Islamayah; and two Filipino organizations: Abu Sayyaf and the Bangsamoro Islamic Freedom Fighters. In addition, the Malaysian government arrested 19 individuals that plotted to bomb several pubs and a brewery outside of Kuala Lumpur (Regencia 2014). ISIL affiliates also issued bomb threats to the largest Buddhist temple in the world, in Java, Indonesia. A myriad of individuals, such as Firman Hidayat Silalahi, from Indonesia, have been arrested for demonstrating their support of ISIL by flying ISIL flags. Videos on YouTube demonstrate various Filipino groups' support of ISIL. A plethora of groups and individuals, the largest from Indonesia, Malaysia, Philippines, and Singapore, have pledged their support to ISIL, which poses significant threats to the region.

These threats are real and require action. For such an effort, the role of ISR stands paramount. PACOM's ISR capabilities should be leveraged to ensure sufficient response times to potential dangers. Admiral Locklear stated, "USPACOM's success depends on our ability to accurately assess the theater security environment with penetrating and persistent ISR and domain awareness…[and] assured means for *sharing critical information with our allies, partners, and our forces [emphasis added]*" (2014). Admiral Locklear also stated the desire to enhance military to military engagements with partner nations. ISR provides another means through which these military to military engagements may be incorporated as a component of building partner capacity. ISR and intelligence sharing will provide PACOM and U.S. allies an asset through which Asian terrorist activity may be mitigated.

Contrarian View

Alternate arguments include the claim that Southeast Asian nation economies are much stronger today than they were during the Soviet occupation in the Middle East, which garnered significant Asian support and will counterbalance a robust Asian response in the present conflict. Additionally, the cultural distinctions between Asian and Middle Eastern Muslims is sizeable and includes fluency in Arabic and overarching religious fervor, which will make the two groups incompatible.

Despite the veracity of the aforementioned claims, ISIL has attained a minimum of 1,000 Asian jihadists traveling to the Middle East, while the previous conflict with the Soviet Union achieved only 800. Additionally, Asian extremist organizations have already pledged allegiance to ISIL. Neither economic prowess nor cultural ambiguities have impeded the response from Asia.

Conclusion

ISIL is playing a significant role in the PACOM area of responsibility. Asian fighters are traveling to Iraq and Syria, secondary effects of these travels present serious risks, and Asia proper is witnessing increasing support of ISIL. The following actions will assist in mitigating said threats: the formulation of a combatant command coordinating council will facilitate the countering of threats posed by those traveling to the Middle East, building partner capacity will reduce the risk of secondary effects, and ISR and intelligence sharing will minimize potential terrorist activity in Asia proper. The threats in Asia are real and merit the attention and action necessary to quell ISIL's footprint in the region.

Chapter 5

Missing Political Front in Afghanistan

Clark Johnson

First Published 21 January 2015

Abstract: *US efforts in Afghanistan since 2001, and especially since the surge of 2010-2011, have emphasized military and to a lesser extend donor aid operations, while side-stepping political and cultural complexities. The policy has failed, as evidenced by both persistence of the insurgency and by acknowledgement of Coalition leaders that they do not know how to reinforce credibility of GIRoA (Government of Islamic Republic of Afghanistan). Going back to 1989, and certainly since 2001, the US has failed to construct a coalition of moderates that might be able to enhance legitimacy and increase stability, and hence to begin to defuse military tensions. Indeed, the US has often supported factions that tended to undermine stability and energize insurgent activity. An improved political strategy going forward would look for ways to collaborate with and strengthen moderate tribal and religious leaders, and to support GIRoA structures already in-place for neutralizing extremists and warlords. In line with Afghan historical precedent, the US and Coalition should also seek to decentralize government finance and appointments, in order that some insurgents might choose to compete politically (non-militarily) in provinces and districts. This can be accomplished over time even without negotiations between GIRoA and Taliban leaders, and with a minimum of Coalition military support.*

President Barack Obama's decision to authorize military action on the part of US forces in Afghanistan after the end of 2014 reopens strategic questions often thought to have been closed. Despite the peaceful transition of power to Ashraf Ghani, who is perceived as a moderate reformer and internationally-minded, as President, the war is not going well. Reports indicate that Afghan Army and Police casualties in 2014 were the highest since the 2001 intervention, and civilian casualties, the majority of them inflicted by the insurgency, were the highest since the United Nations began reporting them in 2009.

In Iraq, a military "surge" in 2007 initially brought an upward spike in Coalition and Iraqi casualties, but it was followed by a decline that lasted for several years. In contrast, the parallel surge in Coalition forces in Afghanistan in 2010 and 2011, according to Department of Defense (DoD) data, resulted in no durable downturn in the volume of security incidents.[i]

Senior US and other Coalition leaders routinely identify lack of legitimacy of GIRoA (Government of the Islamic Republic of Afghanistan) as the greatest danger to a successful mission outcome. The shortfall in legitimacy derives from obvious corruption, clientelism, dependence on warlords and unsavory power brokers, and a culture of impunity for human rights and financial crimes. It also follows failure to include traditional tribal and religious leaders. The government's writ often does not extend far beyond Kabul. Even if the new President turns out to be as directed, motivated and "clean" as many hope, he will be able to surmount only a portion of these legacies. To some extent, he is bound for non-Pashtun support to his Vice-President Abdul Rashid Dostum, the Uzbek leader, who by reputation was one of Afghanistan's most violent warlords; and the delay in forming a Cabinet indicates that Chief Executive Abdullah Abdullah has a separate agenda. In any event, transformative action would likely stir considerable opposition.

Policy Vacuum

However much International Security Assistance Force (ISAF) leaders acknowledged GIRoA's legitimacy gap, they seemed not to know what to do about it.[ii] Afghan scholar Thomas Barfield has described counterinsurgency (COIN) in Afghanistan as "a military operation without a political front."[iii] Karl Eikenberry, former US Commander and later Ambassador to Kabul, criticized the surge strategy in 2009. He subsequently explained in *Foreign Affairs* that it was based on "spectacularly incorrect" premises, including: 1) that the COIN goal of protecting population was clear and would prove decisive; and 2) that foreign support and assistance would substantially increase GIRoA's capacity and legitimacy. But rather than offer an alternative to the failed COIN effort, Eikenberry then generalizes that we should try to learn from our mistakes.[iv] Retired Army three-star general Daniel Bolger, who was active in Iraq and Afghanistan, acknowledges that we have "lost" in both, and says US generals failed repeatedly to reconsider basic assumptions, and "failed to question our flawed understanding of our foe or ourselves." Then, however, he punts: far from suggesting a way to proceed in Afghanistan, he volunteers that younger officers will in the future "figure out" how to fight such wars.[v]

Robert Gates, US Secretary of Defense during 2006-2011, recounts a strategic dead-end. He reports that President Obama lost confidence in Coalition war strategy during General McChrystal's tenure as ISAF Commander in 2010, and again during General Petraeus's tenure in 2011. Gates adds that Obama asked him in January 2011 to develop a strategy to "work around" President Karzai in Afghanistan and General Kayani in Pakistan, but he leaves the impression that no such a strategy was ever provided.[vi] Succeeding Commanders Allen, Dunford and Campbell have been occupied with transition of control to the ANSF (Afghan National Security Force} and winding down the US involvement. Rather than seek new understanding of Afghanistan's complexities, their Commands have been marked by drawing back from engagement with Ministries and others ISAF staff label as "non-priority."

What has seldom wavered, from the Bonn Conference of December 2001 through plans for disengagement at the end of 2014, is the diplomatic- and donor-agency-driven commitment to the vision of Afghanistan as a democratic, pluralistic state where the central government's credibility is felt even in distant provinces. This is the way the 2004 Afghan Constitution is written, it is the gist of the Tokyo Mutual Accountability Framework (TMAF) for donor conditionality, and it is even in the language of military planning documents. However, such observers as Barfield and former Ambassador and Special Envoy Peter Tomsen have sharply questioned this view; and Henry Kissinger has similarly described nation-building in Afghanistan as "inherently implausible."[vii] The highly regarded Report on the Wilton Park Conference (2010) offered:

> Other [participants] noted that success does not necessarily lie in Western notions of what a state should look like. The current predatory behaviour of many people within the [Afghan] state apparatus suggests that the international community should be looking to all forms of political governance in the country, including structures which do not conform to Western expectations.

But without a path to achieve such centralized credibility, US and Coalition efforts have focused instead on development, including on institutional capacity building, and on military operations and training. A shortfall of political legitimacy, in contrast, can be addressed only be demanding change, that is, by confronting Kabul on reform and realignment of domestic power, and by energizing groups or forces heretofore dormant. This means reducing the President's power to appoint provincial and district officials, while increasing the role of provincial and district councils; weakening warlords residual powers, while energizing moderate elements among traditional tribal leadership; and, in a country with an Islamist insurgency, finding ways to reinforce religious moderates. But we typically refrain from such hardball diplomacy—and have instead posited that institution-building, or foreign assistance more generally, will itself create legitimacy. [viii] Such Coalition premises reflect strategic confusion.

If the Ghani-Abdullah administration is able to boost the central government's acceptance among Afghans, it will be good news indeed; but the US and Coalition should no longer stake the outcome of the mission on having that happen. GIRoA's growing national visibility in the decade after 2001, far from bringing stability to other regions of the country, did much to re-energize the rural and Pashtun insurgencies, including of the Taliban. Peaceful periods in Afghan history, for example from 1929 into the late 1970s, saw weak central governments that left effective autonomy to the regions. In contrast, both the modernizing Amanullah government of the decade before 1929 and the various Communist governments after 1978 failed, and provoked harsh counter-movements. The presumption should be that GIRoA must first enhance its credibility as a provider of security, dispute resolution and non-corrupt administration, and only then seek to extend its authority.

Some Recent History

The US needs to think like a superpower, rather than like a hired army on the verge of withdrawal. Much of what might have been accomplished during the past quarter-century did not require ground troops; and the fact that forces are being withdrawn does not cause US interests in Afghanistan to vanish. A superpower ought to be in a position to influence outcomes, to shift international financial support, and to leverage credibility in international fora.

Former Ambassador and Special Envoy Peter Tomsen argues that the US has enabled the wrong Afghan leaders and groups ever since the Soviet departure in 1989.[ix] During the anti-Soviet war of the 1980s, the CIA used the Pakistani Inter-Services Intelligence (ISI) as a conduit for supplying the Afghan Mujahideen. Following the Soviet exit, the US, through the CIA, essentially outsourced its Afghan policy to the ISI. The ISI was (and largely remains) under direction of hardline jihadists, and has consistently provided resources to strongly Islamist leaders and factions in Afghanistan. It was not a necessary consequence of US support for the earlier anti-Soviet war that US resources during the 1990s would be pitted against moderate and less sectarian Afghan groups. Journalist Charlotta Gall reports, for example, that "the vast majority of mujahideen were moderate and did not support terrorism."[x]

An Afghan civil war raged from 1992 until the Taliban, to whom the ISI had shifted support, acceded to power in Kabul in 1996. The ISI initially supported demagogue Gulbuddin Heckmatyar and consistently opposed more moderate alternatives, including prominently the Tajik Ahmad Shah Masood in the North and independent-minded Pashtun leaders including Abdul Haq, who sought to organize tribes through traditional Jirga (tribal council) settings. As a result, such leaders received only droplets of financial support from the US through the civil war and the period of Taliban rule to 2001. The civil war itself undermined traditional tribal leadership to the advantage of the sort of warlords who rise in power vacuums.

Western interests were damaged early. Tomsen cabled to Washington as early as 1991 that if Pakistan allies Heckmatyar or Abdul Rassoul Sayyaf were to reach Kabul, then Arab terrorist organizations would relocate their bases to Afghanistan, from which they might "stoke Islamic radicalism" in central Asia and the Middle East.[xi] The civil war era government, headed by Burhanuddin Rabbani and seeking allies—and acting with the approval of the ISI—admitted Osama Bin Laden and Al-Qaeda following their expulsion from the Sudan in 1996. In predictable sequels, Al Qaeda and the Taliban assassinated Masood and Haq as the most viable threats to their power in 2001.

Afghan governance frameworks, and US selection of allies, have improved only slightly since 2001. At the Bonn Conference that December, Hamid Karzai, understood to be a moderate Pashtun, was anointed as leader by US diplomats, with the intention that he would lead a state-building effort. But King Zahir Shah, who had been in exile in Italy since the 1970s and was a natural unifying figure for Afghans exhausted from decades of Communist and Islamist governors—was given a few minutes on the podium, then shown the exit. The US Defense Department, working at some cross-purpose to the State Department—not to mention cross purpose to President George W. Bush's call in April 2002 for a new "Marshall Plan"—then undermined Karzai's position by advancing massive resources on various warlords during 2002 and 2003, among them Ismael Khan, Mohammed Fahim, Dostum, and Gul Agha Sherzai. Deputy Defense Secretary Paul Wolfowitz argued that DoD's warlord-centered policy recognized Afghanistan's natural region-by-regionl autonomy.[xii]

Unfortunately, the DoD-led American policy undermined both centralized state-building *and* recovery of regional stability. Much of the Taliban's original appeal lay in the alternative they offered to the warlord chaos and depredations of the civil war period. But as Karzai was frequently deserted by US backers, he turned to many of the same warlords, his erstwhile opponents, for support at least a *modus vivendi*. The US embrace of warlords in the years after 2001 neglected, and further weakened, potential networks of traditional tribal leaders and village elders—which might otherwise have become moderate and influential allies of the new Karzai government.[xiii] In consequence of these ill-advised moves, the Taliban were on the way to recovery by 2006.

Karzai's role shifted from potential reformer to *de facto* power-broker-in-chief, from strategic nation-builder to tactical deal-maker. He maintained enough authority to be able to balance interests of warlords, tribal leaders, his own political appointees, and legislators. While he was keen to protect his warlord base, he also wanted to be able to bring pressure against the same people; for example, the Amnesty Law, passed in 2007 and gazetted in 2010, protects those who might be accused of past crimes, but without shutting the door to all legal redress. Karzai's transformation was a large setback. The US sought course correction with a fairly open effort to defeat Karzai in the 2009 presidential election. Karzai, who by then had become vocally anti-American, doubled down on his working alliance with various regional power-brokers, and was re-elected with the help of a massively corrupt vote count.[xiv] But while the international community's modernizing agenda was undermined, GIRoA has neither shown interest in boosting traditional tribal and religious leadership, nor been willing to loosen control over budget or appointment power in provinces and districts. (Foreign assistance agencies reinforced GIRoA's centralizing effort with their preference for administration through Kabul.) The base of support for the ISAF effort, and for GIRoA, has palpably narrowed.

Where to Go from Here

Perhaps the most basic rule of war strategy is to expand the breadth of one's support, to boost allies, and to discourage uncommitted forces from joining the enemy. The US has done nearly the opposite since 2001—undermining host country allies, even turning them against us, and ignoring potential new allies.

It is late, but perhaps not too late. The US and Coalition allies have a long-term interest in the stability of Afghanistan: a restoration of Taliban control might make the country again a haven for jihadist activity; and Taliban advances will likely weaken GIRoA, and strengthen regional warlords. A return to warlord rule would mean domestic interference and influence-seeking from most regional neighbors. Whatever Afghanistan's internal dynamics, the US and Coalition allies should also undertake more persistent efforts to involve foreign powers—most of which have ethnic or religious minorities mirroring those in Afghanistan—in finding a regional balance that will endure.[xv]

Emphasis on military support and development aid efforts inside Afghanistan reflect the weight of defense and foreign assistance bureaucracies in Washington and other Coalition capitals; but they have thus far had limited strategic results. The only way forward for Afghanistan's domestic troubles is to build the political front long neglected, in order to put ourselves on the side of and to nurture forces for moderation and stability. The Coalition's course should be to use influence on an array of issues to increase GIRoA's legitimacy in some areas and to reduce its presence in others. Here are some specifics, based in part on meetings with GIRoA officials during 2013 and 2014.

Tribal Engagement. Senior people at the Ministry of Borders and Tribal Affairs (MBTA) repeated a theme in a variety of ways: tribal leadership can play a crucial role in creating social adhesion, and thereby in undermining insurgent appeal. They told us that insurgents (Taliban, Haqani Network, etc.) cannot gain a foothold where tribal networks and loyalties are strong. Where decisions are made by tribal shuras (consultative councils), "extremists would not be part of the culture." More expansively, we were told that tribal jirgas—which bring together leaders of smaller groups on a district, provincial, or even regional basis, in order to reach consensus—can help us to achieve broader goals. These might include: bringing the Taliban into peaceful processes; enhancing border security; and even discouraging consumption and production of poppies.

Westerners tend to think of tribal structures as a barrier to the kind of modernizing, open societies they wish to encourage. But a different, and often superior, strategy is to build on a foundation of tribal leadership, with its built-in legitimacy, and then to absorb tribal leaders and customary law into newer administrative and legal structures. African legal scholar Charles Mwalimu argues that this absorption strategy has worked to advance both constitutionalism and human rights protection in a number of countries in Sub-Sahara Africa—and has certainly been more effective than approaches that sought to discard such traditional structures.[xvi]

We heard repeatedly that the Coalition "was not dealing with the real leaders of Afghanistan"—that is, for its strategic engagement, the Coalition has largely confined itself to dealing with officials in Kabul, many of whom had little standing among Afghans, while neglecting tribal and religious leaders. (In this, we were warned, the US has replayed the Russians' error from the 1980s.) Further, the practive of seeking warlords' backing directly rather than dealing through tribal elders was a serious mistake. The pattern changed to some extent during 2010-2011 when Commanding General McChrystal sought broader engagement, but such discussions mostly ended not long after his departure. Officials at the Human Rights Commission told us that "real" tribal leaders are respected, and are a key to exercising soft power. President Karzai, they told us, often avoided dealing with tribal leaders because they had the potential to break up his patronage network—and certainly *not* because he was a "modernizer." On the other hand, Karzai did frequently deal with his preferred tribal leaders, and to the point of circumventing the Ministry of Interior and other GIRoA structures.

Unlike the situation elsewhere, for example in Iraq, where a few tribal leaders sit atop of large hierarchies, traditional authority in Afghanistan is scattered among almost innumerable tribal and clan groupings. To have a strategic impact—to become part of a political front—they have to be brought together. Going forward, we should look for ways to encourage tribal jirgas—perhaps with advances to MBTA from military or diplomatic budgets—and we should encourage such government departments as the Independent Directorate of Local Governments (IDLG) and the Ministry of Rural Rehabilitation and Development (MRRD) to engage the MBTA—as a conduit to tribal leadership—in their sub-national framework initiatives.

Engaging Religious Leadership. For its optics, engagement with Afghan religious leadership might be sensitive, as Islam has come to be associated in Western minds with extremism, and many younger mullahs have offered support to insurgent groups. Indeed, we heard a credible account of a past US Ambassador to Kabul who told the Minister of Hajj and Islamic Affairs (MHIA). "If I work with you, they [in Washington] will put me in handcuffs."

That premise is wrongheaded, to say the least. Mullahs have a natural leadership role in an Islamic society, and they, more than anyone else, are in a position to affect views and practices on human rights, the status of women, the role of education, the practice of Islam, and—especially—the doctrinal credibility of Islamist insurgents. Outgoing MHIA leadership was especially interested in these matters; indeed, they expressed much dismay at what they considered the frequent uninformed practice of Islam in Afghanistan. One point of MHIA influence is in overseeing training of mullahs, including choice of learning materials and selection of religious teachers. A source of leverage could be payment of stipends to cooperative mullahs; this practice is frequent in other Moslem countries, including in the Levant; in Saudi Arabia, a carrot-and-stick approach helped to restore order after spectacular extremist attacks a decade ago. For example, at $60 dollars/ month for 17,000 mullahs, $1 million/ month (a drop in the bucket against a war budget) might buy a lot of influence.

MHIA could have been a natural ally for the US and the Coalition, one with the potential to deliver a great deal of soft power. But—again, except for some contacts during McChrystal's tenure—it has been neglected, and below the Western radar. With the new Ghani-Abdullah Administration, change is underway in leadership at MHIA, as in most Ministries. Enough is at stake that the US and allies should not leave this succession to chance, and should look for active engagement with the next leadership.

Engage the Human Rights Commission. While bringing traditional leadership into governance is critical, we should also look for ways to improve the legitimacy of the centralized structure in Kabul. The Afghan Independent Human Rights Commission (AIHRC) was established in 2002 pursuant to the 2001 Bonn Conference, and is outlined in Article 58 of the Afghan Constitution. The opinion of many AIHRC officials is that President Karzai, through his appointments, sought to weaken the Commission. He certainly had reason to do so, as AIHRC has investigated war crimes and lesser rights violations from the 1990s, often including those committed by the warlords who came to comprise Karzai's base of support. With assistance from foreign human rights NGOs, the Commission, probably in 2012, completed—but has not released—an 800 page *War Crimes Mapping Report.* In part because of the political sensitivity of this investigation, and concern that Afghan political counterparts might be undermined, or threatened, the US State Department has stayed clear of meetings at policy levels of AIHRC.

Once again, US policy has been misdirected, as AIHRC could offer crucial support toward meeting Coalition objectives. The post-2001 role of many civil war participants, often accused of serious rights violations from the 1990s, has been a large barrier to establishing GIRoA's legitimacy. In our discussions, AIHRC officials indicated that they would advise that the Afghan government is now too weak to release the *Mapping Report,* or to introduce any criminal proceedings based on the investigation. Were GIRoA to take such action, they told me, those named in the *Report* might retaliate with extensive violence, which would have the potential to push Afghanistan back into civil war.

But what AIHRC should be able to do is vet human rights records of candidates for political and administrative positions. AIHRC officials told us that "a credible government is a government without warlords." President Karzai did not wish such second-guessing of his choices for provincial or district governors, or for Ministerial positions. Neglect of closer collaboration with AIHRC has been a large gap in the Coalition's years-long anti-corruption initiative. If GIRoA (with Coalition encouragement) could screen out even some of those whose credibility is heavily compromised, we could begin to undermine the post-2001 Afghan culture of immunity for human rights and financial crimes. It could be much more effective than allowing such people into official positions, then looking for case-by-case evidence of wrong-doing.

A couple of high-profile occasions are illuminating. AIHRC did not vet Presidential candidates for the 2014 election; in consequence, of the top five, one was Qayum Karzai, President Karzai's half-brother, and two were warlords understand Karzai's political allies, one of whom, Sayyaf, has been accused of large-scale war crimes. The warlords apparently had in mind to gain some bargaining leverage in the formation of a post-Karzai cabinet. A more active role by the Commission could have made for a higher-quality Presidential field—and it might have kept Dostum off the winning ticket. (The other two of the leaders, Ghani and Abdullah, presumably would have been vetted fairly easily.) In another incident, Karzai overcame objections from the Coalition to release 65 insurgent detainees in early 2014. AIHRC officials told us that, had they been invited into the process, they had sufficient information on insurgents' human rights violations to have set up a further obstacle to their release.

Sub-National Governance. Afghanistan historically has been a land of different languages, geographic separations, and difficult travel. While GIRoA should find ways both to increase its credibility among Afghans, and to find subnational and tribal allies, it does *not* need to bring all groups and factions into a national governmental structure; indeed, such an inclusive Afghan structure has never existed. But governance can continue outside of the formal structure of GIRoA. The best the Coalition should hope for, going forward, is that armed conflicts will be low-grade and localized. A goal should be to induce some insurgents to pursue their objectives through political channels. Successful innovation in sub-national governance measures could contribute to answering the highest strategic question: how to shift some competition with insurgent groups from the military to the political arena—even in the face of ongoing inability of GIRoA and insurgent leaders seriously to negotiate.

Insurgents who seek to influence local events have little reason to compete for a voice in subnational councils as they now exist, because their power is so limited. Provinces and districts are blocked by Article 42 of the Afghan Constitution from raising their own revenue, which must instead come from Kabul. Currently, all governors are appointed by the President—which makes uncertain their responsiveness to provincial concerns. It would be consistent with the Constitution to have governors selected by elected provincial and district councils. We could insist on a larger role for provinces and districts in spending choices as a condition for ongoing external budget support. And we should look for a way for provinces, and perhaps for districts, to raise revenue, if necessary through legal changes.

Building sub-national governance structures with real powers has the potential to degrade the Taliban's military wing. Barfield, with co-author Nojumi, merits quoting again:

> While non-Pashtuns are particularly opposed to granting Taliban a role in the national government, they have few objections to their serving in local positions if they are

popular there. Those who come to hold such positions would have far less incentive to remain loyal to the Pakistan-based Taliban leadership, particularly its goal of seizing power nationwide, because it would conflict with their own local interests. Similarly, the need to deliver services and patronage to their own districts would increase their cooperation with Kabul and its international allies, which can provide such aid.[xvii]

Coalition leadership has not yet grasped this nettle. For example, the Tokyo Framework, which sets conditions for continuation of foreign non-military assistance to Afghanistan, calls for "de-concentration" of power, rather than for "de-centralization." The former provides for some sharing of decision-making with Kabul, but offers little push for subnational autonomy. While it apparently reflected the wishes of some around President Karzai, it was also favored among donor agencies used to dealing with centralized administration. As more than one Afghan has explained to us, IDLG creates the appearance of decentralization, while preventing it from actually happening. More rudely, IDLG has been called Karzai's coordination post for countrywide patronage. The institutional deference that many in the international community have shown to IDLG suggests strategic confusion.

Some reporting suggests that President Ghani seeks a more substantial role for subnational governance. On an optimistic scenario, such an initiative could over time weaken the Taliban and other insurgents.

Conclusion: The New Administration

Despite the drawdown of foreign troops, the strategic dynamics of the conflict have changed little—although the Taliban's position on the ground appears to be improving. And no matter what the Coalition does, or how effective the new GIRoA Administration becomes, we should not expect a rapid change in the military or political balance.

The key to stabilizing Afghanistan over the next few years lies in the political dimension—and this paper walks through four elements of what might become a political front. All of them push against what President Karzai's priorities were—or what they became after his remake as power-broker-in-chief.

The Ghani-Abdullah government may see things differently. They are not beholden—or are much less so—to Karzai's power-broker network. Neither campaigned for President as a de-centralizer, but they may move in this direction now, particularly as international interest in and material support for Afghanistan slacken—and as the limits of GIRoA's writ become clearer. At the same time, they may look for ways to strengthen moderate tribal and religious leaders. Similarly, neither said much about the Human Rights Commission, but both might now show more interest in laying building blocks for a more responsive and legitimate government. Should the new Administration turn in these directions, they will surely face opposition from domestic factions dependent of GIRoA's *status-quo*. Indeed, scuttlebutt has it that Karzai himself now serves as a gathering point for recalcitrant factions. The role of the US and the Coalition must be to use statecraft, including aggressive diplomacy, to help to overcome such opposition. The US might even move away from a decades-long pattern of undermining moderates and shrinking the domestic coalition.

Chapter 6

Unmasking the Executioner: What This Gesture Means and How It Can Help in the Fight Against ISIS

Holly Hughson

First Published 23 January 2015

Abstract

There are important lessons to be drawn from the November 16 ISIS video. Its slick production of the unmasked execution video displayed one of ISIS's strengths and also presented a powerful clue to governments looking to exploit its inherent structural liabilities as well as the challenges that it faces from within. The assembled force of ISIS is a composite of individuals all fighting for different reasons. Western governments seeking to defeat ISIS and its capacity for "franchise jihad" must recognize and understand this diversity and exploit it. This strategy requires the West to orient itself to the composite that ISIS presents and avoid the catastrophic pitfall of trying to create the enemy it wants to fight at the expense of the one presented.

Article

On November 16, ISIS released its fifth execution video featuring a murdered Western hostage. The video contained several points of departure from the previous execution videos; most notable were its content, structure and length.[i] The American, Peter (Abdul Rahman) Kassig, did not appear alive; rather, his severed head was displayed at the end of the 16-minute video.[ii] Also featured were the choreographed, simultaneous executions of 22[iii] Syrian soldiers. Despite these variations on an established theme, the most dramatic and revealing departure in this video is that the executioners performed their duties unmasked.

The Unmasking: A Statement of Confidence or an Act of Desperation?

Intelligence experts and the media have so far focused their interpretations of the unmasking as either a statement of confidence or an act of desperation.[iv] The fighters appear unashamed of their role; their expressions and swagger filmed in dramatic slow motion are staged to suggest they are convicted to the cause and committed to participating in the mass execution about to take place. Additionally, several if not all of the unmasked executioners appear to be foreign fighters.[v] By unmasking the executioners ISIS flaunts its global appeal and demonstrates progress towards its stated goal of establishing a transnational Caliphate.

Analysts at the U.S.-based Terrorism Research and Analysis Consortium (TRAC) and the U.K.-based Quilliam Foundation have examined each frame of the 16-minute video and using clues in the lighting, shadows and overall production, suggest that it took up to 6 hours to film.[vi] This is not the hasty effort of a group trying to flip the script to remain relevant. Rather it is a deliberate and purposeful effort to broaden their appeal and demonstrate resolve to their cause.

Furthermore it boasts of their ability to recruit jihadists from the international community.

Within 24 hours of the fifth video's release, French authorities identified one citizen, Maxime Hauchard from Normandy. Within two days, medical student Nasser Muthana, from Cardiff, Wales, was tentatively identified by his father, and French authorities identified a second citizen, Mickael Dos Santos.[vii] Previously, Nasser Muthana appeared in a recruitment video, stating that ISIS has "brothers from Bangladesh, from Iraq, from Cambodia, Australia and UK."[viii] That ISIS has clearly accomplished its goal of international recruitment is at this point self-evident from their own use of social media.

Regardless if the video reveals desperation or confidence, it is also true that in unmasking its executioners ISIS has ensured that they cannot go home. The unmasking was an instrument of control. There is little doubt that both ISIS and its foreign fighters are aware of the actions governments are taking to prevent their own citizens from both joining and returning from fighting with jihadist groups. By having foreign fighters turned executioners appear unmasked and complicit in murder ISIS has done just as much to ensure that they cannot go home as Western nations have done to try and prevent would-be jihadists from joining ISIS. Regardless of the intention behind the unmasking, the question posed to governments is now: How can the presence of foreign fighters be leveraged against ISIS?

Unmasking Diversity and Revealing Liabilities

In unmasking their executioners, ISIS has displayed one of its great strengths, the ability to compel foreign individuals to abandon their former lives, risking death for the promise of a glorious resurrection in a new state. The unmasking also presented a powerful clue to governments looking to exploit its inherent structural liabilities. ISIS's diversity has revealed three distinct vulnerabilities in the narrative surrounding the reality of international jihad. First, the foreign fighters motivated to defend the Sunni population in Syria's civil war are not just battling the Syrian government as the recruitment videos and other propaganda that led them to jihad suggested. Rather they find themselves slaying and brutalizing other civilians—the vast majority of them Muslims—in an increasingly fracturing region as ISIS struggles to control the territory it has gained. Secondly, foreign fighters are not experiencing the romanticized jihad they have dreamed of. Instead, many have found themselves conscripted into a jihad of bureaucracy attempting to provide services to non-combatants in the very power vacuum which they helped create. Finally, under the rubric of ISIS there is no room for the concept of meritocracy that foreign fighters who have lived in the west have seen or experienced. They are, and will always remain, second class jihadists.

The Near Enemy is Other Muslims

ISIS information campaign captured the imagination of potential foreign fighters by utilizing social media platforms like Twitter and Facebook to deliver daily propaganda to tens of thousands of subscribers. Through a fully integrated social media campaign, ISIS initially presented the narrative that it was defending the Syrian Sunni majority against a brutal Shia minority regime.[ix] This campaign was all the more effective for showing decisive action, in contrast to Western governments whose rhetoric of outrage and war crimes of the Syrian government had begun to ring hollow.

However, ISIS created expectations of jihad which do not accurately convey the reality of combat on the ground. As the fractures developed amongst the opposition groups, so the targets shifted with fellow Sunni fighters now in their sights. Social media posts revealed internal debate between foreign fighters over whether martyrdom can be the result of being killed by intra jihadist group fighting. Other posts reveal disillusionment that the once honorable resistance of the mission had been lost. One British fighter, claiming to represent 30 other British citizens, told the International Center for the Study of Radicalization and Political Violence (ICSR), "We came to fight the regime and instead we are involved in gang warfare. It's not what we came for but if we go back [to Britain] we will go to jail."[x] Several French jihadists have also echoed this disillusionment with not fighting in a heroic battle, rather battling amongst jihadist factions.[xi]

Furthermore, ISIS exists on the potency of the Sunni-Shia divide. With limited exceptions, the governments and population standing in the way of its goal of a caliphate are Muslim. This divide will be keenly felt and understood by the fighters who have grown up in Muslim countries. The perception that Shia are the mortal enemy of the Sunni will have been a regular feature of extremist ideologues and will have been reinforced through a long history of violent clashes, national identify, and socio-economic conditions. For many of the foreign fighters from Western countries, their minority religious status will have diminished the sectarian divide, and rather focused their motivation to fight along Christian–Muslim lines. These foreign fighters are likely unprepared for the scale of brutality required to gain control of territory by killing other Muslims.

A Jihad of Bureaucracy

The second vulnerability in ISIS media campaign is a function of the changing nature of the battle. Once again, the strength of its ability to inspire and recruit fighters contains an inherent weakness. The slick video productions with dramatic soundtracks and staging as seen in the fifth execution video appeal to a violent video game playing generation.

Following its rapid series of territorial gains, ISIS is now at pains to demonstrate it can equally succeed at governance, including humanitarian assistance, basic services, and rule of law. This "mission creep" includes population control, a task which ISIS approaches the only way it knows how: by instilling fear and terror through the brutal tactics of public executions, beheadings, crucifixions, and torture.[xii] It also involves micromanagement. The German journalist, Juergen Todenhoefer, was recently given permission for safe passage to visit Mosul. He found the militants in control confident, relaxed and even boastful about their brutality. They were also very young, and even adolescent boys were armed.[xiii] He saw professionally produced leaflets and posters instructing men how to pray, women how to dress, and how to treat slaves. Todenhoefer was clear that ISIS motivation to allow him to visit and film was to show their Islamic state is indeed working.

Social media serves the population of Mosul and presents a very different picture. In a series of "diary entries" to the BBC, residents describe constant water and power and shortages, poisoning from contaminated water and anger that ISIS has banned sports and painting from schools, even the use of colored pens.[xiv] The work of governance has to be done under the constant threat of attack. This existentially heightened paradigm where martyrdom and need to keep sewage out of the water supply fosters something of a schizophrenic requirement of its fighters.

To heed the call to jihad in Western countries represents the ultimate rejection of any and all opportunities that can be imagined in their known context. The promise of starting over in a new life in an Islamic Caliphate presents an alluring vision, less the daily experience. The foreign fighters from Western countries have the steepest learning curve, and the gap between the idea and the reality has begun to reveal itself, as evidenced by communications between British and French fighters within ISIS. In letters published by the newspaper *Le Figaro*, complaints included being bored, "I've basically done nothing except hand out clothes and food," annoyed, "I'm fed up. They make me do the dishes," and missing the comforts of life in France: "I'm fed up. My iPod doesn't work any more here. I have to come back."[xv]

Second Class Jihadists

In every institution, there are fault lines which form along natural leadership and personality boundaries. In the Muslim world, there is another, disproportionately weighted hierarchy to overlay: ethnicity. Not all Salafist Sunnis who have committed their fate to ISIS are equal. Without question, Arabs, have the closest connection to the Prophet of all Muslims, and yet it is still a critical point that ISIS's leadership has to demonstrate.

There is a distinct hierarchy within both Sunni and Shia Islam. Just as there are certain formulaic rules used to validate a Catholic saint, there are rules within Islam for claiming the legitimacy of your ideology or authority: the closer you can demonstrate your bloodline to the Prophet Mohammed, the more likely it is that your ideas and leadership will be accepted and elevated. When the self-proclaimed leader of ISIS, Abu Bakr al-Baghdadi, announced the expansion of his emirate to Syria in 2013, Turki al-Binali wrote a biography supporting Baghdadi's claim as the Caliph. Binali examined Baghdadi's family history providing evidence that he is a descendant of the Muslim Prophet Muhammad's Quraysh tribe.

Every non-Arab Sunni, even a Salafist jihadi, ultimately represents a convert at some point in his or her personal history. This means their ability to claim relationship to Muhammad is an inherent limitation on their leadership and influence. This reality is not a concept consistent with being raised in Western democracies and may well pose a long-term threat to the organization. However marginalized the foreign fighters might have felt in their own countries, they are still products of the education system and certain western cultural norms. This will be a distinct attribute that will set them apart from their Arab counterparts.

By showing the faces of foreign fighters who appear to be from Southeast Asia, Southern Russia and Europe, ISIS makes its case for a globally supported jihad, but one with an inherent, unspoken religious hierarchy. This hierarchy will naturally compete with the assigned social hierarchy of its individual fighters. Although converts cannot as easily demonstrate their lineage to the Prophet, it does not stop them from trying. While operating as a humanitarian aid worker in Darfur from 2004 to 2005, I spent time in Khartoum and became aware of notable consistencies in perspectives as I visited some of the more privileged families of the establishment. Invariably, as part of their introductions, each family would at some point attempt to demonstrate their lineage to the Prophet Mohammed. Over time, I became aware of an entire industry in Sudan and elsewhere, which supports this attempt for Muslims to trace lineage as close as possible to the Prophet and his extended family.[xvi]

This hierarchy of honor and ethnicity will have a dynamic role in ISIS operations, and it is something that must be managed. In the unmasking of its foreign fighters, ISIS's leadership is exerting its control over its own rank and file, limiting their options within the organization and effectively removing any opportunity for returning to life in a Western country.

Conclusion

With the decision to release an execution video with unmasked executioners ISIS made a bold statement. It also exposed its underbelly. This last video offers significant clues to the makeup of the organization as well as the challenges it faces from within. The assembled force of ISIS is a composite of individuals all fighting for different reasons. Inherent in this spectrum, of self-defense, defending an adopted homeland against a record of perceived American-led occupation, or Bashar al-Assad's brutal regime, is a diversity that will complicate effective command and control. Both foreign and domestic fighters are also fighting for their own personal reasons, from ambition and glory to curiosity, to a need to belong and religious conviction.

ISIS's self-proclaimed "state" and their dramatically staged presentation of a bold, confident, multi-national force is easy to film but tougher to realize. Managing the diversity of an international jihad is a whole other ballgame. Governments combating ISIS should exploit its diversity and the inherent potential for mistrust and internal discord. The unavoidable requirement of effective command is consensus.

Regardless of what its social media campaign proclaims, this consensus will be an ongoing, dynamic challenge for ISIS.

The West must understand this and orient itself to each aspect of ISIS, avoiding the catastrophic pitfall of trying to create the enemy it wants to fight at the expense of the one presented. ISIS has made it clear that it is not one enemy; it is a composite. The strategy for the defeat of ISIS can be found in seizing upon the organization's diversity. Success may well come in transforming their boast into their downfall.

Chapter 7

Boko Haram's Resiliency Spells Trouble for West Africa

Jeff Moore

First Published 23 January 2015

As the world mourned for the victims of an Islamist jihadist terror attack in France, a mass casualty attack in Baga, Nigeria by Boko Haram killed scores of men, women and children—low estimates say possibly 500 were killed; high estimates say 2,000. Regardless of the exact casualty count, the attack triggered no mass marches, no speeches by international heads of state, and no outward signs of solidarity from the White House or Congress. Why? Nigeria's attack was done by Islamist jihadists, just like France. And if the high the body count is true, it's about 1,000 less than the September 11th attacks, which is astounding. Regardless of the lack of international condemnation, the Baga attack signifies the genocidal nature of Boko Haram's violence, and the group will undermine West Africa's security unless Nigeria can quickly improve its counterinsurgency (COIN) operations.

So what happened in Baga? On 3 January, a large Boko Haram light infantry force attacked Baga town and 16 other villages in Borno State. As previously reported by *Small Wars Journal*,[i] one of Boko's targets was the base of the Multinational Joint Task Force (MNJTF) in nearby Doro Gowon town. The MNJTF, made of soldiers from Niger, Nigeria, Cameroon, Benin, and Chad, has a both border security and counterterror missions.[ii] This was a military target. The rest of Boko's objectives were apparently civilian.

Multiple accounts of the attack suggest Boko Haram fighters waded into the Baga area from multiple avenues of approach and applied grazing fire to fleeing civilians and peoples' homes. They also reportedly rounded up scores of people and raked them with assault rifle and machine gun fire. Some of the dead were found tied up. Thousands of homes were set alight during the carnage.[iii] Tactically, it was calculated and methodical mass murder. Strategically, it facilitated Boko Haram's control of vast tracts of Borno state.[iv]

While the scale of destruction in Baga was new, the target set and tactics used weren't. Boko Haram has been carrying out attacks on civilians for more than a year now. On 10 November 2014, for example, a Boko Haram suicide bomber killed 50 students and teachers at the Government Senior Science Secondary School in Potiskum.[v] It barely made international headlines, but a December 2013 Taliban killing of 132 schoolchildren in Pakistan caused a global outcry and garnered plenty of press.

Other dramatic moves by Boko Haram have rarely made major news outside West Africa despite it being one of the biggest insurgent wars in the world. The group established a caliphate in August 2014, claiming all of northern Nigeria as its own.[vi] Since April, Boko Haram has seized and occupied more than 24 towns through a series of light infantry offensives.[vii] Along the way, it has kidnapped 276 schoolgirls from Chibok[viii]—a rare episode that did make headlines—and murdered people house-to-house in Gwoza.[ix] On 21 November, Boko Haram assaulted Azaya Kura village, killing 45 people. Villagers report that the militants tied their captives' hands behind their backs and slit their throats.[x] On 20 December, Boko Haram released a video of its fighters massacring droves of what it called "infidels"—reportedly just elderly people—in a bloody frenzy at a school dormitory.[xi] Attacks like this have killed 13,000 people since 2009.[xii] 2014 was the bloodiest year of Boko's war with approximately 9,000 killed and some 1.5 million displaced.[xiii]

Nigeria is in Bad Shape, to Say the Least

What's Boko Haram's up to with all this? One of Nigeria's popular retired military officers, Colonel Abubakar Umar, asserts that Boko Haram isn't just aiming to take over parts of Nigeria. It's setting its sights on Nigeria's neighbors, too. "The insurgents intend to use a conquered Northeast as a launch pad on which to invade and conquer the rest of the country and possibly the whole of the West African sub-region," he says.[xiv]

Alarmed at Boko Haram's progress, the government recently launched a new COIN campaign, "Operation No Mercy Against Terrorists," which has experienced some success. The military retook four towns in Adamawa State,[xv] and it claims to have retaken Chibok in Borno State—where the sensational kidnapping of 276 girls happened in April.[xvi] Most of the girls remain captive, and some appear to have been married off to various jihadist fighters. So much for the flaccid, "Bring back our girls" twitter campaign meant to shame Boko into releasing them.

A side note to the American president—Islamist jihadist terrorists that kidnap and murder schoolchildren without hesitation won't be intimidated by a shame campaign on twitter and Facebook.

At any rate, where the Nigerians have had real success comes from a combined military and civilian approach where the former works in close junction with the latter to apply continual pressure to the insurgents. The latter consists of two parts: the Civilian Joint Task Force (CJTF), and local hunters.[xvii]

The CJTF, or "Yan Gora," is a government-supervised local youth force that provides intelligence to the military on Boko Haram's field activities and its agents inside villages and towns. These youth have intimate knowledge of the goings on in their own areas, so they know who the outsiders are—specifically, the Boko Haram infiltration agent provocateurs. Aside from reporting, the CJTF sometimes eliminates the insurgents they find, so they are what's politely referred to as an "intelligence-force application unit." U.S. Special Operations Forces call it "targeting," and it has been used to great effect against al Qaeda in Afghanistan and other areas. While Nigeria's local force targeting appears to be cruder than that of U.S. Special Forces, it is, nevertheless, making progress.

Local hunters play a similar role. They have intimate knowledge of the countryside surrounding the villages, so their guide services are immeasurably helpful to the military for reconnaissance and sweep operations. Hunters also know how to move seamlessly through the woods, so they add an element of stealth to these operations.

The big picture here is that Nigeria is beginning to make more use of local forces, which are vital to success in COIN.

It's not enough, however. Nigeria doesn't seem to have a counter political warfare program to refute Boko Haram's propaganda. Some soldiers are poorly trained and equipped, and others have fled while engaging Boko Haram in battle.[xviii] Accusations of rampant government corruption don't inspire the population's support,[xix] yet another vital ingredient for successful COIN.

Feeling the pressure, Nigeria is just now apparently trying to fix some of these issues, but are the remedies appropriate? Only time will tell. The military recently indicted a brigadier general and 14 other officers, apparently for negligence, and it sentenced 54 soldiers to death for refusing to fight Boko Haram. The accused, however, say the army hasn't provided them with the right weapons and equipment to engage in combat,[xx] and assertions of incompetence in the officer corps are not uncommon.

Another glaring problem is a failure to protect the population from Boko Haram, which seems to strike whatever civilian target it wants, whenever it wants. This would include open-air markets, cell phone vendors, buses, busy streets, and entire villages such as Baga.

Additionally, some villagers that have reported on Boko Haram have been left unprotected, a death knell for informants.[xxi] COIN won't work unless the government has plenty of informants, and when they get murdered, it dissuades others from joining COIN efforts.

As an aside, the government's local force program is likely one reason Boko Haram attacked Baga. An intimidated and bludgeoned population is less likely to provide its government with help. So Baga was not only force application on a soft target, it was a message to the people of Nigeria not to align with the government.

Aside from all this, the political impact of the insurgency is taking its toll. The ruling People's Democratic Party and the challenging All Progressives Congress have turned the war into a political blame game ahead of the February 2015 general elections.[xxii] More than 650,000 people have been driven from their homes,[xxiii] and Boko Haram is threatening to attack the elections.[xxiv]

Nigeria Bar Association's president, Mr. Austine Alegeh, accuses the government of abandoning its constitutional responsibilities of providing for the welfare and security of the population. "The question agitating our minds now is whether the government charged to protect lives and property of Nigerians no longer has the capacity to do so."[xxv]

The war is spilling over onto Nigeria's neighbors, too. Over 100,000 Nigerians have fled to Niger, 44,000 have crossed into Cameroon, and 2,700 have escaped to Chad.[xxvi]

Boko Haram has been using Cameroon as a sanctuary where it secures weapons and food, and it has also staged attacks there.[xxvii] It kidnapped the wife of the deputy prime minister in July,[xxviii] it carried out raids against the Cameroon military in October,[xxix] and it slaughtered villagers in Mokolo in November.[xxx] On 22 December, Cameroon announced it had discovered and dismantled a Boko Haram training camp on its territory.[xxxi] Then on 28 December, Boko Haram attacked and overran a Cameroon military base at Assighasia. Cameroon responded with ground forces backed by close air support, which drove out the attackers.[xxxii] For Cameroon, this raid represents the writing on the wall: Cameroon has become a definite Boko Haram target, and it has moreover become a combatant nation in Boko Haram's war. To punctuate the point, Boko Haram fighters raided Maki and Mada villages (near Mokolo city) in Cameroon on 18 January 2015, taking 80 some hostages, many of them women and children. The Boko raiding parties set the Cameroon homes alight as they left. Cameroon troops pursued via a series of running battles, and about 24 hostages were released or escaped along the way.[xxxiii] The situation there remains fluid.

Alarmed at the growing pandemonium, Chad is getting into the fight. It moved infantry forces, including 400 some odd vehicles backed by attack helicopters, into Cameroon just after the mass kidnapping. Colonel Djerou Ibrahim of the Chadian army made his aim clear, "Our mission is to hunt down Boko Haram, and we have all the means to do that."[xxxiv]

Niger is also troubled at Boko Haram's progress and is no stranger to its advances. Niger security forces arrested 24 Boko Haram operatives in December 2013 bent on carrying out bombings and kidnappings there,[xxxv] and they have reached out to Niger's criminal gangs. One gangster said, "If [Boko Haram] tell you to set off a bomb and it succeeds, if it kills a lot of people, they will pay you a lot of money."[xxxvi] Niger has joined Cameroon and Chad in coalition military planning to deal with the threat.[xxxvii]

What's it All Mean?

Virginia Comolli, a Research Fellow for Security and Development at the International Institute for Strategic Studies (IISS), weighs in. She is a renowned Boko Haram expert, and her book on the subject, *Boko Haram: Nigeria's Islamist Insurgency*, is due out in April.[xxxviii]

Regarding territory, Comolli says that it doesn't appear that Boko Haram recently seized territory with a governing and services plan, "So it is not yet clear whether the group has the ability or desire to administer these territories."

Additionally, Comolli says that Nigeria's military improvements might keep Boko Haram geographically in check. "For all its shortcomings, the military is indeed capable of regaining territorial control, indicating that maintaining an Islamist state in north-eastern Nigeria is not sustainable in the long term."

This doesn't mean that things are looking up, however. Says Comolli, "Boko Haram does not need to control territory to pose a national security challenge." It has proven that it can adapt and apply violence where needed, she says. "They can move their fight from rural to urban environments and vice versa, deploy female or disabled suicide bombers, and they have disguised fighters in female clothes." Comolli says these type tactics are imaginative and indicate resilience.

Regarding the election, President Goodluck's victory is not assured. True, his forces have recently pushed Boko Haram back, but the population needs to see more legitimacy from its government, and it needs some inspiring national security news, a big win against the insurgents, for example. At present, the people have none of this.

And Boko Haram will get to vote, too—with violence. Says Comolli, "Boko Haram rejects the concept of democracy. It's a Western imposition and incompatible with Islamist law. Boko Haram carried out violence around the 2011 elections, and for 2015, attacks are likely to escalate. Targeting will likely include polling stations and political candidates in northern and central Nigeria in addition to the usual targets such as markets, schools, places of worship, and the military."

Nigeria's neighbors aren't optimistic. Niger is watching for pending attacks, and Cameroon border patrol commander Leopold Nlate Ebale asserts, "We're convinced that the establishment of a 'caliphate' [by Boko Haram] is aimed not only at Nigeria but also at Cameroon."[xxxix]

Comolli sums it up by saying that Boko Haram's "Adaptive traits, ideological drive, and the sub-optimal conditions in which military forces are often deployed suggests that violence is unlikely to abate regardless of a caliphate being in place or not."

So Boko Haram can just keep killing and fighting, because that's what it's good at. Saying it has a caliphate and actually setting one up and managing it as ISIS is doing in Syria ands Iraq is another proposition altogether. But this fighting and killing could turn Nigeria into a failed state. The only way forward is for Nigeria to improve its COIN abilities, not only for the sake of its own stability, but for West Africa's as well.

Chapter 8

Urban Siege in Paris: A Spectrum of Armed Assault

John P. Sullivan and Adam Elkus

First Published 2 February 2015

In 2009, we laid out a conceptual model of terrorist "urban siege" based on the Mumbai attacks.[i] As noted by several observers, the recent terrorist attack in Paris on the *Charlie Hebdo* offices may have succeeded due to the unfortunate fact that security officials expected other attack modes (such as airline bombs), not a run and gun in the heart of an urban center.[ii]

While it would be tempting to posit Paris as another bloody data point explained by our conceptual schema, Paris is in fact cause for broadening and expanding it. Unfortunately, the world faces urban security threats that span a spectrum of organization and lethality. Future threats may look like Mumbai (as has been seen in the Mumbai-like operation against the Westgate shopping mall in Nairobi) or they may resemble Paris.[iii] And there is a large spectrum of threats that occupy the threat envelope in between.

Here we review the timeline of the attacks, analyze continuities and complications with urban siege schemas and relevant incidents, review relevant analysis that could inform a more robust analysis of urban siege, and close with a set of our own questions for researchers and practitioners about what assumptions we need to make in planning for, training to stop, and red-teaming urban siege scenarios.

Urban Siege in Paris

In France, the new year opened with a horrific urban siege. This latest installment of urban guerilla action involved armed assault and massacre, execution of police, a massive manhunt and two hostage-barricade situations. Three days of terror saw the deployment of 88,000 personnel from the French Interior Ministry—ranging from community police to specialized gendarmerie, augmented by a large military contingent.[iv]

On Wednesday 7 January, a car pulled up in front of the offices of *Charlie Hebdo*, a satirist magazine in Paris' 11th Arrondissement. Two men—the Kouachi brothers, Cherif and Said—got out of the car; they were dressed in black and carried automatic weapons. After making inquiries the made way to the office and opened fire, killing one. When they arrived at the office they again opened fire killing the editor and 9 others including a police officer guarding the editor, as well as a police officer Ahmed Merabat, the first responding officer to the scene.[v]

After the attack the self-styled Mujahideen fled the scene. The next day (8 January) they robbed a gas station near Villers-Cotterets. The same day a female police officer, Clarissa Jean-Phillpe was killed in Montrouge, a Paris suburb by Amedy Coulibaly (who has been linked to the Kouachi brothers. On 9 January, the Kouachi brothers robbed a car in northeast Paris. A few minutes later the Kouachi brothers took a hostage and the suspects were chased by helicopters in a massive manhunt. Area schools and businesses were put under lockdown and large numbers of officers from the National Police and Gendarmerie (including GIGN and RAID respectively) were deployed with support from the Army.[vi] The suspects settled in for a hostage-barricade situation (the second siege) at a printers suite in Dammartin-en-Goele. The suspects boasted they would become martyrs.

A third incident at the Hyper Cacher, a kosher grocery, was conducted by Amedy Couliby to support the Kouachi brothers.[vii] This siege, which resulted in the death of Couliby and four hostages, was terminated by a police counter assault. The counter assaults were coordinated, simultaneous actions with the taketown of the Kouachi brothers to limit risk to the hostages at the grocery since Couliby said he would execute them if police assaulted the Kouachis' location.

The aftermath of the assaults includes questions about intelligence failure, fear of follow-on attacks conducted by activated sleeper cells, threats to police, and the threat of attacks in The United Kingdom and United States.[viii] Finally, the conflict has both physical and virtual dimensions as seen by a wave of attacks against French websites. Hackers, responding to the French public's defiance in the face of terror, hit 19,000 French websites with denial-of-service attacks.[ix] A group of pro-Syrian regime hackers briefly commandeered the French newspaper *Le Monde*'s Twitter account, tweeting a message mocking the post-attack hashtag #JeSuisCharlie.[x]

Analyzing the Paris Urban Siege: Continuity and Complication

On one end of a spectrum of urban assault lethality and sophistication is the Mumbai attacks. The attackers belonged to a cohesive and organized terrorist organization and received guidance, direction, and real-time information support from an offsite handler. On the lowest end is a garden variety "active shooter" more akin to the Columbine school shooters—no training, no guidance, no resources, no contacts but nonetheless possessing an willingness to kill and die. The organized terrorist group type of attacker is obviously capable of waging urban siege. Operating in small squads, they can challenge police command and control and on-site response through dispersion, firepower, and entrenchment.

As David Kilcullen observed in an application of our work to the Westgate mall attack, the Mumbai attack also was terror by "remote control"—the attackers utilized Skype, cellphones, and satellite phones to connect to an offsite operations team in Pakistan monitoring social media and news reporting concerning the ongoing attack. The Nairobi attack exhibited similar characteristics.[xi] Six suspects affiliated with al-Shabaab executed a hostage-barricade assault against the mall complex.[xii] Multiple squads executed a coordinated attack and successfully entrenched within the mall complex for four days. 72 people died before Kenyan security forces could retake the mall.

As with Mumbai, the Kenya attackers prepared for an entrenchment scenario, fused various weapons and teams, and thwarted a disorganized and bureaucratically disjointed security force response long enough to exact a gruesome toll. The attack, though novel in its ferocity, sophistication, and toll, was preceded by a drumbeat of urban terrorist attacks in which al-Shabaab demonstrated urban assault capabilities. The catastrophic impact of poor command and control cannot be overstated. An extensive *Guardian* report suggested that disputes over police and military command and control delayed response. Not only were attackers able to entrench and kill more victims, but a friendly fire incident also occurred and militants were able to foil a first joint police-army counterattack with sniper fire.[xiii]

Nor has Kenya been the sole instance of a suicide commando assault since Mumbai. In December of last year, the Pakistani Taliban launched a gruesome attack on a school for children of Pakistan army officers.[xiv] In a repeat of previous urban siege patterns, attackers provisioned for a long attack quickly pushed into the school. However, unlike in Beslan there would be no entrenchment and hostage situation. Pakistani forces responded within 15 minutes and killed all of the attackers. However, the security forces were too late to save the 132 children and 10 school staff slaughtered by the terrorists during the initial attack. Pakistani Taliban, Afghan Taliban, and al-Qaeda urban operations continue within urban centers in South Asia, a site C. Christine Fair has noted is one large "urban battlefield."[xv]

While we do not suggest that older hostage and armed attack scenarios were simple, the operational challenges associated with these types of attacks dwarf the typical single-site, hostage-barricade assumptions seen in terrorist operations such as the 1970s Munich Olympics incident or the spate of aircraft hijackings seen during the wave of terror that preceded the current wave of radical Islamist terror. As J. Paul D. Taillon noted in his study of hijacking and hostages, successful counterterrorist operations involved forward base access, cooperation, and specialized units capable of dislodging attackers.[xvi] In contrast, modern urban sieges will require first responders to meet attackers head-on, regardless of sophistication and armament. Such direct police action is necessary to stop the 'kinetic momentum' and minimize casualties.[xvii]

For example, in June 2014 a team of heavily armed Pakistani Taliban militants assaulted the Jinnah International Airport in Karachi.[xviii] Attackers disguised themselves as airport personnel and were successfully held off by security personnel and finished off by military reinforcements. They were provisioned for a long siege, but failed to survive long enough to inflict major damage.[xix] Whatever damage (material, human, and symbolic) they inflicted, it could have been far worse had airport security officers not immediately responded to the incident.

For police, responding to simple, single site attacks requires a high degree of tactical proficiency. Larger, more complex, area-wide simultaneous assaults require a high degree of coordination and the employment of operational art. Urban operational art for the police demands integration of patrol, special operations (tactical response including SWAT, bomb squad, riot/crowd control, media/public information, detectives and investigation, and intelligence, as well as synchronization with the fire service, emergency medical services (EMS), emergency management, civil authorities, and potentially the military. Such coordination may be needed at multiple locations in a single jurisdiction or among authorities spread across multiple jurisdictions.

Our ability to comment on the Paris attacks is limited and based on details currently known in the open source. However, we can observe several important similarities and distinctions to the urban siege model we have outlined in prior work.

Some aspects of the Paris attacks had at least superficially to other observed urban terrorist attacks. While the main actual attack itself was relatively brief, the attackers themselves hid out in the Paris metropolitan area, lengthening the period of terror and fear. The incident reached a bloody climax when the assailants—seeking martyrdom and desiring a fight to the death—holed up in a small warehouse with a hostage and subsequently died at the hands of French law tactical responders.[xx] Both gunmen received tactical training related to basic weapons usage, and one gunman may have visited Yemen to receive further instruction and financing.[xxi]

The distribution of the siege is also relevant. The *Charlie Hebdo* incident must be understood as an integrated whole, with the opening assault against the newspaper offices just one (high-profile) component. For three days, attackers went on a killing spree, distributing their attacks in time and space around Paris and its environs. During this time, the French security authorities were forced to deploy an enormous force to find, fix in place, and neutralize the suspects before they could accumulate a larger kill count. The attacks were synchronized to achieve maximum impact, and police faced enormous difficulties handling both situations simultaneously.

The Hyper Cacher hostage taker, for example, demanded that authorities cease their pursuit of the Kouachi brothers. While the police raid that broke the siege at the Hyper Cacher may seem improvised and amateurish to some observers, it was also conducted under extremely unfavorable conditions.[xxii] Both police raids had to be synchronized for hostages to survive. Moreover, coordinating a massive interagency response is complex and should be considered an operational success for the French security authorities given that difficulties in interagency coordination are an impediment to many operational responses and notably operational response to the Nairobi mall attack in 2013.[xxiii]

While these elements may be familiar to those that respond to, cooand, or analyze urban siege, other elements of the attack were more novel. Analyzing the Paris attacks, Clint Watts argued that the future of jihad was "inspired, networked, and directed:"

> The jihadi movement may have finally become what its original luminaries always wanted it to be—and in Paris of all places. The amorphous connections between the Charlie Hebdo attackers, the Kouachi brothers—who attributed their actions to "al Qaeda in Yemen"—and kosher market attacker Amedy Coulibali – who pledged allegiance to the Islamic State in a recently released online video—may reflect exactly what some early jihadi strategists intended: broad based jihad via a loose social movement. …. Years ago, Bruce Hoffman rightly proposed a spectrum approach to understanding al Qaeda comprising of a core, affiliates, and locals. His framework was appropriate but now needs some updates with the rise of the Islamic State. With two competing poles and a spectrum of adherents littered throughout at least five continents, jihadi plots and their perpetrators might best be examined through the blending of three overlapping categories: 'directed', 'networked' and 'inspired'. These three labels should not be seen as discrete categories but instead as phases across a spectrum—some plots and their perpetrators will bleed over these boundaries.[xxiv]

Counterterrorism analysts have often argued over whether the future of jihad lies with centralized, hierarchal (if not completely top-down) groups capable of organized and lethal attacks or small groupings of alienated, mostly self-directed local attackers.[xxv] Watts suggests that this dichotomous understanding is ultimately misleading—it may be possible for an attack to feature such strange incongruities as terrorists belonging to two rival organizations (the Islamic State in Iraq and al-Qaeda) cooperating together.

Indeed, Islamic State supporter Coulibaly (with logistical support from other men that French authorities have detained) operated alongside al-Qaeda-identifying gunmen.[xxvi] All three were part of a known network of French domestic extremists that orbited around a charismatic yet amateur and unofficial religious figure.[xxvii] We leave discussion of what this means for the global terrorist threat landscape to counterterrorism specialists who will be informed by additional data. However, these debates, typologies, and considerations have practical meaning for operational authorities tasked with preparing for and countering urban attacks.

The three-day Paris siege complicates the assumptions of the conceptual schemas we and others have laid out regarding urban siege and urban terrorism.[xxviii] Attackers did not belong to a single group—they were part of a common network that somehow received inspiration and possible direction from two ideologically opposed terrorist organizations. Investigators are still hunting for possible leads, but it is safe to say that the attacks were a "tangled" mess that involve uncertain connections between the attackers, local terrorist connections in Europe and external organizations in the Middle East.[xxix]

The threat of simultaneous attacks, follow-on attacks, and the tangled web of influence this situation involves complicates operational response. Police must assume from now on that attackers might derive logistical support, inspiration, funding, and/or direction from a diverse combination of local, regional, and extra-regional sources. Moreover, they cannot also assume that one large attack by an attacker group is all they must contend with—synchronized attacks may occur designed to augment the execution and impact of one attack mission. Campaigns containing multiple simultaneous (or near-simultaneous) and/or sequential attacks (including attacks or engagements during exfiltration and escape) must be accounted for and demand the development and employment of operational art for urban battle.[xxx]

While much of the urban sieges since Mumbai demonstrate continuity, complications and change suggest the need for new thinking, including full-spectrum policing, operational art, including operations-intelligence integration to support command.

Diagnosing Urban Siege: Towards A Spectrum of Armed Assault

Deriving problem classes of urban siege requires a look at both the organizational dimension of the attack and the actual means of operational preparation, planning, and execution.

As per Watts' typology of terrorist organization and influence, we believe that the organizational dimension of the attack matters a great deal in creating reasonable assumptions for training, response planning, and wargames/red-teaming efforts. We summarize his typology below. While we make no claims that Watts' typology is the only or necessarily the most accurate template for analyzing jihadist organization, we believe it at least illustrates many of the analytical challenges involved.

First, there are obviously the most traditional kind of attack organization. "Directed" attacks, Watts notes, assume a large degree of central organization by an external group and high lethality and capability. These attacks have become seemingly less likely as improved Western law enforcement, intelligence, and military efforts have made it difficult for attacks to be organized from the top-down. However, as Gartenstein-Ross and Leah Farall have noted, one should not count these attacks out.[xxxi] Moreover, hierarchal organization does not necessarily assume a rigid, military-style command and control structure, and Gartenstein-Ross has noted that our understanding of the global jihad remains too fragmented and incomplete to make sweeping judgements about the likelihood of directed attacks.

"Networked" attacks will assume fighters with some degree of training (perhaps derived from overseas conflicts) and some degree of connection to overseas terrorist organizations or communities of terrorist practice. But, in contrast to elaborately planned directed attacks, Watts notes, networked attackers will constitute a "swarm" that brings together operatives, resources, and perpetrators as needed. Key variables in networked attacks include the local strength of foreign fighter networks, availability of weaponry, and the Western security environment that jihadists must contend with. Watts has suggested elsewhere that the chain of foreign fighters and radicals that being funneled to and from Western states to foreign battlefields may be modeled with the collective intelligence optimization technique known as ant colony optimization.[xxxii]

Finally, "inspired" attacks feature "bungled plots and random violence" by "jihadi wannabees." While directed attacks and networked attacks demand a complex interagency operational response, "inspired" attacks may not typically not fit the urban siege conceptual schema. Competent law enforcement should be able to handle it, as "inspired" but often incompetent jihadists are frequently just as much of a danger to *themselves* as they are to their targets. However, one cannot rule out that directed or network attacks may spawn copycat inspired attacks, complicating security response, intelligence, and investigation before, during, or after an urban siege scenario. It is possible that future "inspired" cells may develop sophisticated capacity on their own or through interaction with other cells over time (although it is expected that this is difficult to achieve).

Next, we summarize Gartenstein-Ross and Daniel Trombly's October 2012 report on the use of small arms by terrorists.[xxxiii] Gartenstein-Ross and Trombly note that the use of small arms figures highly in terrorist strategic thought and must be analyzed as a function of a larger jihadist war of attrition. Al-Qaeda documents outline a strategy for a war of attrition rooted in a combination of complex, multi-member operations and smaller attacks. Complex and large-scale missions force the target to expend significant resources to prevent future attacks of that type, while smaller operations create a constant threat stream and foster an atmosphere of fear and paranoia while driving up costs gradually.[xxxiv] A vehicle for this is the use of firearms and armed assault:

For both large-scale and small-scale attacks, firearms figure prominently in al Qaeda's strategy. A considerable corpus of written works underlies the significant role given to small arms. For years, al Qaeda and other jihadi organizations have published documents on the value of these weapons. In Abd al Aziz al Muqrin's A Practical Course for Guerrilla War, a book based on writings that first appeared in al Qaeda's online journal Mu'askar al Battar, multiple chapters describe tactical and operational planning for urban warfare. Techniques covered include assassination, hostage taking, attacking motorcades, assaulting and clearing fixed targets, and setting up ambush positions. Additional volumes cover the acquisition and maintenance of small arms.[xxxv]

Having outlined the strategic aim behind al-Qaeda contemplation of armed assault, Gartenstein-Ross and Trombly create a typology of urban assault types. Assasination attacks involve terrorist targeting of a high-profile individual. Single-shooter attacks aim for a symbolic target or location of importance to the enemy. Two-shooter teams allow terrorists to conduct more sophisticated attacks over extended periods of time. Mass attacks and frontal assaults denote terrorist operations against fixed targets. Finally, complex urban warfare attacks include multi-man teams and hybrids of the aforementioned attacks. Terrorists may also mix hostage taking, robberies, and defensive siege combat with any one of these attack types.[xxxvi]

Both the Watts and Gartenstein-Ross and Trombly typologies address essential aspects of an urban siege scenario. The organizational capacity and style in one of the categories Watts outlines may dictate the nature of the small arms attack drawn from Gartenstein-Ross and Trombly's study. Moreover, as we have previously suggested, an attack of one Watts type may lead to follow-on and/or concurrent attacks featuring another Watts organizational attack type and multiple possible Gartenstein-Ross and Trombly small arms attack types.

Murky and ill-structured incidents like the Paris incident suggest the need for greater integration between the levels of analysis in both surveys. Both cover core elements of the problem—operational direction and mechanism of attack respectively—but understanding organizational capacity and the causation of attacks may help explain the overlaps between attack execution types that Gartenstein-Ross and Trombly note at the conclusion of their report. "With firearms attackers have great flexibility," Gartenstein-Ross and Trombly rightly note. Once an attack has begun, they can select new targets and counter law enforcement."[xxxvii]

This, when coupled with the potential for a more unpredictable attacker set composition, suggests that conceptual integration is of more than just academic or high-level policy relevance. It matters very much for operational preparation for countering armed assaults. In order to train, prepare, red-team, plan, and allocate resources properly *before* the attack, police and other security agencies need to have scripts, scenarios, and models of how an attack is organized, rehearsed, and executed.

Questions about Future Urban Siege

While we do not propose our own typology, the Paris attack and newer research and analysis by Watts, Garteinstein-Ross and Trombly, and others suggest some pressing questions for both researchers and operational responders to consider when pondering urban siege post-Hebdo. In pondering these questions, we hope that researchers and operational responders can grope towards some conceptual synthesis between the levels of analysis that Watts and Gartenstein-Ross and Trombly cover in their analyses. We list them below:

1. *What kind of organizational assumptions should we utilize when building urban terrorism scenarios?*

Both the Mumbai and Paris urban sieges had similar results—prolonged mayhem by multiple groups of attackers. However, in one operation (Mumbai) the terrorists belonged to one group distributed into multiple teams. During the Paris attack the terrorists belonged to a loose common network but only loosely coordinated their synchronized operations. This created two different kinds of command problems for the first responders. Of course, the police may not and likely won't know which type of adversary they are facing during the initial course of an actual attack sequence and must rely upon real-time intelligence and operational reports to develop situational assessments.

During the Mumbai operation first responders struggled to handle the command and control problem of countering a distributed operation. But in the Paris attack state capacity was high and this was not as grave of a challenge. Rather, the primary challenge was locating the perpetrators, connecting disparate incidents, and later during the hostage situations dealing with the new problem of an attacker that synchronized an attack to coincide with a main operation. This demanded synchronized police response, which was achieved.

The command implications most relevant for an urban siege problem will depend greatly on what kind of organizational assumptions we make about the connection between attacks in the urban terror scenario. But this question also pertains very much to the prevention of attacks before they happen.

A Mumbai-like scenario requires extensive preparation, planning, a forward base, and attack vector that might expose planners and operatives to vulnerability. The terrorist "kill chain" in this case may be amenable to detection and penetration. In contrast, a Paris-like scenario does not have to be analyzed by the familiar recourse to "intelligence failure" explanations—it is perfectly possible that an attack like Paris might occur absent the systemic intelligence-sharing and indications and warnings flaws observed after Mumbai.[xxxviii] Here the terrorist "kill chain" may be more obscure and difficult to penetrate.

2. *How should we weight maximum casualties and maximum disruption in the assumptions we make about terrorist mission planning?*

One issue that Gartenstein-Ross and Trombly implicitly raise is the dichotomy between disruption and casualties as objectives in an urban siege scenario. Certainly, killing a lot of people can induce disruption and disrupting a key site or system can lead to a substantial amount of casualties. But they ought not to be regarded as interchangeable.

One can induce a substantial amount of disruption and fear without Mumbai or Peshawar kill counts—the toll of the Paris attack sequence was small compared to those incidents yet it also induced a massive mobilization of French security forces and led to fear, suspicion, and a backlash that may complicate future counter-terrorism efforts.[xxxix]

This raises some core questions about urban siege scenarios from the point of view of the attacker. Is there a tradeoff between casualties and disruption? How many casualties are necessary for disruption? Is one kind of objective easier to achieve than the other in an urban siege? Do attacker objectives change dynamically during the middle of an incident in response to new information? It should be noted that attackers themselves also may not see a distinction between casualties and disruption or heavily consider it in their planning. Enough casualties automatically suggest disruption, and disruption may be a primary objective with casualty count as a side effect.

All of these questions bear heavily on organizational assumptions and choice of attack tactics and weapons. As Gartenstein-Ross and Trombly note, firearms allow tremendous flexibility both prior to and during the prosecution of an urban siege. Police will be better able to model, red-team, and train for urban siege scenarios if they have a greater idea of how terrorists themselves view success and failure conditions for urban sieges.

3. *How should we think about social media information and operational security during urban sieges?*

We devote the most space to this issue due to the fact that operational security (OPSEC) in response has become more acute due to changes in the social media landscape since we last wrote on urban siege.

The issue of social media and OPSEC is by no means new. The Mumbai attacks were one of Twitter's first real-time crises, with both locals and foreigners giving contradictory and confused play-by-play as the event unfolded. However, the increasing saturation of social media platforms and the ubiquity of Twitter and other social media platforms are increasingly bringing uncertainties about social media and OPSEC to the fore.

In this attack sequence, social media played a significant role for police, the media, the community, and terrorist organizations alike. Jihadists and their supporters used social media to praise the attacks, and the #JeSuisCharlie meme went viral extremely quickly.[xl] Additionally, Twitter became a tool for tracking terrorists and developing situational awareness (for all actors), and social media became a key operational security concern as the tactics, techniques, and procedures of security forces are now broadcast in real time by both new and conventional media and terrorist can track that presence as seen in the warning for police to keep a low profile on social media minimize the potential for terrorist ambush.[xli]

Both everyday citizens and major news media organizations maintain social media presences. Social media increasingly drives news during crises, and fusing social media information has grown easier over time due to the increasing maturation of third party client applications. It has become easier for perpetrators of incidents to monitor feeds, as long as they have manpower to spare or are suitably entrenched in a manner that allows them to monitor feeds unimpeded.

While it is important to remember that attackers (if they successfully infiltrate) begin with the advantage of surprise and responders face an uphill challenge in sorting through contradictory information, so do attackers as well. More research and assessment needs to be done about cognitive and organizational limitations on how attackers receive, process, and utilize social media information during crisis scenarios.

The human factors and emergency response literature is replete with analysis about how the incident commander's situational awareness challenges, but we know comparatively little about that of the attacker group.[xlii] It is plausible that information fusion and processing difficulties may be negated by external support and planning (like the Mumbai attack's handlers), but it also may just add yet another information channel to process as an extra burden. It is only by modeling the information processing challenges attackers face (and how technology may help or worsen them) that law enforcement organizations can gain an realistic idea of OPSEC considerations in future crisis scenarios and justify them to external audiences.

Conclusion: Are We Charlie?

The first question routinely asked after every major terrorist attack is "can it happen here?" Until more information is available about the *Charlie Hebdo* attacks, it is hard if not impossible to even offer informed speculation about the answer. Our own work is based on news reports and others' analyses and we will eagerly monitor how well they hold up as more detailed information continues to emerge about the attacks.

Our purpose in writing this piece, however, is not to argue about the potentials for urban siege. We know that armed assault and urban siege is likely to remain a dangerous threat in both the developed West and the developing world.[xliii] However, noting that the possibility for urban siege exists is no longer sufficient or useful. What increasingly matters is *how* the attack will occur, and we hope that our analysis and questions will spur others to move forward in intensely studying and wargaming the variations and permutations of urban siege.

We titled our first piece on urban siege: "Postcard from Mumbai: Modern Urban Siege." It is our sincere hope that, whatever the tangled aftermath of Paris, we do not see too many more lethal "postcards" of urban siege from any more cities.[xliv]

Chapter 9

The ISIS Beheading Narrative

Doyle Quiggle

First Published 26 February 2015

In this article, I apply Jonathan Matusitz's insights from *Symbolism in Terrorism* to identify and isolate the plotline of the ISIS beheading narrative.[i] If we want to undermine and neutralize ISIS internet recruitment propaganda (the E-jihad), then we need to understand how and why their symbols appeal to their target audience. Narratives kick symbols into motion. ISIS are excellent narrators. We must find ways to counter-narrate and neutralize their group-forming narratives.

> Qu'ran 47:4: "When you encounter the unbelievers on the battlefield, strike off their heads until you have crushed them completely; then bind the prisoners tightly."

Because ISIS communicators legitimize beheading by reference to *Islamic history and Islamic theology*, local Islamic authorities who do not share ISIS's interpretation of Sura 47:4 will need to take careful heed of how ISIS have made beheading into a powerful symbol and narrative of their jihad.[ii] Beheading an enemy, an Islamic terrorist symbolically links his (increasingly *her*) Jihad today to the sword-driven rise of Medieval Islamic Empire and to the late Medieval and Early Renaissance blood-soaked contest between Christendom and Islam for control of Europe. A symbolic connection is made objectively visible in the beheading by the use of the most important Islamic Salafic weapon—the sword. Therefore, to understand the full symbolic energies of Islamic beheadings today, we must also understand the past symbolism of swords and blood in Islam. Here, I will introduce only the symbolic structure of the ISIS *beheading narrative.*[iii]

Timothy Furnish, a leading scholar of Islamic beheadings, notes:

> "Islam is the only major world religion today that is cited both by state and non-state actors to legitimise beheadings… In contradiction to the assertions of apologists, both Muslim and non-Muslim, these beheadings are not simply a brutal method of drawing attention to the Islamist political agenda and weakening an opponent's will to fight. Zarqawi and other Islamists who practise decapitation believe that God has ordained them to obliterate their enemies in this manner."[iv]

The ISIS beheading narrative derives its moral, legal, and theological authority directly from Islam.[v] But it swipes some of its aesthetic appeal from non-Islamic sources, such as comic books, film, and video games. These non-Islamic sources have long circulated images of beheading in popular culture and have kept decapitation actively present in the visual fields and cultural imaginations of potential ISIS recruits, especially of gamers.

Biologically, neurologically, and anthropologically understood, narrative performs the primary social function of creating cohesion and cooperation among in-group members. Creating cohesion and cooperation and activating the altruistic pre-adaptations of group members is why we evolved narrative as a primary social tool of our species. Out of the feeling of cohesion created by shared narrative there emerges powerful, neurologically compulsive feelings of reciprocal altruism, commitment to the group—trust. Neurologically, we encode narrative-induced cohesion-trust as *courage*. And courage is as indispensable a virtue to small hunting parties on the ancient Savannah as it is to SF operators storming a qalat compound in Afghanistan or to ISIS fighters in Iraq.[vi]

The ISIS beheading narrative performs all primary, primal social tasks for group members, beginning as communal blood ritual and ending as a personal trophy that increases a member's sense of pride in his group membership.

The Beheading Plotline

In her book on beheadings in literature, LOSING OUR HEADS: BEHEADINGS IN LITERATURE AND CULTURE, Regina Jones (2005) identifies these four categories of beheading: Judicial; Sacrificial; Presentational; Trophy.

Judicial: Citing a Wahhabist interpretation of Islamic justice, SAUDI ARABIA beheads criminals it has found guilty of murder, drug trafficking, rape, burglary, witchcraft, and apostasy. The state of Saudi Arabia thereby symbolically and jurisprudentially legitimises ISIS beheadings. And we may wonder if the international community indirectly legitimises beheadings because it recognizes the legitimacy of Saudi Arabian state-conducted decapitation—JUDICIAL beheading.

Sacrificial: Borrowing legitimacy from Saudi Arabia, ISIS beheadings participate in all four beheading categories. However, ISIS beheadings begin as a form of RITUALISTIC murder. All ritual is a kind narrative that derives its meaning largely from sequence, doing things in the correct order at the correct moment, just as narrative creates meaning by having characters do things (events) through time.

ISIS beheadings begin as COMMUNAL BLOOD RITUALS. As with any ritual, the beheading ritual is performed to create cohesion and loyalty among ISIS members. The fear and outrage that beheading creates among non-ISIS onlookers often obscures the "group-building" aspect of the beheading narrative. Creating terror, however, is not the main goal of beheadings at this stage in the narrative plot. The social goal is to create group cohesion.[vii]

Beheading as communal blood ritual is also used as a *rites of passage* to initiate newcomers, to mark their identities as "timeless" Jihadis, to link them to an eternal, timeless, "sacred" space. Beheading as communal blood ritual cleanses European-born ISIS of "Westoxification." That term (in Persian, *Gharbzadegi*) was first used by the Ayatollah Khomeni during the Islamic Revolution in Iran (1979) to mean "the state of being inebriated with Western culture and ideas."[viii] ISIS beheadings represent a symbolic severing with Western ideals, beliefs, culture—the main source of the spiritual toxins that infect Islam, according to all-known varieties of modern Salafism. Beheading an infidel, the ISIS executioner symbolically cuts off his own "Western" head. He sacrifices an Infidel's head to re-gain his Islamic identity.

Communal blood ritual inculpates ISIS members in the same crimes as their fellow Jihadis, a technique of coerced loyalty typically practiced by criminal gangs. Beheading represents a point of no "legal" return. Moreover, beheading as communal blood ritual transforms a ritual participant's neuro-network/brain chemistry. Beheading may embody a point of no psychological return as well.

> *My hypothesis: As a communal blood ritual, beheading is a potently addictive psychotropic agent that radically and permanently alters the neurology of ritual participants. Corollary: The limbic system of ritual practitioners is permanently altered by the communal blood ritual of beheading. We must account for this neurological transformation when assessing any ISIS defector's claims about rejecting violence as a form of religious practice.*[ix]
> (When displayed on YOUTUBE, a beheading video can also act as a remote communal blood ritual.)

We need more information about who gets to perform beheadings within ISIS. Are beheadings "permitted" only to privileged members?

Are ALL initiates required to attend beheadings? Are women allowed to participate directly in this ritual?

Presentational: The beheading plotline enters the mediation stage when the beheading becomes PRESENTATIONAL, a sign of victory in the Jihad. Presenting the decapitation is an assertion of success on the battlefield, even as the presentation is also meant to create terror in infidels. According to the logic of magical thinking, the blood spilled during the beheading and presented to a remote audience has the power to cleanse all of Islam, starting with the Infidel-contaminated territory (i.e. Libya) onto which the beheading blood is directly spilled. In this magical sense, the blood sacrifice presented and projected to a global Caliphate cleanses the mythic map of the greater Islamic Caliphate, which the ISIS Jihad purports to be re-conquering. When GPSed on today's map, recent ISIS beheadings become a key part of ISIS mythic cartography, which corresponds to the imperial landmass of the Islamic Empire of Harun Al Rashid (ca. 800). Blood cleansing of the Salaf's imagined Caliphate sets up the presentational use of the beheadings as a tool of recruitment, and the presentation of beheadings becomes a weapon in the Electronic Jihad (E-Jihad).

There's a distinct aesthetic quality to ISIS beheading presentations. ISIS communicators clearly design beheading videos to maximize aesthetic pleasure for an ISIS audience, for example, making the executioners of the Coptic victims appear seven feet tall, as if they're larger than life, like comic book and video game heroes. In mediation, such as Youtube, ISIS beheadings provide remote ISIS members, ISIS sympathizers, or the ISIS-curious a source of voyeuristic pleasure.

As noted above, the beheading narrative borrows its aesthetic appeal from non-Islamic sources that have primed today's youth to critically "appreciate" beheading, especially blood on swords. The blood-dripping beheading sword resonates not only with slasher films but also with popular "sword & blade" films like *Lord of the Rings* and with even more popular video games like SKYRIM and the METAL GEAR SERIES (i.e. REVENGANCE) that feature decapitation as a regular part of gameplay. Video games do not create terrorists. My point is that decapitation had been implanted as a common feature of the cultural imaginary of game players and filmgoers long before ISIS began producing its version of Islamic snuff film. ISIS communicators exploit the decapitation pre-implantation of popular culture.

In its presentational mode, the beheading narrative announces victory on the battlefield, projects the blood cleansing of the ISIS mythic map (the global caliphate), and, with the aim of recruitment, exploits a pre-existing popular blood aesthetic in which the contemplation of beheading is source of pleasurable entertainment. ISIS recruits have likely been primed to become decapitators both by Islamic and by non-Islamic imagery of beheading.[x]

Trophy: The beheading plotline is consummated when the severed heads are made into personal possessions by ISIS members, to increase their status and prestige among fellow Jihadists. The heads become TROPHIES. They perform all of the typical cultural functions of other kinds of trophies. They mark the completion of a rites of passage.

Does the accumulation of heads, Colonel Kurtz style, increase status and prestige among ISIS members?

In sum, the ISIS beheading narrative begins at a primal, neuro-biological level, as a blood ritual meant to link ISIS members horizontally to each other, backward to an Islamic past of sword-driven imperial conquest, and vertically up into a timeless space of eternal Jihad. At the ritual stage, the narrative performs the primal evolutionary function of all narrative/ritual—to create group cohesion and loyalty. Specific to ISIS beheadings is how the "West-toxified" self of the ISIS member is sacrificed in order to gain or re-gain a purified Islamic identity. In cutting off the head of an infidel, the ISIS member heals himself of Occidentosis.

The communal blood ritual is then presented, via mediation, to a remote global audience, to signal victory in the Jihad and to project to the blood cleansing of the terra sancta of the caliphate. As a form of presentation, the beheading becomes an object of aesthetic contemplation (a source of pleasure) and a recruitment lure that exploits non-Islamic imagery of beheadings.

Finally, the severed heads become trophies used to increase prestige and status among ISIS members.

We need further investigation into the neuro-psychology of communal blood ritual.[xi] We also need to know the neurological implications of viewing blood rituals in mediation: To what bio-psychological extent does one participate in this ritual (experience the same neuro-peptide buzz) remotely, through the internet? We also need to contrast the beheading narrative/ritual to other, more pragmatic forms of ISIS violence.

Chapter 10

ISIS For The Common Man

Keith Nightingale

First Published 22 March 2015

Understanding ISIS is fairly simply, resolving it as a matter of National interest is a lot harder. At present, an effective US policy for the elimination of ISIS and retention of a reasonably democratic Iraq is a riddle with the combined complexity of the Gordian Knot and an eight-sided Rubik's Cube. For those of you who are on long subway, bus or train commutes-Here is an ISIS Issues for Dummies.

WHAT IS THE ISSUE?

This is a religious issue between the Sunni's and the Sh'ias on a large scale. On a smaller one, ISIS is a Sunni based organization that has occupied significant parts of Iraq and Syria and is viewed as a terrorist organization by the West. They would say they were religious purists acting in the name of their God as they interpret the Koran. Others say they are just simple terrorists in a religious disguise who kill anyone who disagrees with their position.

WHAT IS ISIS?

ISIS is a Sunni outgrowth of the "Sunni Triangle" in Iraq-the home area for the late less than great Saddam Hussein. It grew out of the disaffection the local Sunni population had with how the central Iraq Sh'ia-dominated government was denying them their rights and ruling with a very hard hand.

When the US and Allied forces left Iraq due to, inter alia, the lack of interest by then Prime Minister Maliki-a Sh'ia-in signing a Status of Forces Agreement-our absence allowed Maliki to restructure his emerging democratic government into a traditional Sh'ia based one man band. He purged all the competent Sunni military leadership and replaced them with mostly proven incompetent Sh'ia thereby significantly weakening the new army we had struggled so hard to build. He trumped up charges against his Vice Premier, a Sunni, and chased him into the desert. He created a local monolithic Sh'iadom with the tacit and sometimes overt support of Iran-the Sh'ia heartland as Saudi Arabia is the heartland for the Sunni. The Sunni population of Iraq was disenfranchised and pretty much left to their own devices but at a distinct disadvantage compared to their Sh'ia bretheren. From this condition, ISIS arose.

HOW DID THIS ALL GET STARTED?

Using the Wayback Machine, return to the end of WW I and the Treaty of Versailles. One of the outgrowths was something called the Sykes-Picot Agreement. This was a treaty between France and England that divided up the newly available Middle East in order to resolve mutual interests-primarily oil access. The present day political boundaries of much of the Middle East were drawn by the treaty committees without regard to existing cultural and religious lines and we have been suffering the internal frictions ever since.

The schism between Sunni and Sh'ia was ignored as was the Balfour Declaration granting the Jews a Home state and the inferred agreement between Britain and Faisal brokered by Lawrence where Faisal would rule most of the Moslem populations of the old Ottoman Empire less Turkey and Egypt. In sum, Sykes-Picot has resulted in a very bad land deal.

Over time, the various brokered rulers managed their internal frictions with a somewhat iron hand. Note that Saddam, a Sunni, controlled his majority Sh'ia population and gave everyone a bit of something in return for loyalty. Maliki rejected that approach by essentially declaring the Sunni's societal outcasts. ISIS is a direct outgrowth of the disaffection.

HOW DOES ISIS MANIFEST ITSELF?

The heart of ISIS-land is the Iraqi Sunni population in the Tikrit Triangle-Saddam's family base. It spreads into portions of Syria and roughly resembles the 1848 Caliphate which encompassed those areas prior to Western political cartography. ISIS governance is extremely well-organized with the infrastructure of a relatively mature nation. It manages social services, revenue collection, security, military operations, religious management/interpretation and suicide elements. It is a real government albeit religious-based-at least from the public view.

Its occupation is marked by strict Sharia law, taxation, impressment and expulsion of non-believers. People viewed as unwilling to provide 100% loyalty are either beheaded, otherwise executed or forced out. Compromise and assimilation are not ISIS words. Extreme purity of cause is stated as the basis for the style of occupation.

It has considerable wealth from a combination of Iraqi and Syrian oil, local taxation and revenues received from other Sunni elements-primarily Saudi Arabian. It has a very sophisticated global social network engagement program which demonstrates considerable psychological and cultural awareness to attract foreign fighters and support from disaffected members of Western nations. So far, they are credited with attracting more than 20,000 foreign personnel to the cause. These newly available ISIS assets range from sex slaves to frontline fighters to suicide bombers-no one is more enthused about a cause than a recent convert.

HOW DOES THIS GET RESOLVED?

The best solution, from our Western perspective, is that the Government of Iraq, retake ISIS-Land and reconstitute a government that includes Sunni assimilation into the mainstream of life. Presently, this is not possible due to a combination of military ineptitude and lack of interest in Sunni assimilation. The present PM of Iraq has pledged to resolve both issues but it will take time. Meantime, how do we contain ISIS and prevent its/their leakage to other parts of the world? At present, in this regard, we have failed utterly, as shown in Libya, Tunesia and Egypt.

WHO ARE OUR FRIENDS AND OUR ENEMIES REGARDING RESOLUTION?

The countries that our logical friends, may not be for a variety of reasons. The countries that we may consider enemies could be our friends but won't be for a variety of reasons. We would like to ally with both enemies and friends to focus on ISIS but can't get there from here. It's a mess. Reviewing our regional friends and enemies list we find…………..

IRAN

Because Iran is strongly supporting the Baghdad government against ISIS, one would assume Iran is an ally in being in our efforts to control/eliminate ISIS. Not so. Iran is the central religious focus of the Sh'ia branch, has strongly supported the Sh'ia majority within Iraq and was the mainstay of the Sadr Militia with which we had major combat issues in our tenure. The Sh'ia's are naturally aligned against the Sunni ISIS and have made the point whenever they re-occupy previous ISIS controlled Sunni populations to the detriment of long term assimilation.

Recall that Iran fought a major war with Saddam's Iraq but that all was forgiven with Saddam's demise and worked very hard to insure a Sh'ia-centric Iraq emerged regardless of US desires for a more mixed democracy. Iran is also a strong supporter of the Assad regime in Syria- another Sh'ia based government the US desires to go away.

Iran is strongly supporting the Iraqi efforts against ISIS to include provision of its quality Qud Brigade and primary military commander, Gen Sulemani. Sulemani has been officially declared a terrorist by the US. Visualizing him working in close association with our in country Lt General is a stretch.

Concurrently, the US is mano a mano with Iran over nuclear proliferation. It is going to be extremely hard for the US to develop any support associated with Iran regarding Iraq with these issues extant. Within Washington, Iran is viewed as perhaps our most significant problem in the region with its nuclear development program and potential to create a major confrontation with Israel. Getting help or helping here is pretty doubtful.

KURDISTAN

Probably our strongest ally in the area and the one most engaged and successful against ISIS. On the surface, we should be supporting them all the way as we did when Saddam was in power. They know how to fight well and hate ISIS even though they are essentially Sunni-centric.

Problems……..because they are good and essentially independent from Baghdad, Baghdad does not want us to help them in any meaningful way that will assist their independence. Ditto Turkey.

TURKEY

Turkey-ostensibly our strongest NATO ally in the conflicted zones, has officially requested we not provide any support to the Kurds-specifically arms, uniformed trainers or US military units in any form. Turkey has been battling Kurdish factions for years and is adamant they not establish an independent nation.

Turkey also benefits financially from the now-ISIS exported oil from a portion of the petroleum crescent via the petroleum pipeline going from Iraq to the Mediterranean. The present government's desire to weaken the Kurds as a priority issue severely limits any steps the US may wish in the northern region against ISIS.

SAUDI ARABIA

The Kingdom is the religious center of the Sunni religion. It is also, ostensibly, our strongest and most consistent ally in the region. Internally, this is a highly conflictive situation. To overtly counter ISIS, is to potentially destabilize the present royal line which is the greatest concern of both the Royals and ourselves.

Much of ISIS' funds are derived from private Saudi sources and the largest single citizenry exporting itself to ISIS is Saudi. In sum, like it or not, Saudi Arabia is ISIS strongest albeit private supporter of ISIS.

SYRIA

The Assad regime is a Sh'ia based government. One third of the country has been occupied by ISIS and the inflicted government would seem a natural ally in the war against ISIS. BUT……..we are on record to overthrown the Assad regime and have been supporting the rebel movement with varied assets ranging from intelligence to air strikes to covert operations.

Our rebel allies are predominately Sunni-based and include a healthy dose of Al Quaida-our sworn enemy in Iran and Afghanistan has somehow managed to be on our side in Syria. Complicated world out there.

JORDAN

The least wealthy and most vulnerable of our allies, is at present, our strongest ally in the anti-ISIS effort-in no small measure due to the public torching of its F16 pilot by ISIS. In return for Jordanian support, the US has provided more than 1.2B$ in aid this year to the King. They need it.

In return, the King has significantly engaged his air and ground forces on the Syrian border and within Syria. He also houses and supports the largest group of Syrian refugees even though it could be potentially destabilizing. His voice and presence is the bridge between the Western and Middle Eastern culture clashes.

There is only so much the King can do before running out of reserves. Supporting the refugees-both Palestinian and Syrian is a major effort. Assisting US interests with close integration of military assets consumes most internal resources and capabilities. Going after ISIS within Iraq, is presently a bridge too far.

IRAQ

The elephant that owns the phone booth. It was PM Maliki's actions that created ISIS and its now PM al-Abadi's task to fix what's broken. His problem is that to be truly effective in ISIS-Land, he needs to place a number of competent Sunni's within the re-occupation government elements, the Iraqi military and the Iraqi governing bodies. Further, he has to seriously build credibility with inclusion of Sunni interests within the fabric of the entire nation and society. Presently, this is a slow process.

Whatever elements of the government manage to re-occupy ISIS-Land, they must engage the locals with a helping and supportive hand. This has not yet been the case. On the contrary, when Sh'ia-dominate government forces have secured ISIS areas, they have spent most of their time extracting their version of religious justice by killing Sunni's and keeping them isolated from any benefits. Until this changes, ISIS will continue to prosper and any efforts to support the Greater Iraq and our interests will be for naught.

OK—WHAT CAN WE DO?

Not a whole lot in a meaningful way without some help. At present, we are conducting highly selective and possibly effective but not decisive air strikes from aircraft and drones. To be really effective with air, we need people on the ground with intimate knowledge of immediate local targets. That means either local Iraqi's we have trained or our own people.

Placing US forces on the ground requires both an invitation from the Iraqi government as well as a signed Status of Forces Agreement (SOFA)—neither of which have been received yet. To place actual combat units requires all of the above and a lot more.

10,000 troops requires in excess of 50,000 support personnel to keep them fed and oiled with the machinery of war. The US public as well as the White House has not indicated this is an acceptable option.

To imbed US advisors within the Iraqi structure requires the same invitation and SOFA plus rules that allow them to accompany their Iraqi counterparts and share the same risks-advisers that cannot accompany can observe and report but not be a credible improvement.

Presently, we have a US Lieutenant General and around a thousand personnel in a Baghdad compound training newer elements-including Sunni soldiers. That may be as good as it gets.

We can hope/train/encourage non-US military to support the Iraqi government. So far that means the Iranian military which we do not view favorably.

Ultimately, the best answer is a credible Iraqi military with Sunni and Sh'ia and an inclusive government that provides for Sunni interests. Some assembly and a lot of time required.

IN SUM

In the region, our enemies ought to be our friends. Our friends are often our enemies due to local circumstances and very little is simple. To engage is one thing. To effectively engage is quite another.

You may now work the Sudoku puzzle. It will be more rewarding.

Chapter 11

Nigeria's Critical Juncture: Boko Haram, Buhari, and the Future of the Fourth Republic

Matthew Blood

First Published 23 May 2015

The recent success of the Nigerian government and the international coalition in the fight against Boko Haram is a welcome development for a country whose citizens have watched helplessly as Islamist militants have killed tens of thousands of civilians and displaced millions more since 2009.[1] With the recapture of Gwoza in northeastern Borno state, Boko Haram has now been driven out of most of the territory it once controlled.[2] After more than a half decade of an official response characterized by alternating bouts of indifference, incompetence, and indiscriminate reprisals, the Nigerian government has managed to do in six weeks what it had seemingly been unable or unwilling to do in six years.

The speed with which the Nigerian military and allied forces were able to retake territory the size of Belgium held for months and even years by Boko Haram is less surprising than might appear at first glance. Much of the early fighting in the campaign relied on hundreds of South

African and ex-Soviet bloc mercenaries using helicopter gunships and armored vehicles in nighttime attacks on Boko Haram encampments. Nigerian security forces would then claim responsibility for the victories, occupying the already-cleared areas only after most of the fighting was over.[3] At the same time, a nearly 10,000-strong coalition force led by the Chadian military, one of the most effective in the region, attacked Boko Haram positions elsewhere in cooperation with Cameroon and Niger, backed by training and intelligence supplied by the United States and its European allies.[4]

Unfortunately, the violence that has plagued northern Nigeria is unlikely to end anytime soon. Significant numbers of militants appear to have been killed only in the early stages of the offensive. As the coalition advance has gained momentum, Boko Haram members have increasingly chosen to retreat rather than risk conventional set-piece battles with superior forces.[5] Thousands of the movement's fighters remain at large, including nearly all of the insurgency's leadership.[6] U.S. and UN officials have both warned of a strategic withdrawal on the part of the militants with a high likelihood of protracted insurgent violence for the foreseeable future.[7] Large numbers of Boko Haram members have already melted back into towns and cities among their ethnic kinsmen or fled deeper into the vast, 23,000-square-mile Sambisa Forest along the Cameroon border.

The Boko Haram Complex

From the start, Boko Haram was poorly adapted to holding and governing significant amounts of territory. In common usage, the Boko Haram label actually describes a complex, multifaceted insurgency composed of a number of different factions, cells, and criminal groups exhibiting varying degrees of coordination with the wider movement.[8] Significant uncertainty exists about almost every aspect of the insurgency. What is clear, however, is that the rebellion is considerably more amorphous and less hierarchical than many accounts in the international media suggest.

The maniacal Abubakar Shekau and his lieutenants head a core organization that might usefully be thought of as Boko Haram proper. But Shekau's group coexists with perhaps three to five other militant factions that, despite their operational autonomy and occasionally serious conflicts over ideological and tactical differences, maintain some degree of cooperation within the umbrella-like Boko Haram structure.[9] The splinter group Ansaru, headed by Mamman Nur and Khalid al-Barnawi, who broke with Shekau over the indiscriminate targeting of Muslims, is the most well-known of these factions. Nur and al-Barnawi are believed to possess the most significant ties of anyone in the Boko Haram network to international terrorist organizations like al-Qaeda in the Islamic Maghreb (AQIM), Ansar Dine, MUJAO, and al-Shabab.[10]

The operations of these Boko Haram factions are regularly outsourced to criminal groups and local gangs that function as paid auxiliaries of the Islamist militants and whose members can be hired or activated and deactivated as needed. Many fighters are therefore part-time, drawn from the vast lumpenproletariat of northeastern Nigeria and the nearby border states. The resulting insurgent mosaic spans the range from jihadist true believers to ex-Nigerian military personnel, organized criminal groups, youth gangs, unemployed young men, and those forcibly conscripted under threat to themselves and their families.[11] The movement is "further complicated by [criminal] imitators… who commit violence under the guise of the group" for illicit, for-profit purposes of no relationship to any religious or political goals.[12] The end result is that the Boko Haram insurgency is not entirely under the control of Shekau or any other single actor. And the exact degree to which the different factions and criminal entities coordinate among each other is often unclear.

Despite the declaration of a caliphate in northern Nigeria, the militants appear to have had little or no plan for programmatic governance and statebuilding of any equivalence to that currently being carried out by the Islamic State (IS) in Iraq and Syria, with which Shekau has recently, at least formally, aligned the Boko Haram movement.[13] Towns and cities under Boko Haram control were mainly turned into rebel military bases, staging grounds, and large prison camps for the multitudes of abducted civilians held hostage by the militants. What passed for governance under the movement appears to have been a mixture of draconian social control, based on the uneven application of medieval punishments mandated by the group's extremist interpretation of Islam, combined with violent predation and anomic violence directed toward the civilian population.[14] The movement lacks the necessary political cadres and administrative personnel for even the most rudimentary social provision.[15] It appears to contain no specialists in anything whatsoever other than indiscriminate violence. In this sense, Boko Haram operates in a manner resembling Mancur Olson's classic roving bandits, extracting resources from civilian populations in a scorched-earth campaign of wanton brutality that has destroyed much of the popular support the insurgency once had.[16]

Journalists travelling with government soldiers entering the black-flagged territory formerly controlled by the militants report finding mass graves on the outskirts of towns and cities emptied of their inhabitants.[17] Markets were systematically looted and shuttered. Most military-aged men and boys appear to have been killed outright with the lucky ones given the opportunity of being forcibly conscripted. Women and girls were distributed among the fighters as sex slaves.[18] The youngest children were collected in Boko Haram madrassas for indoctrination and grooming, presumably for later use as child soldiers, sex slaves, suicide bombers, and human shields. Elderly women, left unmolested, were confined to their homes and neglected. Food was reportedly scarce.[19]

Lack of organizational coherence was always going to be a weakness for Boko Haram's ability to hold and defend territory from competent military opponents. At the same time, the diffuse nature of the insurgency has largely been a strength for the movement's capacity to sow violence across a vast expanse of weakly governed territory. In retrospect, the large area controlled by the group was more a function of the Nigerian government's ineptitude and wholesale abandonment of its sovereign obligations than any deliberate strategic military plan on the part of Boko Haram.

Muhammadu Buhari

The election of retired general Muhammadu Buhari of the opposition All Progressives Congress (APC) is a significant development in a country that has regularly witnessed large-scale electoral fraud and post-election violence since its ostensible return to democratic rule with the establishment of the Fourth Republic in 1999. Outgoing President Goodluck Jonathan, whose government has been widely criticized for a range of abuses and failures, deserves credit for a courageous concession that likely preempted a violent political crisis that would have seriously weakened the Nigerian government and inflamed Muslim opinion in the north at a critical moment in the fight against Boko Haram.

Until recently, many northerners have viewed democracy as synonymous with secular, western-imposed corruption, impoverishment, and government abuse. This perception has grown dramatically since 2011, when Jonathan abandoned the power alternation scheme that voluntarily rotated control of the presidency between northern Muslims and southern Christians. In the near term, Muhammadu Buhari's victory may help ameliorate some of the suspicion held by many Muslims that the national political system is rigged against them. Buhari enjoys widespread popular support across his native north where people celebrated in the streets at the announcement of his victory. His election opens the way for major policy changes in the government's approach to the ongoing Boko Haram crisis and the wider problems facing Nigeria as a whole. As Gallup recently reported, "unlike... past elections, Buhari will govern with a clear mandate from voters and must rule with the goals of his electorate in mind to meet heightened expectations for change."[20]

The escalating crisis in the north was at the center of Muhammadu Buhari's presidential campaign and was a key factor in his victory over the incumbent Jonathan, who is widely believed to have mismanaged and neglected the conflict.[21] The 72-year-old former general's biography contains suggestions he may well be better placed to advance the fight against Boko Haram than his predecessor. Buhari is himself a northern Muslim who promises to be more oriented to the marginalized region's concerns and realities. In the mid-1970s, he served as military governor of Borno state and has firsthand knowledge of ground zero in the contemporary conflict. A decade later, Buhari oversaw the suppression of the Maitatsine uprising, regarded by many as one of the present insurgency's radical Islamist antecedents.[22] This time around the battle against the extremists will also be somewhat personal for the incoming president. In 2014, he survived an assassination attempt by Boko Haram militants during an attack on a campaign event that killed dozens.[23]

Buhari's credentials as an anticorruption reformer are by all accounts unimpeachable. After seizing power in a military coup in 1983, he led an aggressive, if authoritarian, crackdown on the large-scale government corruption for which the Nigerian elite had become infamous. The effort was at times misguided and ultimately short lived, but "[t]he motives for Buhari's authoritarian response to Nigeria's political, economic, and social crises are largely considered to have been pure."[24] Whatever his shortcomings, the new president understands the way official graft has alienated Nigerians from the government, strangled the country's economic potential, and fed into the spiraling discontent and militancy of marginalized groups.

As a former general, Buhari is also acutely aware of the way corruption has crippled the Nigerian military, which has been plagued by problems qualitatively similar to those that led to the collapse of the Iraqi armed forces during the Islamic State's breakout offensive last year. The Nigerian elite has grown accustomed to cannibalizing a $6 billion annual defense budget while poorly trained and equipped security forces consistently underperform in the face of the Boko Haram onslaught.[25]

But ending militancy in northern Nigeria will require more than an effective fighting force. Reigning in the atrocities and human rights abuses regularly committed by the security services must be a key short-term priority. As former U.S. ambassador to Nigeria John Campbell has observed, "the Nigerian security agencies may have killed as many Nigerians as Boko Haram in certain time periods."[26] Extensively documented reports of war crimes and crimes against humanity routinely committed by government forces make for harrowing reading.[27] The conduct of the government and its civilian vigilante proxies has helped fuel the conflict spiral in the north, generating whatever popular support currently exists for the otherwise morally bankrupt Boko Haram movement while enhancing the militants' ability to recruit among victimized populations.

Buhari is no liberal; he is a religious conservative and one-time military dictator who supported the controversial drive to institute sharia law across the north during the early 2000s. His previous victory over the Maitatsine rebellion was purchased at a heavy cost in civilian lives.[28] During the bitterly-contested 2011 elections, both Buhari and Jonathan engaged in divisive appeals to ethnic and religious identity.[29] This time around, such appeals were less prevalent and Buhari gained greater backing from parts of the Christian community alarmed at the government's inability to address the deepening security crisis. Supporters of the former military ruler claim his beliefs about the importance of democracy and human rights have evolved since the 1980s. The extent to which this is true remains to be seen. Whether Buhari's authoritarian personality will prove to be an asset or a liability in Nigeria's contemporary cut-throat politics is another open question.

Nigeria's Critical Juncture

Nigeria's Fourth Republic has arrived at a critical juncture: a moment in which options for the embattled country are comparatively open in a way they have not been in the recent past and will not be in the near future. The immediate prospects for Africa's most populous state contain great uncertainty and considerable danger, but also significant potential. Indeed, one of Buhari's first challenges will be managing the popular expectations for rapid change he himself helped create. But successful elections combined with the recent coalition offensive have bought the government time to consolidate security gains while starting to implement desperately needed short and long-term reforms.[30] The actions of Buhari and the Nigerian government will be the key determinant of the security environment in the coming months and years.

Boko Haram is bloodied but not beaten. The militants are still capable of inflicting massive violence. Going forward, the insurgents can be expected to return to the strategy of guerilla warfare, terrorism, and unbridled atrocity that has characterized the recent past. A renewed campaign of violence targeting government officials, security forces, and civilian soft targets is already underway. Within the apparent chaos, Boko Haram will seek to exploit existing social cleavages by fomenting ethnic and religious conflict and provoking government retaliation against northern civilians. The militants aim to polarize the country and terrorize those with whom they disagree by creating an ethnically and religiously-based security dilemma that will force fence-sitters to choose sides in a war between supposedly "good" Muslims, as defined by Shekau and his fanatical comrades, and everyone else.[31]

Reclaiming the territory once held by Boko Haram is a significant victory nonetheless, one that has disrupted the movement's operations and paved the way for further gains. A key question is the extent to which the Nigerian state will be capable of holding the reconquered ground once its foreign allies withdraw. Buhari has promised to redirect the government's strategy, but exactly how remains unclear. Countering the militant threat will require a broad package of military and non-military measures aimed at degrading Boko Haram, increasing human security, and beginning the difficult work of reforming Nigerian institutions.

Good Enough Counterinsurgency

After more than a decade of bitterly contested warfare in Iraq and Afghanistan, population-centered counterinsurgency has fallen out of favor in many policy circles where it is said to be too difficult and, ultimately, unrealistic.[32] Critics of counterinsurgency doctrine, instead, favor more limited counterterrorism measures aimed at disrupting and dismantling terrorist groups. For comparatively secure countries fighting foreign wars of choice, this may or may not be the preferable option. Unfortunately, a strategy that relies solely on counterterrorism measures is not possible for states facing powerful homegrown insurgencies like Nigeria.

For Buhari's government, the alternatives to population-centered counterinsurgency are limited to the wholesale abandonment of large parts of the national territory to millenarian Islamist rebels and domestic anarchy, or else scaling up and doubling down on the dirty war presently being waged by the Nigerian military. Both of these options guarantee escalating violence and further alienation of the Nigerian people. In short, for Nigeria, there are no alternatives to a population-centered approach in the fight against Boko Haram. Counterinsurgency is difficult, but not insurmountably so. In the near term, the Nigerian government does not need to be good; it needs to be good enough. Nigeria and its security services will not be transformed overnight, no matter who is in charge. The immediate goal should be to establish a secure enough environment in which to begin an ongoing process of reform.[33]

In the short term, the Nigerian government must continue cooperating with the international coalition to press its advantage in the current offensive against Boko Haram. The formidable terrain of the Sambisa Forest offers significant benefits to the insurgents, but it has the virtue of being far from civilian populations, other than those hostages still held captive by the militants. Elsewhere, the Nigerian government should capitalize on the present momentum by securing cleared areas with a greater and more effective official presence across the north capable of protecting local civilians from insurgent reprisals.

Those in the security services responsible for serious human rights violations must be identified, removed, and punished. Ultimately, Buhari and the military leadership must be made to understand that doing so will strengthen the war effort, not weaken it. If the human rights practices of the Nigerian security forces can be sufficiently improved, the door will be opened to increased training and support provided by the United States, which is currently barred by law from doing so under the Leahy amendment.[34] If Buhari wants to establish a virtuous cycle leading to the improved effectiveness and professionalism of the security services, this is the place to start.

If the government can consolidate recent gains in the north, the composition of the insurgency can be exploited to separate irreconcilable jihadist true believers from those who can be deterred or convinced to defect in a context of more secure conditions. The latter categories include for-profit Boko Haram fighters, criminals, gang members, child soldiers, and the unemployed as well as the forcibly conscripted. This cannot happen, however, so long as militants wishing to surrender, defect, or return to civilian life expect torture and summary execution at the hands of government forces.

An amnesty program for low and mid-level insurgents like the one that helped reduce violence in the Niger Delta is one possibility.[35] Though not without risks, the moral hazard associated with such a program might be considerably less in the north, given the lack of critical infrastructure like oil wells and pipelines some militants in the south have used to establish what amount to de facto protection rackets. The government should start making early plans for appropriate disarmament, demobilization, and reintegration (DDR) measures that can be implemented with the help of the international community as a complement to any amnesty program or other bid to bring Boko Haram's reconcilable fighters in from the cold.

The government should also work with the international community to increase humanitarian support to civilians displaced by the war or otherwise deprived of their livelihoods.[36] Conditions in the refugee camps of northern Nigeria and neighboring countries are increasingly dire and government officials have been implicated in the exploitation, sale, and trafficking of refugees in cooperation with criminal groups.[37] An effective humanitarian operation would be a forceful signal to northern Nigerians that the government can help resolve social problems, not just create them. Addressing the growing humanitarian crisis would serve to increase the government's legitimacy while alleviating increasingly desperate human suffering.

The Future of the Fourth Republic

Even if Buhari's regime can improve security and stem the immediate bleeding from the Boko Haram insurgency, the deep, long-term issues of statebuilding and economic development in the north and throughout the rest of country will remain. The fundamental failures of the Nigerian government have been among the most important drivers of the religious radicalism that has metastasized throughout the country since the 1980s.[38] Countering violent extremism will require addressing root causes, the majority of which lack readily available military solutions. Maneuvering the levers of a deeply troubled bureaucracy to accomplish those ends promises to be the more difficult component in the fight against Islamist militancy. In the absence of deeper reforms, however, even the total military eradication of the present insurgency cannot prevent the emergence of successor groups and reincarnations. Boko Haram is only the latest manifestation of growing ethnic and religious violence in Nigeria. Without tackling the underlying causes of extremism, it is unlikely to be the last.

In the long term, reforming Nigeria and its institutions will require rooting out corruption, transforming the country's mafia-like political culture, building government capacity, undertaking comprehensive security sector reform (SSR), institutionalizing the rule of law and respect for human rights, developing the non-oil economy, reducing poverty, and increasing educational enrollment. Buhari's government will also need to counter the radicalizing messages that have become increasingly common in the country's mosques and madrassas, influenced by the globalized Salafism exported from Saudi Arabia since the 1970s. In tandem with other reforms, promoting legitimate and popularly supported representatives of Nigeria's comparatively more tolerant Sufi tradition of Islam might be one part of the necessary war of ideas.

Reversing fifty years of decay in the heart of the Nigerian state is more than a tall order for even the most committed and able of reformers. Buhari is no saint, and much about how he will govern remains unknown. There will be limits to what he can accomplish, and those who benefit from the status quo will continue to resist change, perhaps violently. If significant reform does come, progress will be measured over the course of decades, not years.

Nigeria has arrived at a critical juncture nonetheless. The recent coalition offensive and successful elections have cracked open the door for the start of that reform process. Buhari's job is to jam in his foot and hold for his successors before the door slams shut for good. If he fails, if government and insurgent violence is allowed to spiral upward, the opportunity for significant progress could be delayed by a generation or more. If that happens, the viability of Nigeria as a unified country would not be guaranteed.

It is an open question whether or not Buhari will be up to the task before him. Given the weight of Nigeria's history, there should be no illusions about the likelihood of success. The war in the north will almost certainly get worse before it gets better. And yet, it remains that the current moment offers the single best chance in years to make inroads against the violence of Boko Haram.

Chapter 12

On Self-Declared Caliph Ibrahim's May 2015 Message to Muslims: Key Problems of Motivation, Marginalization, Illogic, and Empirical Delusion in the Caliphate Project

Paul Kamolnick

First Published 4 June 2015

Introduction

On May 14, 2015 a 34-minute audio message was released by the self-proclaimed Islamic State's media arm al-Furqan. This latest message, "March Forth Whether Light or Heavy," from self-appointed caliph Ibrahim ibn Awwad al-Husayni al-Qurashi (birth name: Ibrahim ibn Awwad Ibrahim Ali Muhammad al-Badri al-Samarrai; aka: Abu Bakr al-Baghdadi; Abu Du'a),[1] was the first issued in six months: a 17-minute audio was last uploaded November 14, 2015 announcing recent declarations of loyalty and expansion into new environs.[2] Probably designed to reassure potential followers that despite reports he suffered shrapnel wounds to his spine in a recent bombing attack he remains in charge, a careful reading of this message supplies potential insight into present critical vulnerabilities confronting the Islamic State Organization's (ISO) quest to found and lead a Muslim caliphate.

The Caliph's 'Islamic Problem': Islam *Is* Ultra-Jihadism

One would expect the caliph of 1.6 billion Muslims to expound on the fullness of what is demanded of Muslims as exemplars of righteous faith and deeds. Instead, for Caliph Ibrahim, Islam is equated with what might be termed ultra-jihadism. There is here nothing of prayer, alms, fasting, or pilgrimage; nothing of compassion or mercy, humility or reflections on righteousness. This caliph instead proclaims: "[W]here are you O Muslim in relation to the command of your Lord, who commanded you to fast in one verse, and commanded you with jihād and fighting in dozens of verses?"

One could ask, however, what about the *thousands* of verses on prayer, alms, righteous deeds, honoring covenants and promises and oaths; on forgiveness of sins, and honoring one's mother and father; of hospitality and generosity; on security, prosperity, rights, and honor?

No. Islam *is* war. Islam *is* jihad. Worship *is* fighting. Fighting *is* proof of faith.

O Muslims, Islam was never for a day the religion of peace. Islam is the religion of war. Your Prophet (peace be upon him) was dispatched with the sword as a mercy to the creation. He was ordered with war until Allah is worshipped alone. He (peace be upon him) said to the polytheists of his people, "**I came to you with slaughter.**" He fought both the Arabs and non-Arabs in all their various colors. He himself left to fight and took part in dozens of battles. He never for a day grew tired of war. He (peace be upon him) passed away during the period he was preparing the expedition of Usāmah (may Allah be pleased with him). (emphasis in original).[3]

Caliph Ibrahim supplies quotes from authoritative sources, as do most other 'jihadis,' to prove that fighting in the path of Allah (*jihad fi sabil Allah*) is enjoined on righteous Muslims (e.g. *Qur'an* 2:216; 4:74; 9:38-39). One can declare that expansive military jihad is obligatory until the Day of Judgment. This 'jihad-realist' premise is well-supported in all authoritative sources, and must be conceded by those who do not seek to avoid genuine scholarship.[4] But it is another matter entirely, to *equate* Islam with this superlative form of obligatory duty, or to demand that this obligation must be immediately operationalized without exception, everywhere and unconditionally. Despite this martial dimension in Islam, rules *do* apply, and among these rules for fighting in the Way of Allah, is the requirement that the authorized war leader (e.g. emir, caliph) very carefully evaluate the conditions, abilities, and opportunities available; the potential benefits versus costs of violent armed struggle; the possible loss of life, for believers and non-believers alike; and other less costly alternative means (in blood, honor, property, and other sanctities upheld in Islam) available to expand receptivity to the Call (*Da'wa*) to Islam, and for enjoining good and forbidding evil conduct (*al-amr bil-ma'ruf wa'l-nahy 'an al-munkar*).[5] Baghdadi reveals, and at the same time conceals one of these shari'a requirement of lawful jihad: capacity and power relative to one's opponents.

And we call upon every Muslim in every place to perform hijrah to the Islamic State or fight in his land wherever that may be. And **do not think that we are calling upon you to march forth out of weakness or incapability,** for we are strong by Allah's bounty, strong by Allah, strong by our faith in Him, our seeking of His aid, our seeking refuge with Him, our reliance upon Him alone without any partners, and our good expectation of Him. This is because the battle is one between the allies of the Merciful and the allies of Satan, and so Allah (the Mighty and Majestic) will support His soldiers, grant His slaves authority, and preserve His religion, even if the days alternate between victory and loss, even if war is competition, and even if wounds afflict both parties. **We do not call upon you O Muslim out of weakness or inability.** We call upon you out of advice for you, love for you, and compassion for you. We remind you and call you so that you do not attain Allah's anger, torment, and punishment, and so that you do not lose this good that the mujāhidīn for Allah's cause obtain.[6] (emphases supplied)

Another explanation for this unconditional demand to fight everywhere and immediately without condition is this caliph's apocalypticism, hinted at above in his reference to battle between Allah and Satan. This shall be further explored in a concluding section.

The Caliph's 'Muslim Masses' Problem

A more mundane explanation for this caliph's appeal to ultra-jihadism is available, however: a relative failure of the Muslim masses to be roused to fight for, or really even understand, this ultra-jihadist Islamic State project. It is clear from a careful reading of this message that the Muslim masses exhibit reluctance and have failed to 'buy in' to this caliphal project. "Why will you not fight *for your state*?! Why will you not fight *for our Caliphate*?!," he seems to scream. The caliphs manipulative employment of fear, guilt, and also insinuations of cowardice and unmanliness, are then fully displayed.

So **where are you O Muslim** in relation to the command of your Lord, who **commanded you** to fast in one verse, and **commanded you** with jihād and fighting in dozens of verses? **Where are you** in relation to your Prophet (peace be upon him), **whom you claim to emulate**, and who spent his whole life (peace be upon him) as a mujāhid for the cause of Allah, fighting His enemies?[7] (emphases supplied)

Muslim! O you who claims to love Allah (the Mighty and Majestic), and **claims to love** His Prophet (peace be upon him)… *If you are truthful in your claim, then obey your beloved and fight* for the cause of Allah, and emulate your beloved (peace be upon him), and do not die except as a mujāhid for the cause of Allah.[8] (emphases supplied)

> **Muslims! Do not think the war that we are waging is the Islamic State's war alone.** Rather, *it is the Muslims' war altogether. It is the war of every Muslim in every place*,

and the Islamic State is merely the spearhead in this war. It is but the war of the people of faith against the people of disbelief, *so march forth to your war O Muslims. March forth everywhere, for it is an obligation* upon every Muslim who is accountable before Allah. And *whoever stays behind or flees*, Allah (the Mighty and Majestic) will be angry with him and will punish him with a painful torment.[9] (emphases supplied)

So *there is no excuse for any Muslim* who is capable of performing hijrah to the Islamic State, or capable of carrying a weapon where he is, for Allah (the Blessed and Exalted) *has commanded him* with hijrah and jihād, and has made fighting obligatory upon him."[10] (emphases supplied)

The Caliph's Jewish, Christian, and "Crusader" Problem

Baghdadi cites the standard quranic verses that supposedly prove that Jews and Christians are, and will forever remain, unreservedly hostile to Muslims and Islam generally (2: 105, 120, 217). However, this caliph faces two serious obstacles. Merely citing a few quranic passages is insufficient to fully justify a contemporary ruling (*hukm*) on whether relations among Muslims, Christians, and Jews, are *today* permissible. Second, the evidence he does cite actually tells *against* his position. What Baghdadi shows is that the United States and its allies in the anti-IS coalition, and majority-non-Muslim populations throughout Europe, have given Muslims very little to fear, and much to hope for. It is easy to feel Baghdadi seething since the demonology he requires is unsupported by contemporary facts. Baghdadi's invective is first stated, and then accompanied by the key quranic passages referenced above.

Muslims! Whoever thinks that it is within his capacity to conciliate with the Jews, Christians, and other disbelievers, and for them to conciliate with him, such that he coexists with them and they coexist with him while he is upon his religion and upon tawhīd (monotheism), then he has belied the explicit statement of his Lord (the Mighty and Majestic), who says, {**And never will the Jews or the Christians approve of you until you follow their religion**} [Al-Baqarah: 120]. {**And they will continue to fight you until they turn you back from your religion if they are able**} [Al-Baqarah: 217]. {**Neither those who disbelieve from the People of the Book nor the polytheists wish that any good should be sent down to you from your Lord. But Allah selects for His mercy whom He wills, and Allah is the possessor of great bounty**} [Al-Baqarah: 105]; (emphases in original).[11]

The illogic of Baghdadi's position emerges, however, when he tries to infer from states of fact, what he claims *will* and *must* inevitably happen in the future. Consider these *non sequiturs*.

And **if** the Crusaders today claim to avoid the Muslim public [i.e. meticulously avoiding Muslim non-combatant civilian casualties] and confine themselves to targeting the armed [i.e. IS] amongst them, **then** soon you will see them targeting every Muslim everywhere.[12] (emphases supplied)

And **if** the Crusaders today have begun to bother the Muslims who continue to live in the lands of the cross by monitoring them, arresting them, and questioning them, [i.e. enhanced employment of intelligence and law enforcement assets due to IS-inspired criminal terrorist actions] **then** soon they will begin to displace them and take them away either dead, imprisoned, or homeless. They will not leave anyone amongst them except one who apostatizes from his religion and follows theirs. [13] (emphases supplied)

From the premise that the US *does* deliberately *minimize* loss of Muslim life, one is to infer that the US*will* necessarily seek to *maximize* the loss of life. From the premise that many societies *have*, (owing to IS-inspired terrorist actions) increased surveillance and law enforcement, one is to infer these same societies *will* necessarily force persons out of their homes, into prison or force them to apostasize. Really? This is the logic followed by the caliphate's *leader*? The illogic of Baghdadi's rant against the broader anti-IS coalition is similarly on display.

America and its allies from amongst the Jews, Crusaders, Rāfidah (Shiites), secularists, atheists, and apostates claim that their coalition and war is to aid the weak and oppressed, help the poor, relieve the afflicted, liberate the enslaved, defend the innocent and peaceful, and prevent the shedding of their blood. They also claim to be in the camp of truth, good, and justice, waging war against falsehood, evil, and oppression, alongside the Muslims! Rather, they claim to defend Islam and the Muslims! Indeed, they lie. And Allah spoke the truth and His Messenger (peace be upon him) spoke the truth.[14]

That is *it*? This is the caliph's proof? Argument a*d hominem* is produced—"Rather, they claim to defend Islam and the Muslims! Indeed, they lie [but I do not!]."—but not a shred of evidence or actual fact is offered that disputes or refutes what he himself asserts that this coalition claims for itself. According to him this coalition "aid[s] the weak and oppressed, help[s] the poor, relieve[s] the afflicted, liberate[s] the enslaved, defend[s] the innocent and peaceful, and prevent[s] the shedding of their blood". According to him, this coalition claims to be "in the camp of truth, good, and justice, waging war against falsehood, evil, and oppression, alongside the Muslims!" Yes, indeed, that is what is claimed by the anti-ISO coalition. And it is not surprising that this could be "alongside the Muslims" because Islam as civilization and faith, faith and deeds, stands for precisely *those* Abrahamic-derived moral imperatives as bequeathed by priests, lawgivers, prophets, and righteous communities of faith.

The Caliph's 'Iraqi Problem': 'Ahlus-Sunnah,' Shi'a, and Kurdish Iraqi

The Ahlus-Sunnah ("People of the Sunnah") refers to the Sunni Muslim world. In its Iraqi setting, it refers to the specific reality of approximately 25% of the population, and their future within the present Iraqi state. The destruction of that state is the IS's declared goal, and enmity and fomented civil war among Iraq's constituent religious communities, an essential method for accomplishing this subversion.

The caliph's message evidences desperation, however, since this has not happened, and is not happening on the scale it must. This section of Baghdadi's speech also nicely illustrates the caliph's 'demon theory' of Sunni dis-empowerment. Instead of referencing the ISO's own violent subversion and occupation of Sunni lands, villages, and homes, by a strangely twisted logic he instead, rails against demonic "evil scholars" and other wayward religious culprits. Moreover, he admonishes the Ahlus-Sunnah for daring to seek and find refuge among those communities for whom the ISO harbors only vitriolic hatred. The denial of IS atrocities; the demon theory of emigration; the denial that non-Sunni hospitality is possible; and by default, the presentation of the Islamic State as exclusive safe harbor, are all on display here.

And what saddens us and eats at our souls is to see some of the women, children, and families of Ahlus-Sunnah seeking refuge in the areas controlled by the Rāfidah [Shi'a] and Kurdish atheists in Iraq. They stand at their doors, humiliated, disgraced, and displaced in the lands. And there is no might nor strength except by Allah. **Those who carry the blame for the displacement of these Muslims and their humiliation are the *evil scholars* from the supporters of the apostate tyrants, *the callers* [preachers] at the gates of Hellfire, those who confuse those poor people and portray the Islamic State to them as being the cause of evil and the source of hardships. *They* say,** "If not for them, you would live in safety, extravagance, luxury, and peace." ***They* portray** the Crusaders, Rāfidah, atheists, and apostates to them as being people of good, justice, mercy, and compassion, and that they are the peaceful defenders of Ahlus-Sunnah! There is no doubt that these are the years of deception.[15] (emphases supplied)

Ahlus-Sunnah in Iraq, and specifically our people in al-Anbār, be certain that our hearts are broken on account of your leaving of your homes and your lands, and your seeking of shelter in the territory of the Rāfidah and the Kurdish atheists, and your being forced to wander the lands. And even if some of your relatives are apostates waging war against the religion of Allah and allied with the Rāfidah and the Crusaders, then we don't hold you accountable for their crimes. So return to your lands, and remain in your homes, and seek shelter—after first seeking shelter with Allah—with your people in the Islamic State, for you will find therein, by Allah's permission, a warm embrace and a safe refuge. For you are our people. We defend you, your honor, and your wealth. We want you to be mighty and noble, we want you to be safe and secure, and we want your salvation from Hellfire.[16]

So seek shelter—after Allah—with the Islamic State. What do you wait for after the truth has become clearer than the day and after the spiteful Rāfidah exposed their reality? Here they are today slaughtering everyone considered from Ahlus-Sunnah in Baghdad and elsewhere. No one was saved from them, even their allies, supporters, aids, tails, and dogs from the apostates who had once belonged to Ahlus-Sunnah, those in the Sahwah, army, police, and elsewhere, **those whom the evil scholars confused into fleeing the implementation of Allah's law in the territory of the Islamic State.** So they became homeless, humiliated, fearful, and worrisome of the Rāfidah's cruelty, whereas the Muslims live in the territory of the Islamic State with might and honor, secure by Allah's bounty alone, with a life of comfort, going about the affairs of their business, livelihood, and trade, enjoying the grace of living under the rule of their Lord's law, and all praise and grace is Allah's. Therefore, O Muslims, seek shelter—after Allah—with the Islamic State.[17] (emphases supplied)

The Caliph's Wahhabi (Muhawiddun) 'Kingdom of Saudi Arabia Problem'

The conservative Wahhabi kingdom may be accused of many things, but the caliph's charges border on grossly caricatured agitational propaganda at best, delusional thought at worst. It would have been smart for Baghdadi to follow a tried and true path of accusing the

Kingdom of Saudi Arabia (KSA) of failing to fully implement the strictest elements of the comprehensive shari'a, or of ostentatiousness, lavishness, sinfulness and decadence: the sins of the corpulent wealthy monarchies whom the preachers and prophets of all faiths have condemned for their iniquities and sin. Baghdadi states, for example: "[T]he rulers of the Arabian Peninsula are not people of war nor do they have the patience for it. Rather, they are people of luxury and extravagance, people of intoxication, prostitution, dances, and feasts. They have become accustomed to the defense of the Jews and Crusaders for them and their hearts have drunk humiliation, disgrace, and subservience."

But Baghdadi's shifts to a riskier path and accuses the Saudi Wahhabi monarchy of two things: being servants and slaves of the Crusaders, Jews, and Shi'a and thereby failing to lead Ahlus-Sunnah to destroy the Shi'a; and, turning a blind eye to many sources of oppression afflicting Sunni Muslims. Several paragraphs are devoted to denouncing and delegitimizing Saudi leadership of the Ahlus-Sunnah for abandoning Muslims on every key front, and being subservient to their true masters, the Crusaders, Shi'a, and various other apostates. One discussion in particular is exemplary of Baghdadi's approach.

Āl Salūl, [a derogatory name for the House of Saud; Kingdom of Saudi Arabia] the slaves of the Crusaders and allies of the Jews, do not wish that any good should be sent down to the Muslims from their Lord. They [1] remained for decades not caring about the tragedies of the Muslims all over the world generally, and in Palestine particularly. Thereafter, they [2] remained for years allied with the Rāfidah of Iraq in a war against Ahlus-Sunnah (the Sunnis). Thereafter, they remained [3] observing the barrel bombs of death and destruction in Shām for years, enjoying and taking delight in the scenes of Muslims being killed, imprisoned, slaughtered, and burned, and their honor raped, their wealth plundered, and their homes destroyed, all at the hands of the Nusayriyyah.[18] [derogatory term for Syrian ruling Alawites, founder Ibn Nusayr]. (numbered brackets supplied)

Abandonment of Muslims in general, and Palestinians in particular? Opposing the Sunnis in Iraq and Syria? "[T]aking delight in the scenes of Muslims being killed, imprisoned, slaughtered, and burned, and their honor raped, their wealth plundered, and their homes destroyed"? One is left to ponder how far this caliph feels he can traffic in allegations so contrary to fact. Again, one may accuse this Wahhabi kingdom of insufficient application of shari'a; decadence; and any number of defects. But to claim that Saudi Arabia has abandoned the cause of orthodox Sunni Islam throughout the world, including the unmentioned (by Baghdadi) theatres of Afghanistan, Bosnia, and Chechnya, or to deny they actively promote a worldwide Da'wa and philanthropic mission; to deny the historic Saudi role in the Israel-Palestine conflict; is contrary to known fact. If this caliph seeks to win this particular contest for leadership of the Ahlus-Sunna, known facts of history will be essential; hyperbole or wildly inaccurate claims, a deadly liability.

The Caliphate's 'Universal Muslim Rulership Problem'

But it is not just "Al-Salul" but the entire planet that must be cleansed of its supposed apostasy. This Caliph's universal pretensions appear to demand universal delegitimizing. And he has 'discovered' such in all of the places that Islam now presently exists. In stark contrast to the shari'a of lawful jihad that requires a prudent calculation of costs and benefits, and also adherence to a classical legal tradition amounting to an Islamic law of warfare, what this caliph appears to call for and condone is a virtually unconditional universal theatre of violent confrontation.

Muslims, the apostate tyrannical rulers who rule your lands in the lands of the Two Holy Sanctuaries (Mecca and Medina), Yemen, Shām (the Levant), Iraq, Egypt, North Africa, Khorasan, the Caucasus, the Indian Subcontinent, Africa, and elsewhere, are the allies of the Jews and Crusaders. Rather, they are their slaves, servants, and guard dogs, and nothing else. The armies that they prepare and arm and which the Jews and Crusaders train are only to crush you, weaken you, enslave you to the Jews and Crusaders, turn you away from your religion and the path of Allah, plunder the goods of your lands, and rob you of your wealth. This reality has become as obvious as the sun in the middle of the day [noonday's sun]. No one denies this except for one whose light Allah has obliterated, whose foresight Allah has blinded, and whose heart Allah has sealed.[19]

Apocalypse Now

Several academic analyses confirm that apocalyptic prophecy is one key ingredient underpinning the creed, method, extravagant violence, and killing in masse exemplifying the Islamic State's will to power.[20] Baghdadi in his latest message further illustrates this prophetic apocalyptic dimension. What is key here is the sense of emergency, imminence, and End Times that transforms what under normal historical circumstances demands rational, logical, empirical, and careful investigation, into an eschatological demonology demanding immediate, urgent action. Ethics are radically suspended, or transformed, to fight and win these final battles of human existence: battles from and through which sins are to be fully and completely expiated. Jihad here makes its appearance as an ultimate sacrificial offering that cleanses and readies one for that prized, superlative verdict on the Day of Resurrection.

> His [Prophet Muhammad's] companions after him and their followers carried on similarly. They did not soften and abandon war, until they possessed the Earth, conquered the East and the West, the nations submitted to them, and the lands yielded to them, by the edge of the sword. And similarly, this will remain the condition of those who follow them until the Day of Recompense. Our Prophet (peace be upon him) has informed us of ***the Malāhim (bloody battles) near the end of time.*** He gave us good tidings and promised us that we would be victorious in these battles. He is the truthful and trustworthy, peace be upon him. ***And here we are today seeing the signs of those Malāhim and***

we feel the winds of victory within them.[21] (emphases supplied)

Discussion

Several critical vulnerabilities threaten the foundations and future expansion of the self-proclaimed caliph Ibrahim's ISO caliphate project. First, the Islamic faith in its totality is illicitly equated with a single though superlative dimension: jihad. Though a superlative form of duty and sacrifice—even the superlative form (whether an individual duty (fard 'ayn) to assist in collective defense, or collective duty (fard kifaya) to expand the Islamic sphere of authority and hegemony), it is indefensible to the vast majority of Muslims to equate all of the rights, duties, and obligations of Islam to this supreme but single dimension. Moreover, the lawful waging of jihad in the path of Allah (jihad fi sabil Allah) demands the most careful, exacting legal and prudential judgments. The Islamic faith and its rule of law are here in direct contradiction with this caliph's demand that Islam is only warfare, and that warfare is now to be waged by all in every Muslim-majority and Muslim-minority land.

Second, this caliph is at present deeply marginalized from a broad range of observant Sunni Muslims—whether the conservative orthodox Wahhabi Saudi kingdom, the Ahlus-Sunnah of Iraq, every existing Muslim government, or the Muslim masses generally. Demonized within this Sunni faith are also those Sunni scholars and mosque preachers who deny the ISO the legitimacy it seeks, and who call into question the ultra-jihadist sectarianism and killing in masse *modus operandi* of the ISO.

Third, Baghdadi is marginalized from the non-Sunni Muslims in Iraq—whether observant Shi'a or secular ("atheist") Kurds—and his call to fratricidal civil war and sectarian carnage has in general been resisted. To the contrary, these people and lands have made their abodes available to Sunni's fleeing the ISO caliphate project. Fourth, though rare exceptions exist, Jews and Christians do not seek to force Muslims to apostasize, nor do they harbor an eternal enmity that precludes amicable co-existence on the basis of recognized covenants, shared interests, and earned respect. The empirical refutation of Baghdadi's archaic position will continue to threaten any rational comprehension of potential and actual alliances. Fifth, deeds done: facts, actions, empirical realities, all tell *against* the caliphate project. Baghdadi's obvious recognition that the anti-ISO coalition claims with much success to *defend* Muslims, vividly contrasts with ISO's own record of atrocities, displacement, treachery, subversion, crucifixion, immolation, and killing in masse. Fighting a "war of deeds" against ISO should pay great dividends.[22] Finally, apocalyptic prophecy—whether Zoroastrian, Jewish, Christian, or Muslim—supplies an erroneous and extremely dangerous foundation for human action, particularly ethical-moral action. One direction this may take—wanton destruction meted out by fanatics seeking to expedite the End Times, and win their station in an Eternal Heavenly Abode—has a natural half-life, and must eventually reckon with the stubborn facts of human nature, and history. It appears, in short, caliph Ibrahim has taken on the world—Muslim and non-Muslim—and also history, in his sure faith that he is right, and we are wrong. It will be sooner rather than later, that a verdict shall be rendered. I believe the caliph will be quite disappointed.

Chapter 13

America's New Strategic Reality: Irregular World War

Jeff M. Moore

First Published 24 June 2015

Congressman Devin Nunes[1] (R-CA 22nd District)[2], Chairman of the House Intelligence Committee, said on CBS's Face the Nation this past Sunday[3] that ISIS posed a severe and pending threat to the United States. The FBI, on June 17th, told ABC News that it's in the midst of[4] attempting to disrupt ISIS operations in all 50 states, an historic first for domestic terror threats. This follows similar and recent warnings about ISIS from Homeland Security Secretary Jeh Johnson[5] and former CIA head Mike Morell[6]. While all these warnings are prudent, none have provided the strategic context behind the threat environment, which is this: America is embroiled in an irregular world war with Islamist jihadists. If it doesn't rise to the occasion and confront the threat more effectively, America runs the risk of international strategic decline.

This war is indeed global. Every region on earth is bearing the brunt of Islamist jihad terrorism and insurgency: Asia, Africa, Europe, North America, etc. Even areas that haven't seen jihadist attacks as of late like

Latin America have at least seen Islamist jihadist intelligence, financing, and logistics activities[7].

As for "irregular war," in basic terms, it means wars without front lines, fighters without uniforms, terrorism and political warfare as tactics, and counter-status quo political and/or religious goals. It is the opposite of a conventional battlefield such as WW II in Europe where uniformed Allied armies battled Nazi armies for key terrain on well-designated battlefields.

The Islamist jihadist threat has much in common with the Nazis in other areas, however.

Islamist jihadism is a radical, political-religious ideology defined by a Muslim Brotherhood founding father named Sayyid Qutb[8]. In his book, *Milestones*[9], Qutb asserts that an ultra-conservative, political version of Islam should rule the world, and that Islamism cannot coexist with democracy and capitalism. War on all non-Islamists, says Qutb, is a religious duty to clear the way for his version of a perfect, holy society. ISIS, al Qaeda, and like groups all over the world follow this philosophy. Even when they disagree over leadership issues such as the apparent ISIS-AQ spat, they still adhere to the same end goals.

Sound cartoonish? It's happened before. Adolph Hitler did it. His autobiography, *Mein Kamph*, laid out the core ideology of the Nazis. He inspired millions into battle and the genocide of over 10 million[10].

In this global irregular war, however, instead of a Hitler figurehead as the center of gravity, the driving force is an ideology—Islamist society under a Caliphate. And it's now a deadly fad that's caught on like wildfire.

Regarding military forces, instead of a single, unified army like Hitler's SS troopers and Wehrmacht, the Islamist jihadists have four types of forces all over the globe.

First are the major terror and insurgent groups with global or regional caliphate goals like ISIS, AQ, and Southeast Asia's Jemaah Islamiyah.

Second are country-specific insurgencies such as Somalia's al Shabaab[11], Nigeria's Boko Haram[12], the Philippines' Bangsamoro

Islamic Freedom Fighters[13], and Pakistan's Taliban[14]. These organizations fight for their own version of Islamist jihad, and some have pledged allegiance to ISIS or AQ over the years.

Third are the highly networked terror cells such as those that carried out the 2005 Tube bombings in London[15], the 2015 Charlie Hebdo attacks in Paris[16], and the ISIS-inspired militants that were planning attacks in Malaysia[17] in April.

Fourth are the lone wolves, the individual jihadists such as Oklahoma man Alton Nolen[18] who in September 2014 beheaded a female coworker, and Mohamed Mohamud[19] who in 2010 aimed to bomb a Portland Christmas gathering. Scores of fighters like these seem to materialize[20] all over the world on a monthly basis now.

And it's not just the "West vs. Islamists," either. There's scores of Muslim countries involved in this fight, too. Tunisia, Iraq, Jordan, Indonesia, Saudi Arabia, Pakistan, Bangladesh, Egypt, Kazakhstan, the UAE, and Yemen are all fully engaged against Islamist jihadist fighters in some form or another.

What's it all mean?

First, the Obama administration doesn't understand the threat. National Security Advisor Susan Rice told a crowd at the Brookings Institution in February 2015, "Still, while the dangers we face may be more numerous and varied, they are not of the existential nature we confronted during World War II or during the Cold War."

She's wrong.

ISIS and its cohorts, aside from their irregular nature, are just like the Nazis. They are driven by a radical cultural and politico-religious ideology. Their end goal is to subjugate others under this ideology. They use terrorism and gruesome violence as a tool as demonstrated by their mass executions to "cleanse" society of their enemies. They're violently intolerant of "incompatible" social and cultural norms. Finally, they intimidate and murder their own kind. This is exactly what the Nazis did.

It's also important to note that AQ killed more Americans *on U.S. soil* on 9-11 than the Nazis ever did.

Second, if you don't understand the threat, you can't plan defensive and offensive ways to mitigate it.

Third, since America's foreign partners and allies see no leadership coming from Washington on this global irregular world war, they're forced to go it alone.

To be sure, it's a good thing when other countries ante up and fight the Islamist jihadists so America doesn't have to expend excessive blood and treasure. But it's a bad thing when America won't coordinate and lead a global irregular counterattack when it both could and should. America is the only country with the international clout, technology, and counter terror/counterinsurgency know how that can rally so many diverse partners against this Nazi-like threat reborn. Merging this prowess with partner nations' local knowledge would make a powerful force multiplier.

What to do? In WW II, President Roosevelt met with his counterparts such as Winston Churchill, Joseph Stalin, and Charles de Gaulle through various conferences to plan policy for countering the Nazi onslaught. More than feel-good regional conferences packed with scores of diplomats and photo ops, these small groups of leaders decisively defined the threat and set end goals to defeat it. This would be appropriate now.

Also in WW II, America and the UK established a Combined Chiefs of Staff of their top military officers to coordinate the war. A similar command—beyond global Special Forces coordination—would be appropriate. Indonesia, Saudi Arabia, Jordan, and like countries would be necessary participants. Aside from decisive military and covert action, top priority should be given to worldwide, counter politico-religious warfare.

But it all begins with defining the threat. If that doesn't happen, the counterattack won't begin, and we'll just float along from crisis to crisis, applying half measures and saying we're not at war when we certainly are. Tackling this global irregular threat takes international defense and security savvy, realpolitik capabilities, and seeing world as it is, not as politicians want it to be.

Chapter 14

Al Shabaab Resurgence

Arnold Hammari

First Published 29 July 2015

In 2012 the militant Islamist group Harakat al-Shabaab al-Mujahidin[1], commonly known as al Shabaab, was at its peak of power. It had just declared allegiance to al Qaeda, controlled the majority of Somalia, and was institutionalized as a government collecting taxes, adjudicating legal cases, and implementing sharia law. Al Shabaab enjoyed robust support from abroad with new technologically savvy recruits, funding from Islamic charities, and remittances from individuals. Their success on the battlefield and exploitation of jihad videos online brought in more influence, power, and funding.

When al Shabaab first began to operate in Somalia as the former youth wing of the Islamic Courts Union, it fought using guerilla tactics such as suicide bombers, ambushes, and small unit operations. Its leadership was trained in Afghanistan and Pakistan and adapted the tactics used against Soviet troops to fight the Transitional Government troops in Somalia. As the group swelled in membership and it assumed the governance of regions, al Shabaab changed its tactics to fight as a more conventional force using formations, dug in fortifications, and heavy weaponry. This change in tactics led to the downfall of al Shabaab.

Rise of AMISOM

The African Union Mission in Somalia (AMISOM)[2] was created in February 2007 and finally started to gain some traction in 2011 when it gained control of the Mogadishu International Airport and established a beach-head for the inflow of additional troops, supporting equipment, and materials. Slowly the United Nations backed AMISOM troops expanded their areas of control to control Mogadishu. Western powers provided advisors, intelligence, and air strikes to assist the AMISOM troops in finding and destroying al Shabaab conventional forces. Western security assistance programs also provided air power with attack helicopters and jets to the AMISOM troop contributing countries and this air superiority decimated large al Shabaab military formations.

AMISOM launched Operation Indian Ocean[3] in 2014 that liberated the remaining towns in Somalia from al Shabaab. The remains of al Shabaab displaced to northern Kenya, Puntland, and Somaliland to reorganize. As al Shabaab was portrayed as defeated in the international press many international jihad recruits chose to join other organizations that were enjoying success such as the Islamic State, Boko Haram, or other groups fighting in Syria. Donors also shifted their resources to other groups and with the loss of the ports and taxes the financial resources of al Shabaab were drying up.

Failure of the Somali Government

Success on the battlefield was supposed to provide space for the Somali people to develop a government that could control the conquered territories. The Transitional Federal Government gave way to the Federal Government of Somalia (FGS) in August 2012, however, the new government continued to be plagued by problems of clan politics and corruption.

Multiple international donors worked to create the Somali National Army (SNA)[4] which is still largely composed of units operating independently as clan-based militias with questionable loyalty to the FGS. The Somali National Army is not able to stand on its own against a resurgent al Shabaab and SNA leadership does not have effective control over units with different clan leadership. Often SNA units from rival clans are seen by the local population more as invading forces than as a liberating or protecting force, lessening their effectiveness.

The glacial political progress in the FGS and persistent conflicts with local governments and clan elders as well as the ineffective SNA have caused stagnation on the battlefield and given an opportunity for al Shabaab to regroup and re-attack. Survivors of the al Shabaab leadership returned to their guerilla tactics and began to quietly reassume power in remote areas not under the control of the FGS.

Operation Indian Ocean also culminated the AMISOM forces and stagnated the battlefield. AMISOM troops were reluctant to leave their secure outposts in southern Somalia and grew complacent in their security. The African Union did not authorize an increase in the AMISOM force cap and the AMISOM troops were obliged to police large areas that were without a SNA or SFG presence. As the American troops in Iraq learned with the 2007 Surge, an occupation army requires more troops than an invading army. AMISOM was unable to effectively police their areas of responsibility with their limited numbers of troops, which allowed al Shabaab to fill the power vacuum.

International Support Failures

AMISOM leadership was consumed with political infighting among the troops contributing countries with Ethiopian and Kenyan military and political leaders trying to position themselves to take advantage of the Somali regions that bordered their own countries. The United Nations Support Office for AMISOM (UNSOA) has been unable to fulfill its mandate to provide support, movement, and payment to the troop contributing countries. The failure of UNSOA has resulted in delayed payment of troop salaries[5], lack of transportation for troops into Somalia during troop rotation, and the degradation of AMISOM vehicles and equipment as replacement parts were slow to arrive.

International donors sponsored multiple conference abroad to try to unify the SFG and pledged millions to the government but with weak results. As in the former days of the TFG, Somali delegates were willing to attend the conference, eat the food, and absorb the per diem but made little progress.

Rebirth of al Shabaab

Al Shabaab conducted devastating attacks in Kenya in 2013-14, the most famous being the killing of 67 civilians at the Westgate Mall[6] in Nairobi in September 2013 and 37 Christian workers in December 2014 near Koromey in northern Kenya. In April 2015, al Shabaab killed 147 students at Garissa University College in northern Kenya.

In Somalia, the rising crescendo of attacks included frequent attacks in Mogadishu on fortified hotels and compounds. Al Shabaab mounted a coordinated attacks on the Presidential Compound, Villa Somaliain[7] February and June 2014. In 2015 hotels in Mogadishu were subject to sophisticated al Shabaab attacks in February 2015[8] killing 40 civilians including the Somali Ambassador to Switzerland, March 2015[9] killing six civilians, and a coordinated attack on two separate hotels[10] June 2015 killed ten more civilians.

Al Shabaab has also started taking the fight to AMISOM troops in their fortified compounds. On Christmas day in 2014 al Shabaab troops raided the African Union military compound at the Mogadishu International Airport[11], killing 14. On 26 June 2015, between 500-1500 al Shabaab troops overran the AMISOM base in Leego[12],

Somalia. AMISOM reinforcement troops took over 48 hours to respond to the attack and the al Shabaab fighters escaped with additional weapons, uniforms, and equipment. AMISOM has also withdrawn[13] from nine towns in southern Somalia and is consolidating its presence in larger bases in order to protect against further al Shabaab attacks.

Future of Somalia

Unless the Federal Government of Somalia is able to arrive at a political solution and consolidate control of the country future military victories on the battlefield will accomplish little. The Somali National Army needs to gain control of all units and develop a clan-integrated force in order for it to serve as an effective fighting force. The international community that is already suffering from donor fatigue will be reluctant to continue to fund a Somali government and military that are not working towards consolidating control in the near future.

The failure of support institutions such as UNSOA to resupply, transport, and pay AMISOM troops will result in the weakening of the force and troop contributing countries to withdraw their forces. AMISOM forces will continue to be stretched too thin to effectively police southern Somalia unless the African Union increases the size of the overall force. Further AMISOM losses will lower morale among AMISOM troops and further decrease their effectiveness, providing greater opportunities from al Shabaab to regain power and reestablish itself in southern Somalia.

In 2012 the militant Islamist group Harakat al-Shabaab al-Mujahidin[14], commonly known as al Shabaab, was at its peak of power. It had just declared allegiance to al Qaeda, controlled the majority of Somalia, and was institutionalized as a government collecting taxes, adjudicating legal cases, and implementing sharia law. Al Shabaab enjoyed robust support from abroad with new technologically savvy recruits, funding from Islamic charities, and remittances from individuals. Their success on the battlefield and exploitation of jihad videos online brought in more influence, power, and funding.

When al Shabaab first began to operate in Somalia as the former youth wing of the Islamic Courts Union, it fought using guerilla tactics such as suicide bombers, ambushes, and small unit operations. Its leadership was trained in Afghanistan and Pakistan and adapted the tactics used against Soviet troops to fight the Transitional Government troops in Somalia. As the group swelled in membership and it assumed the governance of regions, al Shabaab changed its tactics to fight as a more conventional force using formations, dug in fortifications, and heavy weaponry. This change in tactics led to the downfall of al Shabaab.

Rise of AMISOM

The African Union Mission in Somalia (AMISOM)[15] was created in February 2007 and finally started to gain some traction in 2011 when it gained control of the Mogadishu International Airport and established a beach-head for the inflow of additional troops, supporting equipment, and materials. Slowly the United Nations backed AMISOM troops expanded their areas of control to control Mogadishu. Western powers provided advisors, intelligence, and air strikes to assist the AMISOM troops in finding and destroying al Shabaab conventional forces. Western security assistance programs also provided air power with attack helicopters and jets to the AMISOM troop contributing countries and this air superiority decimated large al Shabaab military formations.

AMISOM launched Operation Indian Ocean[16] in 2014 that liberated the remaining towns in Somalia from al Shabaab. The remains of al Shabaab displaced to northern Kenya, Puntland, and Somaliland to reorganize. As al Shabaab was portrayed as defeated in the international press many international jihad recruits chose to join other organizations that were enjoying success such as the Islamic State, Boko Haram, or other groups fighting in Syria. Donors also shifted their resources to other groups and with the loss of the ports and taxes the financial resources of al Shabaab were drying up.

Failure of the Somali Government

Success on the battlefield was supposed to provide space for the Somali people to develop a government that could control the conquered territories. The Transitional Federal Government gave way to the Federal Government of Somalia (FGS) in August 2012, however, the new government continued to be plagued by problems of clan politics and corruption.

Multiple international donors worked to create the Somali National Army (SNA)[17] which is still largely composed of units operating independently as clan-based militias with questionable loyalty to the FGS. The Somali National Army is not able to stand on its own against a resurgent al Shabaab and SNA leadership does not have effective control over units with different clan leadership. Often SNA units from rival clans are seen by the local population more as invading forces than as a liberating or protecting force, lessening their effectiveness.

The glacial political progress in the FGS and persistent conflicts with local governments and clan elders as well as the ineffective SNA have caused stagnation on the battlefield and given an opportunity for al Shabaab to regroup and re-attack. Survivors of the al Shabaab leadership returned to their guerilla tactics and began to quietly reassume power in remote areas not under the control of the FGS.

Operation Indian Ocean also culminated the AMISOM forces and stagnated the battlefield. AMISOM troops were reluctant to leave their secure outposts in southern Somalia and grew complacent in their security. The African Union did not authorize an increase in the AMISOM force cap and the AMISOM troops were obliged to police large areas that were without a SNA or SFG presence. As the American troops in Iraq learned with the 2007 Surge, an occupation army requires more troops than an invading army. AMISOM was unable to effectively police their areas of responsibility with their limited numbers of troops, which allowed al Shabaab to fill the power vacuum.

International Support Failures

AMISOM leadership was consumed with political infighting among the troops contributing countries with Ethiopian and Kenyan military and political leaders trying to position themselves to take advantage of the Somali regions that bordered their own countries. The United Nations Support Office for AMISOM (UNSOA) has been unable to fulfill its mandate to provide support, movement, and payment to the troop contributing countries. The failure of UNSOA has resulted in delayed payment of troop salaries[18], lack of transportation for troops into Somalia during troop rotation, and the degradation of AMISOM vehicles and equipment as replacement parts were slow to arrive.

International donors sponsored multiple conference abroad to try to unify the SFG and pledged millions to the government but with weak results. As in the former days of the TFG, Somali delegates were willing to attend the conference, eat the food, and absorb the per diem but made little progress.

Rebirth of al Shabaab

Al Shabaab conducted devastating attacks in Kenya in 2013-14, the most famous being the killing of 67 civilians at the Westgate Mall[19] in Nairobi in September 2013 and 37 Christian workers in December 2014 near Koromey in northern Kenya. In April 2015, al Shabaab killed 147 students at Garissa University College in northern Kenya.

In Somalia, the rising crescendo of attacks included frequent attacks in Mogadishu on fortified hotels and compounds. Al Shabaab mounted a coordinated attacks on the Presidential Compound, Villa Somalia[20] in February and June 2014. In 2015 hotels in Mogadishu were subject to sophisticated al Shabaab attacks in February 2015[21] killing 40 civilians including the Somali Ambassador to Switzerland, March 2015[22] killing six civilians, and a coordinated attack on two separate hotels]23] June 2015 killed ten more civilians.

Al Shabaab has also started taking the fight to AMISOM troops in their fortified compounds. On Christmas day in 2014 al Shabaab troops raided the African Union military compound at the Mogadishu International Airport[24], killing 14. On 26 June 2015, between 500-1500 al Shabaab troops overran the AMISOM base in Leego[25], Somalia. AMISOM reinforcement troops took over 48 hours to respond to the attack and the al Shabaab fighters escaped with additional weapons, uniforms, and equipment. AMISOM has also withdrawn[26] from nine towns in southern Somalia and is consolidating its presence in larger bases in order to protect against further al Shabaab attacks.

Future of Somalia

Unless the Federal Government of Somalia is able to arrive at a political solution and consolidate control of the country future military victories on the battlefield will accomplish little. The Somali National Army needs to gain control of all units and develop a clan-integrated force in order for it to serve as an effective fighting force. The international community that is already suffering from donor fatigue will be reluctant to continue to fund a Somali government and military that are not working towards consolidating control in the near future.

The failure of support institutions such as UNSOA to resupply, transport, and pay AMISOM troops will result in the weakening of the force and troop contributing countries to withdraw their forces. AMISOM forces will continue to be stretched too thin to effectively police southern Somalia unless the African Union increases the size of the overall force. Further AMISOM losses will lower morale among AMISOM troops and further decrease their effectiveness, providing greater opportunities from al Shabaab to regain power and reestablish itself in southern Somalia.

Chapter 15

A War With ISIS is a Battle Against Ideologies

Chelsea Daymon

First Published 31 July 2015

Time and time again the concept of being at war with the Islamic State of Iraq and Syria (ISIS) is echoed in print, the media, and talks throughout Washington, D.C. Granted ISIS, or the Islamic State (IS) as they like to call themselves, is a formidable foe on the frontlines however, when contemplating the issues at hand, we are not "at war" with ISIS. We are "at war" with an ideology.

This poses the questions: how can we be at war with an ideology, what is it that attracts its members, and can an ideology really be combated?

Presently, some intellectuals propose that healing the socio-political issues facing the Middle East will eventually help eradicate the scourge of radical ideologies in the region. Nevertheless, we also heard this theory when al-Qaeda (AQ) was brought to our attention in the 1990s.

Additionally, when the Arab Spring broke out in 2010, it emitted a feeling of hope across nations that perhaps this was the catalyst of socio-political change that would spark a new era where brutal ideologies could not flourish. The hope that truly democratic nations would be formed in Middle East and North African (MENA) nations lead some to believe[1] that it could put a cap on the growth of extremist notions such as those of AQ's. Yet over two decades later since AQ came on the scene and subsequently the Arab Spring fizzled out, we are still faced with violent ideologies. Furthermore, the ideology of ISIS has been described[2] as more radical than its predecessors.

The concept of healing a country's socio-political woes to eradicate extremists view such as those of AQ and now ISIS, at first seems like a valid notion until contemplating the present, past, and some of the motivations behind these radical outlooks.

Both AQ and ISIS have visions of liberating the Middle East from unjust, un-Islamic, and what they identify as apostate rulers in order to create their versions of "true" Islamic systems. Yet the two groups have different ideas on where the root causes of these unjust governments stem from. AQ focuses on what has been describe as the "far enemy" with the bedrock of Middle East transgressions deriving for the west; in this case the United States and its policies in the Middle East. On the contrary, ISIS views itself as liberating the Middle East from itself, the "near enemy", by cleansing the region of what it views as apostate regimes and replacing them with its own vision of an Islamic governorate.

One of the things that stands out when comparing ISIS as opposed to AQ, is the desire to hold territory. In order to have an Islamic State, territory must be held. This is a top priority for ISIS. AQ on the other hand, had long-term goals of setting up an Islamic State but holding territory was not one of its immediate objectives unless it was an area for refuge or training camps.

An ideology that plays a key factor in ISIS's rise to power is this concept of creating an Islamic State and holding territory in its name. By creating a "state", this accomplishment has provided members with a sense of affinity, status, and a group identity to be associated with. A recent report[3] by Quantum Communications found that out of forty-nine testimonies of ISIS members the majority had joined the group seeking status or identity. 77% of internal fighters, categorized as fighters recruited by jihadist organizations in the same country where they lived, in this case Syria and Iraq, were found to be seeking status. Only 8% of Western external fighters and 15% of Arab external fighters were found to be seeking status. While 63% of Western external fighters sought identity with 25% of internal recruits and 12% of Arab external fighters seeking the same thing.

The report also highlights that the majority of interviewed western recruits were facing an identity crisis with a need to find meaning in their lives. "The transnational Islamic identity (*Ummah*) offers them a pre-packaged identity in a context of anti-Western culture" the report stated.

For recruits this "pre-packaged" identity and the idea of making an emigration (*hijra*) to ISIS's Islamic State, evokes a recreation of the Prophet Muhammad's flight from Mecca to Medina due to an assassination plot against his life. There is no doubt that this semblance adds weight to ISIS's "state" as being a refuge from a land perceived to be full of disbelievers just as Medina was for the Prophet Muhammad.

A Canadian woman in her early twenties, going by the name Umm Haritha, traveled to Syria to "live a life of honour" under Islamic (*sharia*) law rather than the laws of the "kuffar," or unbelievers. In an interview[4] she told Canada's CBC news "when I heard that the Islamic State had sharia in some cities in Syria, it became an automatic obligation upon me since I was able to come here." Her words echo a statement that ISIS's leader Abu Bakr al-Baghdadi issued[5] via audio recording in the summer of 2014. "Rush O Muslims to your state. Yes, it is your state. Rush, because Syria is not for the Syrians, and Iraq is not for the Iraqis," he stated. "O Muslims everywhere, whoever is capable of performing hijrah (emigration) to the Islamic State, then let him do so, because hijrah to the land of Islam is obligatory," he declared.

Another ideological factor that plays heavily into the common narrative of ISIS's jihad, is the idea of assisting one's fellow Muslim brothers and sisters in a righteous battle against the "other". In this case the "other" would be considered the al-Assad regime, Shiites, minority groups, and anyone else ISIS views as misbelievers. In his summer of 2014 message, al-Baghdadi also alluded to this idea: "So listen, O ummah of Islam. Listen and comprehend. Stand up and rise. For the time has come for you to free yourself from the shackles of weakness, and stand in the face of tyranny, against the treacherous rulers—the agents of the crusaders and the atheists…"

This notion of aiding the *ummah* applies to internal recruits, i.e. those from Syria and Iraq, as well as recruits from other MENA and western nations. The concept of helping the Syrian people, which can be viewed in the greater context of aiding the *ummah*, resonates strongly in the initial radicalization of individuals. Yasmin Qureshi, a British lawmaker told CNN[6] that individuals joining ISIS "erroneously believe they are going out to help people".

There have been numerous events throughout recent history which have fed into this desire to help the *ummah*. Afghanistan, Palestine, and Bosnia presented strong cases. Currently Syria provides the perfect catalyst with the brutal atrocities inflicted on the Syrian people by the hands of its own government. A Twitter message posted[7] by Muhammad Hamidur Rahman, a twenty-five-year-old from Portsmouth, U.K. stated that his reason for traveling to Syria was because he was "called by God to help Muslims being killed by President Bashar al-Assad". Rahman was killed fighting for ISIS in the summer of 2014 during a firefight with forces loyal to the al-Assad regime. His family received news of his death via text message.

On another degree, the desire for survival in an unstable region fuels many to join ISIS. Survival on many levels both basic and arbitrary can be a practical and seductive reason to align with a group. In Syria a country rocked by mass-destruction and violence and Iraq, a country on the verge of potentially greater bloodshed than seen in the past, the basic concept of survival and aligning one's self with a discerned winner can be a strong factor in recruitment. As human nature shows us, many people will find a way to survive no matter what the costs.

ISIS offers an enticing package to recruits looking for a livelihood. According to[8] Aqsa Mahmood, a young woman who left her family home in Glasgow, Scotland to join ISIS in 2013, who has been a strong supporter of the Islamic State, and a recruiter of young women over social media; the ISIS rewards package includes "a house with free electricity and water provided to you due to the Khilafah (the caliphate or state) and no rent included". When the ideology of survival factors in, the thought of a paid roof over one's head is an appealing attraction especially to individuals seeking status and identity.

Some Syrian refugees driven by desperation have offered an oath of allegiance (*bay'ah/baya'ah*) to ISIS. Accounts of refugees who fled to the Turkish border town of Akcakale, flanking the Syrian town of Tel Abyad which has become a border crossing into the Islamic State, are entering back into Syria to live under ISIS rule. Scarcity of work, low wages, and a desire to return home are driving some refugees to take their chances with ISIS.

Mohammed, a former leader of the FSA's *Omar bin Khatib* brigade and a refugee stated in an interview[9] that, "If you see us on the side of ISIS you should not blame us". Pointing to a fellow ex-soldier with an injured foot that needed attention, Mohammed expressed that the FSA let them down and that "If you are injured then no one cares for you. I would rather live in an ISIS area. In 15 days I will go back and give them *baya'ah*."

Likewise, twenty-two-year-old Abu Hussein, complained that, "There are no jobs here, I have no money". Hussein, fought against ISIS in Tel Abyad before escaping to Akcakale. Considering his desperate situation and ISIS's decrees on atonement, he said[10], "They have declared that anyone who wants to repent can come. They have some negative sides and some positives ones. Tel Abyad is very safe now because people are afraid of them—before it was chaotic. But I have not seen with my own eyes yet how they are applying Shariah (Islamic law)."

Taking all of this into consideration, can an ideology really be combated? The only feasible answer is no. There are no measures to completely eradicate a mind-set, particularly one that is complex on many levels, both personal and socio-political. Currently we are witnessing an ideological war that is being set for generations to come.

Prevention is the only way to reduce the growth of what we are observing with ISIS. Many of today's generation can be described as a disenfranchised group that saw powerful authorities sitting by while innocent people were harmed by either their own governments or what they viewed as influential players who lacked action. Consequently, anger grew towards harsh regimes such as al-Assad's as well as powerful Western governments like the U.S., Britain, and Canada. Due to this idea, there is a conviction that there was a lack of actions and policies that have helped the innocent, in this case the *Ummah*, on the part of these governments. For some, this indignation has morphed into radical ideologies that ISIS now thrives on. AQ also fostered this ideology but, in recent times the organization has come across as frozen to those seeking a group to belong to. ISIS, on the other hand, is viewed by many as taking action. ISIS, just as AQ has fought the al-Assad regime but, ISIS now holds territory, and they have created a caliphate which provides its members with a sense of status and a belief of being on the side of a winning team.

As stated above, prevention is the only means of cutting back on the amount of individuals drawn to radical ideologies such as those of ISIS. There are a number of prevention methods available, from utilizing law enforcement, community elements, outreach, and countering violent extremism (CVE) programs. Law enforcement can be good at intercepting individuals from traveling to Syria to join ISIS and potentially inhibiting attacks on their home countries but, it is not built to thwart radical ideologies. Community programs in at-risk neighborhoods that apply interactive and interpersonal group activities that foster real discussions on grievances, personal experiences, and interpretations on how individuals perceive ISIS with the reality of life under ISIS, are valid methods to potentially sway individuals from glorifying the ideologies of the group. Outreach initiatives to counter these views through youth programs, school workshops, online interaction methods, and campaigns such as Extreme Dialogue[11], all add to reducing and bringing awareness to radical views and the motives that form them. Lastly, CVE programs that take a hands-on approach to the root-causes of violent extremism are important entities in the battle, although many are new and have yet to be proven effective. Still, these programs need to be implemented, worked on, and perfected because, tomorrow's radical generation are the children of today's ISIS recruits.

Chapter 16

Interview: Thinking About ISIS in Strategic Terms

Robert C. Jones

First Published 9 August 2015

It was recently my privilege to conduct an interview as a subject matter expert with the Strategic Multi-Layer Assessment (SMA). SMA is led by Hriar "Doc" Cabayan, Ph.D., and is accepted and synchronized by the Joint Staff J-39 has partnered with the United States Advisory Commission on Public Diplomacy, a body authorized by Congress and based at the State Department, to conduct a series of interviews with experts to explore what the Middle East will look like in 5-15 years. The focus of this interview was ISIS and the current crisis is Syria and Iraq. While the actual interview will be made available by SMA in their official channels, I am providing the answers I prepared in advance for the interview here. The interview was conducted by Ms. Sarah Canna, a principle analyst at NSI.

The positions, insights and thoughts that I am about to share are my own, and in no way reflect the positions of USSOCOM, the US Department of Defense, or the US Department of State.

Canna: *In an email you sent Doc (Dr. Hriar Cabayan), you mentioned that the Iraq/Syria conflict is a "populace-based conflict" at heart. Could you explain why that is so, and how that should impact USG strategies and plans?*

Jones: When the US devised a political solution for Iraq we assumed the inherent "rightness," "goodness" and legality of what we offered could overcome the inherent lack of popular legitimacy that any political solution imposed by a foreign power naturally has—not to mention the historic and cultural differences of our two nations. A mix of hubris and naiveté, and the end result was that we gave political power to the Shia (and de facto influence over the region to Iran); we gave a degree of autonomy to the Kurds (but that increased the revolutionary pressure on Turkey from their own restive Kurdish population). This left the Shia and Kurds with something tangible they could place their trust in, but we only offered the Sunni-Arabs money and promises wrapped in a culturally inappropriate package of governance. The money is gone, the promises fell flat, and the one significant population without a chair when the music stopped was the Sunni-Arab populations of Syria and Iraq. While we agonized over how to solve this problem without abandoning our elegant solution, the hard fact is that ISIS emerged and "stole the march" on both AQ and the US. What AQ offered was too slow and theoretical; and what the US offered was too inappropriate. *The only one offering a tangible, viable political alternative to the Sunni-Arab populations of the region was ISIS.* It is not too late to address this problem, but to simply "defeat" ISIS only removes ISIS governance from the emergent de facto Sunni-Arab state and turns this back into a fragmented mess of competing revolutionary groups; does nothing to address the underlying political driver of revolution; and does much to restore AQs credibility and legitimacy in the region. To get to stability the US must first be willing to abandon our original solution for the region, and frame a new solution that offers a tangible, viable political alternative to Sunni-Arabs that they can actually trust. No small task. But all of that is a bold leap from conventional wisdom, so let me back up a bit and lay some foundation:

I'd like to talk to three broad concepts that I believe are critical to getting to better strategic results in situations like the one we currently face in Syria and Iraq. These are bundled under:

1. How we think about problems;
2. The position that political conflict within a single system of governance if fundamentally unique from political conflict between two or more such systems;
3. And lastly; what all of this means to the United States today.

How we think about problems. We tend to bundle things by how they are tactically similar; I think it is far more productive to disaggregate things by how they are strategically unique. Classic examples of this type of tactical bundling by the US military in the post 9/11 era are "irregular warfare," "Al Qaeda and its Affiliates and Adherents (AQAA")," and more recently "Violent Extremist Organization (VEO)." Equally problematic for the US military is that we tend to be very Clausewitzian in our perspectives. We are too quick to classify political conflict as some type of "war" and to then bring a "warfare" solution that seeks to sustain some particular government, defeat the threats to that government, and at the same time enable much of the interagency community to rationalize that this is not a problem they somehow contributed to the creation of, or that they can really get to the business of their portion of the solution until after the military has solved the military problem. While this approach can indeed suppress the symptoms of conflict and create bubbles of artificial stability, once the energy sustaining those bubbles is removed they quickly return to their natural state and instability, illegal competition and conflict resume. The effects of the surge in Iraq and the subsequent rise of ISIS are the most recent example of this effect.

<u>Conflict Within</u> is a different genus and species than <u>Conflict Between</u>. Based on my study and experience, I think we need to consider the very real possibility that political conflict *within* a single system of governance is fundamentally unique from political conflict between two or more systems of governance. I specifically do not say "state" as a system of governance can be as small as a family or as large as a nation, with many variations, formal and informal, foreign and domestic. In fact, it is not inaccurate to look at the US policy of global leadership in the post-cold war era as the largest example of a "system of governance." I find Clausewitz's social trinity of "Government-Army-People" as a helpful simple model of a system. So long as one has leadership, enforcement, an affected population and some defined space where that leadership and enforcement is applied, one has a system of governance. So, I think we do not error when we apply our Clausewitzian instincts when we deal with political conflict between two or more such systems—but that doing so to a political conflict within a single system has proven to be a huge error over and over again, and counterproductive to resolving the root drivers of instability. If conflict within emerges from the grievances of some identity-based population (rather than a coup by some small party seeking power) within a system of governance, it is what I call a "populace-based conflict." This is the essence of revolutionary insurgency and the tremendous source of strategic energy tapped into by historic revolutionary leaders such as Washington, Lenin, Mao, King and Gandhi—and is also the source of energy that fuels AQ and ISIS today.

What this means to the United States today. This means several things for US strategy and plans. First and foremost it means we have a glaring hole in our understanding of political conflict that we must recognize, discuss, study, and ultimately capture in doctrine and begin to incorporate into our institutional culture. It means we should purge our current doctrine, strategies and plans of strategically dangerous constructs such as the aforementioned Irregular Warfare and AQAA and VEO. If a grouping or name does not suggest a family of solution that applies to everything within that bundle, then it is too superficial and strategically dangerous. After all, our actions tend to follow our words, so when our words are inaccurate, our actions tend to be inappropriate. This is true when we call a government such as that of Iraq "legitimate" and "democratic" when in fact it is fundamentally neither; and also when we throw simplistic tactical bundles around strategic problems and seek to apply a "one size fits all" solution. There are important questions I think we should ask that we currently do not:

1. **Is this conflict <u>within</u> a single system; <u>between</u> two or more systems; or is it some fusion of the two taking place <u>among</u> the populations in some mix?** (At SOCOM we think of this as "within"—"between"—or "among" and roughly matches up with the less strategically useful "continuum of conflict" of State, Hybrid, and non-state conflict employed in the latest National Military Strategy).
2. **For any particular actor or organization, what is their <u>primary purpose for action</u>, and what is their <u>relationship to the population they operate among</u>?**
3. **For any particular identity-based population with political grievance, <u>how do they feel</u>, and <u>who do they blame</u>?**

Armed with the answers to these questions one can begin to understand a conflict and its participants in strategically significant ways that allow one to answer that most critical of Clausewtizian questions: *"What kind of conflict am I in"*??

These are also questions one must ask continuously as one works to affect a solution, as the answers—and the nature of the conflict—can change as one's own actions begin to impact the system. Many organizations and individuals lumped under AQAA are more accurately nationalist or regional revolutionary groups (AQAP, AQIM, Al Shabab and Boko Haram to name but 4). These types of problems do not respond well to counter terrorism, or to Counterinsurgency approaches as we currently define and apply them. Equally, a Saudi member of AQAP is a nationalist revolutionary when in KSA or taking physical sanctuary in Yemen—but when he travels to a foreign place to serve as a foreign fighter or to facilitate a Unconventional warfare campaign his status changes along with his purpose for action and relationship to the population he operates among. So, a "terrorist" who one can reasonably to CT against in one situation is no longer a terrorist and demands a very different approach when his situation changes. In short, we must become more sophisticated in our understanding of the problems we seek to address, and more refined in the approaches we apply to those problems. Changing how we think is the first step in that evolution.

Canna: *You also say that in order to get to a durable solution, there are two "primary sources of strategic energy" that must be addressed. What are these and how do we go about finding solutions?*

Jones: In political conflict between two or more systems of governance I believe the "strategic energy" is a combination of <u>power and interest</u>. In political conflict within a single system of governance I think this energy is best thought of as a combination of <u>power and grievance</u>. In what the US military currently thinks of as "hybrid conflicts" there is typically a fusion of both types of energy at work. Certainly this is true in Syria and Iraq. There are many systems of governance and populations acting on their own distinct and unique strategic energies of power and interest/grievance in this particular conflict.

I believe this strategic energy is fueling two major and distinct dynamics at play in Syria and Iraq. The **first** of those is the larger Sunni-Shia competition for influence. A major strategic side-effect of the US removal of the Saddam regime in Iraq was that it also removed a fairly stable line of Sunni-Shia competition along the Iraq-Iran border, dropping that line down to the northern borders of Kuwait, KSA, Jordan, and Israel. This extended Shia influence in a manner that Shia in general wish to sustain, and that equally Sunni in general wish to restabilize farther north, perhaps along the Euphrates River. The **second** dynamic is the increasing belief among Sunni-Arab populations of Syria and Iraq that they have no viable future under the Shia dominated governments in this newly formed Shia band of influence. A wide array of strategic power has been brought to bear by this situation. The US could recognize a Sunni-Arab State that addresses both drivers in one fell swoop (with no need to recognize ISIS as the government of that state in the process, by the way)—or we can cling to those problematic policies and seek to defeat all of the threats to our current political solution for the region.

Distant powers, like Russia and the US perceive interests in this region and have the power to pursue. Non-state systems of governance like AQ and ISIS also see tremendous opportunity to advance their respective interests here and tap into the power of the Sunni-Arab population. Several regional powers, like Turkey, Iran and the KSA all have major interests at stake, and obviously the governments of the two states directly involved. In this "Field of Nightmares," *we built it, and they came.*

Population-based strategic energy is equally important and even more diverse and distributed. There are the many diverse Sunni-Arab populations of Syria and Iraq whose rising power relative to the governments over them, coupled with their powerful grievances with those governments that is the core of the revolutionary energy that ISIS and AQ compete for influence with in order to advance their own agendas. There are also the broader global Sunni and Shia populations who perceive powerful interest in either sustaining the current line of competition or in restoring the old one. This, not radical Islamist ideology, is the powerful magnet drawing "foreign fighters" of Sunni and Shia alike into this region. Then there are the identity-based populations within the many state actors involved who have their own grievances with their respective governments. The big ones being the Kurds in Turkey; Shia and Sunni the KSA and in Yemen; but many others as well who all see opportunities for change. Any successful approach to restoring durable stability to the region must take into account all of these sources of energy. To overly focus on "threats" is symptomatic, simplistic, and will either fail completely, or only achieve suppression of the symptoms in a manner that most likely makes the negative energy across this trans-regional system worse.

The Challenge with the current US position is that our policy is to preserve the current line of Shia-Sunni competition that is putting so much state and population-based energy into this system; and also to preserve the government of Iraq that is the primary grievance of the

Iraqi Sunnis. To say that we are swimming against a very powerful current is an understatement. The US energy necessary to create and sustain those unnatural conditions far exceeds the potential benefits. Can we compromise to policy ends that are more natural, and therefore both easier to attain and more durable, and still secure US interests in the region? I think the answer is a resounding yes.

By simple analogy, we are attempting a football type defense, which seeks to give no ground and prevent the big play. We are probably better served by more of a martial arts mindset, that channels one's opponent's energy in a direction he generally wants to go, but that is least likely to harm our own position. This is the essence of seeking a position of influence *across* a region, rather than a position of control *over* a region.

Canna: *A recent SME told me that in Iraq, there are three fragments: Shiastan, Kurdistan, and ISIL. This is in opposition to US political discourse that the region is broken into 4 segments: Shiastan, Kurdistan, Sunni Arab tribes, and ISIL. The expert stated that without a viable alternative, the Sunni Arab tribes are already in ISIL's hands. Do you agree with this assessment? If this is true, then Arab Sunni tribes perhaps can't be the cornerstone to the US's effort to defeat ISIL.*

Jones: First of all, it is important to note that historically and across cultures, when revolutionary challenges to governance occur, while the grievances against governance may be widely held, the majority of the population will attempt to remain neutral until the dust settles. A classic example of this is the scene in that Clint Eastwood Classic, "The Outlaw Josey Wales," where the ferry operator sings "Dixie" while transporting Wales across the river, but quickly switches to "The Battle Hymn of the Republic" once returning to pick up the Cavalry unit in pursuit. Nowhere is the adage "The tallest blade of grass is the first to be cut" more true than being caught in the middle of political revolution.

The US position is heavily biased by our belief that our solution for the region is the correct one; by our inability to empathize with the inherent grievance Sunni-Arabs have with our solution; and perhaps most of all by our misunderstanding of the fundamental nature of AQ and ISIS as independent exploiters of political grievance.

ISIS is not the Sunni-Arab Population. ISIS is best thought of as the government of an emergent, de facto Sunni-Arab state. They stepped up to offer the Sunni-Arabs of Syria and Iraq a tangible, viable political alternative to political conditions perceived as intolerable. Equally ISIS has stepped up to lead the charge to restore stability to the Sunni-Shia line of competition in a location perceived as far less dangerous to Sunnis everywhere than where that line currently exists due to US actions in the region. Increasingly ISIS is also growing in influence with the revolutionary Sunni populations and groups around the region who have grown weary of AQ's more patient approach. To defeat ISIS most likely fragments the revolutionary insurgencies in Syria and Iraq, but in no way resolves them. It also re-empowers AQ in an "I told you so" kind of way as they point out how their way was the right way all along. I don't see how that is good for US interests in the region. Also important, is that while ISIS is not the Sunni-Arab population, they come from and their forces are of that population. To attack ISIS can only be perceived as an attack on the Sunni-Arab population itself. Any Sunni-Arabs we seek to recruit are placed in an unwinnable conflict of interests, and are expected to support *our* interests against those of their own people. In short, we are probably working with opportunists driven more by self-interest than patriotism.

Questions we must ask ourselves are:

- *How can the US help restore a more acceptable and durable line of competition between Sunni and Shia?*
- *How can the US become the champion of the Sunni Arab populations of Syria and Iraq and help to offer and attain for them a more acceptable, viable political alternative?*

Our current goals are not <u>acceptable, suitable or feasible</u> with so many powerful sources of strategic energy operating in this current conflict. We need to step back from our preconceived notions of what "right" looks like, and frame new outcomes and approaches that score better in those three tests.

Canna: *Should the USG "do nothing" in the region? Some say this is a fight we cannot win or really influence and that we are supporting an unnatural balance in the region. The only way to arrive at a durable solution is for all sides to exhaust themselves before coming to the table.*

Jones: "Do nothing" is always an option, and certainly has some merit. I think Colin Powell's "Pottery Barn rule" is very applicable in this case though, after all, we really are the primary reason this is broken, and probably have a duty to in some way atone for those actions. Actions designed to facilitate a new Sunni-Shia line of competition would be very appropriate and helpful to getting to stability. Along with that, also appropriate are actions designed to help the Sunni Arab populations of Syria and Iraq get to political situations they find more tolerable.

We need to do these things, however, with a full awareness of the limitations of military power. The military can disrupt the worst actors. The military can mitigate the high end of violence against vulnerable populations and critical infrastructure. Most importantly, the military can help create the time and space necessary for civilian leaders across the range of stakeholders to address the changes necessary to facilitate a future stability.

The military cannot, however, "fix" this. At this point, suppressing revolution is unlikely to produce a durable result at reasonable costs. We can, however, help set the conditions for evolving to new political parameters designed to allow a new stability, and ultimately trust, to emerge.

Canna: *You highlighted the tension between the USG wanting to drag this conflict where we want it to be versus guide it to where it needs to be. Could you explain what you mean?*

Jones: We are overly wed to our solution for the instability caused by our removal of the Saddam regime. We are certain of the rightness of our efforts, and are quick to rationalize away their failure to perform as intended onto external factors. We blame the failures of that solution on the host nation for not working hard enough to make it work or to secure it against challengers; we blame it on the challengers; we blame it on the ideology employed by those challengers—but we are reluctant to admit we misunderstood the problem and applied an inappropriate solution.

I read a piece on strategic culture by Professor Jeannie Johnson that described a unique aspect of American strategic culture that is appropriate to this question. The article described the uniquely American belief that if we just work hard enough, and apply enough resources, we can make anything work. This mindset built our nation, it built the Panama Canal, it drove our approach to WWII, and it put a man on the moon— but it cannot shape the perceptions necessary to make a population believe that the US foreign policies that affect their lives are appropriate, or that the governments we create for, or protect from, an affected population are appropriate. We have a clash of American culture, and an associated "American Way of War" with the types of conflicts we are currently in.

In the Civil War or WWII,—war **between** two systems of governance, the US approach to war and warfare works. Destroy completely, then lift up and dust off. But in a conflict **within** a single system of governance, the *"we had to destroy the village to save the village"* approach we have applied in varying degrees in Vietnam, Iraq and Afghanistan has been strategically out of step with the type of conflicts we were actually in. In Vietnam we deluded ourselves with the Western fiction of "North" and "South" states created by and for the West midway through an ongoing Vietnamese revolutionary movement for independence. In Iraq and Afghanistan we deluded ourselves by our belief that we were liberating people from governance as inherently bad, and offering them new governance that was inherently good. Also problematic is that our doctrine of military phases does not recognize a **presumption** of *resistance* insurgency to any intervention; or a presumption of *revolutionary* insurgency against any government protected or created by our efforts. It should. The **nature of those actions** drives the nature of the response. But by recognizing this nature, we can plan the **character of our actions** to mitigate the character and scope of the response.

Canna: *If this is a battle for influence, not dirt, how does the USG shift its perspective and objectives in line with the real goal? What is the real goal? Is it stability? And if ISIL is the only one really providing stability, do we work with them? Is there a way for the USG to also help provide stability working with regional partners in competition with ISIL?*

Jones: This goes back to recognizing and truly appreciating the difference between political conflict between two or more systems of governance and conflict within a single system.

We report gains and losses in Syria and Iraq as if we were tracking Patton's progress across France and Germany in WWII. In such conflicts the **sum of tactical actions**, regardless how poor the strategy, will ultimately add up to strategic success or failure. But the lesson of Hamburger Hill in Vietnam still applies—it does not matter who controls any particular hill, what matters is how our competition for that hill shaped the perceptions of relevant identity-based populations about the systems of governance that affect their lives. The Vietnamese tactical defeat during the Tet Offensive of 1968 sealed their strategic victory in 1975.

This is why a successful drone strike that takes out a top AQ leader can be both a tactical success and a strategic disaster at the same time. **How** we conduct the mission, and **what messages** that mission sent to local, regional, global and domestic audiences is far more important than the removal of one problematic actor.

The US is founded upon principles of the right of people everywhere to self-determination of governance and the right and duty to revolution when governance is perceived as fatally flawed. Shifting to **influence operations** from **control operations** is consistent with our founding principles, but demands that the US become more agnostic about what type of governance emerges in places where we have interests. So long as we can establish working relationships with those governments, and are not perceived by the populations affected by those governments as being the source of its legitimacy; or as somehow protecting it from having to listen to the concerns of the people affected by it, our interests will be served. This demands we become more of a *neutral mediator* of best possible compromises in the terms of those who are truly a party to the agreement, rather than being an arbitrator of what we believe is best. That is a significant paradigm shift from our Cold War containment approach - but when there was a perceived common threat (and therefore shared interest), people were more willing to compromise on these types of sovereignty issues. Today, no such perceived threat exists for most. Of note, we see an opposite effect taking place in the Pacific, where US influence is rising on the tide of Chinese power and where partners are more open to compromising on points of sovereignty for their own security that they would not even discuss 10 years ago.

Canna: *USG mission is to defeat and degrade ISIL, but by defeating it organizationally, we may be forcing it to evolve into ISIL 2.0—a tougher and harder to beat opponent. What are the implications of an organizationally defeated ISIL for the region?*

Jones: A mission to "facilitate regional stability" is probably better for also facilitating our strategic interests in the region. A broader strategic focus provides our senior leaders with much more flexibility and options for success than a narrow focus on any particular threat. If the mission is "defeat ISIL," we make it very easy to "lose" even though our interests are met. We defined the mission in Vietnam as "defeat North Vietnam" and we failed to do that, but the unified Vietnam that emerged serves very well to block the domino spread of Chinese influence into SEA that drove our intervention to begin with. Imagine the impact on US history if we had supported a liberated, unified Vietnam at the end of WWII? Our relationship with them would be very much like our relationship with Thailand. We missed the inherent opportunity in the strategic energy in the people of Vietnam because we were overly fixated on perceived threat of China. What truly are our interests in Syria and Iraq today? What opportunities are we potentially missing because we did not learn the strategic lessons of Vietnam, Iraq and Afghanistan?

Canna: *How do we get to a viable alternative for Sunni Arabs in Iraq and Syria?*

Jones: First, recognize that our diagnosis of the problem and prescribed solution for the region was inappropriate and probably had no feasible approach to make it work.

Second, accept that we do not need to control the outcome to secure our interests, or to avoid appearing weak.

As Thucydides observed, *"Of all the manifestations of power, restraint impresses men the most."*

Chapter 17

ISIS and the Sex Factor

Thomas McNamara

First Published 12 August 2015

The exact number of Americans who have joined ISIS is unknown, but in late February, the Director of National Intelligence, General James Clapper, testified in front of Congress that roughly 180[1] Americans have traveled or have attempted to travel to Syria in order to fight with extremist organizations. This marked a steep increase as six months prior to his testimony the number was estimated to be only 100[2]. As of April, over 30[3] people had been charged with trying to join terrorist groups in Syria over the previous 18 months.

Also of note is the fact that since the beginning of 2013, a mere seven American residents are known to have conducted a grand total of five terrorist attacks[4] inside the United States that were possibly linked in any way to either ISIS or some other form of Islamic extremism (the April 2013 Boston Marathon bombings, the October 2014 hatchet attack on four NYC police officers, Ismaaiyl Brinsley's December 2014 murder of two NYC police officers,*[i] the May 2015 attack in Garland Texas, and most recently the July 2015 shootings in Chattanooga).

If we accept the above numbers to be generally correct, we can then make several useful deductions. First, likely between 75% and

90% of Americans who attempt to join Jihadi organizations in Syria are successful in doing so. Second, only a small fraction, less than five percent, of Americans who do decide to wage Jihad end up doing so within the United States. The pertinent question to analysts is not merely why individuals decide to travel to Syria to wage jihad. Equally, if not more important is the question of why these individuals are deciding not to wage jihad in the United States. This question is particularly puzzling since ISIS leadership has repeatedly called for potential jihadists inside the United States to do just that, wage Jihad inside the United States. Keep in mind that the lowest standard for carrying out such a terrorist attack is obtaining a hatchet and swinging it at random people while yelling Allah al-Akhbar, a far easier feat than linking up with jihadists in Syria. Why then do more than 95% of said jihadists not follow this call?

The Sex Factor

To answer this question, I offer a Mancur Oslen-esque Rational Choice Theory based answer. Sex (and also not dying so that one can enjoy such sex) is likely a largely overlooked primary explanatory factor that lies towards the top if not at the top of the long list of explanatory factors associated with the perceived splendor of the jihadi experience in Syria. Simply put, Americans who have decided on jihad have two main options. First, they have the option of traveling to Syria, fighting in the jihad, and enjoying up to four wives and countless sex slaves while doing so. If they die, then they will enjoy 72 virgins in paradise. The other option is to stay in the United States, forgo the multitude of wives and sex slaves, wage the jihad, enjoy a near 100% chance of death while waging such jihad (of the seven individuals cited above, only one survived the attacks, Dzhokhar Tsarnaev, and he has since been sentenced to death), and then enjoy the 72 virgins in paradise. To over 95% of those Americans who have entered the jihad, option one seems to be the preferred option, and one can certainly appreciate why.

ISIS's "Pamphlet on Female Slaves"[5] (released on 4 December 2014) coincides with the swell of American jihadists into ISIS's and other Islamic extremist organizations' ranks. In it, the rules of dealing with sex slaves are outlined. It explains that having sex with prepubescent females who are "fit for intercourse," partaking in coitus interruptus with them, having sex with female virgins immediately upon their capture, having sex with non-virgins once their uteruses are cleaned, and beating sex slaves are all permitted within ISIS's caliphate. Another circulated document with similar effect is the actual price list[6] of such sex slaves. It outlines the price of Yazidis and Christians between the ages of one and fifty and the policies regarding their sale as sex slaves. These documents, whether intended to or not, seem to have been far more effective in pushing potential recruits into joining the jihad in Syria than ISIS's repeated calls to wage jihad in the US were in convincing potential jihadists to stay inside the United States.

Of course, documents alone can only be marginally effective in influencing people's decisions. Sadly enough, a morose reality accompanies such pamphlets. We continually hear and read accounts of mostly Yazidis and Christians, either in Iraq or Syria, being captured and sold as sex slaves. Just last Friday, ISIS captured more than 200 Syrian Christians near the town of Qaryatain[7], many of whom will likely become sex slaves. These accounts confirm the viability of the "wage jihad in Syria" option to potential jihadists.

Implications

It is extremely important to understand the potential threats that the U.S. faces and the magnitude of the sex factor. When ISIS captures large swaths of people and converts many of them into sex slaves, the act is not merely a representation of ISIS's barbarism and the suffering of its victims. ISIS's sex slave trade both demonstrates its success as well as creates more success. ISIS's sex slave trade helps to fund the organization, but more importantly it very likely has a tremendous impact on recruiting. The ranks of ISIS are swelling as a result.

Changes to any of three components within this paradigm (changes to the "wage jihad in Syria" option, changes to the "wage jihad in the U.S." option, or changes in perceptions of either option) will likely bring about fundamental change to current trends as jihadists decide how to wage jihad. A more permissive environment for deviant behavior or increased terrorist survival rates within the United States could lead to more potential jihadists selecting the "wage jihad in the U.S." option. The continued expansion of ISIS's caliphate and its sex trade could lead to jihadists continuing their influx into Syria. However, the end of hostilities in Syria and Iraq however, would lead jihadists to pursue other options, and the "wage jihad in the U.S." option very well may be one of them. Finally, changes in extremist indoctrination practices (increased isolation or potency), both in the United States and abroad, could alter jihadi actors' perceptions. As a result, they might be more apt to tolerate higher risks, forego potential pleasures, or not be able to correctly identify and evaluate such utility.

As we continue to formulate strategies to defeat ISIS and protect the homeland, understanding how potential jihadists think is of paramount importance. I submit that sexual factors likely play a key role as potential jihadists decide both what they will do and what they will not. Our strategies should reflect this reality.

Chapter 18

Why is Turkey Attacking the Kurdish Militants Instead of ISIS?

Feryaz Ocakli

First Published 28 August 2015

Turkey's recent transformations caused a surprising degree of conflict. Economic growth was accompanied by the looting of public spaces, leading to social unrest[1]. A bold new foreign policy[2] saw Syria replaced by ISIS as Turkey's southern neighbor. A peace process with the Kurdish National Movement raised expectations for reconciliation. But they crashed with the collapse of the ceasefire[3] last month. The inability of the parliament to agree on a coalition government[4] further increased tensions. The Turkish Lira fell to record lows against the Dollar and the Euro. Turkey is waging two wars: a low intensity war against ISIS and a high intensity war against the PKK. Meanwhile, there is no elected government in Ankara. How can we make sense of these dizzying transformations?

One way to clear the fog is to consider the main actors, their interests, and their interactions. There are five significant actors operating in two interlinked political landscapes. Their changing relationships in response to events outside of any single actor's control limit the range of available options each could pursue. Their behaviors are not predetermined per se, but influenced by the changing context within which they try to realize their interests.

These actors are Recep Tayyip Erdoğan (Turkey's elected president), the AKP (Erdoğan's moderate Islamist party), the PKK (the illegal militant wing of the Kurdish National Movement), the HDP (the legal political wing of the Kurdish National Movement, which recently absorbed some leftist and liberal Turks), and ISIS. The first four of these actors are operating in the Turkish political arena. All five are operating in the broader regional politics of the Middle East.

Erdoğan's priority is regime change[5] in Turkey. He seeks a new system that will confirm him as a super-charged president. Comparisons with Russian President Vladimir Putin may not be too far off the mark. His authoritarian ruling style[6] and cultivation of a large network of crony-capitalists[7] already show that Turkey may be closer to a competitive authoritarian[8] regime than a lackluster democracy.

In my recent article[9] published in *Politics & Society*, I argue that the AKP gained support from non-Islamist voters and won consecutive elections by recruiting center-right politicians, businessmen, and other economic and social elites. It has now built a sufficiently large elite network to reap the benefits of crony capitalism. I show in another article[10], recently published in *Democratization*, that even Turkish civil society is in the business of seeking patronage from the AKP through insider party connections. Erdoğan no longer competes against his rivals in a level playing field. He uses all the might and wealth of the Turkish state, the crony capitalist class, and government-friendly media conglomerates to campaign against his opponents. Neither does he shy away from politicizing the presidency by overstepping constitutional boundaries. His party's recent loss of parliamentary majority frustrated his designs.

The AKP has been undergoing a slow-motion purge under Erdoğan's leadership. The alienation last year of Abdullah Gül, the previous president and one of AKP's founders, made it clear that the new president does not tolerate rivalry. Dengir Mir Mehmet Fırat, another AKP founder, switched over to the pro-Kurdish HDP. Current Prime Minister Ahmet Davutoğlu seems unable to chart his own path. His failure to form a coalition government was partly the result of Erdoğan's unwillingness to accept the current election results. New elections will likely take place in November.

The PKK is the Kurdish militant group that has been waging a war against the Turkish state since 1984. Its current demands[11] from Turkey are rather vague. They range from "free Kurdistan" and a "democratic republican Turkey" to Kurdish cultural rights, local autonomy, and Turkey's intervention against ISIS. The group agreed to a ceasefire in 2012 while negotiating a peace process with the AKP. Both recently fell apart. It is important to note that the PKK ended the ceasefire on July 11. The militants declared a new "revolutionary peoples war," killed a soldier and two policemen. Turkey then launched airstrikes against PKK positions. PKK's main motivation for its new policy was the changing natural environment in Kurdistan. The Turkish state is arguably shaping nature as a weapon. Dam construction projects that depopulate the Kurdish landscape, new roads designed for the military to improve its logistics, and the building of the "kalekol," a neologism that combines the words "castle" and "military station," led the PKK to renew its armed conflict with the Turkish state. The PKK leaders likely believed that a prolonged ceasefire benefited the state and disadvantaged them. But, the PKK also benefited from the ceasefire. It was able to redirect its military muscle to help the Kurds gain more territory in Syria. It also became a more robust actor in the politics of Northern Iraq[12].

The HDP is the pro-Kurdish party that recently increased its vote-share to 13 percent. Besides Kurds, it appealed to leftist and liberal Turks. This cost the AKP its parliamentary majority and frustrated Erdoğan's ambitions. There may be some disagreements between the HDP and PKK as the former incorporates non-Kurdish voters. The PKK is demanding a more active confrontation with the state. But the HDP seems intent on building electoral support via regular political channels.

ISIS was the biggest beneficiary of Turkey's policy towards Syria. The Turkish government rejects the claim that it helped ISIS. But the swift censorship[13] of news covering weapons shipments to Syria raises uncomfortable questions. Turkey hesitated to engage ISIS directly despite the international calls for action. But ISIS always regarded Turkey as a legitimate target in its propaganda. When Turkey agreed to help the U.S. in Syria, ISIS threatened attacks[14] inside Turkey.

Ankara is keeping its operations against ISIS quiet. Ankara's main target is the PKK, and Erdoğan's is the HDP. He recently accused the HDP politicians of conspiring with terrorists[15]. According to Erdoğan, the liberal intellectuals who support the HDP are "traitors[16]." He may be looking forward to a repeat election after a process of bloody conflict with the PKK. It might presumably provoke Turkish nationalists to support the AKP, lead Turkish HDP supporters to abstain in response to PKK violence, and scare the public into voting for a one-party government. The likelihood of this scenario actually playing out is debatable.

The PKK seeks to deny the state the rewards of a prolonged ceasefire. The state's military construction projects makes the conflict zone less hospitable to the militants. It also reduces confidence in the peace talks. But the PKK also benefited from the ceasefire. It expanded its military and political clout in Syria and Northern Iraq. The lack of violence enabled the HDP to broaden its appeal to Turkish voters. The PKK is a more vigorous organization than before. This reduces the state's confidence that it will agree to a negotiated solution. If the PKK can reap more rewards later, why would it make a deal now?

The conflict between the two parties was avoidable. Both the PKK and Erdoğan could have chosen to take more political risks and reduce the tension. But, they didn't. And the constellation of structural factors made conflict more likely.

Meanwhile, ISIS remains a sideshow form Ankara's perspective. One of its militants killed 32 people in a bomb blast[17] in July. Bus drivers, like the one I recently met, discover potential bombers among their passengers. Still, the Turkish government keeps its operations against ISIS at a policing level. And bombs that do not blow up are not yet making the news.

Chapter 19

Status Quo in the Sinai

Daniel Glickstein and John Miller

First Published 8 September 2015

Egyptian Decisions

In light of the growing strength of the Sinai Province after swearing allegiance to the Islamic State, what actions can General Sisi and Egypt's leaders take to counter the strength of the group?

The core of support for the Sinai Province (SP), and its earlier iteration as Ansar Beit al-Maqdis, was the unpopularity of the Egyptian Security Forces in the Sinai as well as the effects of economic austerity measures taken by the Sisi regime. These issues have been exacerbated since the overthrow of Mohammed Morsi. What measures can the Egyptian government take to diminish the support of SP? The most obvious answer would be to institute good governance. That is, reform the security forces, especially the police, into a law-abiding institution that does not resort to torture and which treats its citizens equally with respect to the law.

However, this is not a likely scenario. The security forces have been instrumental in assuring the rule of the military and economic elite in Egypt since the time of Nasser, and they were instrumental in overthrowing Morsi and installing Sisi. Members of the security forces will expect to be rewarded for their loyalty and this level of power and patronage are essential to the "Deep State" that rules Egypt.

The second scenario involves an increase in troop levels in the Sinai in order to pursue a more traditional COIN scenario which protects the civilian population and "degrades and destroys" the ability of militants to operate in the area. However, this scenario is also complicated by Egypt's history.

First and foremost, the terms of the Camp David Accords allow Egypt to keep only a small force in the Sinai and the Egyptians will need Israel's permission to increase their force levels in the region. Israel granted Egypt permission to do so in 2013 and 2014, as Israel has an interest in securing its own border against SP. Unfortunately, Israel's willingness to allow additional Egyptian forces in the Sinai provides a propaganda boon for SP; they are able to portray the Egyptian state as being complaint with Zionists. Additionally, it is not clear that Egypt is willing to pursue the level of effort necessary for a true COIN operation. Instead of dispersing their troops amongst the local population, they remain cloistered on large bases and static checkpoints along major highways.

So, what choice is Egypt likely to make? At present, it seems most clear that they will accept the status quo. The Egyptian government will continue to attempt to degrade the capabilities of SP without committing the overwhelming force needed for a COIN campaign to succeed. It is unlikely that this campaign will destroy the ability of SP to operate in the Sinai, as the state has been using this same strategy for years with little to show for it.

American Involvement

The American perspective is grim as well. Key interests are threatened: namely the stability of the Sisi regime which America has a strategic (albeit strained) relationship with, the security of Israel, and the security of the United Nations Multi-National Force of Observers (MFO) mission in the Sinai. Despite diplomatic flare-ups in recent years, the U.S. still stands to benefit from continued relations with the largest Arab state.

The U.S. currently has nearly 700 soldiers deployed to the Sinai to observe and maintain the peace between Egypt and Israel. Recently the MFO force has had to contend with insurgent aggression. The MFO Commanders' annual reports clearly lay out a growing trend towards violence. On 27 May 2011, an MFO vehicle was struck by an Improvised Explosive Device (IED). By 2012 the MFO reported repeated instances of violent demonstrations and armed blockades. On 14 Sep 2012, insurgents assaulted an MFO base camp with Molotov cocktails, broke through the perimeter, and burned a fire truck. On 13 April 2013, three MFO workers were grabbed off of a bus at gunpoint and kidnapped. In a separate incident other employees were stopped in traffic, forced to lie on the ground, and put through a mock execution by the insurgents. On 17 Jun 2013, insurgents breached the Colombian battalion's operating base, exhibiting continually brazen and reckless behavior.

This pattern culminated recently in an IED strike which wounded four American service-members. The attack was a complex ambush; two peacekeepers were wounded in an initial strike, and insurgents laid a second IED nearby to target first-responders which hit the U.S soldiers. This tactic has been used often in Iraq and Afghanistan by various belligerents, and suggests SP's tactics, techniques, and procedures are trending upwards in complexity. Nevertheless, the attack failed to inflict critical casualties against the Americans, suggesting that SP is still in a learning-stage with regard to execution and lethality.

The Way Forward

Unfortunately the U.S. does not have a selection of viable options available regarding SP. As counterinsurgency canon makes eminently clear, one of the fundamental requirements in a successful COIN campaign is host government legitimacy. Any additional aid the U.S. offers negatively impacts Egyptian legitimacy. Increased materiel support from the U.S. augments Egyptian military effectiveness, but also feeds into SP's narrative painting Egypt as a puppet of the West/Israel. And given SP's propaganda capabilities, they will quickly identify and capitalize upon any further opportunities.

The only significant change the U.S. can make is to update the MFO peacekeeping mandate to better reflect the increasingly violent operating environment. The original mandate spawned out of the original peace treaty and fails to address self-defense capabilities for the MFO. An updated legal mandate would remove the legal gray area regarding escalation of force and kinetic responses the peacekeeping forces can take when aggression. In addition, the U.S. can better fortify MFO bases and close those bases which are most vulnerable, such as those monitoring the Straight of Tiran.

The opinions expressed here are the authors' alone and do not reflect those of their employers, or the United States military.

Chapter 20

Islamism, Islamofascism, and Islam?

G. Murphy Donovan

First Published 12 September 2015

Internet journalism could be the ideal public forum. Anybody with a computer can write, read, or comment on what is written. *Disqus.com* now captures commentary, authors, and content links. Print journalism, in contrast, looks like a one-way mirror. Conventional journalists write, you read. Problem? Write the editor where most mail gets tossed in the circular file.

All literature should be a conversation of sorts. With the internet, critical readers and real-time feedback, over time, should make for better writers. Maybe even better ideas. Of course, the democratization of essaying is not without hazard.

You have a regular opportunity to make a fool out of yourself in public. Alas, the internet is also a bit like a school report card, a military record, or a rap sheet—matters of permanent record.

Then there are trolls! Loosely defined, a troll is a reader who surfs the web looking for an argument. Their commentary is often, but not always, abrasive, rude, and hostile. Comments, like content, usually have editors to screen the obvious abuses. Sometimes the commentary is simply arbitrary. Nonetheless, objection to a single word might spawn a comment thread or a fusillade of like-minded vitriol. "Islamism" is one of those words.

Words matter. Alas, neologisms come into the language all the time, especially when the drama index is high. Ironically, polemicists on the Right and Left abhor words like "Islamism."

Liberals think the word unfairly links radicals or terrorists with religion. Some on the Left, team Obama for example[1], would have you believe that mayhem in Mohamed's name has nothing to do with Islam, a little like claiming that the Crusades were sponsored by Rotarians. The thought police at the White House, at CIA, and even at the Associated Press (AP) have stricken words like Islamism from their vocabularies by fiat.

The American Left, traditionally believes that candor, or the action that truth might require, will make a problem worse. Appeasement is an honored liberal idiom.

American conservatives, on the other hand, suspect the "ism" is a hedge, a reluctance to say that Islam itself is the problem. Alas, blanket attributions, give a part of culture too much credit, implying a kind of terror, rhetoric, and religious monolith.

With the Right, ends are confused with means. The objective of imperial Islam may be monoculture[2]. Yet, with 1.5 billion followers, realities will always be at odds with utopian dreams. The Shia/Sunni schism, for example, has plagued the *Ummah* for 1300 years. To suggest that all Muslims are militant radicals, or terrorists, is a little like confusing bulls with dairy cows.

No matter the culture, the majority are usually inert anyway. Or as Kafka put it, "It is often safer to be in chains than to be free." Hyperbole aside, the loudest voice in any culture, including Islam, is likely to be stasis or inertia.

Islamism, as opposed to Islam, suggests movement and militancy. You might think of Islamists as Muslim crusaders. Such distinctions are self-evident when militants are parsed from the so-called "moderate" majority. That majority in turn are happy to be separated from the swords, shooters, and beards. Unfortunately, none of these distinctions do anything to moderate the menace.

If only ten percent of Muslims (150 million) are militant, then the threat is substantial by any measure.

Neologisms are born when ordinary language fails to capture a phenomenon or an idea. Terms like Islamism and "Islamofascism" fill a void of meaning. Yes, the majority are not terrorists. They are worse! Passive aggressors, not moderates, might be a better description for most of the silent Muslim majority.

How many Russians were Communists and how many Germans were Nazis in the beginning? The numbers never have to be large. Militancy and terror are usually a minority and minorities still prevail. A kinetic vanguard can always depend on the silence and apathy of majorities. The Islamist menace is no different today.

Indeed, the propagandists and the swords are the lesser of two evils. We know what they believe, what they fight for, and we see what they do on a daily basis. Militants make no secret of their religious motivation.

Whatever the number of radicals, they will never be as numerous, or as guilty, as the larger *Ummah* which is routinely disingenuous, routinely apathetic, routinely absolved, routinely hypocritical, and routinely given a pass on accountability.

Most Americans and Europeans believe that most Muslims are innocents. How is this different than what most Muslims believe? Sadly, the great crimes of any century are more a function of apathy and appeasement, and less a product of militancy.

Apathy and denial about the Islamism problem is as much a problem in the East as it is in the West.

A malignant force, once set in motion, tends to stay in motion unless confronted by an equal or superior force (hat tip to Isaac). The real strength of Islamists is the apathy of 59 Muslim nations worldwide, a sixth of the world's population. Islamofascism is an *Ummah* community problem. The secular West cannot save the Islamic East from itself.

Calling Islamists criminals, militants, radicals, fundamentalists, or even terrorists might be necessary but not sufficient. These are half-truths, euphemisms at best. Proselytizers, apologists, and jihadists must be linked precisely, directly, and routinely to the ideology, communities, and culture of origin. That culture is Islam! Culture is the primary culprit midst DCI James Clapper's host of "nefarious" characters.

So let's be clear when we speak of the enemy, the foe in all those small wars and the larger global *jihad*. As long as contemporary Muslim wars last, there are probably three relevant semantic distinctions to be made.

Islam is the big tent, the culture, for the most part an apathetic, apologetic, passive, or mostly bovine majority. **Islamists** are the proselytizing militants or financiers, missionaries, domestic or immigrant clerics who believe they act in the name of God, a prophet, or a "great" religion. **Islamofascists** are the kinetic Muslims, those who oppress or kill in the name of Mohamed, the Koran, or imperial Islam. The terms are related, though not necessarily interchangeable.*

The necessity to distinguish militants from moderates is not trivial. The so-called moderate is the more difficult problem, demographically and ideologically.

Islamism is in the end a political, religious, cultural, now kinetic, quest to reverse the vector of Emanuel Kant's social optimism. There is more than a little history to support irredentist cultures. The passage of time is not progress. Dark ages are still possible. The vector of history moves forward—or backwards. Contemporary Islamism and Islamofascism is a very large sanguinary bet on door number two, the recidivist option.

And yes, Islamists claim that their aggression is actually defense, a victim's posture. Let's allow that historical delusion in the name of consistency. Muslim scholars and clerics have been looking to the past in search of the future for centuries.

Recidivism withal, if not political naiveté, is the fatal flaw of all utopias, especially fascism. Unfortunately, the predicate of all fascism, religious or secular, is also coercion, if not brute force. The Islamic State and *Abu Bakr al-Baghdadi*, like their National Socialist doppelgangers, are the logical products of a viral Islamism unchallenged.

Abu Bakr al-Baghdadi
Source: Islamic State Social Media

There is no question that imperial Islam will fail—implode or be defeated. The question is how much masochism, denial, and damage the *Ummah* and the non-Muslim world will endure before that day arrives.

* Some of the best defenses for using terms like Islamism and Islamofascism often come, ironically, from serious writers on the American Left. See Christopher Hitchens seminal essay[3] in *Slate* or almost anything written by Paul Berman[4] on the subject. Daniel Pipes, on the Right, recently hosted a symposium on the subject which pretty much covered the semantic[5] landscape on Islam.

* Icon translation: "I have been ordered by Allah to fight against the people until they testify…etc."

Chapter 21

The Problem with Proxies: Ideology is No Substitute for Operational Control

Yelena Biberman and Orr Genish

First Published 27 September 2015

The US strategy of selecting reliable proxies against the Islamic State of Iraq and Syria (ISIS) based on their ideological leanings is proving to be disastrous. The latest headlines about US-trained Syrian rebels handing over military equipment to al-Qaeda-linked fighters highlight the serious and enduring problems of outsourcing war.[1] Recruitment of proxies based on their ideology has taken more time and resources than anticipated—it is hard to measure one's commitment to a set of ideas when the bullets are flying. The approach has also shown to be misguided. Without effective operational control, the "moderate" rebels are unlikely to bring victory against ISIS.

The United States began the program of arming Syrian proxies at a base in Jordan in April 2013. It later expanded it to Saudi Arabia. In February 2015, Washington signed an agreement with Ankara to train and equip "moderate" Syrian rebels.

While the Obama administration debated whether to get involved in Syria, the CIA conducted several studies of the effectiveness of its past operations. Many of the findings remain classified, but the *New York Times* reported that one of the conclusions was that many of the state-sponsored militias "had a minimal impact on the long-term outcome of a conflict," especially when "no Americans worked on the ground with the foreign forces in the conflict zones."[2]

Using proxies in Syria was supposed to help the United States avoid placing the regular forces in harm's way while benefitting from the former's local knowledge. However, without the regulars on the ground, the few US-sponsored rebels who are actually engaged in combat are proving ineffective and even counterproductive. They are also becoming a target for groups against which they were not originally intended.[3]

Delegating the fight against ISIS in Iraq to Iran-backed militias, without direct involvement, has been no less precarious. In a March 2015 interview, former commander of US troops in Iraq Gen. David H. Petraeus identified the Shia militias as "the most serious threat" to Iraq's long-term stability. He cautioned that they "could emerge as the preeminent power in the country, one that is outside the control of the government and instead answerable to Tehran."[4] The Human Rights Watch linked the militias, along with the regular Iraqi forces, to looting and even destroying entire villages *after* ISIS had passed through them.[5]

The "Birdcage Dilemma" of Effective Operational Control

In 1982, Communist Party elder Chen Yun compared the relationship between China's economy and central planning to that between a bird and its cage: "You mustn't hold the bird in your hands too tightly or it would be strangled. You have to turn it loose, but only within the confines of a cage. Otherwise it would fly away."[6] Chen's birdcage analogy can be applied to the delicate and dangerous relationship between states and their proxies. In order for the proxies to be effective, states must keep them under control while simultaneously turning them loose. They must construct a kind of a "birdcage" that would allow proxies to be both useful and manageable.

The violence states typically outsource to proxies ranges from mostly defensive (e.g. guarding installations) to offensive (e.g. targeted killings). Proxies have been widely viewed as a Cold War relic: the United States and the Soviet Union used them to wage wars across the Third World without succumbing to direct, apocalyptic confrontation. Ultimately, the victory of the former was facilitated by US-supplied rebels waging an "anti-Soviet jihad" in Afghanistan during the 1980s.[7]

The practice of employing third parties for war-making is millennia-old. Egypt used mercenaries, including the Nubians, for seven centuries starting in 1479 BCE. So did the Israelites around 1250 BCE "so that local citizens would be free to maintain the economic output necessary to support both the kingdom and the army."[8] In the 18th century, all the major European armies relied heavily on foreign fighters, while privateering played an important role in naval warfare.[9]

State outsourcing of war has survived and thrived in the post-Cold War era, not least due to the increased reliance on private contractors for combat-related activities.[10] Many states continue to use nonstate partners—from farmers to warlords—to counter as well as to foment insurgencies.[11]

The effective use of proxies requires the state sponsor to strike a delicate balance between freedom and control. Both too little and too much of either renders the proxy useless, and even dangerous, to its sponsor. Moreover, states that fail to use their nonstate partners effectively face the threat of other state and nonstate actors poaching them (and their equipment) or introducing their own, as did Iran. Rather than holding the proxy too tightly or letting it act freely, the state must construct a sort of a "birdcage"—a strategy for effective operational control. By "operational control" we mean the exercise of command authority over the irregulars: designating their operational objectives and providing authoritative direction for accomplishing those objectives through the tactical application of force.

The following case studies represent two different scenarios in which the state exercised too little and too much operational control for the proxy to be useful. Pakistan provides us with multiple cases of proxy warfare that include significant success in Afghanistan against the USSR as well as failures in Kashmir, India.[12] We can learn from Pakistan's mistakes in proxy use by analyzing the dynamics of militia control through the lens of the bird cage dilemma.

The "Free Bird" Scenario: Pakistan's 1947 Covert Operation in Kashmir

The Muslim-majority princely state of Jammu and Kashmir (henceforth referred to as "Kashmir") was ruled by a Hindu maharaja, who sought independence following the British withdrawal from India in August 1947. Neither Pakistan nor India shared this vision. In October 1947, Pakistan covertly armed and transported Pashtun tribesmen to take control of Kashmir. The panicked maharaja turned to Delhi for assistance, but was told first to sign an Instrument of Accession to India. He had little choice but to oblige. The tribal invasion turned into the first India-Pakistan war. Since then, Kashmir has been a major source of rivalry between the two regional powers. When both countries acquired nuclear weapons in 1998, the Kashmir conflict made South Asia, as then-US president Bill Clinton put it, "the most dangerous place on earth."[13]

Pakistan's ineffective proxy strategy in Kashmir in 1947 was indeed very costly. This section examines why the *lashkars* (tribal raiding parties) failed to serve their purpose. It shows that the problem lay in the birdcage dilemma: the Pakistani sponsors gave the *lashkars* too much freedom.

Neither the currently dominant narrative of uncontrollable *lashkars* nor the original British estimation of them being "under highly competent leadership"[14] are entirely correct. The tribesmen enjoyed high, but not total, autonomy. Pakistani Prime Minister Liaquat Ali Khan signed off on the plan, North-West Frontier Province authorities mobilized the Pashtun tribesmen in their region, and the Pakistani army equipped and transported the invaders. Some Pakistani soldiers turned a blind eye when boxes of .303 ammunition mysteriously disappeared from armories. A number of regulars took leave, or became technically "deserters," to join the fray. Several of them took it upon themselves to assume senior responsibilities. However, they were not fully in control of the tribesmen, especially once the latter arrived in Kashmir.

Having to swear on the Koran "to refrain from killing any neutrals and from individual looting"[15] did not prevent many of the tribesmen from "massacre arson and loot to the very gates of Srinagar."[16] Srinagar was the summer capital of the princely state and the site of an airport, which the tribesmen failed to secure by the time the Indian troops arrived on October 27.

Journalist Andrew Whitehead traces the story of a convent ransacked by tribesmen on their way to Srinagar. It is a story of Muslims who greeted the tribesmen as liberators from the unpopular maharaja, only to be violated on par with their non-Muslim counterparts; and of a Christian mission assaulted and terrorized.

Upon arrival, the raiders pillaged the convent, shot hospital patients as well as a British officer and his wife, and raped and killed nuns. Those who survived the initial onslaught were ordered by the raiders to line up. They were told that they would be shot. However, as the nuns were prepared to be killed, a Pakistani army officer suddenly appeared. One of the nuns recounted him saying something to the tribesmen in their language, and they put down their arms.[17]

Striking about the Pakistani officer is both the conspicuous presence and absence of his authority. On the one hand, he was able to stop the tribesmen from executing innocent civilians. On the other, he was unable to redirect them toward Srinagar, where the first Indian troops were landing that very day. The tribesmen stayed at the convent for over a week, looting and assaulting. When nothing was left to take, many of them headed back home. Had the *lashkars* been under tighter operational command, they would not have been preoccupied with the type of gratuitous violence they displayed at the convent. The Indian troops could then have been prevented from landing in Kashmir and, thus, mounting a rapid offensive. The outcome of the ensuing war between India and Pakistan may have been very different.

Once the Indian troops landed, the *lashkars* were ill-prepared and organized for confronting a regular army. The Pakistani planners erroneously assumed that what their proxies lacked in operational command they would make up for in enthusiasm. The *lashkars* were at their best in hill battles. Usually relying on ambush and surprise attacks, they avoided set-piece battles and exposed positions on the plains. The execution was frequently haphazard. The tribal warriors were also highly prone to turning back after acquiring sufficient booty or when they saw the raid running into trouble. Even their fervent supporter, Pakistan's Brigadier-in-Charge in Kashmir Akbar Khan, was baffled by the *lashkars'* response when Indian troops began coming out of Srinagar: "The withdrawal of the tribesmen had not been a step by step falling back, but a breaking away and a total disappearance. A spectacular advance coming to such an abrupt end was most bewildering."[18] Whitehead explains: "The glory of taking part in the raid was much greater motivation than territorial conquest. Often fighters would simply head home without any attempt at coordination within the *lashkar*."[19]

While Whitehead attributes the ineffectiveness of the *lashkars* to their culture, Akbar Khan identifies the strategic flaws in Pakistan's proxy plan. In his memoir, he laments that not even "ex-servicemen" of the Pakistani army were there to support and command the *lashkars* upon the arrival of the Indian troops. He points out that the *lashkars'* ineffectiveness was primarily the result of the inadequate preparation and backup by the Pakistani regulars:

They [the tribesmen] had, of their own free will, agreed to come and fight in Kashmir but only against the [Kashmiri] State Army. In this they had done more than expected of them. But no one had arranged with them to fight also against the regular Indian Army with artillery, tanks and aircraft… they had naturally expected that, in the changed circumstances, the Pakistan Army would be coming up to support them. And soon they had been shocked to find that no troops, no artillery and no aircraft were coming to help them. Indeed, not even the most elementary requirements of something like a secure base behind them as being provided by them.[20]

Pakistan's 1947 covert operation in Kashmir offers two important lessons about the state-proxy relationship. First, proxies require on-the-ground support and command. Moral hazard and lack of professionalism may otherwise prevent them from carrying out their mission in an efficient and timely manner. When Mao Tse-tung advised that "there must be no excessive interference" with the activities of guerrilla units, he did not mean that there should be absolutely no interference. All guerrilla units, he observed, require "political and military leadership" to discipline them: guerrilla warfare is not about "banditry and anarchism," but about "severe discipline."[21]

The second lesson of Pakistan's 1947 covert operation is one which also appears in Mao's guerrilla warfare manual: nonstate proxies may slow down or weaken the enemy, but they are insufficient for achieving "ultimate victory." Regular troops are necessary. As Mao put it, "while we must promote guerrilla warfare as a necessary strategical auxiliary to orthodox operations, we must neither assign it the primary position in our war strategy nor substitute it for mobile and positional warfare as conducted by orthodox forces."[22] Had the *lashkars* been better supported and commanded by Pakistani regulars, they would have unlikely exhibited high desertion rates and committed as many atrocities, thereby alienating the local population, much of which was initially sympathetic to their cause. They not only failed to prevent the arrival of the Indian troops, but also facilitated India's recruitment of local collaborators.

The "Smothered Bird" Scenario: Pakistan's 1965 Covert Operation in Kashmir

Operation Gibraltar represented Pakistan's second attempt to take Kashmir through a combination of proxies and regular forces. This time, however, the traumatic experience of 1947 led the military planners to keep their proxies too constrained to be effective. What resulted was, again, a botched operation and an inter-state war, as well as the re-freezing of the Kashmir conflict.

While, in 1947, Pakistan's proxies consisted of tribesmen with martial experience, in 1965 they comprised ordinary civilians from Azad Kashmir. Azad Kashmir was the roughly one-third of the princely state that was awarded to Pakistan following the 1947-48 war, with the rest given to India. The roughly 7,000 civilian recruits had the local knowledge that their 1947 counterparts lacked, but they were far less militarily skilled. Their training period was only three to seven weeks, with the main focus being guerrilla fieldcraft. Prisoner of war interrogation reports revealed that although the Azad Kashmir recruits were supposed to have been volunteers, "an element of coercion" was involved in their recruitment.[23] Some appeared to have known very little about their mission. They were told that they would be involved in "an ordinary hit and run exercise in the enemy territory."[24]

In 1947, it was not uncommon for the Pashtun units to contain only one regular. In 1965, a unit ("Company") typically contained an officer, several junior commissioned and non-commissioned officers, key personnel from the Azad Kashmiri battalions or units of the Northern Scouts, and several other ranks. The degree to which the proxies were constrained from exercising any significant role in the operation is illustrated by a story recorded in a secret 1966 report by the Criminal Investigation Department of Jammu and Kashmir.[25]

On August 4, 1965, a group of grazers were tending to their cattle on a pasture located in the high mountains of Baramulla District. Suddenly, they encountered armed men coming from the mountain passes. The commanding officer of the column of the infiltrators collected and addressed the herdsmen. He told them that his force had come from Pakistan to liberate the Kashmiri Muslims from the yoke of Indian imperialism, and that this was the beginning of a "Jihad" in which every Muslim had to participate. The herdsmen were sworn to secrecy and given money. Some of them were directed to go down and collect provisions for the infiltrators, while others were questioned about the disposition of the Indian Army units and other strategic information.

Towards the evening, the Pakistani infiltrators permitted several of the herdsmen to go down to their village, called Darakasi, to run some errands. One of the herdsmen, a young man named Mohammad Din, insisted that the villagers find a way to alert the Indian authorities. In order not to arouse suspicion of the infiltrators, he told his companions to carry on as usual, while he himself set out on a marathon run to the nearest Indian defense post.

What is particularly telling about this story is that it was the commanding officer, not the Azad Kashmiri guerrilla, who addressed the herdsmen. Had it been the latter, the story may have had a different ending since the guerrillas shared the same regional identity as the locals. The Pakistani forces faced a similar outcome in the rest of the region—rather than collaborating with them, the locals reported the infiltration to the Indian authorities, which soon led to the second India-Pakistan war.

While, in 1947, Pakistan exercised too little control over its proxies, in 1965, the Azad Kashmiri guerrillas were far too inhibited to be effective. They lacked not only the necessary military skills and information about their mission, but also the freedom to deeply engage with the local population. The benefits of their local knowledge were, consequently, squandered, and the mission failed.

Conclusion

Proxy warfare requires effective operational control. Ideology is insufficient for predicting how proxies will behave during important military (and civilian) engagements. The advantages of outsourcing war cannot be realized without striking a delicate balance between freedom and control. If effective operational control is not an option, neither should be the fight.

Chapter 22

Why ISIS is Winning in Iraq

Johnny Lou and Patrick O'Connor

First Published 19 October 2015

On May 17th, as the few remaining defenders of Ramadi collapsed and withdrew back to Baghdad in the face of massive attacks by ISIS fighters, officials and observers across Iraq and the United States were asking one question: how? How did the Iraqi defenders of the city, armed and trained by the most powerful military on earth get defeated in a pitched battle against an insurgent terrorist group armed with stolen weapons?

Analysts devised a number of explanations. Many Iraqi officers and political officials blamed a lack of supporting air-strikes from the American-led coalition. Observers in the US blamed the "lack of resolve" amongst the Iraqi defenders, a charge that outraged Iraqi Army officials. Other US officials believed that the defeat was due to an equipment mismatch: the Iraqi defenders lacked the heavy firepower needed to counter the stolen American-made weapons and vehicles ISIS deployed.

The existing explanations almost exclusively focus on tangible assets such as equipment and weapons or the problems within the Iraqi army. What has so far been missing from this discussion is the impressive military skill ISIS has exhibited. This is a level of tactical skill foreign to most terrorist groups, but familiar to any conventional military officer and to Stephen Biddle, who outlined the impact that skill plays in modern warfare.

The Battle of Ramadi

Nowhere was ISIS's incredibly high level of skill better showcased than the Battle of Ramadi. The Battle of Ramadi began on May 14th with an assault by ISIS forces on the government compound at the center of the city. After four days of fighting in and around the city of Ramadi, the few remaining Iraqi defenders of the city fled from their positions in the face of relentless assaults[1] by ISIS militants. Important buildings in the city were soon adorned with the flags of the victorious Islamic State and people suspected of loyalty to the government were put to death[2]. This was a humiliating defeat for the Iraqi forces and the US military advisors who had trained them, as a vastly outnumbered ISIS force managed to capture Ramadi in less than four days with no more advanced weaponry than waves of suicide bombers in stolen vehicles. This victory was due not to any numerical or armament advantage, but ISIS's mastery of what Biddle terms the "modern system" of warfare.

Firepower and the Problem of Modern Warfare

The advent of long-range rapid-fire weapons in the modern era fundamentally changed the way soldiers attacked their enemies. As generals (and soldiers) painfully learned in the First World War, massive ranks of infantry charging a defensive position would be torn to pieces by rapid-fire machine guns, long-range artillery, and precision rifle fire. In the face of such formidable firepower, armies throughout the world had to fundamentally alter the way in which they went on the offensive. No longer were the principles of offensives centered on massed ranks of infantry; any such force would be annihilated long before taking their objective. Armies of the modern system would need to be nimble and efficient; leveraging training and skill instead of brute force to achieve victory.

Combined Arms Integration

The key to the modern offensive is the principle of combined arms integration. Infantry, now organized into smaller assault units to take advantage of cover, were still responsible for taking ground. To get them to their targets unmolested, other troops and artillery would fire upon defensive positions, not to destroy them, but to suppress their fire. This principle of combining attacking infantry with supporting fire is the basis of Biddle's "modern system" and has been the key to modern military offensives from the Western Front to Ramadi.

Although the Islamic State also fields a significant amount of artillery, their weapon of choice on the offensive has been the suicide car (or truck) bomb. In the battle of Ramadi, a number of massive vehicle born suicide bombers were deployed in the attacks on government held positions. The attack on the Ramadi police headquarters on May 15th is a textbook example of ISIS's offensive methodology: an armored bulldozer packed with explosives[3] destroyed the barriers surrounding the western entrance to the government complex to clear the way for two more suicide truck bombers to destroy the entrance and stun the defenders. Immediately after the bombs went off, ISIS fighters swarmed through the breach, overwhelmed the defenders of the compound and took the position[4]. Similar tactics were deployed in attacks on all of the government positions throughout the Battle of Ramadi, and we observe similar tactics in other cities such as Kobane and Mosul. Although they deploy suicide truck bombers instead of long range artillery, ISIS's tactics hew closely to Biddle's modern system: heavy firepower (in the form of suicide bombs) clear the way for a closely coordinated infantry assault via suppression.

Deliberate Moderate Tempo

Though the implementation of the modern system provided a way for offensive forces to overcome the firepower of modern defenders, it required a different sort of offensive pacing. Attacking infantry now needed to wait for slower suppressing units to get in place before their attack could begin. No longer was the speed of an offensive dictated solely by how quickly infantry could be moved from one engagement to the next. The modern system, though effective, demanded a deliberate and moderate tempo to allow for all the requisite elements to get in place.

This sort of deliberate tempo was on display in the May assault on Ramadi. ISIS forces took over four days to take a city just over 5.5 miles across. The modern system necessitated this moderated pace through the city: ISIS commanders knew that infantry assaulting a position had to wait for the requisite suicide car bombs to be set up and launched before they could begin. This led to the pattern we observed in Ramadi of focused attacks to capture select targets before moving onto others.

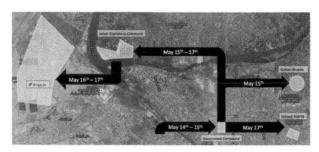

Timeline of ISIS Attacks in Ramadi

The Need for Skill

These new combined arms offensives dictated by the modern system required a much higher level of training and planning on the part of militaries. Suppressing fire from the rear had to be timed precisely: if they stopped too early, the defenders would regroup and destroy the attacking infantry; too late and fratricide would ensue. This meant that leaders and officers across the chain of command needed to possess an unprecedented level of training and skill in order to carry out these attacks.

ISIS's skills and mastery of the modern system were on full display at Ramadi, as well as battles across Iraq and Syria. The question remains as to where ISIS managed to find these all-important skills that are lacking in almost all other terrorist organizations. The answer lies in the events of the US invasion of Iraq in 2003 and the subsequent toppling of Saddam's Baathist party.

The Saddam Connection

In the weeks after the attack on Ramadi, it was discovered that the leaders of the ISIS fighters that had taken the city were former Baathists[5] loyal to Saddam Hussein. In fact, fully four out of seven[6] of the members of the Shura council, including Abu Muslim al Afari al Turkmani, the second in command of ISIS, are former Baathist military commanders. Former Baathist military members also serve as fighters and lower level commanders of ISIS forces.

These Saddam loyalists can be traced back to after the fall of Saddam's regime, when the Baathists that made up the core of his government and followers were swiftly removed from power. Following the collapse of Saddam's regime, official US government policy under Ambassador Bremer called for the "de-Baathification" of Iraq. All individuals affiliated with the Baath party were purged from government positions, the military, and schools. It's been estimated that over 500,000 Baathists in Iraq's military and intelligence services alone were dismissed and stripped of their pay and pensions[7]. Many of these former soldiers then joined Al Qaeda in Iraq and fought coalition forces non-stop during the insurgency period.

These de-Baathification programs were continued even after the end of the interim government. In a decision sanctioned by the

US government, all members or affiliates of the Baath party were subsequently banned by Prime Minister al Maliki[8] from running in the Parliamentary elections in 2005 and 2010. Dismissal of civil servants, including doctors, teachers, and engineers, over charges of being affiliated with the Baathist party continued well after the initial purges.

The Road to ISIS

When AQI gradually evolved into ISIS, many of these Baathists joined the new organization. Former Saddam army officers and soldiers, barred from service in the new Iraqi army, began to fight for the Islamic State. This infusion of military leaders and personnel was the key to ISIS's acquisition of skill necessary for the combined assaults observed in Ramadi and elsewhere.

The rise of ISIS and its military successes are a direct result of the de-Baathification policies of the US interim government and the new Iraqi government. The continued alienation of former Baath party members, whom number in the hundreds of thousands and include Iraq's most capable civil servants and military leaders, cannot continue if ISIS is to be effectively combated. The expertise and experience that they lend to ISIS is the key to their ability to use advanced military tactics like the ones we have seen in Ramadi and other major battles and these tactics have given them an unprecedented amount of campaign success.

A Baathist Awakening

Though the Baathists and the Islamic State are currently working together, their relationship is more a marriage of convenience rooted in the exclusion of the Baathists from the new Iraqi government and military. ISIS continues to be viewed as extremely radical, even in the

Arab world, and it is easy to see how their plans for a global Islamic Caliphate clashes with the views of the nationalist and relatively secular Baathists. The surest way for the Iraqi government to strike at the fighting capability of ISIS is to cultivate relations with the former Baathists and bring them back into the fold of normal Iraqi life, including its political processes. Not only would this deprive ISIS of capable leaders and battle commanders, but it would allow us to use the Baathists to bolster the fighting capabilities of the Iraqi armed forces, which can only be for the better given their recent performances.

Nor is this kind of reconciliation without precedent. During the Sri Lankan civil war, the Sri Lankan government reached out to Col. Karuna, commander of the LTTE in the eastern provinces, who then defected with a third of the LTTE's fighting forces. Not only did Karuna abandon the Tigers, but his men actually joined the Sri Lankan army in fighting the remaining insurgents. This proved to be the key to taking down the Tamil Tigers, who collapsed five years later. Coalition forces followed a similar strategy with the Anbar Awakening, in which Sunni tribesmen were recruited to help eventually defeat AQI. Now that AQI's remnants have evolved into ISIS, we need a Baathist Awakening to turn the tide.

Chapter 23

Disrupting the MFO: ISIS in Sinai

Matthew J. McGoffin

First Published 20 October 2015

Background

On September 3, 2015, Reuters reported[1] that four American soldiers were wounded when an improvised explosive device detonated near their convoy in Egypt. The soldiers are part of a little-known United States Army mission in support of the Multinational Force and Observers (MFO), an independent international force established following the Camp David Accords of 1978 and subsequent Egyptian-Israeli Treaty of Peace.

The mission[2] of the MFO is to "supervise the implementation of the security provisions of the Egyptian-Israeli Treaty of Peace and employ best efforts to prevent any violation of its terms." Accordingly, the American observers focus attention on Egyptian and Israeli military concentrations and troop movements, seeking to prevent violations of the security provisions of the peace treaty. The September 3 attack, however, was initiated not by a conventional military party, but by a local insurgency—previously known as Ansar Bayt al-Maqdis, now known as the north Sinai branch of the Islamic State of Iraq and al-Sham (ISIS). This threat, in other words, exists outside the mandate, or purpose, of the MFO. In light of the deteriorating security situation, "the Obama administration is quietly reviewing the future of America's three-decade deployment to Egypt's Sinai Peninsula, fearful the lightly equipped peacekeepers could be targets of escalating Islamic State-inspired violence. Options range from beefing up their protection or even pulling them out altogether[3], officials told The Associated Press."

Apart from these two extremes, is there a way that the American force in Sinai could continue to accomplish its three-decade-old mission, but through alternative means? One solution would be to reorganize the current US presence into a smaller force, augmented with remote sensing equipment.

Discussion

First let's define terms. The MFO is an independent international organization[4], not a United Nations force. Its narrow support—primarily split between the US, Israel, and Egypt—means the MFO's future is more precariously balanced than that of a similar UN force. With fewer state sponsors and stakeholders, the MFO could be more susceptible to unanticipated shocks and changes in the local environment. Corroborating this, Colonel Thomas O'Steen, a former commander of the US task force in Sinai, wrote a paper in 2013—prior to the rise of ISIS in Sinai—which states that "although the MFO still keeps the peace between Egypt and Israel, it does not address key changes in the environment such as Bedouin unrest, the emergence of violent extremist organizations, and the trafficking of weapons throughout the Sinai".

Noted counterinsurgency theorist and former Australian Army officer David Kilcullen wrote in *Out of the Mountains* that "even where policy makers' intent is to resolve a conflict, monitor a truce, or police a cease-fire, putting peacekeepers into an urban conflict zone amounts to laying out an attractive array of targets for terrorist groups, local insurgents, street gangs, organized crime, or just commercial kidnapping networks, and this can force peacekeepers into combat at short notice" (Kilcullen, 2013, pg. 267). In a parallel to north Sinai, radical Islamist insurgents[5] in Syria have overrun peacekeepers of the United Nations Disengagement Observer Force (UNDOF), commandeering the force's armored vehicles and repurposing them as vehicle borne improvised explosive devices (VBIEDs). If the recent IED attack in Sinai is any indication, sending more American soldiers to beef up force protection within the MFO could very well result in an exacerbation of attacks on peacekeepers, with potentially catastrophic results.

ADRP 1-02[6] defines *disrupt* as "a tactical mission task in which a commander integrates direct and indirect fires, terrain, and obstacles to upset an enemy's formation or tempo or interrupt his timetable." What happens when conventional peacekeepers are disrupted by domestic insurgents, as in Sinai? The mission of the peace operation, its purpose, and its endstate must be reevaluated. At this juncture, the temptation is to stay the course, with familiar tactics and predictable results. Instead, military leaders and policymakers must recognize the need to adapt to the challenges that a flatly networked insurgency presents. Without an offensive mandate, but with the need to fulfill a critical regional security requirement, those responsible for the US mission in Sinai must evaluate policy alternatives outside of the typical Manichean options of withdrawal versus an increase in troop strength.

Recommendation

In Sinai, why change a formula which has worked for so long? Because the Egyptian-Israeli security relationship is evolving[7], as the common threat of ISIS in Sinai brings both governments together. New amendments to the security provisions of the peace treaty enable greater troop movements against the insurgents—the enemy of my enemy being my friend. In light of such cooperation, one alternative to the current peacekeeping arrangement would be for the US to consider substituting remote sensing equipment for some of the American observers, obviating much of the need for a distributed, overt US troop presence.

Of course, such a change should be the result of cooperative dialogue with the Egyptian and Israeli governments. Policymakers must weigh the relative costs and benefits of replacing these Soldiers, and the resulting net impact on regional security, the preservation of which is the sole reason for the MFO's existence. However, one fact stands clear: if we are to succeed in achieving outcomes in this mission, we must periodically revisit the conduct of our operations in light of the changing environment, threats, and available technology. This can only occur by bringing focused attention and constructive conversation to the issue of the future of US peacekeeping. A lack of focused attention on this mission—indicated by much of mainstream media's inability[8] to accurately report what kind of force the MFO is—casts into doubt the potential for the development of the sort of change that needs to occur.

Chapter 24

Mujahideen: The Strategic Tradition of Sunni Jihadism

Brett A. Friedman

First Published 28 October 2015

The world is in the grips of the group known as ISIS. Unable to look away but equally unable to fathom the group's extreme violence, the civilized world marvels at a terrorist threat that is seemingly al Qaeda cranked up to eleven. Its media blitzkrieg has recently been described by Jessica Stern and J.M. Berger and its apocalyptic vision by William McCants, but its military strategy too is an outgrowth of earlier trends in jihadi thought. The military strategy of the mujahideen can be traced back to a jail cell in Egypt in the early 1960s.

Few have looked at jihadi groups in the context of classical military strategy but perhaps surprisingly the jihadis themselves view their ideas through exactly that lens. As Western national security experts deny the utility of Carl von Clausewitz's *On War* in an age of jihadis, insurgents, and terrorists, the jihadis themselves seem not to have gotten the memo as his ideas appear repeatedly in their texts and he is even directly cited in jihadi instructional videos. Perhaps less surprisingly, the ideas of Mao Tse-Tung (another theorist who cited Clausewitz) are even more influential as his three stages of protracted warfare appear repeatedly in slightly modified form. Other names familiar to the student of strategic studies appear in their tracts on military issues, "Che" Guevara and Ho Chi Minh to name two. Other concepts are clear parallels to theorists like Hans Delbrück and J. C. Wylie although they go uncited. If we better understood the terrorists' theory of victory, perhaps we may better understand how to counter it- or at least how not to play into it.

The Sunni tradition of jihadi strategy exhibits three crests or waves of thought. The first began with the publication of Milestones by Sayyid Qutb from the depths of that Egyptian jail cell. The second is exemplified by al Qaeda, its visionaries like Osama Bin Laden and Abu Musab al-Suri, and the numerous jihadis who turned away from the Muslim Brotherhood after its failures in Egypt and Syria. The third wave is breaking on us right now as the Islamic State runs farther and faster with jihadi military strategy than their forebears ever have.

The First Wave

The first wave of modern jihad began with Sayyid Qutb, an Egyptian member of the Muslim Brotherhood. The Muslim Brotherhood was founded in 1928 by Hasan al-Banna and while it always wanted a society guided by Islamic principles, it was not initially as extremist as it later became. Al-Banna's group did want to institute *shariah*, but a version of *shariah* modified for modern times. In the 1930's and 1940's, the organization was focused on social welfare but became a popular political force.[i] By the mid-1950s when Sayyid Qutb was a member, however, the organization took a violent turn. In 1954 members of the organization, including Qutb, attempted to assassination Gamel Abdul Nasser who would become the first President of Egypt. Nasser's crackdown drove the organization underground and Qutb, among others, was imprisoned.[ii] Qutb was born in 1906 and his family was able to provide a good education for him, including two years of studying abroad in the United States in 1949 and 1950.[iii] He was negatively affected by his view of the West and his religious conservatism, always strong, was deepened by the experienced.

In 1964 he while imprisoned for his participation in the assassination attempt, he published *Milestones*, his most influential work. In it, he attacked the idea of secular authority and any separation between Islam and politics. Qutb viewed such ideas as a tool for state leaders in the Middle East to "… use state structure and power to prevent their people from following God's governance…"[iv] Since state power was inherently opposed to the people in this way, violence was, "necessary to break down this human-imposed order so that the people held under it would be free to serve God alone."[v] In this vein violence, even offensive violence, was justified as self-defense and thus was incumbent for the faithful Muslim as part of jihad. He stated that jihad was, "the defense of man against all those elements that limit his freedom."[vi] That freedom, however, was only the freedom to follow God as following other men was "enslavement."[vii] His summation of these ideas is important: "It [Islam} has the right to destroy all obstacles in the form of institutions and traditions that limit man's freedom of choice. It does not attack individuals, nor does it force them to accept its beliefs; it attacks institutions and traditions to release human beings from their poisonous influences, which distort human nature and curtail human freedom."[viii] Qutb subsumes individuals in institutions, justifying their deaths as an attack on "obstacles" vice individuals. Like the communist thinkers of the 20th Century such as V. I. Lenin, Qutb believed that a vanguard of the faithful would perform such deeds in order to "free" the masses.[ix] His ideas on violence, politics, and religion have parallels in military theory. His belief in the use of violence for political ends is reminiscent of Carl von Clausewitz's assertion that war is the continuation of political intercourse with the addition of violent means and Mao Tse Tung's statement "political power grows out of the barrel of a gun." For Clausewitz and Mao though, violence and war were controlled—and limited by—policy, politics, and party but for Qutb politics was dominated by Islam. "It [modern politics] transfers to man one of the Greatest (sic) attributes of God, namely, sovereignty, and makes some men lords over others."[x] In other words, the only legitimate sovereignty is God's. Qutb's marriage of politics, violence, and religious jihad forms the base of the modern Sunni jihadi movement and greatly influenced the military strategy of early Islamic extremist military strategy.

The Muslim Brotherhood was so popular amongst Sunni Muslims that it spread beyond Egypt. In Syria in the late 1970's and early 1980's, Sunni opposition to the Alawitte-dominated regime of President Hafez al-Assad escalated despite harsh regime crackdowns.[xi] The opposition, spearheaded by the Syrian Muslim Brotherhood amongst other Sunni and jihadi groups, seized the city of Hama in 1982. The Assad regime responded with extreme violence, virtually destroying the city and killing some 10,000 Syrians.[xii] Many members of the Muslim Brotherhood were also killed or were forced to flee the country, including one Abu Musab al-Suri.

The Second Wave

As time went on after Sayyid Qutb's execution in 1966 and its failure in Syria, the Muslim Brotherhood shifted again towards more peaceful methods to achieve their vision, working through political structures rather than attempting to overturn them. Although sidelined by the Musharraf regime in Egypt, they were still an influential force in jihadi circles. Some of its members would leave the organization due to its more moderate turns and would end up participants in the second wave of the Sunni jihad which took form in al Qaeda. Al Qaeda's founder and leader Osama bin Laden was also its primary strategic visionary. Whereas Sayyid Qutb envisioned the ground swell of a vanguard from within a state, al Qaeda would take a more global view based on a conception of the "near enemy"—secular Arab states- and the "far enemy"—the United States, Israel, and the West.

Frequently portrayed as a cave-dwelling malcontent, Bin Laden had a sophisticated strategic vision for his jihad. Drawing on his significant business expertise, Bin Laden added economic warfare to Qutb's cocktail of religious politics and violence. The son of a successful businessman, Bin Laden clearly saw an economic connection between the Soviet Union's failure in Afghanistan and its subsequent collapse. Bin Laden's strategic vision is clear from his own statements. In a letter to Mullah Omar, the late Taliban leader, dated 3 October, 2001, Bin Laden stated that the imminent US invasion of Afghanistan, "will impose great long-term economic burdens leading to further economic collapse, which will force America, God willing, to resort to the former Soviet Union's only option: withdrawal from Afghanistan, disintegration, and contraction."[xiii] In subsequent interviews Bin Laden talked at length about the damage done to the American economy, in each case comparing it to fall of the Soviet Union.[xiv] Thus, al Qaeda's theory of strategic victory is that of cumulative strategy or a strategy of exhaustion. In Military Strategy, US Admiral J. C. Wylie described a cumulative strategy as "…a type of warfare in which the entire pattern is made up of a collection of lesser actions, but these lesser or individual actions are not sequentially interdependent."[xv] Rather than seek large battles one after the other in a long campaign, the pursuant of a cumulative strategy counts on the ever-increasing effect of small but disparate defeats to eventually overcome the enemy's will to continue. A strategy of exhaustion, *Ermattungsstrategie*, is a concept from German historian/theorist Hans Delbrück. When pursuing a strategy of exhaustion, the strategic will choose to fight only when it is advantageous but may also delay, avoid, or otherwise force the opponent to expend time and resources until his will to continue is depleted.[xvi]

The military aspects of al Qaeda's strategy was captured by one of his protégés, Abu Musab al-Suri, sometimes referred to as "al Qaeda's mastermind" or "the professor of jihad." Al-Suri is the nom de guerre of Mustafa Setmariam Naser who was born in Aleppo around 1958. He became a member of the Syrian Muslim Brotherhood before joining the jihad in Afghanistan. As a member of al Qaeda, Suri worked in the west writing and publishing jihadi tracks and establishing cells in Spain and England. Upon returning to Afghanistan prior to 9/11 as an instructor in its training camps, he began work on *The Call to a Global Resistance*. After al Qaeda was ejected from Afghanistan, Suri joined one of his students, Abu Musab al-Zarqawi, in Iraq. In October of 2005, he was captured in Pakistan. He was allegedly repatriated to Syria and al Qaeda figures claim he remains in prison there.

The Call to a Global Resistance is a unique document in that it is a relatively honest critique of jihadi military methods from an instructor in the craft. At 1,600 pages, it is a detailed window into the thinking of Sunni militants. Al-Suri builds on the ideas of Qutb, echoing that secular institutions—and those that support them—violate *shariah* and thus deaths of supporters are justified. Where al-Suri goes further is in the codification of al Qaeda's global cellular structure that ensures the organization's secrecy and durability in the face of attrition. His description of the decentralized nature is presented as a means to correct "errors" committed by previous jihadis and he criticized the Muslim Brotherhood of which he was a former member.[xvii] Al-Suri goes on a worldwide "tour" of Sunni terrorist and insurgent groups, describing their successes and failures. He blames the Syrian Muslim Brotherhood's efforts at moderation for the failure of the revolt the al-Assad regime in the early 1980's, for which he was present.[xviii] While still referring to Sayyid Qutb in reverent tones, he accuses the Muslim Brotherhood of losing sight of jihad.

Another evolution from the Qutb era is his focus on the use of media, or information operations. Despite al-Suri's justification of targeting civilians, his work reflects al Qaeda's greater concern with the messaging of violence; civilians are not randomly targeted but violent acts are planned to both send a message and amplify that message. An entire chapter in *Call* is essentially a treatise on jihadi rhetoric and details how to craft various media efforts. He recommends to his audience that such messaging be rooted in "Islamic history"[xix] and "the history of the Crusade expeditions," an oblique reference to jihad as self-defense.

The name "al Qaeda" means "the base" and this vision of al Qaeda as a foundation to a global revolution is evident throughout al-Suri's book. He writes, "Therefore, the first lesson we must learn from these equations is that we must return the Muslim nation to the battlefield so that the battle becomes once again a battle of a nation and not just that of a few, as it has become these days. The first thing required in this matter is that these "few" must convince the rest that those who stand by the enemy become the enemy. They must be convinced that confronting the enemy is at the core of jihad and it is not something off the path of righteousness."[xx]

Al-Suri's vision of a global revolution catalyzed by a group of dedicated devotees is reminiscent of the foco concept, most widely associated with Ernesto "Che" Guevara. Guevara believed that guerrilla warfare, insurgency, or any type of revolution rested on the support of the population. A revolutionary vanguard would be necessary to provide focus—the *foco*—to a population which would then rise up in support. For Guevara, this support was necessary: "The guerilla band is an armed nucleus, the fighting vanguard of the people. It draws its great force from the mass of the people themselves... Guerrilla warfare is used by the side which is supported by a majority but which possesses a much smaller number of arms for use in defense against repression."[xxi] Al Qaeda would later adopt this belief in the sense that the "vanguard" most not move towards seizing political control until it had broad popular support; both Osama Bin Laden and Ayman al-Zawahiri would recommend against moving too fast and condemn any jihadi group that moved without such popular support. While the United States adopted a theory that the support of the population was necessary for success, al Qaeda would too. As we shall see though, later jihadi movements would dispense with such gentility.

Guevara is not the only communist guerrilla fighter to influence jihadi military strategy. Another al Qaeda theorist, Abd al-Aziz al Muqrin, wrote a more militarily-focused tract that shows the influence of Chinese communist leader Mao Tse-Tung especially. Al-Muqrin was a Said born in 1979. He was pious from an early age and grew up in a conservative neighborhood near Riyadh.[xxii] He joined the jihad in Afghanistan in 1990 against the wishes of his parents.[xxiii] There, he saw combat against the Soviets and then continued to travel and work in jihadi circles in Africa and Europe throughout the 1990's. He returned to Afghanistan after 9/11 to participate in the fighting there but was dispatched back to Saudi Arabia by Osama bin Laden to establish an al Qaeda presence.[xxiv] As a founding member of Al Qaeda in the Arabian Peninsula (AQAP), he was an instructor for other members in fighting and warfare and wrote for AQAP's media efforts. At some point in 2003 or 2004 he became the organization's leader until he was killed in a gunfight with Saud security forces in Riyadh in June of 2004.[xxv]

Only thirty years old at the time of his death, al-Muqrin nevertheless was steeped in military and jihadi theory. In his book, *A Practical Course for Guerrilla War*, al-Muqrin uses the teachings of Yusuf al-Ayyiri, another member of AQAP. Al-Ayyiri's videotaped lectures, produced by AQAP, included lectures on the ideas of Prussian theorist Carl von Clausewitz and Mao Tse-Tung. They also mention guerrilla leaders like Ho Chi Minh, "Che" Guevara, and Fidel Castro. Al-Muqrin builds on those lectures in his book though, providing a synthesis of military theory relevant to the jihadi.

The book is filled with such influences, taking as its core the idea that organized violence is essentially political from Clausewitz and Mao. Al-Muqrin's definition of war reflects this: "War is a state of conflict that erupts between two communities, factions, or states, or between two individuals and, in general terms, between two armed camps, with the purpose of achieving political, economic, or ideological gains or for expansionist goals."[xxvi] Throughout the book, al-Muqrin discusses ways to break the enemy's morale or will, another concept with Clausewitzian connections. Where he part with Clausewitz and leans more towards Mao is in his recommendations to court the support of the civilian population. Like Bin Laden and al-Suri, al-Muqrin believes that jihadis compete with opposing forces for the allegiance of civilians. This leads him to a similar focus on information operations and the use of terrorism as messaging. He writes: "Attacks within cities are considered diplomatic-military. This type of diplomacy is normally written in blood, decorated with corpses, and perfumed with gunpowder. It has a political meaning connected to the nature of the ideological struggle." [xxvii]

The most obvious connection between al-Muqrin and Mao and Vietnamese guerrilla leaders like Ho Chi Minh and Vo Nguyen Giap is his practical plagiarism of Mao's three stages of guerrilla warfare. Al-Muqrin names the phases Attrition, Relative Strategic Balance, and Military Decision but the differences end there.[xxviii] The first phase involves small-scale but widespread attack by "mujahidin" cells. These attacks are continued in the second phase but coexist with developing "conventional" forces which seize control where enemy forces are weak.[xxix] The third phase features victory over the enemy using conventional forces that are "completely familiar with conventional war and with an army's order of battle and how it operates in the field." [xxx] Like Giap, al-Muqrin believes that the phases may occur concurrently vice sequentially. He also connects each phase with political conditions that parallel the military efforts. He depicts a slowly-contracting ability on the part of the enemy forces to maintain political control in the region.

The significant contributions of this second wave of jihadi thought is the injection of more advanced strategic concepts without regard for their origin under the justifications put forth by Sayyid Qutb. Osama Bin Laden's focus on economic warfare combined with the focus on persistent small-scale attacks shared by him, al-Suri, and al-Muqrin combine to form a cumulative strategy a la J. C. Wylie which they hope will deplete the United States' wealth, will, and strength. They apply this same strategy to regional conflicts as per al-Muqrin, whose work focused on insurgencies against regional powers. The cellular structure first proposed by Qutb but used by Bin Laden and codified by al-Suri should not be discounted: it is this structure that provides al Qaeda and similar groups with a depth of resistance to strategies of decapitation that target their leadership. Although this structure was lifted from successful guerrilla movements, al Qaeda managed to institute it on an unprecedented global scale. It has made al Qaeda particularly resistant to the attrition of its leaders, including Osama Bin Laden himself. But al Qaeda has failed to transition from their base of dedicated fighters to a more formal political force with all the benefits of total mobilization that they hoped to gain. As Jessica Stern and J. M. Berger have described an example of al Qaeda's media campaigns: "...the video's simple problem/solution formulation did not off al Qaeda as a political force, only as a paramilitary force multiplier for the hypothetical Muslim silent majority waiting to be mobilized."[xxxi] The creation of a true political force has been the major success of the third wave of jihadi military thought and its brutal avatar, the Islamic State.

The Third Wave

The history of the doctrinal dispute within al Qaeda that spawned the third wave of jihadi military strategy goes back to the foundation of al Qaeda in Iraq (AQI) by Abu Musab al-Zarqawi in 2002 and 2003. Al-Zarqawi was a Jordanian protégé of Abu Musab al-Suri whom we met above, but al-Zarqawi never adopted the concern for winning over the population that the mentor showed. His strategy was to provoke the Shia population of Iraq into a civil war, presumably to unite the Sunnis behind his banner. He succeeded in provoking the war, but was repeatedly upbraided by al Qaeda leadership including Bin Laden and Ayman al-Zawahiri, then Bin Laden's deputy and now leader of al Qaeda. His tactics also alienated the Sunni tribes of Iraq who eventually turned towards the United States and against AQI after al-Zarqawi's death in 2005.

Subsequently, AQI leadership declared the existence of an Islamic State and renamed the group the Islamic State in Iraq (ISI). This was done in direct violation of Bin Laden's guidance to wait. Despite advice to the contrary, however, Bin Laden refused to cut ties with the group until his death. By that time the group was led by Abu Bakr al-Baghdadi, an Iraqi former Islamic Studies student. Importantly, the group was also stiffened by an influx of Baathist military officers barred from joining the post-Saddam Hussein Iraqi Army.[xxxii]

The break with AQ came after al-Zawahiri ordered the group to expand its efforts in Syria as that country plummeted into civil war. The group sent to Syria by ISI called itself Jabhat al-Nusra. Simultaneously, ISI started to expand into Syria as well, attempting to seize political control of territory whereas Jabhat al-Nusra focused on defeating the regime of Syrian President Bashar al-Assad alongside Syrian rebel groups.[xxxiii] The two groups were subsequently at odds regarding revenue sharing from captured oil fields.[xxxiv] Jabhat al-Nusra seceded from ISI (now renamed the Islamic State in Iraq and al-Sham, or ISIS) with al-Zawahiri's blessing. After a blistering response to the al Qaeda leader from al-Baghdadi, al-Zawahiri cut ties with ISIS in February of 2014.

Beyond the bureaucratic spats that led to the schism, the major doctrinal dispute between al Qaeda in regards to military strategy is the intense targeting of civilians and rapid implementation of *shariah* exhibited by ISIS. Their methods bear the imprint of the book *The Management of Savagery: The Most Critical State Through Which the Umma Will Pass* by Abu Bakr Naji. The name is a nom d'guerre and the true author is unknown but the book appeared at roughly the same time as al-Suri's *Call*. Whereas al Qaeda and its affiliates (including Jabhat al-Nusra) lean more towards al-Suri's vision of local and global popular uprisings led by jihadis and a more phased imposition of *shariah*, Naji's conception is different. Naji dispenses with any requirement to woo the population and instead recommends the exploitation or creation of regions engulfed in violent chaos and societal disarray—a state of "savagery." Jihadis can then seize political control of such areas. A state of savagery is a prerequisite to the political control of jihadis since the population of the afflicted region will desire security over everything else. The brutality of harsh control becomes not a weakness as al-Suri believed but a strength; the population will welcome the strongest horse. In *Management,* Naji states: "The region of savagery will be in a situation resembling the situation of Afghanistan before the control of the Taliban, a region submitting to the law of the jungle, whose good people yearn for someone to manage this savagery. They even accept any organization, regardless of whether it is made up of good or evil people."[xxxv]

Like Mao and al-Muqrin, Naji envisions three stages of warfare. The first is "[T]he stage of "the power of vexation and exhaustion.""[xxxvi] In this stage jihadis perform the typical small-scale attacks, recruit more followers, and generally displace existing political structures. In the second stage, that of "the administration of savagery," Naji describes typical insurgent actions like the provision of services and increasing the ranks and "combat efficiency" of the fighting force. Interestingly, at this point Naji launches into a long description of drawing the United States into the conflict in order to place it, "in a state of war with the masses of the region."[xxxvii] Naji never goes into depth regarding the third stage—"the establishment of power" but does state that it is "establishing the state."[xxxviii] In some regions, Naji believes that only the first and third stages are necessary.

Like other jihadi military thinkers, Naji describes a military strategy of overextending and exhausting the enemy and a coordinated information strategy using media to attract recruits and project legitimacy. Where Naji differs is in a section entitled "Using Violence." In it, he takes other jihadis to task for "softness": "Those who study theoretical jihad will never grasp this point well... One who previously engaged in jihad knows it is naught but violence, crudeness, terrorism, frightening (others), and massacring..."[xxxix] Naji believed that modern Muslims are not like the Arabs who fought with the Prophet who "used to fight and know the nature of wars"[xl]; they must be trained to be violent. Internet videos depicting ISIS fighters having children present for and even performing executions underscores this point. He uses historical examples to explain that extreme violence is a necessary ingredient of success. He specifically cited examples of the immolation of victims and said it was used by early Muslims, "... because they knew the effect of rough violence in times of need."[xli] Such violence can only be decreased when acceptance of their version of Islam is achieved, but never against "the enemy," referring to apostates and the West. He describes a concept called "paying the price"[xlii] which is essentially achieving deterrence by responding to any attack with brutal violence. (Not really that different from our own conception of deterrence.) The execution of hostages is also described as a way to "send fear into the hearts of the enemy and his supporters."[xliii]

The use of violence is directly connected to the next section titled "Achieving "Power"": "The great "power" and that which causes the enemy to reflect one thousand times are a result of the "powers" of the groups [jihadi fighters], whether they are groups of "vexation" [the first stage] or groups of administration in the regions of savagery [the second stage]. The tie of religious loyalty between all of these is embodied in a covenant written in blood. The most important clause (of this covenant) is: "Blood for blood and destruction for destruction." Attaining a great "power" makes the enemy unable to oppose it."[xliv]

What Naji is describing as "power" is the devotion and moral cohesion exhibited by the Islamic States fighting units in both Iraq and Syria. It is a bloody mix of unbridled violent urges and religious fervor that provides the fighters with a will and capability that Syrian rebel groups and Iraqi Army units cannot match, as shown in the rapid expansion of ISIS and even more rapid collapse of heavily-armed and American backed Iraqi Army units. It is, in short, the Islamic States' center of gravity. Carl von Clausewitz described the strategic center of gravity as, "the hub of all power and movement, on which everything depends."[xlv] It could be a capital city, a particular army, or an influential leader but in any case it is—like in physics—the point which gives a strategic actor its cohesion as a singular unit. Napoleon, for example, was a center of gravity because of the force of his personality and military reputation for victory. For the Islamic State, it is their ideology of ultraviolence mixed with an aura of religious credibility projected by their communications strategy.

The ideas of Naji appeared again in a document written by ISI militants in late 2009 when the group was at its nadir. That document, "The Strategic Plan for Reinforcing the Political Position of the Islamic State of Iraq," was a comprehensive strategy for the group to assert itself once US troops were withdrawn from the country.[xlvi] It included plans for coopting the Sunni tribes, fighting Iraqi security forces, a media campaign, and even quoted Sun Tzu.[xlvii] It is essentially a practical application of Naji's theories, and ISIS has followed it faithfully.

Thus, the ultraviolence of the Islamic State is not blind barbarism but a calculated component of their military strategy. The violence interacts in a feedback loop with their media strategy: slick videos depicting such acts demonstrates their strength to and intimidates local audiences and appeals to potential recruits, thereby increasing their military power. Fear and terror is another component: Iraqi troops tasked with defending Mosul fled rather than face the Islamic State's fighters. Lastly, it is a premeditated means to drawing the United States into the conflict which expends American resources and lends legitimacy to the group as defenders of Islam while depleting the credibility of the United States so long as the group continues to operate despite its best efforts. This lofty goal has already been accomplished.

Total War

The three waves of jihadi military strategy have been ever increasing in their totality. Qutb envisioned a small group of jihadi cells that would seize control from regional Arab government leaders. Bin Laden and al-Suri envisioned more popular revolutions, both regional and global, led by a jihadi vanguard. Naji and ISIS leadership envisions a movement: the mobilization of the entire population towards the singular goal of establishing and expanding the Islamic State. This is demonstrated by repeated calls from ISIS to Muslims of any kind, including administrators, engineers, and doctors as well as fighters to join their banners.[xlviii] This vision is no less than a repetition of the French Revolution's somewhat successful attempt to mobilize the entire nation of France to further the goals of the Revolution and thus is a significant change in the stream of jihadi military thinking. For Clausewitz, the total mobilization of French society was the political change that spurred an advancement in warfare towards his theoretical concept of absolute war which Napoleon came the closest to reaching. Like the revolutionary cockades of France, the Islamic State fastens its black flags to anything it can: police cars, ambulances, traffic cops, bureaucrats, even in its nursing homes.[xlix] The Revolutionaries rewrote history, designing a new calendar and outlawing legacy institutions like the Church. The Islamic State recently destroyed a local, older version of France's *arc de triomphe*, rewriting history with bombs rather than laws. ISIS is not a vanguard of eventual societal revolution as is al Qaeda. It is the revolution.

This trend towards an attempted application of absolute war along with the apocalyptic vision of the Islamic State (a vision shared by, among others, Abu Musab al-Suri) is a worrying development. ISIS has taken jihadi military strategy the along the spectrum towards absolute war. They have adopted ideas of their predecessors and rejected others while learning from their mistakes and failures. Whether the Islamic State ultimately succeeds or fails, they have pushed the envelope of jihadi military strategy to heretofore unprecedented heights and those that come after them will go even further. The overriding concern for policymakers then must be that the Islamic State and similar groups do not under any circumstances acquire weapons of mass destruction as their rationality after such an acquisition is unpredictable. Furthermore, a simplistic strategy of attrition—whether of Islamic State fighting cadres or their leadership—will be ineffective due to both the decentralized nature of their organization inherited from al Qaeda and the obvious fervor of their adherents, exemplified by their self-professed "love of death." Lastly, it is no mystery that a central pillar of jihadi strategy is their goal of drawing the United States into intractable conflicts that expend its blood and treasure. Why the United States has walked into this trap is the only mystery.

Chapter 25

Friday the 13th in Paris

G. Murphy Donovan

First Published 16 November 2015

"The influence of the (Islamic) religion paralyzes the social development of those who follow it."
—Winston Churchill

Islamic fanatics struck another blow for cynicism last Friday night in Paris; wholesale and gratuitous slaughter in the name of some sanguinary Muslim god. History teaches few lessons these days.

We say "Muslim" god because most other religions forsook ritual religious slaughter centuries ago. Indeed, the nearest historical comparison is actually political. Before contemporary *jihad*, the Nazis were the last imperial movement to use industrial scale pogroms to underwrite an ideological message. Ironically, the EU now opens its borders to religious fascism[1], more virulent than the political strain that led to the Holocaust and associated carnage of WWII. Angela Merkel[2] and the European Union do the ironic walk of shame here.

Alas, any distinction between politics and religion in a Muslim context is now moot. Politics are mostly religious in the *Ummah* and dystopic religion seems to be the only relevant politics permissible in much of the Muslim world.

Indeed, the irony is compound. The most egregious exporters of religious hate and sharia bigotry are putative EU/American "partners;" or allies; i.e. Pakistan, Afghanistan, Arabia, and Persia. Withal, Europe and America are fatally impaled on the horns of the Shia/Sunni dilemma—by choice. Judeo/Christian tolerance now has all the earmarks of a suicide pact. Body counts, as Stalin prophesied, are now just another statistic.

Indeed, Islam today is both sword and shield. Terror strikes and then retreats to sanctuary under a burka of global religious immunities. Somehow the larger bovine Muslim majority has no moral or civic responsibility for terrorists, passive aggressors (nee moderates), or those unassimilated and indigestible Muslim refugees. The EU and America are paralyzed by guilt and restraint that has no meaning for Muslim shooters and bombers. The new law of international war is now made by religious zealots while the "best" in the West assume the defensive crouch of infidel catamites.

In the after-orgy of post-Paris apologetics, few western leaders dared to mention Islam, Islamism, or the global *jihad*. The enemy is still the undifferentiated local, militant, terrorist, or criminal as if the ideology or motive that binds them all doesn't matter. In the not too distant past, the threat was atomized as local phenomena like Black September, *Fatah*, *Hamas*, *al Qaeda*, or *Boko Haram*. The flavor of Islam *du jour* at the moment is ISIS or the Islamic state.

No matter the body count or venue, Europe and America refuse to recognize *jihad* as a global Islamic assault. And as with the Charlie Hebdo atrocity, the best response that Francois Hollande and France can muster now is a karaoke *Marseillaise,* a knee-jerk hymn[3] to irrelevant if not discredited notions of *liberté, égalité,* and *fraternité*.

Fey responses to terror are now routine in the West. Call it cultural appropriation. Summary executions are accepted by Islamist butcher and infidel victim alike. Atrocity has been routinized, now hallmarks of 21st Century practices in the East and tolerance in the West. Suicide bombers and their victims are joined by the same moral vacuity. The former have no moral compass and the latter are loath to exert any prudence.

Excuses[4] are epidemic. Bernie Sanders on the looney Left actually believes that global warming[5] and ISIS are wingmen. The Sanders pronouncement is of a piece with team Obama's flawed assessments where ISIS has been described as the "junior varsity."

Exaggerating a threat might be a no lose hedge but underestimating an existential threat can be fatal. Just ask Paris.

Maybe Parisians should build a monument to terror too as New York and Washington did after the Saudi Muslim attack against lower Manhattan and the Pentagon. Appeasement, withal, seems to be the new deterrence.

For those with the attention span to notice, global Islamic terror is the most obvious symptom that globalization is not working. Democratic civility and "one-world" comity are not ascending stars, especially in the Muslim world. Societies that venerate 7th Century absolutist monoculture[6] or cult prophets are impervious to fact or reason—much less democracy.

With the possible exception of Kurdistan and a few of the former Soviet Muslim republics, the *Ummah* is morphing into universal dystopic theocracy.

The quest for Islamic monoculture is facilitated by three trends: a weak or indecisive West, dishonest assessments[7] of the threat, and a generation of leaders in the West who fail to appreciate or defend the virtue, indeed, superiority of their own culture. Indeed, of the three, the most pernicious is the last, the notion that all cultures and religious beliefs are morally equivalent.

Culture is the synergistic interplay of positive national values which allow independence, civility, cooperation, tolerance, and peaceful productivity. None of these virtues can be attributed to most of the Muslim world today. Indeed, much of the *Ummah* is a cesspool of human depravities. Friday the 13th in Paris is just one of too many examples.

Days before the latest Paris slaughter, the President of the United States declared[8] unequivocally that ISIS had been "contained." Here again we have another triumph of false hope over experience. The White House, the Pentagon, and the American Intelligence Community still treat Islamism as a public relations problem to be "managed" largely with hyperbole, wishful thinking, and domestic mendacity. The Islamists win in places like New York, London, and Paris because they understand that real victories in real wars war come from the barrel of a gun—not the mouths of fools.

Huntington was correct; the "clash of civilizations"[9] is here. If the latest Muslim massacre in France does not underline that clash, it's difficult to imagine what kind of losses or atrocity might have to be endured to convince the West.

Immigration, nonetheless, is not the only Trojan horse in the Muslim kit. The pathologies of Islamic culture are well recorded at the expense of women, children, ethnic and non-Muslim minorities. Alas, there is no single Islamic Trojan horse; the phenomenon today is more like a diseased herd at full gallop. *Allahu akbar*!

Chapter 26

The Starfish Caliphate: How ISIL Exploits the Power of a Decentralized Organization

Stewart Welch

First Published 20 November 2015

Until recently, Islamic terrorist groups generally adapted themselves to one of two models. The first model was an underground resistance network that could appear anywhere and carry out spectacular attacks. This was Al Qaeda, who sought to inspire jihadists to their cause. The second model, used by groups like the Taliban, was hierarchal and geographically centered, but did little to recruit outside their location.

Today a hybrid has emerged, and that is ISIL. The recent Paris attacks demonstrate how they have managed to combine these two models to deadly effect. ISIL utilizes a leadership structure necessary to hold territory and implement Sharia law, but their real strength comes from an ability to operate as a decentralized network that helps them project power on the battlefield and in the information sphere.

In their 2006 book, *The Starfish and the Spid*er, Ori Brafman and Rod Beckstrom describe starfish organizations as those that survive without leadership. Centralized organizations are like spiders: cut off the head and the spider dies. Decentralized organizations are more like starfish, which multiply when you try to cut them to pieces. Groups like Napster, Wikipedia, or Alcoholics Anonymous have strength in their decentralized, leaderless nature. ISIL is a spider organization that acts like a starfish. It is a formidable challenge because it utilizes the power of the starfish and exploits advantages of decentralization, while maintaining a hierarchy of leadership. ISIL possesses aspects of all five legs of decentralization that are common to open system organizations:

1. *Circles*—Open networks thrive on circles of common community. ISIL has created circles of interest and support by using the internet and by sharing shocking videos of graphic executions on social media. These forums enable a virtual identity for any would-be jihadist. This has allowed ISIL to propagate their message and recruit tens of thousands of followers. It also allowed supporters and sympathizers to follow ISIL with a certain degree of anonymity, even if they are not actively participating. Thousands of disenfranchised Muslims living in Europe, the Middle East, and America have been inspired not only to support them, but also to move to Syria to be part of the new Caliphate.
2. *Catalyst*—Typically, a person initiates a movement and then steps aside to let it develop. However, in the case of ISIL the catalyst was an event: the *declaration* of a caliphate. The re-establishment of a Muslim caliphate has energized the jihadist imagination and sparked a flood of immigration to Iraq and Syria. This declaration put ISIL on the map as the premier Sunni Jihadist group, likely because no one had been so bold with words and actions until then. This went beyond killing Westerners, to challenging the entire world order and nation-state system.
3. *Ideology*—Justifying violence with Islamic texts is a core tenant of ISIL's ideology, and it is one of the most difficult aspects to counter. ISIL reads in the Quran and Hadith an obligation to

subjugate or kill anyone who does not share their narrow views, including fellow Muslims. They are also apocalyptic, stressing end-times theology far more than Al Qaeda ever did. Muslims must challenge and correct these interpretations, and non-Muslims must reject ISIL's actions without alienating the vast majority of the Muslim world who do not share this perspective.

4. *Pre-existing Network*—Al Qaeda in Iraq operated for years before it morphed into what is now ISIL. Members exploited an already existing network of Bath'ists from Iraq. The U.S.-run Camp Bucca detainee prison in Iraq was a training ground for future ISIL members detained there during 2004-2005. Abū Bakr al-Baghdādi was a leading organizer in that prison. He went on to capitalize on Sunni grievances against corrupt Shia governance in Baghdad to cast ISIL as the people's choice. Without this pre-existing network, it is doubtful that ISIL would have organized and spread their message so effectively.

5. *Champion*—Abū Bakr al-Baghdādi declared the world-wide Muslim Caliphate on 29 June 2014, which energized the movement. He elevated the plight of Sunni Muslims against the West to a degree above the nation-state system, realizing dreams of a caliphate that has been absent since Attaturk abolished it in 1924. Al Baghdadi is the advocate who started the movement and then took a relative back seat to allow it to flourish.

While ISIL fits the criteria for a starfish organization, it still maintains a hierarchical structure among members of the Caliphate in Iraq and Syria. Brafman and Beckstrom call this a hybrid organization, but ISIL is far more of a starfish than a spider. Many of the strategies suggested to stop them will be ineffective or counterproductive altogether because they fail to address the decentralized nature of the threat.

"Pull them up by the roots"—Some favor deploying an overwhelming military force to Syria and Iraq to defeat ISIL. This might work initially, but the networked nature of the organization will allow it to re-spawn elsewhere. The question of 'what next' in Syria also lingers,

and this has kept us from pursuing an open-ended course of action, and wisely so. This military-centric option leaves the underlying ideology unaddressed, and it plays into their hand. A Western invasion is precisely what ISIL wants, because it would realize their jihadist fantasies of a grand apocalyptic battle with the Western forces in Dabiq, Syria that will supposedly bring about the end days. Fighting the apocalyptic battle would only encourage, bolster its recruitment efforts, and incite sympathizers or would-be soldiers to conduct lone-wolf attacks.

Decapitation—Some advocate killing leadership, but this will be ineffective as well. It is highly unlikely that killing Baghdadi would trigger the collapse of the caliphate, because the movement is not dependent on his personality. The hydra does not die, it just grows another head. The starfish limb grows into another starfish. While hierarchical leadership is necessary to manage a pseudo-state earning millions of dollars a day in oil revenue and implementing sharia law over large swaths of territory, targeting that structure will only slow them down at best. A decentralized movement that has already catalyzed is not dependent on leadership. Al Quaeda did not collapse after UBL was killed, and much less so the Islamic state. In fact, Baghdadi's death will function as a martyrdom and further catalyze the group to push to achieve the Caliphate and its preexisting goals.

Don't worry, the world has never been safer—Some argue that ISIL is not a vital U.S. national interest because they are effectively a problem 'over there'. The Paris attacks demonstrate how they are metastasizing, and how this threat has no effective borders. The Islamic state has already established "providences" in Egypt, Libya, Algeria, Nigeria, Yemen, Russian Caucuses and the Philippines. They are taking their brutality to Europe by cultivating support through a rapidly growing population of disenfranchised Muslim refugees. This expansion North exemplifies how disaggregated and decentralized ISIL has become. Labeling them a peripheral national interest is a mistake that will eventually cost innocent American lives.

While each of these strategies targets specific aspects of ISIL, none of them addresses all aspects of the organizational structure. These strategies fail to respond one of the primary successes, the ideology as spread by networked messaging and branding. Therefore, we must adapt our thinking in order to compete with this threat.

Renewed Focus on Counter-Messaging

Countering a starfish requires becoming one. As retired Gen Stanley McChrystal has stated, *it takes a network to defeat a network*. By definition, a transnational threat requires a coordinated transnational response. To counter the spread of ISIL messaging, we need to organize and synchronize messaging efforts among all groups, nations, and individuals who oppose their visceral, radicalized propaganda. This applies to kinetic as well as information operations. We must take this starfish thinking to the information sphere in order to defeat ISIL at their own game.

Creating an information infrastructure to prevent the spread of ISIL involves identifying ungoverned, under-governed, or refugee-laden areas where Islamic extremism is likely to spread. It also requires identifying and synchronizing governmental, religious, individuals to speak to those target populations about the dangers of this ideology, and the misery of living under their oppression. The more Muslim voices the better, since this is largely an internal Islamic dispute regarding how to best interpret Muslim texts. No group is more qualified to focus messaging efforts than moderate Muslims themselves.

ISIL's brutality disgusts everyone in the world, and that is to our advantage. The widespread rejection of their ideology and brutality establishes single unifying factor for multiple different groups and nations. Consider the fact that U.S., Sunni Gulf states, Iran, and Russia are actively fighting ISIL ideology and seek to limit their influence and expansion. We should use this confluence of interests to develop a multi-faceted information effort highlighting the dangers and moral bankruptcy of their ideology. Our unified message should focus on universal rejection of their oppressive and murderous worldview.

Our brand should be simple: *the whole world is against ISIL*. This requires connecting opposition voices and proactively messaging audiences that are susceptible to this toxic ideology. By multiplying nodes, sharing counter-messaging information and focusing our efforts, the international community will become a more expansive, diverse network than the jihadist sympathizers can muster.

These efforts to coordinate messaging are currently underway, but networks take time to develop. The sheer number of nations, groups and individuals that reject ISIL is an untapped advantage that we need to exploit. Messaging alone will not solve the problem, but it is a critical aspect to countering any decentralized organization fueled by an ideology of violence. Peaceful, freedom-loving people around the world will be dealing with this threat for generations. We need to start to see ourselves as a bigger, stronger starfish with more tentacles and a far greater reach than our enemy.

This article represents the author's views and not necessarily the views of the U.S. Air Force or Department of Defense.

Chapter 27

Jihadist Narratives: Democratized Islam and Islamic Nation Building

Caleb S. Cage

First Published 10 December 2015

The driving storyline of extremist Islam, often referred to simply as the Narrative, states that the West and its allies are continuing in a historical effort to destroy Islam. More particularly, the Narrative states that the U.S., Israel, and puppet Islamic leaders, are continuing the historic efforts of outsiders conspiring to eradicate, exploit, and humiliate Muslims. That some westerners view this proof that jihadists are freedom fighters and others bristle at this characterization does not matter: variations on the Narrative are some of the most powerful tools wielded against the West by extremist Islam, providing a common ideological reference point, powerful recruitment tools, and justification for their violence.

A cursory examination of the literature of extremist Islam reveals overt references to the Narrative. In his 1996 manifesto, *A Terrorist's Call to Global Jihad*, Abu Musa'ab al-Suri states, "the modern Crusader-Jewish, American-led campaign against the Arab and Islamic world has clearly announced its goals: total elimination of the civilizational, religious, political, economic, social, and cultural existence of Muslims." In his 1996 *fatwa*, as translated in *Princeton Readings in Islamist Thought*, "Declaration of War Against the American Occupying the Land of the Two Holy Places," Osama bin Laden writes:

> It is no secret that the people of Islam have suffered from aggression, iniquity, and injustice imposed on them by the Zionist-Crusaders alliance and their collaborators, to the point where Muslim blood has become the cheapest and their wealth as loot in the hands of the enemies.

But it is not only in the writings of the major jihadist leaders that you find the Narrative. Through invoking it through mass communication, the Narrative has come to permeate parts of the broader Islamic worldview. It is common in the media communications of extremist Islam and even in their abundant rumors.

Anti-terror leaders have long noted the importance of understanding and combating the Narrative in postmodern warfare. After the rise of the Islamic State of Iraq and Syria (ISIS) in 2015, President Obama addressed it directly, saying, "that narrative becomes the foundation upon which terrorists build their ideology and by which they try to justify their violence," as he outlined a plan to defeat the Narrative through a campaign that includes counterterrorism operations, social media, and encouraging Islamic clerics to weigh in. Shaykh Abdullah bin Bayyan, a prominent but controversial Islamic scholar, was among the first to issue a *fatwa* against ISIS in late 2014, which some have seen as a step toward an effort to weaken the narrative over time.

Scholars and strategists have examined the sources of the Narrative's power for years, but to limited measurable outcome. Extreme Islam remains active and aggressive; the reform movement within Islam remains unpersuasive; and the U.S. and its allies remain as much on the brink of war as they were in 2001 before they invaded two Islamic nations bent on democratization.

In his *Atlantic* essay, "What ISIS Really Wants," Graeme Wood asserts that two key misunderstandings of the Islamic State are the reasons for the West's failures. The first error, Wood writes, is that "we tend to see jihadism as monolithic" when it really consist of many factions. Second, and specific to ISIS, Wood asserts that westerners are misled by a "well-intentioned but dishonest campaign to deny the Islamic State's medieval religious nature."

Wood's assertion that extremist Islamic groups have diverse ideologies and strategic goals is a crucial first step. Although his focus is ISIS, he alludes to a major difference between ISIS and Al-Qaeda: where ISIS wishes to establish a Caliphate based on original Islam, Al-Qaeda has focused on a more amorphous goal of decentralized terrorism prosecuted through a global network. Stated differently, ISIS aims to establish a premodern state while Al-Qaeda aims toward a postmodern movement. Both rely on narratives to achieve their goals and to erode the modern political and religious barriers, respectively, they confront.

Scholars' efforts to understand and combat extreme Islamic narratives have yet to provide a full picture. The shortcomings in understanding narratives are precisely for the reasons Wood describes: they tend to view jihadism as monolithic, namely, that all jihadist organizations desire a geographic caliphate, and they fail to recognize that the extraordinary difference in strategic outcomes are driven by extremely different philosophical worldviews. In doing so, theses scholars have attempted to understand the narrative in modern or postmodern terms instead of applying those lenses to the various philosophical foundations of extremist groups.

The 2012 book, *Narrative Landmines: Rumors, Islamist Extremism, and the Struggle for Strategic Influence*, Daniel Bernardi and his co-authors examine Islamic narratives through their most basic element, rumors, while Jeffry Halverson and his co-authors study the hierarchy of narratives in their 2013 book, *Master Narratives of Islamist Extremism*. Both books largely agree that narratives operate rationally within formal frameworks and that they are used to achieve the jihadist goal of establishing a global caliphate. However, they disagree on nearly all the particulars, from whether narratives can be strategic tools to the appropriate use of modern or postmodern theories when understanding them.

Narrative Landmines studies how narratives manifest locally through rumor, and how rumor drives broader beliefs. For them, "rumor is a shorthand term for speculation, half-truths, and misinformation in the form of stories that, to some groups, appears to offer rational cause-and-effect explanations of events." Previous scholars argued that rumors are non-narrative in nature, an idea that these authors contest, arguing instead that rumors "are, in essence, local stories that participate in larger narrative systems that, given the right mix of cultural references and ideological formations, end up volatile when placed in the service of either an insurgent or counterinsurgent agenda." To them, rumors are actually "narrative IEDs," mimicking the cheap and effective tactical weapons insurgents use in Iraq and Afghanistan.

If rumors are tactical weapons, then they are most effective when they complement narratives used as strategic communications. In a broad sense, a narrative is "a system of interrelated stories that share common elements and a rhetorical desire to resolve a conflict by structuring audience expectations and interpretations." For their study of rumor in wartime, they define the concept as "a continuous process of understanding in which external data are constantly ordered and re-ordered into patterns that make sense to people." A "narrative landscape," then, is "a system of narratives" that refer "to the complex array of narratives that circulate within a specific social, economic, political, and mediated environment—the narrative context that gives rise to rumors and in which rumors compete for prominence."

Unlike rumors, narratives are comprised of stories, which they argue, "consist of sequences of events involving characters in setting and are recounted for rhetorical purposes." There are three components to stories that make them meaningful and understandable to audiences: archetypes, story forms, and master narratives. These components are crucial for successful narratives as they are derived from "larger cultural systems."

In narratives, archetypes represent easily identifiable shorthand for versions of people, places, and events the Muslim world has interacted with throughout history. They range from Tyrants and Hypocrites, to Crusaders and Colonizers, Martyrs and Champions, and include the oppressive Pharaohs of Egypt, to the Mongolian military leader Hulaga Khan, who sacked Baghdad in the 13th Century, and others. Archetypes act through story forms, or "recognizable patterns of storytelling that are easily comprehended because of their familiarity." Common story forms include Invasion, Noble Sacrifice, Reward, and Deliverance, which are intended to persuade the audience that they are an aggressed underdog, and dying and even killing for their cause is just. Master narratives move "across historical boundaries, resolving archetypal conflicts through established and literary and historical forms," and include the Crusades and Colonization, which depict westerners invading Muslim territories to "exert their political power to extract natural resources (Islamic wealth and property) from the rightful Muslim owners."

Master Narratives of Islamist Extremism provides an alternative understanding of narratives. Its proposed structure operates through "vertical integration" between three levels of narratives, with communication at the lowest level being more "concrete" and "manifest" and moving toward the more "abstract" and "latent" at the highest level. Vertical integration of narratives allows Islamic extremists to achieve their primary goals, which the authors refer to as resistance, rebuking, and renewal.

The rumors described in *Narrative Landmines* are most closely aligned with "personal narratives," or "systems of stories experience, remembered, and told by individuals." Personal narratives integrate with "master narratives," which the authors describe as "narratives whose component stories, by virtue of being widely shared and repeated across time, have become deeply embedded in a particular culture." The majority of their work is a detailed analysis of 13 master narratives that they have identified in extremist literature, including the Crusader and Hypocrites narratives.

Contrary to the central argument of *Narrative Landmines*, Halverson and his co-authors argue that master narratives are not strategic. Instead, master narratives combine "at the highest level of abstraction" to form a "rhetorical vision," which is similar to the "narrative landscape" defined in *Narrative Landmines*. A rhetorical vision uses story forms and archetypes to integrate "master narratives in an emotional and logical sense," providing common "resources for constructing personal narratives and developing goals for actions and behaviors."

While both sets of authors base their arguments on highly structured narrative models, they have opposite views when it comes to addressing modernism and postmodernism when understanding Islamic narratives. The authors of *Narrative Landmines* see modern rigidity as the fundamental source of the West's communications failures. Conversely, the authors of *Master Narrative of Extremist Islam* favor a decidedly modern approach.

The authors of *Narrative Landmines* provide important analysis of the concept of objective truth in wartime rumors. "The standard in rumor studies has been for many years to define, and thus study, a 'rumor' as information or belief about a situation that is of dubious veracity, a statement that does not meet 'secured standards of evidence,'" they write. "Although dubious veracity and unclear origins are central characteristics of rumors, an overemphasis on veracity and truth claims isolates rumors categorically, rather than recognizing their impact and dynamic functions, especially with regard to strategic communications contexts."

Instead, they call for rumors to "be understood in their cultural contexts." This means that "the truth of a situation presented to any given individual has more to do with how that individual organizes available data than any objective and idealized 'truth.'" It is the primary function of narratives, therefore, "to make sense of that body of data," which narratives do by offering "a means of uniting culturally provided templates to include story forms and archetypes with data such as stories, rumors, histories, and the like." In the end, "'truth' becomes less about facts and evidence and more about coherence with pre-existing and prevailing understandings." This is a postmodern understanding of rumor and narrative, making them a highly subjective force that actively deconstructs modern structures and beliefs.

Master Narratives of Extremist Islam builds its case for a modern understanding of narrative on a modern understanding of Islam. In modern Islam, they argue, being able to "quote extensively from the Qu'ran by memory creates an aura of knowledge and piety in a speaker and establishes a hierarchical position that situates the speaker apart from (or above) the audience on the basis of his or her knowledge of the sacred text, infusing or encoding his or her words with transcendent authority." Modern Islam allows those in higher positions to dispense doctrine and adjudicate legal matters in accordance with the various sacred texts of Islam.

Islam's master narratives, then, "are thoroughly 'modern' (in a macro sense) and their ideological uses are definitively 'modernist.'" They concede that "some readers may ask why [they] are relying on elements of modernist notions of narrative" when so many in their field have "moved beyond modernist conceptions like 'master narratives'" to understand the way narratives work. They respond that "while postmodern theories may well represent attractive resources for how we might learn to *counter* extremist arguments (in the same ways that postmodern theories provide rich textual resources to counter modern conceptions of narratives) it is vital to remember that Islamist extremists emphasize the articulation of 'transcendent' values derived from a 'grand' or authoritative text."

These distinctions highlight the shortcomings of these works, which are the same shortcomings proposed by Wood. First, they view Islamic terror organizations as a monolith, at the very least implying that they all seek the establishment of an Islamic Caliphate. Second, central to both works are misapplications of the modern and postmodern lenses to the narratives themselves. Narratives should simply be seen as tools used to achieve the different strategic goals of organizations like ISIS and Al-Qaeda. Because modernity and post-modernity describe philosophical foundations, these lenses are better applied to understanding the organizations and to their movements.

In an article entitled, "A Tale of Two Jihads: the Al-Qaeda and ISIS Narratives[1]," Naureen Chowdhury Fink and Benjamin Sugg suggest that this monolithic understanding of extremist Islamic organizations is understandable due to their many surface similarities. Through their examination of the official publications of Al-Qaeda and ISIS, *Inspire* and *Dabiq*, respectively, they note that both organizations demand jihad from all Muslims and that they rely on the broad use of the Narrative to justify their actions. However, beyond those surface similarities, Al-Qaeda and ISIS have vastly different "ultimate aims," which are reflected by the narratives that they generate.

The authors identify the driving narratives found in Al-Qaeda's *Inspire* revolve around three recurring themes. First, the magazine glorifies "militant activities and terrorism"; second, *Inspire* provides a "DIY guide for weaponry"; and third, it encourages "'lone wolf' acts of terror by individuals that can have absolutely no formal association with Al-Qaeda." All of the elements of Al-Qaeda's narrative appear to empower independent, uncoordinated action toward achieving Bin Laden's one-time goal of a "defensive jihad, a battle to promote and protect the *Ummah*, or global Muslim community, from the onslaught from the West."

Unlike Al-Qaeda's narrative, the authors show that ISIS's narrative revolves around a centralized, organized plan for the establishment of a formal Islamic State. *Dabiq* calls for support of the Caliphate through appealing "to doctors, engineers, and professionals to make *hijrah* (migration) in order to assist the construction of an Islamic government," the authors write. It also advances the narrative of political Islam by highlighting the type and level of "social services, defense, and dignity" that Muslims will be able to enjoy once protected from by the newly-established Caliphate.

These strategic differences between ISIS and Al-Qaeda complement their philosophical differences. ISIS is driven by a pre-modern worldview toward the establishment of a pre-modern, medieval Caliphate, while

Al-Qaeda is driven by a postmodern worldview toward the facilitation of perpetual global jihad. Narratives play a key role within these strategic and philosophical frameworks, with ISIS using narratives to replace the constraints of modern political constructs, and Al-Qaeda using narratives to replace the constructs of modern Islamic jurisprudence and doctrine to justify their actions as Islamic.

If ISIS's strategic objective is the establishment of a premodern Caliphate, then it is akin to movements political Islam, the greatest distinction being ISIS's reliance on a premodern worldview. Regimes within Islamic states have long used official or national narratives to rally their people in support of their vision for the future, to rise up against continued enemies and challenges, or both. In her book, *Official Stories: Politics and National Narratives in Egypt and Algeria*, Dr. Laurie Brand studies the creation, evolution, and circulation of these narratives, and in a subsequent essay, she argues that ISIS has already developed similar national narratives.

According to Brand, national narratives are the nation's story as it is told and understood by the people. They amount to the nation's collective social, ethnic, religious, and cultural identity, especially as they relate to the nation's understanding of its story through historic trials, victories, enemies, and heroes. They establish legitimacy to rule for the regime, and once implemented, regimes can select and shape elements of their national narrative to adapt to the current challenges the regime faces.

"No political leader or elite, even in authoritarian states, rules solely through the threat of coercive violence," Brand writes. Additionally, they require "some level of support, or at least acquiescence, from the people over whom they rule." This support is often developed not entirely through formal levers of power like the military, the courts, and other institutions, but through "less tangible elements" organized in a "complex configuration of values, customs, political principles, and social relations accepted throughout society and its institutions at a given historical moment."

According to Brand, attempts by regimes to control these variables have often come from the efforts to control public discourse, especially as they attempt to establish official narratives. They can be seen in a regime's investment in cultural productions, such as plays and literature, through asserting control over educational texts, through speeches, policy programs, charter documents, or other official statements. Brand places the use of official narratives by states or state actors within the literature of propaganda, which historically has been effectively used to shape public opinion in times of crisis.

Establishing a national identity and unity are major goals of national narratives, but Brand argues that they are not desired ends. Regimes use narratives to establish their legitimacy, which she describes as "the process by which a leadership secures the people's acknowledgement of its right to rule." This process is accomplished through using narrative by obscuring their "state-building efforts intended to serve the citizenry in general," on one hand, and policies intended to sustain and reinforce the regime's hold on power, on the other. Without linking the interests of the people with the actions in support of sustaining the regime's power, Brand argues, "a key part of the narrative's legitimizing project will fail."

If such a linkage is created through national narratives, then the regime is able rely on the narrative to rally support for their vision for governance. That is, by establishing themselves as legitimate leaders, the regime can further legitimize their "guiding ideology and the policies that flow from it." By fitting their current existential threats or challenges into their established national narratives, regime leaders can further use narratives to provide the populace with a rationale for their personal responsibility to their nation, and "exhorting the people to serve, protect, and even die for them."

While *Official Stories* is exclusively about the use of national narratives by Egypt and Algeria in the 20th Century, it also provides a remarkable overview of how and why Islamic states have circulated official narratives to establish their legitimacy and build their nations. Because ISIS is a derivative of political Islam, her argument regarding the use of national narratives found in *Official Stories* can be applied as well. Brand does exactly this in a piece in the *Washington Post*, entitled "The Islamic State and the politics of official narratives[2]," written only a few months after the establishment of the Islamic State was declared in 2014.

Brand argues here that the earliest actions of ISIS suggest that they are poised to develop a national narrative to legitimize their own government and build a case for national unity around the concept of a pre-modern Caliphate. Brand points out that ISIS established "its first major seat of power" in Mosul, Iraq, where "the basic institutions of its nascent state can be most effectively observed." These institutions consist broadly of the basic civil services aligned with the tenants of Islam: prisons and courts, mechanisms for complaints and tax collection, and even "morality patrols" intended to ensure that the populace lives up to *sharia* law.

In addition to these formal efforts, Brand also notes an early move by ISIS to establish the criteria for "legitimate education." Examining an August 2014 release from the Islamic State's Bureau of Curriculum entitled, "General Directive to all Educational Institutions," Brand analyzes ISIS's efforts to establish the initial model for educational instruction under the Islamic State. According to the directive's first order, schools should immediately remove from their curriculum all training in humanities subjects, such as music, art, civics, social studies, and history, but also in mathematics and religious studies, to include Christian and Islamic education. Brand notes that the directive allows for these subjects to be replaced, which she concludes to mean "what is underway is not the wholesale abolition of most courses of study, but rather the first stage in a massive reworking of the curriculum."

This reworked curriculum will establish a new national narrative for the Islamic State. This new narrative will "'correct' the history and mission promulgated by the former colonial power" and in its place, "an heroic story would be constructed, aimed at building a unified national identity, establishing the vision of that nation, and – crucially – consolidating power through reinforcing the regime's legitimacy to rule." Specifically, the directive calls for the reworked curriculum to replace national symbols and identities with Islamic ones, to remove photographs that defy *sharia*, and to replace references to evolution with attributing all acts of creation to Allah.

These early actions, especially when combined with the Islamic State's expressions of violence, can fairly easily be seen as efforts to legitimize a conservative, authoritarian, pre-modern state. However, they should also be seen as efforts to delegitimize and erode support for competing modern political structures and practices through actions that directly support their narrative. In addition to those cited above, they have reportedly commandeered oil production facilities in order to sell the commodity and fund their efforts; they appear to continually disregard global treaties and practices by exacting a ransom for foreign hostages, and even murdering some on video for the largest response; and, Brand points out, ISIS has destroyed the border crossing between Syria and Iraq, "which the Islamic State framed in terms of overturning the legacy of Sykes-Picot, demonstrated its ideological rejection of existing state boundaries as it extended its own realm." Unlike other Islamic nations determined to gain legitimacy through establishing and using national narratives, inherent within the ISIS narrative and actions is the message that it cannot exist alongside competing practices, beliefs, or even states.

Unlike ISIS, Al-Qaeda's objective is maintaining a disruptive global jihadist movement. In order to accomplish this, Al-Qaeda has applied a form of postmodern thought to Islam, deconstructing Islam's authority structure and replacing it with a more subjective and democratized forms. Though it is not a formal study of narratives, Al-Qaeda's postmodern form of Islam is explored in great detail in Faisal Devji's book, *Landscapes of the Jihad: Militancy, Morality, Modernity*.

Landscapes of the Jihad draws a significant distinction between political Islam and global jihad, though because it was written in 2005 it does not consider the rise of ISIS. To Devji, political Islamists aim to create a geographic Caliphate, while global jihadists aim to create a metaphysical one. Within the deconstructed Islam of global jihadist movements like Al-Qaeda, narratives have replaced traditional Islamic doctrine as the central authority of Islam, and are also used to justify their tactics.

Although Devji never uses the term "postmodern," his argument suggests that he is referring to a deconstructed Islam created through efforts by global jihadists to "wrest the jihad away from the juridical language of the state and make it a strictly individual duty that is more ethical than political in nature." Global jihadists have focused on the "destruction of the traditional forms and distinctions of Islamic authority," which has resulted in "the democratization of such authority among all manner of groups as well as individuals." Decrees and decisions once dictated by Islamic doctrinal and juridical authorities are now "given over to individual rather than collective examination."

The fragmentation of traditional Islam influences the structure and language of the movement as well. Instead of Islamic groups committed to political change, the jihad has instead provided an umbrella cause and organizational structure for various groups and various interests, creating an "extraordinarily diverse membership, one that is not united by way of any cultic or ideological commonality, to say nothing about that of class, ethnicity or personal background." For Devji, global jihad operates almost exclusively as a loosely affiliated network, diminishing the centrality of the Arabic culture and language, and has even replaced traditional Islamic architectural references like Islam's five pillars with Sufi imagery.

As with all forms of postmodern philosophy, this entails rejecting claims to objective truth and claiming instead a necessary tolerance for the individual or subjective truth experienced by others. Devji addresses this directly, claiming, "militant Sunnism has abandoned the theological disputes of the past, based as these were on differing claims to the truth, and adopted a democratic narrative of enmity instead." By this he means "it is no longer arguments about truth that animate such militants, only a desire for the recognition and respect of their neighbors, who are accused of insulting their sanctities while at the same time claiming to be fellow Muslims."

Although Devji does not go into great detail into what he means by jihadists adopting a "democratic narrative of enmity," his assertion here is at the center of his disagreement with the authors of *Master Narratives of Islamist Extremism* and *Narrative Landmines*. To these authors, narratives are defined as important communications tools used to drive their fellow believers toward an Islamic state. But to the global jihadists, narratives have replaced Islam's fundamental objective truths. They are used to explain the world in terms that are aligned with the Narrative, but that are interpreted subjectively by the individual jihadist.

This subjective interpretation is available because of a belief in mystical engagement with the divine allows leaders of the global jihad to interface directly with God. "Everything we know about Al-Qaeda as a religious movement compares favorably with Sufi or mystical brotherhoods," Devji writes, "even if these happen to be disapproved of by members of the movement itself." This results in a significant reliance on the occult, on dreams as direct contact with God, and a view of Al-Qaeda's leaders as a type of Prophet archetype "as spiritual authorities endowed with a grace that is unrelated to bookish learning of the kind that would mark a traditional cleric or even a fundamentalist." This not only provides an easy way to circumvent the traditional authorities of Islam, but is also an enhancement to a democratized Islam in that it is used to reinforce the personal and ethical expectations of postmodern Islam.

Deconstructed Islam coincided perfectly with the new media age, Devji argues, with the Internet allowing beginners to have the same voice as established authorities. The new media age also assists in making the jihad available globally and impossible to ignore. Devji argues that, for most, the jihad "is experienced visually, as a landscape initially made available by way of the international media and then redacted in conversations, posters, literature, art-work" and so on. Acts of jihad are the primary visual associated with the religion, and through these depictions, "the jihad's battlefields become sites of a global Islam." This media focus on Islam's violence not only drives jihadist attention and resources, but it also creates a new standard of personal and ethical Islam and unites "Muslims and non-Muslims alike in a common visual practice."

Devji argues that this media dynamic within global jihad creates a universal, metaphysical caliphate, which is the ultimate goal for global jihadists. Through media representations of jihad, a "generic Muslim" is created, "one who loses all cultural and historical particularity by his or her destruction as an act of martyrdom." This allows the jihad to achieve universality, allowing all viewers, even future martyrs, to experience the jihad in ways that are "entirely abstract and individual," allowing them "to break with locally available forms of Islamic authority." It also forces all who view martyrdom "into an ethical choice to support either its Muslim victims or their infidel oppressors—and all who make this choice are held responsible for it, having become participants in the jihad irrespective of their knowledge about its truth." That is, it is not the truth behind the cause of global jihad that requires its viewers to make this choice, but the "spectacle of martyrdom" itself.

It is this notion of truth within global jihad that clearly defines it as a postmodern movement, one that is made especially possible because of these new media characteristics. "Media images of martyrdom have no epistemological status," Devji writes, because truth is subjective and is never "a subject for discussion in the holy war." Truth, then, in true postmodern form, fits a similar definition for narratives provided in *Narrative Landmines*: it is subjective, self-referential, and ultimately as flexible as it needs to be to justify their tactics.

If it is true that ISIS is driven toward a Caliphate through a premodern philosophy and Al-Qaeda toward global jihad through a postmodern philosophy, then they are extraordinarily different organizations. It may be true that Al-Qaeda laid the groundwork for ISIS to exist and has since faded, but each organization's ongoing appeal cannot be understated. Because both have successful rallied followers to their causes through narratives, any future combination of their worldviews among extremist Islam will result in disastrous outcomes.

The Islamic State appears to be aggressively on the march. Western efforts to combat them through kinetic and non-kinetic means have yielded poor results, just as poor as the results from similar efforts to defeat Al-Qaeda. Though ISIS will certainly present a more static target than Al-Qaeda's loose network, definitive strategies remain elusive.

This could result in a dangerous new phase in the battle against extremist Islam. If ISIS continues to build its case against modern political structures in favor of a Caliphate, and the remnant of Al-Qaeda continues its efforts to strip modern Islam in favor of global jihad, then the West will be faced with a worst-of-both-worlds scenario, with ISIS providing a clear vision for the future of Islam and Al-Qaeda providing methods for individual involvement everywhere. Indeed, it appears that this melding is already well underway, and narratives are key to each effort.

Chapter 28

Justifying Jihad: A Case Study of Al-Shabaab and Boko Haram

Daniel Pesature

First Published 26 December 2015

Jihad—Today this ancient Arabic word has near universal recognition, but also near universal misunderstanding. In the non-Muslim world jihad erroneously conjures images of masked gunmen and televised beheadings. Fundamental misunderstanding relating to jihad are not confined to non-Muslims however. A perversion of Islam known as jihadi-salafism attempts to justify monstrous atrocities through the establishment of a pure Islamic State (Caliphate) and a return to the pristine version of Islam practiced in the age of the Rightly Guided Caliphs (Salaf).[i] Al Shabaab and Boko Haram are two jihadi-salafist groups that manipulate the tenets of jihad to justify violence on an immense scale. Their actions, and those of other jihadi-salafist groups, threaten to shape America's perception of Islam. At its core, jihadi-salafism is an ideological perversion, and the long-term solution is a counter narrative true to the tenets of Islam.

Drone strikes and commando raids will not solve this issue. The United States (US) must understand the problem of jihadi-salafism so that the policies it enacts do not alienate the vast majority of good, law-abiding Muslims. The cure cannot kill the patient. Islam is the antidote to the poison of jihadi-salafism. Al Shabaab and Boko Haram both manipulate Islamic law (Sharia) to justify their jihads in Somalia and Nigeria. They use genuine transgressions like the collapse of order, foreign invasion, corruption, and oppression to sanction cruel, primal, reciprocal violence. Analyzing the false jihads of Al Shabaab and Boko Haram provides a window into the minds of jihadi-salafists, and it also offers recommendations on countering this spreading and imminent threat.

Sharia regulates jihad. Sharia is far more than a criminal code, as it influences every aspect of Muslim life. Sharia is mainly derived from the Quran and from the sayings or actions of the Prophet Muhammed (Hadith). The Quran is best divided into two sections: the Meccan period (before hijra), and the Medinan period (after hijra). The two periods are written with different perspectives, and there are often contradictions. The Quran is contextual. It is based on the specific enemies and situations present during the time of Muhammad.[ii] The Hadith provide even less clarity. Some Hadith were recorded in the time of Muhammad, while others were recorded much later. Islamic scholars (ulama) loosely codify the numerous Hadiths based on strength, veracity, probably authenticity, and consensus (ijma).

In the past, the ulama could also apply reasoning (ijtihad) to the Quran and Hadith, but in the ninth century the Abbasid Caliphate proclaimed that all pertinent guidance was extracted from these sources and closed the gates of ijtihad. Today the ulama can only consult the Quran, Hadith, and prior rulings to reach ijma and issue a religious ruling (fatwa). It is difficult for the ulama to apply dated sources and interpretations to the situations of a modern, globalized world. For example, there is a Hadith that forbids women from traveling one day's travel without a male escort. During the age of reasoning, the ulama's ijma was that this distance could not exceed fifty miles. In the modern age, however, a woman can travel that distance in less than an hour by car and in mere minutes by plane.[iii] Jihad originates from Sharia, and like Sharia it can be misinterpreted or misapplied in the modern age.[iv]

Jihad is derived from the Arabic root that means to struggle or strive in the service of God. War is not simply jihad and jihad is not simply war.[v] There is the greater jihad and the lesser jihad. The greater jihad is the ever-raging battle within the hearts and minds of all Muslims to stay true to the teachings and tenets of Islam. This greater jihad was called the "jihad of the tongue" because Muslims were ideologically struggling to overcome disbelief (kufr) and polytheism (shirk). Muhammad stressed the importance of greater jihad repeatedly throughout the Quran. Muhammad stated, "The best struggle is to struggle against your soul."[vi] The greater jihad is a peaceful jihad, and it is the most esteemed version of jihad in the Quran.[vii]

The lesser jihad dominates the headlines today. This jihad is war, albeit war in the name and service of God. The Quran emphasizes order because Islam is a communal religion and cannot thrive in chaos.[viii] Accordingly, strict laws govern the violence inherent in lesser jihad. [ix] Only the legitimate ruler of an Islamic State can declare jihad.[x] Jihad, however, cannot create an Islamic State because only an Islamic State can sanction jihad in the first place. Muhammad did not use the force of arms to establish the Islamic State in Medina. God provided for the peaceful establishment of this Islamic State through the Charter of Medina.[xi]

The Quran advises Muslim leaders on the criteria for jihad, and the intended audience is not every Muslim.[xii] Jihad must restore order and provide justice. If this is not the purpose of jihad, then it is just violent anarchy which the Quran forbids.[xiii] Furthermore, a just end can never be achieved through unjust means. Muhammad Tahir Al Qadri, the founder of Minhaj Al Quran International and a fierce opponent of extremism, preaches pure acts for pure goals. A Muslim cannot finance the construction of a mosque by robbing a bank.[xiv]

Islam prefers order to chaos, even if that order is not perfect. Jihad to overthrow rulers is extremely difficult to justify. Muslims who live in non-Muslim societies cannot use jihad to overthrow non-Muslim rulers who do not implement Sharia. A non-Muslim ruler who protects the religious rights of Muslims and does not force them to act against Sharia cannot face jihad.[xv] The Quran advocates peace and dialogue in the face of oppressive rulers. Muhammad said, "The best jihad is a true word spoken in the presence of a tyrannical ruler."[xvi] God granted Muhammad permission to wage jihad only after he migrated to Medina and the Meccans pursued him.[xvii] Quranic verse 22:39 is the first verse that approves violence. It reads, "Permission is given to those who are fought against," but it comes only after seventy previous verses forbidding violence.[xviii]

It also difficult to justify jihad through claims of disbelief. In Islam there is a huge difference between disbelief and sin. The Quran advises all Muslims to assume sin and let God be the judge of disbelief. Anything short of a public denouncement of Islam fails to justify a jihad to overthrow a Muslim ruler, and an uprising against a non-Muslim ruler is only permissible jihad if that ruler blatantly oppresses the practice of Islam. For example, if a Muslim ruler announces publicly that Ramadan is forbidden, then that is disbelief and worthy of jihad. However, if that ruler simply fails to fast, then that is laziness and merely sinful.[xix]

There are many additional laws that control that conduct of jihad. The false jihad of the Islamic State flies in the face of true and legitimate jihad. Massacres on the streets of Paris, suicide bombings in Beirut, and pressing captured Yezidi girls into sexual slavery are not jihad. Muhammad set the precedent for true jihad during the conflicts of the Medinan period and the Quran clearly demarcates these rules.[xx] Sharia prohibits the killing of the elderly, sick, women, or children. The deliberate destruction of animals or fruit producing trees is also forbidden. The Quran specifically inhibits the mistreatment of prisoners, the mutilation of fallen enemy warriors, and reneging on treaties or agreements.

Saladin is perhaps the most accepted exemplification of righteous jihad in Islamic history, excluding the Prophet. Saladin waged a defensive jihad at the behest of a legitimate Muslim ruler to regain the holy city of Jerusalem. In 1099 Christian Crusaders sacked Jerusalem and put the Muslim residents to the sword. Saladin avenged this conquest, and reconquered Jerusalem, in 1187. Saladin, however, followed the tenets of jihad and spared the Christian inhabitants of the city. The wives and daughters of killed Crusaders even asked for his mercy, which he granted by giving them gifts, money, and protection.[xxi] Saladin honored all treaties, truces, and agreements with the Crusaders and ensured that prisoners were treated in accordance with Sharia.[xxii] Saladin is considered the standard in Islam for just, righteous jihad.

The jihads of Al Shabaab and Boko Haram do not live up to Saladin's standard. The jihadi-salafists today use Al Qaeda's interpretation of jihad, which stems from the Wahhabism of Saudi Arabia. The gradual exposure of Somalia and Nigeria to Wahhabism made their populations more susceptible to the militant tenets of jihadi-salafism. Saudi Arabia used their significant finances to export their particular strain of Islam. In the 1990's, Saudi Arabia provided over $70 billion to fund over 1500 mosques, 210 Islamic Centers, 202 Islamic Colleges, and roughly 2000 Islamic schools all over the Muslim world.[xxiii]

Al Shabaab's and Boko Haram's ideological ties to Wahhabism explain how fundamentalist jihadi-salafist groups sprung from the largely Sufi landscapes of Somalia and Nigeria. When Al Shabaab emerged in 2006 fully half of their eight-man Shura council were veterans who fought under Al Qaeda's banners in Afghanistan against the Soviets in the late 1980s.[xxiv] Boko Haram's origins stem from the ideological founder of the Salafist Izala movement in Nigeria, Sheikh Abubakar Gumi. Gumi worked in Saudi Arabia and established a network of Wahhabi financiers who bank rolled his Izala movement. Boko Haram's founder, Muhammad Yusut, was a former member of Izala.

The militant ideology of jihadi-salafism stretches back to the thirteenth century Islamic scholar Ibn Taymiyya. Ibn Taymiyya preached a return to the pure Islam of the Prophet, and he argued that a lack of Muslim piety caused the calamity of the Mongol invasion. Ibn

Taymiyya released a fatwa which stated that multiple emirates, or Islamic states, were permitted, and that each ruler could proclaim jihad.[xxv] Hassan Al Banna, the founder of the Muslim Brotherhood, brought Ibn Taymiyya's militant jihad into the twentieth century. Sayyed Qutb, Muhammad Abd Al Salam Faraj, and Abdullah Mawdudi continued to expand on this unique and controversial interpretation of jihad.[xxvi]

Abdallah Azzam merged the disparate militant interpretations into today's modern version. Azzam issued a fatwa in 1979 titled, "In Defense of Muslim Lands," that really championed the notion of non-state sanctioned jihad.[xxvii] He supported the claim that the famous "sword verse" of the Quran abrogated all the preceding verses which promoted peace. Azzam ushered in the age of Islamic terrorism by giving groups like Al Shabaab and Boko Haram the doctrine they needed to lay a false claim to justified jihad.

Azzam provided the Islamists in Somalia the ideological doctrine to wage jihad, but the iron regime of Said Barre prevented them from actually acquiring power. The complete collapse of order in 1991 provided the opening for the Islamist groups waiting on the periphery, Al Shabaab among them, to rise to prominence in Somalia. Al Shabaab existed as an organization long before they officially became a distinct group in 2006.[xxviii] The Sharia Islamic Courts Union (ICU) in Mogadishu served as an incubator for the fledgling group. The years following the collapse of the Barre regime were filled with chaos and corruption. Islam requires order to flourish, and Somalis were tired of the constant conflict. Somalis experiences the failures of authoritarianism, clannism, nationalism, socialism, and warlordism. The powerful and influential Mogadishu businessmen were especially desperate for order, and they turned to the Islamists.[xxix] The Sharia courts appeared in Mogadishu in 1998, and they merged in the street battles of 2006 to become the Islamic Courts Union.

The ICU, Al Shabaab, various militias, and the Transitional Federal Government (TFG) all controlled certain areas and neighborhoods of Mogadishu. Al Shabaab suddenly experienced the opportunity to govern and administer actual territory. The disparity in governance between Al Shabaab's area and the areas under the control of the TFG or militias quickly became apparent to the residents. The international community trained the majority of the TFG-militia members, but the Somali government lacked the resources to actually pay these fighters a fixed, predictable salary. As a result, these militia members preyed on the local population through corruption and extortion to acquire the fixed income that their government could not provide.[xxx] The TFG-militia forces alienated the people under their administration, and many of these people began to support Al Shabaab.

The price of Al Shabaab's order was far from cheap. Al Shabaab prevented theft and corruption, but in the process they altered the very fabric of daily life. They destroyed Sufi tombs and assassinated Sufi clerics under charges of heresy. Al Shabaab ruthlessly applied a draconian interpretation of Sharia law that was totally alien to the local population. Sheikh Abdallah Ali, a senior cleric in the ICU, release a fatwa in 2006 which stated, "He who does not perform prayers will be considered an infidel and Sharia law orders that person be killed."[xxxi] Somalis, however, were willing to pay Al Shabaab's price to eliminate corruption and chaos. A unanimous Somali man told the Human Rights Watch, "A human being always strives to get independence and freedom, but the Shabaab administration brought peace and stability."[xxxii] Al Shabaab initially justified their jihad by proclaiming that they reestablished order, stability, and rule of law.

The collapse of order gave Al Shabaab their initial opportunity, but foreign intervention enabled them to continuously justify their jihad. Al Shabaab played off traditional Somali xenophobia by claiming a defensive jihad, and by tying Somalia into the Muslim clash of civilization with the West. Ethiopia was wary of a potential Islamist state on their border, and they executed a relatively limited incursion into Somalia in 1996 to secure their borders. In December 2006, Ethiopia raised the stakes substantially by conducting a large-scale invasion to prevent the Islamists from conquering the TFG capital of Baidoa. Ethiopian forces proceeded to occupy parts of Mogadishu and Kismayo, two of the largest cities in Somalia. The African Union created the Somalia Mission (AMISOM) and deployed roughly 1,500 Ugandan troops to Mogadishu in March 2007. Kenya followed in 2011 with an additional deployment of troops. Meanwhile, the United States conducted near continuous drone strikes targeting Al Shabaab leadership.[xxxiii] Somalis watched as foreign forces poured into their homeland.

None of the forces that intervened in Somalia originated from Muslim majority countries, and these attacks enabled Al Shabaab to advertise a defensive jihad against infidel and apostate forces attacking Islam. The very fact that the TFG received support from Ethiopia and Kenya tainted them in the eyes of the Islamists and prevented any potential peace negotiations. In June 2006, the leader of the ICU, Sheik Hassan Dahir Aweys, said, "As long as Ethiopia is in our country, talks with the governmental cannot go ahead…if the government cares about the Somalis it should remove our enemy from the country."[xxxiv]

Foreign intervention justified Al Shabaab's jihad and provided a steady stream of recruits. Ethiopian forces followed a Soviet Doctrine which relied on heavy artillery bombardments. They adhered to this doctrine even when operating in the heavily populated urban areas of Mogadishu.[xxxv] These bombardments caused massive civilian casualties and collateral damage, and Al Shabaab stepped in to market themselves as defenders and avengers of Muslim blood. Consequently, the clans with the most exposure to Ethiopian forces provided the most recruits to Al Shabaab.[xxxvi]

Foreign intervention did more than justify the jihad in the eyes of Al Shabaab, it also changed the very nature of their jihad. In his book *Chechen Jihad,* Yossef Bodansky coined the term "Chechenization" to describe the process of jihadi-salafists co-opting a localized conflicts and steering it toward global objectives.[xxxvii] Today, Al Qaeda pursues this same objective when it seeks to "unify the jihad." Lorenzo Vidino applied this concept more directly to Somalia in his article, "Bringing Global Jihad to the Horn of Africa." Vidino uses the term "sacralization" to describe conflicts where religion goes from being irrelevant or secondary in the initial phases to becoming the driving force in the later phases.[xxxviii] Al Shabaab exploited the feeling within the broader Muslim community (ummah) that Islam was under siege worldwide from Somalia to Iraq, Palestine to Afghanistan to tie the struggle in Somalia into the conflicts raging across the Muslim world.[xxxix]

Al Shabaab worked with Al Qaeda to globalize the Somali jihad. In 2006, Usama Bin Laden released a video in which he called the TFG leader an "agent of foreign apostates," and promised the international community that all true Muslims would "fight your soldiers on the land of Somalia and will fight you on your own land if you dispatch troops to Somalia."[xl] The ideologue of Al Shabaab, Sheikh Shongola, released a statement in 2007 tying Al Shabaab to the struggles in Jerusalem, Gaza, Iraq, and Afghanistan.[xli] Muktar Robow, a key Al Shabaab leader, further embraced the concept of a global jihad when he said, "Al Qaeda is the mother of holy war in Somalia."[xlii]

Al Shabaab and the ICU did not share a vision for a global jihad, and this difference led to severe tensions. In their official magazine, *Millet Ibrahim*, Al Shabaab attacked the leader of the ICU for simple nationalism when they wrote, "He had a different opinion about Ethiopia and its war, and about America and its aggressiveness. Rather, he is nothing more than a Somali nationalist, pure and simple. The global jihad means nothing to him."[xliii] Al Shabaab altered the purpose of the Somali jihad by aligning it with the global aims of Al Qaeda. This alignment became official in 2012, when Al Shabaab formally merged with Al Qaeda. In truth, this merger simply formalized in name what was already occurring in practice.

The Somali ulama were slow to condemn Al Shabaab. In 2006, when Al Shabaab emerged, no one was really certain of their aspirations or intentions. Over time, Al Shabaab clearly demonstrated to the ulama that they were manipulating Islam and perverting the concept of jihad to help them consolidate power. On 12 September 2013, after years and years of wanton violence and bloodshed, 160 Somali ulama finally convened and released the first fatwa against Al Shabaab. This fatwa prohibited violence against the legitimate Somali government, joining or supporting Al Shabaab, and urged Somalis to fight the group. The fatwa stated, "Al Shabaab has strayed from the correct path of Islam, leading the Somali people onto the wrong path. The ideology they are spreading is a danger to the Islamic religion and the existence of the Somali society."[xliv] Al Shabaab confirmed the danger they posed only a week later when they stormed the West Gate Mall in Nairobi, Kenya and massacred dozens of innocent shoppers.

When Said Barre fled Somalia in 1999 he found sanctuary in Nigeria. The chaos and conflict for which Somalia is infamous followed him there. By 2011, the Nigerian academic professor Pat Utomi remarked, "We've arrived in Somalia…the average Nigerian now seems disconnected from the Nigerian state (like the Somalis). He doesn't feel he is worth much. If his life means nothing, the lives of others means nothing to him also."[xlv] Theophilus Danjuma, a former Nigerian Minister of Defense, coined the term "Somalisation" to describe Nigeria's rapid descent into chaos.[xlvi]

Nigeria contains about 20% of Africa's entire population, and it is the largest country in the world that is almost equally divided between Muslims and Christians.[xlvii] Nigeria has a long history of inter-religious and inter-communal violence which is exacerbated today by the earning potential of massive hydrocarbon resources.[xlviii] Nigeria is a different case than Somalia, but it is similar in that it also under siege by violent jihadi-salafists. In Somalia, Al Shabaab used a lack of governance to initiate jihad and foreign intervention to sustain it. In Nigeria, Boko Haram used the corruption of an existing government to begin jihad and unrelenting government brutality to spread it.

In 1999 Nigerians looked to a restored democracy to solve their problems and realize their hope for a better future. Nigerians yearned for better living conditions, and for Nigeria to take her rightful place among the industrialized nations of the world. They were soon disappointed. Today about 75% of Northern Nigerians live on less than a dollar a day. Oil revenues increase yearly, but so does the percentage of Nigerians living in poverty.[xlix] Less than 54% of men can read and half of all children under the age of five are stunted due to malnutrition. Only one house out of four has access to electricity.[l] All of this abject poverty is present in Northern Nigeria despite Nigeria earning over $86 billion in hydrocarbon exports in 2011 alone.[li]

Northern Nigerians saw the quality of life improve in the non-Muslim south. Southern Nigerians today fare better in every economic and educational statistic. Democracy failed the Nigerian Muslims, and bereft of other options, they looked to their religious history to secure their future. The implementation of Sharia law began in the Zamfara state in October 1999, and it quickly swept across the North. Life, however, did not improve under Sharia for the majority of Muslims. The elite used Sharia to consolidate power, enrich themselves, and continue to oppress the masses.[lii] The misapplication of God's law and continued corruption propelled the rise of Muhammad Yusuf and the organization he founded: Boko Haram.

Boko Haram began as an Izala splinter group which sought to implement Sharia law and eliminate the endemic corruption in Nigeria. Corruption was culprit for the disparity between horrid living conditions and massive hydrocarbon wealth. Government officials at every level siphoned off hundreds of billions of dollars since the discovery and exportation of Nigerian hydrocarbons.[liii] Bribes were part of the rhythm of everyday life. Bribes initiated criminal investigations, and bribes determined the eventual outcome of those investigations. Corruption permeated everything, from school admissions to road construction. Extortion was also rampant. The police organizations were pyramid schemes. Low-level police officers made payments up the chain to the highest levels. This organizational demand for cash pushed policemen to relentlessly extort the local populations.[liv]

Boko Haram's message of a return to the pristine Islam of the Prophet and the equal justice of Sharia law resonated with the corruption weary populace. The membership and influence of Boko Haram soared. A Nigerian journalist interviewed Yusuf and wrote, "His teaching was easily accepted because the environment, the frustrations, the corruption, and the injustice made it fertile for his ideology to grow fast, very fast, like wild fire."[lv] An arrested Boko Haram member shouted to journalists in the crowd, "Our objective of fighting corruption by institutionalizing Islamic government must be achieved very soon."[lvi] The government grew wary of Boko Haram's growing reach and influence.

Corruption enabled Boko Haram to craft a message that resounded with the Muslim population and attracted new members. Heavy-handed government oppression, however, handed Boko Haram the provocation they needed to declare jihad. Nigerian Security Force (SF) members conducted Operation Flush in June 2009 to oppress a growing and alarmingly influential Boko Haram. They stopped a Boko Haram funeral procession in the Boko Haram stronghold of Maiduguri because several motorcyclists within the procession were not wearing helmets in accordance with local laws. The Boko Haram members refused to comply, and the SF opened fire on the procession, wounding seventeen people.[lvii] Yusuf demanded a public apology and a transparent investigation, but the government did not concede to Yusuf's demands. In response, Boko Haram's jihad began in earnest on 26 July 2009 with attacks across Bauchi, Kano, Yobe, and Maiduguri.

The SF's brutality continued to sustain Boko Haram's jihad by alienating the population and providing Boko Haram with the manpower and motivation to continue. Yusuf warned his followers against surrendering to the mercies of the government and told them, "If we give ourselves up, or they get us or me, they will kill me."[lviii] It was a prophetic revelation. Police captured Yusuf alive on 30 July 2009 and summarily executed him while he was in police custody shortly thereafter. The police executed at least twenty-four suspected Boko Haram members in Maiduguri alone between 28 July and 1 August 2009.[lix] Yusuf's father-in-law, Babu Fugu Mohammed, sent a letter to the Borno State governor prior to the attacks warning him of the impending violence. After the attacks, Babu turned himself in to the local authorities at the behest of his lawyer, and the police promptly shot him dead.[lx]

The government failed to restrain their forces or investigate extrajudicial killings. In a colossal display of short-sightedness, the Information Minister said that Yusuf's murder was, "the best thing that could have happened to Nigeria."[lxi] The Nigerian government learned a lesson that the United States would learn years later after the raid on Abbottobad: killing the leader does not always kill the organization. The government's brutality validated all of Yusuf's teachings and turned him into a martyr. Boko Haram went underground for about a year, but then they reemerged with a vengeance in 2010 under the leadership of Yusuf's more extreme protégé, Abubakar Shekau.

Under Shekau's leadership, Boko Haram attacks have increased in frequency, scope, and sophistication every year since 2010. Government forces continue to answer violence with violence. The government holds suspects indefinitely without charges or trials. They execute suspects, burn homes, torture detainees, and use rape as a weapon. Human Rights Watch estimated in 2012 that government forces caused as many casualties as Boko Haram.[lxii] Today, the jihad of Boko Haram is in danger of transitioning to a full-fledged local insurgency under the banner of the Islamic State. Boko Haram continues to rely on government brutality to recruit and sustain its membership. In 2012, Shekau stated, "Everyone has seen what the security personnel have done to us. Everyone has seen why we are fighting them."[lxiii] Government oppression continues to fuel the false jihad of Boko Haram.

The Nigerian ulama, unlike the Somali ulama, quickly attacked Boko Haram publicly with fatwas and statements. The Nigerian ulama challenged the legitimacy of Boko Haram's ideology even before the violent outbreaks. The salafist Ja'far Adam publicly attacked Yusuf's ideology and Islamic pedigree.[lxiv] Muslim leaders like the Sultan of Sokoto labeled Boko Haram members as common criminals. The prominent Nigerian cleric, Dr. Muhammad Abdul Islam Ibra him, issued the most damning fatwa in 2012. Dr. Ibrahim said, "Terrorism, in its very essence, is an act that symbolizes infidelity and rejection of what Islam stands for…Only the victims of ignorance, jealousy, and malice go for militancy. Islam declares them rebels. They will abide in hell."[lxv] The global ummah was largely silent on Boko Haram until they kidnapped two-hundred school girls in April 2014, and today the entire ummah universally condemns Boko Haram.

The ulama across the Muslim world are finally awakening to the dangers of jihadi-salafism and the threat that groups like Al Shabaab and Boko Haram pose to the world at large. The issue is that the ulama will often condemn atrocities, but refuse to condemn the individuals who committed those atrocities. A former Kuwaiti official lamented in 2004 that the ulama did not issue a single fatwa calling for Bin Laden's death.[lxvi] There is bitter struggle within Islam between the educated ulama and unqualified criminals for the authority to issue fatwas. If charismatic leaders with scant Islamic educations like Yusuf can issue religious rulings with no repercussions, then the system of Islamic jurisprudence is threatened with irrelevance. A true Islamic education is a powerful for force for counter-radicalization, which is why few jihadi-salafist leaders are true members of the ulama.[lxvii] The ulama must wage relentless jihad against the legitimacy and ideology of jihadi-salafism in order to take the narrative of Islam back from the hands of criminals and psychopaths.

Muslim democrats are also leading the ideological fight against jihadi-salafism. Abdullahi Al-Naim adovcates a return to the Islam of the Meccan period. "Meccan Islam" puts a premium on reasoning, the peaceful celebration of God, and upholding the moral responsibilities of the faithful.[lxviii] A return to the Islam of the Meccan period would also open the gates of ijtihad, which is critical because this would give the ulama the right to apply logic and reasoning to modernize the applications of Islam. Without ijtihad unqualified terrorists will continue to deliberately manipulate and misapply Sharia by exploiting loop-holes to justify bloodshed.

Misapplying Sharia is not uncommon, and cunning, charismatic leaders like Yusuf can selectively edit the Quran or Hadith to justify almost any action. This is not a new trend. In the thirteenth century the Islamic scholar Ibn Qayyim Al Jawziyya made an observant that remains relevant today: "As for the fanatics, they can place any problem upside down. When they turn to the Sunnah they borrow only what corresponds to their pronouncements and contrive tricks to push away evidence that does not suit them."[lxix]

There are true heroes within the ranks of the ulama, but not enough to turn to tides of this ideological war. Jamal Al Banna actively disputes the ideology of his brother and founder of the Muslim Brotherhood, Hassan Al Banna. Jamal compares the militant Islamists today to the Kharijites who killed the Caliphs Uthman and Ali.[lxx] El Fadl, Al Na'im, and Qadri are among the ulama who aggressively undermine the legitimacy of jihadi-salafism, and the jihadi-salafists who continue to commit heinous crimes in the name of Islam. The Islamic State conducts mass executions, sells captured girls into a life of sexual slavery, and destroys ancient relics all while waving a black flag emblazoned with the name of God. The question is, will mainstream, moderate Muslims confront these corruptions, or will they continue to let a bloodthirsty band of radicals define Islam for the non-Muslim world?

Jihadi-salafism is an Islamic problem, and it requires an Islamic solution. Dr. Ibrahim, when speaking of Boko Haram, said, "They are in the minority in the Muslim ummah, but as is often the case, such forces are always the most vocal. It is time now in our dear country for the voice of the majority who have always been against extremism and terrorism to move away from silence and let their voices be heard."[lxxi] If the majority remains silent, then it is likely violence will continue to escalate and transcend international borders, as it has most recently in France and Kenya. Eventually the non-Muslim world, be it France, Russia, or the United States, will seek to impose a non-Muslim solution through the force of arms. This will only add more fuel to an already blazing fire. Will the ummah respond?

The opinions expressed in this article are solely the author's and do not necessarily represent the views of the U.S. Army or Department of Defense.

Chapter 29

ISIS is Not a Terrorist Organization

Ajit Maan

First Published 29 December 2015

Given the climate of U.S. public opinion about U.S. intervention in the Middle East it is not surprising that the current administration has focused its foreign policy objectives on counter-terrorism.

But that priority limits our position to a defensive one. Further, the term "terrorist organization" offers little insight and limits our understanding and approach. ISIS is an insurgent organization using terrorism as a tactic.

The American public is wary of getting into what it views as quagmires, particularly in the Middle East, but is less hesitant when it comes to fighting terrorists who we view as a direct threat to the US. As a result, we have intervened in Syria to fight ISIS but not Assad.

While ISIS certainly employs terrorism as a tactic, and the label is one that de-legitimizes an opponent, the label also obscures the facts. To call it a terrorist organization is to mislabel it.

Traditionally, groups were identified as terrorist groups if their goal was ultimately to effect policy through intimidation. The policies in question were regionally specific: Ireland, Israel, even as specific as the green line separating Muslims and Christians in Beirut. What we are witnessing now is something closer to criminal psychopathology than terrorism. And the aims of these groups are not regionally specific but often international in scope. Moreover, the tactics have gone beyond intimidation to affect policy.

Terrorist organizations do not typically hold territory. They are generally comprised of small numbers, and they cannot prevail in a military confrontation. They pose an asymmetric threat. ISIS, however, has impressive military capabilities, has an estimated 30,000 man army, and conducts itself as a global criminal enterprise looting its victims, exchanging hostages for millions in ransom, stealing and selling antiquities, imposing taxes, routinely engaging in extortion, creating and imposing laws. It has demonstrated a disregard for national borders and is holding territory in Iraq and Syria. In the first six months of 2014 it took Fallujah, Ramadi, Mosul, Tikrit, and al Qaim, while the world watched in disbelief.

And ISIS has a decidedly genocidal aspect. Its victims are not just means to an end. The "end" of the mass executions by ISIS is to rid the earth of targeted populations—never mind the effect on the rest of us. Terrorism is just one tactic groups like ISIS employ in addition to conventional military operations, unconventional warfare techniques, state-building and even humanitarian aid. ISIS has even issued its own currency.

If we understand ISIS as an insurgency using terrorist tactics, their goals are comprehensible. Insurgency is the strategy; terrorism and guerrilla warfare are its tactics.

Because ISIS is not simply a terrorist organization, what is required to deal with this threat goes beyond the CT strategies of any one country. It is going to require joint military tactics to contain its expansion on the ground and to protect soft power initiatives designed to counter its media appeal, stem recruitment, and ensure diplomatic progress.

A light military footprint may be tactically advantageous in short-term local conflicts, but our focus on counter-terrorism strategy leaves us unfocused on other forms of instability in the region that can undermine our interests in the Middle East.

In order to get ahead of the game we should focus on preventing and mitigating regional conflicts. Regional instability and non-functional states create a vacuum that terrorist organizations are ready to fill. Even if it were possible to kill off every member of ISIS, new groups would form to take its place as long as core grievances are not addressed. When governments are too fragile to operate, and when fringe groups have greater capacity to address the needs of populations than their governments, some organization is going to take advantage of that vacuum.

Robust diplomacy combined with conflict resolution and mitigation strategies can potentially disrupt conflicting tensions and reduce the level and scope of the antagonisms and civil disorder that extremist groups require in order to flourish.

We should not think of the marker of success as having the solution to every problem. Success would be the reduction and containment of conflict. And it is not our job to do this alone but we have a vested interest in partnering with vulnerable states, like Yemen and Iraq, to help invigorate their governance and defense capacities. Insurgency happens when governance fails.

The real threat from these groups to the US isn't the acts of terror they perpetrate. The real threat results from the regional instability they create or take advantage of. When they become insurgencies or function as states we are in big trouble. And that is where we are now. Containment from here on means stabilizing the region through partnerships and protecting civilian refugees.

Now is the time to take preventative action. This does not mean exporting democracy. It means resolving, or at least mitigating, conflict with the goal of making states less vulnerable to civil war and promoting regional stability by providing local support and capacity building to regional allies and creating new ones.

The situation in Syria has left over 12 million people displaced, has de-stabilized much of the Middle East, has created an unprecedented refugee crisis that has not been addressed—and the situation rages on with no end in sight.

The refugee crisis threatens to become something more if not for intervention.

Sustained military attacks kill a few fighters, more civilians, and heighten the instability that generates mass exoduses and the desperation that ISIS capitalizes on. It also reiterates the narrative of extremist Sunnis that they are under attack. Military attacks presented on social media and the instability they create on the ground as well as the feeding they do to the extremist narrative provide a perfect breeding ground for further recruitment.

ISIS's real or imagined attractions may fail to deliver but so have countries like Syria failed to deliver. Removing ISIS militarily, even if it were possible, without removing the elements that enable it to flourish is not a good strategy.

Frustrated with the complexity of the problem, some voices have called for a conventional war. But to fight a conventional war against an unconventional enemy is a losing proposition that would deplete our resources and the majority of the American public simply would not get behind such a move. We would not win. Do we withdraw and take an isolationist stance? We cannot. Our own stability and security is too interdependent on the rest of the world's stability and security.

We must cooperate with other countries that are equally or more threatened by ISIS's advance and advocate joint diplomatic endeavors to assist refugees and local forces like the Kurdish Pesh Merga. And together we must wake the UN out of its slumber. When millions of people are ousted from their homes by a global criminal enterprise it is time for the UN to act.

U.S.-Allied Policy and Counter-Jihadi and Counter-Islamic State Strategies

Chapter 30

Adam Smith's Invisible Hand vs. The Taliban: Bottom-Up Expeditionary Diplomacy in Fragile States—Best Practices from the Civilian Surge in Afghanistan

Melinda Hutchings

First Published 20 January 2015

Abstract

The U.S. civilian and military surge in Afghanistan is over and the process of transition to full Afghan Government control and eventual withdrawal of conventional forces has proceeded according to the 2014 timetable agreed upon by the Afghan Government, U.S. policymakers and the international community. There is much public debate on what has been accomplished or not in the last thirteen years as the U.S. and international community counter a complex insurgency, a violent attempt to overthrow the democratically elected Afghan government. Academics, foreign aid critics, think tank analysts, journalists, media pundits, military officials and former civilian and military surge participants are contributing to this growing Revisionist and negative debate, arguing that the U.S. Counterinsurgency (COIN) strategy was a sustainability failure and Afghanistan will inevitably return to the pre-2001 levels of insurgent control and instability. The COIN strategy operated along a three-pronged assistance: security, governance and development. The emerging and continuing revisionist debate maintains that this strategy incorporating economic growth, agriculture, governance, health and education into COIN's clear-hold-build-transition timeline has been a wholesale failure. Realistically there are numerous instances of failure to bring about the desired COIN end state goal of legitimizing and strengthening Afghanistan's central government and extending its writ outside the capital, Kabul. However, as the COIN revisionist bandwagon grows in popularity with America's weariness of the Afghan war and trepidation over involvement in possible future conflicts, it is imperative to pause and take a more balanced view of what was achieved in the early stages of COIN and apply those lessons learned and best practices to current and future U.S. Government deployments in fragile states. Those critics who don't believe the United States and international community will find themselves in the not too distant future, confronted with challenges in strategic countries or regions where populations are ethnically and tribally fractured, poor, terrorized by threats from various sources and vulnerable to terrorist organizations, may want to reassess their perception of current world realities.

The primary purpose of this paper is not to determine directly whether or not the billions of dollars spent in Afghanistan in governance and development were well spent in relation to COIN results on the ground. Rather, this paper sheds light on that key question by providing compelling evidence of how setting conditions and promoting free market enterprise, as theorized by the father of modern economic theory, Adam Smith, stabilized conflict zones in Afghanistan, a fragile state. This paper documents the experiences of four civilian-military units involved in the surge, representing joint teams of U.S. Army, and experts from the U.S. Department of State, U.S. Agency for

International Development, and the U.S. Department of Agriculture during the early COIN phase of operations, 2009-2011.

These joint civilian-military units conducted *"Expeditionary Diplomacy"* outreaches with Afghan partners to promote the generation and growth of Afghan human institutions and institutional processes in the form of: traditional Afghan tribal decision making bodies called jirgas; traditional (tribal) forms of representational community leadership, i.e. village mayors (*maliks*); Afghan government-led district level agricultural extension agents and their services; and creation of village level farmers and traders associations *(cooperatives)*. These culturally appropriate *human institutions and institutional processes* provided the framework from which Afghan villagers were able to pursue their own economic gain and thus reject the insurgent (i.e. Taliban) influence which discourages participation in a free market economy.

Given the fundamental change in the economic behavior, institutions being promoted, it is useful to step back at this point and review some of the basic premises of modern capitalistic thought. In his 1776 classic, *"An Inquiry into the Nature and Causes of the Wealth of Nations,*[i]*"* Adam Smith theorized that as people pursue their own individual economic self gain in the marketplace, their individual actions are guided by an *Invisible Hand* resulting in *Beneficial Social Orders* for the entire society. In a sense, this is what the programs under review sought to achieve. Led, as it were, by an *Invisible Hand,* each of the four communities represented in these case studies experienced the *Beneficial Social Order* of stability; a reduction in violence and a return to the "normal" function of society. How? By crafting inclusive economic development opportunities through Afghan institutions which not only develop the Afghan government's capacity to deliver services to its people, but also keeps Afghan government accountable to its citizens. This is the key to strengthening a fragile state.

The U.S. and international coalition of 67 International Security Assistance Force (ISAF) member nations had some resounding successes stabilizing traditional, insurgent influenced societies through dialogue, community empowerment, job and market creation, and empowering Afghan provincial and district governments to delivery services and be accountable to their citizens. Though lost in the emerging revisionist debate to dismiss the Afghan COIN experience a failure, these stabilization intervention success stories need to be documented, analyzed and applied to future deployments in regions of the world experiencing violent conflict among poor and ethnically fractured societies. These best practices illustrate what "right looks like" during those initial steps to analyze and build successful governance and development program interventions, offering the best chance of stability in fragile states and for effective transition to democratically elected national governing authorities in insurgencies.

As 2014 draws to a close, the United States and international community are carefully considering how best to craft interventions in response to several complex, sectarian, ethnically and tribally divided fragile states in strategically important regions around the world. Perhaps the principles of Adam Smith's *Invisible Hand* can illuminate for diplomats, aid workers and military commanders how best to craft effective expeditionary diplomacy efforts in strategically important areas before crisis flashpoints emerge using the lessons learned and best practices from the Afghanistan fragile state experience.

Introduction

During my last tour in Afghanistan at Embassy Kabul, I was tasked with interviewing departing civilian field staff who participated in the historic 2009-2011 Civilian Surge to collect and document their best practices and lessons learned. Though I was not able to conduct exit interviews with all deployed staff consisting of well over 1,000 civilians, I was able to conduct a solid representational sampling. In my estimation, four of these exit interview case studies illustrated a common thread of success as impoverished Afghan communities caught in conflict zones, were allowed to participate in their own economic and security destiny against the forces of a resilient and intimidating Taliban insurgency.

All four case studies from 21st century Afghanistan mirrored the 18th century economic principles of Adam Smith explaining human behavior in another emerging economy of a weak and violence ridden state, the United States of America during its Revolutionary War. Specifically, Smith, wrote in the 1776 (and fifth edition in 1904) *"An Inquiry into the Nature and Causes of the Wealth of Nations"* that as individuals in the marketplace focus locally on pursuing their own economic self gain, the *Invisible Hand* guides the actions of farmers/traders and merchants in socially beneficial ways. Modern economic theorist, Dr. Jonathan Wight of the University of Richmond, expands on Smith's analysis stating that the pursuit of economic self gain must be channeled through "appropriate human institutions" and "institutional processes" in order for beneficial social order to emerge[ii]. The four case studies presented in this paper illustrate what appropriate human institutions and institutional processes looked like in Afghanistan, 2009-2011, and the resulting beneficial social order that emerged. Each case study demonstrates COIN's desired end state: enhancing the government's legitimacy, by connecting the people to their government and the government to their people. Specifically, the five appropriate human institutions and institutional processes included:

- The creation of *jirgas*, ethnically and tribally inclusive community decision-making body working in tandem with an existing non-inclusive Afghan government sponsored decision making body.
- Resurrecting the traditional leadership model of the village mayor, i.e. the *"malik,"* to represent local citizens' interests to their government.
- Consolidating farmers' economic bargaining power by creating agricultural co-operatives for villagers and local business owners to advance economic development opportunities.

- Injecting Afghan company sourced improved vegetable seeds into insurgent held areas through Afghan District level agricultural extension agents thus jump starting the role of the Government's agricultural service delivery to its citizens.

In each case study, Adam Smith's *Invisible Hand* guided the actions to individual farmers, traders and merchants to produce the unintended "beneficial social orders" of stability: individual economic advancement; strengthening the capacity of the Afghan government to deliver services to its people; making the Afghan government more accountable to its citizens; reduction of inter-tribal and ethnic tensions and increasing citizens participation with their local government on issues such as governance, development and security.

ADAM SMITH'S 18TH CENTURY "INVISIBLE HAND" AND 21ST CENTURY CIVILIAN SURGE IN AFGHANISTAN

As the President said last night, the United States is meeting the goals he set for our three-track strategy in Afghanistan and Pakistan. The military surge has ramped up pressure on al-Qaida and Taliban insurgents. The <u>civilian surge</u> has bolstered the Afghan and Pakistani Governments, economies, and civil societies, and undercut the pull of the insurgency. The diplomatic surge is supporting Afghan-led efforts to reach a political solution that will chart a more secure future[iii].

By preferring the support of domestic to that of foreign industry, [a farmer/trader] intends only his own security; and by directing that industry in such a manner as its produce may be of the greatest value, he intends only his own gain, and he is in this, as in many other cases, led by an <u>invisible hand</u> to promote an end which was no part of his intention[iv].

Published in 1776, the same year the young United States of America ratified its Declaration of Independence from the British Empire, Adam Smith presented his analysis of how emerging nations build wealth (*and Stability*) through division of labor and wages, agricultural productivity and trade. Smith is forever immortalized for his assessment of how the

Invisible Hand leads to an overall, though unintended, beneficial social order as individuals focus on pursuing their own economic self interest. Per Wight's study of Adam Smith, the metaphorical *Invisible Hand* represents the unseen instincts of human nature that motivate and direct behavior. Channeled through appropriate <u>human institutions (*and institutional processes*),</u> the *Invisible Hand* can generate a spontaneous and beneficial social order. Wight defines an appropriate institution as one that aligns incentives of the individual with those of society.

Sometimes, however, appropriate institutions can be disastrous for the society since societies change with time. For example, 18th Century Europe had in place the human institution of property rights ensuring that sons would inherit property, not daughters. Such a human institution was appropriate for the time to ensure adequate defense against invaders. Wight continues; however, as time progresses and societies change, Europe changed its outdated property rights (human institution) to better serve society's interest to have resources flow into the most productive hands. Therefore, Smith's *Invisible Hand* does not ensure the best outcome will result if the wrong institutions for the times are in place.[v]

At first glance, Smith's analysis of the *Invisible Hand* fits nicely into the narrative of emerging Western, democratic societies, not a historically isolated tribal society such as Afghanistan with a small minority of the population belonging to an ultra-conservative form of Islam, i.e. the Taliban. However, Smith's 18th century analysis of the *"Invisible Hand"* in emerging societies can provide insight for Expeditionary Diplomats to understand human behavior and how to set conditions in fragile states which promotes the equitable pursuit of individual economic interests, a force stronger than the chaotic insurgent attraction. For traditional societies, the hope of increasing personal economic gains to better the lives for families is stronger than the insurgent authoritative worldview which stifles commerce and collective, ethnically inclusive decision making. As communities look to their government to represent their interests in pursing emerging economic advancement, governments are forced to be more accountable and transparent, less likely to favor one ethnic group over another.

WHAT WAS THE CIVILIAN SURGE IN AFGHANISTAN?

*Our overarching goal remains the same: to disrupt, dismantle, and defeat al Qaeda in Afghanistan and Pakistan, and to prevent its capacity to threaten America and our allies in the future. To meet that goal, we will pursue the following objectives within Afghanistan. We must deny al Qaeda a safe haven. We must reverse the Taliban's momentum and deny it the ability to overthrow the government. And we must strengthen the capacity of Afghanistan's security forces and government so that they can take lead responsibility for Afghanistan's future... These are the three core elements of our strategy: a military effort to create the conditions for a transition; a **civilian surge** that reinforces positive action; and an effective partnership with Pakistan*[vi].

Whether at the District Support Team (DST), Provincial Reconstruction Team (PRT) or the Regional Platform level, creating and sustaining gains in governance and economic development will take creative solutions, and given the level of investment over the past ten years, a mechanism for measuring the effectiveness of our efforts[vii].

We need to work with the Afghan government to refocus civilian assistance and capacity-building programs on building up competent provincial and local governments where they can more directly serve the people and connect them to their government[viii].

Following President Barack Obama's December 1, 2009 directive to conduct joint civilian and military surges in Afghanistan to defeat al-Qaeda, over 1,200 civilians representing nine US government agencies continued to deploy to Afghanistan to work joint governance and development operations with US and NATO military units throughout Afghanistan. Most of Afghanistan's 34 provinces had a provincial level civilian-military team, a Provincial Reconstruction Teams (PRT.) By late 2009, a new initiative sent civilian-military units to remote "key terrain areas" representing the lowest reach of the Afghan Government, the district level. District Support Teams, or DST's, though a construct from the US experience in Iraq, were reminiscent of the 1960's Vietnam experience under the US Government's Civil Operations and Revolutionary Development Support program, or CORDS program. This unique hybrid of a civilian-military structure was used by the United States in its "Pacification" counterinsurgency program to strengthen the South Vietnamese Government from the Communist North Vietnamese Government. Not since the Vietnam CORDS program, have so many US civilians been deployed with military units to conduct governance and development counterinsurgency operations (COIN.) Ideologically, the Afghanistan Civilian Surge followed Secretary of State Clinton's priority to elevate the role of Diplomacy and Development along with Defense—a "smart power" approach to solving global problems

During his June 22, 2011 evening address to the nation, President Obama announced the beginning of the US troop withdrawal from Afghanistan. The next day, Secretary of State Clinton announced the civilian surge had reached its height, at 1,200 civilians, on track to achieve its goals. Of note, the 1,200 civilians participating in the surge brought expertise in: agriculture, development, infrastructure, health, economic development, rule of law, stabilization and sub-national governance capacity building programs. The Special Inspector General for Afghanistan Reconstruction (SIGAR) in its September 8, 2011 audit estimated that the cost of the civilian surge cost U.S. taxpayers nearly $2 billion since 2009.[ix]

By 2012, in response to the gradual drawdown of US military forces and the corresponding closure of District Support Teams (DST's), civilians were gradually pulled back to regional capitals where their focus was one of "Transition" and capacity building of Afghan Government officials in provincial budget planning, formulation and execution. By 2013, the closure rate of Provincial Reconstruction Teams (PRT's) has accelerated more rapidly than originally planned, due to conversations and commitments beyond this author's purview. The Afghan Government leads the Transition process stemming from concerns that PRT's and DST's functioned as "Shadow Governments," thus weakening the Afghan State's ability to plan, formulate and execute their national budgets down to the provincial level, impeding Afghan sovereignty. By the end of 2014, if not sooner in reality, the final PRT will close and the historic civilian surge will be a subject in future foreign affairs history books.

A CASE FOR EXPEDITIONARY DIPLOMACY

This paper documents the efforts of four joint U.S. civilian and U.S. Army elements working with their Afghan counterparts to create "appropriate human institutions and institutional processes" during the civilian-military surge campaign in Afghanistan, 2009-2011. Hence, these appropriate human institutions and institutional processes provided a framework from which Afghans dialogued to make collective decisions on the distribution of scare aid resources, express their grievances, compete and obtain a fair price in the agricultural marketplace, received agricultural advice and assistance and gained a voice in their economic destiny.

Not having a previously written script to follow in Afghanistan, these four civilian-military units worked in different geographical areas devoid of any significant Afghan government control or influence beyond that of a district governor. Further, most district governors had no budget from Kabul from which to fund a staff or programs. Significant tribal tensions, insurgent intimidation, basic subsistence farming, and an absent operating commerce-based economy to speak of, were typical of all four operating areas in the early stages of COIN operations.

PRESENTATION OF THE EXPENDTIONARY DIPLOMACY CASE STUDIES

The term "Expeditionary Diplomacy," though not a trademark, is a buzzword used by former Secretaries of State, governance and development professionals describing the need for diplomats to move out from the walls of the embassy and engage with the local population to find creative solutions in complex, conflict zones. From my experience, "Expeditionary Diplomacy" is the most effective form of diplomacy needed in today's complex operating environment calling on unique individuals who possess not only practical technical skills sets but who also possess the interpersonal skills necessary to understand a complex operating environment and communicate effectively with key stakeholders in complex operating environments.

Case Study One[x]

The district of Spin Boldak, in Kandahar Province's southeastern corner, was an anomaly in Afghanistan's turbulent south during the course of 2010. Despite its location astride key lines of communication for coalition, as well as insurgent, resupply in and out of neighboring Pakistan, the district had little to report in terms of coalition-insurgent activity and, most fortunately, not a single serious coalition casualty that year. The relative calm of the border district permitted coalition commanders to focus troop strength elsewhere in the south.

With fewer NATO troops at its disposal than might otherwise be deemed necessary for a border region with a population standing officially at 100,000-150,000, our coalition strategy was to enjoy the fruits of Spin Boldak's stability and relative calm.

According to a prevailing view in the field, district stability was dependent on a tribal equilibrium underpinned by the force of personality, and numerous troops, of the local Afghan National Security Force (ANSF) chief. This narrative held that the ANSF commander was himself an Achekzai tribesman, a traditional tribal leader possessing the prestige and authority with which such a position is endowed.

Supporting this analysis was a local governance arrangement that recognized a distribution of shares among the two dominant, traditionally violent tribal rivals, the Achekzai and Noorzai. Perceived to reflect demographic realities, the balancing of each tribe's claims in both the community decision making bodies, i.e. the District Tribal Shura and District Development Assembly, was held as a pillar of local security. This perceived demographic reality demanded equal apportioning of any development assistance only between the two tribes, the Achekzai and the Noorzai.

Often justified as necessary to ensure the delicate balance between the Achekzai and Noorzai, the position of District Governor was held by an outsider; since 9/11 primarily a member of President Karzai's Popalzai tribe. The local tashkeel (civil service organizational chart) was thereby satisfied but with marginal impact on local affairs.

This was the accepted view of Spin Boldak when our civilian-military District Support Team (DST) was established in late 2009: a stable, representative tribal arrangement reflected district government, supported by a capable local Afghan National Security Force finding authority in the tribal basis of its command. Though coalition challenges to this analysis emerged during the last quarter of 2009, the basic narrative remained intact despite questions about the integrity and tribal favoritism of the local Afghan National Security Forces, in particular.

Within this analytical framework, the DST was forced to confront a number of contrary findings, primary among them:

- The Achekzai and Noorzai after thirty years of conflict and internal displacement could no longer claim tribal exclusivity in Spin Boldak district.
- The main local Afghan National Security Force element and its Achekzai commander, Colonel Abdul Razik, rather than viewed as a tribal authority was felt by many, including within the Achekzai, to be a divisive factional leader.

As allegations surrounding Spin Boldak's Afghan National Security Forces commander have been widely reported on[xi], this paper will look at the demographic realities of the two unrecognized and unrepresented tribes in Spin Boldak district, a sizable population of internally displaced persons (IDPs) and the Kuchi nomadic tribe numbering according to some estimates at over 100,000.

Having settled in Spin Boldak, either while fleeing post-911 violence in neighboring provinces, or attracted by the border's economic opportunities while returning from earlier exile in neighboring Pakistan, the district's IDPs of diverse ethnic and tribal origins to include the quasi-settled nomadic Kuchis, were a substantial community. To the Achekzai and Noorzai, however, they were "outsiders" presenting a competing claim on resources and privileges. If these communities harbored deep mutual suspicions, they could at least agree on one thing: the imperative to restrict others from decision making circles and thus receipt of what limited government and donor assistance existed.

For our DST, a significant but disenfranchised population posed not only a latent threat to local stability, but also to efforts for the Afghan government to connect and extend its authority to the Spin Boldak district population. It was failure to date in the latter arena that was partly fueling the insurgency in the South and sustaining insurgent freedom of movement thought the district. This was particularly so in outlying communities where the narrative of tribal harmony was found wanting. Addressing the enfranchisement of IDPs and Kuchis thus became a priority for our DST.

It was determined that a first step for our DST was reducing reliance on the District Shura and District Development Assembly, both of which institutionalized existing monopolies favoring the Achekzai and Noorzai tribes. Imposing reform on these community groups was not an option and would have risked direct confrontation with Achekzai and Noorzai elders, whose continued cooperation was critical. On an occasion when the issue of Shura reform was raised, the District Development Assembly chairman proclaimed, "not over my dead body will they (the IDP's and Kuchi) sit in my Shura."

Though reducing reliance on the District Shura and District Development Assembly was as an internal matter for our DST, a local vehicle was still necessary for prioritizing development needs and obtaining indigenous approval-ownership of community development projects. Marginalized to a certain extent by his outsider status in Spin Boldak and lack of support from higher levels in the Afghan government, our DST turned to the Afghan District Governor for support.

Not beholden to the district's status quo of Achekzai-Noorzai tribal dominance[xii], the Afghan District Governor proved sensitive to IDP and Kuchi needs; whether out of a desire to gain leverage over established local power brokers or a desire to better the community remained an open question.

Under the District Governor's leadership, a new advisory committee was established called the "Commission". The Commission's stated purpose was not to replace either the District Shura or District Development Assembly's, but rather to offer the district governor his own venue in which Spin Boldak district residents could have their needs heard through their own representatives.

To this new community forum, the heads of the District Shura and District Development Assembly along with other influential Noorzai and Achekzai elders, who either could not be ignored or were seen as forces for change, were invited by the District Governor to participate in the Commission. More importantly, so were representatives of the communities making up the IDP population and the Kuchi camps; their first official recognition by the local Afghan district government.

Henceforth, it was "Commission" endorsement, rather than the District Shura-District Development Assembly Shura which held weight with our DST, particularly where U.S. Military funded community development projects were concerned. To further the normalization process, our DST ensured IDP and Kuchi representation at coalition events, attended their respective community-level shuras accompanied by district officials, and coordinated their attendance at relevant Government of Afghanistan sponsored activities, especially those involving provincial or national level officials from the Kabul.

Not long after the Commission was operational, the chairmen of the District Shura and the District Development Assembly attempted to influence the composition of the Commission, but their efforts fell short.

The number of tribal elders seeking inclusion in the new Commission, even from within the two dominant Achekzai and Noorzai tribes, exceeded the capacity of the old guard to resist. Finding himself increasingly redundant in local circles, the head of the District Development Assembly soon vacated his position, his departure allowing for more accommodating attitudes to emerge. Still a challenge, but with his main partner in obstruction gone, the district Shura leader was more easily managed.

The lifespan of the "Commission" was not long, reaching its natural limits by October 2010 due to a number of factors (e.g. It had no official Afghan Government recognition from Kabul.) However, with the environment seemingly more permissive, the District Governor decided to tackle reform of the District Shura. The District Governor was emboldened by an earlier announcement from the Kabul central government that "Shura Reform" would be a feature of a new Kabul governance initiative. In time, the reformed Spin Boldak District Shura opened up new seats for the previously disenfranchised IDP and Kuchi populations and received official recognition from Kabul. Though not a perfect reflection of the population demographics, leaders of the newly enfranchised IDP and Kuchi groups were satisfied with the outcome.

Gauging the immediate impact of Spin Boldak's District Shura expansion in quantifiable terms would be difficult. In some respects, it was a remedial step, rather than a real advancement; in the early days of the civilian surge, addressing decade-old neglect was par for the course. But if measurable dividends were still to be seen, our DST's efforts engendered tremendous goodwill within the newly enfranchised communities, and the profile of the district government was increased. More significantly, within the directly affected communities, the prestige of elders was immeasurably enhanced by the District Shura outcome.

Case Study Two [xiii]

Dand, a rural district of 165,000 residents, is located between Kandahar City and the Registan desert bordering Balochistan Province,

Pakistan. Dand District is an arid to semi-arid agrarian region with some small plot agriculture and erratic irrigation via underground canals and wells allowing one wheat growing season per year. Dand district is comprised of Durrani Pashtuns, chiefly the Popalzai (over 50%) of President Karzai's tribe, Barakzai, Noorzai, Alikozai as well as several permanent and nomadic Kuchi population centers.

As of June 2010, Government of Afghanistan's Dand district officials held little sway south of the Tarnak River, which slices Dand district in half. The Dand district government consisted of: the District Governor; three government line directors representing health, agriculture, a law clerk and six (6) "maliks," the equivalent of village mayors in traditional Pashtun society. International Coalition forces in Dand included the U.S. Army's 1-71 Cavalry unit of the 10th Mountain Division providing security, development and governance assistance following handover from Canadian Forces.

Unity of Effort—Team Dand: In order to function successfully, how we as civilian-military Team Dand were to work together was the precursor to reaching our strategic and tactical goals in Dand district. There could only be one guiding mission: clear the Dand of insurgents, hold the cleared space from insurgent control and infuse economic development project strategies behind clearing operations. Once stability (i.e. reduction of violence and a return to society's normal function) held, these economic development strategies such as agricultural production for sale, engine repair, tailoring, and related jobs would solidify the security gains allowing Team Dand to transition out of the district. I overlaid what I brought to the effort as a "soft effects" (as opposed to kinetic operations) enabler within the bigger picture of successfully connecting the local population to the Afghan Government. To connect the Dand population to the Afghan government, Team Dand had to focus efforts to drive a wedge between the population and the insurgency and fill that void with a new perception for the average villager that they can withstand and defeat the insurgency. Team Dand were seamless and holistic in our process of working together. Unified, Team Dand was a group of civilian-military enablers focused on bringing the villages of Dand into the fold of the Dand district government. We began by building relationships with traditional village leaders through the process of working with these villages to improve their local conditions in security, governance and development. We focused on controlling the perception of the population by customizing our approach based on what they showed us, intentionally and unintentionally, and enabling them to decide to work with us.

Identifying and building an Afghan appropriate Human Institution: Early on in our interactions with the Dand population, Insurgents planted Improvised Explosive Devices (IED's) placed along strategic roads leading to Team Dand's forward operating bases. The high rate of IED emplacement was an indication of Team Dand's lack of influence on the local villages. Dand's District Governor held little influence outside the Dand district administrative center. Insurgents intimidated Dand district officials by sending harassing "Night letters" threatening district officials to leave their posts or face insurgent reprisal. Less than five schools were open in the vicinity of the district administrative center and only six villages were represented by their village mayors, the "maliks" responsible for bringing news, needs requests and grievances to the Dand District Governor and his staff of line directors.

Team Dand began to exert influence through daily, regular, dismounted patrols, speaking with village elders, local representatives and merchants to gathering information on local security and economic conditions, grievances of the local population and who the population trusted to solve their problems. Within two months, the data we collected on local conditions revealed that assisting local communities with infrastructure project assistance could facilitate better dialogue with communities, spontaneously generate economic growth opportunities and elevate local leaders back to their traditional roles in this Afghan society as those who represent their communities to the local government.

For centuries, the Pashtun tribes of Dand district have always prided themselves as shrewd businessmen, responsible for delivering negotiated rewards back to their clans and villages. However, thirty plus years of civil war and a religious extremism had torn the social and traditional fabric of Afghan society. Experience showed that "wanting to help the Dand people" did not provide a return on the investment. Doing development projects for the Dand community never resulted in a "magical return of appreciation." Doing "top down" development projects belittled the Pashtun Dand communities. We had to find a way to bring Dand leaders to a perceived negotiation table with us as we elevated the role of their District Governor. If we were to provide projects, we needed to receive something of equal or greater value to us in order to gain the respect of the elders, per the Pashtun worldview. A Pashtun elder would take all that is provided to him and offer nothing in return if his counterpart is perceived as weaker or not respecting that which he has to offer. It was our position that presenting weak terms early in the relationship building process would handicap our efforts in the long run. If you are deemed as an equal, with something to offer, "business" can expedite and solidify the relationship through the perception from the average villager as being one who is worthy, conveyed by the malik in bringing home the negotiated rewards. Our review of the culture, history and human nature show us these patterns of behavior and this dynamic has been studied, indirectly, in social psychology and organizational behavior literature[xiv].

Team Dand conducted the first local community meeting, i.e. *Jirga*[xv], allowing the U.S. Army Dand Commanding Officer to speak directly to local Dand elders on issues related to security and eventually larger buy-in decisions from villagers on economic development projects. Regular jirga meetings were conducted at the district center, receiving motivated village elders and eliciting their help in forming a representational government. Farmer focused jirgas were conducted in the villages and eventually a district-wide farmer jirga was held at the Dand district center drawing the largest gathering ever at the Dand government center. Farmer Shuras here were even conducted south the Tarnak River, in concert with clearing operations, in areas which had no history of Afghan government contact. In such isolated communities previously untouched by the Afghan government, local villagers lived as subsistence farmers with food deficits and life-threatening disease and water contamination.

The role and influence of the traditional malik, or village mayor, has greatly diminished over the past thirty years of war and subsequent extremism. Ideally, the malik's role is held in high regard as the "voice of the people." Distinct from a village elder, the trusted malik position is vital for connecting the population with Afghan government at the district and provincial levels. Team Dand worked with respected elders and district political leaders to mentor maliks in their dealings with the district government to bring goods and services to the Dand communities. Election of maliks became one of Team Dand's metrics of stability, determining which villages were cooperating with their district government. If a holdout village was denied inclusion due to a questionable malik whose activities may be in support of the insurgents, we leveraged projects to a neighboring village in an effort to isolate the population and force them to change their leadership. When Maliks or village elders tried to play games with Team Dand to unduly enrich themselves during project implementation or if insurgents returned to the area and IED's showed up again, all projects would be halted until cooperation was restored.

Team Dand partnered with the Dand District Governor to conduct the first District Development Assembly (DDA) meetings, modeling for maliks and other village leaders how to nominate projects for their representative villages. DDA's represent the Afghan central government's initiative to establish a mechanism for mobilizing communities into the forefront of development planning and implementation. As Dand DDA groups became more comfortable in their new roles, they were provided a budget of $2,000 U.S. dollars with which to nominate, collect bids and close out their community infrastructure improvement projects. The District Governor and line directors would meet with the DDA's on a weekly basis to achieve regular population interaction allowing the general population to receive benefits and services from their local, representative government.

Evidence of Smith's *Invisible Hand* guiding the actions of those seeking economic self gain in the market place producing the unintended consequences of *beneficial social orders:* As stability increased in Dand, benefits that positively affected economic self gain such as seed distribution, trade establishment, market development and training in mechanics, repair and other trades were introduced at different times along the timeline, depending on the psychological state of the village. Farmers were provided improved seed, fertilizer, tools and other facilitators that would make it possible for them to begin to achieve self- sufficiency in crop production and, eventually, produce a surplus. It was here, with stability within sight, that the forward inertia of farmer's actions began to dictate outcomes. No longer burdened with fear or security/ safety concerns, farmers biggest concerns took the shape of universal business concerns. How large is my surplus? What are the current market price levels? How can I get more of my product to market? What are my neighbors growing? Can I expand my market? Can I increase shelf- life of my products to get a better price in the future?

Dand District Transformed: Shortly after the start of 2011, (approximately 6 months after arrival), all of Dand's 32 schools were open, all 50 of Dand's villages were represented by a Malik and a fully functioning district government was meeting weekly to hear grievances and represent the interests of its people. Dand District became the model of stability in all of Kandahar Province and was the first Kandahar district to transition to full Afghan security control in July 2012. It remains Afghan secured and Afghan led. It's all about relationships and how business is conducted.

Case Study Three[xvi]

As the United States Department of Agriculture (USDA) Advisor in Regional Command East's province of Wardak, USDA's mission was strengthen the emerging Afghan government's capacity. To accomplish this mission, I worked with my U.S. Military and Civilian colleagues to mentor and guide Afghan civil servant officials of the Directorate of Agriculture, Irrigation, and Livestock (DAIL—the provincial arm of the Cabinet level Ministry of Agriculture, Irrigation and Livestock) in creating a provincial strategy for agricultural-based economic growth. This Afghan government led provincial strategy included: creating export opportunities; increasing the quality and quantity of crop yields through vocational trainings and the introduction of improved farming practices; to strengthening private sector agribusiness job options.

USDA worked with the DAIL Director and his team to assist receptive farming communities, the municipal capital and "stable enough" adjacent districts, by hosting farmer jirga meetings with a view to stand up farmer associations among population groups demonstrating a strong desire to participate in economic expansion. Afghan government led agricultural extension service delivery improved the overall image of the Afghan central government as the Wardak population witnessed their government delivering services to them.

Location and Security Conditions: Wardak province of roughly 500,000 people is fairly unique, situated less than an hour's drive to Kabul, close in proximity to the largest airport in the country for export, semi-reliable electricity, and large domestic consumer base for agricultural goods. Kabul has an expanding population of at least 4 million people in need of agricultural produce.

Insurgent presence and kinetic activity in Wardak has had adverse economic impacts: inability to capitalize on abundant and inexpensive energy from the hydroelectric project in Chak district; constant road repair due to improvised explosive devices (IED's) in the roadway culverts which cripple economic trade routes; and the constant insurgent intimidation of government officials preventing officials from reporting for duty and fulfilling their tasks. Tribally, Wardak province is predominantly Pashtun with Uzbeks, Hazaras and Tajiks people groups represented. Some levels of tribal tensions exist, stemming from past history of tense tribal relations.

Building Afghan Government Capacity to Manage and Direct the Donor Aid Deluge: Wardak province, like many provinces in Afghanistan, received millions of dollars of international donor assistance over the past decade to rebuild their infrastructure, enhance economic development opportunities and deliver some level of basic services to the population. As the Afghan government matured, the challenge became how to quickly build the capacity of Afghan civil servants in Wardak to effectively manage and direct all donor funded agricultural-based economic development activity in *their* province. To assist, USDA mentors and DAIL officials created a Provincial Strategy which required international donors, like the U.S. Agency for International Development (USAID) and the U.S. Military's Commanders Emergency Response Program (CERP) to seek approval from the DAIL before any agriculturally-related projects were implemented, such as "Cash-for-Work" projects.

Traditionally, Cash-for-Work projects were conducted to offer fighting age males the opportunity to work for wages at a higher rate than insurgents were offering them to place Improvised Explosive Devices (IED's). Further investigation, however, proved this theory erroneous. Cash-for-Work was indeed a potential tool that could be leveraged to reduce the susceptibility of fighting age males working with the insurgency, though not completely eliminating the economic incentive to accept insurgent employment. Simply employing hundreds of fighting age males to dig ditches or rebuild village structures for eight hours a day would only feed a village for a day. Upon further investigation, existing Cash-for-Work projects were undermining the historical and social traditions of the Wardak people; work they had organized for themselves without receiving financial remuneration. Cleaning and maintaining the traditional irrigation canal systems (kareez[xvii]), rebuilding mosques and common use buildings, and digging deeper and new wells were all examples of historic traditions the USDA and DAIL officials decided against endorsing as Cash-for-Work projects. Instead, USDA and DAIL officials advocated Cash-for-Work projects with a heavy vocational training element to move villages toward economic self sufficiency. Thus, a trend toward village economic self sufficiency was in line with the Afghan government's strategy for agriculture-based economic growth.

Farmer Cooperatives, an Appropriate (Afghan) Human Institution:

One of the objectives of the Afghan government's Provincial Strategy for Economic Growth was creation and expansion of export opportunities for Wardak Province produced agricultural goods. To achieve this objective, DAIL, USDA and the U.S. Agency for International Development (USAID) launched Wardak farmers' associations, a low-cost, high impact program to unite farmers in getting the best price and developing new markets for their crops. The challenge, however, was overcoming the worldview held by Afghan farmers that "collectivizing" had negative implications due largely to the Communist legacy of involuntary land re-allocation and state control of agricultural markets during the Soviets era in Afghanistan, 1979-1989. Any mention of farmers' associations, collective bargaining or mixing yields with neighboring farmers for efficient transport was viewed skeptically. It was unfortunate as this destructive and defeatist line of thinking does not allow a farmer to capitalize on the extremely advantageous opportunity that an association affords a typical farmer. If an Afghan farmer were a member of an association, he would have the bargaining power to demand higher prices from the trader or, ideally, ban together with other farmers to share transportation costs of delivering goods to pre-determined buyers, much as modern agricultural associations function in other parts of the world.

Added to the fear of "collectivizing," the DAIL Director and his staff feared a 3,000 member Wardak farmers' association would pose a challenge to his legitimacy as the director of DAIL. Instead of looking at the famers' association as complementary to his goals as the director, he viewed the association with fear and frustration. To help the Director overcome his fear, I leveraged my relationship with him to help him understand the proper role of a government institution in agriculture and the need for a quasi-private association to spur economic growth from my personal experience as an almond farmer belonging to a farmer's association in central California. The DAIL Director and I shared a common knowledge of agricultural issues in Afghanistan, and I used this trust to push him toward acceptance of the concept of an association in spite of his high level of trust and skepticism.

The *Invisible Hand* guides the actions of farmers and merchants in the marketplace to produce unintended *Beneficial Social Orders*: Eventually, a strong farmers' association was stood up in Wardak province's very diverse Jalrez District. Primarily Pashtun in makeup, the Jalrez farmers' association was multi-tribal led by a Hazara man with Uzbek and Tajik members. The Jalrez farmers' association experienced tremendous cooperation among its leaders to get their agricultural produce to outside markets. With the economic incentive of export economic potential as the communal goal, the Hazara, Pashtun, Uzbek, and Tajik members were extremely cooperative in putting their tribal squabbles behind them and a layer of tribal stability in the district emerged as a by-product of their drive toward economic self gain. In addition, other farmers and merchants benefited economically from the newly formed farmers' association business activities as demand grew for expanded goods and services in Jalrez.

Preventing the Donor Aid Hangover: To civilian USDA Advisors and U.S. Military leaders alike in Wardak Province, security evolved first from governance capacity building, which then led to economic development opportunities. As farmers benefitted economically from greater access to markets for their agricultural produce, overall security increased in various districts of Wardak Province. When U.S. military leaders and company level soldiers witnessed the direct correlation between "functional local governance" and "economic growth" to achieve "stabilization," civilian agricultural advisors were able to conduct comprehensive government capacity building programs down to the district level to effectively administer the Afghan government's strategy for agriculturally-based economic growth. As the International Security Assistance Forces (ISAF) draw down in 2014, Afghanistan will undoubtedly have areas that slide back into insurgent control, an obvious threat to the Afghan government leaders in those districts. Civilian and military advisors should, therefore, remain focused on Afghan government capacity building programs, and bottom-up economic development and growth opportunities for farmers to avoid projects that create an "donor aid hangover." Without functioning Afghan government agricultural assistance programs in place to deliver services to the population as donor aid assistance shifts directly through the central Afghan government system during this time of Transition, an "aid hangover" will lead to localized economic recession and other destabilizing impacts.

Case Study Four[xviii]

I love farmers. I have been working for over twenty years with farmers in some of the poorest and most violent countries of the world. My initial thought before joining with Special Forces' efforts in Afghanistan as an Agricultural Advisor was... how can my team and I replicate the success we had in Iraq in a unique operating environment in Afghanistan, the third poorest country in the world, where roads are inadequate, the terrain is difficult to transit and the rural areas are very kinetic with insurgent activity. It was my job to help Special Forces elements connect with the local population on the village level, in an effort to strengthen and encourage the local population to reject the Taliban insurgents and side with the democratically elected Afghan government. When we are successful in the rural areas of a "Rural-based Insurgency," then we will be successful in the urban areas; but the opposite does not hold true. One of the best ways to gain influence in the rural areas is to assist the farmers and growers that live there. During a conflict farming may be reduced but, in most instances, farmers do not abandon their land. This is why farmers are such a rich source of information and influence in siding against insurgent forces. Also, farmers know their home areas; they know who belongs and who the insurgents are. Famers also closely guard their investments and profits while pursuing their individual self gain in the agriculturally-based market place, thus their actions create other economic development opportunities for merchants and business owners who feed off the agricultural economy.

What is one of the basic building blocks of agriculture? Seed, I imagine. The U.S. Agency for International Development (USAID) had a large scale security program in southern Afghanistan that provided seed and hand tools to farmers. However, the seed for this project was purchased from local markets; most of this seed originated from Afghan farmers saved from the previous year's harvest. This seed was at least one or two generations old and lost much of its ability to germinate. As one farmer told me, "If I wanted local seed I could go purchase it myself from the local market." I contacted Monsanto, the international agricultural services company in Saint Louis, Missouri for assistance in finding and procuring improved vegetable seeds appropriate for the growing conditions in southern Afghanistan. Monstanto introduced me to their Director of Operations in India who then introduced me to a small Afghan seed company with an office in Kandahar City. This seed company had access to the improved vegetable seeds I was seeking and was this particular seed company was willing to deliver the seed to Kandahar Airfield, the sprawling desert airbase in southern Afghanistan where I stayed between deployments into remote areas of southern Afghanistan with my Special Forces colleagues.

Four weeks later the first shipment of vegetable seed sourced from the U.S. (California), France and The Netherlands was delivered by taxi to the main gate at Kandahar Airfield. This shipment was significant for several reasons:

- The Afghan seed company used Monsanto connection to procure a new source of improved seed specifically designed for the growing conditions in Afghanistan.

- The seed was paid for in local currency thus stimulating the local economy.
- The Afghan seed company, with its local office in Kandahar City, represented a sustainable Afghan-process for procuring improved vegetable seeds for local Afghan farmers.
- The initial and subsequent shipments assisted an American company, Monstanto.
- The improved vegetable seed proved more valuable than money to local farmers since the seed was not readily available.

In early May 2010, we launched a Village Stability Operations (VSO) project in the Gizab District of Oruzgan and Daikundi Provinces, designed in part to halt the flow of Taliban fighters into the vulnerable and strategic Kandahar city. The Village Stability Operations Methodology is a bottom up approach that employs U.S. Special Forces Operations Teams and partnered units (*like the U.S. Department of Agriculture civilian agricultural advisors*) embedded with villagers in order to establish security and to support and promote socio-economic development and good governance[xix]. All farmers in the district were considered subsistence farmers unable to produce surplus produce to sell in the marketplace. Further, Gizab District residents had never seen an Afghan government official, much less receive assistance from an Afghan Government official. Our team began distribution of the improved vegetable seeds to farmers who expressed an interest in cooperating with us to secure their lands of insurgents. The seed was not given away, rather the seed was used as a catalyst for building relationships with local Afghans. These same farmers revolted against the Taliban insurgents, fearing insurgent presence and influence would limit the Special Forces team's ability to work with farmers due to the poor security conditions. Thus farmers were not willing to give up their prospect of future profits generated from the infusion of the improved vegetable seeds and so they denied insurgent lodging, feeding, hiding in their villages and transiting their lands.

News of the improved vegetable seed project spread quickly from the Hazara farming communities to other areas including Pashtun communities. What was remarkable, was that the insurgents were mostly of Pashtun origin and now these Pashtun farming communities were choosing to participate in the vegetable seed project and rather than choosing the side of the Pashtun insurgents. We also used the injection of improved vegetable seed project also create a need for the role of the emerging Afghan-led district agricultural extension service to teach farmers new farming methods and practices. Farmers were anxious to learn new techniques in cultivating the improved vegetable seeds and once we trained the Afghan agricultural extension agents, the local people were able to see their government actually delivering agricultural assistance services to them. We were fulfilling our mandate to build the capacity of the Afghan government outside the capital; connecting the Afghan people to the Afghan government and vice versa.

Conclusion

By late 2010, testimonial field reports from civilian *Expeditionary Diplomats* started coming into Embassy Kabul about the progress, or lack of progress, in achieving the U.S. Counterinsurgency objectives in Afghanistan. These objectives involved security activities to clear areas of insurgents while governance and development activities were conducted to hold, build and transition Afghan districts and provinces to full Afghan security responsibility by the end of 2014. I conducted and documented 100-plus testimonial field reports from fellow civilian surge participants to track trends in best practices and lessons learned while meeting the counterinsurgency objectives. What emerged to impact me the most, were the experiences of four civilian surge participants who, with their U.S. Military and Afghan counterparts, worked with their respective Afghan communities in ways which caused the Afghan government to connect with its people and the Afghan people to connect with their government; the defined end state of the

U.S. Counterinsurgency strategy. Realizing this and wanting to know what that common link was to explain the spark of interest in these communities to reject insurgent influence, collaborate with each other and their local government and enthusiastically participate in their local economy, I spent the next year and a half dissecting these four distinct case study experiences. I found the explanation in the writings of economist Adam Smith, first published in the year 1776 when Smith wrote about the dynamics of another emerging economy in a fragile state, the original 13 American colonies.

Final analysis of the four case study experiences:

Only when Afghan appropriate human institutions and institutional process were created or strengthened to promote advancement of economic development opportunities, could the market's *Invisible Hand* guide the actions of those seeking economic self gain to produce intended beneficial social orders.

Simply put, U.S. civilian-military teams with their Afghan counterparts collaborated to create or in some cases strengthened what was perceived by local populations as Afghan appropriate human institutions and institutional processes. These institutions and processes included: tribally inclusive or tribally neutral community decision making forums; reinvigoration of role of the village mayor, strengthening the role of the often times fledgling District Governor; creating farmer cooperatives; and strengthening and validating the role of the government agricultural extension agent to bring agricultural assistance services to the local population.

Once these Afghan appropriate human institutions and institutional processes were set in place, the Afghans felt a sense of ownership and security in their political and economic destiny further emboldening them to reject the insurgent pull to move away from the central government system. As farmers, traders and merchants participated in the market place seeking their individual economic gain, the *Invisible*

Hand guided their actions to produce *Beneficial Social Orders*. Though the environment in each case study was unique, similar *Beneficial Social Orders* emerged: tribal tensions reduced as such groups had a representative voice in social and economic issues of concern to them; tribal and ethnic groups began working together to achieve greater economic gains than acting independently; security increased as insurgents lost their leverage with disenfranchised tribes and farmers were fearful insurgent presence would adversely affect their pursuit of economic self gain; villages started looking to their traditional village mayors, village leaders and Afghan government officials to hear their grievances and resolve their disputes vice the insurgents; and local government officials gradually became more accountable due to the fact their constituents were becoming more actively engaged to protect their economic gains and required greater local government accountability.

Foundational to all of these case study experiences was the creation and strengthening of another Afghan human institution, the Afghan National Security Forces providing protection for the local population.; a core principle of the Counterinsurgency strategy.

Application of the final analysis in fragile states:

Just as the United States prepares to move beyond its historically longest war experience to date in Afghanistan, the revisionist and other anti-foreign aid advocates are declaring the U.S. Counterinsurgency strategy a wholesale failure with an inevitable takeover by insurgent forces after 2014. Firstly, the U.S. Counterinsurgency strategy, conducted with 48 other member nations of the International Security Assistance Force (ISAF,) created space for the Afghan government and civil institutions to establish and free themselves from the ultra-Islamic fundamentalist Taliban regime. The space has been created, now it is up to the people of the sovereign Afghan state to decide their level of vulnerability to insurgent takeover after 2014 when the U.S. and international community's drawdown is complete.

Secondly, it is imperative to pause and assess what was accomplished in the U.S. Counterinsurgency strategy and apply those lessons to future scenarios as the U.S. contemplates future involvement in other fragile or failing states. For those who don't think the United States and international community will find themselves today confronted with how to react in fragile strategic countries or regions where populations are ethnically and tribally fractured, poor and terrorized by threats such as from insurgencies or terrorism, may want to think again. Specifically:

- When fragile country or region specific human institutions and institutional processes are established, Adam Smith's theorized *Invisible Hand* guides the actions of merchants and traders pursuing their individual economic gain in the marketplace resulting in unintended *Beneficial Social Orders* of stability, further economic expansion and the tendency toward greater governmental accountability and responsiveness to its citizens.
- 21st century Expeditionary Diplomats (civilian or military) must have a solid understanding all ethnic groupings, have an understanding of the tendency of dominant ethnic groups disenfranchise minority ethnic groups in scare resource environments, and the ability to successfully navigate ethnic and tribal dynamics. Therefore, aid assistance must attempt to break down barriers to access such assistance for all ethnic groups. When all ethnic groups are given a voice in the distribution of scare resources, these ethnic groups have the tendency to persuade governments to be more accountable. Simply put, tribes matter; ethnic groups matter. When minority tribes or minority ethnic groups are continually disenfranchised in accessing scare resources, flash points erupt causing the world community to react in some form.
- 21st century Expeditionary Diplomats must have a solid understanding of how to strengthen or create if absent, appropriate human institutions and institutional processes specific to the fragile state they are working in. Counterinsurgency strategies

or traditional aid assistance strategies conducted outside appropriate human institutions or institutional processes will fail to achieve local buy in.
- Foreign aid assistance, especially targeted economic development aid assistance, provides a stabilizing force in fragile countries and regions. Strategic economic aid can set into play the free market dynamics of Smith's *Invisible Hand* which is capable of directing people's behavior in productive ways.

Chapter 31

AFPAK Hands:
A Template for Long-Term Strategic Engagement?

Mike Coleman, Jim Gannon, Sarah Lynch and Reggie Evans

First Published 24 May 2015

Introduction

Afghanistan-Pakistan (AFPAK) Hands (APH) represents a non-traditional application of military talent. The Department of Defense (DOD) has yet to establish a long-term plan for preserving this innovative approach to strategic regional engagement used during Operation ENDURING FREEDOM (OEF). Further, it ought to be expanded in this fiscally constrained environment and extended to other Agencies. An evaluation of the historical origins of the program and its derivation from Joint strategic doctrine lead to recommended courses of action that justify the extension of the capability attained by the program since beginning in 2009. The program should exist independent of contingency operations, remaining instead as an established and enduring military contribution to what should be a long-term, low-signature, approach in regions deemed to hold strategic importance to the nation and require understanding and relationships.

Background

In 2009, the President of the United States (US) shifted strategic focus in Afghanistan due to the deteriorating situation. It had become apparent the US lacked regional understanding of the operational environment (Decade of War, 2012). APH was DOD's response to this national shift in approaching Central Asia. In launching the program in August 2009, Chairman of the Joint Chiefs of Staff (CJCS) Admiral Mike Mullen stated that peace in Central Asia would not likely be, "achieved down the barrel of a gun but rather through the lens of understanding" (Stavridis, 2010). The US formally adjusted its National Security Strategy (NSS) to approach issues from a regional perspective, acknowledging the issues threatening Afghanistan stability were not solely Afghan issues and possessed global implications (White House, 2009, par 5-8). This was an attempt to strategically adjust the way policy-makers defined and approached problems that threatened US interests in the Central Asia region, namely Afghanistan and Pakistan. It was in concept a multi-departmental approach; DOD called their portion the APH program.

After Assistant Secretary of State Richard Holbrooke publically used the phrase "AFPAK" to describe the new regional approach, DOD officials took the phrase and added the "Hands" in part tracing back to the namesake program, the China Hands. The US leveraged the China Hands with their Chinese cultural, language, and personal exposure during the 1920-1940s. They collectively tended to the US interests in China before, during, and after the country's transition to the People's Republic of China.

Ironically, the DOD name for the program to bring regional understanding to its operations actually offended the region it was supposed to help, demonstrating the challenge the US has as a super power in relating to other cultures. The "AFPAK" phrase resulted in public outcry from both Afghanistan and Pakistan, so the phrase became an internal program name only. Once 'in country' Hands were referred to as either Afghan Hands or Pakistan Hands respectively.

Within the first two years, over 180 Service members deployed as Hands throughout Afghanistan and Pakistan (Stavridis, 2010). As of January 2012, there were 700 Hands in the three phases of the program (Stavridis, 2010). As with any new initiative, despite the Services' support, they encountered difficulties synchronizing resources with requirements (Stavridis, 2010). This ad hoc program competes with established programs for the same talent base. Because of its demands, nominees ideally must have regional experience and should be familiar with counterinsurgency principles, physically fit, intellectually curious, culturally adaptable, entrepreneurial, and highly motivated (Stavridis, 2010).

The program was created as a means to develop a cohort of counterinsurgency experts with regional understanding. Unfortunately, the program remains funded as a contingency program and is not supported by the base funding sources of the Services. It is noteworthy the APH remains an ad hoc Joint program, with no permanent Joint positions established and contingency resources to fund it. Additionally, APH personnel remain managed outside the normal Service assignment processing channels. Neither the Joint Staff nor the Services categorize them as much more than language proficient and have struggled to fit them into their respective Service specific personnel systems. Furthermore, the designation as a Joint program with permanent Joint positions cannot occur due to legislative restrictions on the number of Joint positions in relation to the overall Service manning. Arguably, this limitation needs to be revisited given current fiscal constraints and the ongoing force reductions to overall end strength.

Initially, the program training focused on three areas: language, cultural immersion, and tactical security. The languages trained were Dari, Pashto, and Urdu, and the continuously phased approach to language development extended the duration of a service member's assignment to the program, usually three to five years. Once trained, however, APH personnel were very proficient in language, culture, safety, and security.

Hands were trained to fill an undefined gap between traditional DOD interfaces in the region such as Foreign Area Officers (FAOs) and Special Operations Forces (SOF). FAOs focus on relationships at the Mil-Mil level as it affects other nations. SOF's regional expertise has capacity limits. The Hands, at the inception, were specifically not staff officers, rather technical experts equipped with the language skill sets and cultural awareness to effect change where those in the region needed it most.

Linkages to Presidential Policy and National Security Strategy

The National Security Strategy (NSS) guides the use of the Nation's instruments of national power to focus energies on security interests ranging from strengthening our national defense to increasing global health security. The NSS points out there are no global problems that can be solved without the US and few problems that can be solved by the US alone (NSS, 2015). This establishes the Nation's requirement for partnering. The operating environment is a complex world with many security problems that cannot be fixed quickly or without partners. For the US to achieve its security objectives it must partner.

How the US navigates this complex world requires it to lead with partners at all levels. This leadership requirement demands a human interface that may misalign with traditional military platforms. A program like APH supports the national security policy because it enables the US to partner at all levels through a human interface of a person that understands the cultures involved in the region.

Additionally, Presidential Policy Directive (PPD) 23: US Security Sector Assistance (SSA) Policy, describes the US policy and approach to partnering in the global security sector. PPD 23 states by building our partners' capabilities and capacities our partners can better share the costs and responsibilities of global leadership. Clearly the US can't strengthen its partners at all levels without developing relationships at those same levels. Partners and coalitions require trust to operate effectively to accomplish these goals. Trust is formed through relationships. APH provides an example of a program that supports PPD 23 by developing technically competent individuals that can operate throughout this spectrum from tactical through strategic. Leveraging an APH-type program's culture and language expertise, aids development of long-term relationships, increasing effectiveness of partners and coalitions safe-guarding of collective strategic interests.

Regional Security to National Security

World Affairs Journal organized a virtual symposium on "what US policy in the AfPak theater would yield in the next ten years" (Hanson, et al, 2011). According to Hanson, et al (2011), the AFPAK 2020 Symposium concluded that total withdrawal from Afghanistan would be a serious mistake. In scaling back the counterinsurgency (COIN) effort, the perception of yet another abandonment of Afghanistan by the West must not occur. Instead, the US, NATO, UN, and neighboring nations must make a long-term commitment to the well-being of the Afghan people. Thus, policy-makers must negotiate the path between the large-scale COIN that works on paper and the primacy of homeland security that a disgruntled public demands. As such, a COIN-lite doctrine emerges acknowledging that efficacious strategies provide very little instant gratification and no shock or awe, and rely on fewer troops and more diplomats, aid officials, and civil society bodies (Hanson, et al, 2011).

Moreover, the AFPAK 2020 Symposium (Hanson, et al, 2011) highlighted that the vast majority of insurgents fight because their family and tribal networks have been alienated by the government, or they are incentivized economically to capture income from foreign spending or the drug trade. The symposium cohort concluded that ending the conflict will empower ordinary Afghans who are caught between the two sides driven by the corruption and predation that flourish during war. Two prime initiatives in achieving this goal include the de-escalation of spending along with enhanced contracting oversight, and a genuine peace process that does not pay lip service to the need for a political solution (Hanson, et al, 2011).

Linkages to Joint Doctrine

The APH program is an excellent application of Joint Doctrine. Joint Publication 3-0 identifies 12 principles of Joint operations formed around the nine traditional principles of war. The three additional principles, restraint, perseverance, and legitimacy, are relevant to how the US military applies combat power across the range of military operations (Mullen, 2011). APH is particularly effective in applying these three additional principles.

The purpose of restraint is to limit collateral damage and prevent the unnecessary use of force. Because a single act could cause significant military and political consequences, judicious use of force balances the need for security, the conduct of military operations, and the national strategic end state. Additionally, the excessive use of force may indirectly damage legitimacy (Mullen, 2011). In applying the Joint principle of restraint, APH adheres to the small footprint requirement of today's wars, ultimately saving money in a constrained fiscal environment. The program exhibits restraint in its approach to attain solutions through culturally aware negotiation tactics.

The purpose of perseverance is to ensure the commitment necessary to attain the national strategic end state through the provisioning for measured, protracted military operations. Since the root causes of crises can be elusive, some Joint operations may require years of patient, resolute, and persistent pursuit to reach the termination criteria. Further, they may involve diplomatic, informational, and economic measures to supplement military efforts (Mullen, 2011). APH exemplifies the application of perseverance in its long-endurance nature, suitable to the Phase 0 shaping objectives of theater campaign planning. Thus far, the program has displayed perseverance in its commitment to achieving end states in the Afghanistan-Pakistan region, but it must continue to endure globally despite the continuing fiscal constraints and its current contingency-only application.

Finally, the purpose of legitimacy is to maintain legal and moral authority in the conduct of operations. Legitimacy can be a decisive factor in operations. It is based on the actual and perceived legality, morality, and rightness of actions from the various perspectives of interested audiences. Thus, all actions must exhibit fairness in dealing with competing factions where appropriate (Mullen, 2011). In Afghanistan, the program has boosted US legitimacy by recognizing and acting within the contextual worldview of the Afghan people. By synergistically harnessing the benefits of restraint and perseverance, the APH program enhances legitimacy by showcasing US commitment and earning the trust required to maintain access in strategic regions, ultimately bolstering stability and security.

Future Risk and the Counter Argument

In the current US economic environment and projected forecasts with defense spending reductions, military personnel drawdowns are forcing the Services to focus on core competencies. A program like APH remains an outlier not aligned to Services' core competencies and placing further strain on the military by adding to its task list. This results in the reduction of the number of Joint Duty Assignment List (JDAL) positions. If APH transitions from a contingency program to a permanent requirement for the Joint Force, it will compete for traditional JDAL positions. Additionally, APH does not support the traditional military career timeline which officers must follow to be competitive for future operational assignments and promotion which the Services have established to support their personnel.

While the US moves to lessen its interaction in current areas of conflict in the midst of looming budget cuts, one should expect to see more resistance from the Joint Staff and the Services about manning (or the existence of) a Hands-type program. As Federal Departments seek to retain their most competent and talented leaders, Hands-type programs draw attention from the Services as they attempt to recapitalize and rebalance their respective manning priorities. With competing demands for funds, Services may opt to prioritize traditional platforms as they refocus on core competencies. Objections will only grow in a post-overseas contingency operations funding environment. To the Services, 'Jointness' is an esoteric goal; their core competencies will be their priority. They will argue that assuming risk to Service priorities is a risk to national security.

However, this attitude is shortsighted. The economic realities and diminishing human resources the US can leverage into areas with strategic national interest will require new approaches to long-term foreign area engagement. To limit the application of US resources, to include DOD manpower and resources to traditional core uses, limits the options available to US decision makers. The understanding of the problems and how to engage with most of the non-Western strategic partners should not be limited to only contingency type operations or short-term exercises. These restrictive approaches do not promote understanding of the environments required in these regions and the emerging global threats.

Additionally, the limits on the number of Joint positions as a percentage of overall Service manning limits and reduces the ability and bandwidth of the Joint programs at the same time they should increase. To restrict Service manpower use to only traditional Service core approaches in the new emerging world limits the options and understanding of non-Western cultural problem sets. It further limits the level of DOD participation to national policy makers as they consider non-traditional innovative approaches for engagement in these regions.

The Services fund several graduate degrees yearly, many of which cover a broad range of education disciplines. If the Services refocused some of these funded graduate degrees programs the Services with no additional costs could produce the education baseline for a Hands type program.

Recommendations

If APH goes away, the nation will lose vital engagement opportunities and capability gained since the program was started. The Joint, Interagency, Intergovernmental and Multinational approaches require cultural understanding and expertise to effectively partner. There is an African proverb, "If you want to go fast, go alone. If you want to go far, you must go together." In the present climate we must influence, not control; convince, not coerce; inspire, not rebuke; and we must launch better ideas than those promulgated by our foes. Broad regionally-focused programs such as APH can help the US face increasing global challenges by:

- Strengthening international partnerships between the US and other countries, both in military and civilian enterprises. This includes non-governmental organizations, inter-governmental organizations, and private charities.
- Encouraging interagency integration from the tactical level through the long-term strategic level.
- Shifting the interagency cooperative focus forward. "Less tail at home, more tooth forward" means that by sending our best and brightest Service members and civilians into Hands-type programs, we move the brainpower to the fields of the future.
- Understanding the culture of both war and peace. While it is vital that we retain our global combat capabilities, the most powerful and influential means of attaining regional security will come from understanding the environment through personal engagement.

- Maintaining excellent strategic communications. Everything we do depends on our strategic communication efforts. It is the main effort for launching ideas to compete in a complex world (Stavridis, 2010).

Some have recommended relocating the Hands program under another Department. Now that the benefits of a Hands-type program and the need to use it in other regions is established, an assessment is needed as to whether the DOD should lead this effort or if the Department of State (DOS) and its subordinate organization US Agency for International Development (USAID) are best suited to the task. (Walker, 2012)

In either case, DOD should contribute to the effort. Warfighting in the 21st century goes beyond combat[1] to include providing basic services, building infrastructure, encouraging the development of civil society, and democratic governance. The DOS and USAID are the nation's experts at diplomacy and development and should be in the lead, with the DOD supporting. A regional Hands-type program contributes to the understanding of strategically significant regions, and policy makers need DOD and DOS[2] to build civilian-military cohorts to fill the gaps in the face-to-face interactions that are required over the long-term in these strategic areas. These cohorts will serve as visible demonstrations of the nation's commitment to these areas that are required to achieve success. (Walker, 2012)

Lastly, the model may apply in other regions such as Latin America, the Caribbean, East and West Africa, Asia-Pacific, and even Eastern Europe which can benefit from intensely focused expertise. So, instead of losing years of training and expertise, the Joint Staff should begin thinking strategically and develop efforts to establish Africa Hands, Europe Hands, or Asia-Pacific Hands, just to name a few.

Chapter 32

What Is the Counter-Daesh Strategy?: A "Cohenian" Exercise

Kevin Benson

First Published 13 July 2015

> *"So tonight, with a new Iraqi government in place, and following consultations with allies abroad and Congress at home, I can announce that America will lead a broad coalition to roll back this terrorist threat. Our objective is clear: We will degrade and ultimately destroy ISIL through a comprehensive and sustained counterterrorism strategy."*[i]

Many pundits and politicians decry America and the Obama administration's lack of a strategy on how to deal with ISIS. For example, Sen. John McCain, the new chairman of the Senate Armed Services Committee said the Obama administration is "delusional" to think it is winning the fight against these terror groups. "I'm afraid that (White House chief of staff Denis McDonough) and the president have lost touch with reality," McCain told CBS's "Face the Nation."[ii] Accepting the political nature of this on-going scenario highlighted by the latest presidential news conference and following commentary thereon, President Obama said the United States does not have a complete plan to train and equip Iraqi forces to fight the Islamic State in Iraq and Syria (ISIS), saying Baghdad needs to show a greater commitment to building a fighting force.

"We don't yet have a complete strategy," Obama told reporters during a news conference at the G-7 summit of leading industrial nations in Germany.[iii] Michael O'Hanlon of Brookings said, "our Iraq policy is solid but under resourced and flawed. [The President] does admit distinct and emerging frailties: The anti-ISIS game plan is stumbling enough "that it risks failing," just like our Syria policy. "We have some serious work to do."[iv] The pressure for action is great. Presidential guidance, above, remains the start point for understanding the strategy to confront Daesh.[v]

Degrade then destroy ISIL is fairly straightforward guidance. In the February 2015 National Security Strategy the guidance changed to, "We have undertaken a comprehensive effort to degrade and ultimately defeat ISIL."[vi] I would not ask for much more than this statement as it allows plenty of freedom of action to design a strategy. The president also put a constraint on the use of US ground forces to wit; no US troops in direct combat. US ground forces in both Iraq and Jordan serve as trainers for Iraqi military units and selected Syrian organizations.

There are whispers among military circles, uniformed and retired we are pursuing a "Strategy by CONOPS" that is a piecemeal effort built upon the perceived and real results of the effects delivered during a series of short duration contingency operations. We are better than all of this. After years of war I am convinced there is a strategy based on politically aware military advice which is focusing our military efforts on attaining the objectives of our policy vis-à-vis Daesh. Using the Eliot Cohen model for 21st century strategy and only open source information I offer what I think our strategy contains.[vii]

The Cohen model of strategy, broadly stated, requires assumptions, a discussion of ends-ways-means, articulation of accepted risks, priorities, and a theory of victory. I begin with what I believe are the extant assumptions associated with our strategy. Assumptions take the place of facts which are necessary to continue planning. Assumptions made must be checked because if they do not become fact then the strategy is undermined and will definitely demand a new effort.

Our assumptions appear to be; 1] coalition interests will remain in confluence, 2] basing and over flight permissions will remain in effect, 3] airstrikes will work to encourage Iraqi security forces to fight, and 4] the counter Daesh policy will remain in effect in next administration. The first two assumptions require constant vigilance and discussion between senior US diplomats and military leaders with their counter-parts within the anti-Daesh coalition. Sustaining a broad coalition, even one brought together by mutual revulsion of Daesh's barbarity, requires continuous dialogue. Diplomats and military leaders must reassure each other and most especially those front line nations directly engaged with Daesh about the solid commitment to the cause of degrading and defeating Daesh. A rush of doubt or the development of friction points between competing interests would undermine the coalition. A denial of overflight rights completely disrupts the delivery of aerial fires which support ground forces. The third assumption demands constant validation and challenge. The final assumption is a US political assumption.

The diplomatic and military efforts to degrade and ultimately defeat Daesh demands firm commitment by the US government, irrespective of which party holds the White House. The proposed authorization for the use of military force, AUMF, currently before the Congress contains the prudent clause of a reconsideration of the effort after three years. This period carries the AUMF into the next administration. This is prudent as strategy must always be assessed, adjusted and reconsidered based on whether or not we are attaining our desired results. Nonetheless this is a necessary assumption as it serves as a forcing function for our government. Each administration must represent the will of the people regarding the application of force against the threat Daesh represents. The application of force leads to the consideration of the relationship of the ends-ways-means of our strategy.[viii]

A discussion of ends, ways, and means is by no means a relic of 19th and 20th century strategy. The means and ways committed to attaining our policy and strategic ends must be equal to the task. If they are not we are limiting ourselves to a "Strategy by CONOPS" and risk squandering any tactical success we attain. Our ends are stated and unstated, in my view.

The stated end of our strategy is Daesh defeated. The unstated ends are, 1] Iraq secure as a nation-state, 2] Iranian ambitions in the greater Middle East checked, 3] Israel reassured, 4] the Jordanian kingdom supported, and finally 5] the US position in the Middle East strengthened. The president announced our stated end in his speech of 10 September 2014; "Our objective is clear: We will degrade and ultimately destroy ISIL through a comprehensive and sustained counterterrorism strategy." The unstated objectives come from an analysis of media reports, written and video.

There are two distinct theaters of operations for the counter-Daesh strategy; Iraq and Syria. The self-proclaimed Daesh caliphate consists of territory occupied in both countries. A stable and whole nation-state of Iraq is in the interest of the United States. The same is true of Syria with the additional end of the Assad regime replaced. Attaining this end requires a separate strategy but the counter-Daesh strategy contributes to attaining this goal.

Checking Iranian ambitions in the greater Middle East is a worthwhile end for our strategy. On the one hand, in Iraq, the Iranian military contributions on the ground will assist in attaining US objectives. On the other we must ensure Iranian "success" diminishes Iranian standing by emptying Iranian coffers of treasure and tying up Iranian conventional and unconventional military forces for an appreciable amount of time. The final three unstated ends are obtained enroute to attaining the previously stated ends.

The Jordanians are steadfast allies and deserve our support. Daesh provided the motivation for Jordanian participation. US operations in support of this end must be designed as support only with clear Jordanian leadership in the fore. Israel, rough as our relations are at the moment, also deserves our support. The Israeli people and government must know our one of our ends is a more secure Israel. Finally the ultimate end of our strategy must be an improved situation for the United States in the Middle East and the world. The ways of our strategy must reach conditions which assure attaining theses ends.

The ways of our strategy, some of them at least, were sketched out in the president's 10 September 2014 speech. He stated,

> "First, we will conduct a systematic campaign of airstrikes against these terrorists." "Second, we will increase our support to forces fighting these terrorists on the ground… Across the border in Syria, we have ramped up our military assistance to the Syrian opposition." "Third, we will continue to draw on our substantial counterterrorism capabilities to prevent ISIL attacks." "Fourth, we will continue to provide humanitarian assistance to innocent civilians who've been displaced by this terrorist organization." [ix]

Another "way" which must be included in the execution of our strategy is a focused inform and influence operations/campaign. Much is made of Daesh's social media campaign, how it uses social media to attract a flow of volunteers into Syria and Iraq which sustains its fighting strength as well as filling its coffers. Knowing people who work in the cyber domain I am convinced we are waging counter actions in the social media. For example two stories from Reuters, published in the Hartford Courant cite living conditions in the region held by Daesh and condemnation of Daesh by Pope Francis.

> "Services are collapsing, prices are soaring and medicines are scarce in towns and cities across the 'caliphate' proclaimed in Iraq and Syria by the Islamic State, residents say, belying the group's boasts that it is delivering a model form of governance for Muslims." [x]

And,

> "Pope Francis on Thursday condemned the 'brutal persecution' of minorities by Islamic State insurgents and

said the joy of Christmas was marred by the suffering of children in the Middle East and around the world... He condemned Islamic State fighters who have killed or displaced Shiite Muslims, Christians, and others in Syria and Iraq who do not share the group's ideologies...he spoke of 'contemporary Herods,' with blood on their hands."[xi]

The struggle in the cyber domain for an information high ground must be a considered part of a holistic strategy to counter Daesh. The other "way" which must be incorporated into our strategy is the Iranian presence in Iraq.

Iranian military operations in Iraq can be useful in reaching US policy and strategic objectives. This will not be easy but Iranian actions must be considered in our overall strategy. Where our interests coincide our strategy must allow us to take advantage of Iranian efforts. Where our interests are at odds, in Syria, there must be active-overt and covert- actions to frustrate Iran. As the Chairman, JCS stated during testimony to the Senate Foreign Relations Committee on Wednesday, 11 March, "anything anyone does to counter IS is a 'positive thing.'"[xii] The challenge in executing our strategy is ensuring success on the ground in Iraq also serves to attain US policy objectives for the country.

Broadly stated the strategy is designed around three major lines of effort. The first, "the struggle over the legitimacy to govern, make laws, and enforce them." This contest is between Daesh and the legitimate Iraqi regime and the regime which follows Assad in Syria. The second line of effort is the defense of the populations in Syria and Iraq from the barbarity of Daesh during the fighting over each community. The third line of effort is the offensive designed to defeat Daesh in occupied Iraq and Syria, literally a town-by-town and village-by-village effort.[xiii]

The means of our strategy, broadly stated, are, the US training mission in Iraq, coalition training missions in Iraq, the US training mission for Syrian resistance, Coalition air forces, and the ground forces consisting of the Iraqi military and Syrian resistance. Information operations conducted in the cyber domain contest this space with

Daesh. We must also consider the committed air and ground forces from Iran as additional means of our strategy.

The constraints on the US missions are a fact therefore use of these means must abide by them. There are no reports of similar constraints on the reported Canadian, German or Australian trainers. Chances are the undoubtedly highly skilled Soldiers from these countries can perform other roles nearer the line of contact with Daesh in conjunction with Iraqi units and the *pesh merga*.

The available means contribute to build and maintain the coalition. The US-led Combined Joint Task Force provides an organizing framework designed to integrate capabilities and amplify coalition efforts. The forty-plus nations contributing to the effort provide a strategic advantage.

The means of the coalition will pursue Daesh to degrade and destroy its capabilities and defeat its efforts. On 18 December 2014 the coalition air forces conducted 1,361 air strikes. For example the 53 precision air strikes in support of Iraqi security force operations around Sinjar and Zumar resulted in allowing Iraqi forces to regain approximately 100 square kilometers of ground from Daesh.

Coalition means work to deny Daesh safe haven and sanctuary. The coalition uses more than precision strikes, but also enables Iraqi forces to expand their areas of control on the ground. Coalition information operations remove the opportunities for Daesh to manipulate youth, harm citizens, deny basic services and recruit fighters.[xiv]

The risks attendant to our strategy are clear. The Syrian resistance fails to coalesce into a force effective enough to defeat Daesh AND Assad. The *pesh merga* reinforces gains in Iraq and Kurdistan becomes a reality. The Kingdom of Saudi Arabia's interests are threatened forcing more Saudi action counter to the coalition. Finally, Iran's interests are threatened and the ayatollahs act to strengthen their hand in the region.

Execution of our strategy demands constant attention is paid to these array of risks and actions are adjusted to fit the needs of attaining our policy and strategic objectives. The National Security Council clearly plays the leading role in overseeing the execution of the strategy and its military, diplomatic, informational and economic aspects.

The priorities of the strategy can suggest a strategic sequencing, as was seen by the initial focus of air operations to disrupt Daesh's advance in Iraq. The first priority is degrade then defeat Daesh, all efforts must support this priority. Second are the efforts to train/support the Iraqi military and the Syrian resistance. Finally, but certainly not the less, are the associated international and regional diplomatic efforts to sustain coalition.

Managing the efforts associated with the strategic priorities is a full time job, a statement of the obvious perhaps. The information operations to confuse Daesh and sustain public support, American and international, must be prudently conducted. The counter-position to prudent management is a willingness to react to opportunity as opposed to trying to adjust while executing an information plan which may not be attuned to shifting conditions. An effort along these lines demands an extremely agile group of information specialists. This team must operate in the depth and breadth of the cyber domain and reinforce news that harms Daesh while sustaining positive news which sustains the home fronts.

The theory of victory, why we believe our strategy will work is not overly complicated. The strategy plays to US strengths, Special Forces and Special Operating Forces training, air delivered precision fires, a depth of diplomatic experience over years of war in the region and a confluence of interests among the countries of the region.

A Daesh action which plays to our strength is the drive to acquire territory. MAJ Ian Fleischmann observed,

> "By ceding terrain to an ideological adversary, we grant ourselves freedom of action to reform the front in a way that is more advantageous to ourselves. In this instance, we've allowed them to coalesce into a recognizable force. In Sun Tzu's terms, the formless adversary has taken form. This gives two key advantages: First, it gives our tactical actions moral weight they didn't have in the past...Now,

tactical defeats can be arranged in time and space for the purpose of manipulating ISIS morale, as defeats are clear and recognizable. Second, it has begun the process of redrawing the ideological front and shifting bases of political support."[xv]

The barbarity of Daesh actions in ruling its "caliphate" offer stark evidence of cruelty which can be used to influence a wider audience away from supporting this group.

It is an understatement to say getting this strategy right is important. We study the theory of strategy and its relationship to policy in staff and war colleges. We know, "What matters most is the ultimate perception of the situation, not the facts. And the perception will be of the effects, not the effort-there is no credit for trying hard. Different people, depending on their perspective, can legitimately differ in their assessment." We understand, "[W]inning a war (as opposed to a battle or campaign) is a political condition. If war is a political act, victory at the highest levels must be defined in political terms. That is a fairly uncontroversial assertion today, but one with enormous implications… The implication is that military victory (tactical or operational victory) without favorable political outcomes is sterile, and by any reasonable assessment that is true."[xvi]

It is also true, especially for the American people we serve winning and victory goes beyond achieving an esoteric political condition. The expectation of the people of our Republic is our Army and the joint force reach a definitive, conclusive result, a result which defeats an opponent and ensures we do not have to repeat our efforts and expend our blood and treasure, at least in the near term. As COL (ret) Rick Sinnreich succinctly observed, "Americans are accused of being war-weary. We're not war-weary—we're failure-weary."[xvii]

Chapter 33

Narrative: The Critical Component of Counter-Terrorism Strategy

Ajit Maan

First Published 14 July 2015

The shock and awe campaign being waged by ISIS is one we did not predict when we orchestrated our own variety of shock and awe over Bagdad. And while debate about the effectiveness of airstrikes against ISIS continues, those of us focused on the narrative battle are pretty much in agreement about one thing: we are losing. We are losing badly.

President Obama's recent remark, on June 8th, that we "do not have a complete strategy" to defeat ISIS, is an acknowledgment that military strikes and humanitarian aid are not enough to curtail ISIS's momentum and its recruitment capabilities. What we are missing is an effective narrative strategy. And without a narrative strategy, a military victory will be short lived.

Strategic narrative is not some sort of pretty accessory to add on to a military campaign to soften the effect. It is a core component of a comprehensive strategy to defeat ISIS. The ISIS narrative with the title "The Crusader/Zionist Alliance is Waging War Against Islam" is able to draw recruits from around the world faster than we are neutralizing key targets. And it will be our narrative strategy, or lack thereof, that will determine whether we win the war or just cut off a few snake heads.

ISIS has been winning the narrative battle because they put the narrative first and then design operations on the ground to deliver the message. That is an effective strategy. Meanwhile we have ineffectively been using communications after the fact to explain counter-ISIS coalition operations. We are all listening to their story. And the misguided among us are heeding the call to action.

The real power of narrative goes untapped if we think of narrative as mere messaging or communication. "Islam is under attack" is deceivingly simple. That's because it is not their narrative. "Islam is under attack" is the *title* of their narrative. The narrative itself is comprised of the myriad of messages and activities that support the title. The narrative is complex and messy and full of contradictions and mis-steps and irony.

War remains a human endeavor despite advanced technologies like cyber capabilities, and narratives are the way people understand any endeavor. A well-crafted narrative strategy should have two components: 1) A **Military and Development Narrative** explains the necessity for military activities and development strategy for our domestic audience, although it will be heard world-wide. 2) A **Counter-Terrorism Narrative** provides a protective function against the story expressed by our adversary by complicating their narrative and discouraging the enemy's potential recruits.

These two components must be interactive and mutually supportive to be effective. Additionally, they must support military and development efforts: analysis of the narrative landscape (of the stories being told on the ground) will be used as a predictive analysis tool that will support military and development activities. And the stories collected will add complexity to the conflict narrative and will foster the crafting of collaborative narratives with our allies and civilians on the ground.

Both types of strategic narratives *should:*

1. Focus on the suffering of civilians caused by ISIS and extremist groups like it.
2. Explicitly state that our military, development, and aid efforts will support civilians regardless of ethnicity or religious orientation.
3. Emphasize the inter-national collaborative nature of our efforts.

Both types of strategic narratives *should not*:

1. Bring our values (including democracy and human rights) to the areas in which we fight.
2. Contain any religious overtones.
3. Try to camouflage our own self-interests. Rather, our general strategy should be transparent.

Military and Development Narrative

Our own narrative ought to describe what is happening, what we are trying to do, and justify our strategy with moral and emotional triggers. It should describe why the need for military intervention has arisen. For example:

> "The brutality of ISIS and their violence against civilians demonstrate the moral depravity of their leaders who recruit and exploit vulnerable people to use as pawns. We recognize that we played a part in Iraq that allowed ISIS to develop. It is therefor the moral responsibility of the United States and an international coalition to intervene and stop the spread of ISIS militarily and to offer humanitarian and development assistance to those effected. There is a better alternative to the miserable future ISIS envisions for the territories it seeks to dominate. The people of this region, regardless of religion or ethnicity, deserve stability and security."

The audience will pull together elements of a story they hear that are consistent with the story they are a part of—the parts that cohere with their experience. So the experience of suffering should be a part of our narrative, not our values, human suffering.

This military/development narrative strategy being proposed proceeds from an understanding of communications as multi-dimensional and global in scope. That means messages are not hermetically sealed and sent from messenger to receiver in-tact. Rather, narratives are strategically crafted for influence and sent through channels that will necessarily distort the message, changing the meaning as it goes. And that process doesn't stop when the message reaches the intended audience. We cannot target a particular audience in the current communications environment. Our audience is our own domestic audience, coalition partners, those impacted on the ground including our own fighters, our adversaries, the potential recruits of our adversaries, as well as a world-wide viewing audience.

Counter-Terrorism Narrative

One of the reasons we have been ineffective in countering the ISIS narrative is because we are not the right messengers. Our counter-terrorism narrative strategy ought to proceed by identifying those stakeholders within the effected population who are hostile, or at least unsympathetic, to ISIS's message and then amplify their voices. The resulting counter-narrative will not come from us, but from inside communities effected by violent extremists. We will simply encourage them to tell their stories and ensure that they are heard.

Conclusion

In terms of Information Operations, it is strategically imperative that we stop running around trying to plug the holes ISIS blows in our narrative, and get out in front of their messaging. We need to undermine the appeal of the ISIS narrative in order to stem the flow of recruits and thereby not only weaken their military capacity at present, but also, address the threat that will continue to creep back up if we don't address it at a foundational level now. We can kill bad guys with drones but bad ideas don't die that way. The narrative strategy proposed here will accomplish what drones cannot.

Chapter 34

'Confronting ISIS in Libya: The Case for an Expeditionary Counterinsurgency'

Nader Anaizi, Frederick H. Dotolo, III
and Merouane Lakehal-Ayat

First Published 30 July 2015

Introduction: ISIS in Libya

In February 2014, scattered news reports placed ISIS aligned fighters in the Mediterranean city of Derna in eastern Libya. However, these sightings were dismissed as returning Libyan jihadists from Syria until November, when after months of intensive ISIS terrorism, targeted assassinations, murders, and street battles, ISIS had taken control of the city. Derna was promptly incorporated into The Barqa Province of The Islamic State, an ominous portent for what ISIS intended to do to the rest of Libya.[1]

ISIS took Derna while the international community was focused on The Second Libyan Civil War, which had started in May 2014 and pitted the nation's newly elected government at Tobruk against the prior Islamist controlled regime at Tripoli. Furthermore, both sides had foreign state supporters: Egypt, The United Arab Emirates, Saudi Arabia, The United States, and Europe recognized Tobruk, while Turkey and Qatar supported the Tripoli faction. The consequences of the civil war, with its associated international politics, prevented a unified response to ISIS.[2] This was a critical oversight because initially ISIS was very weak and its presence tentative. The group had no prior activity in North Africa let alone Libya, and Derna was traditionally controlled by rival Islamists. ISIS was also not even the main foreign terrorist group in Libya. Al Qaeda in the Maghreb (AQIM) had been in Libya for over a year with strong ties to the Tripoli government. Thus, ISIS faced considerable opposition from these groups. The Martyrs of Abu Salem Brigade, which was a *jihadist*-nationalist group, rejected the international character of ISIS's political goals while The Libyan Shield Force, an alliance of tribal militias loyal to Tripoli, dominated western Libya. Even the new Libyan government, which was backed by The Libyan National Army was, despite being degraded during the recent revolution proved a viable adversary its 35,000 soldiers.[3]

Unlike the groups fighting in The Second Libyan Civil War, ISIS posed a unique threat because it seeks to destroy and incorporate Libya into The Islamic State, and then use Libya as base to further spread throughout North Africa and portions of Europe. Abu Bakr al-Baghdadi, the leader of ISIS, proclaimed the existence of a caliphate in June 2014, and subsequently divided Libya into three provinces—Cyrenaica, Tripolitania, and the Fezzan—with the ultimate goal, according to ISIS activists, of erasing the borders of Libya, Tunisia, and Egypt.[4] The existence of a caliphate benefits ISIS in other ways. In November 2014, al-Baghdadi ordered a Yemeni ISIS commander, Abu al-Baraa el Azdi, to Derna to lead military operations. By March 2015, ISIS had expanded into Benghazi and Sirte, and received the allegiance of two larger insurgency groups—Ansar al-Sharia, based in Benghazi, and Boko Haram in Nigeria.[5]

ISIS is seizing, governing, and exploiting Libyan territory. It intimidates the population into complacency, imposes on them the harsh laws of The Islamic State, and thereby attracts younger Libyan jihadists, who are either disenchanted by the lack of opportunity in the post-revolutionary period or who see ISIS as the best means of achieving an Islamic caliphate. Currently, it fields 5,000–7,500 fighters, a number which will likely continue to grow the longer ISIS controls Libya.[6] If unchallenged, ISIS will dominate the entire country, and use it to become a staging ground for the return of tens of thousands of Algerian, Tunisian, and Western jihadists currently in Syria and Iraq.[7] If left unchecked, ISIS will threaten the stability of North Africa, the Middle East, and Europe.

ISIS has, as Mao Tse-tung argued any successful insurgency must, transitioned from guerrilla war into a regular military force that aims to complete the armed struggle with a final political transformation.[8] ISIS fighters wear military uniforms, use standardized equipment, and employ control and communications methods that resemble a regular force. Its tactics include mobility and firepower. It operates a full range of ground military vehicles, including armored fighting vehicles to main battle tanks to which its fighters gained access after overrunning military supply depots and arms' caches.[9] Other heavy weapons include artillery and attack helicopters, all of which, according to a U. S. State Department assistant secretary, qualify ISIS as an army.[10] While observers might point out that ISIS lacks the technical knowledge to maintain these forces, it could easily obtained the necessary expertise, parts, and ammunition in a relatively short time because of the assets—the oil fields—that ISIS controls in Libya, and elsewhere.

However, for the time being, ISIS remains largely a light infantry force, although a well-financed, experienced, and competently led one, and is following a coherent national strategy—the establishment of a caliphate.[11] An analysis done by the Institute for the Study of War observed, 'ISIS is pursuing a phased campaign design...the evolution of ISIS's strategy in light of these reports resembles these same control phases, with ISIS behaving as a proper military organization.'[12] It concluded, 'ISIS is not simply a terrorist organization, but rather an armed insurgency moving to control territory.'[13] Its theater decentralized military command structure, directed by a central political authority, is geared toward seizing, holding, and exploiting key economic and political terrains in the service of a discernable goal pursued through terrorism, fear, and military conquest.

The very strength of ISIS in Libya—gaining, holding, and governing territory—also provides a key vulnerability that can and should be exploited. Once ISIS takes territory, it must allocate logistical support, infrastructure, and manpower resources to hold and administer it. These resources seem to come, at least initially, from outside of the immediate area of operations, from other parts of the IS. A highly mobile counterinsurgency focus could interdict, destroy, and ultimately allow local military units to hold these strategic components. International security and development aid could also be employed to end, or mitigate the effort of the chaos of failed or collapsed states, including those undergoing civil war, and strengthening the institutions of the state (security, political, and economic), whilst also providing political legitimacy and economic development to prevent the recurrence of ISIS after military operations. At the same time, ISIS's rigid ideological adherence to an uncompromising religious understanding, to the detriment of local religious groups and practices, must render it vulnerable to becoming delegitimized in the eyes of Muslims coming under its control, provided a viable, permanent, alternative solution is presented.

Setting the Stage for the ISIS Insurgency: The Outbreak of Second Libyan Civil War, May 2014

The civil war in Libya was finally precipitated when, after many abuses by the Islamist dominated government and amid widespread violence and lawlessness, the Chief of Staff, General Khalifa Hiftar, returned from retirement and threatened the government with military action unless it resigned. However, his actions were interpreted either as an attempt to restore elements of the older regime or implement a military dictatorship. He seemingly pointed in this direction when he declared that all Islamists were terrorists, and vowed to rid Libya of them by launching Operation Libya Dignity. Militias from the city of Misrata, members of The Muslim Brotherhood, and those persecuted by the former security forces allied with each other and The General National Congress (GNC). Aided with material and political support from Turkey, they launched Operation Libya Dawn in July to liberate Libya from Gaddafi-era leaders.[14] Their forces seized Tripoli and western Libya, and reinstated the GNC. A second government, elected shortly after the launch of Libya Dignity, the House of Representatives, was established in Tobruk, and was soon recognized by The United Nations, Egypt, Saudi Arabia, and The United Arab Emirates.

The civil war derailed any future constitutional stability in Libya and spread anarchy, allowing local Islamists in eastern Libya, notably Ansar Al Sharia, the opportunity to assert control. Armed groups clashed over control of the nation's oil facilities, leading the petroleum industry in Libya, the National Oil Corporation (NOC), to declare *force majeure*.[15] This pronouncement signaled to the world that Libya had lost control of its oil resources, and provided ISIS the later opportunity to seize, hold, and sell the nation's oil to finance its operations.

The Arrival of the Islamic State in Libya, 2014–5

Thousands of Libyans who had gone to Syria to fight Assad joined the Islamic State, and when they returned, spread its propaganda to the local population.[16] The turmoil of post-revolutionary Libya and the spread of civil war created the perfect opportunity for ISIS. The group gained the support of local disaffected Islamists—those who no longer expected the solution to Libya's problems to be found in nationalist solutions.[17] The Shura Council for the Youth of Islam, for example, rejected both Tripoli and Tobruk, and pledged itself to ISIS, an act which granted the foreign-led group a sense of legitimacy and provided ISIS with an infrastructure from which to expand. Another tactic was to use Islamic charities, which were needed to help alleviate the sufferings caused by the economic problems and the depravations of the civil war. In other areas, ISIS used terror tactics to undermine the government and convince the population that it was too dangerous to oppose the group. These maneuvers succeeded, and the numerical strength of ISIS increased considerably. When ISIS reinforcements arrived from Iraq and Syria, the group made its most brutal statements in February and April 2015, by beheading twenty-one Egyptian Coptic Christians and, more recently, twenty-nine Ethiopian Christians.[18]

Security and Economic Implications of an ISIS dominated Libya

The dire issues facing Libya should ISIS dominate the entire country will have broad implications for the security of North Africa and southern Europe. Libya's geographical position means that ISIS would be able to quickly destabilize surrounding states, creating the chaos it needs to expand. ISIS fighters and sympathizers could enter and leave Libya. The borders are wide and difficult to manage, and the desert regions offer vast areas for bases. Even Al Qaeda in the Maghreb was able, from just three desert bases in southern Libya, to attack targets in Algeria and Tunisia.[19]

The continuing war in Syria poses another potential danger for Libya and the region. Nationals from countries like Tunisia and Algeria, as well as the European nations, went to Syria and Iraq to fight. While some of those fighters, especially those who were in Syria genuinely aided the people to free country, many of the others fought alongside the Islamic State militia. In the same way that Libyans returned home to spread ISIS ideals, many of these fighters will eventually return to their own nations and do the same. ISIS has made clear its intentions to invade Europe, portions of which it has claimed for its caliphate.[20] Libya is the key strategic point from which to infiltrate fighters into Italy and southern Europe. The many refugees who fled the chaos in Libya, and risking the dangerous trip across the Mediterranean, would provide the perfect cover for men and women aligned with ISIS to enter Europe, an infiltration strategy that could be executed at little cost to ISIS, as it could send young, minimally trained, recruits on high terror yielding, Mumbai-style attacks.[21]

The ISIS problem in Libya is manageable, but only for a short time. The situation could quickly spiral out of control. The Libyan Army is hindered by its poor training and cannot legitimately acquire weapons because of The United Nations arms' embargo.[22] Europe will face the gargantuan task of trying to mitigate the security risk along 1770 km of Libyan coast line and an additional 2146 km of coastline in Algeria and Tunisia. But given ISIS's current expansion over the past year, with the additional support it has received from the state apparatus of The Islamic State, the conversion of other Islamists groups within Libya, Boko Haram's recent declaration to ally with ISIS, and the return foreign fighters, the security problems would not stop with Libya, but would extend across North Africa and southern Europe.[23]

The Response to the Libyan Crisis: Limited International Counterterrorism Effort, 2011–4

The United Nations Security Council Resolution 1973 provided the framework for international involvement in the Libyan Civil War of 2011. NATO subsequently enforced an arms' embargo and a no-fly zone on Libya, while providing ground attack missions against regime forces for humanitarian purposes in Operation Unified Protector. After Qaddafi fell, a political process was agreed to by the parties, the revolution entered a political phase, and Unified Protector ended.

At that point, some Western nations continued to aid the GNC, by funding low-level counterterrorism efforts in Libya, mainly training or intelligence sharing.[24] The European Union, for example, backed The European Border Mission Libya, (EUBAM), to provide a border guards and a naval coast guard.[25] The Americans provided intelligence support until the murder of Ambassador Chris Stevens and the destruction of the American Consulate in Benghazi in September 2012. They trained Libyan Special Forces, and contributed to Libya's security by helping the French and African Union counterinsurgency and peacekeeping missions in Mali and Central Africa, over the following year.[26]

The outbreak of the Second Libyan Civil War caused these missions to be either modified or outright canceled. The West shifted from direct government contact to providing minimal indirect support through international diplomacy, which was understandable before ISIS began to expand. The problem, however, was not only did the West lack an energetic strategy to deal with the declining political instability in Libya, it also completely ignored the significance of ISIS, facing it only in early spring 2015, when ISIS had already metastasized. In Libya, the international community was not focused on stopping ISIS, but rather in reconciling the two warring sides. The United Nations Support Mission in Libya, for example, sponsored talks that if successful would essentially reward the use of violence and authoritarianism in Libyan political life, furthering the very lawlessness that had led to the civil war and enabled ISIS to spread.[27]

One particular challenge the international community now faces is how to transition from its counterterrorism mentality. ISIS is brutal, its policy of terrorism designed to shock the local population, reinforcing the message that modern Arab governments and the West are weak, and ISIS is now established. Furthermore, the use of retaliatory of force provoked by ISIS's terrorism aids speaks of Western defensiveness, and illustrates a lack of determined effort to dislodge ISIS from Libya. In early March 2015, for example, the Italian navy demonstrated off the city of Derna after ISIS threatened to attack Rome. And while the ISIS fighters fled their positions, because no one really expected sustained Italian military action, one even coordinated with the Libyan National Army, ISIS returned, probably strengthened by having survived another confrontation with the West.

Unilateral kinetic military operations which do not seize ISIS territory, a key area of vulnerability, are not effective. Egypt and The

United Arab Emirates, for example, conducted air strikes against Islamist targets in August 2014, with the Egyptians hit ISIS after the Coptic Christians were murdered outside of Sirte. While these air strikes presumably damaged specific targets, because there was no subsequent ground operation to clear and hold Sirte, either unilaterally or better yet with the Libyans, nor were the air strikes conducted as part of a comprehensive strategy, for example to interdict ISIS supply routes, they failed to damage ISIS. In another case, the government of Tripoli ordered air strikes in support of the guards who were defending oil production sites from ISIS fighters, but these failed to prevent ISIS from overrunning the oil fields, because the guards lacked the ammunition to sustain an active defense, despite the air strike.

A New Response to ISIS: An Expeditionary Counterinsurgency (COIN)

The international community, especially members of those regional powers aligned with the Tobruk government: Egypt, Saudi Arabia, The United Arab Emirates, The African Union, The Arab League, The European Union, and the Western powers led by The United States, needs a comprehensive political and military counterinsurgency to aid the Libyans in restoring their own national sovereignty by driving out ISIS. In this respect, the Libyan National Army would require aid, though its competency is increasing. Over February and March 2015, the army secured the Port of Benghazi from Ansar al-Sharia, and made considerable gains against Islamist held positions outside of Tripoli, though little against ISIS.[28] Therefore, the coalition must be balanced between applying enough power to help the government but, because of Libya's colonial history, cannot overwhelm the nation with tens of thousands of western troops deployed in heavy combat maneuver elements, as did the Surge in Iraq when 30,000 additional troops brought total strength to over 100,000 forces. Rather, the coalition presence should include smaller, mobile, combined arms formations that are heavy-hitting expeditionary units capable of immediately responding to the flow of the battle against ISIS, and correcting operational deficiencies in the Libyan military.

Similarly, the coalition could assist the Libyans with border security and by forming a strategic reserve nearby the country which could respond with overwhelming military force in case of dire military necessity. In addition, Western and regional political assistance to the Libyan government should focus on ending Turkish support for Tripoli, which is perpetuating the civil war and undermining the government's ability to deal with ISIS, a threat not just to the Libyans but also, given the proximity of the Islamic State to Turkey, the Turks as well. The coalition could persuade The United Nations to reevaluate its current arms embargo to allow for a more sensible, case-by-case basis to enable the government to purchase arms and ammunition while preventing the Islamists and ISIS from being resupplied. Also, political and economic aid is needed to strengthen the Libyan state and economy if it is to correct decades of Qaddafi's dictatorial policies that undermined genuine national institutions.[29] The key focus of the coalition, however, must to aid the Libyans in defeating ISIS by striking its vulnerabilities, particularly supply routes and strongholds.

The French experience during Operation Serval in Northern Mail in 2013, for example, might hold some lessons. The French deployed an expeditionary force of air, artillery, airmobile infantry, and tanks, about 4,500 soldiers—augmented by 3,000 men from the African-led International Support Mission to Mali (AFISMA) and 6,000 soldiers from the Malian army—to defeat Al Qaeda in the Islamic Maghreb and other Islamist rebels holding northern and central Mali during Operation Serval. The French operated under a U.N. Security Council Resolution, and were requested by the Malian government. Their forces waged a high tempo operational and logistical offensive backing the Malian army which cleared the various towns and cities along the Niger River, while other African forces held the ground taken from the lighter armed terrorist forces.[30] French operations helped to squeeze AQIM fighters into remote strongholds, where they were subsequently isolated and destroyed.[31] During operations in Gao, for example, Chadian and Nigerian troops seized objectives supported by the French.[32] Afterwards, the French kept 1,000 troops in Mali—with an additional 3,000 based in smaller bases throughout the region—to conduct counterterrorism missions.[33]

However, coalition forces in Libya must understand that ISIS will use any wide-scale, large permanent military presence in the country to appeal to popular opposition, aiding anti-western propaganda and recruitment campaigns.[34] Therefore, coalition forces must be expeditionary in nature, with the capability to maneuver quickly from either over-the-horizon locations, such as amphibious vessels, or limited cantonments. There should be a high operational tempo as coalition forces quickly move into and out of areas of operations in support of The Libyan National Army to throw ISIS off-balance. Only if absolutely necessary would coalition forces be used to unilaterally seize and hold those territories, and then so these might be quickly turned over to the Libyans. Ideally, the coalition supports Libyan operations. Additionally, the coalition needs to see tactical victories as shaping not just the battlespace but more importantly advancing a strategic political goal—the defeat of ISIS held territory, and the destruction of those forces.

In the case of naval operations, because Libya has little if any capability, the coalition forces should be prepared to assume a more direct role. In other words, a naval component must be integral to the overall military mission because Libya currently lacks sufficient naval forces to even patrol its coastline. Also, the coalition must help Libya develop this naval capability as quickly and efficiently as possible. The United States Naval doctrine calls for the Navy to strengthen and stabilize regions, 'by securing and leveraging the maritime domain, with and in support of national and international partners.'[35] There is a history of naval forces performing counterinsurgency missions in North Africa. During the Algerian War, for example, the French employed their navy in a full-range of air/naval/ground combat, support, and reconnaissance missions against The National Liberation Front, successfully denying the FLN resupply of arms and munitions from oversea sources while degrading their enemy's combat effectiveness.[36] The key to the French approach was what one scholar observed, 'Maritime security operations have tended to be implemented randomly. This approach needs to be replaced by a far more robust, proactive, and intelligence-led strategy...'[37]

Given Libya's proximity to existing NATO assets, joint expeditionary forces—naval, air, and ground—would possess the military power and logistical sustainability to maintain operations, and could provide training and support to The Libyan National Army. The mission would require reasonable political and legal agreements with the government, and with tribal associations. It would include a counterterrorism dimension, but this would be more strategically focused than those employed haphazardly in 2012–3. The counterinsurgency should not become involved in the Libyan civil war; the military coalition is an ally of the Tobruk government in its fight against ISIS, and is not to be used against the Tripoli government.

A successful COIN can be accomplished in Libya. One example of what might constitute this COIN effort is The United States Marine Corps Expeditionary Force 21 concept. The Marines focus on conducting littoral operations that could support the Libyan army's operations.[38] The document calls for expeditionary operations to be sea-based, rather than the traditional land-based force. While the concept is guiding Marine Corps planning for the next decade—a sea-based expeditionary force would require 38 naval ships, compared to the 14-16 current for a Marine Expeditionary Brigade (MEB)—contingencies could provide the necessary platforms for a smaller Marine Air-Ground Task Force (MAGTF) to be sea-based in the immediate future.[39] The problems in deploying a smaller force in Libya involves relative combat power, and sustainability, as the equivalent Marine Expeditionary Unit (MEU), is not suitable for counterinsurgency operations. The point is, however, that such a force is available to aid the Libyans in case of a dire necessity.

The ideal expeditionary force structure would be two Marine Expeditionary Brigades (MEBs) for the combat power, sustainability, and operational relief. Still these would have to be supplemented with additional theater forces from other NATO members, regional states, or associated international bodies, such as The African Union, if operations were expected to last beyond sixty days, as they did for The French in Mali. Built around a reinforced marine infantry regiment, a MEB is a joint expeditionary force that includes command, ground combat—infantry, artillery, and armor, and other assets—air, logistical, and support elements, and can operate independently ashore for thirty days. There are two main types of MEBs. An amphibious MEB is housed on amphibious ships, and moves ashore where it establishes positions for combat missions. The other example airlifts troops to a theater of operations, and marries these with prepositioned or maritime deployed ships.[40] A deployed MEB has approximately 14,000–18,000 personnel, which would be sufficient to aid the Libyan military against ISIS, but without the appearance of a permanent occupation.[41] An important component of this expeditionary counterinsurgency would be, while in theater, using smaller Company-sized Landing Teams, (CTLs) to bolster Libyan National Army units, increasing their capability, while maintaining a light 'footprint' for the Americans.

Regardless, a vigorous expeditionary MAGTF unit could deny ISIS access to the sea, severely undermine its ability to initiate operations, while bolstering the Libyan military's operations. Furthermore, the MEBs could also coordinate with French expeditionary forces and their allies on Niger's border with southern Libya, and with Egyptian, Tunisian, and Algerian forces on their respective frontiers to isolate ISIS, ensuring that Libyan operations would be more successful than not intervening, and leaving a *status quo* that is doing long-term damage to Libyan security.

A comprehensive COIN would also include economic and political components. The synergy of smart reforms with the fruits of successful military operations—striking ISIS's vulnerabilities, by demonstrating to the population the weakness of IS—will lead to better political results for the government. The objective of these two components would be to strengthen existing all state institutions, including but not limited to the military, local police forces, legal systems, markets, and property and political protections. Reliance only on active counterterrorism missions, where coalition forces unevenly train Libyan forces or conduct drone strikes fails to address ISIS in a systematic manner, and amount to mere pinpricks that will not strike the vulnerability of ISIS.

Likewise, a population-centric COIN, where coalition forces attempt to secure the population first, would be problematic in Libya. The core of such a strategy is security, a metric that is very difficult to measure and which would require large numbers of foreign troops, at least initially, the number of which might tip the population toward ISIS, or simply allow ISIS to wait out the withdrawal of foreign troops before resuming its insurgency from untouched strongholds. This would also undermine the legitimacy of the Libyan government, which is responsible for securing the Libyan people.

This type of security COIN would confuse the effort, as tactics would replace strategy. Hew Strachan writes that 'in counter-insurgency the distinctions between the levels of war, tactical, operational, strategic and political, are much less clear than in major war.'[42] Therefore, coalition forces must avoid confusing tactical successes with achieving local security, especially if ISIS can wait out the coalition. The other issues with a population/security COIN, is that ISIS would use those areas of Libya it governs to attack government or coalition declared 'safe' areas, gaining political advantage. If the coalition does not address retaking ISIS's territory, then no matter what the coalition did, and no matter how many ISIS fighters were killed, or facilities bombed, ISIS would be seen as having survived, and thus having defeated the coalition.

Likewise, reliance on a counterterrorism response only, although less costly to coalition governments, is largely ineffective as it would only require coalition forces to "engage with nations' military or civilian security forces and authorities,"[43] and not seize ISIS's key political and military terrain. This strategy would not be effective in stopping further ISIS expansion.[44] Reliance on an air strategy, where coalition forces just bomb ISIS targets, even in support of local militia, would also not be very effective. The U.S. has already flown over 5,000 missions against ISIS in Iraq and Syria, and ISIS has still expanded.[45] In those instances in Iraq in which coalition air strikes have aided Shia militias in taking ISIS strongholds, the resulting sectarian violence unleashed by the militiamen has undermined the populace's political support for the government.[46] Airpower alone cannot take territory and because it cannot be applied in a broadly sustained manner it presents ISIS with military opportunities to exploit. During the recent air campaign in Iraq, for example, even though ISIS was on the defensive throughout Anbar Province, it still managed to overrun an advanced Iraqi brigade headquarters at Thar Thar.[47] Despite having expelled ISIS from Tikrit, the situation in more recent weeks remained strategically grim as ISIS forces switched operations to Ramadi.[48]

One argument for the use of air strikes in counterterrorism missions is that it spares 'boots on the ground,' while supporting the ground forces of host government. But even this is problematic: During operations in Tikrit, ISIS defenders inflicted considerable casualties on the attacking poorly trained Shiite militias, the bulk of the government force retaking the city. The offensive was halted for days before it resumed and secured the city.[49] Likewise, in its wake, there are no indications the Iraqi government is interested in developing any institutions beyond security forces in Tikrit that will prevent the return of ISIS, let alone address those concerns that led to the Sunni revolt in the first place. Similarly, relying on militia forces to conduct a ground war is troubling given the rise of sectarian violence associated with militias. Out of 24,000 men conducting operations in Tikrit, for example, 20,000 were militiamen, a disparity that could easily contribute to the return of social conflict and ethnic cleansing, thereby increasing the popular support for ISIS among Iraq's Sunnis.[50] There is also the question of whether such ground force are efficient. At Kobanî in Syria, for example, only after four months of coalition air strikes and brutal ground combat between ISIS and Kurdish militia, were the Kurds able to finally drive ISIS from the town

Based on experiences in Iraq and Syria, it would seem that neither a counterterrorism approach nor relying on untrained, or ill-trained and equipped militia are ways forward against ISIS in Libya. An expeditionary counterinsurgency led by the west could succeed if the coalition supplements, supports, and trains the Libyan army, which has proven itself in limited engagements against Islamists and ISIS fighters. As the situation in Libya deteriorates, the window for action is closing fast. There are a multitude of factors that must be assessed when considering any commitment, but to do nothing or to do too little, would only increase the costs for action later when the threat from ISIS has metastasized.

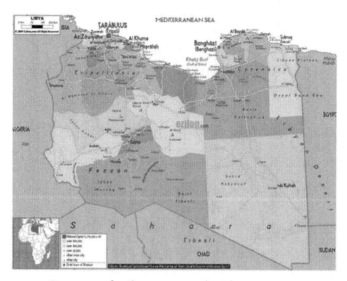

Courtesy of ezilon.com, used with permission

Islamic State Social Media; June 2014
English Version of Arabic Map
[For Public Distribution]

Chapter 35

The 21st Century Answer to "Burning their Crops and Salting their Fields": Interdicting and Destroying The ISIS Financial Network

Greg Kleponis and Tom Creal

First Published 1 August 2015

The enemy of terrorism has evolved particularly over the past decade in terms of organization, resourcing, public relations and above all tactics. I have written on several occasions that today's terrorist organizations more resemble organized criminal organizations rather than the strictly political or military organizations they once were.

We have seen ISIS or the so called "Caliphate" organized in such a way that they keep organized records, have accountants, bankers and budget directors—all to keep track of the money which is the life blood of their organization. Their income, not unlike any other organized criminal element comes from the sale of commodities (in this case oil), protection rackets, human trafficking and out-right robbery. Sound familiar?

The point is that we are essentially fighting organized criminal gangs like we would be waging war on military insurgents and this is just the wrong approach. Instead of tasking just the military to deal with the problem as they will simply address it in the only way they know how, we should start thinking like crime fighters and like the FBI and other federal law enforcement in the US and in Europe, hit the terrorist and insurgents (criminal gangs) where the live and that's at the bank.

Most criminal organizations do not have an apocalyptic ideology—this much is true. I would suggest that too much is made of this so called radical ideology. There is no doubt that it is the animating force behind some of their most obscene crimes carried out by the "true believers" but like the Taliban whose ideologically pure are estimated to be a number less than 10%, they are in most senses a criminal business enterprise run by and controlled by the cynical who control the most fanatical.

What most criminal enterprises want and cherish above all is money. Though it may not have been the motivating force at the beginning, it slowly corrupts the organization from within so that so called radical terrorists become nothing more than corrupt conflict entrepreneurs. Just check out the $7,000 Rolex Oyster on the wrist of Abu Bakr Al Baghdadi the self-styled leader of the new Caliphate.

While focusing on training, drones and airstrikes may be necessary and may degrade their abilities, the lifeblood of their organizations is money. For example, their jihadis don't jihad for free—they get a monthly salary. Weapons, ammunition, salaries, and other overhead all cost money.

Where does the money reside and how to they access it? The simple answer is—the same as we do. They use banks and other financial intermediaries. Knowing this puts us a long way forward in using another arrow in our quiver toward defeating organized criminal terrorist groups. We must follow the money trails backwards and also forwards to every single set of hands that touches the movement of these funds. As with all legitimate businesses, in any monetary chain of custody there are individuals and organizations involved and all of these can be considered "aiders and abettors."

Tracing the sources of money as well as those who act as conduits, agents and advocates and prosecuting them is just the start of the unravelling of the money web that finances them. This is not unheard of as, for example, under the former Bank Secrecy Act of 1970 (now the Patriot Act) has put in place requirements for banks currently to report monies that are dubious which can result in large fines or in some cases jail time for those who fail to report suspicious activity and are caught so in a way in the US, they have deputized, albeit unwilling financial institutions in the fighting of financial crimes. In Britain as an additional example, financial crimes have come to the attention of the authorities and similar requirements of made of financial institutions, broker dealers and money service providers all overseen by the Financial Conduct Authority. In each of these instances there are rules, regulations and authorities in place not only to prosecute those to "aid and abet", the actual criminals themselves but also to seize these funds under private forfeiture statutes.

The movement of money around the world by organized criminal terrorists and their enablers is what and where the focus needs to be. I am working with Tom Creal who is a Forensic Accountant and Panel Expert for the United Nations. His specialty is the tracking of ill-gotten monies and those who aid and abet the disposition of those monies. His efforts have led to the tracking of Charles Taylor, the former President of the Republic of Liberia monies from businesses he ran to fund what were deemed war crimes from the International Court of Justice. His bank dealings stretched from the British Virgin Islands to China to Citibank in New York. Through the civil forfeiture statute and other legal means his tens of millions were confiscated.

Creal was also part of Task Force 2010. This Task Force set up by the US DEA to combat corruption in contracting. While I was in Afghanistan with Tom he was able to uncover enormous corruption within the Host Nation Trucking Vendors contracts. Creal was the forensic accounting expert that dug deep into the finances, traced the fast movement of large sums of money using Hawaladars (a type of informal money transfer system used in the Middle East and Asia), and then through banks around the world. One of these conflict entrepreneurs was making $34 million a year funnelling money to the Taliban. In this perverse way the US Military was actually funding the very enemy they were combatting on the ground nearly every day!

One of the individuals we worked on together was a minor security contractor and low grade gang leader named Rohullah. A petty criminal and drug addict, he nevertheless managed to become the security contractor of choice among many of the trucking companies largely because by hiring him your loads would be not be attacked. Once we attacked his money, he changed teams and provided information then used for military operations. Thus, what was once a liability became an asset.

Fighting ISIS is something that will require not brute force only but a certain sublime cleverness that we in many ways have failed to do in the past. The idea "if it don't fit get a bigger hammer" did not serve us well in Iraq nor Afghanistan and when we realized that and started to fight smarter rather than harder we made progress. I advocate that a significant part of the effort in fighting ISIS involve a counter-finance operation or directorate. It would include bank analysts, oil industry subject matter experts, organized crime subject matter experts, logisticians, web and social media experts and accountants. This organization would focus on the sources of IS income as well as tracing from the sources to the disposition of assets. For example, the logisticians and oil industry SME's would focus on the current practice of ISIS transporters moving oil on the main road from Baihi to Mosul then north onto Turkey and elsewhere. Baiji is a major industrial center and is home to the most expansive oil refinery infrastructure in Iraq. We know from aerial photos, we are able to obtain the trucking companies names and track the monies to various end users and other financial sources from there. This is just one example of an IS income stream that can be traced and attacked from source to end asset state.

The other Subject Matter Experts on the team would be internet and social media professionals. We know that ISIS uses Twitter both to raise funds to support their acts of terrorism and recruit. Twitter accounts can be traced, the money raised through social media can be tracked and the data points along the movement of the monies can be identified and dried up. One example is Hajjaj bin Fahd al-Ajmi. He raises money via Twitter and funds ISIS and the al-Nusrah Front from his base in Kuwait, but the funds raised move through weapon dealers, suppliers, hawalas, money carriers or through trade routes.

Lastly a concerted effort must address what Creal has named the "aiders and abettors" These are, as have been mentioned, the banks, investment advisors broker-dealer institutions, money transmitter and real estate developers. In addition, as noted above they can be commodity suppliers, those in the service industry, local informal and formal power brokers and other. In short they all conspire to aid and abet organized criminal terrorist activity and should themselves all be targeted.

Many of the most nefarious international war criminals were only successful because they were served by quite literally an army of enablers from a multitude of different locations and service platforms. All of this was possible for two reasons, first the financial rewards for doing so were great, the second was that they were greater than the risk of being caught and prosecuted.

The international community has both the resources as well as the body of international law to support an cooperative effort to not only trace these tainted monies but more importantly to confiscate them. This international task force if you might call it that, could establish a financial command center to coordinate attacks on those providing, moving, and holding assets for ISIS. As mentioned not only could the alliance of nations opposed to ISIS put into action processes to check monetary transactions of ISIS but to freeze and ultimately confiscate those assets to be used to raise, train and sustain forces that are actively fighting ISIS on the ground at present. This would not be dissimilar to the US indirectly funding the Taliban as mentioned earlier-only this time in reverse!

The time has come for the US and its allies in the fight against terrorism to begin to think more creatively about how to degrade and ultimately defeat organizations like ISIS. The face of international terrorism is changing and they have proved that they are not only sophisticated, brutal and above all "wired." Fighting a sophisticated 21st century enemy is going to take more than mid-20th century tactics. In other words we are not going to be able to bomb them into submission. Rather the fight we have on our hands now is going to require us to think less like soldier and more like crime fighters, bankers, logisticians, IT Geeks and Anthropologists. We must not only understand the enemy but also have a firm grasp of how the enemy not only operates but how it feeds itself. Throughout history, armies burnt the enemy's crops and slaughtered their animals to literally starve them into submission. Now is the time to start starving organizations like ISIS by taking away their financial resources.

Chapter 36

"Channeling": The United Kingdom's Approach to CVE-A Plan Americans Deserve But Will Never Receive

Ryan Pereira

First Published 5 August 2015

Responding to a perceived increase in radicalization among American Muslims, the White House recently convened a summit on Countering Violent Extremism (CVE). However, the concept remains poorly defined and places a disproportionate emphasis on preventing radical beliefs instead of violent behavior, making it nearly impossible to quantify success. Despite the fanfare, the United States has yet to develop a sophisticated prevention and de-radicalization infrastructure to counter the myriad push-and-pull factors that draw susceptible individuals towards violent extremist organizations like the Islamic State (ISIS).

To date, over 150 U.S. residents have attempted to travel to Syria to join Sunni jihadist groups; to counter ISIS' recruitment successes, the FBI must exploit ISIS' social media networks to identify supporters in the United States, use disinformation to sow doubts about Western recruits' loyalty, and counter ISIS' narrative that "the State is a state for all Muslims"[i] by elevating criticisms from aggrieved members and Muslims living in ISIS-controlled territory. For the purposes of this strategy, CVE entails the use of non-coercive means to reduce the overall number of American residents attempting to join ISIS.[ii] Congress should authorize and fund an intervention program along the lines of the United Kingdom's Channel Program. The program will try to encourage 'law abiding supporters'[iii] to disengage from extremist networks by offering positive alternatives to violence. The analysis concludes by showing how the plan might be implemented.

While this strategy would improve upon US counter-terrorism policies and help initiate a more constructive dialogue about the "lone-wolf" terrorism threat, the pendulum has already swung away from CVE towards "preventive prosecution."[iv] In the last five weeks alone, the FBI has arrested more than 10 suspected ISIS sympathizers;[v] unfortunately, this is a proposal that Americans deserve but will never receive.

Intelligence: The government could try to limit the availability of ISIS' propaganda by pressuring private companies to suspend supporters' social media accounts. However, efforts to do so are unlikely to succeed, set a dangerous precedent in regards to free speech, and conflict with the government's imperative to gather intelligence. Trying to remove ISIS' propaganda from social media platforms represents an impractical game of "whack-a-mole;" popular disseminators usually maintain backup accounts in case one is flagged and suspended.[vi] Because ISIS' propaganda is so widely available on the Internet, those extremists who wish to find it will still be able to. Even if social media companies were willing and able to identify and suspend most ISIS propagandists' accounts, doing so would be counterproductive, eliminating a valuable supply of intelligence.

Instead, we should exploit social media networks to gather intelligence on supporters in the United States. Western foreign fighters are rather unsophisticated operatives, often posting incriminating photos of themselves on social media.[vii] Because of this, the FBI has a better opportunity of identifying potential recruits who might otherwise have gone undetected. Once American foreign fighters are identified, the FBI should prioritize investigating these individuals' social networks to try to identify other ISIS supporters. The FBI can map out known recruits' social media networks to identify any US residents who are openly celebrating ISIS propaganda or 'following' the group's official accounts or popular disseminators.

Once recruits are identified, the FBI should try to gain access to these individuals' private social media accounts. Although companies have incentives to protect users' privacy, this is not an insurmountable obstacle. In 2014, Twitter cooperated in roughly 80% of the cases in which authorities requested access to Americans' accounts.[viii] Since these foreign fighters' social media posts, activities, and geo-location indicators will have already demonstrated their membership in a Foreign Terrorist Organization, it is expected that social media companies will comply with these specific requests for information.

The government should highlight information gathered from recruits' private social media conversations to spread disinformation about the level of infiltration by Western security services. By sowing doubts about Westerners' loyalties, intelligence agencies might encourage ISIS leaders to recruit fewer Americans.[ix] Disinformation can help to weaken the group's solidarity and exacerbate tensions between Middle Eastern and North African fighters and Western recruits. If US recruits are seen as potential spies, local fighters might assume that they can mistreat them without being punished. This may increase the number of Western members who are mistreated, become disillusioned, defect, and choose to speak out.

Turn Away: This intervention program aims to dissuade 'law abiding supporters' from attempting to travel to Syria to join the Islamic State. If social media 'friends,' peers, or family members suspect that an individual is radicalizing, they can refer that person to "Turn Away." A designated Turn Away employee from the nearest FBI field office will be responsible for assessing whether the supporter should enter the program or, in serious cases, FBI informants should be used. Similar to the Channel Program, "Turn Away" uses a vulnerability framework to assess extremists along three dimensions: their degree of engagement with ISIS' networks or ideology, their intent to cause harm, and their capability to do so.[x] Possible indicators of capability include having a history of violence or crime, having military training, and having occupational skills like civil engineering that can enable acts of terrorism. When these dimensions are considered together, they provide a rounded view about an individual's vulnerability to recruitment and the likely security risk that he or she poses to other US residents.

Many of the individuals who openly celebrate terrorist propaganda online would now fall under "Turn Away's" jurisdiction. This allows the FBI to distinguish more serious threats that will require confidential informants from less-serious threats in which local authorities would approach the supporter and suggest that they enter "Turn Away." Informants should only be used against extremists who are deemed most vulnerable to recruitment or violence and those individuals who are referred to but refuse to participate in "Turn Away." Rather than trying to build criminal cases against non-violent extremists who might support terrorism *if given the right encouragement and support,* informants will only target extremists *whose vulnerability assessments suggest that they are least likely to be dissuaded.* This allows the FBI to apportion scarce intelligence and law enforcement resources more effectively.

Since "Turn Away" enables the FBI to be more selective in its use of informants, the number of indictments filed against ISIS supporters may decrease. These frequent indictments attract media attention and reinforce the perception that ISIS is the preeminent threat to the homeland.[xi] This may have the unintended effect of encouraging supporters to join or conduct homegrown terrorist attacks; sympathizers might feel that they're missing out on a chance to be a part of a larger cause. Even if aspiring recruits are arrested, sensationalized media coverage may increase their status among jihadist fan boys.

If an individual is referred to "Turn Away" and agrees to participate, support packages will be tailored to resolve participants' unique motivations for supporting ISIS; potential services include but are not limited to anger management, substance abuse interventions, housing support, and theological and peer mentoring.[xii] Once Congress establishes "Turn Away," it should earmark funds to finance support providers. Ideological or theological mentors must *currently* oppose violence; repentant terrorists and non-violent extremists are eligible.

In fact, these 'formers' and non-violent radicals are more credible messengers. They are more likely to understand the unique emotional and psychological push factors that may have primed an individual to extremist ideologies, be able to connect with susceptible young adults by highlighting their own experiences with disengagement, and build the trust and rapport needed to pull these individuals away from violent extremist networks.

Support providers do not need to be experts in counter-radicalization but should at least be informed about the indicators "Turn Away" uses to assess vulnerability so that they can assess participants' progress. Local "Turn Away" police practitioners will be responsible for approving support providers, supervising the delivery of the support package, monitoring high-risk participants, assessing participants' progress with his or her providers, and updating extremists' vulnerability assessments.[xiii] If the risk of criminality related to terrorism increases, the police practitioner will determine whether the intervention should continue or the case should be referred to the FBI.

Counter-Messaging: Because the vast majority of homegrown jihadists were radicalized, in part, through interactions on the Internet,[xiv] any counter-terrorism strategy must attempt to contest the messages that the terrorists use to try to encourage supporters to travel to Syria. While 'formers' and non-violent extremists acting as mentors can provide theological counter-arguments to 'Turn Away' participants, any large-scale counter-messaging campaign conducted over the Internet and social media should not wade into the thicket of religious debates. Instead, the counter-messaging effort will try to delegitimize some of the non-religious narratives that might motivate Westerners to join the Islamic State.

One way to do so is to de-romanticize the notion of 'jihad cool.' Counter-messaging should highlight Western defectors' complaints about being mistreated by local fighters, forced to perform menial tasks like cleaning toilets and washing dishes,[xv] and living without electricity, clean water, and access to medical care.

Pragmatic arguments that highlight the hardships that Western recruits will experience might dissuade some supporters from attempting to travel to Syria. When ISIS' media outlets claim that they're winning military battles only to be defeated, these statements can be juxtaposed against images of ISIS' insurgents fleeing, leaving dead and wounded members behind. These counter-narratives may help to dissuade aspiring recruits who are searching for excitement, a sense of purpose, or solidarity.

Rather than framing recruits as committed terrorists motivated purely by religious ideology, the government should investigate other possible explanations. If recruits have a criminal history, known mental illnesses, or substance abuse problems, authorities should publicize this information. If supporters suspect that they will be framed as confused teens or petty criminals, they might be less willing to risk arrest by trying to join or plotting lone-wolf attacks.

We must crystallize the difference between ISIS' words and deeds. While humanitarian motivations may be becoming less important for Westerners trying to join ISIS, we must contest the group's claim that it is defending the *ummah* from repressive governments by showing that Muslims will be the greatest victims of ISIS' expansion. If the intelligence community intercepts communications between senior leaders and emirs that reveal disagreements over how fighters are treating local Muslim populations, the government should declassify this information. We can also exploit the infighting within the global jihadist movement, pointing out that even al-Qaeda condemns ISIS for its wanton violence against Muslims.

While a counter-messaging campaign can discredit ISIS' narratives by elevating criticisms and stories of hardships posted on social media by current members and Muslims living in ISIS-controlled territories, it is incumbent on 'Turn Away' practitioners to provide alternative narratives for US sympathizers. Mentors interacting regularly with

ISIS sympathizers, discussing their own previous feelings of alienation, inadequacy, or emotional distress, and explaining how their lives improved after disengaging from violent extremist networks offer powerful alternative narratives; mentors can demonstrate that they found meaning, belonging, and solidarity as devout Muslims living in the United States. When they chose to disengage from violent extremist networks, these individuals were able to find purpose in the West by building relationships with other Muslims who had similar experiences and worldviews, and helping to encourage these wayward youth not to throw away their lives.

If vulnerable individuals participating in the 'Turn Away' program are judged to have disengaged from violent extremist networks and de-radicalized, the government can solicit their support as mentors. This can provide a positive outlet for these 'formers' to talk about their own experiences and disengagement from violent extremist networks and ideologies and gain their own sense of self-worth and belonging. By employing these individuals as mentors, the government can gradually scale up its intervention infrastructure by increasing the number of credible messengers willing and able to connect with ISIS sympathizers.

Counter-Messaging Implementation: ISIS sympathizers are unlikely to view agencies like the US Department of State as credible messengers so the government's primary role should be to encourage private companies to elevate existing counter-narratives. Public officials should solicit help to establish an initiative similar to Google's Network Against Violent Extremism. The idea would be to lobby social media companies to establish a global network of Westerners who defected from ISIS and Muslims who survived its attacks and wish to share their experiences. The government should frame social media companies' participation in the program as a way to discredit allegations that they have not done enough to prevent terrorists from using their platforms to communicate and proselytize.

To have any hope of influencing sympathetic fence sitters, activists must produce material that can compete with ISIS' high-definition, flashy propaganda videos. The Department of State can organize competitions and provide grants for start up companies who design the most compelling music videos, short films, or comedic skits challenging ISIS' narratives. The intelligence community can help these companies to identify and connect with defectors and survivors so that they have a larger platform to broadcast counter-narratives.

Assessment/Feasibility: The government has a role to play in convening activists to counter the Islamic State's narratives. However, those messengers whom ISIS' supporters are most likely to listen to are the same individuals who the government would be least willing to partner with. Defectors are credible messengers but amplifying their criticisms might require working with individuals with blood on their hands. Similarly, officials might decide not to provide grants to online activists who wish to publicize al-Qaeda ideologues' condemnations of ISIS; doing so could expose the administration to allegations that it is giving these jihadist ideologues attention and publicity and connecting them with a wider audience.

The government can try to solicit social media companies' participation in a counter-messaging campaign by framing it as a form of corporate social responsibility. Nevertheless, most companies will be unwilling to invest large amounts of equity in the program and even if they do, this will be insufficient without significant financial support from the central government. However, this is unlikely to materialize. Most government funding goes towards kinetic solutions to terrorism, interdicting or killing terrorists, as opposed to preventive measures.[xvi]

Additionally, it is unclear how effective a counter-messaging campaign can be. Many fence sitters will not be dissuaded by a counter-messaging campaign unless they decide to disengage from violent extremist networks. Inserting counter-narratives into ISIS' online networks does not guarantee that they will have the desired impact. Since ISIS' online social networks are incredibly interconnected,[xvii] they act as 'echo chambers'[xviii] in which sustained interactions with other supporters may reinforce radical views. In these ideologically segregated free spaces, accepting counter-narratives is costly because doing so will expose an individual to vocal criticism from within the network and may lead to the loss of valuable relationships.

By requesting that social media companies partner with the government to provide access to known foreign fighters accounts and private conversations, civil libertarians would likely protest that innocent, law-abiding residents might be caught up in the government's surveillance drag-net. These advocates offer compelling counter-arguments in the debate between security and civil liberties; if the government inadvertently violates Muslims' civil liberties it not only legitimizes many of the Islamic State's criticisms of the West but also forfeits the core values that American society is built upon.

However, these criticisms are unlikely to apply in these specific requests for additional information. By gaining access to and analyzing foreign fighters' private conversations, intelligence agencies can distinguish between those US residents who have reached out to known ISIS members for research purposes or cursory curiosity and those Muslims who are actively committed to the group's extremist ideology and deemed most likely to support violence.

Providing higher-risk extremists who have not yet broken the law with the opportunity to enter an intervention program enables the government to more effectively balance the national security-civil liberties pendulum than the FBI is with its current "preventive prosecution" approach. Rather than using confidential FBI informants to target every known extremist who might resort to violence if given the right encouragement and support, the government would prioritize providing higher-risk individuals with an opportunity to disengage from violent extremist networks and turn around their lives before they crossed the boundary between protected speech and criminal activity.

Nevertheless, federal, state, and local law enforcement will vigorously lobby against an intervention program. Building criminal cases against "law-abiding supporters," regardless of their competence or the likelihood that they will join ISIS, increases public concern about the possibility of domestic terrorism and helps the FBI to demonstrate its role in protecting Americans and make the case for budgetary increases. From the FBI's standpoint, it is risky if ISIS supporters, even incompetent ones, enter "Turn Away." The agency would not receive any credit for successful interventions but would shoulder a large part of the blame if one of the program's participants went on to attack the United States.

While local governments across the United States have established intervention programs for gang members, it is unlikely that there would be political support for similar programs designed to dissuade aspiring terrorists. Since most of the public perceives non-incarcerated terrorist supporters as irredeemable,[xix] American voters would likely oppose an intervention program. It is psychologically reassuring to know that the FBI is disrupting terrorist plots. Americans will remain convinced that trying to interdict *all* supporters is the least risky approach; they are unlikely to be swayed by arguments that some terrorists might not have acted without informants' encouragement and support. Thus, an intervention program will remain a political non-starter. There are few benefits but significant risks for voting for the program. If one of "Turn Away's" participants attempted or succeeded in carrying out a terrorist attack, it is likely that most of the politicians who authorized the program would lose reelection.

If Congress authorizes "Turn Away," there are limits to what it can achieve. Some youth will spend long hours online interacting with ISIS supporters but will successfully conceal their ongoing radicalization from family members and peers. In other cases, parents or friends might suspect that an individual is radicalizing but choose not to bring the case to authorities' attention. Some parents might assume that preventive measures, taking the teen's passports or monitoring his or her computer access, will resolve the issue. In other cases, parents might ignore the problem, fearing that intervention will fail and their child will end up in prison.

Even if an individual is accepted into to the program, the government cannot force non-incarcerated extremists to participate.[xx] Inevitably, some people who are referred to the program will decide not to participate. Furthermore, interventions will only succeed if extremists remain convinced that the potential costs of joining the Islamic State outweigh the benefits. By offering support packages and reminding participants about the criminal consequences of supporting terrorism, the government can somewhat influence extremists' cost-benefit calculations.

However, the likelihood that interventions succeed or fail is greatly influenced by factors largely outside of the government's control. Interventions will work best when individuals and their families "fully engage with the program."[xxi] In cases involving minors, parents can monitor teens' activities, reprimand children if they are caught interacting with extremists on the Internet, and emphasize the emotional pain that the child's support for terrorism would cause his or her family. Nevertheless, if extremists do not disengage from the networks that are pulling them towards terrorism, even the most supportive families might not be able to dissuade sympathizers.

While beyond the scope of this analysis, another concern is that by making it seem less attractive to travel to Syria to join ISIS the government may unintentionally make other behaviors more attractive. To illustrate, an ISIS supporter might accept the argument that life in Syria will be miserable, that local fighters will treat him poorly, and that he will be forced to perform unexciting, menial chores. However, this may make it seem more attractive to conduct a terrorist attack in the United States.

It will be difficult to measure the program's efficacy. In the vast majority cases in which extremists who participate in "Turn Away" do not try to join ISIS, there is no way to prove that the intervention itself is the reason why. On the other hand, if one of the participants carries out a terrorist attack or is arrested for trying to join ISIS, the public will likely deem the program a failure and demand that it be ended.

Conclusion: Congress should authorize "Turn Away." By providing support packages to address extremists' unique motivations for joining terrorist groups, we may be able to prevent some wayward individuals from ruining their lives. "Turn Away" may encourage the FBI to be more selective in its use of informants, allowing the agency to focus on more serious domestic terrorism threats.[xxii] However, the politicized nature of the terrorism debate means that this strategy will not be implemented.[xxiii] Despite the recent attention devoted to Countering Violent Extremism, talk goes a lot further than action in Washington.

Chapter 37

Cultural Heritage Preservation and Its Role for Paving the Way Toward Peace

Marc A. Abramiuk and Wilem S. Wong

First Published 7 August 2015

[U.S. Government; For Public Distribution]

Approaching archaeological site designation CHCP-12 with Marines in Garmser District (Helmand Province, Afghanistan). Visible in the distant foreground of this image is the top of a large retaining wall behind which protrudes a massive structure with a series of smaller walls on its summit.

373

Introduction

The purposeful destruction and ransacking of cultural properties has been with us probably for as long as there has been war. Among the several reasons cultural properties are deliberately destroyed in war, two in particular come to mind: the first is for loot,[i] and the second is to erase the cultural significance the properties may have for one of the engaged parties. These reasons are not mutually exclusive, for the actors involved might be driven by both of the aforementioned motives. For example, the Taliban in Afghanistan and ISIS in Iraq and Syria aim to loot as well as erase any vestige of an unfamiliar early Islamic past or pre-Islamic past. The consequence has been the destruction of these nations' patrimonies. Such destruction, it is argued in this paper, has ramifications that go far beyond the first-order effect it has for scientists and historians who study cultural properties. The destruction of cultural properties effectively eliminates the fixtures behind which local communities can rally and thereby use to support some semblance of stability. In what follows, we propose that there is a significant role that the military can play in curtailing the destruction of cultural properties[ii] which has far-reaching effects for conflicts in general.

The purpose of the 1954 Hague Convention was to establish rules of conduct that would protect cultural properties during war. The problem that we are faced with today, however, is that such rules are not being followed. One reason is that many actors involved in war today, such as the Taliban or ISIS, are administratively organized in a manner in which responsibility for such destructive actions carries little weight, since it is diffused across a group rather than directed at individuals in the group. As a result, refusal to adhere to the rules of the Convention carries few, if any, realizable repercussions for the perpetrators. But perhaps the more significant problem is that such rules governing battle etiquette are a western construct that few outside the US and Europe care to recognize. Indeed, it is precisely the western values embodied in these rules that many anti-government actors today imagine themselves resisting and in some cases upturning. As for the local civilians who could be regarded as mostly neutral in their loyalty, they are often ambivalent to protecting cultural properties which they too see as serving western interests and values.

Defenseless though cultural properties may be during wartime, they are not passive "actors," as preservation advocates—ourselves included—would like to think. At war, cultural properties become strategic objectives, and it is naïve to think that they do not pose an existential threat to certain groups and that in desperate circumstances that they will be spared by these groups. Although salvage operations can play an important role in protecting cultural properties just before they are destroyed,[iii] in this paper, we propose an aggressive preemptive strategy in which cultural properties are used to build community solidarity well before threats of war become realized.

The idea we put forward is that cultural properties constitute a *special kind* of actor ("special" in so far as they are vulnerable and merit our protection), but an actor nonetheless. Seen in this light, the role of cultural properties acquires much more centrality in the theater of war than it is conventionally depicted as having. According to this view, although salvage operations are important, there are preventative actions that can be taken well ahead of considering salvaging. Drawing from our work in Afghanistan, we provide an operational example of this preventative strategy which we undertook as lead social scientist and team leader, respectively, for HTT AF07[iv] in 2011. We then discuss what some of the anticipated outcomes of that work meant for developing regional solidarity and, by implication, additional protective measures for cultural properties.

Central Helmand Archaeological Study

By 2011, the illicit trade of antiquities looted from archaeological sites in Afghanistan was on the rise and becoming a backing source for insurgents as well as terrorists throughout Afghanistan.[v] Operation Enduring Freedom not only had to contend with devising ways of reducing the poppy industry, which was bankrolling the Taliban, but with curtailing funding derived from the looting of archaeological sites. Although certain efforts were going on at that time to freeze financial accounts linked to insurgents and religious extremists, these labors were only effective at preventing money laundering and cash transactions between non-state actors. Ultimately they were proving ineffective in preventing these actors from being subsidized.[vi] This is because many non-state actors were being subsidized not through cash transactions but through a traditional promissory system known as *hawala*. Accordingly, artifacts looted from archaeological sites likely would have served as one of many honorary forms of collateral being jostled about to support insurgents and terrorists. By *promising* rather than transacting, insurgents like the Taliban could avoid the conventional bank system where illicit monies might be more easily detected and vigilantly monitored by authorities.

Appreciating that the central Helmand River valley was replete with archaeological sites that were unrecorded, unmonitored and therefore at risk, HTT AF07 took preemptive measures to prevent them from being exploited by insurgents. The result was the Central Helmand Archaeological Study (CHAS), a study facilitated by and in support of the U.S. Marine Corps in conjunction with the Afghan government. The CHAS was one of several ambitious studies undertaken by HTT AF07 under the auspices of RCT-1 and RCT-5. Its goal was to cut off a prospective funding source deemed to be the artifact trade, while protecting archaeological sites at risk of being damaged. Furthermore, it strove to connect the various peoples of eastern Rig and Garmser Districts through their territories' copious archaeological sites.

In the course of the fieldwork phase of the CHAS, HTT AF07 identified and recorded thirteen archaeological sites. None of the sites surveyed exhibited any unquestionable traces of looting. Holes if any were to be found were insignificant and could have been the result of animals burrowing just as much as people digging opportunistically with rudimentary equipment.

On the surface, all sites appear to be early Islamic, the large preponderance of which are medieval, most likely fortresses dating to the Ghaznavid period (A.D. 977-1186). These determinations were made based on certain characteristic retaining wall features, general layout, and ceramics diagnostic to the period. Although, we could not determine whether underlying the early Islamic period phase there were earlier phases, we do know that the sites identified were used in later periods. As we were informed by locals, several of the sites were used as burial mounds as recently as two generations ago. Also, based on the cartridges and other debris dating to the 1980s that littered the summits of some of the sites, it seems that some of the sites were used as vantage points or combat posts for the Soviets and Mujahedeen.

Implications of results for curtailing looting

Whatever the precise chronology turns out to be for the sites that HTT AF07 identified and recorded, the issue is perhaps incidental to the operational relevance of the cultural property protection work undertaken by HTT AF07 and to which we now turn. In 2011, early Islamic artifacts were in substantial demand by collectors and therefore carried significant value on the black market.[vii] Thus, the fact that an early Islamic phase was identified in the course of the site surveys undertaken by HTT AF07 now meant that there was a legitimate risk of these sites' exploitation in subsidizing the insurgency.

With the potential looting risk now made clear through the site survey, HTT AF07 proceeded to the next step of the study which was to present the details on the sites and their importance to the Marines at the regimental and battalion levels. In particular, details on the sites' locations were critical so that the Marines could periodically monitor the sites and, in so doing, deter their looting and destruction. In relaying the required information and advocating a plan for these sites' policing, the CHAS took a preemptive role by depriving looters access to the sites, thereby removing a major motive for systematically destroying these sites, namely economic incentive. In other words, by removing the economic incentive, the systems for subsidizing the insurgency and consequently the recurrent damage done to archaeological sites were weakened. Potential operational funds that could be acquired immediately through transactions and deposited into and disbursed from bank accounts, as well as potential funds that could be funneled through alternative funding mechanisms (e.g., *hawala*) would effectively be curtailed.

Engaging with the population and its proposed effects on the insurgency

The CHAS provided the platform to thwart looting which could have funded insurgent activities; however, it also provided a starting point for engaging with the local population to foster community solidarity and resistance to insurgent recruiting and intimidation. Regarding this latter point, it follows that protecting these archaeological sites served a dual reinforcing function, both as a cultural preservation measure and *unavoidably* as a counter-insurgency measure.

Taliban influence was still weighing heavily on the people of the central Helmand River valley and this was deemed by HTT AF07 to be the result of two issues: 1) a lack of cohesion beyond the tribal or village unit (e.g., little district-wide, provincial-wide, or nation-wide sense of solidarity) and, 2) the ambivalence of a tribe's or a village's sympathies—whether it be for the Taliban or the Afghan Government. These issues both contributed to a sense of alienation requiring that the village or tribe survive on its own by aligning with whatever influence was strongest or in the group's best interest. This state of affairs was especially detrimental at a time at which insurgents and religious extremists, through their decentralized make-up, close ties to local communities, and adept use of social media were able to influence not only local sentiment but western media outlets in a bid to appeal to those who might join their ranks.

To defend against a swelling insurgency and its destructive consequences, a proposed extension of CHAS involved community outreach to show the local communities the value in preserving their cultural properties rather than being intimidated by the Taliban into engaging in destructive behavior. Falling directly in line with counter information operations strategies that seek themes that resonate with local communities,[viii] it was believed that through such outreach archaeological sites would begin to be seen as part of the communities rather than abstracted from them.

The first proposed step in engaging with the local communities would necessarily involve incorporating the Afghan Government in the engagement process so that communities would see that it was not their tribe or village alone that was pitted against the Taliban. Indeed, HTT AF07 made certain headway in this regard by offering to act as a bridge between the MoIC based in Kabul and the local district governing bodies of Helmand Province. The intent of this offer was to help educate local Afghans about their shared cultural heritage, and to encourage locals to invest in their cultural heritage. Through investing in their cultural heritage it was hoped that locals could begin building a much needed sense of solidarity within the central Helmand River valley that might serve to deter internal dissidents as well as foreign fighters from posing a threat to local communities. Although unfortunately HTT AF07 made little progress on this latter front, in retrospect, it is believed that over the long term the proposed strategy might have been realized with more lobbying and more resources than HTT AF07 had at the time.

Implications for the Middle East

It is our contention that a lesson can be drawn from the problematic situation that HTT AF07 dealt with in Afghanistan in 2011 which, in turn, can be used to relate to ongoing events in Iraq and Syria. In Iraq and Syria, archaeological sites are being demolished because of their symbolic significance as well as for their loot. Armed extremist groups, such as ISIS, in their attempts at intimidation and demonstration of their radical values, have gone to significant lengths to destroy numerous archaeological sites throughout the region. Some of the sites that were damaged are internationally renowned. Examples of such sites include Hatra and Palmyra, both UNESCO World Heritage sites, and Nimrud, a World Heritage site nominee.[ix]

The indiscriminate destruction of cultural properties seen in Iraq and Syria is different than the situation observed by HTT AF07 in Helmand where looting and destruction were anticipated and effectively prevented. Thus, while the lesson drawn from our experience in Helmand on the issue of direct intervention might not be applicable in the context of Iraq and Syria, we feel that our proposal for engaging with the population *is* extremely relevant to the situation in Iraq and Syria. As discussed in the previous section, HTT AF07 anticipated that in order to prevent site destruction from recurring, significant work would be needed to foster cultural heritage appreciation. One way HTT AF07 proposed to do this was to advocate direct, vertical engagement between the national government and district-level local communities. In the case of Iraq and Syria, we believe that a similar direct, vertical engagement strategy is warranted.

To exemplify how a direct, vertical engagement strategy might work on armed extremist groups, we look at ISIS in Iraq and Syria. ISIS poses a serious threat to the citizens of Iraq and Syria as well as to these nations' cultural properties. ISIS recruits members from abroad by the thousands through their extensive social networks, while also exerting an influence over locals much like the Taliban managed to accomplish at their height in Afghanistan. This is to say that, like the Taliban in Afghanistan, most ISIS members rely on local sympathy and apathy to achieve their cause. The problem that lies at the heart of these cases is the fundamental disconnection between the government and the people. Any hope at resolution therefore entails encouraging the government to engage with locals regarding their regional history and making them feel a part of this history rather than disenfranchised from it.

UNESCO plays an enormous role in elevating the recognition of sites. However, international recognition is a doubled-edged sword. In times of relative peace, an international spotlight on archaeological sites can help attract tourism and research which can, in turn, positively affect the economic conditions of the region, as well as draw international interest in protecting the sites. However, at times of war, this two-edged sword can cut the other way. International recognition is something that many locals cannot relate to because they cannot legitimately and economically benefit from it, particularly when violence is erupting. It goes without saying then that international stature of certain archaeological sites in the midst of such conditions does little to encourage locals to value their heritage. Rather, it could have the opposite effect and serve to alienate locals, especially when locals see that more attention is being paid to archaeological sites than to them.

Recommendations

United Nation Security Council resolutions 2139 and 2199 are recent manifestations of the international community's response to the ongoing volatility that has embraced Syria and Iraq.[x] The latter of these resolutions is directly relevant to the issue discussed in the paper, as it constitutes an attempt to cut off funding to groups such as Al Qaeda and ISIS derived from, among other activities, the antiquities trade. In resolution 2199, UNESCO encourages its member states to cooperate with INTERPOL and UNODC (via their databases, IMoLIN/AMLID) in identifying illicit dealing in art and antiquities, and reporting these violations while seeking to prosecute the offenders.[xi]

In addition to these direct efforts at stymying the subsidization of these groups, the fight for ideas (i.e., information operations) is underway. The electronic publications of Al-Qaeda's *Inspire* and ISIS' *Dabiq disseminate* many views, one of which is the espousal of flagrant disregard for cultural properties, as these properties are deemed idolatry. Such views pose a significant challenge to moderate Muslims and western countries[xii] and several counter narratives have been launched in response.

One recent counter-narrative initiated by UNESCO, for example, is #UNITE4HERITAGE, which is a program that seeks to support the protection and preservation of cultural property in Iraq and Syria. However, although UNESCO[xiii] and, in particular, #UNITE4HERITAGE[xiv] publicize local efforts to preserve cultural properties, one still gets the sense that the audience for which such news is intended is the global community at large rather than the local community. This is a step in the right direction, but more can be done to connect local people to their cultural properties, and awaken in them a sense that these properties are their heritage and should be preserved.

What is missing from this picture, we feel, are the efforts on the ground at the local level that could be significantly enhanced by enlisting the help of specialized non-combat troops in the armed forces. This is to say that the armed forces have the logistical capabilities in opening up channels to locals who live near the cultural properties that are at risk. They, furthermore, have the know-how to assist UNESCO in reaching out to the people on the ground through their direct engagement with host nations, inter-governmental organizations, and inter-agency partners. On this latter point, the United States Army Civil Affairs and Psychological Operations Command (USACAPOC), for example, can play a vital role in offering up the military personnel with military as well as civilian acquired skillsets and expertise to assist in circulating information to locals where it is needed most. Finally, this command would be ideally positioned to garner the resources for recruiting specialists in order to assist with salvage operations, as well as to identify and protect cultural properties that are at risk, as HTT AF07 did in Afghanistan. Comprised of what would most appropriately be described as citizen-soldiers, these personnel would bring their critical subject matter expertise in archaeology, museum studies, and restoration in line with the existing regional alignment of military forces in assigned geographical areas. One proposal that seems natural is to recruit modern day "monuments men" (currently scarce) to fill commission officer vacancies in the Civil Affairs branch of the U.S. Army Reserve.[xv]

UNESCO's high-level vision for cultural heritage is certainly necessary, but village-level, grass-roots engagement is more critical than ever in Iraq and Syria at this time. Small numbers of specialized armed forces members from UN affiliated states can make this difference. In the situation of Iraq, it is important that the face of this engagement should be that of the Iraqi government and that the beneficiaries of this engagement be Iraqis. As for Syria, the on-going civil war for the last four years will see no winners if both sides cannot agree to at least protect and preserve their common cultural heritage. The cultural heritage of Iraq and Syria should not be more important to the international community than it is to the citizens of these nations. The cultural heritage of Iraq and Syria is something which all citizens of these nations should feel they have a stake in protecting. Only then will they be able to stand together with common purpose, thus breaking the cycle of perpetual division and antagonism that is responsible for an expanding conflict that is increasingly taking a toll on people as well as things.

Chapter 38

It is Time to Reassess How the US Conducts Detention Operations in the Current Fight and the Need to Incorporate our Regional Partners in the Future—Insurgents are Not Traditional Enemy Prisoners of War

John Hussey

First Published 10 August 2015

The Rand Corporation conducted a study entitled "The battle Behind the Wire, US Prisoner and Detainee Operations from World War II to Iraq." Rand concluded that in each major conflict the US has been involved in from World War II up until present day detention operations, the US has taken in a large number of prisoners or detainees. US military planners and policy makers simply have not prioritized this part of the military plan, and as a result, detention operations became an afterthought which has created various personnel and logistical problems.[1]

Some of these issues have resulted in strategic consequences which have plagued the US and its coalition partners. For instance, the US did not have enough troops to guard the vast amount of detainees that were captured in the initial stages of Operation Iraqi Freedom. The overcrowding and stress were contributory factors which resulted in the abuses at Abu Ghraib. More importantly, the United States simply has failed to capture many of the lessons learned from previous conflicts regarding the tactical through strategic lessons of detention operations. The same Rand study discussed the reeducation and vocational training of prisoners. It should be noted that these programs were nonexistent during the initial stages of military action in Afghanistan and Iraq.

Senior leaders within the US military often view detention operations as a supply problem rather than a challenging and continually changing dynamic with strategic level implications. The concept was simply to build a large area or use preexisting facilities, guard it, and provide a safe and secure environment for the masses. In many instances, US military personnel simply missed or ignored the war or detainee counterinsurgency which continued inside the US detention facilities throughout Iraq and Afghanistan. In many cases it was simply "on the too hard to do list" as a consideration to counter.

The US military must change the paradigm with regard to detention operations. In future operations, US senior leaders must take into account exactly what type of detainee the US has in custody: Is the detainee a fully radicalized insurgent leader or a person caught moving weapons for his local tribe? Part of this process will be to determine how each of these individuals will be assessed, classified, and placed. This process will help determine and shape the programs that will be conducted in an effort to deradicalize detainees and return detainees to the nations from where they came. Consideration must also be given to the fact that there may not be a nation to return them to due to the fact that the government is either fragile or simply nonexistent.

Just Say No to FIFO

FIFO is an acronym which means first-in, first-out. It is an accounting technique used in managing inventory of produced goods, raw materials, parts, components, or feed stocks. Often those in charge of inventory will practice FIFO by ensuring that the first goods purchased are also the first goods sold. Simply stated, under the FIFO method, the earliest goods purchased are the first ones removed from the inventory account.[2]

While FIFO may be an accepted practice in managing inventory, it is not preferred practice when it comes to detention operations. Unfortunately, many leaders view detention operations solely a logistical problem. The belief is to simply capture detainees, house them, feed them, and provide medical care for them. Once the system is full, meaning the facility can hold no more, then detainees may be released. Releasing detainees to make room for new detainees based on the length of time they served in detention is not a common-sense approach to this problem. There should be a system of due process where detainee's cases are heard by a military review board or local judge who may grant release based on local laws and the nature of the allegations. The average incarceration period for a detainee at Camp Bucca, Iraq during Operation Iraqi Freedom was about one to two years prior to being released despite the fact that the detainee may have been involved in insurgent activity against US or coalition forces. There are examples of insurgents who were released from Camp Bucca multiple times despite specializing in improvised explosive devices (IED).[3] While the US does not make this a common practice, US officials have conceded that American-led forces in Iraq had increased the tempo of the releases to foster good will and to free up space in the overcrowded prisons.[4] In retrospect, this approach may have been flawed because several reports have concluded that several key leaders from the Islamic State of Iraq and Syria (ISIS), including the Abu Bakr al-Baghdadi, the head of ISIS, and up to nine members of the Islamic State's top command were confined at Camp Bucca.[5]

COL James B. Brown, the commander of the Eighteenth Military Police Brigade, which oversaw the major detention operations facilities in Iraq during in 2005 gained an appreciation for the ongoing dynamics which occurred inside US detention facilities. Brown noted Camp

Bucca was not just a holding pen but an integral battlefield in the insurgency.[6] The difficulty with this battlefield, as with so many others, is some of the tightest bonds are formed. In this current conflict, these bonds have come back to hinder the US and international community. Unlike wars of the past in which prisoners of war returned to their communities and families and went on with their lives, this new battlefield within detention operations facilities has created new terrorists as well as new insurgent groups. These newly-developed links have continued to morph into more sophisticated insurgent or terrorist networks which the US, and the international community must come to terms with.

A variety of senior military officers categorized the prions in Iraq as "unique settings for prisoner radicalization and inmate collaboration".[7] Al Qaeda in Iraq (AQI) and the Islamic state of Iraq (ISI) weren't only using US-run prisons as "jihadi universities," according to Major General Doug Stone, former commander of Task Force 134, they were actively trying to infiltrate those prisons to cultivate new recruits.[8] Consequently, one may conclude the same indoctrination took place in US prisons in Afghanistan and at Guantanamo Bay. Senior officers in both Iraq and Afghanistan realized that the placement of hard-core jihadist prisoners with everyday, common prisoners would be a mistake and allow for a more indoctrinated radicalization program to develop within the confines of the prison. The difficulty was classifying the detainees by how radicalized they were when they came into US custody. Subsequently, when detainees were transferred to the camp, the US lacked the capacity to monitor and adjust for how radicalized they became while confined in the camp. The lack of this assessment coupled with the placement of these individuals into large style camp settings, communal living, allowed the indoctrination of those less radicalized detainees and also allowed for the forming of new networks to emerge.

The challenge was not only confined to Iraq. The same setbacks have occurred with detention operations in Afghanistan and at Guantanamo Bay, Cuba. Dr. Michael Welner, who is the Chairman of The Forensic Panel and an ABC News Consultant, has extensive knowledge of US detention operations at Guantanamo Bay. He noted that if the US government does not actively deradicalize detainees held in custody then detainees will continue to "soak in hate and find comrades-in-arms who buy into that now-dominant message of Islamist supremacy and entitlement to violence."[9] In Afghanistan the situation is similar in that Taliban and Al Qaeda insurgents were radicalizing noninsurgent inmates in an already overcrowded prison system.[10]

The Current Problem in the Middle East is Not Confined to that Region

As this paper is being written, Iraqi forces are conducting military operations in and around the city of Tikrit, Iraq in an attempt to dislodge ISIS fighters from the city and regain control. The Pentagon has announced that upwards of 25,000 Iraqi and Peshmerga Soldiers will conduct military operations against ISIS in the May 2015, time frame to dislodge these fighters from the city of Mosul and restore Iraqi sovereignty over the population. Based on the sheer number of fighters, common sense should dictate that there may be prisoners captured from ISIS. The question is: What will be done to secure these prisoners? Strategically, the US and its coalition partners must take an active role in the detention operations planning and also serve in an advisory role at the tactical level. If ISIS personnel are captured, there is a possibility that other ISIS members will attempt to free their comrades from captivity similar to the "breaking the walls campaign" of 2012. The "breaking the walls campaign" was a coordinated, well-planned operation in which Abu Bakr al-Baghdadi described its objective to "refuel" his operations with additional manpower. He outlined two campaign objectives, namely, to secure the release of prisoners and to regain control of lost territory in Iraq. The 12-month campaign that ensued was characterized by 20 waves of simultaneous vehicle-borne explosive attacks, eight major prison attacks which resulted in the release of two hard-core veterans who had likely participated in AQI's signature

VBIED network during the period 2006-2007.[11] It was estimated that more than 500 inmates had been set free in the operation.[12] Coincidently, in April of 2015, Al Qaeda fighters attacked a prison in the coastal city on Al Mukallah in Yemen and released 270 prisoners.[13]

While this current dilemma occurred in the Middle East, there are strategic implications for the West and national security concerns for the US. In an effort to deal with this problem, the US should be prepared to discuss and educate those governments affected by the crisis on the different aspects of detainee operations. This should include the differences between correctional detentions which is a secure, safe, and humane environment for detainees to include the opportunity for a successful re-entry in the community versus security detention, the detention in the absence of a criminal charge or trial. Part of any detention program should be preventing the spread of extremism within the broader detainee population.

Conceptually, if the US is to again become involved in the region militarily, the US military will have to revamp and deal with future detainee operations with a much more sophisticated methodology. This will require detailed planning regarding facility construction, detainee assessment, classification and placement, deradicalization programs, rehabilitation and reintegration, and finally monitoring released detainees. These programs will not be successful if they are done unilaterally. Rather, this is a strategic problem with international ramifications, and ISIS exemplifies the challenge. To resolve the conundrum will require input, assistance, and expertise from a variety of regional actors, predominantly by nations being breached by Sunni insurgents.

Those responsible for detention operations must understand that there is a "constant chess game" ongoing within the detention facility. The US, in conjunction with regional and religious experts, must use Military Information Support Operations (MISO) in an effort to change or modify a detainee's behavior. There are a variety of tools available to assist prison officials to change or positively influence a detainee's perception and, thus, his behavior. These PO programs are often inexpensive and they can foster reconciliation, rehabilitation, and support to the US, host nation, or nation where the detainee will be repatriated. Often we allow detainees the opportunity to simply linger and either become frustrated at their detention or to be indoctrinated by a radicalist's viewpoint. This must not be allowed. Overt PO policies and programs must be in place to counter their ever-prevailing "chess game" within the facility.

Assessment, Classification/Placement and Facility Construction

When detainees first arrived at the Abu Ghraib prison they were often placed within the facility according to their behavior after a minimal review. Abu Ghraib was divided into five sections known as levels. Level I was communal living for well-behaved detainees. Levels II through IV were 25 person compounds which were more restrictive and for moderately behaved detainees, and level V were individual cells for poorly-behaved detainees. Detainees were initially placed into a Level III hosing category and then monitored. If they behaved and followed the facility rules, they would be eligible to move to level II or even Level I. Level I was a large compound that housed in excess of 500 detainees. Once in a large compound such as level I, or any of the compounds at Camp Bucca, a detainee could simply "fly under the radar". While his behavior may have met facility rules and, therefore, he may never have been disciplined, his ability to recruit and indoctrinate individuals into a more hard-core radical form of Islam would have been undetected by the average guard. The process in Camp Bucca was very similar. Although the cells at the Afghan National Detention Facility in Parwan (ANDF-P) were much smaller when compared to Camp Bucca and Abu Ghraib, there was insufficient consideration given to the assessment, classification, and placement of detainees at any of the above-mentioned facilities.

The US must reconsider and revamp how it assesses, classifies, and places detainees particularly when engaged in a counter-insurgency operation. When a detainee first enters a US detentions facility, an initial assessment (IA) must be conducted. The IA involves a basic assessment in which detainees are provided the rules, regulations, and roles of the prison authorities. The IA will include a health assessment, a review of the detainee's charges and the evidence seized in an effort to determine what type of detainee is in custody. Upon the completion of the IA, the detainee should be reviewed for classification purposes. Classification systems help both the Military Intelligence (MI) and Military Police (MP) personnel to know the potential for the level of radicalization, influence, misconduct, and escape. Proper classification is critical to reducing the level of radicalization and influence within the prison and, thus, the overall operation and level of cooperation within the facility. Once the IA and classification has been completed, the placement into a facility will occur.

If the US military has targeted a high-level individual and captures that detainee, it would be inappropriate to place this hard-core, committed insurgent in general population with individuals who may be classified as "economic insurgents". (Those individuals who were paid a fee to plant an IED). Those hard-core insurgents should be classified and placed in maximum security prisons that are constructed to isolate and change behavior while the "economic insurgent" should be placed in a medium or minimum facility without the influences of hard-core jihadists. While these classifications may be subjective in nature, one could argue that at least a detainee went through a vetting process and was placed according to an assessment and classification.

If the MI personnel or MP personnel noticed, or learned through some other form of monitoring that a certain detainee was conducting indoctrination programs within the facility, that individual detainee could be relocated from a minimum or medium security facility to a maximum security facility. For those detainees identified as minimum and medium-security risks, the facilities such as Abu Ghraib and Camp Bucca with communal living may be appropriate. For those detainees who wish to continue the fight within the wire and have been classified as maximum-security threats, facility construction will be vital to the success of their rehabilitation as well as the security of US personnel within the facility.

For those detainees who are not classified as extreme radicals and are placed in medium and minimum security facilities, the US must incorporate some form of deradicalization programs in conjunction with vocational training for detainees. Considering the fact that many of the detainees are not educated or simply lack the requisite job skills necessary for employment, it would be cost effective both monetarily and militarily to provide them some form of vocational training. This may help them to be productive members of the community and not reengage in insurgent activity. While these detainees may not be the "center of gravity" in the war within the wire, they can't be ignored for they too may gain resentment against their captors and become radicalized while in detention.

A great deal of planning went into the construction of the Afghanistan National Detention Facility-Parwan (ANDF-P). The construction of the ANDF-P cost approximately $218 million dollars to build. The facility offered the MPs more protection than those detention centers constructed in Iraq while reducing a variety of problems simply by the design and location of the facility. The most notable items that benefited the security of the US guard force and also prevented the radicalization of other detainees are noted below:

- The size of the cells allowed the guard force to house detainees based on a variety of factors, thus having more control over the camp and the population,
- Segregation cells allowed for separation due to investigatory, administrative, or disciplinary purposes as well as hunger strikes,
- Reduced population of the cell allowed the guard force more control of the population to include feeding, escort, medical care, and riot control,

- The concrete pads reduced the detainees' ability to throw rocks/debris at the US guard force,
- The concrete pads reduced the detainees' ability to tunnel out of the facility.

Implementation of Deradicalization Programs

Saudi Arabia has one of the most comprehensive and well-founded deradicalization programs being used today.[14] Saudi Arabian prison officials also realize it would be irresponsible to house large groups of individuals in communal-type settings. They too realize it would be careless to house common criminals with hard-core jihadists.[15] The Saudis are using prisons very similar to the ANDF-P as part of their deradicalization program. The isolation of detainees coupled with their inability to spread jihadist concepts has been beneficial to the rehabilitation of detainees and the program's overall success.

Strategically, the US and Western European powers must come to the realization that the deradicalization of those being held in detention facilities can't be done alone and will require assistance from the regional actors. Any deradicalization program must attempt to gain an understanding of what motivated a particular detainee to join a terrorist organization. The US does not have this expertise and it is simply beyond the scope of the mission of MI or MP personnel within a detention facility. The US will only enhance success if the religious, political, and intellectual leaders of Islamic countries are actively involved in an effort to confront extremist views at a religious and ideological level.[16] The US must involve and incorporate Islamic countries and religious leaders into their detention operations planning and deradicalization programs. While deradicalization is not going to be a "silver bullet" the US simply can't house future detainees as they once had in Iraq and Afghanistan. Most of the detainees that the US has held, and will hold in the future, will be returned to the nation from which they came. There must be a focus in conjunction with allies and

Islamic nations to institute programs within detention facilities to focus on hard-core radical detainees with the goal of deradicalization.

There are several nations throughout the Middle East and Asia which have implemented deradicalization programs within the confines of the prison. Saudi Arabia, Yemen, Indonesia, and Singapore have instituted such programs and have asserted some success in these programs. These nations have used a several prong approach to the deradicalization programs to include respected religious leaders, counseling programs to include mental health treatment, education to include religion, and family members. The concept, once again, is to isolate the radicalized individual keeping him apart from other detainees so they cannot influence their thought process or behavior patterns. Once isolated, both physically and psychologically, the re-education program of the detainee begins. Family and societal norms are key factors in the deradicalization programs and, thus, US military planners will have to incorporate this into their operational plan. The nations whose wayward citizens have crossed the borders to fight the jihad in foreign lands should have a vested interest in providing personnel and funding for this type of endeavor. Nations throughout the Middle East realize that in many instances the detainee will be repatriated back to that nation. Additionally, those nations will understand the cultural norms, have the ability to provide vetted religious leaders, and produce family members and/or tribal leaders who will assist in the deradicalization process and the postrelease supervision process. These programs are not full proof. Saudi government officials were proud to note that the recidivism rates of released security prisoners are only 1–2 percent of 1,400 prisoners who have been released after participation in the program.[17]

Successful elements of the Saudi Arabian deradicalization program are:

- High profile and credible religious leaders,
- The involvement of family members in the deradicalization program,

- Financial, educational, and social programs to assist the detainees, integration back into society,
- Cultural values to include societal, family, and tribal norms,
- The use of social networks to prevent recruitment and radicalization,
- Aftercare and monitoring the detainee after his release.[18]

Conclusion

The failure of the US to alter its detention operations and facilities will enhance jihadist recidivism and potentially allow radicalized detainees to form new networks such as ISIS. Senior leaders within the US military should not view detention operations as a supply problem, rather a challenging and continually-changing dynamic with strategic-level implications and ramifications. The US must truly understand what type of detainee they actually have in their custody. Once determined, the US must have a method to determine how each of these individuals will be assessed, classified, and placed. The US must work with various nations to plan and implement a whole of government and regional-level detention operations policy that incorporates many of the assets that are unavailable to US forces.

The US does not possess the regional, religious, or societal expertise, and most importantly, the credibility to institute these programs. In this regard, the US must use the cultural and regional expertise of the nations in the region to assist in delivering the types of programs to be conducted in an effort to deradicalize detainees and return detainees to the nations from where they came. The failure of the US to work in unison with the host nation and the nations in the region to assist in detention operations within US facilities will have strategic ramifications.

Chapter 39

Global War on Terrorism: How Does the United States Military Counter and Combat the Worldwide Spread of Islamic Extremism?

Richard K. Snodgrass

First Published 15 September 2015

Reviewing the events of the decades preceding the devastating attack on the Homeland on September 11, 2001, reinforces the fact the world in general, the West and the United States in particular, have been subjected to the constant threat of terrorist attacks by groups and individuals espousing a twisted version of Islam through bombings, shooting sprees in public locations and suicide attacks against mostly soft targets. These attacks have been perpetrated by a wide range of state sponsors of terrorism, groups and individuals with varying motivations and aspirations. But they all have one thing in common: Islam. The United States and its partner nations in the battle against Islamic Extremist terrorists must discover new and improved courses of action to combat these extremists and their ability to recruit, brain-wash and train continuing waves of future terrorists.

In the foreseeable future, the dominant challenge facing the United States is the asymmetrical threat of terrorism, especially in the form of Islamic extremism. From the original attack on the Twin Towers in 1993, to the African embassy attacks in 1998, to the devastating destruction of the Twin Towers on 9/11, and more recently the rise of the Islamic State of Iraq and al-Sham (ISIS) and overthrow of the Yemeni government, the United States military apparatus has proven incapable of adequately addressing this threat through the application of predominately conventional warfare. To combat this ever worsening rise of Islamic extremism requires the focused dedication to the creation of hybrid joint forces that are culturally sensitive, religiously respectful and possess enhanced language skills.

Many associated with the military will most likely comment we already have forces that have training in these three areas and that these forces reside in the Special Operations Command. It is true we do have our Special Forces, Civil Affairs (CA) and Psychological Operations / Military Information Support Operations (MISO) forces who are exposed to this training during the process to earn their Military Occupational Specialty (MOS). A result of this training, they are extremely adept at working with host nation security forces and the local populace. However, there are not enough of these forces to conduct their own mission, much less work with the tens of thousands of Soldiers who will deploy to conduct overseas contingency operations. Therefore, it is vital we greatly increase the capacity of this capability so that every squad-sized element has at least one Soldier adequately trained and educated to a specified level. Expanding the cultural awareness capacity of the traditional units normally engaged in missions that put them in constant contact with the local population in foreign lands will serve us well in our efforts to minimize the instances of Soldiers engaging in offensive actions, often accidently, through a lack of understanding of the local customs and traditions, or a basic exposure to the values of respecting other cultures that are most likely very different from those they were exposed to growing up in the United States.

As recently as February 2015, the Army Times reported a huge push to recruit, train and field 5,000 special operations Soldiers, including 3,000 Green Berets, 950 Civil Affairs (CA) Soldiers and 800 Psychological Operations / Military Information Support Operations (MISO) Soldiers. This will be an extremely time consuming process as only a small percentage of recruits are ultimately successful in completing a pipeline taking 43 weeks for MISO, 46 weeks for CA and 67 to 103 weeks for a Green Beret. Another indication of the shortage in these critical specialties is the fact they are eligible for Selective Reenlistment Bonuses up to $72,000.[1]

These are not the forces we have to worry about alienating Muslim populations in the area of responsibility in which the US is conducting operations. It is those young Soldiers, Non-Commissioned Officers and Commissioned Officers who are conducting those day-to-day interactions, key leader engagements and presence patrols in the cities and villages of Iraq and Afghanistan, and whose actions, proper and improper, are being witnessed by the very populace we hope to influence in a positive way.

Culturally Sensitive and Religiously Respectful Joint Forces

On a positive note, our engagements in Iraq and Afghanistan have created recognition among the services of a need for education on culture. However, the methods lack an acceptable effort for interoperability of the needed education, with each service approaching this requirement based on an assessment of their particular needs, instead of a joint perspective. Some of the new programs include, but are not limited to the Defense Language Institute, U.S. Army Training Command (TRADOC) Culture Center, U.S. Air Force Culture and Language Center at the Air University, U. S. Navy Center for Language, Regional Expertise and Culture, U.S. Army Human Terrain System and the

U.S. Marine Corps (USMC) Center for Advance Operational Culture Learning.[2]

Of all these initiatives, it is the Marines who have led the way through the Regional, Culture and Language Familiarization (RCLF) concept. This is a web-based application that breaks down the globe into sub-regions, concentrating on the ethnic groups and languages to that region. The program's mission statement,

> "to ensure that Marine units are globally prepared and regionally focused so they are effective at navigating and influencing the culturally complex 21st Century operating environment in support of the Marine Corps' missions and requirements. The program is based on seventeen regions that may expand as required in the near future. Each region may contain many different cultures but due to some shared cultural traits and geographical proximity, they are bound by common economic, political, and historical or social issues,"

encapsulates the needed focus of all services and the joint community necessary to counter Islamic extremism the US and the West will continue to face.[3]

The RCLF module is the most appropriate approach within the Department of Defense as it not only provides distance learning capabilities in language and cultural emersion, but also ties this training into the Professional Military Education (PME) requirements for Officers and Non-Commissioned Officers. This establishes "blocks" of requirements to be accomplished throughout their career path from Lieutenant / Warrant Officer through Lieutenant Colonel / Chief Warrant Officer 5 and Sergeant through Master Sergeant.[4]

The infamous actions in Abu Ghraib detainment facility, Koran burnings and urination on corpses can be the result of a lack of cultural sensitivity education and an unwillingness to respect religions other than our own. In the book "BlackHearts, One Platoon's Descent into Madness in Iraq's Triangle of Death," Jim Frederick chronicles what can occur when Soldiers who lack this ability to respect local culture and religion, resulting in a view of the local citizens as non-humans, leading to rape and murder of the very individuals we are there to help.[5]

These criminal actions can also impact the relationship with the security apparatus (military and police) our forces are working, training and living with on a daily basis. Cultural insensitivity and a real or perceived lack of respect of Islam obviously creates friction points between our Soldiers and the host nation forces. This friction prevents a synergistic relationship, commitment from our partners, and in extreme instances, is an instigator of insider attacks. In the Department of Defense December 2012 Report on Progress Toward Security and Stability in Afghanistan, there is significant discussion on the dramatic rise of insider attacks (commonly referred to as Green on Blue) between 2007 and 2012. The number of incidents ranged from a low of three in 2008 to 29 in 2012.[6]

The report identifies four probable motives for the insider attacks as:

1. Infiltration (an insurgent is able to enlist in the ANSF);
2. Co-option (a current member of the ANSF is recruited by the insurgency to conduct the attack);
3. Impersonation (insurgent obtains an ANSF uniform and uses it to gain access to the FOB);
4. Personal motives (member of the ANSF acts on their own without guidance from the insurgency).[7]

This represents a tremendous recruiting tool for the insurgency, and further demonstrates a dire need for institutional education through pre-commissioning, initial entry training, Non-Commissioned and Commissioned Officer Education Systems and Professional Military Education. As David Kilcullen, the former Senior Counterinsurgency Adviser to General David Petraeus points out in his article in the Fletcher Forum of World Affairs, the United States is much more likely to face irregular warfare in the future, as opposed to conventional force-on-force conflicts.[8] Moreover, the common thread of our involvement in Iraq, Afghanistan and the Horn of Africa has been battling an opponent who bases their existence on the tenets of Islamic extremism.

Language Capable Joint Force

In the overwhelming majority of school districts throughout the United States, there is a crippling lack of requirement for our youth to learn a foreign language, which of course translates to potential military recruits and leaders who are devoid of this highly valuable skill when serving in a foreign nation, working with host nation officials, local leaders, military partners and the general populace we want to leverage to dry up support to an insurgency. The ability to communicate, at any level of conversation, with someone in their native language is usually considered the most basic sign of respect for their culture and their country. This does not necessarily imply the ability to conduct an entire key leader engagement without the services of a Department of Defense translator or a local hired interpreter, but at least the capability to converse in the pleasantries that are an important component of establishing relationships in the Muslim world: greetings, asking about your counterpart's family, eating and drinking, counting, and the days of the week. Phrases you can expect to use in virtually every key leader engagement. This shows an effort to learn about the locals, their customs and traditions and helps establish a lot of good-will early in the relationship. Will these actions change the mind of the most virulent jihadist? Of course not. But for that part of the population who do not actively or passively support the insurgency, it can help counter any message that U.S. forces are there to disrespect the host nation customs, traditions and religion.

During my 2005-2006 deployment to Iraq working with the Iraqi police forces in the Kurdish provinces of Kirkuk and Sulaymaniyah, I developed a several hundred word capability in Kurdish, instead of Arabic. This effort bought tremendous amounts of good-will with Kurdish government and police leadership, especially with those older and very senior in rank. I was informed that when Sadaam Hussein was still in power, it was illegal for the Kurds to speak their native language in public. So to see a United States Army captain greeting them in Kurdish instead of Arabic, they were simply astonished, and incredibly receptive to any advice I presented, making my deployment an extremely productive and rewarding experience.

Fortunately, there are several tracks we can pursue to develop the language capability of our joint forces: traditional college and universities where our future leaders are participating in the Reserve Officer Training Corps (ROTC) program; the Defense Language Institute, Foreign Language Center (DLIFLC) in Monterey CA where the majority of Army personnel are trained; the United States Army John F. Kennedy Special Warfare Center and School (SWCS) at Fort Bragg, NC; or Command Language Programs operating within units utilizing commercially available systems such as Rosetta Stone software.[9]

Aside from the process of actually identifying future service members with the ability to learn a foreign language and successfully training them for this new skill set, one of the most difficult tasks for our strategic leadership is to correctly identify the needed languages for future needs and contingencies. Chinese, Korean, Arabic and Farsi will easily appear on most planners' radar. The last two administrations have focused a lot of attention on the continent of Africa, integrating all aspects of national power—DIME (Diplomatic, Information, Military, and Economic). Africa has over 1.000 languages and dialects and many strategic fault lines that may flare up and involve a populace that speaks Berber, Portuguese or Swahili, so it is impossible to make perfect predictions.[10] But we can certainly focus on the most likely scenarios, and start with our future leaders attending institutional learning at our nation's military academies and ROTC programs by implementing requirements for basic and intermediate foreign language courses at a minimum, and advanced courses for those demonstrating a higher proficiency. We can also encourage and reward those students who wish to obtain their degree in foreign languages. If a standardized level of foreign language proficiency is established at the academies and ROTC programs, this will create tremendous inroads toward developing a multi-language capable joint force.

The initial process for helping to identify the ability to learn a foreign language is to administer the Defense Language Aptitude Battery (DLAB). This test needs to be administered to all in-coming freshmen to the academies, first year students in the ROTC programs and new recruits who achieved a minimum score on their service's version of the Armed Forces Services Vocational Aptitude Battery. For efficiency, it would be advisable to develop a "pre-test" to the DLAB, and then administer the full battery to those applicants achieving a certain score. The actual DLAB is a web-based test, comprising of 126 multiple choice questions and is scored out of a possible 176 points. Half of the test is audio and half is written. It does not test a current language proficiency, but rather the ability to learn a foreign language.[11]

For Army linguists, Army Regulation 11-6 rates their proficiency on a scale from 0 to 5, with 5 being the most proficient. Basic language training is designed to bring a student to a level 2 proficiency (described as limited working proficiency). Intermediate language training is designed to bring a student to a level 2+ proficiency (described as limited working proficiency, plus) and the advanced language courses are designed to train a student to level 3 proficiency (described as general professional proficiency). The third column, LPIND (Language Proficiency Indicator) is a 4 digit code where the first 2 numbers represent the listening / reading level and the last 2 numbers representing the speaking level.[12] For purposes of this paper's recommendations, a level 2, limited working proficiency will certainly be sufficient to appropriately prepare our joint forces to fully engage their host nation and partner nation counterparts. It will also serve to help qualify the service member for the "Cultural" additional skill identifier (ASI), as well as language proficiency pay.

From a practicality standpoint, based on the limited number of training seats available and the protracted period of time it takes to send a service member through the Defense Language Institute; (over one year for many languages), training via this method alone is not practical, and will require other training approaches. The Special Warfare Center and School already provides language training for Civil Affairs, Military Information Support Operations (MISO) and Special Forces operators at their Fort Bragg, schoolhouse. This is another source to be leveraged, although it will certainly require an increase of civilian and military instructors, web-based training material, support staff and classroom facilities. However, expanding the capacity of a current capability is always more advantageous, less expensive or time consuming than the initial creation of the capability.

Another resource that was previously available to service members, as well as their families, was the Rosetta Stone web-based language training program. This was provided to service members free of charge by simply accessing this software via the Army Knowledge Online (AKO) website where there was a direct link to the Rosetta Stone website. The Army elected not to renew the user contract with Rosetta Stone when the contract ended on September 24, 2011.[13] As someone who effectively used this software, I can attest to its value as a language resource tool. It would need to be reinstated for this proposal to be viable and would certainly be more cost efficient than traditional methods of language learning in a classroom setting.

Additional Skill Identifier (ASI)

Although they may go by different names, the overall concept is basically the same within the various services; identify a need for specialized capability, training and education, then create an alpha-numeric combination to capture this ability for future assignments. Within the Army's personnel structure it is known as an Additional Skill Identifier (ASI).[14] The Navy uses the term Additional Qualification Designator for Officers and the Air Force goes by Special Experience Identifier to match uniquely qualified personnel to specific critical missions.[15] Regardless of the name, the philosophy must be adapted within the construct of establishing a manner in which to identify those who have accomplished this valuable level of learning and ensuring they are assigned to those leadership positions requiring this education for mission accomplishment.

Recommendations

As our military leaders look to the future in an effort to forecast where we will be required to conduct operations and against whom those operations will be conducted, it can be anticipated our civilian leaders will continue to seek out partner nations with which to work to create a coalition, especially in the Middle East with Muslim countries. This was the case with Desert Storm and efforts are in place to achieve the same with the current fight against ISIS. In the 2012 Sustaining U.S. Global Leadership: Priorities for 21st Century Defense, it specifies the following challenge for the military leadership: "U. S. forces will plan to operate whenever possible with allied and coalition forces."[16]

Accordingly, US commanders will be required to not only be aware of the culture, norms and thoughts of the enemy, but will be required to also understand the same when working with partner militaries and government leaders. Failure to establish positive working relationships with senior leadership from different cultures and religious backgrounds at the strategic level will create potentially more difficulties than at the operational or tactical level. To achieve this, the Department of Defense must do the following;

> Codify this concept in all of our strategic documents: National Security Strategy, National Defense Strategy, National Military Strategy, Quadrennial Defense Review and the Quadrennial Development and Diplomacy Review. Fully integrate the value of cultural capabilities into the framework of the various War Colleges and create a curriculum of study designed to offer a Master's level degree to students, both those in residence and distance learning. Senior level buy-in is key for the rest of the force to fully

realize the importance of attainment of this skill-set on our future conflicts with Muslim religious extremism.

Designate Cultural Training one of the most basic concepts of all initial entry-level training for Officers and Enlisted service members. This includes the military academies and all ROTC programs. Develop a curriculum of learning that will enable students to earn a minor in Cultural Awareness, which can be applied to the process of earning their ASI once they are commissioned and achieve other milestones in their culture educational pathway. For our enlisted service members, develop cultural training to become a part of Basic and Advanced Individual Training (AIT) for every (MOS).

Make Cultural Training an integral component of all levels of PME for both the Officer and Non-Commissioned Officer Corps. Make provisions to prevent "grandfathering" for those who have already progressed to higher levels of their military education. These are the leaders who will soon be in elevated positions of leadership and must be more prepared for working in a multinational, multicultural area of operations.

Another component of the cultural education process is language training. Language capability potential must be identified early in a Soldier's career by the development of an abbreviated version of the DLAB that will be administered to those achieving a minimum score on the Armed Services Vocational Aptitude Battery (ASVAB). Those earning an acceptable score will be administered the full DLAB once they arrive at their Basic Training station. Students of the Academies and ROTC programs will go through the same process during their first year. All students will be required to take a minimum of two (2) semesters of a foreign language and those who pass the DLAB will be "strongly encouraged" to earn a minor in a foreign language and be given preferential opportunities to attend further language training upon completion of BOLC (Basic Office

Leader Course). These opportunities must be extended to the Reserve component Soldiers as well.

Soldiers who have already completed their initial entry training will conduct similar language ability testing. Those passing the DLAB will be selected for attendance at an institutional language training facility, such as DLI or SWCS. Until such time as the capacity is sufficiently increased to accommodate this influx of students, Rosetta Stone will be made available in their selected language and they will be assigned to a distance learning cohort with an instructor from DLI / SWCS to monitor their progress and further prepare them for attendance at an actual school.

The attainment of the Cultural Awareness ASI must be viewed by the force as a career enhancer. For the enlisted service member, it must be worth a significant number of promotion points and place the service member ahead of their peers for attendance in their NCO professional development courses. For the Officer Corps, it should be required to serve in various leadership positions during overseas contingency operations that place the leader in positions of frequent interaction with the host nation populace and foreign military advisor roles. Promotion boards must be instructed to view leaders with this particular ASI in a very favorable light, much as was the case in 2006 when there was a concerted effort to get more Officers to volunteer to serve as members of a MITT (Military Training Team) working and living with the Iraqi Army.

No matter what name they go by: Al-Qa'ida, Islamic State of Iraq and the Levant, Al-Qa'ida in the Arabian Peninsula, al-Shabaab, Boko Haram, Ansar al-Shari'a, or most recently, the Islamic State of Iraq and al-Sham (ISIS), all of these terrorist organizations present an existential threat to United States interests and allies around the world, the American homeland and our way of life. Thanks to the operations in Iraq and Afghanistan, the original Al-Qa'ida threat had been greatly neutralized, culminating with the death of Bin Ladin. With the lack of action by the United States toward the recent onset of civil war in

Syria, coupled with the al Maliki-led government's alienation of Sunni populations in Iraq, and Turkey allowing its borders to remain porous to foreign fighters, ISIS has been able to make never before realized inroads to establishing a caliphate in Syria and Iraq. The more success they achieve, the more they are able to recruit and influence around the world, even in America. The United States is losing the battle with radical Islam in general and ISIS in particular. Defeating this threat will require US military intervention. This intervention means more than air combat missions and "boots on the ground". It means those boots need to be filled with US Soldiers, Marines, Sailors and Airmen who are culturally aware, religiously respectful and language capable.

Chapter 40

Deconstructing ISIS: SWJ interview with William McCants on The ISIS Apocalypse: The History, Strategy and Doomsday Vision of the Islamic State

Octavian Manea

First Published 24 September 2015

William McCants is a fellow in the Center for Middle East Policy[1] and director of the Project on U.S. Relations with the Islamic World[2] at the Brookings Institution. He is also an adjunct faculty member at Johns Hopkins University and has served in government and think tank positions related to Islam, the Middle East, and terrorism, including as State Department senior adviser for countering violent extremism.

How should we define ISIS? Is it a state, an insurgency, a terrorist group?

Today I see the group as a proto-state. It offers governmental services, provides security, raises taxes, and does everything that other states do.

And it sees itself as a state. When the organization was founded back in 2006 it proclaimed itself to be a state but was nothing of the kind. It was an insurgent group, and then by 2008 an underground clandestine terrorist group. After 2014, the fact that it controlled so much territory and governed so many people gave credibility to its claim to be a state.

What are the core differences between al-Qaeda and ISIS?

There are at least three major differences between al-Qaeda Central and the Islamic State. In some respect these differences existed from the beginning when Zarqawi's franchise in Iraq joined up with al-Qaeda in 2004. The main difference was that al-Qaeda in Iraq believed in establishing an Islamic State or a Caliphate now, while al-Qaeda Central focused on getting rid of the Western powers in the Middle East and unifying Muslims behind al-Qaeda's cause. The Caliphate would be established in the future. That was a major difference in terms of strategic timing with respect to actually creating an Islamic state.

The second difference was also a question of timing-when is the end of days coming? Bin Laden believed it would be very far in the future, while the Islamic State believes it is right around the corner. That belief almost destroyed the Islamic State in the early days. Now it has made the apocalypse and the end of days an effective recruiting pitch, especially when attracting foreign fighters for its cause.

The third difference is a question of strategy. Al-Qaeda Central always believed that you need to win over the Sunni masses in order to establish an Islamic state. For Bin Laden, popular support was crucial. If the masses didn't agree with your political project, and with the way you were pursuing it, your political project would not endure. Al-Qaeda had a more hearts-and-minds approach in the Sunni world, which the Islamic State fundamentally disagreed with. The Islamic State believed from the beginning that it would be better to be feared than to be loved, and that waging a brutal insurgency campaign not only against their enemy, but also against their fellow Sunnis, would allow them to reach their political objective faster and more effectively than trying to win over popular support.

To what extent did personal biographies and formative experiences of the leaders influence the direction of their respective organizations? The AQ core formed in Afghanistan in the 1980s, while for AQI the formative experience was the invasion of Iraq. Do these experiences and legacies contribute to differences in the organizations?

I think you can go further back in time in their biographies and see how their differences in class influenced their perspectives on insurgency. Bin Laden came from the upper class of Saudi society. So did Zawahiri. He came from an elite family in Egypt. This was not Zarqawi's background. He was a street thug before he became a jihadist. I think if you look at the way they wage insurgencies, you can identify some differences based on their demographic background. Bin Laden and Zawahiri wanted to wage a more high-minded campaign in the Sunni world, versus Zarqawi's street thug tactics.

But I take your point about the differences in how their perceptions on insurgency and the usefulness of violence formed. In Afghanistan you had a broad-based coalition where a lot of Arabs were brought together by Abdullah Azam who wanted to play nice with the other Arab regimes and who saw the fight as a classic defense of the Islamic land against the infidels. The focus was on unity of mission rather than unity of mind. This is in deep contrast with the Iraqi experience, which was a sectarian inter-communal fight between Sunni and Shia deliberately provoked by Zarqawi, whose hatred for the Shia was all-consuming.

What are the reasons for the failure of AQI in 2008?

For Bin Laden, the lessons of the first Islamic State failure in 2008 were that the organization was too brutal, too unwilling to work with other rebel groups, and too insistent that everyone bend the knee to its cause. Again, he wanted to cultivate broad popular support for al-Qaeda's program. Bin Laden also thought that AQI didn't do enough to cultivate the support of the tribes, which were crucial for the success of the jihadist state-building enterprise.

The IS members that survived the killing of their leadership took the exact opposite lesson. Their conclusion was that they failed because they had not been brutal enough. These are two very different readings of the lessons of that period. Where they converge is in coopting and winning over the Sunni tribes in Iraq. There is a fascinating document from 2010 that looks like a Washington DC think tank report but was written by ISIS members in which they conclude that they need to work better with the Sunni Arab tribes. The model they recommended emulating was what the Americans had done in Anbar. They thought that the Americans had coopted the tribes brilliantly and that the Islamic State needed to follow the exact same model, which in some ways they have.

Why did Bin Laden have a fear of governing?

He had two reasons for discouraging the Islamic State and the other al-Qaeda affiliates from establishing Islamic governments. One was that he did not believe that those governments would last; the US would not allow them to last and would destroy them with overwhelming power. Until you got rid of the US from the region, he believed, you wouldn't have the conditions required to establish a lasting state.

The second reason was that he didn't feel that these groups were ready to govern. They didn't have the necessary human resources, and the areas they wanted to govern had acute economic problems that the jihadists would not be able to cope with. Sooner or later the people would blame them for these failures and problems. It's one thing when you are fighting against the government and another thing when you are the government and you have to own all these problems. Bin Laden believed the state-building projects would fail because the jihadists couldn't deliver quickly on services.

Why did AQI fail?

It's hard to say from the outside why the state failed, but it's also hard to say from the jihadist perspective. Did they fail because they were too brutal and were not doing more to win over the population? Or because of outside intervention? This is a problem particularly for the global jihadists. Inevitably global jihadist groups, just by virtue of who they are and what they say, invite invasion and are overthrown because they level threats against powerful nations, particular Western nations. As a result, they can't decide if their failure is a consequence of the outside intervention or if they were terrible at governing. The question is never settled.

To what extent did The Management of Savagery[3] influence the strategy of ISIS?

It's hard to say. It's been around for many years, since 2004, and is highly valued by the leadership of ISIS. But if you read the book and compare it with the strategy that they actually implemented you will see similarities, but also some interesting divergences. The similarities are the focus on taking and holding territory and providing basic services. That is the plan outlined in The Management of Savagery and this is certainly a plan pursued by ISIS. The Management of Savagery talks about the need to coopt tribes or suppress them if they don't cooperate, which is part of the ISIS blueprint. The book also strongly emphasizes the need to wage a brutal insurgency. A major difference is that The Management of Savagery recommends a broad-based coalition with other Sunni rebel groups, which is not a program that ISIS has followed. That's more of a program followed by al-Nusra.

In a time of revolutions that really have shaken the Middle East order, what significance does the Abbasid revolution have on the mindset that ISIS is trying to mobilize?

The Abbasid revolution happened in the 8th century. The propaganda for that revolution called for a restoration of rule by the Prophet's family. They regarded the rulers at the time as usurpers of Mohammed's family. A lot of disgruntled people began to coalesce around the movement and around the idea that everything would be better once a descendant of Mohammed was on the throne.

They also portrayed their movement in apocalyptical terms. The person that would come to the fore to lead the movement would be a savior called the Mahdi who would be the rightful ruler of the empire. There are a lot of similarities between their propaganda and the Islamic State's propaganda today. Apocalypse, caliphate, and revolution were essential for both movements. The Islamic State emphasizes the lineage of its leader Abu Bakr al-Baghdadi[4] as a direct descendant from Mohammed, which has garnered support for the State's program. One additional thing that they emphasize is the centrality of Iraq and particularly Baghdad, which was also important for the Abbasid Caliphate.

What explains ISIS's success under Baghdadi? What made ISIS better at state-building?

It is a confluence of a political context that was favorable to the rise of this kind of organization and the right kind of organization that could capitalize on the political context. If you look at ISIS's strategy and recruitment, it used the same formula it had in 2007 but the politics then weren't favorable to its program. It was acting like a state, but nobody wanted it there. It was facing a powerful US military that was capable of working with the tribes against it, the government in Baghdad was cooperative, and Syria was still under the iron fist of the Assad family, none of which was favorable to ISIS. You compare that with the politics that followed the Arab Spring and the civil war in Syria. The chaos gave ISIS a new strategic opportunity, and its formula all of a sudden worked. Its emphasis on state-building suddenly worked because it focused on taking the Sunni hinterland in Syria and Iraq while every other rebel group focused on overthrowing the Assad government. In short, ISIS's focus on building its own state rather than leading revolution against an existing state worked in its favor.

Then, the apocalyptic recruiting pitch which had nearly destroyed the organization in its early days became critical to its success in attracting foreign fighters to its cause. These foreign fighters have really given the organization an edge in the insurgency because they didn't have many ties with the locals so they can afford to be far more brutal, which coincides with ISIS's strategy of ruling through fear.

The third thing that worked in its favor was that the lack of an American military to stop ISIS from taking over the Sunni hinterland. ISIS did not have to worry about a popular uprising because the population had no strong external parties to turn to for help. At the same time, as a consequence of Baghdad's and Damascus's divisive policies, the restive Sunnis were ripe for the ruling by someone who wanted to establish a state and who had enough manpower and experience to do so.

How sustainable is this extreme brutality as a foundation for long-term state-building?

You would hope not very, but over the course of my research, I had to accept that this is a political strategy that can work. We forget that this terrifying approach to state building has been tried before. Extreme brutality is not incompatible with establishing a state. The Taliban came to power and ruled in a similar way. It was as brutal as ISIS, its state would not have collapsed had it not antagonized a powerful Western nation. We would still be talking about the Islamic Emirate of Afghanistan today. Brutality works and can be durable. The challenge for ISIS is that like the Taliban, they will inherently antagonize foreign nations. Foreign intervention is what poses a threat to ISIS and may lead to its destruction, not the nature of its governing style.

What do you see as necessary to fight ISIS successfully? Degrading—the emphasis that we see today—is definitely not the same as defeating.

This is a hugely complex issue, especially because of the disaffection of the Sunni Arabs living in the land between Syria and Iraq. Until the Iraqi and Syrian governments reach an accommodation with them that is acceptable to all parties, this conflict is going to endure. It may not manifest as the Islamic State, but we will see similar groups emerge to capitalize on this disaffection, whether to channel it against the government or to exploit it as the Islamic State has done. Addressing the underlying politics driving this Sunni disaffection has to be high on the agenda. Even if Baghdad and Damascus reach some sort of political accommodation with the Sunnis, those governments will still have to take care of their material needs. They have to equitably provide goods and services and fairly apply the rule of law.

The difficulty that I see in an international intervention is that it lets the local governments off the hook. The US and its allies may come in and solve the ISIS kinetic problem, but this will not solve the political problem. It will absolve local governments of making the tough political choices required to end the Sunni disenfranchisement that fuels the insurgency.

I am also hesitant to recommend that kind of Western intervention because I don't believe it's sustainable. After more than a decade of war and occupation, the domestic political will is not there. There is no will for these long-term military commitments. We are very focused on maintaining the integrity of Syria and Iraq. That may be the right thing to do, but I also wonder if we shouldn't start contemplating more of a federal system of governance. The current formula is not working.

What made ISIS more popular than AQ in the context of the global jihadist movement? Is the ISIS brand becoming more powerful than AQ?

ISIS has definitely become more popular than AQ and has really seized the imagination of the global jihadist movement precisely because it has been able to take and hold territory and proclaim itself the Caliphate. And it is not an empty claim. By the same token if it were to lose its state, that would put at risk its political program. Since it stakes its legitimacy to control of the land, it makes itself and its political project vulnerable if its land is taken away. The appeal of the Islamic State rests on its ability to endure and expand. Take either of those away and you erode its legitimacy.

Chapter 41

How to Defeat the Islamic State: Crafting a Rational War Strategy

Anthony N. Celso

First Published 24 September 2015

Introduction

The Islamic State of Iraq and al-Sham (ISIS) caliphate declaration is the most significant historical event since the Cold War's end. ISIS' jihadist state has unhinged the Mideast, contributed to destabilizing refugee flows and inspired global terrorism. Military reaction by the United States and its allies to ISIS has been dysfunctional and ineffective.

This essay examines ISIS' caliphate and the security challenges the jihadist state portends. These problems have been poorly addressed by the Obama Administration's *low cost/minimum* risk *containment* policy. Above all the essay is concerned with crafting an alternative war strategy to destroy the caliphate's institutional edifice.

The analysis has four parts. First, the roots of ISIS' formation are explained. Second, the caliphate's emergence and the security challenges it presents to regional and international order are discussed. Third, the failure of Western policy makers to address this problem is presented.

Fourth, an alternative war plan is developed to exploit the strategic vulnerabilities of the jihadist transnational state.

ISIS' Origins

Many analysts blame the 2003 Iraq War for the region's destabilization and ISIS' emergence.[1] While the overthrow of Saddam Hussein's Sunni dominated regime made an important contribution, the 2003 war's impact is often over-stated. A 2014 POMEPS report on ISIS, for example, predominantly blames the 2003 war for the caliphate's emergence.[2] This Iraq war centric argument captures a part of the story that begins earlier and is catalyzed by later events.

Instead ISIS' rise has more varied historical roots. The clash between Sunni fundamentalism and Shi'ite radicalism has been building for a generation.[3] Since the 1979 Iranian Revolution Tehran has exported Shia radicalism across the region.[4] Working through its Lebanese Hezbollah proxy and Syria's Assad regime, Tehran wants to project a regional Shi'ite arc of influence. Threatened by a Shi'ite rebellion in its oil rich eastern provinces, Saudi Arabia countered Iran by fortifying Sunni fundamentalism. Enriched by oil wealth the Kingdom's export of Wahhabism spawned radical jihadist movements hostile to "apostate" religious minorities.[5] Within the chaos of the 2003 Iraq war, Al Qaeda in Iraq (AQI) grew abetted by sectarian antagonisms.

AQI's ethno-sectarian warfare against Shi'ites, Kurds and Christians hoped to force state collapse and a US military withdraw.[6] Beaten back by American counter terror policies and anti-jihadist Sunni tribal militias, AQI and its Islamic State of Iraq (ISI) successor lost ground and by the end of the American occupation ISI was considered defeated.[7]

ISI's resurgence was facilitated by the Obama Administration's post 2010 policies that created a power vacuum stimulating regional rivalries.[8] Especially damaging was the US pivot to Asia, its 2011 Iraq withdraw, and its non-intervention in the Syrian conflict. These actions sent a message to regional actors that America is not a credible power.

Iran, Turkey and the Gulf Arab states intensified their intervention supporting opposing sides in the Syrian conflict.

Regional competition coincided with Arab Spring protests and the weakening of the state system. These forces have been devastating. Parts of the Mideast represent a Hobbesian state of nature where sectarian fratricidal violence rages. The Syrian civil war's carnage fueled ISIS rise undoing the fragile colonial era state system. With no dominant hegemon, regional actors pursued their respective interests igniting proxy wars in Iraq, Syria and Yemen. The Syrian civil war internationalized this conflict by producing the greatest foreign fighter migrations in history.[9] Today Syria is the epicenter of a sectarian shadow war between Iran, Turkey and Gulf Arab states.

The Caliphate Reborn

The resulting chaos set forth two deadly dynamics: one in Iraq; the other in Syria. These events contributed to ISIS transnational jihadist state. Before ISIS no modern extremist group was successful in breaking colonial borders and forming an Islamic Empire. ISIS caliphate is a vindication of late AQI leader Abu Musab al-Zarqawi's anti-Shia war strategy that within the cataclysm of the Syrian civil war succeeded.[10] After the US disengagement events in Iraq were important. Former Prime Minister Nuri al-Maliki contributed to Iraq's unraveling by repressing the Sunni minority.[11] The Obama Administration inability to negotiate a long term US troop presence freed Baghdad from American military pressure. Pursuing sectarian agenda Maliki persecuted Sunni politicians and demobilized tribal militias. Faced with state repression and absent the protective shield of tribal militias, Iraqi Sunnis looked for someone to defend their interests. Sunni anti-government sentiment allowed ISI to rehabilitate its terror network.[12]

Working from Mosul and Tikrit the movement expanded. ISI's *Breaking the Walls* and *Soldiers of Harvest* campaigns freed hundreds of jihadist prisoners and killed thousands of Iraqi army and Sunni tribal militias members.[13] Two years of relentless ISIS attacks shattered Iraqi security forces. ISI terrorism was de-stabilizing. Religious antagonisms and Iraqi security vacuums expanded ISI's territorial reach to Anbar province. Once pacified, Fallujah again became a key jihadist stronghold.

The network's transnational consolidation was propelled by the Syrian conflict. Without the revolt against the Alawite dominated Bashar al Assad's regime, it is doubtful that ISIS would have developed. Beginning in March 2012 as a peaceful protest for democratic change the revolt evolved into a jihadist dominated insurgency. With over 240,000 deaths and ten million refugees the conflict continues. The Syrian civil war reflects past confessional antagonisms. Over three decades ago the Sunni Muslim Brotherhood revolted against President Bashar al-Assad's father in the beleaguered city of Hama. Damascus responded savagely by destroying the city and wiping out the rebels.[14] Avenging Hama has been a rallying cry for Syrian jihadists who now have the opportunity to succeed where the Muslim Brothers failed.[15] Today's jihadist revolt against Damascus is more fortuitous. Global and regional forces favor the Sunni jihadists who benefit from Gulf Arab funds and a permissive Turkish border transit policy.[16] This has globalized the conflict and allowed ISI to benefit from foreign fighter migrations.

Confronted by a popular insurrection Assad consolidated his forces leaving regions lightly defended. Rebels soon dominated remote rural areas. This was especially true of the border area with Iraq that allowed ISI to expand its network into Eastern Syria.[17] By 2012 ISI's network developed a Syrian branch Jabhat al-Nusra (JN) that gained fame for its successful assaults against regime forces. Within eastern Syria ISI began attacking other rebel groups and displacing them. Concentrating its forces around Raqqa, the town soon became ISI's iconic Syrian headquarters that imposed medieval Sharia justice.[18] With its Syrian base of operations strengthened and flush with international recruits, the network announced ISIS' creation merging its Iraqi and Syrian branches.

Sensing a leadership challenge, Al Qaeda emir Ayman al-Zawahiri enjoined the union and ordered ISI's Syrian disengagement. Vexed ISI leader Abu Bakr al-Baghdadi repudiated Zawahiri's order. By January 2014 jihadists turned on each other, thousands died.[19] One month later ISIS was ejected from Al Qaeda's network.[20]

Fortified by its Syrian network, ISIS stormed into Western Iraq seizing Mosul and most of Anbar Province. ISIS' Blitzkrieg demoralized the Iraqi army that either surrendered or retreated. This left ISIS with a vast arsenal of American weapons. ISIS celebrated its victory by slaughtering over 1,200 Shi'ite Iraqi Army prisoners at Camp Speicher, a celebratory slaughter of military prisoners not seen since the Rape of Nanking.[21]

Two seminal events followed. ISI spokesperson Muhamad al-Adnani in late June announced the caliphate's formation, now rebranded the Islamic State (IS). In the fourth issue of the *Islamic State Report* ISIS foot soldiers announce the abolition of the Franco-British treaty and confidently predicted the caliphate's predestined expansion.[22] ISIS's transnational aspirations were fortified by Abu Bakr al-Baghdadi later address at Mosul's Grand Mosque. His July 4, 2014 sermon called for the loyalty of the world's Muslims and he demanded their *hijrah* [emigration] to his caliphate. Renamed Caliph Ibrahim, Baghdadi's address divides the world into heavenly and devilish realms and suggests the inevitability of an apocalyptic struggle where Islam destroys its enemies.[23]

One cannot overstate the significance of Baghdadi's proclamation. IS's formation and its caliphate centric strategy are historic events. The Islamic State acts as a magnet for unprecedented foreign fighter migrations (some 40,000 fighters) and serves as the embodiment of millenarian jihadist aspirations.[24] This is magnified by IS' on-line Twitter campaigns that have generated significant mass support.[25] Some of these on-line participants have headed Baghdadi's call for *hijrah,* while others have committed acts of terrorism in their home countries. With attacks by IS sympathizers in Brussels, Copenhagen, New York, Sydney, Paris, Suisse and Garland, and with thirty provinces worldwide the caliphate is a significant threat to the international liberal order.

The Islamic State's Multi-Pronged War

These achievements should not mask the obstacles confronting the caliphate's *remaining* and *expanding* strategy. The Islamic State's expansive ideology blends takfirist, apocalyptic, sectarian, and Salafi-jihadist values. Though complex IS' vision can be divided into sequential projects that prioritize the extinction of foreign influenced apostasy in Islamic lands and then proceeds to conquer all non-Islamic civilizations.

ISIS' confrontation with Sunni apostates and Shi'ite, Alawite, Druze, and Kurdish heretics is driven by its Salafi-jihadist worldview. These groups' heterodox beliefs are believed by the Islamic State to be source of apostasy that must be eradicated.[26] Despite this enormous challenge, conflicts among IS' enemies and regional religious antagonisms work to the caliphate's advantage. IS believes that it must fortify the Islamic community's religious foundations by cleansing apostates and imposing servitude upon heretical Yazidi and Christian communities. Such actions reflect IS' idealization of Muhammad's Medina community and his immediate successors caliphate. Islamic State ideologues see this formative period in Islamic development as God's will incarnate. Once purified of apostasy, IS believes it will have the divine fortitude to vanquish its Zionist-Crusader enemies.

ISIS June 2014 Mosul conquest threatened a deep advance into Iraqi Kurdistan and the encirclement of Baghdad. IS' success impelled a risk averse Obama Administration into action. IS' conquests were partially a tragic legacy of the Administration's post 2011 neglect. After the American withdraw jihadist military advancement elicited no response from the Obama Administration. Rejecting requests from the Iraqi government to target ISI's network, the Administration, never less, continued to support Baghdad as it brutalized its Sunni political opponents and disbanded the Anbar based Sons of Iraq militias the only effective firewall to prevent ISI revival in Sunni communities.[27]

Obama's Dysfunctional "Containment" Strategy

By August the collapse of Iraqi and Kurdish defense forces forced the Administration's hand. Most critical was the need to stem the jihadists advance toward Erbil and prevent the encirclement of Baghdad. This synchronized with "strategic" needs to defend the US mission in Iraqi Kurdistan and protect the US embassy from ISIS attacks. Soon realism and idealism merged. With a genocidal threat to Mount Sinjar's Yazidi community, American military intervention meshed with the Administration's "responsibility to protect" doctrine forcing the US government into launching limited air strikes.

The Administration stumbled in rationalizing its intervention and explaining the scale of its commitment. A number of factors explain this development. Obama is affected by Vietnam's legacy and above all by his opposition to the Iraq War.[28] His reading of history cripples him and this may explain the anemic US military response.

US war strategy against IS is incoherent and dysfunctional. The Administration has implemented a containment policy composed of four essential components. First, it is a low cost, risk minimization approach that confines US participation to an air support, training and equip mission, ruling out combat troops. Second, it relies on a 60 nation coalition (mostly European and Arab regional powers) to assist in ISIS containment. Third, its' Baghdad centric strategy channels resources through the central government and depends upon it to direct the fight against IS with the assistance of Kurdish, Shi'ite and Sunni tribal allies. Fourth, its Syrian component finances the development of a vetted expat army and provides some limited air and supply support for the Syrian Kurdish Peshmerga.

Harmonizing these four components has proved difficult. The divisions within the coalition have hampered the use of force against ISIS. Mistrust between Kurds, Shi'ites, Turks and Sunnis impedes a unified effort and ISIS has adroitly exploited security gaps in their forces.[29] Progress has been slow and degrading ISIS frustratingly difficult. At best the Islamic State's offensive capacity has been repressed in Iraq and Syria. IS media operations inveigh against the US led alliance and shrewdly juxtaposes the caliphate's unity with the chronic disharmony of it enemies.[30]

The Dangers of *Leading from Behind*

The campaign is hindered by the limited scale of its air strikes. Fearful of collateral damage, the Administration bombing strategy leaves IS's economic and civilian infrastructure intact assisting the caliphate's "remaining and expanding" narrative. Having ruled out US Special Forces to direct laser guided air strikes, the Administration impairs the air campaign's effectiveness.[31]

Relying on a fractured coalition is fraught with problems. Turkey's role and its commitment to fight the Islamic State are problematic. Under the Islamist Justice and Development Party (AKP) government, Ankara has supported Muslim Brotherhood chapters across the world.[32] Hostile toward the Assad regime, Turkey supports jihadist groups fighting the Baathist regime. Its permissive border policy has facilitated the transit of hundreds of thousands of fighters whom have mainly joined ISIS or Al Qaeda affiliated Jabhat al-Nusra.[33] Equally counterproductive is Ankara's efforts to repress Kurdish People's Protection Units (YPG) and Kurdistan Worker's Party (PKK) militants fighting ISIS. Hailed by the Obama administration as an important development, Turkish July 2015 participation in the anti-ISIS campaign has featured only one strike against IS and repeated bombing of the PKK's Iraqi bases.

Arab Gulf financial support for radical jihadists groups fighting Assad compounds the problem. Driven more by ideological hostility against Assad than fear of IS, Sunni nations are contributing to the caliphate's *remaining* and *expanding*. This works to the detriment of coalitional efforts. The Saudis, for example, have not mounted one air strike against the caliphate. Yet they are heavily involved in air and ground operations in Yemen against Shi'ite Houthi rebels. These alliance problems and the constraints of a containment policy explain why scant progress has been made.

The Administration has had some sustained success working with the Iraqi Kurdish government and the Syrian-Kurdish YPG. U.S. air strikes and Kurdish Peshmerga resilience have given IS battlefield losses at Mount Sinjar, Mosul Dam and Kobane. Thousands of ISIS' "lions" were eviscerated by American air strikes defending Kobane. Working with the Free Syrian Army (FSA) the YGP has gained ground against ISIS threatening its iconic Raqqa Syrian headquarters. This success is jeopardized by the Administration's agreement with Turkey to create a security zone along the Syrian-Turkish border, a proposal driven by Ankara's anxiety that YPG offensive could result in independent Syrian Kurdistan.[34]

The Administration stance, moreover, suggests a Cold War era containment doctrine. Defenders of Washington's policies, point to past jihadist insurgencies that imploded once effectively isolated.[35] Some point to the Algerian Armed Islamic Group (GIA) where government forces gave the group the space it needed to govern territory which soon engendered popular resistance.[36] Combined with Government counter- terror operations, local resistance and amnesty deals for repentant militants, isolation contributed to the GIA's implosion.

The GIA experience may not be a viable precedent. While similarities exist, the forces that gave birth to these movements are radically different. Today's proxy war raging in Iraq, Syria and Yemen pitting Sunni Saudi Arabia and Shi'ite Iran plays well into ISIS narrative as a defender of Sunni interests. It is the wellspring of ISI's resurgence and its transnational jihadist state.

The GIA lacked the IS's international connections and it acted predominately within Algeria making containment viable. The caliphate's portable forty thousand foreign fighters, its diverse financial base and on-line communications strategy that reaches millions are not amenable to an isolation strategy. Such an effort would require Turkish and Gulf Arab states cooperation whose permissive policies have facilitated ISIS rise.

IS' proto-jihadist state derives revenue from oil, antiquities and human smuggling operations.[37] Its expansion across the Muslim world features some thirty provinces including powerful Egyptian and Nigerian terror networks.[38] The internationalization of the IS network since November 2014 constitutes potent evidence that containment has failed.

ISIS' Effective Counter Response

IS' war strategy facilitates its strategic objective to *remain* and *expand*.[39] The Islamic State's military and propaganda activities have functional qualities vacant in the current anti-IS campaign. Among these are: (1) a unity of purpose and concentration of force; (2) the use of hybrid warfare that mixes asymmetric and conventional techniques; (3) a divide, conquer and diversion strategy that neutralizes its opponents offensive capabilities; (4) total commitment, brutality and risk maximization; (5) operational dexterity across different battlefields; and (6) the synchronization of media and military policy. All of these qualities have allowed it to effectively counter the international military campaign.

The caliphate is unusual in the jihadist world for doesn't have the organizational and ideological fissures that have hindered past Islamist insurgencies. A contrast with Al Qaeda (AQ) is illustrative. Since the 2001 loss of its Taliban protected sanctuary, the organization has fractured and its affiliates have acted contrary to its parent's wishes. The near enemy, sectarian and takfirist behavior of Al Qaeda in the Islamic Maghreb (AQIM), Al Shabaab and even Al Qaeda in the Arabian Peninsula (AQAP) were criticized by bin Laden in his Abbottabad correspondence.[40] Al Qaeda's inability to control policies it objected to led the late AQ media advisor Adam Gadahn to urge separation from affiliates.[41] By 2011 AQ's *far enemy* strategy was in shambles with only AQAP remotely interested in attacking the US homeland.

The Islamic State of Iraq (ISI) anti-Shi'ite, takfirist, apocalyptic and caliphate centric strategy created strains within AQ's network. Despite these tensions it was not until February 2014 that Al Qaeda expelled ISIS for its failure to heed Zawahiri's decree to abandon its Syrian operations. Unique among AQ's network ISIS progenitor AQI never experienced severe divisions and the network has had a stable command structure.[42]

The Islamic State's hierarchical order has an emir/Caliph, a Shura policy-making council, two media divisions, separate Iraqi and Syrian commanders, and a leadership structure for all of its thirty provinces.[43] United by a barbaric sectarian and takfirist agenda that dates back to Abu Musab al-Zarqawi, IS is fully committed to its program tying resources to its goals. Fragmented between Kurdish Peshmerga, the Iraqi army, and Sunni tribal forces, no single actor leads and coordinates offensive capability against the caliphate. This inhibits the concentration of force needed to break IS and may explain why Ramadi and Baiji are still under the caliphate's control after successive Iraqi army assaults. Whenever its opponents advance, IS opens up another front to divert its opponent's resources. Today few speak optimistically about liberating Mosul soon.[44]

The fragmentation of Iraqi forces has two dynamic effects. First, it creates security gaps in anti-ISIS forces allowing IS to exploit. Second, it permits the Islamic State to divide and conquer its opponents through the inflammation of ethno-sectarian divisions.[45] Each attack against Kurdish and Shi'ite civilians creates tensions between these groups and their Sunni coalitional partners inhibiting force coordination and concentration.

The caliphate's army is skilled at hybrid warfare and has an operational dexterity that its opponents lack. Employing varied attacks ISIS made dramatic advances throughout 2014-2015 including capturing Mosul and occupying Ramadi. The latter is a good example. With its forces shielded by a sand storm ISIS unleashed dozens of massive tanker truck bombs and an infantry charge right out of the movie Road Warrior.[46] Denied air support due to weather and not equipped with enough anti-tank missiles to derail the assault, the Iraqi army retreated. This outcome was sadly reminiscent of the security forces abandonment of Mosul last year that allowed ISIS to capture vast amounts of US supplied weapons.

IS military campaigns feature suicide bombers, improvised explosive devices, human wave attacks and vehicular bombs and its slaughtering of its opponents represent a commitment lacking in its numerically superior adversaries.[47] The caliphate's operational dexterity and dedication go beyond its Iraqi-Syrian base and includes a growing presence in Egypt and Libya.[48] This insures that defeat in one theater does not portent he caliphate's demise.

Its military operations are promoted by propaganda campaigns that attract recruits and terrorize its enemies. Reports of battlefield achievements, grisly execution videos, depiction of the caliphate's charitable activities, destruction of pagan architectural sites and appeals for hijrah are designed to facilitate its *remaining* and *expanding* strategy.[49] Packaged as fulfilling ISIS' prophetic destiny this media campaign attracts fanatics committed to its ideological message. Thousands of videos are posed by hundreds of ISIS Twitter accounts. Dozens of these videos appear daily. The propaganda recruits many foreign fighters (including some three to four thousand Europeans) that it hopes will be able to launch external operations in their home countries.[50]

ISIS brilliantly markets itself. Filmed in Palmira's ruins (now completely destroyed) one ISIS video features child executioners killing Syrian soldiers.[51] Presented in grand operatic style the film suggests that the future generations guarantee that it will *remain* and *expand* and imperial glory awaits these *cubs* of the Islamic State. By destroying Palmira ISIS suggests that not only can it shape the future but it can destroy the past. This does not mean ISIS can be defeated and its state building project destroyed. Doing so is critical but is preconditioned upon examining the caliphate's strategic weaknesses.

Exploiting the *Frontiers of Anarchy* and *Hybrid War*

The US led military campaign is plagued by numerous problems. The Obama Administration's unwillingness to expand the air campaign and to deploy US combat troops cripples efforts to defeat the caliphate. With America leading from behind, no one directs sufficient force to smash IS' jihadist state. Except for the Kurds everyone is pursuing a low cost/risk minimization strategy driven by fear and anxiety. This posture clashes disastrously with ISIS totalistic commitment/risk maximization approach that terrorizes its enemies.

Three years forward ISIS will probably *remain* and *expand*. Terrorism, refugee flows and regional destabilization will increase. We are likely to see more attacks like those in Paris, New York, Suisse, Sydney, Brussels, Copenhagen and Garland. By necessity we will need to abandon this ineffective risk minimization containment policy.

Decades ago Robert Kaplan's *The Ends of the Earth* presciently examined the collapse of the Third World's state system.[52] Since than regime dissolution has proceeded alarmingly. Battered by the Arab Spring's turmoil and sectarian proxy wars, the Mideast state system is withering. Current policy aims to preserve Iraq and Syria's territorial integrity and works through Bagdad and Ankara to contain ISIS. This strategy is unrealistic. Instead, we should encourage ethno-tribal centrifugal pressures, work with non-state actors and disengage from regimes whose interests constrain US policy. By-passing Iraq and Turkey is necessary in any engagement with Kurdish and Sunni tribal forces. The Obama Administration's Baghdad centric policy features a prominent role for Iranian backed Shi'ite militias that impairs any Sunni tribal rebellion, while its deference to Ankara prevents any vigorous engagement with the Iraqi and Syrian Kurds. Only by supporting these groups with a sustained air campaign and Special Forces operations can we upend the caliphate.

British policy toward the Ottoman Empire during the First World War may be a helpful guide on how to defeat the Islamic State. Working with tribal federations London assisted revolts that fragmented Istanbul's imperial integrity contributing to British and French colonization of the Middle East and North Africa.[53] As Ephraim Karsh argues, the caliphate's unity has historically been compromised by ethnic-tribal divisions.[54] Past success working with regional non-state actors, moreover, suggests the need to change course. Successful partnerships with Sunni tribal militias during the US Iraq occupation and currently with Kurdish Peshmerga indicate that this could be a more efficacious approach.[55] Given the collapse of states across the region, this devolution of authority presents opportunities for US policy-makers to work with warlords, militias and private vigilantes that are now not fully untapped.[56]

We need to exploit IS' strategic vulnerabilities and attack it at its weakest points. The Islamic State has four core vulnerabilities (see the table below). First, its visible state structure and governance project requires an open persistent presence. This can be shattered by a prolonged air campaign that makes life in the caliphate unviable. Destroying ISIS' institutional foundation by turning its schools, oil fields, police stations, training camps, dams, grain bins into charred rubble derails ISIS marketing of its jihadist state.

ISIS Strategic Vulnerability	Attack Node
State Building Project	Visible and direct can be smashed with extensive air campaign targeting ISIS security installations, dams, grain bins, Sharia councils, educational and charitable institutional. Amplify leadership decapitation strikes and assassination campaign
Apocalyptic Ideology	Vulnerable to overreach and psychological manipulation by luring them to fight US troops directly. Exploit the cult of the offensive and strategic impatience. Media operations use of apocalyptic language to foreshadow ISIS' doom.
Transnational Takfirist Ideology	Ethno-Tribal Resistance and Revenge directed against caliphate by direct support for Kurdish Peshmerga and Sunni tribal forces by-passing Baghdad. Support for autonomous protests and rebellions
Brutality	Weakening of institutional framework to encourage vigilantism and revenge against ISIS militants

Table: ISIS Strategic Vulnerabilities and Points of Attack

Few will emigrate to live in a caliphate composed of destroyed and smoldering cities and towns. IS version of Muhammad's Medina community Raqqa, should be turned into WWII's Dresden. Today's limited air strikes avoid collateral damage (economic and human) and allows for the caliphate's governance project to persist. This plays into the Islamic State's *remaining* and *expanding* narrative. This needs to end.

Second, IS' apocalyptic ideology and its fixation on fighting Western troops in a predestined battle of *Dabiq* makes it vulnerable to open confrontation. Ending the prohibition on US combat troops engaging the caliphate is vital. At a minimum American Special Forces should be mixed with Kurdish Peshmerga and Sunni tribal militias to coordinate targeted air strikes against IS military positions. Western troops will likely coax the caliphate's *lions* into taking risks and make its forces vulnerable to open engagement. Despite their ferocity and experience IS soldiers are no match for the sophisticated weapons and training US Special Forces possess. Targeted air strikes in support for Kurdish and Sunni allies could lay waste to ISIS forces. Driven by prophetic visions of impending victory, Islamic State commanders take significant risks. Washington Institute scholar Michael Knights labels IS' impetuosity the "cult of the offensive".[57] The battle for Kobane is illustrative. Propelled by images of predestined victory, ISIS repeated assaults against the beleaguered Kurdish Syrian city proved dysfunctional. Thousands of its *lions* were slaughtered by sustained US air strikes and determined Kurdish ground resistance.

This is not the first time an apocalyptic jihadist state embarked on a misguided war strategy. The 19th century Mahdist state in Sudan fought openly against well-armed British troops in the battle of Omdurman emboldened by Caliph Abdullah's "clairvoyant dream" that he defeated crusaders in an open field in broad daylight.[58] Omdurman was one of the greatest military routs in history and served as the death knell for jihadist forces.

Thirdly and relatedly, Sunni tribalism is ISIS' Achilles heel. The caliphate's transnational ideology and its foreign fighters mix uneasily with indigenous populations and customs.[59] Reviving tribal resistance to Baghdadi's state building project is critical. The most promising avenue lies in Syria where the Kurdish YPG and the Free Syrian Army (FSA) work effectively. Direct support for this coalition is necessary but is constrained by the Administration's angst over angering Ankara that fears a Kurdish Syrian enclave. The initial Afghan campaign where American forces worked with Northern Alliance allies that destroyed the Al Qaeda-Taliban terror state could be a viable precedent.[60] With Kurdish Peshmerga and Sunni tribal forces fighting IS across the Syrian-Iraqi border, credible ground forces exist.

The US should funnel advanced arms to this alliance aided by air strikes and Special Forces operations. Such a development could assist a march on Raqqa. The fall of IS' iconic community would be an important strategic milestone. In Iraq more support for tribal forces is necessary and US bombing should be directed to assist any tribal revolt against the caliphate. Failure to support past tribal rebellions led to high profiles slaughter of anti-ISIS opponents.[61] At a minimum, when ISIS brutalizes communities as they are in Rugbah there should be retaliatory air strikes.

Fourthly, ISIS brutality creates many enemies whom seek revenge. Overtime a sustained bombing campaign, Special Forces attacks, and assaults by tribal opponents could assist in the caliphate's weakening leaving its militants vulnerable to vigilantism. Especially impacted will be ISIS foreign fighters whose privileges arouse local animosity. Unleashing this culture of revenge and blood lust in Baghdadi's caliphate sends a potent message to any British, French, Tunisian, Saudi, Libyan or Belgian sympathizer contemplating IS' *hijrah* message.

The US led campaign, moreover, should employ language that ISIS understands. Today's debate on countering ISIS' ideology is mostly pointless and sterile.[62] There is little psychological appeal the US government can make to dissuade an ISIS sympathizer form going to Syria or prevent him/her from engaging in jihadist inspired home-grown terrorism. If Al Qaeda ideologues like Abu Muhammad al-Maqdisi and Abu Qatada have no capacity to prevent young jihadists from joining ISIS, what is the likely success of a US State Department counter-radicalization initiative? Instead, we should use ISIS own apocalyptic narrative against them. Terminology like signs of the hour, Allah's will, God's judgment should be used in Department of Defense (DOD) media operations to foreshadow IS' inevitable doom.

Finally, the metric for success must be simple—that is, the *complete destruction of IS' state apparatus*. Only be eviscerating the caliphate's institutional edifice can we reverse some of today's destabilizing trends. This means taking the war to Libya or any place where no government can effectively fight IS' provinces. In the wake of the caliphate's demise local proxies should be empowered to exact revenge against IS militants. While barbaric, vigilante retribution would be an important impediment to any future caliphate.

Chapter 42

Defeating ISIL in the Information Environment

Alan Dinerman

First Published 22 October 2015

Introduction

After two years, the United States has little evidence that efforts to degrade and subsequently destroy the Islamic State of Iraq and the Levant (ISIL) is working. Although the Iranian aided Iraqi Army liberated Tikrit, ISIL remains firmly entrenched in Mosul and the entire Iraqi Anbar Providence. ISIL continues to consolidate and further gains in Syria in the midst of a fragmented opposition. Most alarming, however, is ISIL's demonstrated ability to recruit a seemingly endless flow of new membership and grow its power through federations with other terrorist groups like Boko Haram. The campaign against ISIL will certainly extend over many years; General Martin Dempsey contends that the effort against ISIL may last 10-15 more years (Mora, 2015). The process of coalition synchronization and resistance group training will not happen quickly. However, the aforementioned efforts are destined to fail if the United States does not effectively strike at ISIL's true center of gravity: its ability to conduct sustained and successful operations in the information environment. Ultimately, well-trained resistance forces and international coalitions will win kinetic fights and achieve operations successes, but strategic success will only spawn from our ability to out maneuver ISIL in the information environment, disrupt their information operations, and conduct an effective offensive information campaign. By first providing a model of the information environment and then establishing two lines of effort, this paper will outline specific effects based policy recommendations, outline obstacles to recommendation achievement, and discuss the potential impact of recommendation failure.

The Information Environment

A necessary prerequisite to an information operations policy discussion is an understanding of information environment. The information environment consists of three domains: The Physical Domain, the Information Domain, and the Cognitive Domain (Romanych, 2005). The Physical Domain represents the physical infrastructure that data transmits from source to destination. Components of the Physical Domain include: routers, switches, cables, wireless spectrum, etc. The Information Domain represents a consolidated format of data into a digestible message for human beings. Components of the Information Domain include: Twitter feeds, newspaper articles, television shows, books, etc. The Information Domain is foundational. Although the Physical Domain transmits data, humans begin their decision making cycle in the Information Domain (Romanych, 2005). The Cognitive Domain represents human internalization. The Cognitive Domain is the apex of the information environment. In the Cognitive Domain, humans synthesize information messages and form opinions / beliefs. Components of the Cognitive Domain are opinions, beliefs, and value assessments. As we begin to examine specific policy positions to defeat ISIL in the information environment, we must remember that ISIL owns little of the Physical Domain. Their information campaign largely traverses commercially owned physical infrastructure. Efforts to kinetically destroy physical infrastructure will probably yield little value. As a result, U.S. effects based policy should not overly focus on destroying architecture but emphasize the message in the Information Domain and how the information is synthesized in the Cognitive information.

Line of Effort I: Discredit ISIL's Message and Create Cognitive Dissonance

ISIL is remarkably adept in propagating a coherent message that attracts new members, focuses their current force, and shapes the cognitive domain in their favor. Unconstrained by the truth, ISIL has a freedom of maneuver in the information environment that the United States does not enjoy. Their ability to imaginatively manipulate print and social media provides them diverse and effective tools to conduct information operations. While unimaginable to many in the West, ISIL is considered a charitable and good will organization to many in the Islamic World. A successful information campaign has allowed them to more effectively shape the cognitive domain than the United States. In June 2014, ISIL began posting a series of videos on You Tube that highlight the organization as a charitable organization, providing care and assistance to the impoverish portions of the Islamic world. ISIS is adept at maintaining a sustained population of devoted twitter followers. In addition to the internet, ISIL uses print media like the Dabiq newspaper to reaches a vast population in Syria (Al Arabiya, 2014). Thus far, the United States has not been able to effectively counter ISIL's ability to focus information and shape human cognitive beliefs.

The United States must more effectively impede ISIL's ability to shape the cognitive domain by creating Cognitive Dissonance in the Islamic community. "Cognitive dissonance refers to a situation involving *conflicting attitudes,* beliefs or behaviors. This produces a *feeling of discomfort l*eading to an alteration in one of the attitudes or beliefs" (McLeod, 2014). By developing Cognitive Dissonance in the Islamic world, in reference to ISIL as a charity / good-will organization, the United States will ultimately achieve the desired effect of shaping the cognitive domain.

This effect will not be easy to achieve, however. ISIL's message is well entrenched and the United States has little creditability within the targeted audience (TA). Additionally, the United States continues to wrestles with finding human information carriers to counter ISIL's message. Nevertheless, a body of reporting that depicts ISIL's true nature is emerging. A series of articles titled "Life in the Islamic State," by Washington Post that was published in the Small Wars Journal, exposes the truth and paints a bleak picture of life under ISIL (SWJ, Oct 2015). The series highlights ISIL's harsh rule over both Islamic and non-Islamic populations. This is the type of information that has not effectively permeated ISIL's TA. Using proxy sources that are more credible in the Islamic World than the United States, we must saturate the Information Domain with this type of information and start to create Cognitive Dissonance. Budding new technology camps and an emerging digital communications hub with the UAE may further this process (Romm, 2015). Thus far, a significant portion of the Islamic world only receives ISIL generated information.

Line of Effort II: Information Disruption via Offensive Cyber Operations

A foundational problem in our attempt to conduct operations in the information environment is the difficulty getting approval for military offensive cyber effects. The United States' offensive cyber approval process is too arduous and too time consuming; the target nomination and approval process has trouble keeping up with ISIL's nimbleness in the information environment. In 2013, the Joint Staff was poised to approve a new set of cyber rules of engagement that provided for limited delegation of approval to COCOM commanders (Fryer–Biggs, 2013). ISIL is a nimble adversary in the information environment; the time from planning to execution when disrupting their information campaign must be short. As discussed previously, information feeds the cognitive domain. ISIL's continued ability to use unfiltered and untruthful information has had a dramatic impact in the cognitive domain. By empowering U.S. forces to use offensive cyber effects, we can begin to disrupt ISIL's information flow and break the chain to from information to beliefs. Opponents of this viewpoint will address the legal concerns of conducting offensive cyber operations and the potential impact of damage to noncombatant computer systems. This is a valid concern. However, through the establishment of strict rules of engagement, emphasis on intelligence based effects, and carefully selected offensive cyber capabilities we can largely mitigate these concerns.

Conclusion

A recognition that ISIL's center of gravity is their ability to conduct effective operations in the information environment is essential. Although the United States is building a formidable coalition that includes Arab partners and training resistance forces, kinetic action will ultimately have little impact if the United States can't thwart ISIL's ability to shape the belief system in the Islamic community. Necessary to this efforts is our ability to both discredit and disrupt their information campaign.

Chapter 43

Information War with the Islamic State in Iraq and the Levant: An Indirect Approach

Brian Russell

First Published 29 October 2015

After bombing Islamic State of Iraq and the Levant (ISIL) forces for more than a year, the United States (US) and its multi-national coalition are locked in an apparent stalemate with this threat to regional and global stability. Within the limits of policy restrictions to the application of hard power (military) to break this stalemate, the US must smartly employ the softer elements of national power, specifically information, to defeat this enemy. While ISIL is widely recognized as conducting a masterful campaign in the information environment to achieve its strategic ends (Talbot, 2015), the US should not strive to compete directly with ISIL in an information war. ISIL defeat requires attacking the root cause of the conflict with all tools of national power and information can best serve as a unifying, and in most cases supporting, element for the other more direct instruments of power in achieving that end. This paper provides recommendations for US actions to counter the ISIL information war at the strategic, operational, and tactical levels of war, as well as within the cognitive, informational and physical dimensions of the information environment.

At the strategic level, the conflict with ISIL is a war between ideas ultimately waged in the cognitive dimension of the information environment. Per joint doctrine, the cognitive dimension is the realm of decision-making and rests heavily on factors such as beliefs, norms, motivations and, perhaps most importantly in this case, ideologies. Unfortunately for the US and its allies, ISIL is waging a jihad, or holy war, based on an ideology that resonates deeply with elements of the regional, and sometimes global, Muslim community. Abu Bakr al-Baghdadi's declaration of a caliphate upon ISIL's seizure of Mosul in 2014 was a deliberate message to Muslims who had been "psychologically primed for a long time to the idea of reestablishing the caliphate" (Talbot, 2015). It is a powerful message to a population long disenfranchised from dictatorial Middle Eastern governments and one that will be difficult to overcome directly. Government officials may decry the lack of national effort (only 20 personnel assigned to the State Department's counter propaganda team) to directly counter this ideology (Tucker, 2015), but unless the counter message offers a viable alternative to what many Muslims see as their principal path to personal or religious redemption, larger efforts will only fall on deaf ears. More personal, peer-to-peer engagement within social media spheres holds promise, but its effects are incredibly difficult to measure (Talbot, 2015) and direct government involvement in the process risks delegitimizing the counter messaging itself.

This latter point makes US government efforts in the war of ideas particularly problematic. Bruce Reidel, a 29-year Central Intelligence Agency (CIA) counter-terrorism analyst, suggests a core portion of broader Muslim dissatisfaction in the Middle East stems from decades of unpopular American policy in the region, particularly US support to oppressive governments (Reidel, 2015). So, while nation-states like Russia agree that ISIL must be defeated by attacking its core ideology (Goble, 2015), the US is forced to take a less direct approach. Such an approach would include both diplomatic, economic and, in limited cases, military efforts to support inclusive and moderate governments in the middle east, all couched in a message that the United States is concerned with improving the lives of Muslims in those affected areas. This requires the appointment and empowerment of a leader and department within the US government to craft an effective strategic communications campaign that synchronizes the intent of these actions and exploits opportunities to broadcast this message. A good opportunity to demonstrate this resolve is more effective *regional and local* broadcasting of the recent hostage rescue operation in northeastern Iraq in which a US special operations member gave his life to save the lives of Muslims facing imminent execution by ISIL (Stewart, 2015). Sadly, to date, there is no mention of this sacrifice in the Center for Strategic Counterterrorism Communications Twitter posts about the hostage rescue. The center's arabic Twitter feed (http://www.state.gov/r/cscc/214420.htm[1]) has just over 4,800 followers anyway compared to an estimated 46,000 ISIL supporting Twitter account holders (Berger & Morgan, 2015). If the government is going to invest *any* time in social media, what it does broadcast should be crafted more effectively along the lines of J.M. Berger and Jessica Stern's *A 6-point plan to Defeat ISIS in the Propaganda War*. The newly appointed State Department "czar" for coordinating the coalition campaign against ISIL should implement those in-house changes immediately but will also need increased authority across the executive branch to affect the broader interagency cooperation required in the anti-ISIL campaign (De Luce & Hudson, 2015), including strategic communications. The risk of such an approach at the strategic level is the amount of time it will take to produce tangible results for disaffected communities in the region and the resultant improved security for the United States and its regional allies.

However, the US can achieve more rapid effects against ISIL in the operational level of war while it implements its strategic efforts. Within the theater of operations, ISIL uses modern information technology for a whole host of functions including recruiting, internal communication, command and control of forces, and financing (Talbot,

2015). In the last category, ISIL is recognized as one of the wealthiest terrorist organizations in existence (Almukhtar, 2015) giving it both operational capacity and legitimacy as a self-professed governing state. Therefore, the US, in conjunction with multi-national partners, should continue to attack this specific aspect of the informational dimension by restricting or preventing the "content and flow" (JP 3-13) of ISIL financial information.

This approach is already a major line of effort for the anti-ISIL coalition since the formation of the Counter-ISIL Finance Group in early 2015 (Levitt, 2015). The group focuses its efforts on restricting ISIL access to the international financial system by isolating banks in ISIL-controlled territory, largely through restriction of electronic fund transfers (EFTs) (Levitt, 2015). These efforts should continue, in addition to implementing measures to identify and restrict other external revenue sources supported by the information environment like crowd funding, electronic currency (Bitcoin), and internet trading. While ISIL revenue generation from internal sources (oil sales, taxation, ransom) is sufficient to meet current operating costs, the demands to provide population services (infrastructure and social welfare) within their territory will become financially untenable without additional external resourcing (Humud, Pirog & Rosen, 2015). Making the Islamic State unsustainable in the near term can also produce a supplemental effect to counter ISIL recruiting propaganda that life under the caliphate is better than other alternatives (Sullivan, 2014). The risk in such a plan of action is concurrent degradation of the financial viability and stability of anti-ISIL populations within or adjacent to enemy territory as well as ISIL using that possibility to bolster their anti-western narrative (Levitt, 2015). This approach, therefore, requires the support of and detailed implementation with regional nation states. Those respective leaders and agencies should be listed at the top of the anti-ISIL czar's key leader engagement program. Additional risk mitigation is possible, if again, the person responsible for the national strategic communications approach also maintains the levers of implementation for the financial (and other) obstacles levied at ISIL during the course of the campaign. The ability to match message to action is no less important at the operational level than at the strategic and a more deliberate focus on this coordination can help unify the entire campaign, in addition to using information war to indirectly but specifically target ISIL economic power.

Waging direct information war with ISIL in the tactical realm as a primary coalition objective is also a mistake. ISIL leadership and personnel have fully embraced the wide range of information technologies and tools that emerged coincident to their rise of power. "Affordable devices, fast networks, and abundant social-media accounts" (Talbot, 2015) are the instruments that dominate the immense physical dimension of ISIL's information environment. Those who argue for attacking this aspect of the environment through increased offensive cyber activities (Dinerman, 2015) run the risk of turning the campaign into an electronic version of "Whack-a-mole." While select cyber (and kinetic) attacks against key leadership and command and control nodes, with appropriate collateral damage mitigation, will always have a time and place to achieve operational effects, the expansive nature of the information infrastructure will make those effects fleeting. Much like you cannot kill your way out of an insurgent movement, you cannot hack your way out of one either.

Instead, the United States and its allies need to take an asymmetric approach in the tactical sphere and view ISIL's prolific and decentralized use of information technology as a weakness. While some may admire ISIL's rapid ability to message and communicate through social media tools, it presents a security vulnerability and intelligence treasure trove for exploitation. Harvesting tactical information from enemy networks and transmissions is a proven United States military capability already being applied against ISIL leadership (Tucker, 2015). The real game changer will come from further employing our national technological advantages from private industry by harnessing the developments in big data analytics. The bane of intelligence professionals in the information age has been the enormous amount, and often latent, information to collect and decipher. But with advanced analysis tools now available to quickly fuse disparate data (often across operational and geo-political boundaries) into actionable intelligence, what practitioners call improving the "signal to noise" ratio (McNulty, 2014), the tactical warfighter can now have a much clearer picture of enemy maneuver in the information environment and apply an appropriate combined arms response. A coordinated, national-level intelligence effort to exploit enemy big data patterns also reinforces strategic and operational information operations to counter ISIL recruiting and illicit finance activities. J.M. Berger and Jonathan Morgan's March 2015 *ISIS Twitter Census* shows the enormous potential of big data to understand the ideology, demographic, and activities of people sympathetic to the terrorist organization from just a single social media tool.

This approach does not discount the need for fighting information fire with information fire at the tactical level, but one should not envision American and partner nation soldiers engaging in Twitter wars with ISIL foot troops. Instead, with large swaths of enemy controlled territory devoid of internet access and cellphone service due to ISIL information control and aggressive psychological operations (Sullivan, 2015), our formations on the ground, even in an advise and assist role, need national-level efforts to give them the tools and authorities to possess true "spectral agility" (Chou, Kim, Shin & Shankar, 2004) to counter enemy information operations. Much like American forces became adept at employing Radio-in-a-box (RIAB) and hand-cranked radio sets through the Iraq and Afghanistan counterinsurgency campaigns, national research and development efforts should be focused on developing the next generation of information dissemination technology, something akin to Internet-in-a-box or distributable hot spots. And when network capabilities are unavailable, they still need to possess the capability and authorities from host nations to broadcast over more traditional airwaves like current efforts in Al Anbar province (White, 2015).

The challenge to an intelligence-focused approach, though, is striking the right balance between exploiting and destroying ISIL's capability within the information environment. Independent hacker organizations, like Anonymous and GhostSec, have essentially taken up cyber arms against ISIL by disrupting or destroying supporting websites through Distributed Denial of Service (DDOS) attacks (Cottee, 2015). While these tactical-level actions may be helpful in degrading enemy operations, they may be devastating to coalition plans relying on those sites for indication and warnings or deception efforts. This kind of cyber fratricide is not a new problem as demonstrated by the Pentagon's 2008 dismantling of a Saudi Arabian government website used by Al Qaeda leaders to plan attacks on American forces in Iraq. The action degraded enemy coordination capabilities within the theater of operations but it also brought a sudden halt to the CIA's use of that same site to collect vital intelligence on global terrorist networks (Nakashima, 2010). While the need for intergovernmental coordination remains in the current campaign, the new wrinkle of private-public convergence in the cyber domain will require additional policy or legal frameworks to ensure adequate coordination, if not cooperation, for this conflict and future ones.

Contemporary and future non-state actors like ISIL are often credited with applying asymmetric capabilities to great advantage against the United States and its allies. It is time to turn the tables and use ISIL's seemingly dominant information advantage to produce its eventual defeat. This can be accomplished through the development of a strong national-level strategic communications capability that can make information a unifying element of the anti-ISIL campaign across the broad coalition and the levels of war by fusing intelligence into synchronized actions and messages amongst all elements of national power. Additionally, instead of going toe-to-toe with ISIL in each dimension of the information environment, the US must attack those enemy capabilities indirectly as in the example of degrading ISIL economic power through the use of information technology. Ceding ground to your enemy in one specific area to gain ground in another through unexpected means is not weakness. Rather, it is the new acme of strategic agility in the information age and a better approach to developing smart power (Nye, 2011) against contemporary adversaries.

Chapter 44

Reevaluating General Order 1X

Tom Ordeman, Jr.

First Published 5 December 2015

Introduction

General Order 1-X (GO-1X) was developed in the mid-1990's to govern American troops' conduct in the Balkans. Its requirements codified orders from prior operations, notably the Gulf War[01], and subsequently proliferated throughout the United States Central Command (USCENTCOM) area of responsibility (AOR). After 9/11, GO-1X enforcement became ubiquitous throughout the USCENTCOM AOR. Uniformed and civilian personnel must abide by its restrictions in an effort to secure popular support through compliance with Islamic cultural norms.

With deployments to USCENTCOM projected to wane, and the joint force incorporating lessons learned from recent operations, now is the time to revisit GO-1X. What is its purpose? Has it served that purpose? Does it present opportunities for improvement?

Version Confusion

GO-1X's initial shortfall is version control. For example, the term "General Order One" competes with General Orders for Sentries. Existing differences between the individual services' general orders notwithstanding, GO-1X's title competes with rote knowledge imparted during recruit training.

Additionally, multiple GO-1X versions exist, issued at various times by overlapping authorities. Casual web searching produces examples dating from 1996 to 2013, issued by at least six different commands. While their proscriptions are broadly similar, numerous variations and inconsistencies breed further confusion. For example, the 101st Airborne Division requires that any found currency be "collected, recorded, secured, and stored until it can be delivered to the appropriate authority".[02] I Marine Expeditionary Force clarifies restrictions on smoking.[03] The 3rd Infantry Division prohibits personnel from intentionally becoming non-deployable for medical reasons, causing redeployment of oneself or another soldier through pregnancy, or circumventing official channels to inform another soldier's next-of-kin of an injury or death.[04] The latest USCENTCOM issuance, May 2013's GO-1C, omits these requirements.[05] The potential for confusion is obvious.

The Proscriptions

GO-1C forbids personnel from: any activities related to, up to and including the consumption of, alcohol or controlled substances; exchanging local currency at unofficial exchange rates; private firearm ownership; gambling; possessing or destroying national treasures; keeping pets or mascots; photographing or videotaping detainees, casualties, sensitive equipment, or security infrastructure; possessing pornography; confiscating private property from host nation citizens; religious proselytization; or violating host nation laws.[06]

Of these proscriptions, only those forbidding alcohol and pornography are actually USCENTCOM AOR-specific. Restrictions on controlled substances, currency, gambling, national treasures, and religious matters are USCENTCOM-relevant, but globally applicable, and either are or should be covered by existing regulations. Restrictions regarding firearms, pets, photography, videography, property, and host nation laws are universal. This arbitrary inclusion of existing regulations into GO-1X undermines those regulations' authority, and provides additional opportunities for confusion.

Understanding Sharia

Reconsideration of GO-1X requires an understanding of the complexities of sharia (Islamic law).

Westerners' perception of Islam is influenced by the Judeo-Christian tradition. Thus, many see the Quran as Islam's ultimate authority, commensurate with the Bible's role in Christianity. Many overlook the Hadith and Sunna, which lack clear Christian corollaries. The Hadith (narrative) consists of statements attributed to the Prophet Mohammed, while the Sunna ("direct path") derives from records of his lifestyle. Judeo-Christian corollaries include Bible editions that render Christ's words in red ink, the Gospels' description of Christ's lifestyle, Roman Catholicism's observance of church tradition, Judaism's consultation of the Talmud, and the writings of early church fathers like Augustine. Together, the Quran, Hadith, and Sunna form the corpus of Islamic authority. Multiple versions of the Hadith and Sunna exist, and an individual collection's authority varies according to its age and proximity to the Prophet Mohammed. Early in Islamic history, the adoption of a given Hadith or Sunna collection led the ulema (Islamic jurists) to establish competing maddhabs (schools) of fiqh (jurisprudence).[07]

Western-style pluralism is a recent novelty for Islamic audiences. "Islamism" represents the traditional view that religious and political authorities are synonymous. Thus, in the Islamic tradition, religious scholars are simultaneously legal scholars, somewhat akin to American Constitutional law experts. The challenges of applying aged legal precedents to modern cultural challenges are broadly similar. In Anglophone nations, distinct national bodies of precedential case law are founded upon English Common Law. Conversely, in the Islamic tradition, the Quran constitutes Islamic "Common Law", while the madhhabs represent "precedent"/"case law". Thus, "sharia" varies throughout the Islamic community (ummah), rather than being monolithic. Fiqh influences many aspects of a Muslim's daily life. Excluding the Sunni/Shia split, differences of fiqh caused most of Islam's ecumenical schisms. Not surprisingly, entire books have been written on this subject.[08]

Unfortunately, the sweeping proscriptions outlined in GO-1X's various versions fail to take these intricacies into account.

GO-1X and Sharia

While many inconsistencies exist, for brevity's sake, three will be examined in detail: dietary restrictions, prohibitions against pets, and personal grooming. GO-1X's most controversial restriction may be its alcohol moratorium. The Quran says:

> "O ye who believe! Strong drink and games of chance and idols and divining arrows are only an infamy of Satan's handiwork. Leave it aside in order that ye may succeed."[09]

Some Islamic nations ban alcohol outright, while others restrict its sale to Muslims, and others are more permissive still. In most Islamic nations, expatriates typically consume more alcohol than locals. These cultural mores inform GO-1X's directive against alcohol. However, despite American enforcement, coalition partners eschew these bans. According to noted Navy SEAL Chris Kyle:

"Being an American, officially I wasn't supposed to be drinking. (And officially, I didn't.) That asinine rule only applied to U.S. servicemen. We couldn't even buy a beer. Every other member of the coalition, be they Polish or whatever, could. Fortunately, the GROM liked to share. They would also go to the duty-free shop at Baghdad airport and buy beer or whiskey or whatever the Americans working with them wanted."[10]

In Afghanistan, German forces notably received a daily beer allowance.[11] An American soldier notes of his French colleagues:

"Many Americans have asked me, 'Is it true the French served wine at dinner and had wine in their MREs?' The answer is yes and no. They not only served wine at dinner, they sometimes served it at lunch as well. The firebase I was on, which wasn't that big, had three bars. The regular French Joes could have all the alcohol they wanted in their tents."[12]

American authorities also forbid alcohol while ignoring other dietary restrictions. Sharia categorizes all food as halal (permissible) or haram (forbidden). Halal observance is often strict: as journalist Michael Yon observed in one Afghan village, potential food is haram unless specifically authorized by the Prophet Mohammed.[13] The Quran specifically forbids pork:

"He hath forbidden you only carrion, and blood, and swine flesh, and that which hath been immolated to (the name of) any other than Allah. But he who is driven by necessity, neither craving nor transgressing, it is no sin for him. Lo! Allah is Forgiving, Merciful."[14]

Several madhhabs prohibit shellfish consumption; others exempt shrimp and prawns. However, since 2001, multiple MRE menus include pork, and at least one— Jambalaya—includes both pork and shellfish.

In Afghanistan and Iraq, dining facilities held regular steak and lobster nights.[15] In USCENTCOM posts where personnel can live on the local economy, pork is a popular commodity at commissaries. American troops strive to avoid exposing Muslims to haram foods—for example, by sending halal MREs to Syrian refugees in Jordan[16], or dropping halal rations to Afghans early in Operation Enduring Freedom. The inconsistency is obvious. Even the alcohol ban is subject to loopholes:

> "As an exceptional matter to recognize special holidays, occasions, or events, the Commander, U.S. Forces-Afghanistan, within the Combined Joint Operations Area Afghanistan (CJOA), has non-delegable authority to grant written, event-specific, waivers to paragraph 2(a)(1), for personnel subject to this Order. The Commander, International Security Assistance Force (ISAF), within the CJOA, has non-delegable authority to grant waivers to paragraph 2(a)(1), for U.S. Service members and DOD civilians assigned to purely North American Treaty Organization billets (i.e., Headquarters, ISAF)."[17]

NATO's incorrectly rendered name notwithstanding, such caveats constitute further inconsistencies. One former soldier speaking on condition of anonymity notes that, while deployed to Iraq, his unit was authorized two beers apiece on Super Bowl Sunday, only to witness the unconsumed remainder being destroyed by TCN catering staff—likely at significant taxpayer expense. Terminal Lance cartoonist Maximillian Uriarte describes a similar incident:

> "I happened to be in Iraq during my second-ever Marine Corps Birthday experience... [W]e were allotted two beers each, which was pretty great considering we were in Iraq. As soon as the day came, Marines were going to the extent of taking aspirin in anticipation for the alcohol so it would have a stronger effect on them. While this isn't recommended by most doctors, pharmaceutical labels, Corpsmen, and people

with common sense; the thought of only ingesting two alcoholic beverages is just too much to handle for some."[18]

The message is clear: alcohol consumption is an egregious affront to Islamic values, to be prevented under threat of disciplinary action, unless it takes place during the Marine Corps; birthday or the Super Bowl.[19] By contrast, while embedded with Omani troops during the 1970's Dhofar Rebellion, British forces were allowed alcohol.[20][21][22] Notes retired Royal Marine Brigadier Ian Gardiner:

> "Alcohol was available in much the same way as in a British officers' mess, and the routine of daily life would have been familiar to British officers serving in a hot climate at any time in the past hundred years or so... There was an acknowledged risk of overindulgence in alcohol. This did happen from time to time, and one was discouraged from taking booze back to one's room and drinking on one's own."[23]

Like present-day Afghans, Dhofaris were conservative Muslims living in austere conditions, and initially distrustful of counterinsurgent forces. The Dhofar campaign is universally recognized as an overwhelming success—despite the alcohol consumed by British troops.

Another example is GO-1X's ban on adopting pets. While counterintuitive to Westerners, sharia looks unfavorably upon dogs. One authoritative hadith reports:

> "Abu Dharr reported: The Messenger of 'Allah (may peace be upon him) said: When any one of you stands for prayer and there is a thing before him equal to the back of the saddle that covers him and in case there is not before him (a thing) equal to the back of the saddle, his prayer would be cut off by (passing of an) ass, woman, and black Dog. I said: O Abu Dharr, what feature is there in a black dog which distinguish it from the red dog and the yellow dog? He said: O, son of my brother, I asked the Messenger of Allah (may

peace be upon him) as you are asking me, and he said: The black dog is a devil."[24]

In another respected hadith, the Prophet Mohammad states that keeping company with dogs voids some of a Muslim's good deeds, and that they should be killed.[25] Sharia deems dogs unclean, but mandates their humane treatment. Two ahadith relate stories of God granting forgiveness to those who offered water to thirsty dogs.[26] [27] In another account, the Prophet Mohammed ordered sentries posted to prevent his army from disturbing a dog and her puppies while in transit. Sharia offers provisions for working dogs, though sources disagree whether dogs may be sold.[28] Muslims typically dislike dogs, though even this is inconsistent. Wilfred Thesiger, writing of his travels in 1940's Arabia, notes:

> "We had a saluki with us... My companions said disgustedly that he was not worth his keep. They had expected great things of him. But they played with him, and allowed him to lie on their blankets and drink from our dishes, for, although dogs are unclean to Muslims, the Bedu do not count a saluki as a dog."[29]

Michael Yon notes:

> "Kuchi dogs have a reputation for ferocity and fighting. This one has slept without bothering a soul. There is something of a caste system for dogs in Afghanistan. Normal dogs often are treated badly, while the fighting and hunting dogs are treated with respect."[30]

Conversely, Westerners love dogs, and utilize military working dogs (MWDs) in spite of Islamic sensibilities.[31] Famous examples include a Labrador/Newfoundland cross that was recovered after a lengthy disappearance in Afghanistan[32], and a Belgian Malinois that reportedly participated in the bin Laden raid.[33] US Army officer Kevin

Hanrahan operates a website about MWDs[34], while Foreign Policy published two photo essays about MWDs after the aforementioned bin Laden raid.[35][36] They work as searchers, crowd controllers, bomb and contraband detectors, and serve as valued companions. MWDs exceed tentative Islamic provisions for dogs' use as shepherds, guards, or for hunting, and cannot be fully reconciled with sharia or host nation cultural sensitivities. Retired US Army Colonel Gerald Schumacher, quoting an American contractor, notes:

> "Part of my mission in Iraq includes conducting dog handler training classes at the Baghdad Police Academy. Given that the Muslim culture views dogs as filthy and unclean, it is very difficult to find Iraqis [who] will even work near them. Sometimes we can find a couple of Christian police cadets [who] don't have a problem with dogs. The Iraqis treat dogs with disdain and often kick and throw rocks at them... Most Iraqi people won't even look at a dog. I think our dogs don't much care for them either. Their hatred of dogs becomes a self-fulfilling prophecy. The dogs probably sense the hostility and are reacting in kind."[37]

Quoting the same source, Schumacher notes:

> "While I can't prove this, I actually think that sometimes I am a lot safer because I'm with Blek. An insurgent suicide bomber takes one look at me and Blek, and he knows that if he detonates his explosives the dog remains will be all over him. I've heard that they believe that if they die spattered with dog parts, they will be considered unclean and unacceptable to enter heaven."[38]

Aside from MWDs, American allies sometimes keep battlefield pets. Journalist Chris Terrill deployed to Helmand Province with the Royal Marines in 2007. He highlighted two adopted local dogs' contribution to unit morale.[39] Robert Kaplan, embedded with American Special Forces in Afghanistan in 2003, reports:

> "The Lithuanians distinguished themselves by their handy decision to bring a pregnant cat along on the deployment, which produced kittens that in turn killed the field mice in their barracks."[40]

Considering Russia's epidemiological challenges in Afghanistan[41] and Chechnya[42], the Lithuanians exhibited uncommon sense borne from experience. However, American forces prohibit such practices. USCENTCOM's 2013 issuance specifically mentions rabies concerns, but nonetheless provides conditions whereby personnel in some locations can adopt pets.[43] (During more than a decade of operations in Afghanistan and Iraq, American forces have sustained only one rabies death attributed to ineffective post-exposure prophylaxis.[44]) The potential benefits of keeping pets at the discretion (and subject to the corresponding discipline) of lower echelon leaders should be obvious.

A third example, not codified in GO-1X, represents a missed opportunity. DoD grooming regulations prohibit beards.[45] Justifications include hygiene, professional appearance, and the ability to maintain an airtight seal when wearing gas masks.[46] Authorized exceptions to policy occur mainly in the special operations forces (SOF). Popular satire website The Duffel Blog parodied this with such articles as "Pentagon Study Finds Beards Directly Related To Combat Effectiveness"[47] and "Soldier Kicked Out Of Special Forces Because He Can't Grow A Beard".[48] However, even SOF troops' facial hair has been targeted in recent years.[49] By contrast, beards are required by many madhhabs.[50] One authoritative hadith states:

> "Yahya related to me from Malik from Abu Bakr ibn Nafi from his father Nafi from Abdullah ibn Umar that the Messenger of Allah, may Allah bless him and grant him peace, ordered the moustache to be trimmed and the beard to be left."[51]

Conservative Muslims encourage beard growth in deference to this pronouncement. Beards can also bridge broad cultural gaps between troops and local nationals. Robert Kaplan, quoting Army Special Forces Major Kevin Holiday, relates one example:

> "The other day I had a meeting at the provincial governor's office... All these notables came in and rubbed their beards against mine, a sign of endearment and respect. I simply could not get my message across in these meetings unless I made some accommodations with the local culture and values. Afghanistan is not like other countries. It's a throwback. You've got to compromise and go a little native."[52]

Other ISAF partners relax grooming standards for troops deployed to Afghanistan, particularly in austere positions. During the aforementioned Dhofar Rebellion[53], British troops grew beards, which facilitated relationships with local actors. Despite multiple justifications to relax grooming standards (particularly in Afghanistan[54]), few American troops are allowed such leeway.[55]

Several additional examples are noteworthy:

- Coalition troops eschew the restrictions associated with the Islamic holy month of Ramadan.
- Multiple GO-1X issuances attempt to regulate troops' sexual urges virtually out of existence. Although troops can purchase softcore men's magazines at USCENTCOM post exchanges, these can be retroactively confiscated as contraband. (These restrictions are often circumvented by deployed troops.[56][57])
- In the Islamic tradition, even wedding festivities are typically gender-segregated. By contrast, USCENTCOM installations have officially sanctioned mixed-gender dance classes[58][59] and massage parlors.[60]
- Citing proscriptions against proselytization, senior personnel have prevented subordinates from holding private religious study groups during non-work hours. In 2009, officials destroyed

Dari/Pashtu-language New Testaments provided to American troops for distribution.[61] By contrast, after a 2012 incident in which Qurans defaced by Afghan prisoners were incinerated in accordance with sharia, the ensuing host nation demonstrations compelled ISAF commander General John Allen to publicly apologize.[62]

- GO-1C details conditions whereby personnel may visit mosques in Egypt[63], raising the question of why prior guidance about being "directed to do so by military authorities, required by military necessity, or as part of an official tour conducted with the approval of military authorities and the host nation"[64] was insufficient.[65]
- From Islam's founding, Islamic authorities granted non-Muslims (dhimmi) latitude to live in accordance with their own beliefs. Acknowledgment of this status may be more productive than mandatory adherence to an arbitrary selection of Islamic practices.

Conclusion

> "[No new technologies or weapons systems] would have helped me in the last three years [in Iraq and Afghanistan]. But I could have used cultural training [and] language training. I could have used more products from American universities [who] understood the world does not revolve around America and [who] embrace coalitions and allies for all of the strengths that they bring us."
> —General James N. Mattis, USMC

GO-1X's mandated sacrifices are premised upon the belief that limited adherence to sharia will secure the coveted human terrain and encourage good order and discipline. It is incumbent upon senior leaders to ensure that troops' sacrifices facilitate the achievement of American strategic goals.[66]

GO-1X fails to meet these criteria. It replicates redundant directives, and appeals to oversimplified stereotypes representing a rudimentary understanding of the diverse cultures within the Islamic tradition. Recent events in Afghanistan and Iraq suggest that any contribution GO-1X adherence may have made to winning the human terrain was nullified by other events. GO-1X undermines morale and breeds contempt for host nation personnel with whom troops must cooperate. For negligible strategic benefit, GO-1X enforces unnecessary deprivations upon troops while sending the signal that their commanders do not trust them to behave like adults.

GO-1X fails to adequately serve its purpose of helping troops to secure the human terrain. To improve upon the current status quo, senior leaders should consider the following recommendations:

- USCENTCOM and other COCOMs should exercise authority for COCOM-specific guidance. Such guidance should be renamed to prevent confusion with General Orders for Sentries.
- Competing issuances should be rescinded. Should subordinate or rotational commands deem additional guidance to be necessary, COCOM-specific guidance and other existing regulations should be referenced, rather than recreated, in memoranda for the record.
- Monolithic COCOM-wide directives are unrealistic. Guidance covering both Egypt and Kazakhstan is every bit as untenable as guidance covering both Australia and Mongolia. COCOMs electing to issue AOR-specific restrictions should do so by country, rather than by region.
- Country-specific guidance should be developed by subject matter experts, such as Foreign Area Officers, Defense Language Institute personnel, or inter-agency partners. Such guidance should be subject to cost/benefit analysis, perhaps utilizing third party think tanks to ensure analytical rigor and objectivity.

- The current bans on alcohol and pornography do disproportionate harm to troops' physical and mental health, and to morale. Wherever possible, and particularly in combat zones, they should be rescinded with the expectation that abuse of either will result in appropriate disciplinary action. Restrictions must remain in place, but the outright bans have proved counter-productive.

GO-1X inconsistently implements conflicting versions of a monolithic approach to cultural sensitivity. Senior leaders should seize the opportunity presented by current strategic conditions to evaluate its effectiveness since 2001, and to capitalize upon that information pursuant to the morale and effectiveness of the joint force.

Chapter 45

Talking to Tyrants, Sharpening Axes

Robert Murphy

First Published 8 December 2015

"Purify your soul from all unclean things. Tame your soul. Convince it. Make it understand. Completely forget something called "this World." Pray the supplication as you leave your hotel, when riding in the taxi and entering the airport. Pray the supplication before you step aboard the plane, and at the moment of death. Bless your body with verses of scripture. Rub the verses on your luggage, your clothes, your passport. Polish your knife with the verses, and be sure the blade is sharp; you must not discomfort your sacrifice."
—Final instructions discovered in baggage of a 9-11 hijacker[i]

America's approach to the threat of global terror has been one dimensional and strategically ineffective. We have slaughtered thousands of terrorist leaders and their adherents with staggering efficiency, yet have failed to be effective in destroying the spawning beast. This is because terrorism isn't a global entity, it defies space and time by living in human imagination. We have neglected the philosophical underpinnings of terror that inspire hate because they float, like a dandelion's seeds, settling in the minds of the world's youth. Under the right conditions, these seeds will either take root or turn into dust.

America must assault the ideologies of terror with the vigor and effort of the targeted assaults on Bin Laden and Al Zarqawi. The contemporary anti-terrorism strategy has largely been a military endeavor, and must expand to harness the power residing in American culture and intellect.

A new strategy increases the resources available to our counter-terror operations, who have proven themselves so effective at destroying near-term, existential threats. These threats include, but are not limited to the command and control elements that plan and direct spectacular attacks against American civilians and interests. Relative to conventional warfare requirements, and given their limited scope, counter-terrorism organizations and their supporting entities are a cost effective means to protect ourselves, and deny the victories essential to terrorist recruitment.

The assault on the ideologies that advocate terror begins with a sober assessment of our own activities to determine which are contributing to the expansion of terrorist ideology. America supports activities and regimes that fertilize otherwise dormant seeds of terror. We encourage harmful ideology through inaction and hypocrisy. We allow weeds to flourish in neglected corners of the earth and express surprise when they flower.

America allies itself and provides military support to nations like Saudi Arabia, whose ultra conservative, Wahabbist madrassas proliferate the globe and generate legions of fanatically anti-western youth[ii]. Pakistan, which encourages and sponsors many of these madrassas also explicitly organized and supported the Taliban, and likely continues to do so surreptitiously[iii].

Saudi Arabia and Pakistan are relatively simple examples. Less flagrant examples include our support for governments in Africa, Central and South America and in Asia. The analysis of our policies toward foreign states and leaders must also account for the type of hypocrisy that contributes to resentment of America's actions. Any legitimacy regarding our obsession with removing Assad from power in Syria is perverted by our open support of totalitarian regimes in Egypt, Saudi Arabia, Azerbaijan, most of the 'stans, Chad, Rwanda, Uganda, to name a few[iv].

Our inaction in preventing Iraqi sectarianism to divide their security forces largely negating any gains made in increasing their capacity and capability. Our further inaction to stem the growth of ISIS, as they steamrolled their way through Mosul and Ramadi revealed our true reliability as security partners, simultaneously enhancing ISIS' esteem among an Arab youth intrigued with the group, and discouraging the commitment of necessary security partners. At least we are consistent. The shi'a and Kurds who rose up against Saddam after the first gulf war, and Ngo Dinh Diem can attest to that.

America also consistently chooses to ignore the places on our earth not illuminated by our immediate vital interests. Somalia, for example, got our attention as a hotbed of piracy and famine, but not to the extent that we appreciated it as fertile ground to raise Al Shabaab. So too the Philippines, where the conditions of weak centralized government control and a pre-existing Islamic militant group spawned Abu Sayyaf[v]. Both Al Shabaab and Abu Sayyaf have succeeded in expanding terror beyond the boundaries of their remote bases.

Adjusting our foreign policy is not sufficient; America must weaponize its intellect and culture. Every terrorist has likely had a coke and a smile, been mesmerized by Star Wars, or been exposed to any number of influential and stimulating emanations from our city on the hill. We have a history of leveraging Hollywood, among others, to help sell what we offer. Our reluctance or inability to do so as a nation has resulted in an inappropriate and overwhelming demand on our military public relations efforts, who are restricted by law and by resourcing from producing content in the volume and quality required to win hearts and minds. Moreover, we've missed an opportunity to engage an ambivalent, yet powerfully influential segment of our society, as partners in this war.

It is overwhelmingly apparent that contemporary terrorists and their aspirants are voracious consumers of social media and online content. Whereas our military employs cyber operations to manipulate this content, it is also constrained by law and resources. A joint effort between our nations' security apparatus, the entertainment industry, commercial marketing organizations and online service providers is a critical element to eroding support for the ideologies that inspire terror.

Our special operators and their supporting cast are doing a magnificent job keeping the barbarians away from the gates, but the odds of eventual success are in the terrorists' favor. Success for a terrorist is ridiculously easy; a bomb that explodes at the first layer of any security system is sufficient to generate intimidation. We must continue to pluck the weeds, but the only way to a long term respite from terror is to disrupt the ideologies that cultivate it, and that lies in the realm of ideas.

Chapter 46

Finding the ISIS Center of Gravity: Why Does It Have to Be So Complicated?

Ian Bertram

First Published 9 December 2015

A recent article from Col Robert Dixon brilliantly detailed the mess of Joint understanding and application of Clausewitz's Center of Gravity (COG).[i] Like others before him, he argued that the concept is confusing to planners and leaders alike, and that the search for this Holy Grail-esque of targets has led to strategic level failures in conflicts since World War II. Dixon is largely correct in that US doctrine has made the COG concept almost unusable, but the question is why do we need to make it so complicated? Perhaps if we remove the need for a COG to be something physical that we can bomb, we can look at an adversary as a system, and seek out a binding element of that system. In the case of ISIS, properly identifying their COG will not only help lead to an eventual victory, but uphold Clausewitz's classic principle once again.

The Prussian wrote "Out of these [dominant characteristics of both belligerents] a certain center of gravity develops, the hub of all power and movement, on which everything depends. This is the point against which all our energies should be directed."[ii] Strategists and armchair theorists are aware of this quote and have been misapplying it for years. LtCol Antulio Echevarria did everyone a service in 2002 when he sheds light on the concept by reminding us that the idea stems from engineering, and that a COG is "not a source of strength, but a factor of balance."[iii] So rather than search for that key ISIS strength or weakness, we should examine what would ultimately push ISIS off balance and knock them over?

The search for an opponent's COG, for that balance point, must use an interdisciplinary process. The myopic antagonist of Stanley Kubrick's *Dr. Strangelove* General Jack D. Ripper framed the idea best, albeit with the wrong conclusion, when he stated that "war is too important to be left to the politicians. They have neither the time, the training, nor the inclination for strategic thought."[iv] However, in modern warfare, the situation has changed to the point that the military may not necessarily have the all-encompassing time/training/inclination for proper strategic thought. When strategists search for a COG, or worse, try to develop multiple COGs, they may not have the broad background needed to accomplish the task. The military specialists become the myopic ones. The search for *the* COG must include detailed analysis of all aspects of an enemies culture, economy, religion, fielded forces and abilities, leadership, terrain and weather, population, internal and external politics, transportation needs and abilities, and myriad other factors. COGs are difficult, elusive creatures to say the least, but that does not mean that they are not worth the hunt, and the personnel developing them should not be limited to the military.

Enter ISIS. The Western strategy for defeating lacks strategic coherence, at least in appearance if not in form. Airstrikes and targeted raids, the functions that the United States performs excellently, are not having the strategic effects desired by the public or politicians. Attacking key leaders and oil refineries make for good headlines, and both targets fall into a Joint understanding of COGs. The West is attacking and destroying these targets along with ISIS's fielded forces, yet the war continues. The West needs to analyze ISIS as a system, and through that analysis a COG will hopefully emerge that we can channel our full efforts against.

So what makes ISIS run? What is their hub of all power and movement? What will throw them off balance? What is their Center of Gravity? Journalist Graeme Wood provided the answer to all of these questions in March 2015 with his article "What ISIS Really Wants."[v] Wood explains how ISIS has rejected modernism, and emphatically embraced a strict interpretation of Islam that many see as medieval. He writes:

> The reality is that the Islamic State is Islamic. *Very* Islamic. Yes, it has attracted psychopaths and adventure seekers, drawn largely from the disaffected populations of the Middle East and Europe. But the religion preached by its most ardent followers derives from coherent and even learned interpretations of Islam.[vi]

The rest of the article fleshes out how deeply rooted ISIS is in their pursuit of not only establishing a caliphate, but in bringing about a final confrontation between "Rome" (think Christianity) and Islam. They publicize that they will suffer enormous setbacks before their final victory. In essence, their very beliefs insist that every time we strike them with bombs, drones, Special Forces, or effective resistance from Iraqi/Kurd/Syrian forces it is simply a logical part of their greater plan. Even when the West succeeds militarily, ISIS still sees it as a twisted victory. Therefore, Wood shows us that ISIS's COG cannot be found on the battlefield. It is not fielded forces, their capital, or anything else physical.

ISIS's COG is their ideology. Whether that ideology is a strict interpretation or bastardization of the Koran is irrelevant to COG identification. What matters is that the message is what is keeping the recruits flowing, the fighters fighting, and the people trapped under their rule in line. The problem to military planners and politicians alike is how to target their COG.

The military obviously prefers targets that can be destroyed with some application of force. This is a natural outgrowth from the fact that militaries exist for the primary purpose of delivering violence. It is harder to channel that violence towards an idea. A military can kill the people who carry the idea, but in today's inter-connected world, the idea will continue beyond the breath of individuals. Indeed, Al Qaeda, the Taliban, ISIS, and numerous other groups have shown just how resilient an idea can be, even in the face of massive and effective violence concentrated on its people. The analogy holds up equally well when one considers how much punishment the Germans, Japanese, and even the North Vietnamese endured.

Naturally, this article is not the first to suggest that combating ISIS's ideology is the key to long term success. Rather, it urges the proper application of Clausewitz's COG principle to help anti-ISIS forces to channel their efforts into the quickest, more assured method of victory. But simply identifying the COG is not enough. A plan to exploit the COG needs to be developed.

Several suggestions have been put forth, but here are some actions that Clausewitz would hopefully agree are useful in concentrating efforts against the ISIS COG. They are culled not only from military thinking and efforts, but from across the spectrum of international and human relations:

1. *Counter-narrative.* The West needs to support not only a counter narrative to ISIS's radical form of Islam, but needs to actively help push the ideas to ISIS's target recruits. This is absolutely the best way to fight their ideology, but offering something different and desirable. The counter-narrative also needs to include messages and support from leading Islamic teachers, leaders, and countries worldwide.
2. *Attack ISIS's ability to spread their message.* The hacker group Anonymous has taken a very public lead on this issue.[vii] Western Cyber Forces need to combine electronic attacks on ISIS's communications to hinder their ability to spread their

message. When fighting an idea, it should prove highly effective to also fight the ability to transmit that idea. The counter-argument is that taking down ISIS sites and accounts that are easy to access is not as useful as monitoring them, but when you're fighting an idea it can be more useful to make the idea more difficult to receive.

3. *Welcome Syrian/Iraqi Refugees.* A key component of ISIS's ideology is that Islam is locked in a deadly confrontation with the West. When Western states deny refugees a safe haven, it plays into the ISIS narrative. Fear mongering amongst Western people and politicians will do more to support ISIS than it will do to secure Western states.

4. *Classic Counter-Insurgency in contested/recently cleared areas.* The West is historically bad at utilizing small teams to fight insurgencies because we typically lack the patience. However, when allowed the freedom and resources to secure small areas, counter-insurgency programs that place small teams directly with local populations have proven themselves repeatedly since Vietnam. In areas of Iraq and Syria, these teams should incorporate volunteers from refugees that are willing to be trained as militia and returned home to fight for their own countries. A local connection to these militias will help the West avoid the appearance and necessity of occupation forces.

5. *Reach out with real economic/social plans to Muslims around the world.* This is one of those options that is outside the militaries hands, but is vital. Support agencies around the world need to reach out to their indigenous Islamic populations and lend a helping hand. They need to help provide economic opportunities and bridge the divide between them and the population majority. Fear and repression are pushing people to seek the message ISIS is spreading.

6. *Share information.* Western states and the US in particular have come a long ways since 9/11 in sharing intelligence. However, intelligence agencies have an almost inbred resistance

to sharing information, and this will hinder response to ISIS and in stopping future attacks like those seen in Paris, Beirut, California, and numerous other locations. Senior military and political leaders need to push information to each other and help build a united front against ISIS.

7. *Target people with capability.* The US loves to publicize successful attacks against "key leaders" in any modern conflict. However, these leaders may not be as important to their operations as we think they are. As Retired General Stanley McChrystal recently suggested, to keep the pressure on ISIS we need to attack the people who are capable of carrying out important tasks.[viii] They may not be leadership, but instead financiers, smugglers, and recruiters to name just a few.

These actions would prove as a logical place to start from to attack ISIS's COG. Proper application of Clausewitz not only demonstrates that COGs are singular and overarching in a conflict, but that they can help us frame a conflict and develop a strategy capable of ending that conflict. In the case of ISIS, their COG is their ideology, and we should focus our efforts to defeat it. A continuing game of global wack-a-mole combined with endless airstrikes will not end this conflict. So for the sake of American credibility, Parisian vengeance, world security, and of Dead Carl's honor, the West needs to put their focus on ISIS's COG.

Chapter 47

Basing Stabilisation Efforts on Evidence of What Works: Lessons from Afghanistan

Jon Moss

First Published 19 December 2015

Summary

The current context of the Middle East demands complex multifaceted strategies that merge hard, soft and smart power. The UK Government has continued its commitment to supporting interventions in fragile states as evidenced in the launch of the GBP 1.3 billion Conflict Stability and Security Fund. It is therefore vital to understand the structures that have to be in place to ensure money is effectively targeted.

Monitoring and evaluation of collective stabilisation efforts is extremely challenging; there have been limited examples of successful approaches. Most approaches for fragile states are predicated on the notion that a complex series of concurrent mutually reinforcing interventions needs to be carefully sequenced and integrated to foster stability. This implies that there is some overarching stabilisation strategy and plan. It also implies that there is a process in place to monitor and evaluate activity to support the continued application of these approaches. Crucially, interventions need to be designed to be capable of modification during implementation, reflecting changes in the context and environment (changes captured through monitoring).

There is limited evidence and experience of how to implement such monitoring and evaluation (M&E) successfully. This paper draws on some recent experience and seeks to identify attributes of a successful approach. It captures the experience of the author through 10 years of working in governance, security and justice in fragile and conflict affected states.

A Short History of Monitoring and Evaluation in Stabilisation

In late 2007, the UK government commissioned a short internal review of about USD 700 million of investment in stabilisation activity undertaken in Iraq from 2003 to 2007. Funds had been used for everything from fish and poultry farms, roads, bridges, power and water distribution schemes to spraying date palms and revitalising the entire date growing industry. The diversity and scale of activity was quite bewildering.

The intent of the review was to establish an evidence base to support a narrative of progress. It rapidly became apparent that there had been no consistent strategy or plan, and that there was almost no effort to systematically evaluate what was working, or what failed, and most importantly why.

It was also apparent that key actors, including the Multi-National Division South East, responsible for security in the south east of Iraq from 2003 to 2009, UK and US development agencies and the government of Iraq had very different perspectives on what should be done. The political pressures on all actors were intense and the incentive was toward action now. Consequently, it was impossible to discern common strategy, let alone a plan, and no way of evaluating impact.

The result of the conflicting pressures and levels of understanding as well as the need to accommodate a variety of actors is frequently a basket of disparate measures— any one of which might be justifiable on its own merits but which collectively falls short of an integrated strategy merging hard, soft and smart power to foster a level of stability that will permit progress toward a lasting political settlement and that will set the conditions for peace growth and prosperity.

Effective stabilisation is about the consistent integration and synchronisation of a range different activities over time. It is understandable that major nations and coalitions are attracted to the idea of overarching M&E programmes that cover an entire theatre, country or region and that attempt to monitor and evaluate various projects with a common goal of improving stability.

Recent examples of such programmes in Afghanistan include the UK government's Helmand Monitoring and Evaluation Programme (HMEP), the Australian government's Uruzgan Monitoring and Evaluation Programme (UMEP) and the US government's Measuring Impacts of Stabilization Initiatives (MISTI). Currently, some donors are looking at possible country-level M&E programmes following on from the success of MISTI. Donors are also considering the feasibility of programmes that can monitor and evaluate the impact of stabilisation support funds, either regionally or globally.

Experiences of the last 20 years do suggest that there are some guiding principles and approaches in the M&E of stabilisation efforts that are likely to deliver a better outcome than others.

Conflicting Agendas, Narratives and Audiences

The stabilisation landscape is complicated by the multiplicity of donors and nations which are a necessary feature of coalition work; each bringing its particular interests and prejudices to the table. There is the classic military-civilian rift, exacerbated when military actors seize on the importance of non-kinetic interventions, sometimes as a substitute for the tougher challenge of getting the security situation right. In doing so they can attempt to railroad host nation governments, security forces, international aid agencies and other actors into strategies they know will be unlikely to succeed.

By contrast, civilian actors are often seen as slow to respond to a dynamic situation and indifferent to the sacrifices of national and international forces. NGOs are understandably, but perhaps not always realistically, concerned about militarisation of aid, the compromising of humanitarian space and being co-opted into supporting overtly political agendas that are inconsistent with their charters.

All stakeholders—be it the putative governments of conflict states, the governments of nations committed to stabilisation, development agencies, NGOs or civil society—have their own narratives to buttress and their own constituencies to inform, influence and maintain the support of to ensure they build and maintain their political licence to operate.

Frequently, the need to cement support at home or ensure collation cohesion takes precedence over the need to understand what is and is not working in the concerned region or country and to apply the evidence to inform future activity. At times, the last thing decision makers want or need is evidence or information that suggests that not everything they have done has been successful, or that a partner's intervention is counterproductive, their dilemma being that to publicly admit mistakes is to deny themselves the ability to continue their intervention. One manifestation of this is that even where effective and impartial monitoring and evaluation is undertaken, the evidence gleaned is often jealously guarded and so the potential benefits in terms of lessons learned and applied are denied to the wider community of practitioners.

It is unrealistic to expect that every decision can or should be taken on the basis of comprehensive evidence and analysis. Paralysis by analysis is an enduring feature of the response to low level conflict and insurgencies in countries as diverse as Afghanistan, Iraq, Pakistan, Somalia and elsewhere. There are times when decisions need to be taken and acted on quickly and perhaps modified later. Effective and comprehensive monitoring and evaluation is one tool that can facilitate this approach.

Features of Effective Monitoring and Evaluation—Conspicuous in their Absence

Effective M&E is normally based on a deep understanding of context and a strong evidence-based theory of change, consistently applied. This needs to be linked in turn to a carefully chosen set of indicators that allows for monitoring of outputs, outcomes and impact to provide a comprehensive measure of progress and achievement at every level of programming.

Most importantly, the M&E framework allows for the testing of the assumptions that underpin the theory of change—and therefore enables lessons learning and adaptation. Given that stabilisation interventions invariably operate in highly complex political and security contexts, it is this feature of an effective M&E approach that is most important. Good M&E is one of the enablers for an adaptive learning approach to programming.

Of course, not all successful examples of complex adaptive approaches are founded on deep contextual understanding and a strong evidence based theory of change. In unstable and violent areas, where there are big political considerations at stake driving the pace of operations, it is often all but impossible to develop a sufficiently deep understanding to craft either the optimal approach or to formulate a theory of change based on strong evidence. Instead, it is necessary to accept that at best it may only be possible to arrive at an interim framework that identifies the most likely entry points and best approaches, and have in place a robust M&E approach that allows for subsequent development of both the theory of change and the approaches adopted.

A good example of an organic adaptive process was seen during the Iraq surge in late 2007. A range of pilot interventions ultimately evolved to deliver a highly effective short term impact in the Anbar Awakening.

In effect, a strategy evolved from a series of rapid experiments. Some of these were abject failures, others demonstrated clearly the drivers of local level political legitimacy and what was required for the US military strategy to win the hearts and minds of the tribal leadership. None of that would have been possible if leaders and decision makers had waited until they had all the relevant evidence in hand to help determine the decisions they made. Today it is easy to deride the US strategy in Anbar, but at the time it transformed a failing campaign. The Anbar example is interesting because it evolved, reflecting a permissive command environment within which licensed experimentation within boundaries was encouraged, as well as an assessment process that identified and scaled up activity that appeared to be working. Critically, it also occurred within the context of a single organisation, so it didn't have to accommodate the interests of multiple actors or the incentives and interests of the Iraqi government.

Get the Context or the Context Will Get You

Contextual understanding is the foundation of everything that follows. As Stanley McChrystal, former US commander in Afghanistan, said in 2011, "We didn't know enough and we still don't know enough." Both Afghanistan and Iraq offer excellent examples of well-meaning interventions that failed to achieve the impact they deserved because they were not designed in the light of a deep contextual understanding.

Poor contextual understanding can lead to disastrous decisions early in a stabilisation effort from which it is hard to recover. In Iraq, the UK government and military consistently underestimated, misunderstood or chose to ignore the complexity of Iranian efforts to influence the Shia population in the Basra, in southern Iraq. The UK discounted the multitude of non-kinetic investments that comprised a combination of soft and smart power which led to the loss of effective control over the security situation in 2006/07 as it became apparent to citizens that the UK narrative lacked substance.

In 2006, the planners of Task Force Helmand (ISAF's military command in Helmand Province, Afghanistan) also failed to consider how their deployment to northern districts such as Sangin Musa Qala and Nowzad would impact on a complex tribal political economy where the population perceived the UK to be taking sides in a long-standing tribal struggle for influence and control of resources. It took ISAF five years and a significant commitment of US military forces to recover from a decision that might have been very different had the context been fully appreciated. Such miscalculations are not unique to the UK or US military, or coalition partners—they also occur in the myriad of civilian agencies and NGOs.

Look at the Whole Picture—Not Just the Piece that Interests You

For some of those working in Helmand in 2008, one of the most useful references on how Pashtun society actually worked was still Frederik Barth's excellent work from the 1950s. This, combined with some interesting contemporary work from the Tribal Liaison Office, an NGO, provided a good theoretical framework to start from. The UK and US governments had also commissioned some useful work on drivers of radicalisation. What was less obvious was an understanding of the extent to which principles of socio-political organisation outlined by Frederik Barth might apply in Afghanistan's Pashtun belt, how they might be translated into practice in Helmand, and what this meant for the practical application of stabilisation and counter insurgency strategies and operational plans. In short, the analysis of the political economy of the area was inadequate. We simply didn't understand enough of the context.

The vogue approach to understanding context in the UK is focused on practical application of the concept of political economy analysis, a brief summary of which is encapsulated in a UK Department for International Development how to note. The basic idea is simple enough—understand the formal rules of the game and the informal realities of doing business, analyse the stakeholders in terms of their incentives, motivation and relative influence, and then use this information to inform the selection and implementation of strategies that are likely to work with the grain of what is uncovered.

Political economy analysis needs to encompass everything from micro-local to national and regional politics. To work effectively in tribal and sectarian societies, it is fundamentally important to understand how political authority is acquired, maintained and utilised to support the interests of key stakeholders and sections of society. This goes to the heart of understanding what contributes to political legitimacy in the eyes of key interest groups.

A strong monitoring and evaluation framework should always be anchored in first class political economy analysis. Critically, such an analysis enables us to understand how information is transmitted and received—especially important in societies where there is limited media penetration. HMEP was able to use techniques based on social network analysis to better understand how information was disseminated and how de-facto power and influence were exercised through a network of hujras (or guest houses) across the various districts. This information was then used to inform the development and implementation of initiatives to support local governance which built on existing practice and custom but also offered a transitional pathway toward the model on democracy set out in the constitution.

In Helmand, in contrast to a comprehensive political economy analysis, ISAF's counter insurgency narrative tended to limit analysis to a small number of key leaders and the machinations of the formal institutions of the state and in doing so missed one of the most valuable sets of insights needed to inform programming, which is that in a land of weak institutions and volatile security the real centres of gravity, contested by the Government of Afghanistan, the Taliban and ISAF, were the enduring tribal networks that controlled central Helmand's agricultural economy. Consequently interventions often targeted the wrong constituencies, which reduced their impact considerably.

Finally, it is necessary to validate and understand key background data, including the location, distribution and size of settlements. This has proved particularly challenging in the Afghan context, but is a feature of working in places as diverse as Pakistan, Colombia and Somalia. Considerable care needs to be devoted to ensuring that individual settlements are clearly identifiable and that basic demographic data is as accurate as possible given the circumstances. Technology is helpful in this respect, and aerial surveys combined with the use of GPS and GIS technology have made this process much easier than it was in the past. Almost by definition, most of the fragile and conflict affected states we are currently concerned with are characterised by very poor information on demographics, and often basic mapping data is considerably out of date and difficult to obtain.

The HMEP programme devoted significant resources to reconciling data collected with existing maps and survey information. Detailed social network analysis conducted by HMEP was preceded by a comprehensive geospatial validation exercise to ensure that data was anchored to an accurate map that reflected the understanding of the local population in terms of where people live and how communities were grouped and chose to associate.

Have a Plan; Remain Engaged

In Helmand, in 2005, an original UK stabilisation strategy was delivered through a cross government planning team. By 2006 the original strategy had gone out of the window as UK forces deployed rapidly out of central Helmand to northern districts, and civilian actors found themselves rapidly overtaken by a deteriorating security situation that constrained their ability to operate.

The Helmand Provincial Reconstruction Team (HPRT) grew in strength and capability, but it was not until late 2008 that there were sufficient civilian resources to provide a credible and consistent input to stabilisation planning. There followed a series of efforts to develop a joint civilian and military multi-national multi-agency stabilisation plan, and the first fully formed plans appeared in early 2009. It was not until 2010 that we saw the first fully worked out product of a joint analysis and planning process. When the HMEP team deployed in 2010, there was neither a strategy nor plan capable of sustaining a tight conventional monitoring and evaluation framework. Instead, it took a series of evolutions of HMEP culminating in the development of a transition readiness template before the potential of M&E could be realised.

Given the very different perspectives of key stakeholders, it is remarkable they were able to agree on a joint planning process that survived significant differences of opinion and operational challenges. One of the more successful features of the subsequent stabilisation effort in Helmand was the way in which senior leaders were able to overcome differences and seek to provide a consistent approach over time.

Collaborate

The stabilisation environment is crowded, and any overarching programme to monitor and evaluate interventions within a particular theatre will only be successful if it is treated as a joint and shared endeavour with the people who are delivering and implementing interventions. Given the pressures on stakeholders and the challenges of the environment it would be unreasonable for an M&E provider to expect full co-operation and disclosure from all implementers from the outset—even when high level direction is consistent and unambiguous.

It is necessary for those charged with implementing countrywide, theatre-specific or fund-specific monitoring and evaluation to work closely with implementers and to establish a strong element of trust from the outset. This is a huge challenge, requiring an approach that is able to flex to accommodate different institutional cultures and agendas and to refrain from overt value judgments as to the relative value of particular activities.

Establish Value—Earn Trust

Effective M&E in a fragile state multi-agency stabilisation context cannot simply be imposed on all actors from the outside. A programme needs to be negotiated and supported at a senior leadership level, but more importantly it must demonstrate value before it can earn trust. Credibility will be hard won and very easily lost.

One of the biggest challenges experienced by the team implementing HMEP in 2010 was to overcome a mixture of scepticism, indifference and downright hostility on the part of various implementers and stakeholders. Key to this was positive messaging that M&E was there not to identify poor or under-performing programmes but to assist implementers in identifying what might work and help them to find ways to deepen the impact of their interventions. Understanding the political economy of the donor and international environment proved as important as understanding the local context.

There are lessons that can be derived from approaches such as Problem-Driven Iterative Adaptation (PDIA) to help in achieving ownership from implementers. PDIA has a strong emphasis on joint problem analysis. An M&E team can add significant value in this process because it is likely to bring broad evidence-based contextual understanding and an awareness of what others are doing in the same space, and because the team can jointly agree indicators and instruments with implementers and can input to programmes at their design and inception phases rather than having to retrofit the M&E approach during implementation.

Share

Insights are only useful if they are widely disseminated and are available in time to influence programme design and implementation. This presents a number of challenges. Stakeholders operate on a number of IT platforms and with varying security policies, which can result in different standards and thresholds for the classification of data. One of the earliest tasks in implementing a common M&E programme is therefore establishing a mechanism that allows suitably anonymised data to be shared across platforms. In practice this is harder than it appears, especially when civilian actors are attempting to work with military, diplomatic and other government counterparts.

One important benefit of adopting an open platform and making as much data as possible available to as wide an audience as possible is that it does much to help establish the credibility of the M&E provider.

Be Responsive, Yet Maintain Consistency Over Time

Just as the external environment changes rapidly over time in an unstable and fragile state, so M&E providers need to flex and adapt their approaches without compromising the quality and integrity of their data sets. It is remarkable how few stabilisation contexts are monitored consistently over time—this is an unglamorous but necessary activity that is sometimes hard to get funded. A good example of an enduring data set in a fragile state is the Asia Foundation's national perception survey in Afghanistan which is used extensively by a wide range of actors but has many well documented limitations, including that it cannot be dis-aggregated by district.

An interesting example of flexible and responsive implementation can be found in the way in which the HMEP team adapted its approach to sampling and survey work to accommodate a fluctuating security situation in some of the more challenging and insecure districts. Once a sampling framework had been established, it became apparent that enumerators would not be able to access all the planned sampling points, and the programme was exhausting its supply of reserve sampling point. One work-around was to group similar districts and pool them to maintain the statistical integrity of the data set. Thus as security became more variable it was possible to continue to sample within a defined group of northern districts and deliver data that was reliable.

HMEP tried to be responsive in a number of ways. The programme was structured around a series of quarterly research waves. Prior to each wave, the team consulted with the end users of data and implementers of programmes to adjust survey instruments to reflect the interests and emerging concerns of the implementers. This process not only ensured the M&E programme remained relevant but was also important in securing the implementers' cooperation.

Clearly, there is a balance to be struck between adjusting the data collection to reflect changing interests and ensuring consistency to allow for inter-wave comparison and the identification of long term trends.

One way of ensuring responsiveness over time is to build in the capability to conduct in-depth focus studies that seek to answer particular research questions that have a direct bearing on an aspect of stakeholder intervention. In 2011, HMEP was able to study political networks in one district which helped to validate donor approaches to support local representative bodies. In 2012, the programme conducted a focus study on the expansion of opium cultivation in Helmand's desert areas. By understanding who was occupying land, how they came to obtain rights to cultivate, how their operations were financed and where they obtained public services it was possible to contextualise data from other sources. In turn, this challenged a number of assumptions around the role of the Taliban in the desert areas and the implications of the ISAF drawdown in security. Finally, also in 2012, HMEP also looked in depth at the fiscal sustainability of investments in infrastructure and what it would cost to support continued provision of basic services after ISAF's drawdown.

Be Honest on Limitations of Data

An interesting feature of the public perception data gathered through HMEP was the public's consistently high levels of confidence in the Afghan Police. Unsurprisingly, there was a temptation for a number of stakeholders to quote headline percentages that appeared to support their particular narrative on the police. The HMEP team was at pains to provide an honest assessment of social desirability bias in perception survey work and to say that individual data points were far less reliable than long term trends (which in effect discount preference bias). HMEP made it clear that it would be wrong to conclude that the police were held in universal high esteem, but that the surveys could show whether public confidence in the police was rising or falling over time and point to why that might be.

HMEP attempted to use regression analysis to help explain how different variables combined to impact on public perceptions. This approach has potential to help explain how and why particular activities might impact on public perceptions, but it needs to be used with care. Firstly, the base sample needs to be statistically significant and fully representative—not an easy task in most stabilisation contexts. Secondly, it is hard to isolate variables in a crowded environment where stakeholders are struggling to share all the information on what they are doing and where. Finally, independent and dependent variables can only be successfully identified by an M&E team that has a deep understanding of the context.

Regression analysis was useful in Helmand in that it did help the planners to weigh and prioritise activities over time. In particular analysis demonstrated a strong and enduring correlation between the availability of quality public information and positive perceptions of local government and security bodies. It also highlighted the importance of interventions in key public services that were perceived to be drivers of government legitimacy.

Data is Interesting—But How You Use Data is What Counts

M&E programming in fragile states has limited utility if it is not used to inform the design, timing and implementation of interventions. A challenge in Afghanistan was that many donors had pre-determined programmes that were rolled out pretty much regardless of what monitoring and evaluation might show. Under such circumstances, M&E has limited benefit—it can provide a snapshot of how a programme is being received, but unless the programme in question has been structured to allow for revisions and mid-course corrections there is a limit to how M&E insights can be applied.

Complex adaptive stabilisation programming will not work unless it includes near real-time M&E and unless the actors owning interventions have the ability to insulate their implementation teams from political pressures. In Anbar in 2007 General Petreaus was able to create just enough time, space and a permissive environment to find what worked. Arguably, in Marja in Helmand in 2010, General McChrystal did not have time on his side and therefore had to run with what was available off the shelf, with a less satisfactory outcome.

HMEP provided a range of insights into how people's perceptions, including perceptions of the army, police, local government and informal governance mechanisms, changed over time and, critically, how public priorities evolved. Some research products were extremely helpful in understanding what was happening on the ground—for example the expansion of opium cultivation into the desert areas or the impact of ISAF base closure on security. What was harder was to change was the nature of the interventions in light of the emerging evidence as to their impact.

Sometimes this was due to stakeholders disputing the validity of the data. More often it was to do with models of programming or decision making that were inflexible or because stakeholders were trapped in narratives that precluded any substantive change in direction irrespective of evidence suggesting that their actions were capable of improvement. Under such circumstances, there are limitations on what adaptive M&E can deliver.

The overwhelming lesson is to design and implement M&E programming at the same time that interventions are being designed and go through inception. A flaw in HMEP was that it did not appear until 2010, by which time many of the stabilisation approaches in

Helmand had become quite fixed. It is inevitable in a multi-donor stabilisation context that the timing will never be perfect for all actors and some element of retrofitting will be necessary, but it is certainly a factor that needs to be borne in mind for the future.

Integrity Matters—Protecting the Process

Given the well documented challenges of working in fragile states it is very easy for the research product to be compromised because data collection protocols have not been observed and enumerators have cut corners or failed to apply their training consistently.

HMEP outsourced some survey work and data collection to a reputable international survey company established in Afghanistan and utilised by a number of other major donors and organisations. In time, it became apparent to the HMEP team that there were occasions where the company was not consistently applying the agreed data collection protocols. The solution adopted was to grow a local network of trained validator teams and apply an external validation process to ensure the integrity of survey processes. A key lesson learned was that it was relatively easy to recruit, train, and deploy independent validation teams that ensured that the sampling frameworks were correctly applied. (Subsequently in Khyber Pakhtunkhwa, Pakistan, the UK funded Aitebaar Programme has taken the M&E function in-house as opposed to outsourcing data collection. This has significantly improved the quality of the M&E process as well as providing a much stronger research capability to inform programming.)

Field researchers face many challenges. Aside from action by insurgents, there is also understandable suspicion from host nation security, intelligence agencies and police forces. The best solutions have been to invest time and effort in preparing the ground with such agencies well in advance to ensure consents are in place and to be as transparent as possible in dealing with authorities, whilst ensuring that research is conducted in accordance with ethical principles and that the confidentiality of data is guaranteed.

Care needs to be taken to ensure that survey instruments are designed to be administered quickly and that enumerators are selected to be representative of the communities in which they are working. Considerable attention needs to be paid to small details such as dress and appearance. Use of smart technology, including GPS equipped mobile phones, is helpful, but it needs to be borne in mind that possession of such equipment in some contexts can be misinterpreted by governmental and nongovernment actors. In practice, there are relatively few locations where remote monitoring by survey teams suitably selected and trained is completely impossible, provided appropriate measures are adopted specific to the context.

With careful planning, clear understanding and preparation of the political environment, experience from Afghanistan suggests that comprehensive M&E can be made to work and can provide valuable insights even in dynamic multi-national, multi-agency contexts, provided basic ground rules are applied. As the complexity of the challenges facing the international community in countries such as Syria and Iraq increases, and resources committed continue to rise, it is essential that these lessons are not forgotten.

Chapter 48

Defeating the Abu Bakr al Baghdadi Gang: A Realistic Strategy

Huba Wass de Czege [i]

First Published 22 December 2015

The militant religious cult led by Abu Bakr al Baghdadi has become more than the scourge of Iraq and Syria, where it is expropriating property, killing civilians, <u>raping and forcing captured women into sexual slavery</u>, and beheading foreigners. The Abu Bakr al Baghdadi Gang (BG), as I prefer to call it, has "gone to war" with the civilized world—using spectacular slaughter to political ends. The civilized powers must respond, but how? The strategy of the American coalition to "degrade, disrupt and defeat " it, and to "defend the allied homelands" from terrorist attacks directed or inspired by this rapacious criminal gang is near-sighted, half-hearted, unsophisticated and most likely to result in an ugly, dangerous, expensive and enduring stalemate. Defenses designed to threaten attackers with near certain death do not deter those who welcome it. And offensives dependent mainly on inflicting losses on an enemy leave crucial decisions of whether and when to quit murdering, looting and enslaving to fanatics. Even when such defenses and offenses are combined, they perpetuate, rather than conclude, war.

We can, and must, do better than respond with measures that satisfy only near-term political pressures to "do something."

But there is no easy road forward. First, al Baghdadi and his gang will win if those who oppose them continue to refer to this criminal enterprise by the descriptive names they apply to themselves, whether in English or Arabic. Doing so advertises their aspirations and assists their propaganda. They chose to frame their "caliphate" as the vanguard of the titanic end-times struggle of the religious pure against the wayward and decadent. We should, instead, speak and think of this as a conflict of the lawful against the lawless, the fanatical against the reasonable, the modern against the medieval, and the civilized against the barbarian. To draw a line between the Muslim, or Sunni Muslim, world community and all others is wrong and the height of folly, when the lawful, reasonable, modern, and civilized among them are the main object of BG "jihad." These millions of Muslims have the most to lose in this struggle. And the vast majority among them who are Sunni can exert the greatest leverage against them.

Second, we must realize that Al Baghdadi and his gang of lawless cutthroats will win if we, and all of our allies, cannot destroy his organization in place; apprehend and bring to trial its criminal leaders, followers, and supporters; and leave behind stable, functioning, and extremist-resistant indigenous communities under a political regime their citizens consider legitimate. And we must lay down a useful precedent for similar challenges in the future. No lesser goals are worthy of a civilized world. *And no lesser goals are practical.*

Third, America must formulate, adopt, and advance the goals stated above and a realistic core strategy to achieve them. This article will explain why and how.

Fourth, America will need a vigorous grand strategy of creative incentives to form a political alliance of the right combination of powers to implement it and resolve the many dilemmas of present national policies that stand in the way. This article will outline the essentials.

Finally, America and its allies must understand that this will require a strong "whole of government" commitment by a large alliance of the "civilized" powers in the Middle East and around the globe. This means visionary politics and dogged diplomacy to lay down the political foundation upon which to build the future of the communities now occupied by BG. It means a coordinated allied military assault in all the dimensions that matter, sufficiently strong to achieve decisive results in minimum time, in which the required tasks are accomplished by the powers best suited. It also means having in place a parallel international effort of coordinated police work, prosecutors, courts, and prisons. Equally important will be a coordinated and parallel allied effort in the wake of operations to establish legitimate local governing bodies to secure the community, facilitate the distribution of humanitarian aid, guide allied efforts to jump-start local economies, and, thus, rebuild viable and safe communities in short order. And to be better prepared for the likely rise of offspring and cousins of this movement the allies must provide a useful precedent of legitimating logic and judicial procedures for similar transnational challenges in the future.

To defeat our efforts to achieve these goals, BG only needs to survive the current angry, shortsighted, overly militaristic, and half-measures of the civilized powers. So far, they have.

There is only one global power capable of convincing the relevant powers, especially those in the BG neighborhood, to join a coalition committed to a realistic strategy. So far, America has not.

This is the third revision[ii] of a work I began in the spring of 2014 when the American administration began serious thinking and planning for a campaign in Iraq and Syria against this group. This version expands, refines and updates my earlier thinking on this subject.

On Preconceived Schemes and Knee-Jerk Responses

Our current "counter terrorism"[iii] approach has undeniably degraded and disrupted the Abu Bakr al Baghdadi Gang (BG). But this degraded and disrupted, even besieged, "caliphate" has been able to increase its recruitment and the number and ferocity of its attacks abroad. We should be impressed by the simple efficiency of their tactics and the brilliance of their strategy. It seems that al Baghdadi, or his subordinate leaders in Raqqa need only suggest broad objectives, provide a little guidance and support, and small parties of pre-positioned followers willingly offer up their lives to wreak havoc in our modern civilized societies. Our efforts at detection and defense will continue to foil many such attempts, but our best efforts will continue to fail to prevent many others.

Their fighters, both in their occupied territories and abroad, are far from equivalent in skills, training, and equipment to the professional soldiers, sailors and airmen of modern states deployed against them. Yet inexpensive and simple weapons and tactics produce impressive global results that add up to a potent strategy for imposing huge psychological, material and political costs on the advanced nations of the world, and retard development in the Middle East, Asia and Africa. In contrast our very expensive sophisticated weapons and tactics appear impressive to us, but add up to stalemate on a global scale and no strategy for moving forward.

In the wake of murderous attacks on North Atlantic Treaty Organization (NATO) homelands, citizens are urging their politicians to respond. This is a natural reaction, and politicians react by doing the first vigorous thing that comes to mind and they have the means to do. The immediate response has been to intensify the pace and number of air strikes and commando raids that constitute the current "counter terrorism strategy" of the allied effort.

Some in NATO Europe may want to replicate the strategy and tactics of the Kosovo Air War—bombing the cities of al Baghdadi's criminal occupation, such as Raqqa. Forcing Serbia to withdraw their forces from Kosovo is not the same as causing these fanatics to stop committing crimes; to give up control of the Syrian and Iraqi territories they forcibly and illegally hold, and to surrender or face the destruction in place of their "army" of thugs. Those politicians who advocate this response should also remember that the pace of airstrikes NATO could muster during the 78 day Kosovo Air War will be extremely difficult to match far away from home and without the larger Air Forces and well stocked nearby airbases available at that time.[iv] Not only that, but the cost of each airplane's flight to and from the target from distant air craft carriers or airbases, and that of the sophisticated munitions expended, is staggering[v] in comparison to the cost of just one terrorist mission in Europe, Asia or North America. Others may want to replicate the NATO air campaign to remove the Libyan dictator Muammar al-Gaddafi. They should think instead about the chaos left behind in that country after the Gaddafi regime was "destroyed." Not even a ten-fold increase in intensity of "counter terrorism" or "Air War" tactics can defeat the so-called "caliphate," and leave behind an acceptable result. Instead a strategy comprised of such tactics can cost dearly without "destroying" the situation that gave birth to the BG, especially when these tactics transform formerly prosperous villages, towns and cities into uninhabitable moonscapes and send former occupants fleeing. But an interim campaign of well planned and precise airstrikes and raids by outside powers can complement, and prepare the way for, a more complete strategy to follow.

The civilized global and regional powers can win (achieve the above mentioned quartet of goals) if they act in concert through a realistic core strategy aimed at these mutually supportive goals. After all, they are states with millions of citizens and vast resources. None of them need to make this effort their top priority. They need only elevate these aims sufficiently high, among their many other interests, to counter balance the very high priority Abu Bakr al Baghdadi and his relatively small number of fervent and focused followers (no more than 150,000) place on their own apocalyptic vision of a final end-time war ahead of a messianic redemption, in which the planet is burned to ash. Compared to slowing climate change this is a very small undertaking, if addressed intelligently. If not, such criminal fanaticism will engulf the Middle East; worsen the flow of refugees from the hell they and we create by the current mode of fighting. And acts of politically motivated spectacular slaughter will continue to regularly punctuate otherwise civilized life around the globe.

What I have in mind is nothing like the two wars against Saddam Hussein. It is more like the war against the Afghan Taliban in late 2001 where local forces on the ground where assisted by US and Allied special and air forces. But where the Taliban was able to escape into the wild country of Afghanistan and the sanctuaries of Pakistan, the BG must be corralled. And where the Taliban was able to return to contest control of various villages, towns, and cities, these would be secured and defended by armed, able and trusted locals with keen incentives to keep the BG out. And finally, while the Taliban was driven out, they never decisively lost the struggle for the legitimacy to govern, especially in the Pashtu inhabited towns and villages some distance removed from Kabul. In fact, a major shortcoming of the strategies for the US and allied interventions of the last decade and one-half, in Afghanistan, Iraq, and Libya, was that most strategizing and planning was devoted to destroying an intolerable status quo by fighting, and very little was devoted to the politics, judicial processes and economics of constructing the favorable one to follow. That is not just unwise, it is unconscionable.

The Heart of the Matter

This situation is so complex that it is easy to lose focus. One must find, isolate, and take aim at the heart of the matter. The aspect of the situation making the summer 2014 status quo intolerable enough to trigger the original American and allied intervention was the rule of al Baghdadi's militant group across great parts of Syria and Iraq, and the threat of this 7th century model of governance spreading further, if not checked at its origin. (A number of smaller scale BG colonies are cropping up elsewhere.) As such a regime swells in territory and membership, not only Middle Eastern, Afghan and North African populations will be at risk, but also those of modern industrialized nations across the globe. In other words, the problem caused by al Baghdadi's militant group should, from the beginning, have been recognized to be, not a Syrian or Iraqi problem, but an international problem. And it needed an international perspective to resolve it, one that exploits common interests and overcomes, mitigates, or resolves differences, of which there are many. Recent events, such as Russia's active intervention in support of the Syrian Ba'athist government, have only underscored this reality.

Moreover, BG is, both structurally and in terms of its aims and methods, significantly different than Al Qaeda. Al Qaeda does not need to control territory to exist. It only needs to promote and work toward a foreordained future caliphate. To be what it is, this group needs to control territory and to rule a population by strict Sharia law, on the 7th century model prescribed by the Prophet Mohammed in Koranic scriptures. And that territory *needs to expand*. It draws a growing stream of immigrants to that territory by offering a place for those who wish to live under such rule, and a regime that rigorously enforces such laws. It particularly attracts from abroad young, unemployed, unfulfilled, single Sunni Muslim men, and new converts to Islam, who feel victimized by local circumstances and fall prey to the vigorous and manly image the movement portrays on modern media. Within Syria and Iraq, it attracts Sunni's who feel victimized by the Shia and Alawite dominated regimes that now rule their home countries. This movement also provides a cause that pursues concrete near-term objectives within the current generation rather than the more distant ones Al Qaeda followers pursue across many generations. And that cause, succinctly expressed, is to defend, sustain, and expand a place and a regime that rules according to the prophet Mohammed's 7th century vision in every respect and actively seeks to bring about the final apocalyptic end-time war in the near term. Finally, because the Prophet has foreordained the ends they pursue, the leaders and fighters of this movement are emboldened to take great risks. This boldness, and the successes they have achieved, combines to attract action-oriented adherents from abroad. Breaking this success-fueled pattern of boldness is one key to their defeat.

One difficulty for the largely modern-minded international community is that this fanatical cult does not advocate a "perversion" of Koranic scriptures. It adheres to a strict interpretation of un-ambiguous prophetic passages of the holy book. And, like other believers of the Muslim faith, its members believe the Prophet Mohammed faithfully recorded the true word of Allah. What religious splits exist between this cult's orthodoxy and most other Sunni Muslim authorities (including Salafists of any stripe) is over methods and timing—gentler methods of the struggle now and a later foreordained caliphate. As a result, it will be difficult to drive a wedge, solely on the grounds of religious principle, between them and other Sunni Muslim believers, including moderate ones and many of Assad's other opponents in Syria.[vi] It is particularly unhelpful for Western leaders to argue that BG's orthodoxy is "perverse." That is framing our conflict with BG as if it were over religion. There are more effective wedge issues than points of religious orthodoxy. For instance, I cannot think of one Cold War debate between Marxist and Capitalist authorities ever bearing fruit! Communist regimes were not transformed or brought down by converting true believers. That happened when average citizens and rulers became convinced that rule based on such beliefs could not deliver the modern life they wanted. What convinced them was hard evidence of a more bounteous life in the West, and not words.

I prefer framing the conflict with BG, not as war (certainly not holy war), but as the fanatical against the reasonable, the civilized against the barbarian, the modern against the medieval, and the lawful against the lawless. I don't honor BG fighters as holy warriors. The operations against them are not "war." They are primarily "police actions" by legitimate authorities to bring criminals to justice. (They will necessarily include applications of military force and fighting in villages, towns and cities to apprehend BG fighters occupying them. Although the term "police action" was applied to the Korean War, that military intervention was war.)

The majority of Arab Sunnis have rationalized their religion with modern life and sensibilities regarding law and order. I believe they would be more trusting and cooperating allies if outside powers reframed the combined operations against BG the way I have.

Beyond that, I think it is a colossal failure of clear thinking for politicians to use the word "war" to garner support for bringing mass murderers to justice. And it is equally unwise to choose the logic of war to combat crime.

War is the last resort for settling existential issues between states. War legalizes killing the enemy by the regular[vii] soldiers of a state in the name of collective objectives. And reciprocally, vanquished enemy soldiers are not held individually accountable for the soldiers they have killed for the aims of the state, only if there is evidence to implicate them in the murder of civilians. War ends when the enemy state quits. Causing the enemy to quit is far more difficult than most people think, especially when the enemy is not a state. If there is no enemy state with which to "make peace," the war continues "under ground." (This is what happened in Afghanistan and Iraq when the Taliban and Ba'athist regimes collapsed.)

Holding individuals accountable for acts all modern states have designated as crimes follows a different set of rules. All states have made murder illegal; therefore it is a crime everywhere. BG members who have murdered abroad have been either killed while committing the crime; killed resisting arrest; or apprehended, jailed, tried, and punished within some system of justice. This ends the process of holding individuals accountable for a crime.

It takes strength and discipline to follow this logic. The reward for doing so is respect for the laws and legitimacy in the eyes of citizens at home and abroad. Weak states cannot maintain the discipline of the process, are tempted into legal short cuts, and suffer loss of respect and legitimacy at home and abroad.

A "police action" to bring the leaders and henchmen of a murderous criminal gang to justice would have the strength of a united and large alliance of states. But it would need to combine the resources of their systems of justice to do it, and share the responsibility. This problem needs an international legal perspective to resolve it.

Another major difficulty for the distant international community to understanding is how to make strategic sense of the relevant territory occupied by BG and adjacent to it. It is easy to see place names, political boundaries, transportation infrastructures, and river lines that demark the territory on a map. But it is more difficult, and more important to understand how the large number of small groups fighting BG and the Syrian government relate to the territory and the tribal communities. An understanding of the history of the people on this land, and their present circumstances, is vital to formulating a sound strategy. It was three years after the 2003 invasion of Iraq that a map of tribal distribution became available.

Another major difficulty to overcome is how to get the neighboring Turks, Iraqi Shia, Syrian Alawites and Christians, and Sunni Jordanians, Saudi Arabians, and Qataris to act in concert on any effective strategy to destroy al Baghdadi's organization in place; apprehend and bring to trial its criminal leaders, followers and supporters; and leave behind stable, functioning, and extremist resistant indigenous communities under a political regime their citizens consider legitimate. The Turks need strong incentives to abandon their suppression of the Kurds and team up with them instead. The Iraqi Shia need strong incentives to share power with Kurds and Sunnis and to permit the Sunni majority provinces as much autonomy as the Kurdish ones have acquired. The Syrian Alawites, Shia and Christians need strong incentives to share power and national resources with Sunnis in the central government, and to allow provinces and districts more self government.

The flow of immigrants into Europe, and the potential for expanding terrorism there, gives the Europeans a strong incentive to offer help and demand solutions. Normally, modes of self-government are strictly internal national concerns, but, in this case, the international community has a strong interest in imposing measures designed to achieve the above mentioned trinity of goals: destroy BG organization in place; apprehend and bring to trial its criminal leaders, followers, and supporters; and leave behind stable, functioning, and extremist-resistant indigenous communities under a political regime their citizens consider legitimate.

On Custom Designing Strategies And Their Tactics

In his book, <u>The Seven Pillars of Wisdom</u>, T.E. Lawrence describes how, during World War I, he conceived of the unique core strategy for combining the fighting potential of the Arab tribes to assist the British Army defeat the Ottoman Army in what is today Saudi Arabia, Jordan, Israel, Lebanon, and Syria. The British had in mind an Arab Army, patterned after their own. What proved successful instead was a tailor-made way of organizing indigenous fighting forces, command structures and logistics. Not only that, but while European weapons were useful, European fighting tactics were not. Lawrence and his Arab allies adapted tactics to the strategy and the local situation. The details of what Lawrence and the Arabs then did to defeat the Ottoman Turks is less interesting than the mode of thinking that created their governing strategy and implementing tactics. What follows is how I have adapted to the current situation how T.E Lawrence thought about his problematic situation in this region one hundred years ago.[viii]

In the rational pursuit of vital interests in any human undertaking, the design of concrete actions to pursue them must subordinate to a conceptual strategic design based on a well-researched theory of the specific situation. Any such theory will be based on a combination of hard data and educated guesses about what those data mean. The underlying research must encompass not only the historic sweep of similar cases (history does not repeat, it educates), but it must also examine the peculiarities and differences of the present situation compared to any that came before. Finally, because of the differences between the present case and those of the past, it must adapt, rather than adopt, past practices. What results from such inquiry and contemplation is a rough but useful strategic framework that can be adapted as learning occurs. At the core of such a framework is a theory of the situation at the very heart of the matter and a strategy for resolving it—a core strategy. Other secondary aspects of the situation are accounted for separately in supporting strategies. Having an explicit consensus among allies on a core strategy aligns costly allied operations.

Such a core strategy should drive the design of tactics and supporting strategies. To my way of thinking, strategies are logical schemes for achieving broad conceptual ends employing conceptual ways and means along several lines of effort. Complex human affairs are usually resolved when a cluster of related, but sometimes very different, conceptual ends are pursued sequentially or in parallel. Tactics are the practical schemes for achieving concrete ends employing concrete ways and means.

As in the past, we have based this intervention to "degrade, disrupt and defeat" this militant movement, on theories of the situation that are, at best, under-informed and always behind the times, basing our action on ends, ways and means derived from old thinking. Under informed because much that is relevant is hidden from view. Behind the times because situations involving humans are always evolving. And old thinking because no two situations are ever the same.

Military force becomes military power only when its application causes humans to react as intended. The purpose of any extended military campaign is to affect the choices and behaviors of specific sets of humans within that dynamic and interactive situation of human complexity.

It is the duty of military professionals to conceive of military strategies (conceptual schemes for applying power in a particular situation) with a high probability of causing specific and relevant humans to react as intended.

One way of evading that duty is to report physical tactical activity and its product as progress. During the Vietnam War progress was famously measured and reported by "body count." Today it is often measured and reported by the number of strikes and raids and their immediate physical product—things destroyed, and fighters or leaders killed or captured.

Another way of evading that duty is to construct strategies from collections of doctrinally enshrined off-the-shelf tactics. Today the favored collections of experience based <u>tactical</u> "best practices" are labeled Counter Insurgency (COIN) and Counter Terrorism (CT) strategies. COIN and CT are not strategies, and there is no wisdom in constructing strategies from a collection of off-the-shelf tactical "best practices." That's reversing the more effective thought process.

Making headway in any extended military endeavor designed to achieve such aims requires periodically making both conceptual choices of how to understand the always-opaque objective situation and practical choices of how to take concrete action to improve it. Progress is measured by evidence of intended changes in human choices and behaviors. And this evidence, while vital, is far more difficult to obtain than progress toward achieving the objectives of tactical actions.

The viability of strategies inherently expires as key circumstances of the situation evolve. Thus strategies require periodic revision, as a matter of course. Leaders must allow for this inevitability.

My own enquiries along this line have led me to the following core strategy for accomplishing the vital and very difficult tasks at the heart of the current crisis. And from the logic of that core strategy emerge the ends of grand strategic lines of effort. And from those emerges the logic of a grand strategy. And, in the other direction, the core strategy also governs the logic of the unique tactics required to make progress.

Summarizing The Core Strategy

Changing any intolerable status quo in human affairs into an acceptable one is ambitious. A useful core strategy needs to be specific about ends, ways and means. For instance, there is nothing ambiguous about destroying BG in place; apprehending and bringing to trial its criminal leaders, followers, and supporters; leaving behind stable, functioning, and extremist-resistant indigenous communities under a political regime their citizens consider legitimate; and laying down a useful precedent for similar challenges in the future. To achieving such complex ends, a useful core strategy must be designed along multiple lines of operations. In this case I suggest four distinct major lines of effort. Each of these can be described clearly in one short paragraph of simple declaratory sentences.

The first line of operations is the struggle over the legitimacy to govern, make laws, and enforce them within the BG occupied territory. It is between Al Baghdadi's group and *the alternative that will follow.* Winning this struggle requires creating stable, functioning, and extremist resistant indigenous communities under a political regime the people living in these communities consider legitimate.

The second is to defend the occupied populations in Syria and Iraq from the "armed propaganda" of the violent BG militants during the fighting for each community *and afterwards.* Winning along this line of effort requires a very disciplined interim political and security regime to provide immediate security.

The third is the offensive effort to destroy BG in place by defeating and capturing its fighters and arresting its agents and officials town-by-town and village-by-village. Winning along this line of effort would require two operational branches. A strong NATO effort is needed to choke off all sustenance from abroad and to destroy all internal logistical and command capability. And a strong and disciplined Sunni Arab led and NATO supported force is needed to destroy the "terrorist army" and its weapons; prevent the escape of its members to organize anew elsewhere; and to retain the moral high ground and legitimacy in the process.

The fourth line of effort is to design, build, and legitimate in global eyes, the judicial processes required for this "police action." This BG problem needs an international legal perspective to resolve it. How the alliance incarcerates, prosecutes and brings BG leaders and other criminal members to trial matters greatly. Not only is legitimacy an important facet of this strategy, but also it will remain so for the future worldwide struggle between and the forces of modernity and the remaining wide spread remnants, offspring, and cousins of this movement. Winning these future struggles will also require framing them as the fanatical against the reasonable, the civilized against the barbarian, the lawful against the lawless, and the modern against the medieval. As important as expeditious and fair disposition of cases is for the success of this "police action, setting a precedent for transparent, impartial and efficient judicial processes for future multi-national "police actions" will provide a great advantage. There is no doubt that large, sophisticated, well-organized, and violent transnational criminal organizations, whether motivated by greed or power, lie in our future.

The power of this strategy derives from synergy among the four major lines of effort, but a weakness in one cannot be compensated by the strength of another. In my mind, all four lines of effort are equally important, parallel, and mutually supporting. But I have deliberately bracketed the two fighting efforts between the legitimizing ones. And I have separated the fighting for keeping the people safe from the fighting against BG, because the logic of their fighting differs. I have separated the struggle for internal legitimacy from the struggle for external legitimacy for the same reason. The power to transform *intentions into desired outcomes* along each of these lines of effort depends on finding and applying an effective causal logic unique to this situation, which is the subject of the following paragraphs.

Winning the Local Legitimacy to Govern

Legitimacy is granted from below not imposed from above. The populations of these communities will be impressed by actions, not promises. An effective interim local replacement regime must be operational immediately in the aftermath of town-by-town and village-by-village fighting. How these communities will fit into a stable Syria or Iraq must be agreed among the intervening powers and the governments of Syria and Iraq from the start. And to meet the principal aim of this line of effort, there must be credible plans and funding to reconstruct economically viable villages, towns and cities in former BG occupied territories. And this work must start as soon as inhabited places are secure.

Any ruler relies on the support of the people for protection, intelligence, supplies, funds, and recruits. They also rely on public support to legitimate the power to apprehend, and bring criminals to trial and punishment. And, no government of outsiders imposed from above will be stable, extremist resistant, and functional in this situation.

Liberators, even if they are not outsiders, will have to win the people's allegiance away from BG. The support of the people is partly coerced through conquest. But many people of these territories chose to live there rather than under the rule of either the Syrian or Iraqi governments because they are better served by BG justice, public safety, and social services than by their former rulers. Some have immigrated there from neighboring provinces for the same reasons. Some would rather risk the deprivations and dangers of emigration to a country of strangers. Many endure BG rule for the sake of being at home and with family. Some become believers in the BG orthodoxy and cause when they are shown scriptural justification. Some immigrants arrive in these territories from abroad already converted to the BG orthodoxy and cause. While some may regret their choice as they experience the "caliphate" first hand, it would be a mistake to assume that it will be easy selling any post-BG regime to a harried and often disappointed people on both sided of the Iraqi-Syrian border.

There are some obvious mistakes to avoid. In the Afghan and Iraqi interventions we saw how quickly the relief of liberation from one oppressive regime can turn into dissatisfaction with the regime of a foreign liberator. Differences in nationality are not all that makes a foreigner. Iraqis and Syrians of a different religion and ethnicity will be judged "foreign" in the communities they liberate.

Also, there is no such thing as "ungoverned space" except when it is unpopulated. Some form of governance takes shape organically, and armed violent groups will either impose their form of order, or influence the existing one to their advantage.

People will favor indigenous governors over foreign ones. This is why foreigners have such difficulty establishing legitimate rule over indigenous people. To the extent BG is seen as foreign, and the replacement regime as indigenous, the better the result.

If a force comprised of allied "foreigners" is necessary to remove fighters from occupied communities and neighborhoods, the allied fighting force must shortly move on to the next fight and an interim indigenous political and security regime must take its place to organize, resource, and develop a functioning community under an acceptable and permanent indigenous governance. It would be unrealistic to expect Sunni communities in Anbar province, for instance, to accept as "indigenous" a Shia militia from anywhere else in Iraq. Likewise the successful relief of Kobani in Syria can be credited as much, or more, to the ethnic affinity of the Kurdish fighters on the ground to the citizens of the town than to the increased allied air support these fighters received.

At present, on the Iraq side of the border, US policy is to recover Iraqi towns and villages to Iraqi sovereign control. If T.E. Lawrence (Lawrence of Arabia) were to organize this effort he would insist, and I would agree, on a bottom up approach—first creating stable, functioning, and extremist resistant indigenous communities under a local political regime they consider legitimate. Lawrence would give members of the nearby Sunni Arab community a visible leading role in this line of effort. (He would probably try to enlist the Saudi rulers to organize and lead this effort.) In some local communities this leadership and public face would be Kurdish, Turkoman, Yazidi, or whatever combination of indigenous people mirrors the community. Others, who would stay out of these communities, could provide important support and backing. In order to be operational for the community immediately in the aftermath of the fighting, he would insist that an effective interim replacement regime be organized town-by-town and village-by-village before the fighting begins.

He would not try to install Western model governance. He would point out that there is no useful objective standard for governance, only a relative one. The governance of the replacement regime and its agencies must be better in the eyes of the people than the previous alternative.

He would then install a layer of autonomy between these communities and centralized nationalistic governance. And when they are incorporated into national political structures, they would have a voice in the government. How this will be done should be of vital interest to all of the allies, and cannot be left undetermined for later resolution. All this would be spelled out in treaty form before this phase of the allied intervention began.

Lawrence would not need to ask permission of the Ba'athist regime to operate on the Syrian side of the border. He would only need to confer with the Russians, informing them of his plans, and of his intentions to install air defenses there. He would then separate the territory still held by the Ba'athist regime of Bashar al Assad from the territories controlled by the various opposition groups.

To do that, he would enlist the government of Jordan to organize the defense of these communities, and the militias operating in and from them, into a self-defense alliance of mutual support. (Lawrence and the Jordanians would probably vet these militias based on the extremity of their actions rather than on their beliefs.) He would then urge the Jordanians, with NATO nation backing and support, to establish "all of government" aid and liaison parties specifically designed to meet the needs of these communities. (The alliance would then have the leverage to bargain with the Ba'athist regime over the future geography and government of Syria.)

This territory could then be used to stage operations against BG occupied villages, towns and cities. A similar bottom up approach, as employed on the Iraqi side of the border, would then ensue— first creating stable, functioning, and extremist resistant indigenous communities under a local political regime they consider legitimate.

Simultaneously to the above, Lawrence would then try to negotiate a cease-fire with the Ba'athists. If the Ba'athists refused, he would entrench the militias along the line of militia controlled territories and enhance air and ground defenses with NATO support.

Russia could be helpful. Lawrence would offer them the opportunity to fully join the alliance against BG if they deliver a Ba'athist ceasefire with the militias, and a treaty guaranteeing a reasonable level of autonomy to the territories held by BG and the various Sunni, Turkoman, and Kurdish militias. Having accomplished this, Russia would not feel obligated to defend Assad's regime from the militias, only from BG attacks. And their air operations could then be fully integrated into those of NATO forces.

If Russia cannot, or will not, then they will be a problem for the alliance. Russian air operations against BG may remain semi-independent and unpredictable. Without a ceasefire, Russia would need to be prepared to defend Ba'athist territory. And they could also strengthen Assad's bargaining power within a rump Syria.

However, the alliance can still meet it's goal of "leaving behind stable, functioning, and extremist-resistant indigenous communities under a political regime their citizens consider legitimate," by other means. These Sunni majority provinces can become independent or be joined to Jordan.

Defending the Population from "Armed Propaganda"

Once again, if T.E. Lawrence were to organize this effort he would insist, and I would agree, that removing BG without immediately securing the aftermath is a wasted effort because the "cancer" would otherwise return. A fearful and exposed population is lost to whoever attempts to govern next. Liberated communities need immediate protection from stay-behind BG elements and re-infiltration of BG fighters and agents.

Violent movements like BG extort intelligence, recruits, money, support, and compliance through fear, threat and cruel example—for example the numerous public beheadings that have been reported under BG rule. Without these enablers, violent movements wither. Once security and governing elements of BG are driven out of the communities they occupy, they will attempt to leave covert cells behind, or re-infiltrate them later. The proverbial "three men and one knife" in an otherwise unarmed community can control the people. The antidote is around-the-clock security, which is costly in manpower and difficult to emplace from the outside and is best done from inside out and bottom up, with motivated and trusted self-defense forces.

It would be the primary task of the interim political and security regimes to provide immediate security, to discover and arrest covert indigenous BG cells, and to recruit and train a competent and trustworthy indigenous self-defense force. Our community by community liberation plans would not only address removing BG control but would also plan for an interim political regime and a disciplined interim security force that rapidly is phased out as a permanent local force under local civilian control replaces it.

Because an interim security force must be immediately capable of discovering and arresting covert indigenous BG cells, a force, even a very professional one, of foreign NATO soldiers would not be our choice for this role. Neither would the community trust a very disciplined force of occupying Shia Arabs. Nor would they trust any *undisciplined* force capable of imposing a tyranny of their own. Best qualified would be *disciplined* members of Sunni Arabs tribes at least familiar to the people of the communities. Next best would be elite Sunni Arab units of neighboring powers. And, they must immediately begin to recruit and train a competent and trustworthy indigenous self-defense force.

Because this line of effort is also the most expensive in terms of trained and armed manpower, there is really no other alternative than local recruitment. Some studies based on rare historical successes in similar unstable situations have judged the price to be no less than 20 security personnel per 1,000 citizens.[ix] And doing this takes advantage of old-fashioned social and political structures to build local security forces.

It is possible to avoid the mistakes of the "Sunni Awakening" and "Son's of Iraq" model of several years ago. The Sunni Awakening of 2007 emerged unexpectedly. The US military command in Iraq took advantage of the willingness of Sunni tribal leaders to ally with US forces against Al Qaeda led insurgents in their home provinces in exchange for arms, pay and promises of power sharing in the central government. A force of nearly 80,000 Sunni fighters made up the "Sons of Iraq" by 2011. The Shia leaders of the government were frightened by the prospect of a nationwide "Sunni Army." As US forces left, so did the money to pay them. Iraqi promises to integrate them into the Armed Forces never materialized, and neither did promises of the Shia to share power with the Sunni.

This strategy proposes a fundamentally different model of local recruitment and political control. First, the local indigenous regimes that finally replace BG in the occupied communities emerge from the bottom up, as communities are "liberated." Second, the local security force they form and recruit (with outside assistance as described earlier) is automatically subordinated to whatever indigenous governmental structures evolve from the bottom-up.

Lawrence and I would facilitate a bottom up evolution of political and security regimes on both sides of the Syria-Iraq border. (This is more like the model of governmental evolution between 1775 and 1785 in America, and the opposite of what happened during the period of the French revolution—governance evolved there from Paris outward and down. The post-Ba'athist Iraqi regime also was reorganized from Baghdad outward and down—a strategic mistake.)

As proposed at the local community level, interim political and security regimes are planned and prepared ahead of time for every district and province. They are activated in the wake of the fighting, as they can begin to influence matters.

The interim security forces assigned at these levels are tailored to the specific needs of the situation. Here would be allied back-up reaction forces, and units with heavier weapons, transportation and support. Once local political regimes are able to appoint responsive representatives, they send them to the next higher level of government. Interim regimes and security forces melt away as indigenous ones take hold.

We should have learned in Afghanistan, and Iraq, that the key to regime change is not knocking down the undesirable one but quickly filling the power vacuum that follows regime collapse before the legitimacy of a "liberator," in many eyes, becomes the illegitimacy of an occupier, in all eyes. Foreign "liberators," even when they are cousins, can fill that vacuum only temporarily. They must waste no time gaining control of population centers, and commencing effective governance and security infrastructure building. The sooner "good enough" indigenous governing bodies and security forces replace foreigners the better the result, and the quicker and the more visible the draw-down of strangers the happier the indigenous community is to see them go and the more pleased people who sent them there are to welcome them home.

Fighting and Defeating the "Terrorist Army"

Thus, if T.E. Lawrence were to organize this effort he would insist, and I would agree, that keeping people safe and getting them on the side of peace under a legitimate local government is not enough, but being able to promise and deliver safety and legitimate alternative rule is an advantage in the fight to defeat the al Baghdadi regime and its "terrorist army." As Lawrence and his Arab allies did one hundred years ago, this mission will need a tailor-made way of organizing indigenous and foreign fighting forces, command structures and logistics. And, as then, they will need to adapt tactics learned earlier and elsewhere to the present strategy and the local situation.

Lawrence would make three relevant observations about the object of this effort. First, to be what it is, BG needs to promote and work toward a foreordained future caliphate. Thus, it needs to rule populated *territory*, and that territory *needs to expand*. BG will fight fanatically for every community and willingly take losses to retain populated ground, using brutal tactics, shielding itself among innocent civilians, and starving the population to remain well fed. Leaders and fighters of this movement are emboldened to take great risks because the Prophet has foreordained their success. This boldness, and the successes they have achieved, combines to attract action-oriented adherents from abroad. Breaking this success-fueled pattern of boldness, stemming the flow of reinforcements from abroad, containing and steadily reversing their territorial expansion are all key to their defeat.

Second, and equally defining of their identity, this movement (small compared to the forces the rest of the world could, and should, array against them) places a high priority on their own apocalyptic vision of a final end-time war ahead of a messianic redemption. Lawrence would ask, if they seek to bring about the final apocalyptic end-time war, not figuratively and some day, but literally and in the near term, how would they (the forces of virtue) stage this show down with us (Satan's corrupt and decadent minions of non-believers)? If what they, and al Qaeda, have done is demonstrate micro versions of the apocalypse in New York, Washington, London, Madrid, Mumbai, Beirut, Paris, elsewhere, and, more recently, in San Bernardino, then how do they intend to stage the main event? It is possible to over-think this. If a micro version of the apocalypse were the martyrdom of a small number of foot soldiers to kill hundreds, would they not be willing to martyr tens of thousands of them (and the citizens of the communities they rule) in exchange for hundreds of thousands of their assailants.

Third, when put like this, only fools would volunteer to assault the communities of the "caliphate." But the wise strategist would exploit some inherent asymmetric vulnerabilities of this "terrorist army." The geography of the "caliphate" the BG army needs to defend is one. They will have difficulty controlling the sandy and rocky empty space between the communities they need to defend. The connecting transportation links between them will also be difficult to defend and easy to interdict. The long and populated Euphrates valley is vulnerable to flanking and dissecting attacks. The size of the "terrorist army" relative to the size and distribution of the population centers it needs to defend is another. And they will have difficulty moving forces from one threat to another, once serious ground operations threaten multiple communities at once. And as every tyrant knows, the attentions of his army must divide between the enemy beyond the gates and the enemy within. Finally, they rule millions, with little opposition. But when they no longer appear invincible, and when the population senses a better alternative than being sacrificed for a fanatical cause, how will they maintain control?

Thus Lawrence would conclude that its "terrorist army" is the heart of the movement led by Abu Bakr al Baghdadi. It is the instrument of territorial control and expansion and for defeating Satan's minions. Because its members welcome death, and because defenses designed to threaten attackers with near certain death do not deter them, they have repeatedly frightened away ill trained and unconfident Iraqi and Syrian troops many times their number. Trained, confident and disciplined soldiers can reduce this "terrorist army's" strength and effectiveness; reverse this pattern of success; and confound their expectations of an apocalyptic end-times battle by disciplined and skilled fighting.

But an offensive against it, dependent mainly on inflicting losses on it from the air and by raiding, will not cause its leaders and members to quit. Such fighting methods leave crucial decisions of whether and when to quit murdering, looting and enslaving to fanatical leaders and fighters, prolonging the fighting, and inciting more of the people to support them. When the civilian populations suffer heavy casualties from air bombardment, the survivors will become enraged and join the defense.[x]

To defeat this "army" Lawrence would confront it with a two-armed approach, both focused and discriminating, so that the lives and property of the people BG has enslaved and impoverished are preserved. Retaining the moral high ground and legitimacy in the process is crucial to success. Together these two arms combine to enforce its destruction in place and prevent its escape to organize anew elsewhere.

One arm of this offensive will choke off all sustenance from abroad, and also destroy all of its internal logistics and internal command infrastructure. The first task will require *external* internationally coordinated police work. The second task will require *internal* military destruction, raiding and interdiction. While planning and executing the latter, it will be important to limit collateral damage to economic infrastructures needed to restore viable communities and their economies in the aftermath of fighting.

The second arm of this offensive enforces the in-place destruction of this "terrorist army" and its weapons and prevents the escape of its members to organize anew elsewhere. This option-eliminating and constricting arm includes: systematic encirclement of separate communities to reduce them piecemeal; simultaneous attacks from multiple directions to divide the "terrorist army's" fighting efforts; closing borders to escaping or reinforcing fighters and leaders; and relentless pursuit into sanctuaries to eliminate safe havens. It also plans and controls operations to constrict, and then stop, all forms of organized motorized movement throughout the "caliphate" except that allowed to provide humanitarian relief, medical evacuation, and authorized civilian traffic. It also shuts down all "terrorist army" support functions to include: the flow of information and orders among leaders; and arms, ammunition, and food for its fighters. It shuts down all BG income generating functions throughout these communities, (such as: taxation; extortion; and smuggling—especially of expropriated oil) and, most of all, the in-flow of immigrants and recruits.

The mission of destroying this "terrorist Army" in place, and preventing the escape of its members, will require a Sunni Arab led, and NATO supported, command. It will need to fight systematically for villages, towns, and cities, and perform the various supporting tasks outlined above. Therefore, it must train up for disciplined fighting, and for success at this specific mission. And this combat force must be large enough to threaten the "terrorist army" from multiple directions and in all relevant dimensions. When these soldiers go into combat they must believe in their cause, their comrades, and their skills.

In principle, this command will allocate tasks to the ally best suited to the mission. Its Sunni Arab assault brigades attach NATO liaison and advisory teams and indigenous military police detachments. To every three Sunni Arab brigades within an allied assault division, Americans and other NATO members can provide a reinforcing combat brigade of four mobile and armor protected battalions augmented with intelligence, artillery, engineers, aviation, and logistics. The mission of this complement of foreigners is to reinforce and support the requests of the Sunni Arab brigades leading the fight for the communities. These reinforcing NATO units would position in easily defensible terrain outside populated areas but within supporting distance of the assault brigades they reinforce.

Lawrence would suggest, and I would agree, that forces be marshaled, trained, and rehearsed months ahead of commitment and outside the combat zone. It will take time to build up such a force. And during their preparations they need to be beyond reach of spoiling attacks. Teamwork and mutual trust is important within multi-national combined assault forces. When ready, these forces assault Abu Bakr al Baghdadi's forces from multiple directions nearly simultaneously, depriving the "terrorist army" the ability to mass fighters against sequential threats.

When the combined assault divisions described above attack the detachments of the "terrorist army" in encircled communities, the method of clearing them of gang members reduces in microcosm to the method of clearing one room. The present method is to guess which rooms the enemy occupies and then to bomb them, hoping the guess is correct and no innocents are killed or hurt. This was also a choice for young American commanders between 2005 and 2007, when the mission was clearing out the earlier version of this gang of cutthroats from Fallujah and Ramadi. These commanders chose to clear thousands of rooms with squads of soldiers or marines.[xi] The leaders and members of these squads chose to fight within the legal strictures of international laws of armed conflict, accepting risk and exercising "due care" for civilian casualties. Advantageous conditions for accomplishing this task were set.

At some point in the defense of a besieged community, the population will realize that their "protectors" are their jailers, and willing to sacrifice their lives. Non-combatants anywhere are clever, bold and inventive when warned of danger and allowed to escape. Thus, fewer civilians are likely to be in the room when the squad enters.

Meanwhile, prior tactics have insured that the armed gangsters in the room are sleep deprived, hungry, ill equipped and low on ammunition. The squad's mission then is to capture those who quit fighting and to kill those who won't. Squads of Sunni Arab soldiers must now perform this mission. Americans can train, advise, support and reinforce.

If al Baghdadi is willing to martyr the lives of tens of thousands of his fighters in defense of his "caliphate," then this approach will give him that opportunity, but it will not grant him the results he desires. A well-trained and disciplined allied army to execute it will confound his expectations. Many of his fighters may choose to fight to their death, as rooms are systematically cleared in the fighting, but the victors' losses will be light in comparison. And most of the people of the community will escape being "sacrificed" in the fighting.

Captured BG fighters and leaders are now handed over to the forward detachments of the legal system we will discuss next. Having "cleared" this community the assaulting forces move on refit and prepare for the next mission, while the community designated interim replacement political and security regime immediately begins to organize, resource, and develop a functioning community under acceptable and permanent indigenous governance. Other forces seal borders and prevent escape to sanctuaries. Still others follow to provide reserves and support. All of them win firefights quickly and decisively through preparation and training, and use disciplined fighting practices designed to avoid casualties and unnecessary collateral damage.

Winning Global Popular Legitimacy Against Transnational Terrorists and Criminals

Having in place a parallel international effort of coordinated police work, prosecutors, courts, and prisons will be essential to defeating this criminal movement. As BG gangsters and suspected collaborators are captured in the operations described above, they are immediately turned over to detachments of Sunni Arab police operating within the specialized Combined Assault Divisions. From there investigators, prosecutors and jailers prepare cases against them and hold them for trial. How the alliance handles the incarceration, prosecution and trials of BG leaders and other criminal members will certainly affect the success of the present global campaign against BG, and the stability of the aftermath in the communities they have ruled. Old precedents will fail in this case. (In an earlier section I have explained why it is unwise to choose the logic of war to combat crime.[xii]) And new ones need to be established to follow in future cases of a similar kind.

Up to this point in the description of this strategy, there is little to distinguish the fighting of a "police action" from the fighting of a war. The difference, if any, is that the object of the fighting during a police action is to overcome the violent resistance to capture and bring individual criminals to trial. During war, the two sides fight primarily to cause the other side to quit. The objects of war have always been to impose outcomes on a collective polity, even before modern states existed. The object of a police action is to hold individuals accountable for crimes they have committed, when normal "policing" doesn't work—especially when criminals band together in great enough strength to challenge the power of the state to stop their crimes and punish them. But more importantly in this case, the transfer of captives is from a military organization that captured them to the organs of a system of justice.

And also up to this point, the soldiers engaged in ridding the world of Abu Bakr al Baghdadi's movement have fought and captured the resisting movement members, as they would have the leaders and soldiers of any state at war with the state they serve. If the capture was done according to the international laws governing the means and methods of war, how much more stringent would be the laws governing the capture of armed criminals in a shootout with police in Paris or San Bernardino? None. The suspected criminal captured by the police would be tried in a civil court for resisting arrest, murder or attempted murder while doing so, and also for any prior crimes that can be proven. The enemy soldier, on the other hand, would not be tried for defending himself, even if he has killed while he did. But, if he had committed wanton murder against non-combatants, a military tribunal would try him for war crimes. So, in our case of Abu Baker al Baghdadi's captured associates, what would be the advantage of choosing to call them "enemy combatants," a category in the gray area between being a soldier and a gangster?

This is what the US Government chose to do with members of al Qaeda captured in Afghanistan after the mass murder by twenty Al Qaeda Members on September 11th, 2001. American authorities chose to "go to war" with a violent movement that wasn't a state and lacked a fixed permanent address. And, as a consequence of that choice, could label al Qaeda captives "enemy combatants."

Creating this category provided two perceived conveniences. Captive "enemy combatants" could be treated as prisoners of war, kept in military prisons, and interrogated more conveniently for intelligence. Military tribunals patterned after the post-WWII War Crimes Tribunals could be used to hear their cases. And, elusive al Qaeda senior operatives could be assassinated when found, if a Federal Judge reviewed the cases against them and judged them sufficient. "Common" criminals can't be held in military prisons and can't just be assassinated.

Were these conveniences really advantageous? America's strategists should abandon this strategy for two reasons: it isn't working; and it's an impediment to moving on to a strategy that will.

The strategy isn't working because responsible military professionals and their political masters are again evading their duty to craft sound strategy as they have historically by confusing successful tactics with strategic progress. Officials responsible for defeating these movements take refuge in doctrinally enshrined <u>tactical</u> "best practices" to justify the present <u>strategy</u>. They also report the results of tactics as progress toward strategic ends, such as "body count" was during the Vietnam War. Today we hear reports of killed or captured terrorists and their leaders and of destroyed weapons and installations, rather than measures of how such tactical results combined to cause desired changes in the size, scope and activities of the remaining movement.

The record of America's military prisons and tribunals, as well as its unilateral and uncoordinated assassination attempts in foreign countries (especially when there has been collateral damage) has de-legitimized its fight against al Qaeda, especially in the region we now need allies the most, the Middle East and Pakistan. For example, already in August 2014 the Grand Mufti of Sunni Islam in Egypt, Shawqi Allam, denounced al Baghdadi's movement as "an extremist and bloody group" that "poses a danger to Islam and Muslims, tarnishing its image as well as shedding blood and spreading corruption." He also added that they "give an opportunity for those who seek to harm us, to destroy us and interfere in our affairs with the (pretext of a) call to fight terrorism." This, clearly, is not an open invitation for Americans to solve this problem for the Muslim people. It would be helpful to shift the discussion with the Sunni Muslim community from intolerable "extremism" within <u>their</u> religion to intolerable crimes and criminals, whatever the religion, and how such criminals can be apprehended and brought to justice.

There is precedent in plain sight. In other cases, both in America and abroad, al Qaeda terrorists were successfully treated as criminals, held in civilian jails, interrogated, and tried in civilian courts, all within the existing laws of the countries that had jurisdiction in the case.

Modern states do not tolerate crimes, no matter what the motivation. They allow people to be passionate about religion, but they draw the line when passion leads to crime. Some Americans Christians may be passionate about what abortion clinics do, but their religious beliefs do not absolve them of burning down these clinics or killing the doctors who staff them. Some Muslims in Middle Eastern countries may be passionate about the invasion of their way of life by Western Culture, but their religious beliefs do not absolve them, in the eyes of most of their fellow citizens, from killing or injuring those who are attracted to it.

We should shift the discussion with the Sunni Muslim community from intolerable "extremism" within <u>their</u> religion to the commission of intolerable crimes against a broader civilized community we share. Then the kind of police action I describe here appears more legitimate from all relevant perspectives—that of the people in the communities al Baghdadi rules, the people in the region who will fight his "terrorist army," and the people outside the region who will support that fight. It is for the first two of these groups to reconcile universal modern laws about murder looting, and enslaving with ancient and revered Koranic scripture. We in the third group and all of our allies of the second should instead be concerned about the legitimacy of our own conduct.

Where BG fighters may claim to be regulated by 7th century Koranic scriptures, the conduct of all allied fighters must be as regulated by international law. When BG fighters bear arms and use them, in modern eyes everywhere, they become common criminals, not even "war criminals." The modern legal logic is this: when BG fighters are captured, they are arrested, tried by legitimate authorities, and punished for their crimes according to the laws of the country where they committed them or under international law. The alliance must decide the particulars of the incarceration, prosecution and trials of BG leaders and other criminal members. And a robust and just judicial system must be ready when BG captives are caught. In principle, legitimate international authorities, the nations who bore the costs of capture, and the people who have been oppressed by BG, must together judge the prisons and courts legitimate.

In Closing

Ridding the world of this scourge will require more than the wishful thinking and half-measures that took America to War in Afghanistan and Iraq. It will require deep commitment, not only by Americans, but it will also require the commitment of a broad coalition to share the burdens and carry it out. Most of all, it will require clear and realistic thinking about warfare in the modern age.

By current means and methods the global struggle with al-Qaeda inspired movements, such as Abu Bakr al Baghdadi's gang, will continue into the foreseeable future. Both they and we will keep learning and adapting. American leaders should learn that the strategy of defending the homeland, while waging an old fashioned war of attrition abroad is a formula for perpetual warfare. This strategy can "degrade," and "disrupt" but not "defeat". We have yet to see the effects of an option-eliminating, constricting, peace-enforcing offensive strategy of "defeat" anywhere. What America must learn to do is to shift the framing of the problem from being a matter of religious beliefs, and thus outlawing and condemning the "extreme" beliefs of one religion in particular, to being a matter of outlawing, condemning, stopping and punishing violent crimes of powerful gang members. And then learn to shape the global strategy and lead a global effort based on the logic of the "quartet" outlined above. This will mean leading while remaining mostly in the background, as the main struggle is fought "by, with, and through" Muslim allies to create stable, functioning, and extremist resistant indigenous communities.

The task, as described here, is immense. If it is undertaken, it will take time and resources. Politicians eager to please the public will either support the current Counter Terrorism (CT) "strategy" in some form or intensity or, if they agree that ground operations are necessary, they will down play the risks of taking on this mission and allocate too little to the effort.

This tendency of political calculation reflects the present public's expectation that it should be able to vent its emotions and not pay the entry fee. A feature of post-Vietnam military interventions by Americans and their Western allies has been freedom from the normal privations a society accepts as a consequence of war. In the modern industrialized countries of the world, like America, small well-paid professional Armed Forces insure that casualties are limited to the small circle of family and friends of the volunteers who serve in combat. Not even the privations formerly meted out by the mandatory "guns versus butter" trade-off are felt due to robust and growing economies, and the ability to finance budget deficits.

There is no safe, scientific way to estimate troop requirements. In this case it is foolish, even reckless, to economize. The larger the force, the more easily it can divide to attack multiple places at once and fix in place the limited number of fighters al Baghdadi can muster. It is better and safer to over-estimate the initial force requirement and send troops home as soon as they are not needed, than to start the intervention short-handed. There will be fewer casualties and quicker mission accomplishment. The reverse is a certain formula for high casualties and a lengthy war.

There will be great temptations to compromise the principles of this strategy in execution. While keeping people safe and getting them on the side of peace under a legitimate local government is not enough to defeat BG's "terrorist army," without the leverage these parallel efforts provide, the sacrifices required to defeat it might be in vain. And none of these aims can be achieved without allied unity, disciplined execution and an enabling grand strategy.

Chapter 49

Kurdistan: The Permanent Solution to Daesh

Joshua A. Perkins

First Published 27 December 2015

Introduction

History has taught us that when an armed conflict arises between two belligerents, countries with interests in the outcome of that conflict either need to pick a winner, a loser, or stay out of the conflict. If containment or maintaining the status quo is chosen it naturally results in perpetual conflicts, e.g., Israel and the Palestinian Liberation Organization (PLO) /Hezbollah. In this scenario, the weaker belligerent is never defeated through armed conflict or forced to recognize that eventuality. They are allowed to carry on in the conflict. The weaker belligerent never has reason to seek peace terms as a part of their surrender, and is free to continue to harass its opponent because a state or non-state actor, like the United Nations, maintains the status quo regardless of how chaotic that is for regional or international stability. The best choice a state can make is to decide which side it supports and *give war a chance*, in order to remove the other belligerent so that true stability can be achieved.[1]

The United States (U.S.) is currently seeking a solution to the problem 'ad-Dawlah al-Islamiyah fi 'I-'Iraq wa-sh-Sham' (Daesh; aka ISIS, ISIL, the Islamic State) poses to U.S. security, its allies, and civilization in general. The answer: recognize and support the state of 'Kurdistan'. Pick a winner, Kurdistan, and a loser, Daesh, and give war a chance. This decision has two affects. In the short-term, this solution halts Daesh's growth and freedom of movement in the region, thus ending their threat to regional stability. In the long-term, it thwarts Russia's influence in the region. In the absence of this support for Kurdistan, Russia will be the victor. Russia will expand its sphere of influence over the entire Middle East because they have chosen a winner in Syria. It is clear that Putin's final goal is not just to save the Assad regime, but "He [Putin] also means to forge a counter-alliance [against the U.S] consisting of Russia, Iran, Iraq, Syria, and Lebanese Hezbollah and demonstrate that his coalition is more effective than the West's."[2]

Why Kurdistan?

As political commentator David Webb noted, "If we [the U.S.] take out ISIS, we have Assad. If we take out Assad, we have ISIS. If we take out both, we have a vacuum."[3] It's clear from U.S. leaders, whether they be executive, congressional, or presidential hopefuls, that U.S. troops on the ground are not the solution the U.S. is seeking. Senator Rand Paul speaking more broadly on terrorism said, "If we want to defeat terrorism…the boots on the ground need to be Arab boots on the ground."[4] NATO General Secretary Jens Stoltenberg revealed to Reuters that NATO will not send any ground troops to combat Daesh.[5] As a result, if the U.S. wants to defeat Daesh, the boots on the ground need to be Kurdish boots, a viable ally for the U.S. to support. There is no need for the U.S. to roll the dice on supporting "moderate" jihadist groups when it has a known partner it has been working with for over a decade in Iraq. This paper discusses Kurdistan's demographics, economy, and, most importantly, its military capabilities which will demonstrate Kurdistan's viability as a permanent regional partner. It also examines the effects recognizing Kurdistan as an independent state to defeat Daesh will have on Turkey, Iraq, other regional allies, and Russia's burgeoning Shia alliance.

Kurdistan

Demographics

What will this new Kurdistan look like? 'Kurdistan' when referred to in this article is Iraqi Kurdistan, an autonomous region that is part of Iraq's federal system.[6] It also refers to what Kurdistan could be if it was an independent state that absorbed the Syrian territory that Syria is unable to govern and is currently controlled by Daesh.

Kurdistan has existed in a similar condition to its current state since 1991.[7] In terms of landmass, Kurdistan currently occupies 30,400 square miles. That's equivalent to the size of the Czech Republic.[8] Estimates of the landmass Daesh controls varies depending on the definition used, e.g., controlling versus influencing, but estimates on the low end put it at 13,000 square miles and estimates on the high end have it at 35,000 square miles.[9] If Kurdistan absorbed the landmass controlled by Daesh that would put Kurdistan on par with Honduras on the low end and Cambodia on the high end.[10]

Kurdistan's population is currently 5.2 million.[11] For terms of comparison, that would be equivalent to Norway's population.[12] Kurdistan has three primary religious groups: Islam, Christianity, and Yazdanism and has a democratic parliament to represent their respective interests. Kurdistan's Parliament has several parties that participate in governing, but there are two ruling parties in Kurdistan, the Kurdistan Democratic Party (KDP), a social democratic party, and the Patriotic Union of Kurdistan (PUK), a moderate conservative party.[13]

Kurdistan is in a unique and key position in the region because, if its military were armed with modern armament, it has a central government capable of administering the Daesh territory that comes under its control.

Economy

Kurdistan's current economy has a gross domestic product (GDP) of $23.6 billion.[14] The energy industry comprises the largest share of Kurdistan's GDP at 22%.[15] The Kurdistan Regional Government (KRG) signed an oil-sales agreement with Iraq's central government in Baghdad that mandates the KRG provide 570,000 barrels per day, 15% of Iraq's 3.8 million barrel daily output, to Iraq's state-owned Oil Marketing Company (SOMO).[16] In exchange, the KRG receives 17% of Iraq's federal expenditure budget.[17]

If Kurdistan annexes the territory controlled by Daesh it would add an additional $40 million per month ($500 million/year) to its national treasury via energy resources.[18] The Omar oil field alone, which is under Daesh control, produces up to $5 million per month in income.[19] In addition to the Omar field there are seven other oil fields controlled by Daesh: the Tanak, El Isbah, Sijan, Jafra, Azraq, Barghooth, and Abu Hardan oil fields.[20]

Prior to the November Paris attack, the U.S. was hesitant to attack Daesh's fleet of fuel tanker trucks because of civilian casualties and environmental damage.[21] Daesh has a fleet estimated to be at least 1,000 vehicles strong.[22] Following the Paris attack, Daesh's distribution network was targeted by the U.S. resulting in 116 trucks being destroyed by the U.S.[23] With the U.S., France, and Russia all targeting Daesh's fuel tanker fleet it's hard to say how many vehicles remain, but if Kurdistan is recognized and afforded the opportunity and support to secure the region, there are enough vehicles to still add to Kurdistan's own fuel tanker vehicle infrastructure in order to boost its energy sector.

Oil is not Kurdistan's only natural resource. If stability were achieved to allow foreign corporations to invest in the region, there are also gold, iron, uranium, and magnesium deposits all waiting to be explored.[24]

Military

Kurdistan's military force is the Peshmerga, which means "those who face death".[25] Last year the KRG's parliament passed reform to bring the Peshmerga forces under KRG President Massoud Barzani's actual control versus his previously nominal control.[26] Prior to this reform the two ruling political parties controlled their Peshmerga forces. The KDP has between 30,000 and 40,000 Peshmerga soldiers and the PUK has 25,000 Peshmerga soldiers.[27] The KRG's own estimates have each party controlling 50,000 soldiers each and having another 50,000 soldiers each as part of their reserve forces.[28]

Those numbers will have fluctuated over the past year with recruitment as their war with Daesh ramps up and with casualties suffered; but with a force of 165,000 soldiers versus Daesh's CIA estimated 31,500 fighters or Baghdad's estimated 100,000 fighters the question has to be asked, "why isn't Kurdistan more successful?"[29]

The reason is because the armament the Peshmerga have to combat Daesh are from the Iran-Iraq war.[30] Kurdish Major General Sirwan Barzani believes that Daesh has up to 10 times the number of weapons available to Peshmerga forces.[31] The weaponry Daesh has includes mines, C4, sniper rifles, mortars, etc.,[32] whereas the weaponry Peshmerga forces use are a hodgepodge of AK-47s, M16s, and DshKs that the fighters bring themselves from home.[33]

Another reason Kurdistan is having limited success combating Daesh is because the U.S. will not arm Peshmerga forces directly and has even blocked other Middle East countries from doing so as well.[34] European countries have banned together to purchase weapons to supply to the Peshmerga, however, the U.S. has blocked the transfer of those munitions too.[35] Any military aid the Peshmerga receive from the U.S. is indirect. The U.S. gives military aid to Baghdad and it is then Baghdad's responsibility to distribute that aid to the KRG.[36] What priority does Shia controlled Baghdad place on transferring that aid to the KRG when Baghdad is still trying to retake areas controlled by Daesh in Iraq, like Mosul? Baghdad is blocking military aid to Peshmerga forces and refusing to transfer money to the KRG to pay Peshmerga salaries in an effort to reduce the size of Kurdistan's forces.[37] How likely is it that the KRG receives those U.S. arms considering Baghdad's current posture towards Kurdish strength? This problem is compounded in light of the arms Baghdad lost abandoning weapons caches to Daesh in previous 'battles'.

Even with the Peshmerga's limited resources they are still having success combating Daesh. In November, the Peshmerga retook Sinjar, located in Kurdistan's Nineveh Province, in an attempt to cut off a key supply route between Mosul and Raqqa.[38] However, without direct military aid the Peshmerga are not able to extend their gains in Sinjar. Daesh located an unimproved route to the south of Sinjar and brought in gravel to reinforce the route to continue its resupply mission between Raqqa and Mosul.[39]

Iraq

It is a real possibility that oil may be the issue that unravels Iraq's federal system without any U.S. involvement. What was agreed to between Baghdad and the KRG and what has actually materialized from the SOMO agreement is that the KRG has started to sell their oil directly to Turkey through the port of Ceyhan.[40] This is due partly because Baghdad has paid the KRG less than half of what was owed to them under the oil-sale agreement.[41] Add to that, Iraq's Ministry of Oil expects revenue to decrease by 27% in 2015 that will affect the 17% of Iraq's budget that the KRG would receive from Baghdad.[42] The KRG is also selling their oil directly to the open market, rather than using SOMO, because they are under a budget crunch from fighting

Daesh and because they were paid upfront by oil traders, whom the KRG must repay, in an effort to support their fight.[43] At the same time, Kurdistan's budget deficit has been amplified because the conflict with Daesh has led to the KRG handling 2 million displaced refugees that has cost the KRG $1.4 billion thus far.[44]

It's time to treat allies as allies and quasi-allies and non-allies as such. All of this leads to the inevitable conclusion that it is time for the U.S. to aid a new ally Kurdistan and decrease or stop funding a quasi-ally, Baghdad. Is Baghdad allied with Iran or the U.S? If the U.S. recognizes Kurdistan, Baghdad will object to its lost revenue, but Iraq's federal system is precarious at best. It's hard to imagine Baghdad is an ally on par with England and France considering their close ties with Iran, a fellow Shia government, whose official position is "Death to America."[45]

Also of concern to the U.S. is Iraq's growing relationship with Iran through its ties with Russia. Iraqi Brigadier General Tahseen Ibrahim speaking about Russia using Iraqi airspace said, "If Russia needs to participate in aircraft reconnaissance flights, it can make a formal request to the Iraqi government and there will be no objection in my opinion."[46] One month after Brigadier General Ibrahim's comments, the U.S. and Russia signed a memorandum of understanding about the use of airspace over Syria and Iraq.[47] The language of the memorandum has remained secret, but one result of the agreement is that after an ultimatum was delivered by Chairman of the Joint Chiefs of Staff, General Joseph Dunford, to Iraqi Prime Minister Haider al-Abadi, Iraq will not request Russia aircraft into its airspace or risk losing U.S. support.[48]

Should the U.S. be concerned with Iraqi objections over Kurdish independence when Kurdistan will be a stronger ally for the U.S. in the region and Iraq's interests only align with the U.S.'s after an ultimatum is delivered by the most senior military officer in the U.S. Armed Forces?

Turkey

Perception in the U.S. is that the biggest obstacle to recognizing Kurdistan as an independent state is Turkey, but is that true? Recent evidence suggests that might not be the case. On December 4, 2015, Turkey sent Turkish troops to the Nineveh Province to train Peshmerga soldiers against the express demands of Iraq's central government that Turkey removes its forces from Iraqi territory.[49]

The misconception about Turkish obstinacy to Kurdish independence is focused around the Kurdistan Workers' Party (PKK). The PKK is listed by the United States and the North Atlantic Treaty Organization (NATO) as a terrorist organization. The PKK is a Kurdish ethnic organization focused on greater political rights *within* Turkey's border not with Kurdistan's independence from Iraq.[50] The PKK formerly carried out attacks in Turkey, but recently declared a cease-fire since their leader has been captured. The reality, as one Middle East analyst notes, is that "relations between Turkey and the Kurdish administration are good, neither side sees the other as a threat."[51] Turkey has a vested interest in seeing Daesh destroyed because Daesh has started crossing into Turkey and killing its citizens.[52]

If the U.S. is in favor of recognizing Kurdistan's sovereignty as a state it is hard to imagine that Turkey would oppose that decision in light of Russia's violation of Turkish air space on November 24, 2015 that forced Turkey to shoot down a Russian Su-24.[53] The U.S. has significant leverage via NATO and Turkey's right to invoke Article V for its mutual defense within that organization. Turkey does not want to jeopardize its U.S. support when Russia now occupies an air base in Latakia, Syria.

The air base in Latakia is only 31 miles from the Turkish border and is oriented north-south, meaning the Russian Su-24 can be in Turkish airspace in the span of minutes.[54] "It could be almost impossible to tell if such a fighter intended to cross into Turkey or turn east to operate against rebels until the very last moment."[55] This prediction was accurate and evidence shows that after Russia's Su-24 was shot it took a 90-degree turn east in an attempt to leave Turkish airspace.[56]

Russia

The greatest misstep made in the fight against Daesh has been delaying to act forcefully. In delaying, the U.S. created an opportunity for Russia to move troops into the region. According to Frederick and Kimberly Kagan:

"The Russian deployment severely constrains Western options within Syria and may come to challenge America's ability to continue to operate in Iraq as well. Russian aircraft flying around Syria give Moscow absolute veto power over any attempt to establish any sort of no-fly zone or ISIS-free zone, unless the U.S. and its partners are prepared to risk aerial combat with the Russian Air Force. Russian planes can escort Syrian Air Force (SAF) aircraft on missions, fly combat air patrols (CAP) to protect Syrian helicopters engaged in barrel-bombing, and harass U.S. or NATO aircraft or drones attempting to enforce ISIS-free zones."[57]

Russian use of the Syrian air base in Latakia is an even bigger risk to U.S. national security because it allows Russia to stalk the U.S. 6th Fleet in the Mediterranean Sea.[58] It also allows Russia to control airspace in the Middle East indirectly because the U.S. and its allies want to avoid putting their aerial assets at risk and they will need to reach out to Russia to de-conflict airspace.[59] In effect, this allows Russia to control airspace because they will have visibility on any U.S. or NATO air missions.

Other Regional Actors

Iran

Iran stands to lose, in terms of the regional balance of power, if Kurdistan is recognized and supported as an independent state. Its ally, Shia controlled Baghdad, will lose a large share of its revenues from oil rich Kurdish territory. Kurdistan has the potential to serve as a bulwark against Iran's objectives in the region similar to the way Saddam Hussein's Iraq did in the 1980s and 1990s. Kurdistan and Iran will become a regional microcosm of the Cold War bipolar balance of power that existed between the U.S.S.R and the U.S. *if* the U.S. provides Kurdistan with direct and substantial military aid.

Saudi Arabia

Similar to how the U.S. wanted to surround Iran with democracies to pressure a change in that state it could be Russia's true objective to surround Saudi Arabia with Shia allies to pressure an economic change in Saudi Arabia's energy policies, which will affect the U.S. economy. With global oil prices reaching new lows, $36 per barrel, it is Russia and Iran who is affected the most because both their economies are heavily dependent on energy prices.[60] Saudi Arabia would likely support Kurdish independence because it diminishes the strength of the Shia regimes in the region.

Syria

If Kurdistan is supported as an independent state and absorbs the Syrian territory controlled by Deash, it stands to reason that Syria's strength would be cut in half and potentially end their influence over Lebanon. Syria would then be between the vise of Israel and Kurdistan and there is evidence that Israel and Kurdistan could become strong allies in the Middle East. Supporting Syrian rebel groups does not permanently solve the problem of Daesh or Assad. The U.S. has provided direct military aid to Syrian rebels[61], but evidence shows that the rebels fighting in Syria don't necessarily disagree with Daesh; they would just rather be the group in Daesh's position of power.[62]

Israel

It is important to remember that Kurds are not Arab. Kurdistan has been selling oil directly to Israel, which is in Kurdistan's interest to keep quite considering the influence Baghdad has over their finances and the influence Iran has over Baghdad.[63] The loss of Syrian influence over Lebanon would decrease the support Hezbollah receives in Lebanon. Thus, decreasing the threat Israel faces against Hezbollah's terrorism. It is no wonder Israel wants to strengthen its relationship with Kurdistan.[64]

Conclusion

Failing to take action against Daesh is a decision to cede influence in the Middle East to Russia. Abdicating U.S. leadership and support in the Middle East will lead to two outcomes: 1) our partners will fall under the Russian sphere of influence, or; 2) Sunni states will turn to Daesh, or other Sunni groups, in an attempt to balance against Russia and its Shia alliance.

In fighting Daesh there is a chain of support that threatens U.S. security. The U.S. continuing to support Iraq, through Baghdad, only increases the power of Iran. Helping Iran aids Syria. Aiding Syria is Russia's goal to keep Assad in power. The U.S. is weakening itself with its current strategy to contain/defeat Daesh.

The choice to break that cycle of self-defeat is to recognize Kurdistan as an independent state and immediately support them with direct military aid. It is military aid that they can afford to finance through their oil revenues and other natural resources. Kurdistan has the will and the ground forces to fight Daesh. Kurdistan needs the modern jets, tanks, armored personnel carriers, artillery pieces, and small arms to be effective. Supporting Kurdistan also strengthens the position of U.S. allies in the region, e.g., Turkey, Israel, and Saudi Arabia.

History has shown the U.S. must pick a winner, and in this case it is Kurdistan. This will allow the U.S. to give war a chance and to show U.S. allies that they have a committed partner in the Middle East and that tepid partners will not receive benefits their actions have not warranted.

Postscript

Ten Endgames of an Effective Counter-Insurgency Against IS

Joshua Sinai

Alexandria, VA

May 2016

As discussed in this volume's Foreword and its 50 chapters, it is crucial to understand the nature of one's adversary in order to formulate an effective strategy to counter it. Moreover, with the Islamic State (IS) as a "complex adaptive system" with multiple centers of gravity (i.e., in its control of territory and administrative services in Syria, Iraq, and cyberspace, as well as in its areas of armed operations that extend into the Sinai Peninsula, the Maghreb in North Africa, and elsewhere, along with those radicalized adherents and operatives spreading throughout Western Europe, North America, and numerous other regions), an effective counter-strategy would have to be comprehensive, multi-dimensional, and multilateral in order to succeed in defeating it militarily, politically, and ideologically/theologically.

With IS being a hybrid military organization that combines terrorism and guerrilla operations in its warfare, its control of substantial swaths of territory—as well as economic enterprises—in Syria and Iraq, and its ability to attract thousands of recruits worldwide to join its fighting forces through its ideological appeal, what are the specific endgames of a successful counter-insurgency campaign against it? Based on the volume's chapters and the literature on effective counter-insurgency, the following ten endgames, which are inter-related, are proposed:

1. Arresting or "terminating" significant numbers of insurgent military and political leaders, their operational managers, and operatives in order to degrade the organization's military capability.
2. Sufficiently degrading the organization's ability to acquire new arms and military materiel to conduct warfare.
3. Defeating the organization in sufficiently important military engagements to render it militarily insignificant.
4. Greatly curtailing the organization's control over economic resources in Syria and Iraq, including cutting off its external funding.
5. Preventing foreign recruits from reaching the organization's areas of operation in Syria and Iraq.
6. Drastically curtailing and shrinking the organization's control over territory, including eliminating its safe havens.
7. Significantly curtailing and eliminating the organization's activities in cyberspace, thereby also reducing its radicalization appeal to new adherents.
8. Preventing the organization's operatives in Syria and Iraq from entering Western countries in order to conduct terrorist operations in those countries.
9. Formulating a counter-narrative that is effective at shutting own the appeal of IS propaganda.
10. Establishing legitimate and popular regimes in Syria and Iraq that are effective at controlling their territories and providing effective social-welfare and judicial services to their populations.

Although these ten endgames of effective counter-insurgency will cumulatively significantly degrade and defeat an insurgent organization such as IS, they are not intended to be implemented in a linear or sequential manner. Moreover, other specific endgames are also likely to prove effective, as the unique environments of Syria, Iraq, and other countries where IS operates may require other tailored counter-insurgency solutions.

Notes

Foreword:
Foreword: The Islamic State (IS) as a Complex Adaptive System

No notes.

Introduction:
Jihadi Terrorism, Insurgency, and the Islamic State in Context

Notes

[1]. Shia radicalism, as it pertains to Iran and Hezbollah as a threat to the U.S. and its allies, has also been focused upon in *SWJ*. See Dave Dilegge, Alma Keshavarz, and Robert J. Bunker, eds., *Iranian and Hezbollah Hybrid Warfare Activities—A Small Wars Journal Anthology*. Bloomington: iUniverse, 2016.

[2]. For a timeline of the Islamic State since 1999, the various names associated with it, and some of its early history, see Daveed Gartenstein-Ross and Bridget Moreng, "Foreword: The Islamic State's Growth and Misrule, and the Future of Violent Non-State Actors." Dave Dilegge and Robert J. Bunker, eds., *Global*

Radical Islamist Insurgency: Al Qaeda and Islamic State Networks Focus Vol. II: 2012-2014—A Small Wars Journal Anthology. Bloomington: iUniverse, 2016: xxvii-xli. For further readings on the Islamic State, see Jessica Stern and J.M Berger, *ISIS: The State of Terror.* New York: HarperCollins, 2015; William McCants, *The ISIS Apocalypse: The History, Strategy, and Doomsday Vision of the Islamic State.* New York: St. Martin's Press, 2015; and Joby Warrick, *Black Flags: The Rise of ISIS.* New York: Doubleday, 2015.

[3]. Cameron Glenn, "Timeline: The Rise and Spread of the Islamic State." *The Islamists.* Wilson Center. 5 July 2016, https://www.wilsoncenter.org/article/timeline-rise-and-spread-the-islamic-state.

[4]. John Lawrence, "ISIS Sanctuary: December 21, 2015." *Institute for the Study of War.* 21 December 2015, http://understandingwar.org/map/isis-sanctuary-december-21-2015.

[5]. John Lawrence, "ISIS Sanctuary: June 19, 2015." *Institute for the Study of War.* 19 June 2015, http://understandingwar.org/map/isis-sanctuary-june-19-2015.

[6]. "ISIS Sanctuary: January 15, 2015." *Institute for the Study of War.* 15 January 2015, http://iswresearch.blogspot.com/2015/01/isis-sanctuary-map-january-15-2015.html.

Jihadi Terrorism, Insurgency, and the Islamic State in Context

Chapter 1:
Legitimate Deliberate Democracy in Transition: Failure in the Democratization of Iraq by the United States from 2003-2014

Bibliography

Barnes, Julian (2014). *U.S. General Decries Spiraling Iraq Violence*. [online] WSJ. Available at: http://online.wsj.com/articles/SB10001424052702303618904579167911247903846 [Accessed 28 October 2014].

Bellin, Eva (2004). The Iraqi Intervention and Democracy in Comparative Historical Perspective. *Political Science Quarterly*, 119(4), pp. 595-608.

Biddle, Stephen, Friedman, Jeffery and Shapiro, Jacob (2012). Testing the surge: Why did violence decline in Iraq in 2007? *International Security*, 37(1), pp. 7-40.

Blumenson, Martin (1974). *The Patton papers*. 1st ed. Boston: Houghton.

Brooks, Thom (2009). A Critique of Pragmatism and Deliberative Democracy. *Transactions of the Charles S. Peirce Society: A Quarterly Journal in American Philosophy*, 45(1), pp. 50-54.

Cohen, Joshua (1989). Deliberation and democratic legitimacy. Reprinted in *Deliberative Democracy: Essays on Reason and Politics*, James Bohman and William Rehg, editors, Cambridge, MA: MIT Press, 1997, pp. 67-92.

Damluji, Mona (2010). "Securing Democracy in Iraq": Sectarian Politics and Segregation in Baghdad, 2003-2007. *Traditional Dwellings and Settlements Review*, pp. 71-87.

Dawisha, Adeed (2005). Democratic attitudes and practices in Iraq, 1921-1958. *The Middle East Journal*, 59(1), pp. 11-30.

Dobbins, James (2006). No Model War. *Foreign Affairs*, pp. 153-156.

Dodge, Toby (2013). State and society in Iraq ten years after regime change: the rise of a new authoritarianism. *International Affairs*, 89(2), pp. 241-257.

Eland, Ivan (2005). The Way Out of Iraq: Decentralizing the Iraqi Government. *International Journal on World Peace*, pp. 39-81.

Fiala, Andrew (2007). The Bush doctrine, democratization, and humanitarian intervention: a just war critique. *Theoria: A Journal of Social and Political Theory*, pp. 28-47.

Green, Penny and Ward, Tony (2009). The transformation of violence in Iraq. *British Journal of Criminology*, pp. 609-627.

Gutmann, Amy and Thompson, Dennis (2009). *Why Deliberate Democracy?* Student Edition, Princeton University Press.

Hamoudi, Humam (2007). My perceptions on the Iraqi constitutional process. *Stanford Law Review*, pp. 1315-1320.

Hill, Christopher (2014). *US Support of PM Maliki following the 2010 Iraqi Parliamentary Election*, interviewed by Brooks, Daniel T. at University of Denver, 29 October 2014.

Khedery, Ali (2014). Why we stuck with Maliki and lost Iraq. [online] *Washington Post*. Available at: http://www.washingtonpost.com/opinions/why-we-stuck-with-maliki--and-los... [Accessed 8 October 2014].

Locke, John (1690). *Second treatise of government*. Raleigh, N.C.: Alex Catalogue.

Manchester, William (1978). *American Caesar*. 1st ed. Boston: Little, Brown.

McLaughlin, Jenna (2014). Was ISIS chief Abu Bakr al-Baghdadi radicalized in a US-run prison in Iraq? [online] *Mother Jones*. Available at: http://www.motherjones.com/politics/2014/07/was-camp-bucca-pressure-cook... [Accessed 17 October 2014].

Mingus, Matthew (2012). Progress and Challenges with Iraq's Multilevel Governance. *Public Administration Review*, 72(5), pp. 678-686.

Moon, Bruce E. (2009). Long time coming: Prospects for democracy in Iraq. *International Security*, 33(4), pp. 115-148.

Neblo, Micheal; Esterling, Kevin; Kennedy, Ryan; Lazer, David; and Sokhey, Aanand (2010). Who wants to deliberate and why? *American Political Science Review*, 104(03), pp. 566-583.

Pei, Minxin (2003). Lessons of the Past. *Foreign Policy*, [online] (137), p. 52. Available at: http://dx.doi.org/10.2307/3183688 [Accessed 22 September 2014].

Petraeus, David and Amos, James (2009). *Counterinsurgency*. 1st ed. Boulder, Colo.: Paladin.

Rathmell, Andrew (2005). Planning post-conflict reconstruction in Iraq: what can we learn? *International Affairs*, 81(5), pp. 1013-1038.

Stradiotto, Gary A. (2004). Democratizing Iraq: Regime Transition and Economic Development in Comparative Perspective. *International Journal on World Peace*, pp. 3-36.

Terrill, W. Andrew (2012). *Lessons of the Iraqi de-Ba'athification program for Iraq's future and the Arab revolutions*. 1st ed. Carlisle, PA: Strategic Studies Institute, U.S. Army War College.

Thompson, Scott (2008). Can Might Make Right? The Use of Force to Impose Democracy and the Arthurian Dilemma in the Modern Era. *Law and Contemporary Problems*, pp. 163-184.

Notes

[i] Enounced: v. 1. To utter or pronounce; 2. To state a proposition or theory in definite terms. Origin: early 19th century: from French *énoncer*, from Latin enuntiare (see enunciate). http://www.oxforddictionaries.com/us/english/enounce.

[ii] Both Thomas Jefferson quotes were Obtained from http://famguardian.org/Subjects/Politics/thomasjefferson/jeff0500.htm; 16 September 2014.

[iii] I define legitimacy here as "consent of the governed." This is not to say that consent cannot be obtained through coercion. In fact, in Counterinsurgency (COIN), consent of the governed is obtained through two primary methods: coercion and providing a non-violent avenue for resolving grievances. The win-condition of COIN through democratization is to progress from the former to

the latter method. The focus of this paper is how "inclusiveness" is crucial to the win-con.

[iv] The execution of De-ba'athification initially fell on US military commanders and the Organization for Reconstruction and Humanitarian Assistance (ORHA). At first, US Army Commanders, such as then Major General David Petraeus in his capacity as commander of the 101st Airborne Division, limited the scope of De-Ba'athification in order to maintain security and key infrastructure upon surrender of Saddam Hussein's army. The US Civilian head of the Coalition Provision Authority (CPA), Paul Bremer, under the direction of Secretary of Defense Donald Rumsfeld and Undersecretary Paul Wolfowitz, went against the advisement of US military commanders on the ground and expanded De-ba'athification to include practically all Iraqi security and government officials under the first several orders of the CPA in 2003 (Terrill, 2012, pp. 13-15).

[v] The 1920s Revolutionary Brigade was a criminal element separate from AQI; however, there was much cross pollination in regards to membership. Ultimately, member loyalty to tribe was stronger than loyalty to AQI, and US exploitation of this drove the crucial wedge in isolating AQI from the Iraqi Sunni population. Of interests, the 1920s Revolutionary Brigade's namesake harkens back to the 1920s Iraqi revolution against British Colonization. Ironically, the time period from 1921-58 was the closest Iraq had ever been to having a historical precedent for democracy (Dawisha, 2005, p. 11). After the Sahwa, the 1920s Revolutionary Brigade resumed more modest levels of criminal activity, and maintained their illegal operations at discrete, acceptable levels that were tolerated by US commanders.

[vi] MAAWS was the later doctrinal term. In FM 3-24, it was described as "money is ammunition." Discretionary funds for SOIz salary was funded through the "Commanders Emergency Response Program." (CERP) that was used for a wide variety

of low budget infrastructure, economic, and security programs managed by tactical commanders.

[vii] From OCT 2008 until the transition of SoIz to Iraqi Government control in 2009, I was the pay agent for CERP in the Ka'nan Nahia of Diyala Province. During this time, I managed a contract for approximately 250 SoIz, and became intimately familiar with the politics of managing SoIz relations with Iraqi Police, Iraqi Army, and Local Nahia Government that was predominately Shiite controlled. I also had the significant challenge of finding ways to negotiate integration of the SoIz into civilian employment upon the transition of the organization to Iraqi government control. When SoIz lacked professional skills or desirability for government employment, my default solution was using CERP to fund small business Micro-Grants as a "severance." Each micro-grant added up to approximately $5,000 in two monthly payments (2-3 years SoIz salary, depending on the generosity of the militiaman's sheik). The micro-grant program under CERP was highly criticized by State Department representatives on PRTs, as they argued the program in general incentivized local national entrepreneurs into not taking small business loans from local banks, thus hurting the economy. By the end of 2009, the CERP program as a whole came under severe criticism of abuse and misuse in an environment of little oversight over tactical commanders and pay agents. Shortly thereafter, the program was shut down, and many half-finished projects were cancelled when the GoI did not continue them following the hand over. Some members of the PRTs saw CERP as US commanders circumventing GOI bureaucratic system, often when Shiite GoI leaders refused to support/maintain projects in Sunni communities, and as such, failed to create capacity and GoI legitimacy. The validity of this criticism varied wildly dependent on the US commander in question, and the amount of by-in he received from GoI on a given project. Additionally, in the example of the SoIz "severance," analysis of the 2nd and 3rd order effects of the program really depended on the analyst

understanding how and why the money was being used, and to what purpose, which wasn't always immediately obvious to those further removed from the execution of the program. Additionally, add to this legal advisors conservatively interpreting the MAAWS SOP in ways that resulted in disapproval of projects due to subjective reasons that were specifically listed as "commander's discretion." Yet commanders, once given legal advice from a SJA, will rarely question it or seek a second opinion. An example of this would be disapproving a SoIz micro-grant due to proximity to a similar establishment or disapproving a micro-grant for a "rent-a-dj" business for a disabled SoIz because the MAAWS says "funds will not be used for entertainment purposes," the intent of which is for business owners to not abuse the funds by buying frivolous items for personal use, instead of suggesting that commanders can't fund businesses that are an entertainment service. Another example would be an Internet Café micro-grant getting disapproved as "entertainment," when the intent is to provide Iraqi civilians internet access to free press (furthering US information operations) and small business owners access to expand into digital markets. These examples are actual cases.

[viii] Not only did the Sunnis learn to vote, they also learned to ally with the Kurdish voting block to gain parity against the Shiite majority who supported PM Maliki. Not only that, but the Sunnis took advantage of the fact that the Shiite vote itself was somewhat split, as the Iraqi Nation Accord had garnered some of the Shiite vote as well. A good explanation for why the Sunnis attitudes towards voting shifted is the counter-argument to the "Stealth Democracy Thesis." The "Stealth Democracy Thesis" asserts that voters become apathetic due to cynicism towards democracy. The Counter-argument is that in fact, voters are less apathetic when corruption is high and overt (Neblo, 2010, p. 570). The 2005 and 2010 Iraqi elections are evidence for both respectively; although the 2005 Sunni boycott was a deliberate act, and not a function of apathy.

[ix] For additional back ground: http://www.politico.com/magazine/story/2014/10/how-the-obama-administration-disowned-iraq-111565_Page3.html#.VDGA7KC9KrV.

[x] Dean Christopher Hill was gracious enough to share an hour of this time with me discussing his time in Iraq as Ambassador. He suggested that two major failures made the reinstatement of PM Maliki inevitable: 1. The Iraqi Constitution did not specify the method of a run off between two leading parties without a majority of seats. Dean Hill suggested that what might have benefited Iraq would have been if the situation had be resolved in a similar fashion to the 2013 Israeli Elections that resulted in a similar situation for PM Benjamin Netanyahu. In the Israeli case, the party with the most seats (but not the majority) was allowed to form the new government. Additionally, the Constitution of Iraq was not constructed in such a way as to have a bi-cameral legislature. During his tenure in Iraq, Dean Hill and others attempted to form something akin to a "House of Lords" or "House of Sheiks" in order to provide a Sunni balance to the Shia Majority (in what would become a "House of Commons") and give teeth to attempts at Iraqi Federalism. Unfortunately, these measures were not in the Iraqi Constitution, as these power-sharing concerns were overlooked at the time the constitution was conceived, and these new attempts never really took hold. 2. Reconciliation Efforts of the US post-surge were not internalized by neither the Shia population as a whole, nor in key Shia leadership such as PM Maliki. Consequently, as the US left Iraq, the Shia controlled Iraq felt few moral qualms against discriminating against Sunnis who were seen as having blood on their hands from the Ba'athist regime and the 2003-05 insurgency. Dean Hill suggested that what the country needed during reconciliation was something akin to the Truth Commission of South Africa, where those Sunni (and Shia militia members) who had done wrong simply confessed their sins and were forgiven (and the offending individual or a third party like

the US paid proper retinue as restitution to victims families). The unfortunate problem was that PM Maliki was neither a Nelson Mandela nor George Washington, and lacked the civic virtue to forgive and forget past wrongs, personal or otherwise, when integrating the SoIz and Sunni population following the exit of the US in December 2011. Dean Hill also mentioned that Iraq was significantly difficult to dominate politically by the US because Local Nationals, Shia especially but also the Sunni, did not see themselves as defeated by the US because they distanced themselves so much from Saddam Hussein. This self-perception would have been a major obstacle to a relationship similar to the one enjoyed by General Douglas MacArthur in Post-WWII Japan where the US had destroyed two major cities with an atomic bomb, and the population willingly acknowledged their complicity with the Emperor Hirohito.

[xi] In 2011, ISI was a primary Sunni terrorist organization on the rise in Iraq. Al-Baghdadi was a person of interest so to speak. Unfortunately, following the June, 30 2009 security agreement, US tactical commanders were ordered to stay out of the cities. Additionally, Brigade Combat Teams still in theater renamed themselves "Advise and Assist Brigades" in order to meet political objectives and legal definitions of US national level leadership. As such, by 2011, the sorts of operations tactical commanders could conduct to effect an organization such as ISI were limited. Consequently, tactical focus at the Brigade level and below at this point shifted mostly to preservation of combat power as logistics officers focused on redeploying equipment and transitioning US forward operating bases (FOBs) over to Iraqi control, eventually leading to the final US withdrawal in December, 2011 after PM Maliki refused to renew the SOFA agreement on acceptable terms to the US. The June 30th agreement was a symbolic event, signifying a return to Iraqi sovereignty, and marked the transition from the US Surge Campaign to "Operation New Dawn."

[xii] The closest the US came to this was the CPA under Paul Bremer. The transitional period was very short lived (2003-05) ending with the ratification of the Iraqi Constitution, which was generated by mostly by Shiite and Kurdish representatives, was heavily influenced by US De-ba'athification policy, and was rushed to ratification due to pressure by the US without solving the inequities generated by lack of Sunni buy-in due to the Sunni Boycott. A much more equitable government could have been formed had it just been drafted by impartial US occupiers and presented to the Iraqis. Occupations by nature are military operations, not diplomatic ones, and therefore should be run by a non-partisan military commander with very wide authoritative latitude as a representative of the conquering nation.

[xiii] For example, Oskar Schindler: http://www.google.com/url?sa=t&rct=j&q=&esrc=s&source=web&cd=2&ved=0CCoQFjAB&url=http%3A%2F%2Ftime.com%2F3462544%2Foskar-schindler%2F&ei=TAdQVIfTMs35yQS464DACg&usg=AFQjCNGiMeHELgLdSXa_XBuRXn9v5JillQ&sig2=hjEdlkmCl4gxOKDbTOKmew&bvm=bv.78597519,d.aWw.

[xiv] I was deployed as a United States Army officer in Iraq from SEP 2008-SEP 2009 (Kan'an Nahia in Diyala Province) and JUL 2011-DEC 2011 (Diwaniyah), and this was my understanding of higher intent.

[xv] The quote from the movie "Field of Dreams" was commonly used by field commanders in Iraq; my critique of it is a reference to Niccolò Machiavelli's definition of strategy as being the matching of means to ends in his work "The Prince." Not all development in Iraq was conducted with a specific objective in mind. On many occasions it was development for development sake, commanders, Provincial Reconstruction Team (PRT) experts from the US Department of State, and organizations like USAID not grasping the implications of power dynamics and second and third order effects on the goal of legitimizing the Democratic Government in Iraq. An example of this would be how PRTs would push building

schools and soccer fields as "low hanging fruit." Oftentimes, there were plenty of buildings/homes schools could be operated out of, and a vast abundance of dirt sufficiently fertilized with raw human sewage runoff for soccer fields and garbage in the street to use as goal posts. The real problems are always harder to fix, but that doesn't mean solving easy non-existing problems is the solution. Another example is using Commander's and PRTs pushing to use CERP funds to dig wells and installing gas pumps for sheiks without buy in from the Nahia water managers; such projects reduced local national dependency on the government for essential services, and consequently, delegitimized the government while giving sectarian sheiks more power and influence. Such decisions were very easy, feel good "low hanging fruit" projects because "at least the people are getting clean water." The interpretation of "The Prince" is inspired by class lectures from DR Paul Viotti, Josef Korbel School of International Studies at the University of Denver.

[xvi] From the US Military Officer Commissioning Oath (DA Form 71, 1 August 1959)
See: http://www.history.army.mil/html/faq/oaths.html.

[xvii] From the United States Bill of Rights.

[xviii] In the original draft of this paper, I Implied an American Style government; however, at the suggestion of DR Paul Viotti, Professor of Josef Korbel School of International Studies at the University of Denver, I have explicitly stated the type of government I have in mind. Democracy in the style of Greek City State Direct Democracy is not be the only form of government considered in the democratization of undeveloped nations, as the term "democratization" seems to suggest. In the case of Iraq, what would have worked best pre-2010 was a Constitutional, Federalist, Republic with a bicameral legislature. Since the Iraqi government settled on a parliamentary system, it would have been better to split the legislative body into a popular house (House of Commons) and a house of sheiks (House of Lords)

to ensure sectarian minority rights. The Iraqi government in fact was established in a federalist system, with the Provinces mimicking what could be compared to US States, but the legislature was not designed with minority protections in mind, nor with any incorporation of sheik leadership in an official capacity. The formation of the US constitution took these factors into consideration when compromising with having both the House of Representatives and Senate. The point is that post-enlightenment political philosophy approached democracy from an analysis of human nature, not European or American nature, and the principles that informed the Founding Fathers of the US government drove their decisions as they created the structure of the US government. The US Founding Fathers neither reinvented the wheel, nor created a system on non-universalizing principles.

[xix] Granted, US military commanders forcing Iraqi leaders to "democratically" do things a certain way is not in the spirit of true democracy; however, in transition, such measures are often necessary until the mores are internalized.

[xx] From the United States "Declaration of Independence."

[xxi] Members of the US Libertarian parties would probably argue that not even the United States Government lives up to this lofty ideal, but the ability of the party members to field a party and make this claim openly and peacefully is evidence enough that there is some truth to British Prime Minister Winston Churchill's statement that "Democracy is the worst form of government, except for all the others."

[xxii] Further discussion in this vein devolves into the realm of Epistemology. This line of reasoning, while it appears tangential, is not, if one approaches rationality from a Coherency Theory of Justification. Suffice to say, logical/rational systems of belief are founded on assumptions, which are beliefs rooted in faith. Philosophy of Science is captive to this, even if an empiricist is an agnostic or atheist (the example being that non-belief or absentia from belief in deity is a belief founded entirely on faith).

[xxiii] Within the scope of this article; the invasion of Iraq is not a moral application of the Bush Doctrine, as explained in the following paragraph.

[xxiv] Defined as the idea in International Relations that democracies do not go to war with one another.

[xxv] The problem Kenneth Waltz identifies with anarchy in "War, the State, and Man" is that anarchy at the international level creates uncertainty. One interpretation is that in a system of uncertainty, war erupts in an effort by states to mitigate risk. Remove uncertainty, and one greatly reduces the incidence of war. One method for removing uncertainty is the monopolization of force by a single governing entity, thus all wars become civil wars and COIN. In the current world system, at best are self-enforcing international institutions, but this is the starting point for evolving the international system into one of international governance. World governance is not inherently evil; it is the specific structure of a given system that may or may not be.

[xxvi] "Be careful when you fight with monsters, lest you become one." —Fredrick Nietzsche.

Chapter 2:
Confusing a "Revolution" with "Terrorism"

Notes

[i] Others argue it should be called Da'esh:
D (dal in Arabic د) stands for Dawla = state
A (aleph in Arabic ا) stands for islamiya = Islamic
'E (ein in Arabic ع) stands for iraq = iraq
Sh (sheen in Arabic ش) stands for Sham = Levant

[ii] George Kennan, July 1947, "The Sources of Soviet Conduct," *Foreign Affairs,* Council on Foreign Relations, Washington DC, p. 581.

[iii] League of Nations 1937 "Convention for the prevention and punishment of Terrorism."
[iv] Edward Luttwak and Stuart Koehl, 1991, *The Dictionary of Modern War: A Guide to the Ideas, Institutions and Weapons of Modern Military Power*, Harper Collins, New York, p. 609.
[v] Bruce Hoffman, 2006, *Inside Terrorism*, Columbia University Press, New York, p. 40.
[vi] *Ibid.*, pp. 40-41.
[vii] Alexis De Tocqueville, 2000, *Democracy in America*, edited by Harvey Mansfield and Delba Winthrop, University of Chicago Press, Chicago, p. 600.
[viii] Peter Amann, March 1962, "Revolution: A Redefinition," *Political Science Quarterly,* Volume 77, Number 1, The Academy of Political Science, p. 36.
[ix] *Ibid.*, p. 38
[x] *Ibid.*, p. 39.
[xi] *Ibid.*, p. 43.
[xii] Chalmers Johnson, 1964, *Revolution and the Social System,* Hoover Institution Studies, Stanford, pp. 3-26.
[xiii] Sheldon Wolin, January 1963 "Violence and the Western Political Tradition," *American Journal of Orthopsychiatry."* pp. 15-28.
[xiv] Johnson, pp. 31-34.
[xv] *Ibid.*, pp. 35-39.
[xvi] *Ibid.*, pp. 40-45.
[xvii] *Ibid.*, pp. 45-49.
[xviii] Lawrence Stone, January 1966, "Theories of Revolution," *World Politics,* Volume 18, Number 2, Cambridge University Press, Cambridge, p. 163.
[xix] Johnson, pp. 49-57.
[xx] Edward Luttwack, 1968, *Coup d'Etat: A Practical Handbook*, Harvard University Press, Cambridge.
[xxi] Johnson, pp. 57-68.

[xxii] Isaac Kraminick, 1972, "Reflections on Revolution: Definitions and Explanation in Recent Scholarship," History *and Theory*, Volume 11, Number 1, Wiley, p. 26.

[xxiii] *Ibid.*, p. 30.

[xxiv] *Ibid.*, p. 31.

[xxv] *Ibid.*, p. 36.

[xxvi] *Ibid.*, p. 37.

[xxvii] Luttwak and Koehl, p. 487.

[xxviii] Clifton Kroeber, 1996, "Theory and History of Revolution," *Journal of World History*, Volume 7, Number 1, University of Hawaii Press, Honolulu, p. 24.

[xxix] *Ibid.*, p. 25.

[xxx] ___, May 2014, *FM 3-24, MCWP 3-33.5, Insurgencies and Countering Insurgencies*, Headquarters, Department of the Army, p. 1-1.

[xxxi] *Ibid.*, p. 4-1

[xxxii] *Ibid.*, p. 4-2.

[xxxiii] We recognize "transitory" is a relative term in this context. As Audrey Kurth Cronin documents in *How Terrorism Ends Understanding the Decline and Demise of Terrorist Campaigns* (Princeton University Press 2009), a terrorist movement can survive a full generation of more than 20 years.

[xxxiv] ___, 10 September 2014, "Transcript: President Obama's speech outlining strategy to defeat Islamic State" *Washington Post,"* Washington.

[xxxv] ___, 16 September 2014, "TRANSCRIPT: Dempsey testifies to the Senate Armed Services Committee on the Islamic State," *Washington Post*, Washington.

[xxxvi] Barrack Obama, 28 September 2014, "President Obama: What America Makes Us," CBS, New York.

[xxxvii] Joel Beinin and Joe Stork, 1997, *Political Islam*, University of California Press, Berkeley, pp. 3-4.

[xxxviii] Graham Fuller, 2003, *The Future of Political Islam*, Palgrave MacMillan, New York, p. xi.

[xxxix] For instance see: Charles Butterworth, 1992, "Political Islam: The Origins," *Academy of Political and Social Science*, Volume 524, Sage Publications, pp. 26-37; Charles Hirschkind, 1997, "What is Political Islam?" *Middle East Report*, Number 205, Middle East Research and Information Project, pp. 12-14; and, ___, 2010, *Political Islam from Muhammad to Ahmadinejad*, edited by Joseph Skelly, Preager Security International, Santa Barbara.

[xl] Moorthy Muthuswamy, 2009, *Defeating Political Islam*, Prometheus Books, Amherst, New York, p. 54.

[xli] Alireza Doostdar, 2 October 2014, "How Not to Understand ISIS," Martin Marty Center for the Advanced Study of Religion, University of Chicago, p. 2.

[xlii] *Ibid.*, p. 3.

Chapter 3:
Reconsidering Religion, Reconsidering Terrorism

No notes.

Chapter 4:
Ignored in Asia: The ISIL Threat

References

Ackerman, Spencer. "Foreign jihadists flocking to Iraq and Syria on 'unprecedented scale'—UN." *The Guardian*. October 30, 2014. http://www.theguardian.com/world/2014/oct/30/foreign-jihadist-iraq-syria-unprecedented-un-isis (accessed October 31, 2014).

Liow, Joseph Chinyong. "ISIS Goes to Asia." *Foreign Affairs*. September 19, 2014. http://www.foreignaffairs.com/articles/142004/joseph-chinyong-liow/isis-goes-to-asia (accessed October 17, 2014).

Locklear, Samuel J. "Testimony before the House Armed Services Committee on U.S. Pacific Command Posture." *House Armed Services Committee.* March 5, 2014.

Locklear, Samuel J. "Department of Defense Press Briefing on U.S. Pacific Command's Area of Responsibility by Admiral Locklear in the Pentagon Briefing Room." Defense.gov. September 25, 2014. http://www.defense.gov/Transcripts/Transcript.aspx?TranscriptID=5507 (accessed October 17, 2014).

Olson, Matthew G. "Prepared Statement at Brookings Institution." *National Counterterrorism Center.* September 3, 2014. http://www.nctc.gov/docs/2014-09-03_remarks_for_the_brookings_institution.pdf (accessed October 17, 2014).

Regencia, Ted. "Islamic State's Support Spreads into Asia." *Aljazeera.* July 19, 2014. http://www.aljazeera.com/indepth/features/2014/07/islamic-state-support-spreads-into-asia-201471392121686815.html (accessed on October 30, 2014).

Shanahan, Rodger. "'Islamic State' poses 'serious threat' to Asia's Muslim countries." *DW.* August 12, 2014. http://www.dw.de/islamic-state-poses-serious-threat-to-asias-muslim-countries/a-17847370 (accessed October 30, 2014).

Chapter 5:
Missing Political Front in Afghanistan

Notes

[i] DoD, October 2012 and DoD *Report on Progress Toward Security and Stability in Afghanistan*, December 2012, p. 151.

[ii] On January 1, 2015, NATO's ISAF mission was succeeded by the Advisory Resolute Support Mission.

[iii] Thomas Barfield and Neamatollah Nojumi, "Bringing More Effective Governance to Afghanistan: 10 Pathways to Stability," *Middle East Policy Council*, Winter 2010.

[iv]   Karl P. Eikenberry, *Foreign Affairs*, September-October 2013; p. 61
[v]   Daniel P. Bolger, "Why We Lost in Iraq and Afghanistan," *Harpers*, September 2014. Also, *Why We Lost: a General's Inside Account of the Iraq and Afghanistan Wars* (HMH, 2014).
[vi]   Robert M. Gates, *Duty: Memoirs of a Secretary at War* (Knopf, 2014); pp. 483, 557.
[vii] "E.g., Barfield, "Afghanistan's Ethnic Puzzle: Decentralizing Power Before the U.S. Withdrawal,"*Foreign Affairs*, September-October 2011; p. 55; Peter Tomsen, *The Wars of Afghanistan: Messianic Terrorism, Tribal Conflicts, and the Failures of Great Powers* (Perseus, 2011), p. 646; and Henry Kissinger, "How to Exit Afghanistan Without Creating Wider Conflict," *Washington Post*, June 7, 2011.
[viii] Stephen Biddle, "Ending the War in Afghanistan: How to Avoid Failure on the Installment Plan,"*Foreign Affairs*, September/October 2013: p. 56.
[ix]   Tomsen (2011), *passim*.
[x]   Charlotta Gall, *The Wrong Enemy: the US in Afghanistan, 2001-2014* (Houghton Mifflin Harcourt, 2014); pp. 122-3.
[xi]   Tomsen (2011), pp. 451-2.
[xii] Ahmad Rashid, *Descent into Chaos: the United State, and the Failure of Nation-Building in Pakistan, Afghanistan, and Central Asia* (Viking, 2008), especially Ch. 7, "The One-Billion Dollar Warlords." Also, Tomsen (2011), p. 597.
[xiii] Tomsen (2011), pp. 646, 656-7, 662.
[xiv] Gates (2014); pp. 358-9.
[xv]   Sherard Cowper-Coles, *Cables from Kabul: the Inside Story of the West's Afghanistan's Campaign* (Harper Press, 2011), p. 200; also Kissinger, *World Order: Reflections on the Character of Nations and the Course of History* (Allen Lane, 2014), pp. 321-2.
[xvi] Charles Mwalimu, *Seeking Viable Grassroots Representation Mechanisms in African Constitutions: Integration of Indigenous*

and Modern Systems of Government in Sub-Sahara Africa (Peter Lang, 2009); p. 79ff.

[xvii] Barfield and Nojumi (2010); pp. 9-10.

Chapter 6:
Unmasking the Executioner: What This Gesture Means and How It Can Help in the Fight Against ISIS

Notes

[i] https://www.youtube.com/watch?v=LUaxyhRfqyk (YouTube clip that stops short of the actual execution)

[ii] http://www.theguardian.com/world/2014/nov/16/isis-beheads-peter-kassig-reports

[iii] http://www.trackingterrorism.org/article/detailed-analysis-islamic-state-isis-video-although-unbelievers-dislike-it-story-expansion-3

[iv] Here we are, come get us," comments Paul Hunter of Canadian Broadcasting Corporation, adding that they are "intentionally unmasked and exposed." "It's just a way of saying, 'We're not afraid,'" comments Firas Abi Ali, a London-based senior analyst at the global intelligence group HIS:http://www.cbc.ca/m/touch/news/story/1.2838106

[v] http://www.trackingterrorism.org/article/detailed-analysis-islamic-state-isis-video-although-unbelievers-dislike-it-story-expansion-6

[vi] http://time.com/3624976/isis-beheading-technology-video-tracquilliam/

[vii] Since then, doubt has been cast on whether Dos Santos and Muthana appear in the execution video, though neither deny fighting with ISIS. http://www.ibtimes.co.uk/isis-french-jihadist-mickael-dos-santos-denies-appearing-beheading-video-1475833

[viii] http://www.ibtimes.co.uk/isis-british-medical-student-nasser-muthana-shown-next-jihadi-john-peter-kassig-beheading-video-1475162
[ix] http://abcnews.go.com/blogs/headlines/2014/09/official-american-may-be-key-in-isis-social-media-blitz/
[x] http://www.independent.co.uk/news/world/middle-east/syria-crisis-british-jihadists-becoming-disillusioned-at-fighting-rival-rebels-and-not-assad-regime-9713279.html
[xi] http://news.nationalpost.com/2014/12/02/joining-isis-has-left-them-bored-disillusioned-and-afraid-french-jihadists-write-in-letters-to-home/
[xii] "Rule of Terror: Living under ISIS in Syria," (2014) http://reliefweb.int/sites/reliefweb.int/files/resources/HRC_CRP_ISIS_14Nov2014.pdf
[xiii] http://www.bbc.com/news/world-middle-east-30585783
[xiv] http://www.bbc.com/news/world-middle-east-29600573
[xv] http://news.nationalpost.com/2014/12/02/joining-isis-has-left-them-bored-disillusioned-and-afraid-french-jihadists-write-in-letters-to-home/
[xvi] There are as many sources debunking this myth as those claiming direct lineage, no less than the national history and arrival of Islam posted on the their website by the Embassy of Sudan in DC: http://www.sudanembassy.org/index.php?option=com_content&id=114&Itemid=217

See also: Jacob K. Olupona, "African Religion: A Very Short Introduction," Oxford University Press, 2014; and for a compelling argument that the Arabization of Sudan is as much a strategic alignment overtime with the power brokers as it is a comment on the centuries old association of "black" with slavery, see: "The Scramble for Arab Genealogies," in *African Writing*, June-August 2007, http://www.african-writing.com/aug/jalal.htm

Chapter 7:
Boko Haram's Resiliency Spells Trouble for West Africa

Notes

[i] Bill Roggio, "Boko Haram overruns Multinational Joint Task Force base, *Long War Journal*, 4 January 2015, http://www.longwarjournal.org/archives/2015/01/boko_haram_overruns_1.php

[ii] Human Rights Watch, "What really happened in Baga, Nigeria?" 14 January 2015, http://www.hrw.org/news/2015/01/14/dispatches-what-really-happened-baga-....

[iii] http://www.thesundaily.my/news/1296987, http://www.telegraph.co.uk/news/worldnews/africaandindianocean/nigeria/11345905/Boko-Haram-raze-Nigerian-towns-in-most-destructive-attack-yet-says Amnesty.html, http://observers.france24.com/content/20150113-boko-haram-survivor-baga-maiduguri, http://www.sfgate.com/news/world/article/UN-condemns-surge-in-Nigeria-killings-6009007.php.

[iv] "Boko Haram Fighters Seize Army Base In Nigerian Town Of Baga In Deadly Attack," *International Business Times*, 5 January 2015, http://www.ibtimes.com/boko-haram-fighters-seize-army-base-nigerian-town....

[v] "Bomb at School in Nigeria Kills Nearly 50 Boys," *The New York Times*, 10 November 2014, http://www.nytimes.com/2014/11/11/world/africa/nigeria-suicide-bomber-boko-haram.html.

[vi] "New video: Abubakar Shekau announces Boko Haram 'Islamic State' caliphate in Nigeria," *The Global Dispatch*, 28 August 2014, http://www.theglobaldispatch.com/new-video-abubakar-shekau-announces-boko-haram-islamic-state-caliphate-in-nigeria-20666/.

[vii] "Nigeria's Boko Haram sets new tone in controlled areas," *AFP*, 16 November 2014, http://www.rappler.com/world/regions/africa/75187-nigeria-boko-haram-controlled-areas.

[viii] "Nigeria's Boko Haram sets new tone in controlled areas," *AFP*, 16 November 2014, http://www.rappler.com/world/regions/africa/75187-nigeria-boko-haram-controlled-areas.

[ix] "New video: Abubakar Shekau announces Boko Haram 'Islamic State' caliphate in Nigeria," *The Global Dispatch*, 28 August 2014, http://www.theglobaldispatch.com/new-video-abubakar-shekau-announces-boko-haram-islamic-state-caliphate-in-nigeria-20666/.

[x] "Nigerian village buries 45 after Boko Haram 'slaughter'," *Reuters*, 21 November 2014, http://www.reuters.com/assets/print?aid=USKCN0J511R20141121.

[xi] "Video shows Boko Haram killing captives," *Agence France-Presse*, 22 December 2014, and http://www.aysor.am/en/news/2014/12/22/Video-shows-Boko-Haram-killing-ca....

[xii] "New video: Abubakar Shekau announces Boko Haram 'Islamic State' caliphate in Nigeria," *The Global Dispatch*, 28 August 2014, http://www.theglobaldispatch.com/new-video-abubakar-shekau-announces-boko-haram-islamic-state-caliphate-in-nigeria-20666/.

[xiii] "Nigeria 2014 sees bloodier, emboldened Boko Haram," *World Bulletin*, 22 December 2014, http://www.worldbulletin.net/world/151389/nigeria-2014-sees-bloodier-emb....

[xiv] "Nigeria: As Another Civil War Looms," *All Africa.com*, 21 November 2014, allafrica.com/stories/201411210272.html.

[xv] "Boko Haram hangs in Hong, routed in 3 villages," *Sun News*, 20 November 2014, http://sunnewsonline.com/new/?p=91761.

[xvi] "Nigeria army says retakes village of abducted girls from insurgents," *Reuters*, 16 November 2014.

[xvii] "Boko Haram hangs in Hong, routed in 3 villages," *Sun News*, 20 November 2014, http://sunnewsonline.com/new/?p=91761.

[xviii] Boko Haram steps up attacks in Cameroon, *News 24*, 20 November 2014, http://www.news24.com/Africa/News/Boko-Haram-steps-up-attacks-in-Cameroo....

[xix] "Why is Nigeria's Jonathan worried?" *Al Jazeera*, 27 November 2014, http://www.aljazeera.com/indepth/opinion/2014/11/why-nigeria-jonathan-worried-20141123104313818965.html, and "Boko Haram hangs in Hong, routed in 3 villages," *Sun News*, villages," *Sun News*, 20 November 2014, http://sunnewsonline.com/new/?p=91761, and "How Nigeria's Stupidly Brutal Cops Botch the Hunt for Boko Haram," *The Daily Beast*, 14 May 2014, http://www.thedailybeast.com/articles/2014/05/14/how-nigeria-s-stupidly-....

[xx] "Nigerian Army to Court-Martial General, Other Top Officers," *All Africa.com*, 22 December 2014.

[xxi] "Boko Haram hangs in Hong, routed in 3 villages," *Sun News*, 20 November 2014,http://sunnewsonline.com/new/?p=91761, and "How Nigeria's Stupidly Brutal Cops Botch the Hunt for Boko Haram," *The Daily Beast*, 14 May 2014, http://www.thedailybeast.com/articles/2014/05/14/how-nigeria-s-stupidly-....

[xxii] "Nigeria's Dangerous 2015 Elections: Limiting the Violence," International Crisis Group, 21 November 2014, http://www.crisisgroup.org/en/publication-type/media-releases/2014/afric....

[xxiii] "Nigeria: As Another Civil War Looms," *All Africa.com*, 21 November 2014, allafrica.com/stories/201411210272.html.

[xxiv] "Insurgency threatens democracy and economic development—NBA," *Daily Post*, 21 November 2014, http://dailypost.ng/2014/11/21/insurgency-threatens-democracy-economic-d....

[xxv] "Insurgency threatens democracy and economic development—NBA," *Daily Post*, 21 November 2014, http://dailypost.ng/2014/11/21/insurgency-threatens-democracy-economic-d...

[xxvi] "Nigeria: As Another Civil War Looms," *All Africa.com*, 21 November 2014, allafrica.com/stories/201411210272.html.

[xxvii] "Boko Haram steps up attacks in Cameroon," *News 24*, 20 November 2014, http://www.news24.com/Africa/News/Boko-Haram-steps-up-attacks-in-Cameroo....

[xxviii] "Senior minister's wife kidnapped by Boko Haram militants in Cameroon as bombs rock Nigeria," *News.*

com.au, 28 July 2014, http://www.news.com.au/world/senior-ministers-wife-kidnapped-by-boko-har....

[xxix] "Cameroon under pressure from Boko Haram," *BBC*, 18 November 2014, http://www.bbc.com/news/world-africa-30078626, and "Nigeria, Boko Haram reach ceasefire deal, kidnapped girls to go free, official says," *CNN*, 27 October 2014, http://www.cnn.com/2014/10/17/world/africa/nigeria-boko-haram-ceasefire/.

[xxx] "Boko Haram steps up attacks in Cameroon," *News 24*, 20 November 2014, http://www.news24.com/Africa/News/Boko-Haram-steps-up-attacks-in-Cameroo....

[xxxi] "Boko Haram camp dismantled in Cameroon, army says," *Associated Press*, 22 December 2014.

[xxxii] "Cameroon bombs Boko Haram positions," *Al Jazeera*, 29 December 2014, http://www.aljazeera.com/news/africa/2014/12/cameroon-bombs-boko-haram-p....

[xxxiii] "Boko Haram crisis: Group of Cameroon captives freed," *BBC*, 19 January 2015, http://www.bbc.com/news/world-africa-30882991

[xxxiv] "Boko Haram frees hostages as Chad enters regional fight," *AFP*, 20 January 2015, http://news.yahoo.com/boko-haram-lets-20-cameroon-hostages-army-chase-00...

[xxxv] "Niger hit by Nigeria's Boko Haram fallout," *BBC*, 22 April 2014, http://www.bbc.com/news/world-africa-27111884, and "Niger fears contagion from Nigeria's Boko Haram Islamists," *Reuters*, 19 March 2014, http://news.yahoo.com/niger-fears-contagion-nigerias-boko-haram-islamist....

[xxxvi] "Niger hit by Nigeria's Boko Haram fallout," *BBC*, 22 April 2014, http://www.bbc.com/news/world-africa-27111884

[xxxvii] "Nigeria's neighbours unite to fight Boko Haram," *The Guardian*, 17 January 2015, http://www.ngrguardiannews.com/news/national-news/194284-nigeria-s-neigh...

[xxxviii] Hurst website for Virginia Comolli's *Boko Haram: Nigeria's Islamist Insurgency*, http://www.hurstpublishers.com/book/boko-haram/.

[xxxix] "Boko Haram steps up attacks in Cameroon," *News 24*, 20 November 2014, http://www.news24.com/Africa/News/Boko-Haram-steps-up-attacks-in-Cameroo....

Chapter 8:
Urban Siege in Paris: A Spectrum of Armed Assault

Notes

[i] John P. Sullivan and Adam Elkus, "Postcard from Mumbai: Modern Urban Siege," *Small Wars Journal*, 16 February 2009, and "Preventing Another Mumbai: Building a Police Operational Art," 15 June 2009.

[ii] Shane Harris, "US Spies Expected Airline Bombs—And Got The Paris Attacks Instead," *The Daily Beast*, 17 January 2015, http://www.thedailybeast.com/articles/2015/01/17/u-s-spies-expected-airline-bombs-and-got-the-paris-attacks-instead.html.

[iii] David Kilcullen, "Westgate Mall Attacks: Urban Areas Are The Battleground Of the 21st Century," *The Guardian*, 27 September 2013.

[iv] BBC, "Charlie Hebdo Attack: Three Days of Terror," 14 January 2015, http://www.bbc.com/news/world-europe-30708237 and Pierre Bienaime, "France Has Mobilized 88,000 Personnel After the Paris Shootings," *Business Insider*, 8 January 2015, http://www.businessinsider.com/france-has-mobilized-88000-personnel-afte....

[v] Emma Graham-Harrison, "Paris Policeman's Brother: Islam Is A Religion of Love. My Brother Was Killed by Terrorists, By False Muslims," *The Guardian*, 10 January 2015, http://www.theguardian.com/world/2015/jan/10/charlie-hebdo-policeman-mur....

[vi] *CBS News*, "The Special Forces Behind France's Rescue Operations," 9 January 2015, http://www.cbsnews.com/news/the-special-forces-behind-frances-rescue-ope....

[vii] Griff Whitte, "In A Kosher Grocery Store In Paris, Terror Takes A Deadly Toll," *The Washington Post*, 9 January 2015, http://www.washingtonpost.com/world/europe/paris-kosher-market-seized-in...

[viii] Ray Sanchez, Laura Smith-Spark, and Hakim Almasmari, "Source: Terror Cells Activated in France," *CNN*, 11 January 2015, http://edition.cnn.com/2015/01/10/europe/charlie-hebdo-paris-shooting/, and Shashank Joshi, "Charlie Hebdo attack: A French Intelligence Failure?" *BBC*, 10 January 2015, http://www.bbc.com/news/world-europe-30760656.

[ix] Christian de Looper, "Post-Charlie Hebdo Attack, "Islamist Cyberattacks' Cripple French Media: About 19,000 Websites KO'd," *Tech Times*, 19 January 2015, http://www.techtimes.com/articles/27228/20150119/post-charlie-hebdo-atta...

[x] *AFP*, "Hackers Took Control of a French Newspaper's Twitter Account and Tweeted 'I'm Not Charlie'", 20 January 2015, http://www.businessinsider.com/afp-syrian-group-hacks-french-newspapers-...

[xi] Kilcullen, ibid.

[xii] For an overview of that operation, see John P. Sullivan and Adam Elkus, "The New Playbook? Urban Siege in Nairobi," *Small Wars Journal*, 24 November 2013, http://www.isn.ethz.ch/Digital-Library/Publications/Detail/?lng=en&id=17...

[xiii] Howden, ibd.

[xiv] Sophia Saifi and Greg Botelho, "In Pakistan, Terrorists Kill 145, Mostly Children," *CNN*, 17 December 2014, http://www.cnn.com/2014/12/16/world/asia/pakistan-peshawar-school-attack/.

[xv] C. Christine Fair, *Urban Battle Fields of South Asia: Lessons Learned From Sri Lanka, India, and Pakistan*, Santa Monica: RAND Corporation, 2004.

[xvi] J. Paul D. Taillon, *Hijacking and Hostages: Government Response to Terror*, Westport: Praeger, 2002.

[xvii] John P. Sullivan and Adam Elkus, "Preventing Another Mumbai: Building a Police Operational Art," *CTC Sentinel*, West Point:

Countering Terrorism Center, 15 June 2009, https://www.ctc. usma.edu/posts/preventing-another-mumbai-building-a-poli...

[xviii] *BBC,* "Gunmen kill 13 at Karachi's Jinnah International Airport," 8 June 2014, http://www.bbc.com/news/world-asia-27757264.

[xix] Taimur Khan, "Karachi Attack Shows Pakistani Taliban Fighting to Re-Assert Itself," *The National,* June 2014, http://www. thenational.ae/world/pakistan/karachi-attack-shows-pakistani-...

[xx] "Cornered French Suspects Vow to Die as Martyrs," *USA Today,* 9 January 2015, http://www.wusa9.com/story/news/nation/2015/01/09/report-hostages-taken-...

[xxi] Scott Bronstein, "Cherif and Said Kouachi: Their Path to Terror," *CNN,* 14 January 2015, http://www.cnn.com/2015/01/13/world/kouachi-brothers-radicalization/Erich Schmitt, Mark Mazzetti, and Rukmini Callimachi, "Disputed Claims Over Qaeda Role in Paris Attacks," *The New York Times,* 14 January 2015, http://www.nytimes.com/2015/01/15/world/europe/al-qaeda-in-the-arabian-p...

[xxii] Some have snarkily compared the operation to the infamous "Leeroy Jenkins" raid in the computer game *World of Warcraft,* mixing the audio dialogue from the failed multiplayer mission with the video of the Hyper Cacher police assault. See, for example, https://www.youtube.com/watch?v=cKw65EN_JtE.

[xxiii] Daniel Howden, "Terror in Westgate Mall: The Full Story Of The Attacks That Devastated Kenya," *The Guardian,* 4 October 2013, http://www.theguardian.com/world/interactive/2013/oct/04/westgate-mall-a...

[xxiv] Clint Watts, "Inspired, Networked, and Directed: The Muddled Jihad of ISIS and Al-Qaeda Post-Hebo," *War on the Rocks,* 12 January 2015, http://warontherocks.com/2015/01/inspired-networked-directed-the-muddled...

[xxv] For an overview of the debate, see Daveed Gartenstein-Ross, "Is Al Qaeda A Global Terror Threat Or A Local Military Menace?," *The Globe and Mail,* 28 May 2014, http://www.defenddemocracy.org/media-hit/

gartenstein-ross-daveed-debate-is-al-qaeda-a-global-terror-threat-or-a-local-military-menace/.

[xxvi] Maia de la Baume and Dan Bilefksy, "France Vows Forceful Measures Against Terrorism," *The New York Times*, 21 January 2015, http://www.nytimes.com/2015/01/22/world/europe/amedy-coulibaly-paris-gun...

[xxvii] Griff Witte and Anthony Faiola, "Suspect In Paris Attack Had 'Long-Term Obsession' Carrying Out Terrorist Attack," *The Washington Post*, 8 January 2015, http://www.washingtonpost.com/world/europe/suspect-in-paris-attack-had-l...

[xxviii] See David Kilcullen, *Out of the Mountains: The Coming Age of the Urban Guerrilla*, Oxford: Oxford University Press, 2013, Anthony James Joes, *Urban Guerrilla Warfare*, Lexington: The University Of Kentucky, 2007, and John Robb, *Brave New War: The Next Stage of Terrorism and the End of Globalization*, Hoboken: Wiley, 2007 for a sampling of academic and practitioner writings on urban guerrilla operations.

[xxix] Mariano Castillo, "Following The Tangled And Treacherous Trail After France Terror Attack,"*CNN*, 15 January 2014, http://www.cnn.com/2015/01/13/europe/france-charlie-hebdo-attack-trail/

[xxx] The Boston Marathon Bombing Attack (2013) was followed by the shooting of an MIT police officer, carjacking, a manhunt, and firefight. See J.M. Hirsh, "Boston Bombing Overview: The Unfolding Of A 5-Day Manhunt For Suspects," *Huffington Post*, 21 April 2013, http://www.huffingtonpost.com/2013/04/21/boston-bombing-timeline_n_31270...

[xxxi] Gartenstein-Ross and Farall's analysis is reviewed in Adam Elkus, "Leader of the Pack," *War on the Rocks*, 31 October 2013, http://warontherocks.com/2013/10/leader-of-the-pack/.

[xxxii] Watts, "Foreign Fighters and Ants: How They Form Their Colonies," *Geopoliticus: The FPRI Blog*, June 2013, http://www.fpri.org/geopoliticus/2013/07/foreign-fighters-and-ants-how-t...

[xxxiii] Daveed Gartenstein-Ross and Daniel Trombly, *The Tactical and Strategic Use of Small Arms by Terrorists*, Washington, DC: The Foundation for Defense of Democracies, 2012.

[xxxiv] Gartenstein-Ross and Trombly, 6.

[xxxv] Garteinstein-Ross and Trombly, 7.

[xxxvi] Gartenstein-Ross and Trombly, 7-8.

[xxxvii] Gartenstein-Ross and Trombly, 21.

[xxxviii] Sebastian Rotella, James Glaz, and David E. Sanger, "In 2008 Mumbai Attacks, Piles Of Spy Data, But An Uncompleted Puzzle," *ProPublica*, 21 December 2014, http://www.propublica.org/article/mumbai-attack-data-an-uncompleted-puzzle.

[xxxix] Steven Metz, "The Paris Attacks and the Logic of Insurgency," *World Politics Review*, 16 January 2015, http://www.worldpoliticsreview.com/articles/14873/the-paris-attacks-and-...

[xl] Ben Hubbard, "Islamic Extremists Take To Social Media To Praise Charlie Hebdo Attacks," *The New York Times*, 10 January 2015, http://www.nytimes.com/2015/01/11/world/europe/islamic-extremists-take-t...

[xli] Noah Ryman, "How Twitter Tracked the French Terror Suspects," *Time*, 8 Jan 2015.http://time.com/3659307/twitter-tracked-terror-suspects/ and Sanchez et al., ibid.

[xlii] See, for example, Alexander Kott(ed), *Battle of Cognition: The Future Information-Rich Warfare and the Mind of the Commander*, Westport: Praeger, 2007, and Christine Owen (ed), *Human Factors Challenges in Emergency Management: Enhancing Individual and Team Performance in Fire and Emergency Services*, Farnham: Ashgate, 2014.

[xliii] David Kilcullen "New terror paradigm after Charlie Hebdo raids," *The Australian*, 17 January 2015, http://www.theaustralian.com.au/in-depth/terror/new-terror-paradigm-afte...

[xliv] Postscript: As we completed this piece another urban siege attack transpired in Tripoli. Libya. This attack on 27 January 2015 involved a combined assault (car bomb and gun attack) against the Corinthia Hotel killing at least three and injuring a half

dozen more. See UN News, "Terrorist attack on hotel in Libyan capital," *Scoop*, 30 January 2015, http://www.scoop.co.nz/stories/ WO1501/S00251/terrorist-attack-on-hotel-i...

Chapter 9:
The ISIS Beheading Narrative

Notes

[i] Jonathan Matusitz, *Symbolism in Terrorism: Motivation, Communication, and Behaviour*, (New York: Rowman & Littlefield, 2015).

[ii] For recondite but instructive discussions of Islamic law, see Bernard Weiss, *The Spirit of Islamic Law* (London, 1998); Hashim Kamali, *Principles of Islamic Jurisprudence* (Cambridge, 1991); Ann Lambton "Changing Concepts of Justice and Injustice from the 5th Century to the 8th Century in Persia: The Saljuq Empire and the Ilkhanate" in *Studia Islamica* (volume 68, 1988) pp. 27-60; Wael Hallaq *A History of Islamic Legal Theories* (Cambridge, 1997); Franz Rosenthal, "Political Justice and the Just Ruler" in *Israel Oriental Studies* (volume 10, 1982) pp. 92-101. I owe these references to Gudrun Krämer, "Wettstreit der Werte: Anmerkungen zum zeitgenössischen islamischen Diskurs" in *Die kulturellen Werte Europas* edited by Hans Joas and Klaus Wiegandt (Bonn: Bundes zentrale für politische Bildung, 2005) pp. 469-493.

[iii] For an overview of Islamic history, see Efraim Karsh's *Islamic Empire: A History* (New Haven: Yale University Press, 2007).

[iv] Timothy Furnish, "Beheading in the Name of Islam" in The Middle East Quarterly, (12 (2), 51-57, 2005).

[v] See Michael Bonner's *Jihad in Islamic History: Doctrines and Practices*. (Princeton: Princeton University Press, 2008).

[vi] For a comprehensive discussion of the evolutionary development of narrative as a social tool, see Brian Boyd's *On the Origin of*

[vi] *Stories: Evolution, Cognition, and Fiction* (Cambridge: Harvard University Press, 2009).

[vii] Dawn Perlmutter, "Mujahideen Blood Rituals: The Religious and Forensic Symbolism of Al Qeada Beheading" in *Anthropoetics* (11-2, 10-21, 2005) and *Investigating Religious Terrorism and Ritualistic Crimes* (Boca Raton: CRC Press, 2003) and "Mujahideen Desecration: Beheadings, Mutilation & Muslim Iconoclasm" in *Anthropoetics* (12, 2, 1-8, 2006).

[viii] Jonathan Matusitz, *Symbolism in Terrorism: Motivation, Communication, and Behaviour*, (New York: Rowman & Littlefield, 2015).

[ix] See Eugene G. d'Aquili, Charles D. Laughlin, Jr., John McManus, et al, *The Spectrum of Ritual: A Biogenetic Structural Analysis* (New York: Columbia University Press, 1979). Victor Turner, "Body, Brain, and Culture," in *The Anthropology of Performance* (New York: PAJ Publications, 1987). Ronald Grimes, *Beginnings in Ritual Studies,* Revised Edition (University of South Carolina Press, 1995). D' Aquili and Andrew B. Newberg, *The Mystical Mind: Probing the Biology of Religious Experience* (Minneapolis: Fortress Press, 1999). Nathan Mitchell, "What Biogeneticists Are Saying About Ritual: A Report," *Liturgy Digest*, 1:1 (Spring 1993). Pascal Boyer Religion Explained: The Human Instincts that Fashion Gods, Spirits, and Ancestors (Wiedenfeld and Nicolson: London, 2001).

[x] Combating Terrorism Center *The Islamic Imagery Project: Visual Motifs in Jihadi Internet Propaganda,* 2014.

[xi] For accounts of the evolutionary development of ritual, see Pascal Boyer's *Religion Explained: The Human Instincts that Fashion Gods, Spirits, and Ancestors* 2001 (New York: Basic Books) and Robin Dunbar's *The Human Story*, 2004 (London: Faber & Faber). For an early but still-useful look at the neurological basis of ritual, see Eugene D'Aquili's *The Spectrum of Ritual: A Biogenetic Analysis*, 1979 (Columbia: Columbia University Press) and *The Mystical Mind*, 1999 (Fortress Press).

Chapter 10:
ISIS For The Common Man

No notes.

Chapter 11:
Nigeria's Critical Juncture:
Boko Haram, Buhari, and the Future
of the Fourth Republic

Notes

[1] Council on Foreign Relations, "Nigeria Security Tracker," http://www.cfr.org/nigeria/nigeria-security-tracker/p29483.

[2] *BBC News*, "Boko Haram HQ Gwoza in Nigeria 'retaken'," March 27, 2015, http://www.bbc.com/news/world-africa-32087211.

[3] Adam Nossiter, "Mercenaries Join Military Campaign Against Boko Haram," *New York Times*, March 12, 2015, http://www.nytimes.com/2015/03/13/world/africa/nigerias-fight-against-boko-haram-gets-help-from-south-african-mercenaries.html; and David Smith, "South Africa's ageing white mercenaries who helped turn tide on Boko Haram," *Guardian*, April 14, 2015, http://www.theguardian.com/world/2015/apr/14/south-africas-ageing-white-mercenaries-who-helped-turn-tide-on-boko-haram.

[4] Adam Nossiter, "Chad Strongman Says Nigeria is Absent in Fight Against Boko Haram," *New York Times*, March 27, 2015, http://www.nytimes.com/2015/03/28/world/africa/chad-strongman-says-nigeria-is-absent-in-fight-against-boko-haram.html.

[5] Aminu Abubakar and Bukar Hussein, "Civilians still targets for Boko Haram despite military success," *Agence France-Presse*, April 28, 2015, http://news.yahoo.com/civilians-still-targets-boko-haram-despite-military-success-135041894.html; and *Agence France-Presse*, "Regional forces retake Nigerian town

from Boko Haram, says Niger," April 1, 2015,http://news.yahoo.com/regional-forces-retake-nigerian-town-boko-haram-says-112004968.html.

[6] Estimates of Boko Haram's size range from 6,000 to 15,000 fighters. *VOA News*, "US Estimates Boko Haram Has Up to 6,000 Fighters," February 6, 2015, http://www.voanews.com/content/boko-haram-attacks-niger-border-town-/2631583.html; and Amnesty International, *Our Job is to Shoot, Slaughter, and Kill: Boko Haram's Reign of Terror in North-East Nigeria*, AFR 44/1360/2015, April 15, 2015, https://www.amnesty.org/en/documents/afr44/1360/2015/en/.

[7] *VOA News*, "Niger President: End of Boko Haram Near," April 1, 2015, http://www.voanews.com/content/niger-president-end-of-boko-haram-is-near/2702500.html; and Lisa Schlein, "UN Calls for Global Response to Stop Boko Haram Terror Threat," *VOA News*, April 1, 2015, http://www.voanews.com/content/un-calls-for-global-response-to-stop-terrorist-threat-by-boko-haram/2702583.html.

[8] Mike Smith, *Boko Haram: Inside Nigeria's Unholy War* (New York: I.B. Tauris, 2015), 12-13, 137-138; and Marc-Antoine Pérouse de Montclos, "Nigeria's Interminable Insurgency? Addressing the Boko Haram Crisis," Chatham House (September 2014), 11-12, http://www.chathamhouse.org/publication/nigerias-interminable-insurgency-addressing-boko-haram-crisis.

[9] Ibid; and International Crisis Group, *Curbing Violence in Nigeria (II): The Boko Haram Insurgency, Africa Report*, no. 216 (April 3, 2014), 22, http://www.crisisgroup.org/en/publication-type/media-releases/2014/africa/curbing-violence-in-nigeria-the-boko-haram-insurgency.aspx.

[10] Jacob Zenn, "Leadership Analysis of Boko Haram and Ansaru in Nigeria," *CTC Sentinel* 7, no. 2 (February 24, 2014), 23-29, https://www.ctc.usma.edu/posts/leadership-analysis-of-boko-haram-and-ansaru-in-nigeria; and John Campbell, *U.S. Policy to Counter Nigeria's Boko Haram*, Council on Foreign Relations,

Special Report, no. 70 (November 2014), 9-10, http://www.cfr. org/nigeria/us-policy-counter-nigerias-boko-haram/p33806.

[11] Monde Kingsley Nfor, "No shortage of recruits for Boko Haram in Cameroon's Far North," *IRIN*, March 5, 2015, http://www. irinnews.org/report/101198/no-shortage-of-recruits-for-boko-haram-in-cameroon-s-far-north; and Thomas Fessy, "Niger hit by Nigeria's Boko Haram fallout," *BBC News*, April 22, 2014, http://www.bbc.com/news/world-africa-27111884.

[12] Smith, *Boko Haram*, 5.

[13] On IS governance, see Charles Caris and Samuel Reynolds, "ISIS Governance in Syria," Institute for the Study of War, *Middle East Security Report*, no. 22 (July 2014), http://www. understandingwar.org/report/isis-governance-syria.

[14] Amnesty International, *Our Job is to Shoot, Slaughter, and Kill*, 15-17. On violent predation, see Nelson Kasfir, "Domestic Anarchy, Security Dilemmas, and Violent Predation: Causes of Failure," in Robert Rotberg, ed. *When States Fail: Causes and Consequences* (Princeton: Princeton University Press, 2004), 53-76; on anomic violence, see Phil Williams, "The Terrorism Debate Over Mexican Drug Trafficking Violence," *Terrorism and Political Violence* 24, no. 2 (2012), 259-278.

[15] For the importance of political and administrative personnel in rebel treatment of civilian populations, see William Reno, *Warfare in Independent Africa* (New York: Cambridge University Press, 2011), 119-162.

[16] Under conditions of anarchy, stationary bandits taxing local production on an ongoing basis have an incentive to limit their own predation and protect populations under their control from other bandits in order to avoid threats to their own source of income. In other words, stationary bandits have an incentive to govern. Roving or mobile bandits, in contrast, have no such incentive and will extract as much as possible, as quickly as possible with no regard for their victims before moving on to the next target group. See Kyle Beardsley and Kristian Skrede

Gleditsch, "Is Boko Haram a Roving Bandit?" *Political Violence @ a Glance*, April 16, 2015, http://politicalviolenceataglance.org/2015/04/16/is-boko-haram-a-roving-bandit/. For a detailed description of a representative sample of Boko Haram raids, see Amnesty International, *Our Job is to Shoot, Slaughter, and Kill*, 33-55.

[17] Kevin Seiff, "I've seen the Taliban's brutality in Afghanistan. Boko Haram might be worse." *Washington Post*, April 12, 2015, http://www.washingtonpost.com/blogs/worldviews/wp/2015/04/12/i-spent-nearly-3-years-in-afghanistan-but-nothing-prepared-me-for-the-brutality-of-boko-haram; and Tomi Oladipo, "Ashes and death: What Boko Haram left behind in Baga," *BBC News*, March 16, 2015, http://www.bbc.com/news/world-africa-31902549.

[18] Ibid; and Amnesty International, *Our Job is to Shoot, Slaughter, and Kill*, 59-76.

[19] Ibid.

[20] Jay Loschky and Robin Sanders, "Nigeria's Big Chance," *Gallup*, April 8, 2015, http://www.gallup.com/opinion/gallup/182345/nigeria-big-chance.aspx.

[21] Ibid.

[22] Philip Obaji, Jr., "Can This Man Crush Boko Haram?" *Daily Beast*, April 14, 2015, http://www.thedailybeast.com/articles/2015/04/14/can-this-man-crush-boko-haram.html; and "Maitatsine Riots," in Toyin Falola and Ann Genova, *Historical Dictionary of Nigeria* (Lanham, MD: Scarecrow Press, 2009), 218.

[23] *BBC News*, "Nigeria's Muhammadu Buhari in profile," March 31, 2015, http://www.bbc.com/news/world-africa-12890807.

[24] Toyin Falola and Matthew Heaton, *A History of Nigeria* (New York: Cambridge University Press, 2008), 215; and "Buhari, Major General Muhammadu (1942-)," in Falola and Genova, *Historical Dictionary of Nigeria*, 68.

[25] Campbell, *U.S. Policy to Counter Nigeria's Boko Haram*, 13; Tim Cocks, "Boko Haram exploits Nigeria's slow military decline," *Reuters*, May 9, 2014, http://www.reuters.com/article/2014/05/09/

us-nigeria-military-insight-idUSBREA4809220140509; and Will Ross, "The soldiers without enough weapons to fight jihadists," *BBC News*, January 22, 2015, http://www.bbc.com/news/magazine-30930767.
[26] Ibid.
[27] Amnesty International, *Nigeria: Trapped in the Cycle of Violence*, AFR 44/043/2012 (November 2012), https://www.amnesty.org/en/documents/AFR44/043/2012/en/; Human Rights Watch, *Spiraling Violence: Boko Haram Attacks and Security Force Abuses in Nigeria* (October 2012), https://www.hrw.org/reports/2012/10/11/spiraling-violence-0; Adam Nossiter, "Massacre in Nigeria Spurs Outcry Over Military Tactics," *New York Times*, April 29, 2013, http://www.nytimes.com/2013/04/30/world/africa/outcry-over-military-tactics-after-massacre-in-nigeria.html; and Michelle Faul, "Nigeria's military killing thousands of detainees," Associated Press, October 18, 2013, http://news.yahoo.com/nigerias-military-killing-thousands-detainees-173718500.html.
[28] Obaji, "Can This Man Crush Boko Haram?"
[29] John Campbell, *Nigeria: Dancing on the Brink* (Lanham, MD: Rowman & Littlefield), 29.
[30] Campbell, *U.S. Policy to Counter Nigeria's Boko Haram*, 23.
[31] On ethnically organized security dilemmas, see Barry Posen, "The Security Dilemma and Ethnic Conflict," in Michael E. Brown, ed. *Ethnic Conflict and International Security* (Princeton: Princeton University Press, 1993), 103-124; and Kasfir, "Domestic Anarchy, Security Dilemmas, and Violent Predation," 53-76.
[32] See Oleg Svet, "COIN's Failure in Afghanistan," *National Interest*, August 31, 2012, http://nationalinterest.org/commentary/coins-failure-afghanistan-7409.
[33] Susan Rose-Ackerman, "Establishing the Rule of Law," in Rotberg, *When States Fail*, 184.
[34] Campbell, *U.S. Policy to Counter Nigeria's Boko Haram*, 17-23; Lauren Ploch Blanchard, "Nigeria's Boko Haram: Frequently

Asked Questions," Congressional Research Service, R43558 (June 10, 2014), 14-16, https://fas.org/sgp/crs/row/R43558.pdf; and *BBC News*, "Boko Haram crisis: Nigeria fury over US arms refusal," November 11, 2014, http://www.bbc.com/news/world-africa-30006066.

[35] Smith, *Boko Haram*, 73-74.

[36] Campbell, *U.S. Policy to Counter Nigeria's Boko Haram*, 21-22.

[37] Charles Dickson, "Grim Tales of Rape, Child Trafficking in Displaced Persons Camps," International Centre for Investigative Reporting, January 29, 2015, http://icirnigeria.org/grim-tales-of-rape-child-trafficking-in-displaced-persons-camps; and Moki Edwin Kindzeka, "UN Refugee Chief: Nigeria Crisis Similar to Syria's," *VOA News*, March 26, 2015, http://www.voanews.com/content/un-refugee-chief-nigeria-crisis-similar-to-iraq-syria/2695111.html.

[38] Kyari Mohammed, "The Message and Methods of Boko Haram," in Marc-Antoine Pérouse de Montclos, ed. *Boko Haram: Islamism, Politics, Security and the State in Nigeria* (Leiden: African Studies Centre, 2014), 23; Daniel Jordan Smith, *A Culture of Corruption: Everyday Deception and Popular Discontent in Nigeria* (Princeton: Princeton University Press, 2007), 219-220; and Falola and Heaton, *A History of Nigeria*, 211.

Chapter 12:
On Self-Declared Caliph Ibrahim's May 2015 Message to Muslims:
Key Problems of Motivation, Marginalization, Illogic, and Empirical Delusion in the Caliphate Project

Notes

[1] English translation available at: https://pietervanostaeyen.wordpress.com/2015/05/14/a-new-audio-message-b..., accessed 18 May 2015.

[2] An Address from Amirul-Mu'miniin [Commander of the Faithful], the Khalifah of the Muslims Abu Bakr al-Husayni al-Qurashi al-Baghdadi, "Even if the Disbelievers Despise Such," 13 November 2014, available at www.gulfup/NuPaRN, accessed on 14 Novembe4r 2014. See also: Rukmini Callimachi, "ISIS Releases a Recording it Says was Made Its Leader," 14 May 2014, available at: www.nytimes.com/2015/05/15/world/middleeast/isis-releases-recording-said..., accessed on 15 May 2015.

[3] Ibid.

[4] See, for example: Paul Kamolnick, *Delegitimizing Al-Qaeda: A Jihad Realist Approach*, Strategic Studies Institute, Carlisle, PA: US Army War College, Strategic Studies Institute, 2012. Available at: http://www.strategicstudiesinstitute.army.mil/pubs/display.cfm?pubID=1099.

[5] Paul Kamolnick. "The Egyptian Islamic Group's Critique of Al-Qaeda's Interpretation of Jihad." *Perspectives on Terrorism*, October 2013, Vol. 7, No. 5, pp. 93-110. www.terrorismanalysts.com/pt/index.php/pot/article/view/293/591.; Paul Kamolnick "Al Qaeda's Shari'a Crisis: Sayyid Imam and the Jurisprudence of Lawful Military Jihad." *Studies in Conflict & Terrorism*, May 2013, 36(5): 394-418. DOI: 10.1080/1057610X.2013.775478.

[6] Ibid.
[7] Ibid.
[8] Ibid.
[9] Ibid.
[10] Ibid.
[11] Ibid.
[12] Ibid.
[13] Ibid.
[14] Ibid.
[15] Ibid.
[16] Ibid.
[17] Ibid.
[18] Ibid.

[19] Ibid.
[20] For important analyses: See, David Cook, *Abu Mus'ab al-Suri and Abu-Musa'b al-Zarqawi: The Apocalyptic Theorist and the Apocalyptic Practitioner*, Unpublished Manuscript, 2007. (15 pp.); David Cook, "Iraq as the Focus for Apocalyptic Scenarios," CTC Sentinel, October 2008, Vol. 1, No. 11, n.p., available at *www.ctc.usma.edu/v2/wp-content/uploads/2010/06/Vol1Iss11-Art8.pdf*, accessed April 21, 2015; Emma Glanfield, "The 1,300-year-old apocalyptic prophecy that predicted a war between an Islamic army and 'infidel horde' in Syria is fuelling ISIS's brutal killers," October 9, 2014, available at *www.dailymail.co.uk/news/article-2786039/*, accessed on May 5, 2015; BBC Monitoring, "Why Islamic state chose town of Dabiq for propaganda," November 17, 2014, available at *www.bbc.com/news/world-middle-east-30083303*, accessed on April 30, 2015; Jessica Stern, "ISIS's Apocalyptic Vision," February 25, 2015, available at *www.hoover.org/research/isiss-apocalyptic-vision*, accessed on May 5, 2015; Jessica Stern and J.M. Berger, *ISIS: The State of Terror*, New York: Ecco, 2015. An important recent exchange occurred with the publication of and commentary on Graeme Wood's article for the Atlantic. See: Graeme Wood, "What ISIS Really Wants: The Islamic State is no mere collection of psychopaths. It is a religious group with carefully considered beliefs, among them that it is a key agent of the coming apocalypse. Here's what that means for its strategy—and for how to stop it," March 2015, available at *www.theatlantic.com/features/archive/2015/02/what-isis-really-wants/384980/*, accessed on February 20, 2015. [6,543 comments as of Feb. 20; 14,163 comments as of May 13, 2015]; Fareed Zakaria, "the limits of the 'Islamic' label," February 19, 2015, available at *www.washingtonpost.com/opinons/the-limits-of-the-islamic-label/2015/02/19/*, accessed on February 20, 2015; Caner K. Dagli, "The Phony Islam of ISIS," (c. February 19, 2015; n.d.), available at *www.theatlantic.com/global/archive/2015/02/the-phony-islam-of-isis/386156*,

accessed on March 2, 2015; Jack Jenkins, "What the Atlantic Gets Dangerously Wrong About ISIS and Islam," February 18, 2015/updated February 19, 2015, available at thinkprogress.org/world/2015/02/18/3624121/atlantic-gets-dangerously-wrong-isis-islam, accessed on February 19, 2015; J.M. Berger, "Enough about Islam: Why religion is not the most useful way to understand ISIS," February 18, 2015, available at *www.brookings.edu/blogs/order-from-chaos-posts/2015/02/18-enough-about-islam-berger*, accessed on February 19, 2015. Various official publications of the ISO are also key: Islamic State News, #1, June 1, 2014, available at *azelin.files.wordpress.com/2014/06/islamic-state-of-iraq-and-al-shc481m-22islamic-state-news-122.pdf*, accessed on December 10, 2014; Islamic State News, #2, June 2014 [Shaban 1435], available at *azelin.files.wordpress.com/2014/06/islamic-state-of-iraq-and-al-shc481m-e2809cislamic-state-news-222.pdf*, accessed on December 10, 2014; Islamic State Report, #2, June 2014 [Shaban 1435], available at *azelin.files.wordpress.com/2014/06/islamic-state-of-iraq-and-al-shc481m-e2809cislamic-state-report-2e280b3.pdf*, accessed on December 10, 2014; Islamic State News, #3, June 2014 [Shaban 1435], *azelin.files.wordpress.com/2014/06/islamic-state-of-iraq-and-al-shc481m-e2809cislamic-state-news-322.pdf*, accessed on December 10, 2014; Dabiq, #1, July 5, 2014 [Ramadan 1435], available at *archive.org/download/…/dbq01_desktop_en.pdf*, accessed on August 19, 2014; Dabiq, #2, July 28, 2014 [Ramadan 1435], available at *azelin.files.wordpress.com/2014/07/Islamic-state-e2809cdc481biq-magazine-2e28ob3.pdf*, accessed on August 19, 2014; Dabiq, #3, August 2014 [Shawwal 1435], available at *archive.org/download/Dabiq03_en.pdf*, accessed on October 6, 2014; Dabiq, #4, c.September/October? 2014 [Dhul-Hijjah 1435], available at *ia601403.us.archiv.org/0/items/Dabq04en/Dabiq_04_en.pdf*, accessed on October 13, 2014; Dabiq, #5, November 22, 2014 [Muharram 1436], available at *ia601407.us.archiv.org/6/items/dbq05en/Dabiq_Issue_5.pdf*, accessed on December 16, 2014; Dabiq, #6, c. December/January

2015 [Rabi' al-Awwal 1436], available at *ia801509.us.archiv. org/19/items/dbq_06/Dabiq_6.pdf*, accessed on January 7, 2015; Dabiq, #7,February 12, 2015 [Rabi' al-Ahkir 1436], available at *ia601506.ur.archiv.org/27/items/Dabiq7/Dabiq_7.pdf*, accessed on February 13, 2015; Dabiq, #8, c. March 2015 [Jumada al-Akhirah 1436], available at *azelin.files.wordpress.com/2015/03/the-islamic-state-e2809cdc481biq-magazine-8e280b3.pdf*, accessed on April 2, 2015; Dabiq, #9, May 21, 2015, available at azelin. files.wordpress.com/2015/05-the-islamic-state-e2809cdc481biq-magazine-9e28063.pdf, accessed on May 26, 2015. For the Black Flag Book Series and Shuhada [Martyrs] Book Series: As of May 13, 2015, all books available on: *archive.org/download/ BlackFlagNShuhadaStoriesEbooks/Black%20Flag%20n%20 Shuhada%Stories%20Ebooks.rar*.The Original Shuhada Series: *Lover's of Maidens of Paradise* [Lover's of the Hur al Ayn]. A copy of Abdullah Azzam's, *The Martyrs of Afghanistan*, Azzam Publications. Covers period 1979-1989. Available at *archive.org/ download/BlackFlagNShuhadaStoriesEbooks/Black%20Flag%20 n%20Shuhada%Stories%20Ebooks.rar*, accessed on May 13, 2015; *Miracles in Syria* (2012-13), available at *archive.org/ download/BlackFlagNShuhadaStoriesEbooks/Black%20Flag%20 n%20Shuhada%Stories%20Ebooks.rar*, accessed on May 13, 2015; *Martyr's of Syria* (2014), [2011-2014] available at *archive. org/download/BlackFlagNShuhadaStoriesEbooks/Black%20 Flag%20n%20Shuhada%Stories%20Ebooks.rar*, accessed on May 13, 2015; *The Undead Warriors*, [Iraq, 2003-2006] *archive.org/ download/BlackFlagNShuhadaStoriesEbooks/Black%20Flag%20 n%20Shuhada%Stories%20Ebooks.rar*, accessed on May 13, 2015; *Revivers of the Khilafah* (Global Caliphate) [2005-2010], available at *archive.org/download/BlackFlagNShuhadaStoriesEbooks/ Black%20Flag%20n%20Shuhada%Stories%20Ebooks.rar*, accessed on May 13, 2015. For the Original series of 6 Conquest works confirmed by prophecy: East, Syria, Arabia, Persia, Rome, Palestine, [then Major End Times Signs, Events]; [#1] *Black*

Flags of the East (1979-2012+), available at *archive.org/download/ BlackFlagNShuhadaStoriesEbooks/Black%20Flag%20n%20 Shuhada%Stories%20Ebooks.rar*, accessed on May 13, 2015; [#2] *Black Flags from Syria*, Revolution 2011-2020+, available at *archive. org/download/BlackFlagNShuhadaStoriesEbooks/Black%20 Flag%20n%20Shuhada%Stories%20Ebooks.rar*, accessed on May 13, 2015; [#3] *Black Flags from Arabia*, available at *archive. org/download/BlackFlagNShuhadaStoriesEbooks/Black%20 Flag%20n%20Shuhada%Stories%20Ebooks.rar*, accessed on May 13, 2015; [#4] *Black Flags from Persia*, available at *archive. org/download/BlackFlagNShuhadaStoriesEbooks/Black%20 Flag%20n%20Shuhada%Stories%20Ebooks.rar*, accessed on May 13, 2015; [#5] *Black Flags from Rome*, available at *archive.org/ download/BlackFlagNShuhadaStoriesEbooks/Black%20Flag%20 n%20Shuhada%Stories%20Ebooks.rar*, accessed on May 13, 2015; [#6] *Black Flags from Palestine*, available at *archive.org/ download/BlackFlagNShuhadaStoriesEbooks/Black%20Flag%20 n%20Shuhada%Stories%20Ebooks.rar*, accessed on May 13, 2015. For Post-Conquest of Raqqa/Mosul: *The Revived Caliphate*, (2014) [The Islamic State, 2003-2014+, *archive.org/download/ BlackFlagNShuhadaStoriesEbooks/Black%20Flag%20n%20 Shuhada%Stories%20Ebooks.rar*, accessed on May 13, 2015; *The Islamic State* (2015), available at *archive.org/download/ BlackFlagNShuhadaStoriesEbooks/Black%20Flag%20n%20 Shuhada%Stories%20Ebooks.rar*, accessed on May 13, 2015; *How to Survive in the West: A Mujahid Guide* (2015), available at *archive. org/download/BlackFlagNShuhadaStoriesEbooks/Black%20 Flag%20n%20Shuhada%Stories%20Ebooks.rar*, accessed on May 13, 2015; *Hijrah to the Islamic State* [2015], available at *archive.org/ download/BlackFlagNShuhadaStoriesEbooks/Black%20Flag%20 n%20Shuhada%Stories%20Ebooks.rar*, accessed on May 13, 2015.

[21] Ibid.

[22] For this approach to counterterrorist counter-messaging see: Paul Kamolnick, *Countering Radicalization and Recruitment to Al-Qaeda: Fighting the War of Deeds*. Letort Papers, Strategic Studies Institute, US Army War College, Carlisle Barracks, PA., June 2014, available at *strategicstudiesinstitute.army.mil/pubs/display.cfm?pubID=1205*.

Chapter 13:
America's New Strategic Reality: Irregular World War

Notes

[1] http://nunes.house.gov/
[2] https://www.google.com/search?client=safari&rls=en&q=california%27s+22nd+congressional+district&stick=H4sIAAAA AAAAAGOovnz8BQMDgxcHnxCnfq6-gZFJSUqxEpiZUlZQ VaJlkJ1spZ-eX5ZalJebmleiXxpfHJ-cn5delFpcXJBaVJyfZ5VcWl QElFLIT0vLTE71X9bROf_g_G7Be392PNVMsnn_PfgNAK7R _upnAAAA&sa=X&ei=d16IVejgFcjcsAWu4oLgBw&ved=0CK EBEJsTKAIwFw
[3] http://www.cbsnews.com/news/rep-devin-nunes-america-faces-highest-threat-level-ever/
[4] http://abcnews.go.com/US/fbi-midst-broad-campaign-disrupt-isis-sources/story?id=31826983
[5] http://www.voanews.com/content/us-security-chief-warns-of-new-phase-in-terrorist-threat/2762237.html
[6] http://www.usatoday.com/story/news/politics/2015/05/10/michael-morell-cia-the-great-war/27063655/
[7] http://www.theguardian.com/commentisfree/cifamerica/2010/dec/05/wikileaks-the-us-embassy-cables
[8] http://www.theguardian.com/world/2001/nov/01/afghanistan.terrorism3
[9] http://www.economist.com/node/16588026

[10] http://www.theatlantic.com/photo/2011/10/world-war-ii-the-holocaust/100170/
[11] http://www.cnn.com/2015/04/20/africa/somalia-violence/
[12] http://www.bbc.com/news/world-africa-13809501
[13] http://news.videonews.us/breakaway-rebels-injure-3-philippine-soldiers-south-0912398.html
[14] http://www.voanews.com/content/pakistan-afghanistan-sharif-ghani-abdullah/2762992.html
[15] http://news.bbc.co.uk/2/shared/spl/hi/uk/05/london_blasts/what_happened/html/
[16] http://www.theguardian.com/world/2015/apr/23/france-foils-five-terror-attacks-says-prime-minister
[17] http://www.straitstimes.com/news/asia/south-east-asia/story/malaysia-pulling-out-all-stops-hunt-bomb-plotters-20150429
[18] http://www.cnn.com/2014/09/29/justice/oklahoma-beheading-suspect/
[19] http://www.foxnews.com/us/2014/10/01/mohamed-mohamud-to-be-sentenced-wednesday-for-plot-to-attack-christmas-tree/
[20] http://www.stripes.com/news/us/texas-cartoon-contest-shooting-fuels-concern-over-lone-wolf-terror-attacks-1.344642

Chapter 14:
Al Shabaab Resurgence

Notes

[1] http://www.cfr.org/somalia/al-shabab/p18650
[2] http://amisom-au.org/amisom-background/
[3] http://amisom-au.org/2014/10/joint-security-update-on-operation-indian-ocean-by-somali-government-and-amisom/
[4] http://www.irinnews.org/report/100141/shortages-clan-rivalries-weaken-somalia-s-new-army
[5] http://www.theeastafrican.co.ke/news/Amisom-relief-as-EU-releases--1b-for-security/-/2558/2390216/-/bt2b0q/-/index.html

[6]   http://www.bbc.com/news/world-africa-33578890
[7]   http://www.bbc.com/news/world-africa-28219681
[8]   http://www.aljazeera.com/news/2015/02/deaths-attack-luxury-hotel-somalia-capital-mogadishu-150220103959237.html
[9]   http://www.aljazeera.com/news/2015/03/somalia-mogadishu-hotel-attack-150327142646865.html
[10] http://www.theguardian.com/world/2015/jul/10/gunmen-storm-hotel-somalian-capital-mogadishu
[11] http://www.independent.co.uk/news/world/africa/alshabaab-militants-attack-african-union-base-near-mogadishu-airport-in-somalia-9944895.html
[12] http://www.voanews.com/content/al-shabab-attacks-expose-amisom-weaknesses/2845768.html
[13] http://somalianewsroom.com/2015/07/03/%E2%80%8Banalysis-amisom-vacates-10-towns-in-somalia-amid-al-shabaabs-ramadan-attacks/
[14] http://www.cfr.org/somalia/al-shabab/p18650
[15] http://amisom-au.org/amisom-background/
[16] http://amisom-au.org/2014/10/joint-security-update-on-operation-indian-ocean-by-somali-government-and-amisom/
[17] http://www.irinnews.org/report/100141/shortages-clan-rivalries-weaken-somalia-s-new-army
[18] http://www.theeastafrican.co.ke/news/Amisom-relief-as-EU-releases--1b-for-security/-/2558/2390216/-/bt2b0q/-/index.html
[19] http://www.bbc.com/news/world-africa-33578890
[20] http://www.bbc.com/news/world-africa-28219681
[21] http://www.aljazeera.com/news/2015/02/deaths-attack-luxury-hotel-somalia-capital-mogadishu-150220103959237.html
[22] http://www.aljazeera.com/news/2015/03/somalia-mogadishu-hotel-attack-150327142646865.html
[23] http://www.theguardian.com/world/2015/jul/10/gunmen-storm-hotel-somalian-capital-mogadishu

[24] http://www.independent.co.uk/news/world/africa/alshabaab-militants-attack-african-union-base-near-mogadishu-airport-in-somalia-9944895.html
[25] http://www.voanews.com/content/al-shabab-attacks-expose-amisom-weaknesses/2845768.html
[26] http://somalianewsroom.com/2015/07/03/%E2%80%8Banalysis-amisom-vacates-10-towns-in-somalia-amid-al-shabaabs-ramadan-attacks/

Chapter 15:
A War With ISIS is a Battle Against Ideologies

Notes

[1] http://www.cnn.com/2011/WORLD/meast/02/21/arab.unrest.alqaeda.analysis/
[2] http://www.npr.org/blogs/thetwo-way/2014/06/13/321665375/isis-an-islamist-group-too-extreme-even-for-al-qaida
[3] https://now.mmedia.me/lb/en/specialreports/565067-understanding-jihadists-in-their-own-words
[4] http://www.cbc.ca/news/world/the-life-of-a-jihadi-wife-why-one-canadian-woman-joined-isis-s-islamic-state-1.2696385
[5] https://ia902501.us.archive.org/2/items/hym3_22aw/english.pdf
[6] http://www.cnn.com/2015/02/25/middleeast/isis-kids-propaganda/
[7] http://www.independent.co.uk/news/uk/home-news/british-primark-jihadist-from-portsmouth-is-killed-while-fighting-with-isis-in-syria-9661869.html
[8] http://www.cnn.com/2015/02/25/middleeast/isis-kids-propaganda/
[9] http://www.dw.de/desperation-drives-syrians-to-isis/a-17786218
[10] http://www.dw.de/desperation-drives-syrians-to-isis/a-17786218
[11] http://extremedialogue.org/

Chapter 16:
Interview: Thinking About ISIS in Strategic Terms

No notes.

Chapter 17:
ISIS and the Sex Factor

Notes

[1] http://www.nbcnews.com/storyline/isis-terror/isis-numbers-foreign-fighter-total-keeps-growing-n314731
[2] Ibid.
[3] http://abcnews.go.com/International/isis-pennsylvania-woman-allegedly-join-group/story?id=30086440
[4] http://dailycaller.com/2015/07/17/seven-islamic-terrorist-attacks-in-usa-in-seven-years-for-obama-administration/
[5] http://www.memrijttm.org/islamic-state-isis-releases-pamphlet-on-female-slaves.html
[6] http://www.businessinsider.com/isis-sells-child-sex-slaves-for-124-2015-8
[7] http://www.nbcnews.com/storyline/isis-terror/hundreds-christians-feared%20-captured-isis-syria-group-n405871

[i] Brinsley's ties to Islamic extremism is questionable, as police believe that he was revenging the deaths of Eric Garner and Michael Brown.

Chapter 18:
Why is Turkey Attacking the Kurdish Militants Instead of ISIS?

[1] http://www.bbc.com/news/world-europe-27649472

[2] http://foreignpolicy.com/2013/08/22/how-turkey-went-from-zero-problems-to-zero-friends/
[3] http://www.economist.com/news/middle-east-and-africa/21659870-truce-between-turkey-and-kurdish-militants-over-turkey-and-kurds
[4] http://www.aljazeera.com/news/2015/08/turkey-coalition-government-150813123140443.html
[5] http://www.ntv.com.tr/turkiye/cumhurbaskani-erdogandan-baskanlik-sistemi-aciklamasi,eUs7_17mF0CQZnJamO46JQ
[6] http://www.tandfonline.com/doi/abs/10.1080/13608746.2015.1046264#.VdX_Z_mqqko
[7] https://books.google.com.tr/books?hl=tr&lr=&id=N-JnAwAAQBAJ&oi=fnd&pg=PR1&dq=bugra+and+savaskan&ots=t6qnVowJre&sig=mhGyWHqjKVLcELl-c2BwRocHB5A&redir_esc=y#v=onepage&q=bugra%20and%20savaskan&f=false
[8] http://researchturkey.org/turkeys-new-path-the-rise-of-electoral-authoritarianism
[9] http://pas.sagepub.com/content/43/3/385.abstract
[10] http://www.tandfonline.com/doi/abs/10.1080/13510347.2015.1013467?journalCode=fdem20#abstract
[11] http://www.ozgur-gundem.com/yazi/133642/yeni-surec-devrimci-halk-savasi-surecidir
[12] http://www.aljazeera.com/news/2015/07/kurdish-leader-asks-pkk-withdraw-northern-iraq-150730193413866.html
[13] http://www.cumhuriyet.com.tr/haber/turkiye/291073/Kararin_anlami_sansur.html
[14] http://www.nytimes.com/2015/08/19/world/europe/isis-video-urges-turks-to-revolt-against-their-president.html?ref=topics
[15] http://www.diken.com.tr/erdogan-yine-hdpyi-hedef-gosterip-teror-orgutu-temsilcisi-ilan-etti/
[16] http://t24.com.tr/haber/erdogana-gore-hayvandan-da-asagi-hain-yazar-ve-sozde-aydin-guruhu var,306809

[17] http://www.bbc.com/news/world-europe-33606291

Chapter 19:
Status Quo in the Sinai

No notes.

Chapter 20:
Islamism, Islamofascism, and Islam?

Notes

[1] http://www.breitbart.com/InstaBlog/2014/09/24/In-U-N-Speech-Obama-Drops-Claim-ISIL-is-Not-Islamic
[2] http://www.islamdaily.org/en/islam/7679.islam-and-monoculture.htm
[3] http://www.slate.com/articles/news_and_politics/fighting_words/2007/10/defending_islamofascism.html
[4] http://www.salon.com/2003/03/25/willis_6/
[5] http://www.danielpipes.org/comments/116335

Chapter 21:
The Problem with Proxies:
Ideology is No Substitute for Operational Control

Notes

[1] Karen DeYoung, "U.S.-Trained Fighters in Syria Gave Equipment to al-Qaeda Affiliate," *Washington Post*, September 25, 2015.
[2] Mark Mazzetti, "C.I.A. Study of Covert Aid Fueled Skepticism About Helping Syrian Rebels," *New York Times*, October 14, 2014.

[3] Anne Barnard and Eric Schmitt, "Rival Insurgents Surprise Syrians Supported by U.S.," *New York Times*, August 1, 2015, p. 1.

[4] Liz Sly, "Petraeus: The Islamic State isn't our biggest problem in Iraq," *Washington Post*, March 20, 2015.

[5] Human Rights Watch, "After Liberation Came Destruction: Iraqi Militias and the Aftermath of Amerli," March 18, 2015.

[6] Daniel Yergin and Joseph Stanislaw, *The Commanding Heights* (New York: Simon and Schuster, 2002), p. 192.

[7] Steve Coll, *Ghost Wars* (New York: Penguin, 2004), p. 16.

[8] Molly Dunigan, *Victory for Hire: Private Security Companies' Impact on Military Effectiveness* (Stanford: Stanford University Press, 2011), p. 6.

[9] Janice E. Thomson, *Mercenaries, Pirates, and Sovereigns: State-Building and Extraterritorial Violence in Early Modern Europe* (Princeton: Princeton University Press, 1994), p. 11.

[10] P. W. Singer, *Corporate Warriors: The Rise of the Privatized Military Industry* (Ithaca, NY: Cornell University Press, 2007); Allison Stanger, *One Nation Under Contract: The Outsourcing of American Power and the Future of Foreign Policy* (New Haven: Yale University Press, 2009).

[11] Yelena Biberman, *Gambling with Violence: Why States Outsource the Use of Force to Domestic Nonstate Actors* (PhD diss., Brown University, 2014).

[12] Author's interviews with military officials, Islamabad, Pakistan, December 2014.

[13] Lowell Dittmer, "South Asia's Security Dilemma," *Asian Survey* 41, no. 6 (November/December 2001), p. 897.

[14] Inward Telegram from India (Govt) to Commonwealth Relations Office, November 1, 1947; War Staff, India Office, "Kashmir" (Top Secret); 7, L/WS/1/1139; L/WS War Staff Papers, 1921-51, Asian and African Studies Collection, British Library, London, United Kingdom.

[15] Top Secret Cypher Telegram from U.S. High Commissioner in India, New Delhi, to Ministry of Defence, London, November

9, 1947; War Staff, India Office, "Kashmir" (Top Secret); 7, L/WS/1/1139; L/WS War Staff Papers, 1921-51, Asian and African Studies Collection, British Library, London, United Kingdom.

[16] Inward Telegram from India (Govt) to Commonwealth Relations Office, November 1, 1947; War Staff, India Office, "Kashmir" (Top Secret); 7, L/WS/1/1139; L/WS War Staff Papers, 1921-51, Asian and African Studies Collection, British Library, London, United Kingdom.

[17] Andrew Whitehead, *A Mission in Kashmir* (New Delhi, Penguin/Viking, 2007), p. 4.

[18] Akbar Khan, *Raiders in Kashmir* (Islamabad: National Book Foundation, 1975), p. 47.

[19] Whitehead, *A Mission in Kashmir*, p. 45.

[20] Khan, *Raiders in Kashmir*, p. 56.

[21] Mao Tse-tung, *Guerrilla Warfare* (1937), "What Is Guerrilla Warfare?"

[22] Ibid., "The Relation of Guerrilla Hostilities to Regular Operations."

[23] Criminal Investigation Department, *Report on Pakistani Organized Subversion, Sabotage and Infiltration in Jammu and Kashmir* (Jammu and Kashmir, India, 1966), p. 31.

[24] Ibid., pp. 36-37.

[25] Ibid., p. 43.

Chapter 22:
Why ISIS is Winning in Iraq

Notes

[1] http://www.nytimes.com/2015/05/18/world/middleeast/isis-ramadi-iraq.html

[2] http://www.nytimes.com/2015/05/18/world/middleeast/isis-ramadi-iraq.html

[3] http://www.dailymail.co.uk/news/article-3083355/Islamic-State-raises-black-flag-Iraqi-city-Ramadi.html
[4] http://www.longwarjournal.org/archives/2015/05/islamic-state-seizes-government-center-in-ramadi.php
[5] https://theintercept.com/2015/06/03/isis-forces-exbaathist-saddam-loyalists/
[6] http://www.pbs.org/wgbh/pages/frontline/iraq-war-on-terror/rise-of-isis/who-runs-the-islamic-state/
[7] Ferguson, Charles. *No End in Sight: Iraq's Descent into Chaos* (United States: Public Affairs, 2008).
[8] http://www.al-monitor.com/pulse/originals/2013/02/maliki-plays-legal-card-to-prote.html

Chapter 23:
Disrupting the MFO: ISIS in Sinai

Notes

[1] http://www.reuters.com/article/2015/09/04/us-egypt-sinai-peacekeepers-idUSKCN0R404G20150904
[2] http://mfo.org/
[3] http://www.haaretz.com/news/middle-east/1.671955
[4] http://mfo.org/
[5] http://www.longwarjournal.org/archives/2014/12/al_nusrah_front_uses_united_na.php
[6] http://armypubs.army.mil/doctrine/DR_pubs/dr_a/pdf/adrp1_02.pdf
[7] http://www.haaretz.com/news/diplomacy-defense/.premium-1.641497
[8] http://www.cnn.com/2015/09/10/politics/us-troops-sinai-egypt-isis/?utm_source=Sailthru&utm_medium=email&utm_campaign=New%20Campaign&utm_term=%2ASituation%20Report

Chapter 24:
Mujahideen: The Strategic Tradition of Sunni Jihadism

Notes

[i]   Cleveland, William L. *A History of the Modern Middle East: Second Edition*. Boulder, CO: Westview Books, 2000. Pages 196-197.
[ii] Ibid, 298.
[iii] Lacey, Jim ed. *The Canons of Jihad: Terrorists' Strategy For Defeating America*. Annapolis: Naval Institute Press, 2008. Page 11.
[iv] Zabel, 4.
[v]   Ibid.
[vi] Qutb, Sayyid. *Milestones* in Lacey, Jim ed. *The Canons of Jihad: Terrorists' Strategy For Defeating America*. Annapolis: Naval Institute Press, 2008. Page 22.
[vii] Ibid, 20.
[viii] Ibid, 25.
[ix] Ibid, 14.
[x]   Ibid.
[xi] Cleveland, 394.
[xii] Ibid, 394-395.
[xiii] Gartenstein-Ross, Daveed. *Bin Laden's Legacy: Why We're Still Losing the War on Terror*. Hoboken, NJ: John Wiley & Sons, 2011. Page 37.
[xiv] Ibid, page 38.
[xv] Wylie, J. C. *Military Strategy: A General Theory of Power Control*. Annapolis: Naval Institute Press, 2014.
[xvi] Craig, Gordan A. "Delbrück" in Paret, Peter ed. *Makers of Modern Strategy from Machiavelli to the Nuclear Age*. Princeton: Princeton University Press, 1986.
[xvii] Al-Suri, Abu Musab. *The Call to a Global Resistance*. In Lacey, Jim ed. *A Terrorist's Call to Global Jihad: Deciphering Abu Musab*

       Al-Suri's Islamic Jihad Manifesto. Annapolis: Naval Institute Press, 2008. Page 15.
[xviii] Ibid, 59.
[xix] Ibid, 193.
[xx] Ibid, 59.
[xxi] Guevara, Ernesto. *Guerrilla Warfare*. Trans. J. P. Morray. Lexington, KY: BN Publishing, 2012. Page 4.
[xxii] Cigar, Norman ed. *Al-Qaida's Doctrine for Insurgency: Abd Al-Aziz Al-Muqrin's Practical Course for Guerrilla War*. Dulles, VA: Potomac Books, 2009. Page 6.
[xxiii] Ibid.
[xxiv] Ibid, 7.
[xxv] Ibid, 10-11.
[xxvi] Al-Muqrin, Abd Al-Aziz. *A Practical Course for Guerrilla War* in Cigar, Norman ed. *Al-Qaida's Doctrine for Insurgency: Abd Al-Aziz Al-Muqrin's Practical Course for Guerrilla War*. Dulles, VA: Potomac Books, 2009. Page 89.
[xxvii] Ibid, 127.
[xxviii] Ibid, 94.
[xxix] Ibid, 99.
[xxx] Ibid, 101.
[xxxi] Stern, Jessica and J. M. Berger. *ISIS: The State of Terror*. New York: HarperCollins, 2015. Page 56.
[xxxii] McCants, William. *The ISIS Apocalypse: The History, Strategy, and Doomsday Vision of the Islamic State*. New York: Saint Martin's Press, 2015. Page 79.
[xxxiii] Ibid, 85
[xxxiv] Ibid, 90.
[xxxv] Naji, Abu Bakr. *The Management of Savagery: The Most Important Stage Through Which the Umma Will Pass* in Lacey, Jim ed. *The Canons of Jihad: Terrorists' Strategy For Defeating America*. Annapolis: Naval Institute Press, 2008. Page 52.
[xxxvi] Ibid, 54.

[xxxvii] Naji, Abu Bakr. *The Management of Savagery: The Most Important Stage Through Which the Umma Will Pass* translated by William McCants for the John M. Olin Institute for Strategic Studies at Harvard University, 23 May 2006. Page 45.

[xxxviii] Naji, Abu Bakr. *The Management of Savagery: The Most Important Stage Through Which the Umma Will Pass* in Lacey, Jim ed. *The Canons of Jihad: Terrorists' Strategy For Defeating America.* Annapolis: Naval Institute Press, 2008. Page 54.

[xxxix] Naji, Abu Bakr. *The Management of Savagery: The Most Important Stage Through Which the Umma Will Pass* translated by William McCants for the John M. Olin Institute for Strategic Studies at Harvard University, 23 May 2006. Page 72.

[xl]   Ibid, 73.

[xli] Ibid, 74.

[xlii] Ibid, 76.

[xliii] Ibid, 78.

[xliv] Ibid, 79.

[xlv] Clausewitz, Carl von. Michael Howard and Peter Paret, trans. On War. Princeton: Princeton University Press, 1989. Page 595-596.

[xlvi] McCants, *The ISIS Apocalypse*, page 79.

[xlvii] Ibid, 81.

[xlviii] Stern, Jessica and J. M. Berger. *ISIS: The State of Terror.* New York: HarperCollins, 2015. Page 86.

[xlix] Ibid, page 114.

Chapter 25:
Friday the 13th in Paris

Notes

[1]   http://www.slate.com/articles/news_and_politics/fighting_words/2007/10/defending_islamofascism.html

[2]   http://www.theguardian.com/world/2015/oct/15/angela-merkel-rejects-criticism-open-door-refugee-policy-germany

[3] http://www.mirror.co.uk/sport/football/news/paris-attacks-watch-football-fans-6830324
[4] http://news.yahoo.com/paris-attacks-show-u-s--surveillance-of-islamic-state-may-be--going-dark-203103709.html?soc_src=mediacontentstory&soc_trk=ma
[5] http://www.cbsnews.com/news/bernie-sanders-doubles-down-climate-change-terrorism-link/
[6] http://www.islamdaily.org/en/islam/7679.islam-and-monoculture.htm
[7] http://www.newenglishreview.org/G._Murphy_Donovan/Broken_Arrow/
[8] http://www.breitbart.com/video/2015/11/13/obama-isis-is-not-getting-stronger-we-have-contained-them/
[9] http://www.washingtonpost.com/wpsrv/style/longterm/books/reviews/clashofcivilizations.htm

Chapter 26:
The Starfish Caliphate:
How ISIL Exploits the Power of a Decentralized Organization

No notes.

Chapter 27:
Jihadist Narratives: Democratized Islam and Islamic Nation Building

Notes

[1] http://theglobalobservatory.org/2015/02/jihad-al-qaeda-isis-counternarrative/

[2]   https://www.washingtonpost.com/news/monkey-cage/wp/2014/09/08/the-islamic-state-and-the-politics-of-official-narratives/

Chapter 28:
Justifying Jihad: A Case Study of Al-Shabaab and Boko Haram

No notes.

Chapter 29:
ISIS is Not a Terrorist Organization

No notes.

U.S.-Allied Policy and Counter-Jihadi and Counter-Islamic State Strategies

Chapter 30:
Adam Smith's Invisible Hand vs. The Taliban: Bottom-Up Expeditionary Diplomacy in Fragile States— Best Practices from the Civilian Surge in Afghanistan

Notes

[i]   Smith, Adam, *An Inquiry into the Nature and Causes of the Wealth of Nations.* Book IV 2.9. Edwin Cannan, ed. 1904. Library of Economics and Liberty. 30 August 2013

[ii] Dr. Jonathan B. Wight, "The Treatment of Smith's Invisible Hand," Journal of Economic Education 38(3)(2007): 341-358.

[iii] Testimony by former U.S. Secretary of State Hillary Rodham Clinton before the U.S. Senate Foreign Relations Committee. June 23, 2011, Washington, DC. Emphasis added.

[iv] *"An Inquiry into the Nature and Causes of the Wealth of Nations,"* Vol. I ed. R.H. Campbell and A.S. Skinner, Vol. II of the Glasgow Edition of the Works and Correspondence of Adam Smith (Indianapolis: Liberty Fund, 1981, emphasis added.

[v] Dr. Jonathan B. Wight, "The Treatment of Smith's Invisible hand," Journal of Economic Education 38(3)(2007): 341-358.

[vi] Remarks by U.S. President Barack Obama in Address to the Nation on the Way Forward in Afghanistan and Pakistan; Eisenhower Hall Theatre, United States Military Academy at West Point, West Point, New York, December 9, 2009.

[vii] Interagency Provincial Affairs (IPA) Field Guidance, U.S. Embassy Kabul, Afghanistan. July 2011.

[viii] White Paper of the Interagency Policy Group's Report on U.S. Policy toward Afghanistan and Pakistan, http://www.whitehouse.gov/assets/documents/Afghanistan-Pakistan_White_Pa....

[ix] "Joint Audit Identifies Civilian Uplift Costs, Recommends Strengthened Management; Civilian uplift key to U.S. transition strategy in Afghanistan," Office of Public Affairs, Special Inspector General for Afghanistan Reconstruction (SIGAR,) September 8, 2011.

[x] "Beneath the Calm," creating an appropriate (Afghan) institution, the "Commission," an ethnically and tribally inclusive decision making representational body in Spin Boldak District, Kandahar Province. Joint U.S. Department of State and U.S. Army 8-1 CAV (8th Squadron, 1st Cavalry Regiment); Spin Boldak District Support Team, Spin Boldak District, Kandahar Province, Afghanistan: October 2009 – October 2010. Owen H. Kirby, Senior Governance Advisor, U.S. Department of State.

[xi] Matthew Aikins, "The Master of Spin Boldak," Harper's, December 2009.

[xii] See also Seth G. Jones and Munoz, "Afghanistan's Local War: Building Local Defense Forces," for other examples of how dominant Afghan Pashtun tribes disenfranchise weaker tribes leveraged by insurgent influence, 2010, 24-25.

[xiii] Creating the appropriate Afghan human institutions of the village Mayor, i.e. the *"Malik,"* and farmer interest groups, *"Farmer Jirgas,"* to connect the Afghan people with the Afghan government. Joint U.S. Agency for International Development (USAID) and U.S. Army 1-71 Cavalry unit of the 10th Mountain Division. Dand District Support Team, Dand district, Kandahar province, Afghanistan: June 2010–May 2011. Keith Pratt, Field Program Officer, U.S. Agency for International Development.

[xiv] Karni, Edi, "A Mechanism for Eliciting Probablities," The Constructionist Principle, Appreciate Inquiry, Ashridge Business School, United Kingdom. 77(2)(2009): 603-606.

[xv] "Jirga" is a term found in Pashtu, Persian (and Dari), Turkish, and Mongolian that appears to be related to the word "circle," the formation used when a *jirga* meets. But regardless of the origin of the word, *jirga* refers to a local/tribal institution of decision-making and dispute settlement that incorporates the prevalent local customary law, institutional rituals, and a body of village elders whose collective decision about the resolution of a dispute (or local problem) is binding on the parties involved. *Shura* is an Arabic word that translates to "consultation" since it is mentioned twice in the Koran as a praiseworthy, it is readily adopted by Afghanistan's ethnic groups, although the term has a religious connection. Tribal Analysis Center, *"Jirga: Pashtun Participatory Governance." Tribal Analysis Center. http://www.tribalanalysiscenter.com.*

[xvi] Creating an appropriate (Afghan) human institution of tribally and ethnically inclusive and neutral Farmer Cooperatives to promote the Government of the Islamic Republic of Afghanistan (GIRoA's) national strategy for agricultural-based economic growth. Joint U.S. Department of Agriculture, the U.S. Army's 73rd Airborne

Division and GIRoA's Directorate of Agriculture, Irrigation and Livestock (DAIL) for Wardak Province, Afghanistan: November 2009–December 2010. Gary Soiseth, Agriculture Advisor, U.S. Department of Agriculture.

[xvii] In arid climates, a kareez canal system of both below and above ground canals, brings water down to a settlement or agricultural fields via gravity from an aquifer, lake or spring of higher elevation. The kareez canal system is an ancient system designed to transport water long distances and prevent water from evaporating before it reaches its intended destinations. Civilizations have developed intricate social systems to maintain and repair the deep kareez canals and equitably distribute the scare water resource.

[xviii] Using improved vegetable seeds as the catalyst to develop the need for emerging district level agricultural extension services for local farmers - an Afghan appropriate human institution. Joint U.S. Department of Agriculture and U.S. Army Special Forces Units; Kandahar, Oruzgan and Daikundi Provinces, Afghanistan: November 2009–November 2010. Paul Heidloff, Special Forces Agricultural Advisor, U.S. Department of Agriculture.

[xix] Rory Hamlin, "One Team's Approach to Village Stability Operations," Small Wars Journal (SWJ Blog), www.smallwarsjournal.com, September 12, 2011.

Chapter 31:
AFPAK Hands: A Template for Long-Term Strategic Engagement?

Notes

[1] http://wpj.sagepub.com/content/28/2/79.extract
[2] http://www.deseretnews.com/article/700146587/Rethinking-civilian-aid-in-Afghanistan-and-its-implications.html

References

James Stavridis. 2010. Teaching the ROPES. Vol. 136. Annapolis: United States Naval Institute.

Mike Mullen. December 14, 2009. Memorandum from the CJCS to the Service Chiefs.

Admiral Mike Mullen, Chairman of the Joint Chiefs of Staff, Landon Lecture Series, Kansas State University, Manhattan, Kansas, Wednesday, 3 March 2010.

Donna Miles. 2012. 'AfPak Hands' Program Pays Dividends in Afghanistan, Pakistan. Washington: American Forces Press Service.

"Rethinking Civilian Assistance in Afghanistan", By Desaix Myers, *The New York Times*. Myers suggests the development of "expeditionary" civilians similar to the AfPak Hands program, http://www.nytimes.com/2011/06/24/opinion/24iht-edmyers24.html January 28, 2012.

"Move the Af-Pak Hands Out of DoD". *Small Wars Journal*. Major David Walker, a US Air Force officer, argues that the AfPak Hands program should be continued but under the Department of State as the lead federal agency, http://www.nytimes.com/2011/06/24/opinion/24iht-edmyers24.html.

http://www.apus.edu/content/dam/online-library/masters-theses/Hart-2012.pdf.

Hanson, Victor Davis, James Traub, Ann Marlowe, and Matthieu Aikins. 2011. "AFPAK 2020." *World Affairs* 173, no. 6: 16-34. *International Security & Counter Terrorism Reference Center*, EBSCO *host* (accessed February 22, 2015).

Mike Mullen. 2011. Joint Publication 3-0, Joint Operations. Washington DC: Chairman of the Joint Chiefs of Staff.

Presidential Policy Directive 23: US Security Sector Assistance (SSA), 2012.

Chapter 32:
What Is the Counter-Daesh Strategy?:
A "Cohenian" Exercise

Notes

[i]   Transcript Obama speech on ISIL Policy 10SEP14 September 10 at 9:37 PM
[ii] Tim Devaney, http://thehill.com/policy/defense/230665-mccain-obama-has-no-strategy-to-defeat-terrorists?utm_source=dlvr.it&utm_medium=twitter.
[iii] Jordan Fabian, *The Hill*, 06/08/15 on line
[iv] James Warren, *The New York Daily News*, on line, Published: Tuesday, June 9, 2015.
[v]   I use Daesh instead of IS, ISIS, or ISIL. Ken Pollack of Brookings first suggested this to me and from the 9 October 14 *Boston Globe*, in an essay by Zeba Khan, "Words matter in 'ISIS' war, so use 'Daesh,'" "The term "Daesh" is strategically a better choice because it is still accurate in that it spells out the acronym of the group's full Arabic name, al-Dawla al-Islamiya fi al-Iraq wa al-Sham. Yet, at the same time, "Daesh" can also be understood as a play on words—and an insult. Depending on how it is conjugated in Arabic, it can mean anything from "to trample down and crush" to "a bigot who imposes his view on others." Already, the group has reportedly threatened to cut out the tongues of anyone who uses the term."
[vi] National Security Strategy of the United States, February 2015. Retrieved from White House.gov blog: http://www.whitehouse.gov/blog/2015/02/06/president-obamas-national-security-strategy-2015-strong-and-sustainable-american-leadership.
[vii] T.X. Hammes mentioned a model for 21st century strategy articulated by Eliot Cohen in a 7 August 2013 essay, "Sorry, AirSea Battle Is No Strategy," written for *The National Interest*. In an exchange of personal e-mail, in 2013, the author asked

[viii] Cohen further explain the model. This essay is built upon that understanding.

[viii] On 27 April 15, at a "town-hall meeting" in Leavenworth, KS with Kansas US Senator Jerry Moran, the author asked SEN Moran when the Senate would take up the President's proposed AUMF. SEN Moran said there was no interest in either the White House or the Senate to take up a new AUMF. Counter-Daesh operations will continue under the authorization of the post-9/11 AUMF of 2001.

[ix] Transcript Obama speech on ISIL Policy 10 September 14 at 9:37 PM.

[x] Title "Living Conditions Deteriorate In Seized Territory" *The Hartford Courant* 26 December 2014 Page A 13 Reprint of an article by Liz Sly, *Washington Post*.

[xi] 26 December 2014 *Hartford Courant* Page A10 Philip Pullella, Reuters.

[xii] 11 March 2015 Deb Riechmann, Associated Press.

[xiii] Huba Wass de Czege, "Defeating the Islamic State: A Commentary on Core Strategy," in *Parameters* 44(4) Winter 2014-15, pp. 64-65. I am indebted to BG Wass de Czege for his review and comments on this essay.

[xiv] Drawn from the transcript of a Department of Defense Press Briefing by Lt. Gen. James Terry in the Pentagon Briefing Room, 18 December 2014, found at http://www.defense.gov/Transcripts/.

[xv] Drawn from a personal e-mail to the author by MAJ Ian Fleischmann, a 2015 graduate of the Advanced Military Studies Program of the School of Advanced Military Studies. Used with his permission.

[xvi] J. Boone Bartholomees, Jr., Chapter 7, A Theory of Victory, *U.S. Army War College Guide to National Security Issues, Vol. 1: Theory of War and Strategy*, pp. 92-93.

[xvii] Electronic mail note written by Rick Sinnreich, 25 February 2015 on PLANSLIST, a distribution list for the exchange of ideas on strategy, the operational art and tactics.

Chapter 33:
Narrative: The Critical Component of Counter-Terrorism Strategy

No notes.

Chapter 34:
'Confronting ISIS in Libya: The Case for an Expeditionary Counterinsurgency'

Notes

[1] Maggie Michael, 'Libyan city is first outside of Syria, Iraq to join ISIS,' *haaretz.com*, 10 November 2014, http://www.haaretz.com/news/middle-east/1.625652 (accessed 21 March 2015).

[2] Fehim Taştekin, 'Turkey's War in Libya,' *Al-Monitor*, 4 December 2014, http://www.al-monitor.com/pulse/originals/2014/12/turkey-libya-muslim-brotherhood.html (accessed 20 March 2018), and Ishaan Tharoor and Adam Taylor, 'Here are the key players fighting the war for Libya, all over again,' *The Washington Post*, 27 August 2014, http://www.washingtonpost.com/blogs/worldviews/wp/2014/08/27/here-are-the-key-players-fighting-the-war-for-libya-all-over-again/ (accessed 20 March 2015).

[3] BBC, 'Guide to Key Libyan Militias,' 20 May 2014, http://www.bbc.com/news/world-middle-east-19744533 (accessed 15 February 2015).

[4] Andrew Engel, 'The Islamic State's Expansion in Libya,' Washington Institute, http://www.washingtoninstitute.org/

policy-analysis/view/the-islamic-states-expansion-in-libya (accessed April 19, 2015).

[5] 'Islamic State (IS) Recruits Terrorists throughout North Africa and Middle East,' *Global Research News* http://www.globalresearch.ca/islamic-state-is-recruits-terrorists-throughout-north-africa-and-middle-east/5396569 (accessed 20 March 2015) and 'ISIL Tightens grip on Libya's Derna,' *Aljazeera.com*, 7 March 2015, www.aljazeera.com/news/2015/03/isil-fighters-grip-libya-derna-150307090237967.html (accessed 16 March 2015) and Noman Benotman, 'Libya has become the Latest ISIL Conquest,' *Telegraph.co.uk*, 24 October 2014, http://www.telegraph.co.uk/news/worldnews/africaandindianocean/libya/11186153/Libya-has-become-the-latest-Isil-conquest.html (accessed 16 March 2015).

[6] Audrey Kurth Cronin, 'ISIS is Not a Terrorist Group,' *Foreign Affairs* 94 (2015): 87-98.

[7] Jack Moore, '5,000 Foreign Fighters Flock to Libya as ISIS call for Jihadists,' *Newsweek.com*, 3 March 2015, http://www.newsweek.com/5000-foreign-fighters-flock-libya-isis-call-jihadists-310948 (accessed 15 March 2015), and 'Libya army Chief warns of ISIL threat against Europe,' *Aljazeera.com*, 20 March 2015, http://www.aljazeera.com/news/2015/03/libya-army-chief-warns-isil-threat-europe-150320050634976.html (accessed 20 March 2015).

[8] Ian Beckett, *Modern Insurgencies and Counter-Insurgencies: Guerrillas and their Opponents since 1750* (New York: Routledge, 2001), 70-3.

[9] Jeremy Bender and Armin Rosen, 'As ISIS continues to gain ground, here's what the militants have in their arsenal,' 17 November 2014, *Businessinsider.com*, http://www.businessinsider.com/isis-military-equipment-arsenal-2014-11 (accessed 20 April 2015).

[10] Janine Davidson, 'ISIS hasn't gone anywhere- and it's getting stronger,' 24 July 2014, *Council of Foreign Relations* http://blogs.cfr.org/davidson/2014/07/24/

isis-hasnt-gone-anywhere-and-its-getting-stronger/ (accessed 20 April 2015).

[11] 'Report: ISIL forming air force with captured fighter jets choppers,' *World Tribune.com*, 20 October 2014, http://www.worldtribune.com/2014/10/20/report-isil-forming-air-force-captured-fighter-jets-choppers/ (accessed 22 March 2015).

[12] Alex Bilger, 'ISIS annual reports reveal a metrics-driven military command,' 24 May 2014, http://www.understandingwar.org/sites/default/files/ISWBackgrounder_ISIS_Annual_Reports_0.pdf. *Institute for the Study of War* (accessed 19 April 2015).

[13] Ibid.

[14] Hatita, 'Libyan jihadists in Syria and Iraq returning home to fight Haftar: security sources,' *Al*-Awsat, *http*://www.aawsat.net/2014/07/article55334325/libyan-jihadists-in-syria-and-iraq-returning-home-to-fight-haftar-security-sources.

[15] Reuters, 'NOC: Libya Declares Force Majeure on 11 Oilfields Due to Insecurity,' Rigzone.com, 5 March 2015, http://www.rigzone.com/news/oil_gas/a/137537/NOC_Libya_Declares_Force_Majeure_on_11_Oilfields_Due_to_Insecurity#sthash.LyQtfiPL.dpuf(accessed 18 March 2015).

[16] Vivienne Walt, 'How ISIS Sprung Up in Libya,' *Time.com*, 26 February 2015, http://time.com/3721927/isis-libya-establishment/ (accessed 20 March 2015).

[17] Tim Lister, 'ISIS atrocity in Libya demonstrates its growing reach in North Africa,' *CNN.com*, 17 February 2015, http://www.cnn.com/2015/02/16/africa/isis-libya-north-africa/ (accessed 20 March 2015).

[18] 'IS releases new killing video of Ethiopian Christians', *BBC.com*, 20 April 2015, http://www.bbc.com/news/world-middle-east-32373166 (accessed 20 April 2015).

[19] Nick Squires, 'Tunisia museum gunmen went to Libya for weapons training', *Telegraph.com*, 20 March 2015, http://www.telegraph.co.uk/news/worldnews/africaandindianocean/tunisia/11484615/

Tunisia-museum-gunmen-went-to-Libya-for-weapons-training.html (accessed 20 March 2015).

[20] Crisina Silva, 'ISIS will spread to Europe if Libya Threat is Not Stopped, warns Libyan Army Chief,' *ibtimes.com*, 20 March 2015, http://www.ibtimes.com/isis-will-spread-europe-if-libya-threat-not-stopp... (accessed 19 April 2015).

[21] Tucker Reals, 'Why Europe should worry about ISIS in Libya', *CBSNews.com*, 23 February 2015, http://www.cbsnews.com/news/isis-in-libya-direct-threat-to-europe/ (accessed 18 March 2015).

[22] 'UN Security Council keeps Libya arms embargo in place', *Aljazeera.com*, 3 March 2015, http://www.aljazeera.com/news/2015/03/security-council-libya-arms-embargo-place-150328111924635.html (accessed 20 March 2015).

[23] Nima Elbagir, Paul Cruickshank, and Mohammed Tawfeeq 'Boko Haram purportedly pledges allegiance to ISIS,' *CNN.com*, 9 March 2015, http://www.cnn.com/2015/03/07/africa/nigeria-boko-haram-isis/ (accessed 20 March 2015).

[24] Gaub, 47.

[25] 'EU 'Civilian' Missions training Paramilitaries,' *euroobserver.com*, 18 November 2013, http://www.euobserver.com/investigations/122134 (accessed 20 March 2015).

[26] Eric Schmidt, 'US Training Elite Antiterror Troops in Four African Nations,' *nytimes.com*, 26 May 2014, http://www.nytimes.com/2014/05/27/world/africa/us-trains-african-commandos-to-fight-terrorism.html?_r=0 (accessed 17 March 2015).

[27] Andrew Engel, 'Libya as a Failed State: Causes, Consequences, Options,' *washingtoninstitute.org*, November 2014, http://www.washingtoninstitute.org/uploads/Documents/pubs/ResearchNote24_Engel-3.pdf 14 (accessed 18 March 2015).

[28] See Lucy Westscott, 'Libyan Army Reportedly Has Taken Back Benghazi Port,' *newsweek.com*, 6 February 2015, http://www.newsweek.com/libyan-army-reported-have-taken-back-benghazi-port-305113 (accessed 18 February 2015) and Alarabiya, 'Libyan

Army Seizes Two Towns near Capital,' *Alarabiya.net*, 20 March 2015, http://english.alarabiya.net/en/News/africa/2015/03/20/Libyan-army-forces-advance-close-to-Tripoli-airport.html (accessed 20 March 2015).

[29] Ishaan Tharoor and Adam Taylor, 'Here are the key players fighting the war for Libya, all over again,' *The Washington Post*, 27 August 2015.

[30] Michael Shurik, *France's War in Mali: Lessons for an Expeditionary Army* (Santa Monica: Rand, 2014), 9.

[31] Murielle Delaporte, 'French Lessons from Mali: Fight Alone, Supply Together,' *breakingdefense.com*, 17 June 2013, http://breakingdefense.com/2013/06/french-lessons-from-mali-fight-alone-supply-together/ (accessed 19 March 2015).

[32] Shurik, 15.

[33] 'France to deploy troops to fight Sahara militants,' *BBC.com*, 8 May 2014, http://www.bbc.com/news/world-africa-27327759 (accessed 20 March 2015).

[34] Dirk Vandewalle, *A History of Modern Libya* (New York: Cambridge University Press, 2006), 2-4.

[35] The United States Navy. 'The U.S. Navy's Vision for Confronting Irregular Challenges,' January 2010, http://www.navy.mil/navydata/cno/CNO_SIGNED_NAVY_VISION_FOR_CONFRONTING_IRREGULAR_CHALLENGES_JANUARY_2010.pdf3 (accessed 15 March 2015).

[36] Bernand Estival, 'The French navy and the Algerian War', *Journal of Strategic Studies*, 25(2002), 93.

[37] Martin Murphy, 'The Blue, Green, and Brown: Insurgency and Counter-Insurgency on the Water,' *Contemporary Security Policy*, 28 (2007), 74.

[38] The United States Marine Corps, 'Expeditionary 21', mccdc.marines.mil, 4 March 2015,http://www.navy.mil/navydata/cno/CNO_SIGNED_NAVY_VISION_FOR_CONFRONTING_IRREGULAR_CHALLENGES_JANUARY_2010.pdf (accessed 20 March 2015).

[39] Ibid., 43-44.
[40] Global Security, 'Marine Expeditionary Brigade,' *globalsecurity.org*, http://www.globalsecurity.org/military/agency/usmc/meb.htm (accessed 20 April 2015).
[41] U.S. Marine Corps Concepts and Programs, 'Types of MAGTFs', *Marinecorpsconceptsandprograms.com*, https://marinecorpsconceptsandprograms.com/organizations/marine-air-ground-task-force/types-magtfs (accessed 20 April 2015).
[42] Hew Strachan, *The Direction of War*, 218.
[43] *Joint Publication 3-26 Counterterrorism*, II-2.
[44] Ibid., II-5.
[45] Scott Vickery, 'Operation Inherent Resolve: An Interim Assessment,' *washingtoninstitute.org*, 13 January 2015, http://www.washingtoninstitute.org/policy-analysis/view/operation-inherent-resolve-an-interim-assessment (accessed 5 March 2015).
[46] Elizabeth Chuck, 'Why the Obama Administration keeps Saying Degrade and Destroy,' *nbcnews.com*, http://www.nbcnews.com/storyline/isis-terror/why-obama-administration-keeps-saying-degrade-destroy-n201171 (accessed 20 March 2015).
[47] Bill Roggio and Caleb Weiss, 'Islamic State overruns Iraqi Army Brigade Headquarters north of Fallujah,' *longwarjournal.org*, 15 March 2015, http://www.longwarjournal.org/archives/2015/03/islamic-state-overruns-iraqi-army-brigade-headquarters-north-of-fallujah.php (accessed 18 March 2015).
[48] Al Arabiya, 'Iraqi army begins operation to expel ISIS from Ramadi,' *al-Arabiya.net*, 18 April 2015, http://english.alarabiya.net/en/News/middle-east/2015/04/18/Iraqi-army-begins-operation-to-expel-ISIS-from-Ramadi.html (accessed April 20, 2015).
[49] Loveday Morris, 'Iraqi Offensive for Tikrit stalls as casualties mount,' *washingtonpost.com*, http://www.washingtonpost.com/world/middle_east/iraqi-offensive-for-tikrit-stalls-as-islamic-state-inflicts-casualties/2015/03/16/258a6dec-cb58-11e4-8730-4f473416e759_story.html (accessed 18 March 2015).

[50] Deborah Amos, 'In Tikrit Offensive, Local Sunnis, Shiite Militias are unlikely Allies,' *kplu.org*, 19 March 2015, http://www.kplu.org/post/tikrit-offensive-local-sunnis-shiite-militias-are-unlikely-allies (accessed 20 March 2015).

Chapter 35:
The 21st Century Answer to "Burning their Crops and Salting their Fields": Interdicting and Destroying The ISIS Financial Network

No notes.

Chapter 36:
"Channeling": The United Kingdom's Approach to CVE-A Plan Americans Deserve But Will Never Receive

Notes

[i] "The Return of the Khalifah," *Dabiq Issue 1,* July 6, 2014.
[ii] Humera Khan, "Why Countering Extremism Fails," *Foreign Affairs,* February 18, 2015.
[iii] William McCants, "Countering Violent Extremism, Pt. 2: Scope," *Jihadica,* March 1, 2012.
[iv] Robert Chesney, "The Resurgence of the Terrorism-Prevention Paradigm for Law Enforcement,"*Lawfareblog,* July 9, 2015.
[v] Greg Miller and Ellen Nakashima, "Recent Islamic State Arrests Include Suspects in Alleged July 4 Plots," *The Washington Post,* July 9, 2015.
[vi] JM Berger and Jonathon Morgan, "The ISIS Twitter Census: Defining and Describing the Population of ISIS Supporters on Twitter," *The Brookings Project on U.S. Relations with the Islamic World,* March 2015, 41-42.
[vii] Stewart Bell, "Kodaimati Criminal Complaint," April 23, 2015.

[viii] "Twitter Transparency Report," *Twitter,* December 31, 2014, https://transparency.twitter.com/information-requests/2014/jul-dec.

[ix] Daniel Byman and Jeremy Shapiro, "Be Afraid. Be A Little Afraid: The Threat of Terrorism from Western Foreign Fighters in Syria and Iraq," *Foreign Policy at Brookings,* November 2014, 26.

[x] "Channel: Protecting Vulnerable People From Being Drawn Into Terrorism," *HMGovernment,* October 2012, 17.

[xi] Tom Porter, "Majority of Americans Believe ISIS Poses Greatest Threat To USA," *International Business Times,* February 14, 2015.

[xii] "Channel," 17.

[xiii] "Channel," 22.

[xiv] Michael Jensen, Patrick James, and Herbert Tinsley. "Profiles of Individual Radicalization in the United States: Preliminary Findings," *National Consortium for the Study of Terrorism and Responses to Terrorism (START),* January 2015.

[xv] John Hall, "European ISIS Fighters Who Are Seen As Cannon Fodder By Their Commanders Desperately Try to Prove Their Worth By Committing The Most Sickening Atrocities, Says Former Prisoner," *The Daily Mail.* April 10, 2015.

[xvi] William McCants, "Don't Be Evil," *Foreign Policy,* June 30, 2011.

[xvii] JM Berger and Jonathon Morgan, "The ISIS Twitter Census," 45-50.

[xviii] Ines von Behr, Anais Reding, Charlie Edwards, and Luke Gribbon, "Radicalisation in the Digital Era: The Use of the Internet in 15 Cases of Terrorism and Extremism," *RAND Europe,* 2013.

[xix] William McCants and Clint Watts, "U.S. Strategy for Countering Violent Extremism: An Assessment," *Foreign Policy Research Institute,* December 2012.

[xx] "Channel," 24.

[xxi] "Channel," 15-19.

[xxii] "Homegrown Extremism 2001-2015," *New America Foundation,* February 2015.

[xxiii] For a discussion of right-wing terrorist attacks being labeled hate crimes Peter see: Bergen and David Sternman, "US Right Wing Extremists More Deadly Than Jihadists," *CNN*, April 15, 2015.

Chapter 37:
Cultural Heritage Preservation and Its Role for Paving the Way Toward Peace

Notes

[i] Marine Colonel Matthew Bogdanos, who was responsible for creating a task force to recover stolen artifacts from archaeological sites and from Baghdad's National Museum in Iraq, has made abundantly clear that antiquities fund insurgents. See "Artifact Smuggling Aids Iraq Insurgents," Marine Corps Community for USMC Marine Veterans, Leatherneck News, 3/19/2008 (http://www.leatherneck.com/forums/showthread.php?t=62688).

[ii] Civil Affairs advise higher echelon commanders (corps or division commander and staff) on protection of culturally significant sites. [Headquarters, Department of the Army (28 Jan 2014) FM 3-57 C1, *"Civil Affairs Operations,"* pp. 2-36, 2-120]

[iii] Civil Affairs core tasks (Population and Resources Control) are to protect and secure strategically important institutions, such as government buildings and archives, museums, religious sites, courthouses, and communication facilities. [Headquarters, Department of the Army (31 Oct 2011) FM 3-57, *"Civil Affairs Operations,"* pp. 3-6, 3-24]

[iv] HTT AF07 was a Human Terrain Team (HTT) deployed in southern and central Helmand province, Afghanistan to conduct unclassified open source and field research, as well as analyze sociocultural information in support of the commander's military decision making process (MDMP). [Wong, W. (2013, Summer) *"Securing the Peace on the Global War on Terrorism."* Inside Homeland Security, volume 11, issue 2, pp. 49–51.]

[v]   Dutch documentary, "Blood Antiquities," directed by Peter Brems and Wim Van den Eynde (2009).

[vi]   The freezing of financial accounts of enemy combatants to curtail their operational funds may also assists in the prevention of money laundering. [Headquarters, Department of the Army (31 Oct 2011) FM 3-57, *Civil Affairs Operations,*" p. 3-6, 3-24]

[vii]   Personal communication with the DoS representative for Cultural Heritage, Dr. Laura Tedesco, and Deputy Minister of MoIC Omar Sultan (MOIC, Kabul, 08/14/2011).

[viii] Information Operations offer counter-narratives that strongly resonate with communities and which help communities resist insurgent or religious extremist propaganda and intimidation. [Headquarters, Department of the Army (31 Oct 2011) FM 3-57, "*Civil Affairs Operations,*" p. 3-28, 3-135]

[viii] UN Security Council Resolution 2199 is a legally binding measure that prohibits the trade of cultural artifacts illegally removed from Syria since 2011 and Iraq since 1990. (https://hyperallergic.com/183201/un-security-council-takes-aim-at-isis-a...). UN Security Council Resolution 2193. (http://www.un.org/sg/ statements/index.asp?nid=7521).

[ix]   Hatra: http://whc.unesco.org/en/news/1245/, Palmyra: http://www.un.org/apps/news/story.asp?NewsID=51336#.VaRWWEZrsr0, Nimrud:http://whc.unesco.org/en/news/1260.

[x]   United Nations Office on Drugs and Crime (http://www.unodc.org/unodc/en/money-laundering /imolin_amlid.html).

[xi]   "UNESCO Director-General to Brief UN Security Council on the Protection of Cultural Heritage." (http://www.Unesco.org/new/en/media-services/single-view/news/unesco_director_general_to_brief_un_security_council on the protection of cultural _heritage).

[xii]   [Not listed; The Editors]

[xiii] An example can be found at the following link: http://www.unesco.org/new/en/safeguarding-syrian-cultural-heritage/national-initiatives/syrians-protect-their-heritage/.

[xiv] An example can be found at the following link: http://www.unite4heritage.org/who_is_acting.php.
[xv] "2014-2015 Civil Affairs Issue Papers: The Future of Civil Affairs" (http://www.civilaffairsassoc.org/pdf/2014-15_Future_of_Civil_Affairs.pdf).

Chapter 38:
It is Time to Reassess How the US Conducts Detention Operations in the Current Fight and the Need to Incorporate our Regional Partners in the Future— Insurgents are Not Traditional Enemy Prisoners of War

Notes

[1] Rand, The battle Behind the Wire, US Prisoner and Detainee Operations from World War II to Iraq.
[2] The First-in, First-out Method (FIFO) | FIFO Inventory Method, http://www.accountingtools.com/fifo-method.
[3] Whiteside, Craig Catch and Release in the Land of Two Rivers http://warontherocks.com/2014/12/catch-and-release-in-the-land-of-two-ri...
[4] Buckley, Cara, 500 Iraqis Freed from Crowded U.S. Detention Center, *NY Times*, 9 November 2007.
[5] McCoy, Thomas, US Prison was "terrorist university" for Islamic State, Waterloo Region Record.
[6] Fainaru, Steve and Shadid, Anthony, In Iraq Jail, Resistance Goes Under Ground, *The Washington Post*, August 24, 2005.
[7] Mcoy, Ibid.
[8] ISIS, Michael Weiss and Hassan Hassan, Inside ISIS.
[9] Welner, Michael, Facing Jihad's Risk a Corrections Issue, Inside Guantanamo and Out, *Good Morning America*, http://abcnews.go.com/TheLaw/terrorism-gitmo-detainees-striking/story?id...

[10] Boon, Kristen E, Huq, Aziz, and Lovelace, Douglas Jr., Terrorism Commentary on Security Documents, Volume 110 Assessing the GWOT, Oxford 2010, p. 416.

[11] Institute for the Study of War, http://www.understandingwar.org/report/al-qaeda-iraq-resurgent.

[12] Spillius, Alex, Al Qaeda claims responsibility for Iraq mass prison break, *The Telegraph*, http://www.telegraph.co.uk/news/worldnews/10197854/Al-Qaeda-claims-respo...

[13] Almasmari, Hakim and Melvin, Don, Officials: Al Qaeda fighters free 270 from Yemeni prison, *CNN*, http://www.cnn.com/2015/04/02/middleeast/yemen-prison-break/.

[14] Christopher Boucek, "Saudi Arabia's 'Soft' Counterterrorism Strategy: Prevention, Rehabilitation, and Aftercare," Carnegie Papers, Carnegie Endowment for International Peace, no. 97 (2008): 23.

[15] Christopher Boucek, "Jailing Jihadis: Saudi Arabia's Special Terrorist Prisons," *Terrorism Monitor*, 6, no. 2 (2008): 4.

[16] Anthony H. Cordesman, "Winning the 'War on Terrorism': A Fundamentally Different Strategy," *Middle East Policy*, 13, no. 3 (2006): 106.

[17] Oucek, "Saudi Arabia's 'Soft' Counterterrorism Strategy: Prevention, Rehabilitation, and Aftercare, p. 21.

[18] Ezzarqui, Leila De-Radicalization and Rehabilitation Program: The case Study of Saudi Arabia, p. 32.

Chapter 39:
Global War on Terrorism:
How Does the United States Military Counter and Combat the Worldwide Spread of Islamic Extremism?

Notes

1. Tan, Michelle, "SPEC OPS needs 5,000 Soldiers," Stars and Stripes (February 23, 2015), accessed May 11, 2015.

2. Simakhov, Vadim Konstantine, "Cultural Competence and the Opertaional Level of War," (Newport, R.I.: Naval War College, 2013): 3.
3. "Mission," USMC Center for Advanced Operational Culture Learning, 2013, accessed May 14, 2015,https://www.tecom.usmc.mil/caocl/SitePagesHome.aspx.
4. Ibid
5. Frederick, Jim, "Black Hearts-One Platoon's Descent into Madness in Iraq's Triangle of Death," 2010.
6. Report on Progress Toward Security and Stability in Afghanistan, 36-38.
7. Ibid
8. David J. Kilcullen, "The City as a System: Future Conflict and Urban Resilience," The Fletcher Forum of World Affairs 36, no. 2 (Summer 2012); 31.
9. AR 11-6, Army Foreign Language Programs, 2013.
10. One World Nations Online-"Official and Spoken Languages of African Countries." Accessed May 11, 2015. http://www.nationsonline.org/oneworld/african_languages.htm
11. AboutMilitary.com, "Defense Language Aptitude Battery," Accessed May 12, 2015, http://usmilitary.about.com/cs/joiningup/a/dlab_3.htm.
12. AR 11-6, Army Foreign Language Programs, 2013.
13. "Army Rosetta Stone Access has Expired." Accessed May 11, 2015, https://usarmy.rosettastone.com/.
14. United States Department of the Army Pamphlet 611–21, Military Occupational Classification and Structure, 2007.
15. Department Of Defense Instruction 1312.01 January 28, 2013.
16. Sustaining U.S. Global Leadership: Priorities for 21st Century Defense, 4.

References

Kilcullen, David J. "The City as a System: Future Conflict and Urban Resilience." The Fletcher Forum of World Affairs 36, no. 2 (Summer 2012): 19-39.

One World Nations Online-"Official and Spoken Languages of African Countries." Accesses May 11, 2015, http://www.nationsonline.org/oneworld/african_languages.htm.

Panetta, Leon E., and Barack Obama. Sustaining U.S. Global Leadership: Priorities for 21stCentury Defense. Washington, D.C.: U.S. Department of Defense, 2012.

Simakhov, Vadim Konstantine, "Cultural Competence and the Operational Level of War," (Newport, R.I.: Naval War College, 2013): 3.

Army Times Newspaper, online. "Spec Ops Needs 5,000 Soldiers." Staff Writer Michelle Tan. February 23, 2015. Accessed May 11, 2015, http://www.armytimes.com/story/military/careers/army/2015/02/23/army-special-operations/23304113/.

United States, Department of the Army. "Army Rosetta Stone Access has Expired." Accessed May 11, 2015, https://usarmy.rosettastone.com/.

United States, Department of the Army. Army Pamphlet 611-21, Military Occupational Classification and Structure. Washington, D.C. 2007.

United States, Department of the Army. Army Regulation 11-6, Army Foreign Language Programs, Washington D.C., 2013.

United States, Department of Defense. Department of Defense Instruction 1312.01, Department of Defense Occupational Information Collection and Reporting, Washington, D.C., 2013.

Chapter 40:
Deconstructing ISIS:
SWJ interview with William McCants on
The ISIS Apocalypse: The History, Strategy and Doomsday Vision of the Islamic State

Notes

[1] http://www.brookings.edu/about/centers/middle-east-policy
[2] http://www.brookings.edu/about/projects/islamic-world
[3] https://azelin.files.wordpress.com/2010/08/abu-bakr-naji-the-management-of-savagery-the-most-critical-stage-through-which-the-umma-will-pass.pdf
[4] http://www.brookings.edu/research/essays/2015/thebeliever

Chapter 41:
How to Defeat the Islamic State:
Crafting a Rational War Strategy

Notes

[1] Patrick Cockburn, *The Rise of the Islamic State: ISIS and the New Sunni Revolution* (New York: Verso, 2014); Loretta Napoleoni, *The Islamist Phoenix: The Islamic State and the Redrawing of the Middle East* (New York: Seven Stories Press, 2014)

[2] "Iraq between Maliki and the Islamic State" POMEPS Briefing#24-July 9, 2014 accessed at http://pomeps.org/2014/07/09/iraq-between-maliki-and-the-islamic-state/

[3] Samuel Helfont (2013), "The Geopolitics of the Sunni-Shia Divide" *FPRI Footnote* December 2013 access at http://www.fpri.org/doc/Helfont_-Hi_-_Sectarianism.pdf; Steven Hydemann (2013), "The Syrian Uprising: Sectarianism, Regionalization and State Order in the Levant" *Fride and Havos Working Paper* No.

119 (May 2013) 1-19 access at http://www.firda.org/descarga/WP_119_Syria_Uprising.pdf

[4] Vali Naser, *The Shia Revival: How Conflicts within the Islamic world will shape the future* (New York: W.W. Norton, 2007)

[5] Walid Phares, *The Coming Revolution* (New York: Simon & Schuster, 2010)

[6] "Letter signed by Zarqawi, seized in Iraq in 2004" reprinted in Jean-Charles Brisard, *Zarqawi: The New Face of Al Qaeda* (Other Press: New York, 2005) Appendix VIII 233-251; Shmuel Barr and Yair Minzili, "The Zawahiri Letter and Strategy of Al Qaeda" available at http://www.currenttrends./op...thezawahirikms./.isn'; Aymenn Jawad al-Tamimi (2014). "The Dawning of the Islamic State of Iraq an ash-Sham" January 27, 2014 *Hudson Institute* access at http://www.currenttrends.org/the-dawn-of-the-islamic-state-of-Iraq-and-ash-sham.html

[7] Assaf Moghadan and Brian Fishman (editors) *Self-inflicted Wounds: Debates and Division in Al Qaeda and its Periphery* (Combating Terrorism Center: West Point, 2010); Brian Fishman (2009)" Dysfunction and Decline: Lessons Learned from Inside Al Qaeda in Iraq *Combating Terrorism Center at West Point* Harmony Project March 16, 2009 access at http://www.ctc.usma.edu

[8] Colin Duek, "The Strategy of Retrenchment and its Consequences" *FPRI e-note* April 2015 accessed at http://www.fpri.org/document/duek_-_retrenchment.pdf

[9] Richard Barrett, "The Islamic State" November 2014 *The Soufan Group* accessed at http/www.thesoufangroup.com/category/research/the-islamic-state/. Barrett calculates some 20,000 foreign fighters have gone to Syria half of whom join Al Nusra or Islamic State

[10] Nibras Kazami (2008), "The Caliphate Attempted" Current editors Hillel Fradkin, Eric Brown, ad Hassan Mneimnah (2008) 5-49 Hudson Institute *Trends in Islamist Ideology* Volume 7;

Anthony Celso, "Zarqawi's Legacy: Al Qaeda's ISIS Renegade" *Mediterranean Quarterly* 26:2 DOI 10,2015/10474552-2914495

[11] Ken Pollack (2013), "The Fall and Rise and Fall of Iraq" July 30, 2013 access at http://www.brookings.edu/research/papers/2013/07/30-fall-rise-fall-iraq-...

[12] John McCary (2009), "The Anbar Awakening: An Alliance of Incentives." *Washington Quarterly* 32:1 43-59; Bing West (2009), *The Strongest Tribe: War, Politics and the Endgame in Iraq* (Random House: New York, 2009)

[13] Alex Bilger, ISIS Annual Reports Indicate Metrics Driven Military Command *Institute for the Study of War Backgrounder* May 22, 2014 accessed at http/: www.understandingwar.org; Jessica Lewis, "AQI's 'Soldiers of Harvest' Campaign" *The Institute for the Study of War* October 9, 2013 accessed at http://wwwundeerstandingwar.org/sites/default/files/BackgroundSoldiersHa...

[14] Thomas Friedman (1998), "Hama Rules" in *From Beirut to Jerusalem 2nd edition* (Harper Collins: London) 76-105; Raphael Lefavre (2013), *Ashes of Hama: The Muslim Brotherhood in Syria* (Oxford University Press: New York, 2013); Aaron Lund (2011), "The Ghosts of Hama: The Bitter Legacy of Syria's Failed 1979-1982 Revolt" *Swedish International Liberal Center Silc Forag* (June 2011) 1-44 access at http://wwwold.silc.se/files/pdf/The%20Ghosts%20of%20Hama%20by%20Aron%20lund.pdf

[15] Nibras Kazimi, *Syria through Jihadist Eyes* (Stanford: Hoover Institution, 2010)

[16] Elizabeth Dickinson (2013), "Playing with Fire: How Private Gulf Financing for Syrian Extremist Rebels Risks Igniting Sectarian Conflicts at Home" Analysis Paper 16 (December 2013) *Brookings Saban Center* access at http://www,brooking.edu/.../06%20private%20gulf%20financing%20syria%20e...0sectarian%20conflcit%20dickenson.pdf

[17] Jeffery White (2014), Assad's Indispensable Foreign Legions Policy Watch 2196 January 22, 2014 Washington Institute access at http://www.wahsingtoninstitute.org/policy-analysis/view/

assads-indispens... Jeffery White (2013), Hizb Allah at War in Syria: Forces, Operations, Effects and Implications *CTC Sentinel* Volume 7: Issue 14-18

[18] Charles C. Caris and Samuel Reynolds," ISIS Governance in Syria" *Middle East Security Report* 22 July 2014 *The Institute for the Study of War* accessed at http://www.underderstandingwar.org/sites/default/files/ISIS_Governance.pdf

[19] Aaron Zelin, The War Between ISIS and Al Qaeda for Supremacy of the Global Jihadist Movement Research Note 20 *The Washington Institute for Near East Policy* (June 2014) accessed at http://www.washingtoninstitute.org/uploads/documents/pubs/researchnote_2...

[20] Thomas Jocelyn (2014a). "Al Qaeda General Command Disowns Islamic State of Iraq and the Sham"*Long War Journal* Feb. 3, 2014 access at http://www.longwarjournal.org/archives/2014/02/al_qaedas_general_cp.php

[21] "Smashing the Borders of the Tawaghit" *Islamic State Report 4 Alhayat Media Center* accessed at http://jhadology.net/.../al-hayat-media-center-presents-a-new-issue-of-t... 3

[22] Ibid.

[23] "From Hijrah to Khalafah" in *Dabiq 1 The Return of the Khalifah* al-Hayat Media Center accessed at http://www.jihadology.net/2014/07/05/al%e%68%sayat-media-center-presents-a-new-issue-of-the-islamic-state-magazine-dabiq1/ 34-40

[24] Candyce Kelshall, "ISIL: the Ultimate Hybrid Enemy" at http://www.defenseiq.com/air-land-and-sea-defense-services/articles/isil-the-ultimate-hybrid-enemy/. The author puts ISI forces between 90,000-200,000 which vastly exceeds the 20,000 figure cited by the CIA and US military sources.

[25] J.M. Berger and Jonathan Morgan, "The ISIS Twitter Census: Defining and describing the population of ISIS supporter on Twitter" Analysis Paper No. 20 March 2015 The Brookings Project on US Relations with the Muslim World accessed at http://www.brookings.edu/-/media/research/files/paper/2015/03/

ISIS-twitter-census-berger-morgan/ISIS-twitter-census-berger-morgan.pdf

[26] John Calvert, *Sayyid Qutb and the Origins of Radical Islam* (New York: Columbia University Press, 2010)

[27] Pollack, ibid

[28] Barak Obama, *The Audacity of Hope* (Edinburgh: Canongate, 2007)

[29] Andrew Watkins, "Islamic State Operations and Iraqi Fault Lines" *CTC Sentinel* 8:5 17-20; Michael T. Flynn "Why the Iraq Offensive Will Fail." POLITICO Magazine. February 20, 2015. Accessed at http://www.politico.com/magazine/story/2015/02/why-the-iraq-offensive-will-fail-115356.html#.VZVGqmYpCAw

[30] "Dabiq 11: From the Battle of Al-Ahzab to the War of the Coalitions" accessed at http:clarionproject.org/fovd/iddur%2011%20%20From%20the%0f20%20Al-Ahzab%20%to%the%20war%20%of%20coalitions.pdf 4-9

[31] Jessica Lewis, "The Islamic State: A Counter Strategy for a Counter State" *Institute for the Study of War* (ISW) July 2014 accessed at http:www.understandingwar.org/sit/default/files/Lewis-Center%20of20%gravity.pdf

[32] Soner Cagaptay and Marc J. Stevens, Turkey and Egypt's Great Game in the Middle East The Washington Institute Articles and Op-Eds March 8, 2015 accessed at http://www.washingtoninstitute.org/policy-analysis/viewturkey-and-egypt-great-game-in-the-middle-east

[33] Richard Barret, ibid

[34] Wladimir van Wilgenburg, "Turkey's New Syria Policy: Preventing the Islamic State and Kurdish Expansion" *Terrorism Monitor* 13:19 6-8

[35] Clint Watts, "Let Them Rot: The Challenges and Opportunities of Containing rather than Countering the Islamic State" *Perspectives on Terrorism* 9:4 156-163

[36] Ibid

[37] Matthew Levitt and Lori Potkin Boghardt, "Financing ISIS (Infographic)' September 12, 2014 Accessed at http://www.washingtoninstitute.org/pilicy-analysis/view/funding-isis-infographic
[38] Daveed Gartenstein-Ross, "The Islamic State's International Expansion: What Does Ansar Bayt Al-Maqdis Oath of Allegiance Mean? *War on the Rocks* February 25, 2015 accessed at http:www.warontherocks.org/; Jabcob Zenn, Boko Haram, the Islamic State and the Archipelago Strategy" Terrorism Monitor 11:24 23-26
[39] "Remaining and Expanding": Dabiq 5 accessed at http://www.jihadology.net/2014/07/05/al%e%68%sayat-media-center-presents-a-new-issue-of-the-islamic-state-magazine-dabiq2/
[40] Don Rassler, Gabriel Koehler-Derrick, Liam Collins, Muhammad al-Obaidi, and Nelly Lahoud (2011), Letters from Abbottabad: Bin Laden Sidelined? *Combating Terrorism Center at West Point* access at http://www.ctc.usma.edu/posts/letters-from-abbattabad-bin-laden-sidelined
[41] Ibid
[42] William McCants, "The Believer: How an Introvert with a Passion for Religion and Soccer became Abu Bakr al-Baghdadi Leader of the Islamic State" Brookings Essay September 1, 2015 accessed at http:www.brookings.edu/research/essays/2015/thebeliever
[43] Charles Lister, "Profiling the Islamic State" *Brookings Doha Center* Analysis Paper No. 13 November 14, 2014 accessed at http://www.brookings.org/research/files/reports/2014/11/profiling%20islamic%20state%lister/in-web-lister.pdf
[44] Stathis N. Kalyvas "The logic of violence in the Islamic State's war" "Iraq between Maliki and the Islamic State" POMEPS Briefing#24- July 9, 2014 accessed at http://pomeps.org/2014/07/09/iraq-between-maliki-and-the-islamic-state/34-36
[45] Michael Knights and Jabbar Jaafar, "Restoring the Iraqi Army's Pride and Fighting Spirit" July 8, 2015 *The Washington Institute for Near East Policy* accessed at http://washingtoninstitute.org/

policy-analysis-restoring-th-iraqi-army-pride-and-fghting-spirit.pdf; Andrew Watkins, ibid

[46] Kirk H. Sowell, "The Islamic State's Eastern Frontier: Ramadi and Fallujah as Theaters of Sectarian Conflict" *Perspectives on Terrorism* 9:4 130-140

[47] Gary Anderson, "Abu Bakr al-Baghdadi and the Theory and Practice of Jihad" *Small War Journal* August 1, 2014 accessed at http://wwwsmallwarjournal.com/author/gary-anderson

[48] Anthony Celso, "Boko Haram and the Islamic State: Fifth Wave Islamist Terror Groups" *Orbis* 59:2 249-267

[49] Aaron Zelin, "Picture Or it Didn't Happen: A Snapshot on the Islamic State Official Media Output"*Perspectives on Terrorism* 9:4 85-96

[50] Richard Barrett, ibid

[51] "ISIS teens execute 25 soldiers in Syria's Palmyra" accessed at http://www.english.alararabiya.net/en/News/middle-east/2015/07/04/ISIS-t...

[52] Kaplan *The Ends of the Earth: A Journey to the Frontiers of Anarchy* (New York: Vintage Books, 1996)

[53] T.E. Lawrence, *Seven Pillars of Wisdom* (London: Aegitas, 2015)

[54] Ephraim Karsh (2006), *Islamic Imperialism: A Short History* (Yale University Press: New Haven, 2006)

[55] Norman Cigar, *Tribal Militias: an Effective Tool to Counter Al-Qaida and its Affiliates?* (Carlisle: United States Army War College Press, 2014)

[56] Dan Danelo, "Anarchy is the New Normal: Unconventional Governance and 21st Century Statecraft" FPRI E-Note October 2013 accessed at http:www.fpri.org/articles/2013/anarchy-new-normal-unconventional-governance-and-21st-century-statecraft

[57] Michael Knights and Alexandre, "Cult of the Offensive: ISIS on the Defensive" *CTC Sentinel* 8:4 1-5

[58] Murray S. Fradin, *Jihad: the Mahdi Rebellion in the Sudan* (Authors Choice Press: New York, 2003); P.M. Holt, *The Mahdist State in the Sudan* 2nd edition (Clarendon Press: Oxford, 1970); Byron

Farwell, *Prisoners of the Mahdi* (W.W. Norton: New York, 1989); Daniel Alan Butler, *The First Jihad: Khartoum, and the Dawn of Militant Islam* Kindle Edition (Casemate: Drexel Hill, 2007)

[59] Kristin M. Blakke, "Foreign Fighters don't always help" accessed at http://www.washingtonpost.com/blogs/monkey-cage/wp/2014/05/28/foreign-fighters-dont-help/

[60] Gary Bernsten, *Jawbreaker: The Attack on bin Laden and Al Qaeda* (New York: Crown Publishing Group, 2006)

[61] Martin Chulov, ISIS kills hundreds of Iraqi Sunnis from Albu Nimr Tribe in Anbar province" The Guardian October 30, 2014 accessed at http://www.theguardian.com/2014/oct/30/mass-graves-hundreds-iraqis-sunnis-killed-isis-albu-nimr

[62] Clint Watts, "Countering ISIL Ideology: keep it Limited, Focused and in Tune with Lessons Learned" accessed at http:ww.fpri.org/articles/2015/countering-isils-ideology-keep-it-limited-focused-and-tuned-lessons-learned

Chapter 42:
Defeating ISIL in the Information Environment

References

Al Arabiya News. (July 10, 2014). ISIS Issues Print, Electronic Newspaper. Retrieved from http://english.alarabiya.net/en/media/2014/07/10/ISIS-issues-print-electronic-newspaper-.html on 14 October 2015.

Fryer–Biggs, Zachary. (May 27, 2013). JCS Ready to Approve Cyber Attack Rules for US Military. Defense News. Retrieved from http://www.matthewaid.com/post/51466931970/jcs-ready-to-approve-offensive-cyber-attack-rules on 18 October 2015.

McLeod, Samuel. (2014). Cognitive Dissonance. Simply Psychology. Retrieved from http://www.simplypsychology.org/cognitive-dissonance.html on 21 October 2015.

Mora, Edwin (July 23, 2015). Gen. Dempsey, Afghan President Discuss 10-Year Counterterrorism Effort Against ISIS. Breitbart. Retrieved from http://www.breitbart.com/national-security/2015/07/23/gen-dempsey-afghan-president-discuss-10-year-counterterrorism-effort-against-isis/ on 17 October 2015.

Romanych, Marc. (Spring 2005). A theory-based view of IO. IOSphere–Joint Information Operations Center. Retrieved from https://ndu.blackboard.com/bbcswebdav/pid-768740-dt-content-rid-1660791_2/courses/IWS16-01/Romanych.%20%282005%29.%20A%20theory-based%20view%20of%20IO.pdf on 21 October 2015.

Romm, Tony. (Febuary, 2015). Messaging. Politico. Retrieved from http://www.politico.com/story/2015/02/white-house-social-media-firms-al-qaeda-isil-115301 on Oct 22, 2015.

Small Wars Journal. (Oct 2015). Life in the Islamic State—Washington Post Five Part Series. Retrieved from https://ndu.blackboard.com/bbcswebdav/pid-1181973-dt-message-rid-1663467_6/internal/courses/IWS16-01/db/_1181973_1/embedded/Small%20Wars%20Journal%20-%20Life%20in%20the%20Islamic%20State%20-%20Washington%20Post%20Five%20Part%20Series%20-%202015-10-01.pdf on 21 October 2015.

Chapter 43:
Information War with the Islamic State in Iraq and the Levant: An Indirect Approach

Notes

[1] http://www.state.gov/r/cscc/214420.htm

References

Almukhtar, S. (2015). ISIS finances are strong. *The New York Times.* Retrieved from http://www.nytimes.com/interactive/2015/05/19/world/middleeast/isis-fina...

Berger, J.M. & Morgan, J. (2015). The ISIS Twitter census: defining and describing the population of ISISS supporters on Twitter. The Brookings Project on U.S. relations with the Islamic World Analysis Paper No. 20. Retrieved from http://www.brookings.edu/~/media/Research/Files/Papers/2015/03/isis-twit...

Berger, J.M. & Stern, J. (2015). A six-point plan to defeat ISIS in the propaganda war. *Time.* Retrieved from http://time.com/3751659/a-6-point-plan-to-defeat-isis-in-the-propaganda-...

Chou, C., Kim, H., Shin, K.G. & Shankar, S. (2004) What and how much to gain by spectral agility. University of Michigan. Retrieved from https://www.eecs.umich.edu/techreports/cse/2004/CSE-TR-494-04.pdf

Cottee, S. (2015) The cyber activists who want to shut down ISIS. *The Atlantic.* Retrieved from http://www.theatlantic.com/international/archive/2015/10/anonymous-activ...

De Luce, D. & Hudson, J. (2015). New US czar for anti-ISIS fight will inherit job from hell. *Foreign Policy.* Retrieved from https://foreignpolicy.com/2015/10/22/new-u-s-czar-for-anti-isis-fight-wi...

Dinerman, A. (2015) Defeating ISIL in the information environment. *Small Wars Journal.* Retrieved from: http://smallwarsjournal.com/jrnl/art/defeating-isil-in-the-information-e...

Goble, P. (2015) New Russian book says only ideological approach can defeat Islamic State. *Eurasia Daily Monitor Vol: 12 Iss: 190* Retrieved from http://www.jamestown.org/

Humud, C.E., Pirog, R. & Rosen L. (2015) Islamic State financing and U.S. policy approaches. Congressional Research Service. Retrieved from https://www.fas.org/sgp/crs/terror/R43980.pdf

Levitt, M. (2015) Here's how ISIS still has access to the global financial system. *Business Insider.* Retrieved from http://www.businessinsider.com/heres-how-isis-keeps-up-its-access-to-the...

McNulty, E. (2014). US military using big data to improve situational awareness. *Dataconomy*. Retrieved from http://dataconomy.com/us-military-using-big-data-improve-situational-awa...

Nakashima, E. (2010, March 19). Dismantling of Saudi-CIA web site illustrates need for clearer cyberwar policies. *The Washington Post*. Retrieved from http://www.washingtonpost.com/wp-dyn/content/article/2010/03/18/ ... AR2010031805464.html

Nye, J. (2011) *The Future of Power*. New York: Public Affairs.

Reidel, B. (2015) *Bruce Reidel talks jihadist terrorism, Islamic State and the war in Yemen*. [Audio podcast]. Retrieved from http://itunes.apple.com

Stewart, P. & Coles, I. (2015) U.S. Commando killed in raid to free hostages of ISIS in Iraq. *Reuters*. Retrieved from http://www.reuters.com/article/2015/10/23/us-mideast-crisis-iraq-operati...

Sullivan, K. (2015) Life in the 'Islamic State.' Justice: A climate of fear and violence. *The Washington Post*. Retrieved from http://www.washingtonpost.com/sf/life-in-the-islamic-state/2015/10/01/ju...

Talbot, D. (2015) Fighting ISIS Online. *MIT Technology Review*. Retrieved from http://www.technologyreview.com/review/541801/fighting-isis-online/

Tucker, P. (2015) Pentagon: State doesn't have enough people tweeting at ISIS. *Defense One* Retrieved from http://www.defenseone.com/technology/2015/10/pentagon-state-doesnt-have-...

United States Department of State (n.d.) Digital Outreach Team [Twitter feed]. Retrieved Oct 29, 2015, from http://www.state.gov/r/cscc/214420.htm

U.S. Joint Chiefs of Staff. (2014) *Information Operations*. Joint Publication 3-13, Washington, D.C.: U.S. Joint Chiefs of Staff.

White, G. (2015) Task Force Al Asad trains Iraqis on broadcast capabilities. Defense Video and Imagery Distribution Service (DVIDS). Retrieved from https://www.dvidshub.net/news/178422/task-force-al-asad-trains-iraqis-br... capability#.VjIAOHr3arU

Chapter 44:
Reevaluating General Order 1X

Notes

[01] Yates, William; What Effect did General Order Number 1 and the Force Protection Measures Have on Task Force Eagle Operations in Bosnia During Implementation Force?; U.S. Army Command and Staff College; Fort Leavenworth; 2003; p. 14; http://oai.dtic.mil/oai/oai?verb=getRecord&metadataPrefix=html&identifie...

[02] Turner, Thomas R. (signatory); General Order Number 1; Headquarters, 101st Airborne Division; FOB Speicher, Iraq; 01NOV2005; paragraph 5.n.

[03] Gurganus, C.M. (signatory); I Marine Expeditionary Force (Forward) General Order 1A; I Marine Expeditionary Force (Forward); N/A; 22MAR2012; paragraph c.4.

[04] Cucolo, Anthony A. III (signatory); General Order Number 1; 3rd Infantry Division; COB Speicher, Iraq; 04NOV2009; paragraph 3.r. to 3.t.

[05] Austin, Lloyd J., III; General Order 1C; United States Central Command; MacDill Air Force Base, Florida; 21MAY2013; http://www.christianfighterpilot.com/articles/files/go1c.pdf

[06] Ibid

[07] Bulliet, Richard W.; Islam: The View from the Edge; Columbia University Press; New York City; 1995; pp. 81-99

[08] Lewis, Bernard; What Went Wrong?: The Clash Between Islam and Modernity in the Middle East; Harper Perennial; New York City; 2002

[09] Quran, Surah 5 (al Maidah), Ayah 90, Marmaduke Pickthall translation, 1930

[10] Kyle, Chris, McEwan, Scott, and DeFelice, Jim; American Sniper: The Autobiography of the Most Lethal Sniper in U.S. Military History; HarperCollins Publishers; New York City; 2012; p. 142

[11] Connolly, Kate; Troops' beer allowance a headache for Germans; The Guardian; Berlin; 15 November 2008; http://www.guardian.co.uk/world/2008/nov/15/germany-afghanistan-beer

[12] Hernandez, Christopher; Working with the French Army; chrishernandezauthor Blog; N/A; 09JUL2013; http://chrishernandezauthor.com/2013/07/09/working-with-the-french-army/

[13] Yon, Michael; Searching for Kuchi & Finding Lizards; Michael Yon Online Magazine; Ghor Province, Afghanistan; 13JUL2009; http://www.michaelyon-online.com/searching-for-kuchi-a-finding-lizards.htm

[14] Quran, Surah 2 (al Baqara), Ayah 173, Marmaduke Pickthall translation, 1930

[15] Graham-Harrison, Emma; US troops in Afghanistan bid farewell to lobster, steak and salsa; The Guardian; 03APR2013; Kabul; http://www.theguardian.com/world/2013/apr/03/us-troops-afghanistan-lobst...

[16] Neumann, Amanda; Beyond Afghanistan; Defense Logistics Agency; N/A; 2014;http://www.dla.mil/Loglines/Pages/LoglinesJF2014Story01.aspx

[17] Austin, Lloyd J., III; General Order 1C; United States Central Command; MacDill Air Force Base, Florida; 21MAY2013; http://www.christianfighterpilot.com/articles/files/go1c.pdf

[18] Uriarte, Maximillian; The Two-Beer Rule; Terminal Lance webcomic; San Francisco; 11FEB2014; http://terminallance.com/2014/02/11/terminal-lance-308-the-two-beer-rule/

[19] A former field grade officer suggests that few senior leaders would support allowing alcohol over concerns regarding good order and discipline, and the desire to display respect for local customs. The use of an unpopular and ineffective appeal to cultural sensitivity to enforce good order and discipline raises a number of concerns as to the morale and discipline of the joint force.

[20] Akehurst, John; We Won a War: The Campaign in Oman 1965-1975; M. Russell; Salisbury, Wiltshire; 1982; p. 90

[21] Gardiner, Ian; In the Service of the Sultan: A First Hand Account of the Dhofar Insurgency; Pen & Sword Military; Barnsley, South Yorkshire; 2007; Kindle Location 649

[22] Higgins, Andrew; With the SAS and Other Animals: A Vet's Experiences During the Dhofar War 1974; Pen & Sword Military; Barnsley, South Yorkshire; 2011; Kindle Location 455

[23] Gardiner, Ian; In the Service of the Sultan: A First Hand Account of the Dhofar Insurgency; Pen & Sword Military; Barnsley, South Yorkshire; 2007; Kindle Location 641, 660

[24] Sahih Muslim, Book 4, Hadith Number 1032

[25] Imam Malik's Muwatta; Book 54, Number 54.13

[26] Ibid; Book 49, Number 49.23

[27] Sahih Bukhari 4.56.673

[28] Watt, William Montgomery; Muhammad: Prophet and Statesman; Oxford University Press; Oxford; 1961

[29] Thesiger, Wilfred; Arabian Sands; Penguin Classics; London; 1959; Kindle Location 4575

[30] Yon, Michael; The AfterWar; Michael Yon Online Magazine; Kandahar Province; 08DEC2011; https://www.michaelyon-online.com/the-afterwar/All-Pages.htm

[31] Haidary, Emal; Man's best friend takes on Afghanistan's enemy; AFP; Kabul; 19NOV2012; http://www.google.com/hostednews/afp/article/ALeqM5g4WiFbxe6X7ybdHE-IJYJ...

[32] Lee, Sandra; Saving Private Sarbi: The True Story of Australia's Canine War Hero; Allen & Unwin; Sydney; 2011

[33] Owen, Mark and Maurer, Kevin; No Easy Day: The Firsthand Account of the Mission that Killed Osama bin Laden; Dutton Penguin; New York; 2012

[34] Hanrahan, Kevin; Kevin Hanrahan (website); N/A; Virginia; 2014; http://khanrahan.com/

[35] Frankel, Rebecca; War Dog (photo essay); Foreign Policy; N/A; 04MAY2011; http://www.foreignpolicy.com/articles/2011/05/04/war_dog?

[36] Frankel, Rebecca; War Dog (photo essay); Foreign Policy; N/A; 12MAY2011; http://www.foreignpolicy.com/articles/2011/05/12/war_dog_ii?
[37] Schumacher, Gerald; A Bloody Business: America's War Zone Contractors and the Occupation of Iraq; Zenith Press; St. Paul, MN; 2006; p. 234
[38] Ibid; pp. 234-235
[39] Terrill, Chris; Commando: On the Front Line: Episode 6 - Operation Sparrowhawk; ITV1; London; 2007; https://www.youtube.com/watch?v=JuVPhu-Z-AA
[40] Kaplan, Robert D.; Imperial Grunts: On the Ground with the American Military, from Mongolia to the Philippines to Iraq and Beyond; Vintage; New York; 12 September 2006; p. 202
[41] Grau, Lester W. and Jorgensen, William A.; Medical Support in a Counter-guerrilla War: Epidemiologic Lessons Learned in the Soviet-Afghan War; U.S. Army Medical Department Journal, May-June 1995 issue; Foreign Military Studies Office; Fort Leavenworth, KS.; 1995; http://fmso.leavenworth.army.mil/documents/afgmed/afgmed.htm
[42] Grau, Lester W. and Jorgensen, William A.; Viral Hepatitis and the Russian War in Chechnya; U.S. Army Medical Department Journal, May/June 1997 issue, and Center for Army Lessons Learned Publication #98 23; Foreign Military Studies Office; Fort Leavenworth, KS; 1997; http://fmso.leavenworth.army.mil/documents/hepatiti/hepatiti.htm
[43] Austin, Lloyd J. III; General Order 1C; United States Central Command; MacDill AFB, Florida; 21MAY2013; paragraph 2.g.
[44] N/A; Imported Human Rabies in a U.S. Army Soldier—New York, 2011; Centers for Disease Control and Prevention; Atlanta; 2012; http://www.cdc.gov/mmwr/preview/mmwrhtml/mm6117a2.htm
[45] N/A; Army Regulation 670-1 Wear and Appearance of Army Uniforms and Insignia; Headquarters, Department of the Army;

Washington, D.C.; 11MAY2012; http://www.apd.army.mil/pdffiles/r670_1.pdf; Chapter 1-8, Paragraph 2C

[46] An Army National Guard Medical Corps officer who deployed to Afghanistan as a defense contractor reports that he and other contractors maintained seals on their gas masks on all occasions despite having grown full beards.

[47] Sgt B (pseudonym); Pentagon Study Finds Beards Directly Related To Combat Effectiveness; The Duffel Blog; N/A; 09 April 2012; http://www.duffelblog.com/2012/04/pentagon-study-finds-beards-directly-p...

[48] Mandaville, Jack (pseudonym); Soldier Kicked Out Of Special Forces Because He Can't Grow A Beard; The Duffel Blog; N/A; 11 March 2013; http://www.duffelblog.com/2013/03/soldier-kicked-out-of-special-forces-b...

[49] Schogol, Jeff; Some special ops troops told to lose the beard; Stars and Stripes; Arlington, VA; 19AUG2010; http://www.stripes.com/news/some-special-ops-troops-told-to-lose-the-bea...

[50] N/A; Are beards obligatory for devout Muslim men?; BBC World Service; N/A; 26JUN2010; http://www.bbc.co.uk/news/10369726

[51] Imam Malik's Muwatta; Book 51, Number 51.1

[52] Kaplan, Robert D.; Imperial Grunts: On the Ground with the American Military, from Mongolia to the Philippines to Iraq and Beyond; Vintage; New York; 12 September 2006; p. 210

[53] Myklebust, Martin and Ordeman, Tom, Jr.; "Six Requirements for Success in Modern Counterinsurgency"; Small Wars Journal; Bethesda, MD; 11JUL2013; http://smallwarsjournal.com/jrnl/art/six-requirements-for-success-in-mod...

[54] Yon, Michael; Red Horse; Michael Yon Online Magazine; FOB Frontenac, Afghanistan; 01APR2010; http://www.michaelyon-online.com/red-horse.htm

[55] While deployed to Kuwait as a security contractor, I grew a beard. I am not a Muslim, but I was frequently asked if I was, which allowed me to build relationships and disarm several tense

situations in a manner which would not have been possible had I been clean shaven.

[56] Kyle, Chris, McEwan, Scott, and DeFelice, Jim; American Sniper: The Autobiography of the Most Lethal Sniper in U.S. Military History; HarperCollins Publishers; New York City; 2012; p. 142

[57] Cannon, Laura; No sex? Permission to speak freely, Sir.; Washingon Post; Washington, D.C.; 23NOV2012; https://www.washingtonpost.com/opinions/no-sex-permission-to-speak-freel...

[58] Burney, Jazz; Deployed Soldier uses Salsa dancing to help cope with combat environment; 3rd Infantry Brigade Combat Team Public Affairs, 25th Infantry Division; COB Speicher, Tikrit, Iraq; 25 September 2009; http://www.army.mil/article/27867/Deployed_Soldier_uses_Salsa_dancing_to...

[59] Madhani, Aamer; U.S. troops in Iraq have time on hands; USA Today; COB Adder, Iraq; 21 October 2009; http://usatoday30.usatoday.com/news/military/2009-10-20-idle-troops-iraq...

[60] Foust, Joshua; Dispatches from FOBistan: The Kyrgyz Magiciennes of Bagram; unknown; Bagram Air Base, Afghanistan; 10 February 2009; http://registan.net/2009/02/10/dispatches-from-fobistan-the-kyrgyz-magic...

[61] Khan, Huma; Bibles Destroyed in Afghanistan... By U.S. Military; ABC News; N/A; 19MAY2009;http://abcnews.go.com/blogs/politics/2009/05/bibles-destroye/

[62] Raddatz, Martha; Gen. John Allen Stands by U.S. Apology for Koran Burning; ABC News; N/A; 05MAR2012; http://abcnews.go.com/International/general-john-allen-regrets-apologies...

[63] Austin, Lloyd J., III; General Order 1C; United States Central Command; MacDill Air Force Base, Florida; 21MAY2013; paragraph k.1.http://www.christianfighterpilot.com/articles/files/go1c.pdf

[64] Abizaid, John P.; General Order Number 1B (GO-1B); United States Central Command; MacDill AFB, Florida; 13MAR2006

[65] While deployed to Kuwait, one of my co-workers, who considered himself a Muslim, occasionally visited a mosque near company housing to pray. Conversely, while vacationing in Oman, I toured the Sultan Qaboos Grand Mosque, though not on "an official tour conducted with the approval of military authorities and the host nation". By the letter of GO-1X, our organization had grounds to discipline both my co-worker and I, though neither of us violated the spirit of GO-1X.

[66] Herman, Michael; Intelligence Power in Peace and War; Cambridge University Press; Cambridge; 1996.

Chapter 45:
Talking to Tyrants, Sharpening Axes

Notes

[i] Aslan, Reza (2009) *How to Win a Cosmic War*, NY, NY: Random House

[ii] Richard Holbrooke, http://www.pbs.org/wgbh/pages/frontline/shows/saudi/analyses/madrassas.html

[iii] http://www.brookings.edu/research/opinions/2013/08/26-pakistan-influence...

[iv] https://en.wikipedia.org/wiki/List_of_authoritarian_regimes_supported_by...

[v] The founders of Abu Sayaff, the Janjali brothers, studied Islamic theology in Saudi Arabia

Chapter 46:
Finding the ISIS Center of Gravity:
Why Does It Have to Be So Complicated?

Notes

[i] Robert Dixon, *Clausewitz, Center of Gravity, and the Confusion of a Generation of Planners*, Small Wars Journal [20 Oct 2015]: http://smallwarsjournal.com/jrnl/art/clausewitz-center-of-gravity-and-th...

[ii] Carl von Clausewitz, *On War*, Index edition, trans. and ed. by Michael Howard and Peter Paret (Princeton: University of Princeton, 1984), 595.

[iii] Antulio Joseph Echevarria, *Clausewitz's Center of Gravity: Changing our Warfighting Doctrine—Again!* (Carlisle, PA: Strategic Studies Institute, 2002), vi.

[iv] *Dr. Strangelove or: How I Learned to Stop Worrying and Love the Bomb*, directed by Stanley Kubrick, Columbia Pictures, 1969.

[v] Graeme Wood, "What ISIS Really Wants," *The Atlantic* [March 2015]: http://www.theatlantic.com/magazine/archive/2015/03/what-isis-really-wan...

[vi] Ibid.

[vii] Dominique Mosbergen, "Anonymous Declares War on ISIS After Paris Attacks," *Huffington Post* [November 16, 2015]: http://www.huffingtonpost.com/entry/anonymous-isis_5649610ae4b045bf3defc173.

[viii] Scott Faith, "GEN McChrystal on ISIS: Four Tips From Someone Who Actually Knows How to Fight Terrorists," *Havokjournal.com* [September 14, 2015]: havokjournal.com/national-security/gen-mcchrystal-on-isis-four-tips-from-someone-who-actually-knows-how-to-fight-terrorists/.

Chapter 47:
Basing Stabilisation Efforts on Evidence of What Works: Lessons from Afghanistan

No notes.

Chapter 48:
Defeating the Abu Bakr al Baghdadi Gang: A Realistic Strategy

Notes

[i] Huba Wass de Czege, Brigadier General, USA Ret., an independent military theorist, is a veteran of ground combat in Vietnam, and command at all levels through brigade and assistant division command. He founded the US Army School of Advanced Military Studies at Fort Leavenworth, KS. As a special strategic policy assistant to the NATO SACREUR and Secretary General, he helped formulate the strategy to end the Cold War. ia. http://blogs.wsj.com/washwire/2014/09/02/isiss-cruelty-toward-women-gets-scant-attention/

[ii] The first version was entitled "On 'Ridding the World' of 'The Islamic State.'" It circulated in August 2014 among acquaintances in military planning circles. The second was published in Parameters, 44(4) Winter 2014-15, p 63, entitled "Defeating The Islamic State: A Commentary on a Core Strategy."

[iii] Counter Terrorism is a doctrine of tactical operating methods, as is Counter Insurgency. Neither constitutes a strategy. Designing a strategy around a menu of capabilities and practices is proceeding the wrong way around.

[iv] NATO's bombing campaign lasted from 24 March to 11 June 1999, involving up to 1,000 aircraft operating mainly from bases in Italy and aircraft carriers stationed in the Adriatic. Tomahawk cruise missiles were also extensively used, fired from aircraft, ships, and submarines. With the exception of Greece, all NATO members were involved to some degree. Over the ten weeks of the conflict, NATO aircraft flew over 38,000 combat missions.

[v] We spend millions daily in military and police operations against BG and al Qaeda or their ilk. We launch aircraft from aircraft carriers and bases so distant that we need to refuel the strike

aircraft coming and going to distant targets. And the munitions they carry on each flight are expensive and precise. But our ability to locate targets worthy of the expense is hampered by lack of good targeting intelligence.

[vi] I would like to acknowledge the comments of Dr. Alice Butler-Smith of the School of Advanced Military Studies on the August 2014 draft. Also see Graeme Wood, "What ISIS Really Wants," The Atlantic (March 2015). Also see Audrey Kurth Cronin, "ISIS Is Not a Terrorist Group," Foreign Affairs 94, no. 2 (March/April 2015): 87-98.

[vii] Then term "regular" stems from "regulated" by international law and reciprocal practices observed by states. During the war of 1812, American soldiers took offense when the British called and treated them as "irregulars."

[viii] While Lawrence and his book have been inspirational for studying insurrections and how to put them down, his lessons are more universal. He describes how, through a close and critical examination of what he knew about the situation, he created a structured logical mental conception—a theory about the situation and how to gain advantage within that unique setting—so that tactical planning and tactical action could proceed on a sound footing.

[ix] James T. Quinlivan, "Force Requirements in Stability Operations," Parameters 25, no. 4 (Winter 1995-96): 59-69. Also see Huba Wass de Czege, "On Policing The Frontiers of Freedom," Army 56, No. 7 (July 2006): 14-22.

[x] Huba Wass de Czege, "Military Power, the Core Tasks of a Prudent Strategy, and the Army We Need," Strategic Studies Institute, August 6, 2014, http://www.StrategicStudiesInstitute.army.mil/index.cfm/articles/Militar....

[xi] 9 to 12 members to a squad.

[xii] See section entitled "The Heart of the Matter" page 4 to page 7.

Chapter 49:
Kurdistan: The Permanent Solution to Daesh

Notes

[1] Luttwak, Edward N. "Give War a Chance." Foreign Affairs. July/August 1999.

[2] Kagan, Frederick W. and Kimberly Kagan. "Putin Ushers in a New Era of Global Geopolitics."Institute for the Study of War. September 27, 2015. Web. Accessed December 5, 2015.

[3] Kasich, John. "Gov. John Kasich's Plan for destroying ISIS." Fox News. November 20, 2015. Web video. Accessed November 20, 2015.

[4] Team Fix. "5th Republican Debate Transcript, Annotated: Who Said What and What It Meant." The Washington Post. December 15, 2015. Web. Accessed December 16, 2015.

[5] Shields, Michael. "NATO Says Won't Send Ground Troops to Fight IS: Report." Yahoo News. December 7, 2015. Web. Accessed December 7, 2015.

[6] "Iraqi Constitution." October 15, 2005. http://www.iraqinationality.gov.iq/attach/iraqi_constitution.pdf. Accessed December 6, 2015.

[7] "Iraqi Kurdistan Profile – Timeline", BBC. August 1, 2015. Web. Accessed December 9, 2015.

[8] "Geography>Land Area>Square Miles: Countries Compared." Nation Master. Web. Accessed December 25, 2015.

[9] Wing, Nick and Carina Kolodny, "15 Shocking Numbers That Will Make You Pay Attention To What ISIS is Doing In Iraq", The World Post, August 11, 2014. Web. Accessed December 16, 2015.

[10] "Geography>Land Area>Square Miles: Countries Compared.ff" Nation Master. Web. Accessed December 25, 2015.

[11] "The People of the Kurdistan Region", Kurdistan Regional Government, December 16, 2015. Web. Accessed December 16, 2015.
[12] "Countries In the World (ranked by 2014 population)." Worldometers. Web. Accessed December 25, 2015.
[13] Gorzewski, Andreas, "Arms for Kurdish Peshmerga to Affect Military Balance", DW: Made for Minds, August 13, 2014. Web. Accessed December 9, 2015.
[14] "Investment Factsheet Kurdistan Region – Iraq." Japan Cooperation Center for the Middle East. http://www.iraq-jccme.jp/pdf/arc/04_krg_Investment_factsheet_en.pdf. Accessed December 16, 2015.
[15] "Kurdistan's Economy." Kurdistan Board of Investment. http://www.kurdistaninvestment.org/economy.html. Accessed December 10, 2015.
[16] Bradley, Matt. "Iraq, Kurdistan Oil Deal Close to Collapse." The Wall Street Journal. July 3, 2015. Web. Accessed December 16, 2015.
[17] Ibid.
[18] Gordon, Michael and Eric Schmitt. "U.S. Steps Up Its Attacks on ISIS-Controlled Oil Fields in Syria."The New York Times. Novermber 12, 2015. Web. Accessed December 2, 2015.
[19] Ibid.
[20] Ibid.
[21] Ibid.
[22] Ibid.
[23] Ibid.
[24] Najib, Fazil. "By All Yardsticks of Development, Kurdistan Beats Iraq." RUDAW. March 18, 2014. Web. Accessed December 15, 2015.
[25] Gorzewski, Andreas. "Arms for Kurdish Peshmerga to Affect Military Balance." DW: Made for Minds. August 13, 2014. Web. Accessed December 9, 2015.

[26] Mahmoud, Nawzad. "Barazani Orders Peshmerga Forces Reformed." RUDAW. August 25, 2014. Web. Accessed December 10, 2015.

[27] Gorzewski, Andreas. "Arms for Kurdish Peshmerga to Affect Military Balance." DW: Made for Minds. August 13, 2014. Web. Accessed December 9, 2015.

[28] Chivers, C.J. and David Rhode. "In Iraq's Kurdish Zone, Anti-Hussein Forces Wait for U.S." The New York Times. March 21, 2003. Web. Accessed December 10, 2015.

[29] Gartenstein-Ross, Daveed, "How Many Fighters Does the Islamic State Really Have?" War on the Rocks. February 9, 2015. Web. Accessed December 17, 2015.

[30] John, Gavin and Crystal Schick, "Converted Tank Seized from ISIS Part of Kurds' Makeshift Arsenal Against Terrorists." Fox News. June 16, 2015. Web. Accessed December 11, 2015.

[31] Ibid.

[32] Ibid.

[33] McKay, Hollie. "Iraq's Peshmerga Desparate for US Arms in Fight Against ISIS." Fox News. January 3, 2015. Web. Accessed December 9, 2015.

[34] Coughlin, Con. "US Blocks Attempts by Arab Allies to Fly Heavy Weapons Directly to Kurds to Fight Islamic State." The Telegraph. July 2, 2015. Web. Accessed December 11, 2015.

[35] Ibid.

[36] John, Gavin and Crystal Schick, "Converted Tank Seized from ISIS Part of Kurds' Makeshift Arsenal Against Terrorists." Fox News. June 16, 2015. Web. Accessed December 11, 2015.

[37] Gorzewski, Andreas. "Arms for Kurdish Peshmerga to Affect Military Balance." DW: Made for Minds. August 13, 2014. Web. Accessed December 9, 2015.

[38] Gordon, Michael R. and Rukmini Callimachi. "Kurds Retake Strategic Highway in Iraq's North From ISIS." November 12, 2015. The New York Times. Web. Accessed December 9, 2015.

[39] Kalin, Stephen. "Sinjar Aftermath Highlights Islamic State Resilience in Iraq." Reuters. December 7, 2015. Web. Accessed December 7, 2015.

[40] Bradley, Matt. "Iraq, Kurdistan Oil Deal Close to Collapse." The Wall Street Journal. July 3, 2015. Web. Accessed December 16, 2015.

[41] Salih, Mohammed A. "Kurdish Government Seeks $5 Billion Lifeline." U.S. News and World Report. June 24, 2015. Web. Accessed December 15, 2015.

[42] Ibid.

[43] Bradley, Matt. "Iraq, Kurdistan Oil Deal Close to Collapse." The Wall Street Journal. July 3, 2015. Web. Accessed December 16, 2015.

[44] Ibid.

[45] Melvin, Don. "Iranian Leader: 'Death to America' Refers to Policies, Not Nation." CNN. November 5, 2015. Web. Accessed December 16, 2015.

[46] Bradley, Matt, Gordon Lubold, and Nathan Hodge. "Deepening Russian Involvement in Iraq Complicates U.S. Airstrikes on Islamic State." The Wall Street Journal. September 30, 2015. Web. Accessed December 17, 2015.

[47] Burns, Robert and Lolita C. Baldor. "Russia, US Sign Deal to Minimize Risks in Syria; Iraqis Vow not to Seek Russian Strikes." October 20, 2015. Star Tribune. Web. Accessed December 17, 2015

[48] Ibid.

[49] Ditz, Jason. "Turkey Refuses to Withdraw Troops From Northern Iraq." Anti War. December 7, 2015. Web. Accessed December 7, 2015.

[50] Phillips, David L. "Remove the PKK From the Terror List." Huffington Post. July 21, 2013. Web. Accessed December 10, 2015.

[51] Gorzewski, Andreas. "Arms for Kurdish Peshmerga to Affect Military Balance." DW: Made for Minds. August 13, 2014. Web. Accessed December 9, 2015.

[52] Ibid.

[53] "Turkey Downing of Russian Warplane – What We Know." BBC. December 1, 2015. Web. Accessed December 20, 2015.

[54] Kagan, Frederick W. and Kimberly Kagan, "Putin Ushers in a New Era of Global Geopolitics", Institute for the Study of War, September 27, 2015. Web. Accessed December 5, 2015.

[55] Ibid.

[56] Andrews, Robin. "Physicists Show Both Russia and Turkey Were Lying About the Downed Russian Plane." IFLSCIENCE!. December 1, 2015. Web. Accessed December 21, 2015.

[57] Kagan, Frederick W. and Kimberly Kagan, "Putin Ushers in a New Era of Global Geopolitics", Institute for the Study of War, September 27, 2015. Web. Accessed December 5, 2015.

[58] Ibid.

[59] Ibid.

[60] Mooney, Chris. "Oil Prices Keep Falling—The Reason Why." The Washington Post. December 21, 2015. Web. Accessed December 21, 2015.

[61] Starr, Barbara. "U.S. Delivers 50 Tons of Ammunition to Syria Rebel Groups." CNN. October 12, 2015. Web. Accessed December 26, 2015.

[62] "Syria War: Third of Rebels Share IS Aims, Report Claims." BBC. December 20, 2015. Web. Accessed December 23, 2015.

[63] Solomon, Ariel Ben. "Israel 'Very Interested' in Strengthening Relations with Kurds." The Jerusalem Post. August 24, 2015. Web. Accessed December 23, 2015.

[64] Ibid.

Postscript:
Ten Endgames of an Effective Counter-Insurgency Against IS

No notes.

Notes on Contributors

The biographies of the contributors were current at the time of the first publication of their articles in 2015. This has been done to place them in historical context. The biographies of the editors and those contributors providing new material for this anthology are current as of mid 2016.

Editors

Dr. Robert J. Bunker was 2015 Futurist in Residence (FIR) at the FBI Academy, Quantico, VA and is an Adjunct Research Professor, Strategic Studies Institute, U.S. Army War College, Carlisle, PA. He holds degrees in political science, government, behavioral science, social science, anthropology-geography, and history and has undertaken hundreds of hours of specialized intelligence and counter-terrorism training. He is a past Office of the Secretary of Defense (OSD) Minerva Chair and has hundreds of publications including numerous books and reports.

Dave Dilegge is Editor-in-Chief of *Small Wars Journal* and serves as a Director at Small Wars Foundation. He is a retired USMCR Intelligence and Counterintelligence/HUMINT officer, and former USMC civilian intelligence analyst, as well as a defense consultant in the private sector.

Contributors

Dr. Marc Abramiuk, Ph.D., is a professional archaeologist and social anthropologist who works in defense, development, cultural resource management, and education. Reconnaissance and salvage, particularly in logistically challenging environments, are his archaeological fieldwork specialties. His research interests on which he has published extensively include cognitive archaeology and applied anthropology among others.

Nader Anaizi is Financial Controller at JP Morgan Chase Bank in Newark, Delaware with research and policy interests in modern Libya.

Dr. Eric C. Anderson is a faculty member with the National Intelligence University. As a long-standing member of the U.S. intelligence community, he has written over 600 articles for the President's Daily Brief, National Intelligence Council, International Security Advisory Board and the Department of Defense. Prior to assuming his current position, Mr. Anderson served on the CIA Red Cell, as a member of Hicks and Associates, and at the Defense Intelligence Agency as a senior intelligence analyst. In addition, he has been a senior intelligence analyst for the Multi National Forces-Iraq in Baghdad and at the U.S. Pacific Command in Hawaii. From 1990-2000, Dr. Anderson was an active duty intelligence officer in the United States Air Force—with assignments in Japan, Korea and Saudi Arabia. He remains on duty as an Air Force reserve officer. He has also taught for the University of Missouri, University of Maryland, and the Air Force Academy. Mr. Anderson has a PhD in political science from the University of Missouri, a MA from Bowling Green State University in Ohio, and a BA from Illinois Wesleyan University.

Gary Anderson is a retired Marine Corps Colonel who served as a pro-bono Special Advisor to the Deputy Secretary of Defense from 2003-5 and as civilian advisor in Iraq and Afghanistan. He is an Adjunct Professor at the George Washington University's Elliott School of

International Affairs where he lectures on Alternative Analysis (Red Teaming)

Dr. Kevin Benson, Ph.D., Colonel, U.S. Army, Retired, is currently a seminar leader at the University of Foreign Military and Cultural Studies at Fort Leavenworth, Kansas. He holds a B.S. from the United States Military Academy, an M.S. from The Catholic University of America, an MMAS from the School of Advanced Military Studies and a Ph.D. from the University of Kansas. During his career, COL Benson served with the 5th Infantry Division, the 1st Armored Division, the 1st Cavalry Division, the 2nd Cavalry Regiment, XVIII Airborne Corps and Third U.S. Army. He also served as the Director, School of Advanced Military Studies.

Capt Ian Bertram is a U.S. Air Force pilot stationed at Kirtland AFB. He is an evaluator in the UH-1N and Mi-17 helicopters. He has prior experience in nuclear security with Air Force Global Strike Command, and was deployed to Afghanistan in 2012 as a Mi-17 Advisor Pilot. He holds a B.S. in History from the United States Air Force Academy and M.S. in Military History from Norwich University.

Dr. Yelena Biberman is an Assistant Professor of Government at Skidmore College, Saratoga Springs, NY. Her research focuses on unconventional warfare and militias in South Asia. She is currently writing a book on the outsourcing of war.

Matthew Blood is an independent political and security analyst. He has a master's degree in human security from the University of Pittsburgh's Graduate School of Public and International Affairs.

Daniel Tyler Brooks is a U.S. Army Captain currently on sabbatical pursuing a MA in International Security at the Josef Korbel School of International Studies at the University of Denver. CPT Brooks made 2 deployments in support of Operation Iraqi Freedom, Operation New Dawn, and Spartan Shield.

Caleb S. Cage is a 2002 graduate of the United State Military Academy and a veteran of OIF. His first book, *The Gods of Diyala: Transfer of Command in Iraq*, was co-authored by Gregory M. Tomlin and published by the Texas A & M University Press in 2009. Since then he has written or edited books largely focused on Nevada, and he is a founding editor of *The Nevada Review*, a journal dedicated to promoting and understanding the literature of his state.

Dr. Anthony N. Celso is an Associate Professor of Security Studies at Angelo State University, San Angelo, Texas. He is the author of *Al Qaeda's Post 9-11 Devolution* (New York: Bloomsbury Press, 2014).

Lt Col Michael Coleman, USAF, is currently finishing his tour as an Afghanistan Pakistan Hand. In this capacity he served in the Afghan theater as a Counterinsurgency Advise and Assist Team member and as a Ministerial Engagement Team chief. He was commissioned through Officer Training School in 1994. He holds degrees from Missouri State University, BA Communications; Webster University, MA International Relations; and National Defense University, MA in Strategic Security Studies. Prior to his AFPAK Hands assignment he served as a squadron commander, in Portugal and the Kyrgyz Republic.

Tom Creal is a Forensic Accountant and Panel Expert to the United Nations for Corruption and Organized Crime. In addition he has been an advisor in a similar capacity to the US Government, The Government of the Islamic Republic of Afghanistan, The Republic of Sierra Leone as well as the Iraqi Government. He is a Certified Public Accountant.

Brig Gen Huba Wass de Czege, USA Ret., an independent military theorist, is a veteran of ground combat in Vietnam, and command at all levels through brigade and assistant division command. He founded the US Army School of Advanced Military Studies at Fort Leavenworth, KS. As a special strategic policy assistant to the NATO SACREUR and Secretary General, he helped formulate the strategy to end the Cold War.

Chelsea Daymon is an independent researcher living in Washington D.C. She holds an M.A. in Near and Middle Eastern studies from University of London's School of Oriental and African Studies, and B.A. in Oriental Studies from Cambridge University (UK).

LTC Alan Dinerman is a U.S. Army Officer with a vast experience in the information environment; these experiences include information and communications technology (ICT) policy, integration, and architecture, Defensive Cyber Operations, and spectrum planning / management. Alan has held positions in both the military and the U.S. inter-agency. He has a BS from the U.S. Military Academy at West Point and a MS from the Missouri University of Science and Technology.

G. Murphy Donovan is a former USAF Intelligence officer, Vietnam veteran, a graduate of Iona College (BA), the University of Southern California (MS), the Defense Intelligence College, and the Air War College. He the former Senior USAF Research Fellow at RAND Corporation, Santa Monica and the former Director of Research and Russian (nee Soviet) Studies, ACS Intelligence, HQ USAF, serving under General James Clapper. Colonel Donovan has served at the Defense Intelligence Agency, the National Security Agency and the Central intelligence Agency.

Dr. Frederick Dotolo is an Associate Professor of History at St. John Fisher College. His research and publications concern Italian colonialism, and modern Small Wars.

David L. Edwards is a Plans and Policy Analyst at the Defense Language and National Security Education Office within the Office of the Secretary of Defense. In this capacity, he authors, drafts, reviews, and analyzes language, regional, and cultural policies and strategies. He previously served as a foreign language and culture analyst in the Office of the Assistant Secretary of the Army (Manpower and Reserve Affairs).

Adam Elkus is a PhD student in Computational Social Science at George Mason University. He has published articles on defense, international security, and technology at *Small Wars Journal*, *CTOVision*, *The Atlantic*, the West Point Combating Terrorism Center's *Sentinel*, and *Foreign Policy*.

MAJ Reginald Evans, USA, is a 25A, Signal Officer attending the Joint Forces Staff College in Norfolk, VA en route to the Joint Interoperability Division at Pope AFB, NC. He was commissioned through the Army ROTC Program. MAJ Evans earned a BS in Mechanical Engineering from Prairie View A&M University in 1999. He is currently completing a MS in Administration with a concentration in leadership. Prior to his current assignment, MAJ Evans served as an Observer Controller in the Brigade Modernization Command at Fort Bliss, TX.

CPT Brett A. Friedman is a field artillery officer in the United States Marine Corps and editor of the book *21st Century Ellis: Operational Art and Strategic Prophecy for the Modern Era* from Naval Institute Press. Views expressed herein do not represent the views of the Department of Defense, the Department of the Navy, or the United States Marine Corps.

LTC James Gannon, USA, is currently serving as the Joint Forces Support Division Chief and the Joint Center for International Security Force Assistance (JCISFA), Joint Staff J-7. He was commissioned through ROTC in 1997. LTC Gannon earned a BS in Mechanical Engineering from the University of Portland in 1999, a MS in Military Logistics from

North Dakota State University in 2007. Prior to his current assignment, LTC Gannon served as a multi-functional logistician.

Orr Genish is a Government major at Skidmore College.

Daniel Glickstein has worked at the Peacekeeping and Stability Operations Institute at the Army War College and studied abroad in Jordan as a Boren Scholar in 2014. He is an Army National Guard veteran and his writings have previously appeared in *Parameters* and *The Strategy Bridge*.

MAJ Arnold Hammari is a U.S. Army Foreign Area Officer currently serving as a political-military affairs officer at U.S. Africa Command. He has served at the U.S. Embassies in Chad, Uganda, and Senegal as well as at CJTF-HOA in Djibouti. Arnold follows regional security issues in the Sahel and throughout Sub-Saharan Africa.

Holly Hughson is a humanitarian aid worker with an extensive background in rapid assessment, program design, management and monitoring of operations in complex humanitarian emergencies and post-conflict development settings, including Kosovo, Sudan, Iraq, Russian Federation and Afghanistan. Presently she is writing a personal history of war from the perspective of a Western, female operating in Muslim conflicts. She works as an instructor and advisor on humanitarian aid and early recovery to joint, coalition and inter-agency civilian-military training exercises at multiple US bases in the United States and Europe.

Brig. Gen. John Hussey was recently named as the commander of the 75th Great Lakes Division. He is a U.S. Army Reserve officer with a Military Police/Civil Affairs background who commanded the 306th MP Battalion at the Abu Ghraib Prison in 2005 and was in charge of detention operations in Afghanistan as the Task Force Parwan commander under CJIATF 435. He has also earned four masters degrees to include a Master's Degree in Strategic Studies from the United States Army War College.

Melinda Hutchings is an "Interagency" subject matter expert for the U.S. Army and the U.S. Marine Corps conducting disaster response/humanitarian assistance training scenarios in live interagency exercises prior to deployment to *"fragile states."* Following almost a decade of experience as a humanitarian aid worker in Africa; Somalia, Rwanda-Congo, Tanzania, Ethiopia and Mozambique, Melinda spent six years (2004-2011) in southern and eastern Afghanistan working for the U.S. Department of State and the U.S. Agency for International Development conducting Governance and Stabilization interventions to strengthen the Afghan Government in countering the insurgent threat. Melinda participated in President Obama's Afghanistan "Civilian Surge" operation in 2009 working jointly with the U.S. Military at the lowest level of the Afghan Government's reach, the District/Community level. In her last tour at U.S. Embassy Kabul, Melinda represented the Embassy in numerous joint Civilian/Military research projects to "measure the effect" of U.S. Government humanitarian assistance investments in Afghanistan.

Dr. Clark Johnson worked in Afghanistan as a civilian for the US Department of Defense during 2010-2011 and 2013-2014. He previously worked on development issues in Iraq, Krygyzstan, Kosovo, and Saudi Arabia. He has a PhD in History (Yale), and is the author of *Gold, France, and the Great Depression, 1919-1932* (Yale, 1997), as well as a number of papers on economic development and history.

COL Robert C. Jones is a retired Army Special Forces Colonel who has recently been hired as the strategic advisor to the USSOCOM J5. His service includes Special Operations positions in Desert Shield/Storm, OEF-Philippines and OEF-Afghanistan. He is a graduate of the U.S. Army War College, Willamette University College of Law, and Oregon State University. He was serving as a Deputy District Attorney in Multnomah County, OR on 9/11 and is a fellow at the Center for Advanced Defense Studies.

Dr. Paul Kamolnick is professor of sociology at East Tennessee State University. He has published articles and reviews in *Perspectives on Terrorism, Terrorism and Political Violence, Studies in Conflict and Terrorism*, and *Small Wars Journal*. Kamolnick has also authored three monographs through the Strategic Studies Institute of the US Army War College, Carlisle, PA: *De-legitimizing Al-Qaeda: A Jihad-Realist Approach* (April 2012); *Countering Radicalization and Recruitment to Al-Qaeda: Fighting the War of Deeds* (June 2014); and, *The Al-Qaeda Organization (Tanzim Qa'idat al-Jihad) and the Islamic State Organization (Tanzim al-Dawla al-Islamiyya): History, Doctrine, Modus operandi, and United States Policy to Degrade and Defeat Terrorism in the Name of Sunni Islam (Ahl-us Sunnah)*. (Forthcoming, Spring/Summer 2016).

Greg Kleponis is a PhD Candidate with the University of Bolton UK and Researcher for the US Army War College. He was formerly the Senior Advisor to the Afghan Deputy Minister of Interior and Advisor the Ministry of Interior for Security and Training in Iraq. He is a retired USAF Colonel and holds a Masters In Diplomacy from Norwich University and a Master of Laws, LLM in International Criminal Justice from the University of London.

Dr. Merouane Lakehal-Ayat, PhD, is a Professor of Finance at St. John Fisher College. His research and publications concern investment theory, corporate finance and market economies.

Johnny Lou is a researcher at the Chicago Project on Security and Terrorism and a student in the College at the University of Chicago studying Economics and Political Science.

Lt Col Sarah Lynch, USAF, is currently serving as a program analyst at US Strategic Command. She was commissioned through the US Air Force Academy in 1999. Lt Col Lynch earned a BSE in Aeronautical Engineering from the USAFA in 1999, a MS in Aeronautical Sciences from Embry-Riddle Aeronautical University in 2007, and a MS in Logistics from the Air Force Institute of Technology in 2012. Prior to her current assignment, Lt Col Lynch served as a pilot in KC-135 and C-17 aircraft.

Dr. Ajit Maan, Ph.D., Vice-President for Research and Analysis, ENODO Global, is author of *Counter-Terrorism: Narrative Strategies*.

Octavian Manea was a Fulbright Junior Scholar at Maxwell School of Citizenship and Public Affairs (Syracuse University) where he received an MA in International Relations and a Certificate of Advanced Studies in Security Studies.

1LT Matthew J. McGoffin is the executive officer for the Headquarters & Support Company, Headquarters & Headquarters Battalion, 1st Cavalry Division. Previously, he led a scout platoon with USBATT 59, Multinational Force & Observers, 2014-2015. His views are his own and do not represent official policy of the Department of Defense or US Army.

Thomas McNamara is a U.S. Army Special Forces Officer with extensive experience in the Middle East. He has a master's degree in International Affairs and is a fluent Arabic speaker.

John Miller holds Bachelors' Degrees in Middle Eastern Studies and Arabic from the University of Oklahoma His research focuses on Authoritarian Resiliency and Terrorism.

Dr. Jeff Moore, Ph.D., is the chief executive officer of Muir Analytics, which assesses insurgent and terror threats against corporations. Dr.

Moore is author of two books: *Spies for Nimitz: Joint Military Intelligence in the Pacific War*, and *The Thai Way of Counterinsurgency*. He is also the purveyor of SecureHotel.US, a terror risk assessment product for hotels the world over.

Jonathan Moss is a Principal, Governance Security and Justice, at Coffey International Ltd.

LTC Robert Murphy is an Infantry Officer and Strategic Army planner. Commissioned in 1995 from The Citadel, LTC Murphy is a graduate of the Army's Advanced Military Studies Program.

COL Keith Nightingale is a retired Army Colonel who served two tours in Vietnam with Airborne and Ranger (American and Vietnamese) units. He commanded airborne battalions in both the 509th Parachute Infantry Regiment and the 82nd Airborne Division. He later commanded both the 1/75th Rangers and the 1st Ranger Training Brigade.

Dr. Feryaz Ocakli is an Assistant Professor of Government and International Affairs at Skidmore College. He teaches and conducts research on comparative politics and the Middle East. He specializes in the study of Islamist and ethnic politics, democracy, and development.

Patrick O'Connor is a researcher at the Chicago Project on Security and Terrorism and a student in the College at the University of Chicago.

Tom Ordeman, Jr. is an American risk management specialist. In addition to several positions in training and risk management in support of several DoD commands, he spent fifteen months forward-deployed as an antiterrorism advisor in Kuwait.

Ryan Pereira is a second-year graduate student at Georgetown Security Studies Program, specializing in terrorism and sub-state violence. A shorter version of this paper was written for Dr. Daniel Byman's Terrorism

Class. Ryan has previously worked for the National Consortium for the Study of Terrorism and Responses to Terrorism (START) on projects focusing on al-Qaeda and the Islamic State's ideologies, homeland security, and threats to international civil aviation.

Joshua A. Perkins is an Armor officer serving with the 1st Battalion, 66th Armor Regiment, 3rd Armor Brigade Combat Team at Fort Carson, Colorado. He earned his master's degree in political science, with a specialization in national security and diplomacy, from the University of West Florida.

MAJ Daniel Pesature, U.S. Army, is a foreign area officer specializing in the Middle East and North Africa. He graduated from the United States Military Academy in 2005 and recently earned a Master of International Public Policy from the Johns Hopkins School of Advanced International Studies. Major Pesature is currently a student at the U.S. Army Command and General Staff College.

Dr. Doyle Quiggle (PhD, Washington University) has had the honor and privilege of being a professor to US Troops downrange, at Camp Lemonnier, Djibouti, Africa and at FOB Fenty, Jalalabad, Afghanistan. He researches the anthropology of war from within the battlespace, focusing on counter-terrorism and counterinsurgency.

Lt Col Brian Russell is a U.S. Marine Corps Artillery Officer with operational experience in Iraq as a combat advisor and in Afghanistan as a special operations planner. He has worked extensively with allied, coalition and host nation partners in both environments and recently gave up command of 1st Air Naval Gunfire Liaison Company (ANGLICO). He has a BS from N.C. State University and a MA from Liberty University. He is currently a student in the Cyber Strategy masters degree program at National Defense University (Information Resource Management College).

Dr. Joshua Sinai is a Principal Analyst at Kiernan Group Holdings (KGH) (www.kiernan.co), in Alexandria, VA., where he specializes in terrorism, counterterrorism, and homeland security studies. Dr. Sinai's specializations include methodologies to forecast terrorist warfare, root cause analysis, and performance metrics in counterterrorism. He has more than 30 years of experience in government (including working at Department of Homeland Security's Science & Technology Directorate and, as a contractor, at a U.S. Government counterterrorism operations center). The 2nd edition of his pocket handbook on active shooter prevention was published by ASIS International in May 2016. He has published more than 100 articles and book reviews on terrorism and counterterrorism related topics, in academic publications, magazines, and newspapers. He holds a Ph.D. in Political Science, with a specialization in Comparative Politics and the Middle East, from Columbia University.

LTC Richard Snodgrass is a Reserve Civil Affairs officer assigned as the Chief of Governance with the 360th CA BDE (Airborne) at Ft. Jackson, SC. He is currently a student in the Advanced Joint Professional Military Education (AJPME) at the Joint Forces Staff College.

Dr. John P. Sullivan is a career police officer. He currently serves as a lieutenant with the Los Angeles County Sheriff's Department. He is also an adjunct researcher at the Vortex Foundation in Bogotá, Colombia; a senior research fellow at the Center for Advanced Studies on Terrorism (CAST); and a senior fellow at Small Wars Journal-El Centro. He is co-editor of *Countering Terrorism and WMD: Creating a Global Counter-Terrorism Network* (Routledge, 2006) and *Global Biosecurity: Threats and Responses* (Routledge, 2010) and co-author of *Mexico's Criminal Insurgency: A Small Wars Journal-El Centro Anthology* (iUniverse, 2011) and *Studies in Gangs and Cartels* (Routledge, 2013). He completed the CREATE Executive Program in Counter-Terrorism at the University of Southern California and holds a Bachelor of Arts in Government form the College of William and Mary, a Master of

Arts in Urban Affairs and Policy Analysis from the New School for Social Research, and a PhD, doctorate in Information and Knowledge Society, from the Internet Interdisciplinary Institute (IN3) at the Open University of Catalonia (Universitat Oberta de Catalunya) in Barcelona. His doctoral thesis was 'Mexico's Drug War: Cartels, Gangs, Sovereignty and the Network State." His current research focus is the impact of transnational organized crime on sovereignty in Mexico and other countries.

Dr. Alexs Thompson received his Ph.D. from the Divinity School at the University of Chicago where he focused on the Qur'an and Islamic theology. He has backpacked through much of the Middle East and subsequently supported U.S. troops throughout Africa and the Middle East.

Lt Col Stewart Welch, USAF, is currently serving as a Middle East Strategist on the counter-ISIL team in the Joint Staff (J5). He earned a BA in Civil/Environmental Engineering from the George Washington University in 2000, and an MA in Religion from Southern Evangelical Seminary in 2008. Prior to his current assignment, Lt Col Welch was an Olmsted Scholar in Tel Aviv Israel, where he earned a Master's Degree in Modern Middle Eastern History from Tel Aviv University.

Wilem S. Wong, CFE, CAMS, is a Major in the United States Army Reserve (USAR) and a Sergeant of Police, New York City Police Department (NYPD).

Global Radical Islamist Insurgency: Al Qaeda Network Focus Vol. I: 2007-2011
A Small Wars Journal Anthology
By Dave Dilegge & Robert J. Bunker, Editors

Price $38.95
Published: 5/29/2015
Format: Perfect Bound Softcover
Pages: 720
Size: 6x9
ISBN: 978-1-49176-639-2
Print Type: B/W

This anthology—the first of an initial two volume set—specifically covers *Small Wars Journal* writings on the Al Qaeda network spanning the years 2007-2011. It will be followed by a planned second volume covering the years 2012-2014 that highlights both Al Qaeda and Islamic State activities. Depending on the receptivity of the readers to these volumes, future anthologies may be published. Conceptually, these volumes have been inspired by the four *Small Wars Journal—El Centro* anthologies published to date between 2012-2015. These new anthologies are meant to contribute to US security debates focusing on radical Islamist global insurgency by collecting diverse *SWJ* essays into more easily accessible formats. This volume is composed of forty-nine chapters divided into sections on radical Islamist OPFORs (opposition forces) and context and U.S.-allied policy and counter radical Islamist strategies, a preface by Youssef Aboul-Enein, a postscript by Hakim Hazim, this introduction, an acronym listing, extensive chapter notes, and short biographies of the forty-five contributors showcased in this work.

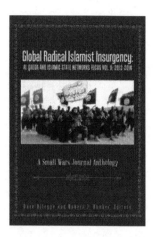

Global Radical Islamist Insurgency: Al Qaeda and Islamic State Networks Focus Vol II: 2012-2014
A Small Wars Journal Anthology
By Dave Dilegge & Robert J. Bunker, Editors

Price: $32.99
Published: 2/12/2016
Format: Perfect Bound Softcover
Pages: 852
Size: 6x9
ISBN: 978-1-49178-804-2
Print Type: B/W

This anthology—the second of an initial two volume set—specifically covers *Small Wars Journal* writings on Al Qaeda and the Islamic State spanning the years 2012-2014. This set is meant to contribute to U.S. security debates focusing on radical Islamist global insurgency by collecting diverse *SWJ* essays into more easily accessible formats. *Small Wars Journal* has long been a leader in insurgency and counterinsurgency research and scholarship with an emphasis on practical applications and policy outcomes in furtherance of U.S. global and allied nation strategic interests. The site is able to lay claim to supporting the writings of many COIN (counterinsurgency) practitioners. This includes Dr.

David Kilcullen whose early work dating from late 2004 "Countering Global Insurgency" helped to lay much of the conceptual basis focusing on this threat and as a result greatly helped to facilitate the writings that were later incorporated into these Al Qaeda and Islamic State focused anthologies. This volume is composed of sixty-six chapters divided into sections on a) radical Islamist OPFORs (opposition forces) and context and b) U.S.-allied policy and counter radical Islamist strategies. The work also contains a preface by Matt Begert, a foreword by Dr. Daveed Gartenstein-Ross and Bridget Moreng, an introduction, a postscript by Dr. Paul Rexton Kan, an extensive notes section, and editor and contributor biographies on sixty-four individuals as well as an acronyms listing and an initial 'About SWJ' and foundation section.

Back Cover Image: An image of Islamic State Wilayah Khorasan branch recruits demonstrating their tactical pistol skills during their graduation ceremony at the the Shaykh Jalal ad Din training camp in November 2015. This image was released by the Wilayah Khorasan in November 2015 via social media (#ISIS #Khurasan) for propaganda purposes [Image Courtesy of the Foundation for Defense of Democracies' *Long War Journal*]. The Islamic State of Iraq and the Levant (formerly al-Qa'ida in Iraq) has been designated a Foreign Terrorist Organization (FTO) by the U.S. Department of State since 17 December 2004, https://www.state.gov/j/ct/rls/other/des/123085.htm.

Made in the USA
Middletown, DE
08 March 2017